The Fate of
the Atlantic Community

Elliot R. Goodman

Published for the
Atlantic Council
of the United States

The Praeger Special Studies program—
utilizing the most modern and efficient book
production techniques and a selective
worldwide distribution network—makes
available to the academic, government, and
business communities significant, timely
research in U.S. and international economic, social, and political development.

The Fate of
the Atlantic Community

PRAEGER SPECIAL STUDIES IN INTERNATIONAL POLITICS AND GOVERNMENT

Praeger Publishers   New York   Washington   London

Library of Congress Cataloging in Publication Data

Goodman, Elliot Raymond, 1923-
    The fate of the Atlantic community.

    (Praeger special studies in international politics
and government)
    Includes bibliographical references and index.
    1. Atlantic Union.   2. International organiza-
tion.   3. North America—Foreign relations—Europe,
Western.   4. Europe, Western—Foreign relations—
North America.   I. Title.
JX1393.A8G66   341.24'3   74-33033
ISBN 0-275-05500-0

PRAEGER PUBLISHERS
111 Fourth Avenue, New York, N.Y. 10003, U.S.A.

Published in the United States of America in 1975
by Praeger Publishers, Inc.

Printed in the United States of America

To my wife
Norma

FOREWORD
Richard J. Wallace

The Atlantic Council of the United States is pleased to sponsor this book by Elliot Goodman since it provides a comprehensive, analytical survey of the problems facing the Atlantic Community. While it should not be assumed that the Atlantic Council agrees with every judgment of the author on all points, it is nonetheless felt that this book presents a stimulating and thought-provoking presentation of the major policy choices and issues that confront the peoples of our Atlantic Community, who must share an essentially common fate.

Professor Goodman displays a striking talent for relating problems of Western organization to the substantive issues of our time. One consequence of this is the realization that some of the problems thrust upon the West are inherently insoluble in the present matrix of Atlantic methods and structure. This leads to the conclusion that improved methods of dealing with those basic problems are urgently required. Ideally, as Professor Goodman suggests, the nations of the Atlantic Community should be able "to solve common problems by means of common policies formulated through common institutions." In many areas actual practice falls far short of this ideal. It is the duty of those who are concerned about the fate of the Atlantic Community to identify these areas that present special dangers and difficulties so that further attention may be focused on them. In this respect Professor Goodman has made a most useful contribution.

The one thread common to all areas of concern that is woven throughout the text also merits special mention. As the author repeatedly emphasizes, movement toward closer union by the Nine of the European Community is a healthy development that deserves support if it does not become divisive and destructive to the unity of the larger Atlantic Community. That is, steps toward tightening the bonds of the Nine must also be accompanied by a strengthening of the trans-Atlantic connection. This will not be easy to accomplish, since some forces leading toward greater European union can provide the pretext for a weakening of the trans-Atlantic link. We must be on our guard to prevent such developments and encourage the common solution of problems, whether they be security, economic, monetary, or other arrangements on an Atlanticwide scale.

Richard J. Wallace
Director General
Atlantic Council of
the United States

ACKNOWLEDGMENTS

A considerable number of individuals, mostly diplomatic figures, deserve acknowledgment for their assistance in helping develop my ideas. I cannot specifically recognize them as I would wish, however, since they have preferred to remain anonymous. I do wish to express my gratitude for the invaluable help given by a group of talented international civil servants who, over a period of years, unfailingly aided me in arranging interviews, supplying documents, and exchanging their considered judgments on a variety of topics: John Vernon of the NATO International Secretariat, Stuart Whyte of the Assembly of Western European Union, Michael Palmer of the European Parliament, and Philippe Deshormes, Secretary General of the North Atlantic Assembly. Senator Claiborne Pell has also rendered innumerable services associated with the writing of this book and I wish to thank him sincerely for his efforts on my behalf. Others who surely deserve mention for their kind assistance include James Huntley, Walden Moore, Livingston Hartley, Lawrence Levy, and Anthony Duynstee.

Research was greatly aided by the receipt of a NATO Research Fellowship and a Guggenheim Fellowship and I wish to express my appreciation for both. I also wish to thank the editors of *Orbis* and *Survey* for their permission to adapt for the book several articles that appeared in these journals.

At the Atlantic Council I wish to express my appreciation to June Haley for supplying documentation and to Richard Wallace and especially Joseph Harned for attending to so many details associated with publication. In this regard I also wish to thank Alvin Singer and Stanley Simon for their efforts to ensure that the manuscript would actually see the light of day.

Elliot R. Goodman
Professor of Political Science
Brown University

CONTENTS

                                                            Page

FOREWORD
Richard J. Wallace   vii

ACKNOWLEDGMENTS   ix

LIST OF ABBREVIATIONS AND ACRONYMS   xvii

INTRODUCTION   xix

Chapter

1 ATLANTIC UNION: PROSPECTS
   AND PROBLEMS   1

      Common Policies and the Nation-State System   1
      Lost Opportunities in Community Building   5
      Europe Confronts America: The Problem of
         Atlantic Federation   9
      Canada and American Power   11
      The Atlantic Union of Clarence Streit   12
      The Dialectics of Atlantic Unification   19
      Streit's Attempt to Accommodate Reality   22
      Atlantic Union and Practical Politics   24
      The Model of Franco-German Reconciliation   26
      Rockefeller and Nixon   28
      Kennedy and Johnson   29
      The Response from Monnet and Eden   30
      Fulbright Joins the Discussion   31
      German Political Leadership Favors
         Atlantic Union   31
      The Atlantic Convention of NATO Nations   34
      In the Aftermath of the Atlantic Convention   37
      De Gaulle and Vietnam   38

Chapter		Page
	Atlantic Unionists Persist in Their Efforts	39
	Notes	43
2	THE POLITICS OF FRAGMENTATION: DE GAULLE THE DISINTEGRATOR	50
	The Unique Quality of Gaullist Nationalism	51
	A "European Europe"—The Arbiter in World Politics	53
	De Gaulle and Atlantic Union	58
	De Gaulle's Singular Atlantic Policy	60
	De Gaulle the Architect of Western Europe	62
	The Machiavellian Style and the European Community	64
	The Franco-German Nucleus for Little Europe	68
	De Gaulle Turns East	71
	Russia and de Gaulle's Europe to the Urals	72
	The Role of Communist Ideology	75
	The Three Steps in Organizing All of Europe	78
	De Gaulle's NATO Policies in Perspective	81
	De Gaulle's Secret Triumvirate Proposals	82
	French Defense vs. NATO Integration	93
	The French Withdrawal from NATO	100
	The Reasons for the Assault on NATO	104
	NATO Integration and Germany	110
	French-NATO Relations When the Dust Had Settled	111
	"Tous Azimuts": The Logical End of Gaullist Strategy	116
	The Gaullist Retreat to Reality and Improved Relations with NATO	120
	Notes	124
3	ATLANTIC PARTNERSHIP: SLOGAN OR SOLUTION?	135
	Who Is a Member of "Europe"?	138
	Atlantic Partnership and Canada	141

Chapter   Page

The Origin of the Partnership Idea: Its
  Broader Basis   146
Partisans of Partnership Redefine Atlantic
  Community   148
Partners, Separate But Not Rivals: Early
  Assumptions   155
Monnet's Europe Not Another Great Power?   158
Britain as a Moderating Influence?   161
The Gaullist Legacy   164
Partnership as a Formula for Stalemate   167
Transformations in America's Self-Image   170
The Call for a New Atlantic Charter   174
The Doctrine of Equality: Atlantic
  Decision Making   177
The Psychological Aspects of Equality   180
Equality and Burden Sharing   184
Notes   186

4 ATLANTIC PARTNERSHIP: ITS FURTHER
   INSTITUTIONAL DEVELOPMENT   193

Partnership in Nuclear Weapons: Problems
  of a European Deterrent   193
Problems of the Double Veto Proposals   197
The Analogy of the U.S.-U.K. Relationship   200
The Costs and Possible Consequences of a
  European Deterrent   204
The Euratom-AEC Relationship as an
  Institutional Model of Partnership   210
The Committee of Entente Idea   215
The Limits of Functionalism   221
Onward to European Union?   224
The Vision Beyond Partnership   227
Notes   234

5 NATO AND DETENTE: THE GAULLIST
   AND SOVIET VIEWS   241

De Gaulle "Discovers" Detente   241

The Gaullist Solution for an East-West
  Settlement   246
Testing the Gaullist Thesis in Eastern Europe   247
Building a New Europe with Old and
  Inadequate Means   250
Soviet Manipulation of Gaullist Detente Themes   252
Europe without NATO   258
Detente and Competition in Nuclear Arms   261
Expanding the Range of Superpower Accords   274
Detente and the Impact of Foreign Trade   278
Detente and the Role of the Soviet Armed Forces 281
Testing the Summit Agreements: The Yom
  Kippur War   285
Notes   289

6   NATO AND DETENTE MANAGEMENT   297

NATO's Future in a Changing Europe   297
NATO and the Euphoria of Detente   299
Detente and the Erosion of the NATO
  Military Position   303
U.S. Force Levels in Europe   305
NATO's Political Role in the Search
  for Detente   316
American Policy Making and NATO's
  Political Functions   323
NATO's Efforts at Long-Term Policy Planning   328
NATO and the "Third Dimension"   332
French Defection and the Adaptation of
  NATO to the Tasks Ahead   336
NATO's Future Institutional Evolution   345
Notes   351

7   POLITICAL ISSUES FACING THE
ATLANTIC ALLIANCE   360

Making Europe Whole and Reuniting Germany   361
Changes in the Approach to German
  Reunification   363

Chapter   Page

    Reunification Redefined   366
    The Brezhnev Doctrine and German
      Reunification   368
    Restructuring the Alliance Systems as a Means
      of Overcoming the Division of Germany   371
    The Search for Accommodation between
      the Superpowers   375
    The Impact of the Non-Proliferation Treaty
      on Alliance Solidarity   377
    Assessing the Limitations of the NPT   383
    Salt and Other Soviet-American Accords
      at the Summit   388
    The Problems of Concerting Global Policies   391
    European Union and More Effective
      Consultation about Global Policies   393
    Notes   397

8 THE NETTLE OF MULTILATERAL
   NUCLEAR SHARING   403

    The Future of Small National Nuclear Forces   404
    The Origin and Agonies of the Multilateral
      Force Idea   408
    The British Counterproposal of an Atlantic
      Nuclear Force   418
    The Duynstee Concept of an Integrated
      Atlantic Deterrent   424
    The Trustee Formula for Nuclear Sharing   433
    McNamara's Initiatives and the Work of the
      Special Committee   435
    Creation of the Nuclear Defense Affairs
      Committee and the Nuclear Planning Group   437
    The Prospects for Allied Nuclear Sharing   443
    Notes   444

9 THE ECONOMICS OF THE
   ATLANTIC COMMUNITY   449

Chapter		Page
The Multinational Enterprise as a Radically New Economic Force		451
The American Challenge and the European Response		455
The Impact of Multinational Enterprises on the Nation-State System		459
The Organization for Economic Cooperation and Development		464
Institutions of the International Monetary System		472
De Gaulle's "Gold War against the Anglo-Saxons"		477
The Effects of the Dollar Crisis on the International Monetary System		483
The Group of Ten and the Committee of Twenty		486
Outline of a Reformed International Monetary System		487
The Creation of a European Monetary Union		490
The Further Liberalization of World Trade		492
The Atlantic Community and Japan		495
Notes		497
10	THE NORTH-SOUTH RELATIONSHIP	503
Giving Aid for the Right Reasons		505
The Definition of "Underdeveloped" States		510
Making Aid Conditional		512
The Multilateral Aid Institutions		515
Aid Leverage through Multilateral Institutions		518
Possible Initiatives by the Developed Countries		523
The Impact of the Energy Crisis on Development Aid		527
Notes		530
11	PARLIAMENTARY ASSEMBLIES IN THE ATLANTIC COMMUNITY	533
The Value of Parliamentary Assemblies		533
The European Parliament		535

The Consultative Assembly of the Council
  of Europe   536
The Assembly of Western European Union   537
The NATO Parliamentarians' Conference   538
The British "Grand Design"   539
OECD and the Consultative Assembly of the
  Council of Europe   542
Plans to Broaden the NPC   544
North Americans at the Consultative Assembly
  of the Council of Europe   549
The Efforts to "Institutionalize" the NATO
  Parliamentarians   552
The North Atlantic Assembly and Its Relations
  with NATO   555
Future Prospects for the North Atlantic Assembly   557
The Place of WEU in the Effort to Rationalize
  Assemblies   566
North American Ties with the European
  Parliament   572
Notes   573

EPILOGUE: A LOOK AHEAD   582

ABOUT THE AUTHOR   584

LIST OF ABBREVIATIONS AND ACRONYMS

ABM	Anti-Ballistic Missile
AEC	Atomic Energy Commission
AID	Agency for International Development
ANF	Atlantic Nuclear Force
APAG	Atlantic Policy Advisory Group
BIS	Bank for International Settlements
CAP	Common Agricultural Policy
CCMS	Committee on the Challenges of Modern Society
CPSU	Communist Party of the Soviet Union
CRU	Composite Reserve Unit
CSCE	Conference on Security and Cooperation in Europe
DAC	Development Assistance Committee
EC	European Community
ECSC	European Coal and Steel Community
EDC	European Defense Community
EEC	European Economic Community
EFTA	European Free Trade Association
Euratom	European Atomic Energy Community
FBS	Forward Based Systems
FOBS	Fractional Orbital Bombardment System
GATT	General Agreement on Tariffs and Trade
GDR	German Democratic Republic
ICBM	Intercontinental Ballistic Missile
IDA	International Development Association
IMF	International Monetary Fund
IRBM	Intermediate Range Ballistic Missile
LDC	Less Developed Countries
MARAIRMED	NATO Maritime Air Forces Mediterranean
MIRV	Multiple Independently Targetable Reentry Vehicle
MLF	Multilateral Force
MOBS	Multiple Orbital Bombardment System
MRBM	Medium-Range Ballistic Missile
NAA	North Atlantic Assembly

NADGE	NATO Air Defense Ground Environment
NATO	North Atlantic Treaty Organization
NDAC	Nuclear Defense Affairs Committee
NORAD	North American Air Defense Command
NPC	NATO Parliamentarians' Conference
NPG	Nuclear Planning Group
NPT	Non-Proliferation Treaty
OECD	Organization for Economic Cooperation and Development
OEEC	Organization for European Economic Cooperation
SAC	Strategic Air Command
SACEUR	Supreme Allied Commander Europe
SACLANT	Supreme Allied Commander Atlantic
SALT	Strategic Arms Limitation Talks
SDR	Special Drawing Rights
SHAPE	Supreme Headquarters Allied Powers Europe
SIOP	Single Integrated Operations Plan
SLBM	Submarine Launched Ballistic Missile
UNCTAD	United Nations Conference on Trade and Development
WEU	Western European Union
World Bank	International Bank for Reconstruction and Development

INTRODUCTION

The Atlantic Community represents the heart of industrial civilization. In the past it has produced the bulk of the world's wealth and has contained the largest reservoir of the world's technical skills and facilities. Moreover this economic and technological prowess has rested upon generally shared political and spiritual values that tend to bind its members together, however imperfectly. For all the stresses in the Euro-American relations, historical experience has clearly demonstrated that their fates are inexorably intertwined.

How this unique grouping of peoples organizes its power is crucial not only for their own futures, but for shaping the direction of world politics. The logic of events has drawn them into increasingly closer cooperative ventures and seems to be moving them toward a more binding community of developed nations. But how far and how fast and in what manner they shall move along this path are the critical unknowns.

At present the Atlantic Community can best be viewed as a community of promise. The nations of the Atlantic Community still remain separate entities, although with different degrees of interpenetration and intensity of interaction. Within it, the nine countries of the European Community have gone the farthest in dismantling the barriers among themselves and in establishing procedures for settling differences and implementing common policies and functions. Whether or not common programs and institutions can or should be spread wider and sunk deeper among all the nations of the Atlantic Community is the subject of this enquiry.

There are a number of competing visions of the future shape of the Atlantic Community. To what extent this community of promise becomes a community of fulfillment depends upon the particular configuration of power that emerges over time.

At one extreme there are those who propose to transform this communion of nations into an intimate political federation. What are some of the problems and what are the likely prospects for realizing this ambitious and far-reaching attempt to seize the future?

At the other extreme are the voices from the past, rooted in the loyalties of traditional nationalism. Even these spokesmen recognize that the future cannot simply reproduce the past, but they remain firmly attached to the building blocks of the nation-state as the ultimate unit of allegiance. How is this tendency to be judged, and what has been its impact upon the Atlantic Community?

There are others who reject outworn nationalism and yet whose aim falls short of a political federation for the whole Atlantic Community. This conception is founded on the premise of a partnership between the United States of America and the United States of Europe. What are some of the merits as well as the shortcomings of this image?

It may, in fact, be as difficult to unite Europe as it is to unite Atlantica, and without a united Europe the bipolar concept of Atlantic relations would remain unrealized. If federation seems beyond realization in the foreseeable future, if reversion to the nationalism of the past is judged unacceptable, and if the partnership scheme is likely to materialize only imperfectly, is the West condemned to resigned inaction? Or are there not many multilateral transactions that can continue to crisscross the Atlantic Community so as to build a strong web of relationships while awaiting the day when further political breakthroughs can occur? Some of these patient but productive experiments in joint enterprises and the sharing of power will be examined.

The basic assumption underlying the survey of all these divergent paths is the rejection of any one "inevitable" pattern of development decreed by the laws of history. Rather than assuming an inexorable and unilinear progression of events, it is presumed that much depends upon historical accident as well as forces beyond our own control, while the rest depends upon the perceptions and will of the power elites who guide the destinies of the various people in the Atlantic Community. If these perceptions can be sharpened by setting in relief various conceivable patterns and the likely dangers, difficulties, and other consequences of pursuing one or another path of development, the aim of this study will be fulfilled.

The Fate of
the Atlantic Community

**ATLANTIC UNION:
PROSPECTS
AND PROBLEMS**

COMMON POLICIES AND THE NATION-STATE SYSTEM

The fundamental task of the West is to generate the capacity to solve common problems by means of common policies formulated through common institutions. The basic difficulty in this proposition arises from the fact that these common policies and institutions must be created from the individual building blocks of separate nations, each with its own deeply rooted historical traditions, memories, and prejudices, each still retaining a high degree of self-consciousness about the differences that set it apart even from its closest allies, each cherishing such distinctions which symbolize values that are to be preserved for posterity.

The gap between the rational requirements for common policies and the separatist tugs of nationalism abounds in every aspect of life. In the missile age it is displayed most dramatically in the realm of national survival. Faced with the almost instant possibility of obliteration from nuclear-tipped missiles, who has the authority to decide a nation's destiny, and under what conditions? Such questions have introduced an element of urgency, if not asperity, into the normal relations among natural allies. The self-appraisal of the North Atlantic Treaty Organization (NATO), undertaken by the "Three Wise Men" and adopted unanimously by the North Atlantic Council in December 1956, pointed to the central contradiction inherent in the attempt to manage nuclear weapons by means of an alliance of nation-states. "The fundamental historical fact underlying development," asserted this NATO report, "is that the nation-state, by itself and relying exclusively on national policy and national power, is inadequate for progress or even for survival in the nuclear age."[1]

Writing before his entry into government, Henry Kissinger characterized the nuclear dilemma facing NATO as arising from the "increasing inconsistency between the technical requirements of strategy and the political imperatives of the nation-state." There is the military need for centralized control over nuclear weapons on the one hand, and the political striving of each major ally, on the other hand, to participate in planning operations, to influence common decisions, and generally to share in the power and prestige connected with the control of nuclear weapons.

> There is no scheme which can reconcile the objectives perfectly so long as the Atlantic Alliance remains composed of sovereign states. The occasional bitterness of the debate is at least in part due to the fact that neither the United States nor its European critics has been prepared to admit that a genuine conflict of interest exists. The only political solution that could dissolve this contradiction is unattainable in the foreseeable future: Turning over *all* the nuclear weapons of the alliance to an authority embracing the North Atlantic area—the supranational political and defense community which would be essentially a federal government. In the absence of such an embracing political structure, a clash of interests is inevitable."[2]

The debate over nuclear policy in the West has assumed its sharpest form in the views advanced by the United States and France. Secretary of Defense Robert McNamara elaborated the need for a centrally controlled nuclear strategy that would be compatible with the technical requirements of the missile age, but he neglected the genuine sharing of political power with the allied nations whose fate would be involved in such central controls. General de Gaulle stood forth as the most adamant advocate of national sovereignty in nuclear affairs, but such a dispersion of national controls over nuclear weapons neglected the military imperatives and techincal realities of the nuclear age. Since the United States was the preponderant nuclear power in the alliance, possessing perhaps 96 percent of the nuclear capability of the West, it was essentially up to the United States to resolve the problem. This could only be done, as Kissinger has suggested, when the United States would be willing "to face the political implications of its strategic views: Central command and control over all the nuclear weapons of the alliance is incompatible with undiluted sovereignty. The United States cannot insist on integration of strategy while jealously guarding its complete freedom of political decision."[3] Or again, "those nations which are being asked to entrust their nuclear defense to the United States will urge, in return, a commensurate surrender of American sovereignty in the political field."[4]

Occasionally, responsible U.S. officials have tried to look candidly at the political implications of the nuclear dilemma. George Ball, when Under Secretary of State, asked: "If the effective nuclear defense of the free world is, in fact, indivisible, then how can the indivisibility of that defense be secured within the present political framework and in such a way as to promote useful progress within that framework?" The present political framework was judged inadequate, since "the dilemma in which we find ourselves is that Western political institutions have not evolved in pace with the advance of our technology. When we face the problem squarely, it seems clear enough that there can be no perfect answer to the management of the nuclear power of the West until the West has achieved a far greater political unity than it possesses today."[5] As Kissinger had made explicit, such "far greater political unity" meant transforming the Atlantic Alliance into an Atlantic federal government.

It was not only the logic of nuclear policies that pressed allies to modify their traditional behavior. "As the founders of the North Atlantic Treaty foresaw," the "Three Wise Men" recorded in 1956, "the growing interdependence of states, politically and economically as well as militarily, calls for an ever-increasing measure of international cohesion and cooperation."[6] They acknowledged that the main urge for creating NATO had been fear of an external enemy, but they insisted there had also been "the realization—conscious or instinctive—that in a shrinking nuclear world it was wise and timely to bring about a closer association of kindred Atlantic and Western European nations for other than defense purposes alone; that a partial pooling of sovereignty for mutual protection should also promote progress and cooperation generally." Those who created NATO agreed that increased "unity was both natural and desirable; that the common cultural traditions, free institutions, and democratic concepts ... were things which should bring the NATO nations closer together, not only for defense but for their development. There was, in short, a sense of Atlantic Community, alongside the realization of an immediate common danger."[7]

The term "Atlantic Community" thus came to symbolize the aspirations to build a new, broader framework for Western civilization, going beyond the existing nation-state system and involving, in the words of the "Three Wise Men," some "partial pooling of sovereignty." Precisely what kinds of institutional changes would be required and how much sovereignty should be pooled were questions that most often were left unanswered. To some the concept meant movement toward the goal of Atlantic Union, a full federal government on an Atlantic scale. To others it implied a less binding association of states, such as existed under the Articles of Confederation in the United States. To others, confederation was too extreme a demand, and they sought only lesser modifications in existing practices, which would nonetheless result in closer forms of alliance. To complicate matters, words like "union," "federation," "confederation," and "community" often have different meanings read into them by different individuals in different national and political settings.[8]

Despite these ambiguities, the cause of "Atlantic Community" has represented a significant movement that deserves serious consideration. It has sought to solve, or at least ameliorate, the whole gamut of problems facing the advanced industrial societies of the West. Not only could a more integrated defense effort be made more rational and better value obtained for the money spent, but the economic and monetary systems themselves would undergo important modifications. If one proceeded to the ultimate goal of Atlantic Union, for example, there would no longer be balance-of-payments and currency crises among the states of the West since these problems would be transmuted into new and presumably more manageable forms through the existence of a single federal reserve system and a single currency. In a like manner, the anomalies of agricultural production, in which each state, or grouping of states in the case of a European Community, erects its own protectionist schemes with absurd and costly results, could be greatly alleviated by rational and uniform policies.

Moreover, the better use of resources could provide the basis for genuinely common development aid programs for the underdeveloped world. Some spokesmen in underdeveloped countries seek to discredit the idea of an Atlantic Community by raising the spectre of a rich, white man's club. An effectively functioning Atlantic Community would not likely generate resentment if the coherent use of its resources could benefit the poor countries on a scale that is not presently possible, since one is now forced to rely upon a number of disparate, relatively unconnected national efforts. In these and many other respects, a better organized Atlantic Community could make an enormous and beneficial impact not only on the lives of its own citizens, but also on those in the underdeveloped non-Communist lands who look to the West for help.

LOST OPPORTUNITIES IN COMMUNITY BUILDING

In retrospect, it is easy to reflect upon the failure to seize unique moments in history.

The United States emerged from the Second World War as the most powerful nation on earth by chance [Hans Morganthau has observed] and it assumed the leadership of the Atlantic Community by virtue of necessity. In consequence, its will and mind were not equal to its power, and opportunity. Had these attributes been the result of conscious choice and deliberate aspiration, America would have been intellectually and morally prepared when what it had chosen and aspired to came to pass. Since it was not prepared, it approached the tasks incumbent upon the paramount power of the Atlantic Community with unbecoming humility and unwarranted self-restraint. It refused to lead where nobody else could.

American involvement in Europe after World War I had ended in disillusionment, and when a Soviet empire was thrust into Central Europe after World War II, the United States was finally forced to respond by creating a barrier to further Soviet encroachment. But the American response was conceived primarily in military terms to counter the military threat from the East. "Thus the Atlantic Community remained an inchoate social fact incapable of becoming a political reality."

Washington did not wish to imitate Moscow and reduce its European allies to the status of satellites. Instead, it chose to revert to the outmoded legal fiction of the equality of sovereign states, all voluntarily cooperating on the basis of some mythical harmony of interests. Experience should long ago have taught all of us that the natural condition among sovereign states is conflict and anarchy.

As Morganthau suggests, however, there was another alternative that apparently was never considered. The United States could have brought its superior power to bear on behalf of the common interests of the West and created "a common framework of permanent and organic cooperation among Allies who would relinquish their equal status in return for the common protection of their essential interests." This would have called for some merger of sovereignty, but at the time it would have seemed a small price to pay. Sovereignty to the despoiled and disheartened European allies had small meaning, in any event. They were, above all, seeking a permanent guarantee for American involvement and protection. For the United States such a merger of sovereignty would have been relatively painless, since its dominant voice would have naturally carried the day in most essential matters. However, American involvement in Europe "carried with it its military and economic power, but not its creative imagination or its constructive will." America could not yet perceive that the values of Western civilization could "no longer be left to the care of individual nations. Three new factors dominating the international scene have made this impossible: The reduction of the nations of Western Europe from world powers to strictly European ones; the obsolescence of the nation-state as a principle of political organization, in view of the technologies of communication, transportation, and warfare; and the pressure which communism exerts from within and without upon Western civilization."9

Following the war it was the United Nations that absorbed the energies of the American leadership and raised the hopes of the American people. Robert Strausz-Hupé has aptly remarked that "since the idea of Atlantic Union never enjoyed such resolute and fervent sponsorship in high places, it is a moot question as to whether the American public would have opted for or against membership in an Atlantic Union. As it was, the American public was never asked. . . . Despite the vague murmurings of those in high places on the beatitudes of closer Atlantic cooperation, the idea of Atlantic Union never got off the ground. Presidents, Secretaries of State, and leaders of Congress agreed that it was a good idea. And that was about as far as they cared to go."[10]

Reluctance of the political leadership to commit one's country to a long-term, constructive program of transforming the nation-state system was similarly found in Britain's postwar attitude toward Western Europe. Britain was the only major, victorious European nation that had escaped enemy occupation and could also boast of an unbroken political tradition. Never was its prestige higher than in the years immediately after the war. Had London taken the lead, which it could have had for the asking, in moving Western Europe toward political union, many later setbacks and the repeated humiliations at the hands of de Gaulle would have been avoided, and a united Europe would have come into existence largely on British terms. But again, when the opportunity presented itself, Britain was not prepared to move. The British still lived under the illusion that it would be possible to maintain their traditional aloofness toward the continent while continuing to play their role as a major independent world power at the hub of the overlapping ties with the Commonwealth, the United States, and Europe.

Many years later, when it became clear that this role was played out and that a new one must be fashioned in the context of a thriving Western Europe, Britain found itself before an unpleasant prospect. The possibility of unchallenged British leadership had slipped away, its belated bid for membership in the European Community was at first crudely rebuffed, and its terms of entry were only arrived at by protracted and painful negotiations.

From this experience can one perceive a rough analogy with the position of the United States in its relation to the Atlantic Community? As already noted, both the United States and Britain were totally unprepared to recognize and make use of a unique but ephemeral moment of history. Both were likewise possessed by an image of their own self-sufficiency and ability to pursue independent policies. In the case of Britain this image was soon shown to be in large measure an illusion, whereas with the United States it still seemed to have substance. When viewed superficially, the overwhelming power of the United States seemed to justify America's retaining its full freedom for independent action. But illusion was also present here.

Secretary of State Dean Rusk once acknowledged,

> We know, and our peoples know that no such thing as absolute sovereignty is to be had in today's world. For compelling and practical reasons the notion of national independence each day gives more ground to the principle of interdependence. At least as it appears to us in the United States, we have never been less sovereign, less independent in our history, because our freedom of action is rigorously circumscribed by our responsibilities and the interests of others in what we do or we do not do. And so we are coming to the point where we almost cannot understand the revival of the notion of independence in dealing with the affairs of the free world, because we have almost none of it ourselves.[11]

One suspects that at the time this statement was aimed more at de Gaulle's irritating pretensions of national independence than meant as an accurate description of the state of mind then prevailing in Washington. Yet assuredly Secretary Rusk had articulated a basic truth that must sooner or later gain wide acceptance in American thought and action.

"Atlantic Union," the Dutch political observer J. L. Heldring remarked, "is a logical and sound idea, but the initiative must come from the United States. It would be a cheap proposal for a European to advance, since the United States seemingly has so much more to lose."[12] A recurrent theme with all Europeans, except the Gaullists, is that Europeans already feel dependent on others and are aware of the impossibility of self-sustained action. When the day comes that the United States feels a genuine sense of dependence on others in order to accomplish its own purposes, then might it not be ready to consider a merger of some of its sovereign prerogatives in a supranational body that will be capable of pursuing the greater common interest?

When this time arrives, will an American overture to form a greater union be rebuffed as were Britain's opening bids to join the European Community? In the interim, might not Europe have taken shape, discovered a new sense of its own strength, and have gone its own way? In effect, might not the British experience be repeated by the United States, only on a larger scale and with a greater time lapse?

EUROPE CONFRONTS AMERICA: THE
PROBLEM OF ATLANTIC FEDERATION

Even though Europe has not yet coalesced politically, there has already been a sufficient rebirth of vigor and pride to make such an accommodation with the United States difficult. The sharpest anti-American sentiment, of course, has come from the Gaullists, who reject the concept of Atlantic Union on principle. Those who propose to transform the Atlantic Alliance into an Atlantic federation, a Gaullist deputy warned, must recognize the consequences of this act. "A real federation, if the word is accepted in its full meaning, supposes, in fact, a federal, and hence, a single political authority. To set up such a system would be to consecrate within the Alliance the political authority of its most powerful member—the United States." Such a solution would be unacceptable since "it would be based on the assumption that Europe has no political interests of its own."[13]

The insistent Gaullist demand of "Europe for the Europeans" has had an influence far beyond Gaullist circles. It has aroused an awareness of separatism that has permeated European public opinion and which finds frequent expression even by those Europeans who are friendly to American purposes, in the sentiment that, after all, "Europe is still Europe."

Many of the "good Europeans" have long shared the aspect of Gaullism that draws a clear line between Europe and America. Typical, perhaps, of this school of thought is Hendrik Brugmans, long-time rector of the College of Europe at Bruges. As a Dutchman who has devoted himself to the cause of European federalism, he abhors the Gaullist glorification of national sovereignty in general and French nationalism in particular. Yet Brugmans has not been a partisan of Atlantic federation because of his fear that Europe would lose its identity and be swallowed up by an overpowering United States. In his view "it is unlikely that the medium states in Europe are prepared to enter a federation where one power—America—is predominant. Naturally enough, they consider such an enterprise an attempt to institutionalize American hegemony, whereas the United States would not unnaturally argue that no effective administration can work without an executive who is able to decide and carry out its decision. Whereas America is a 'nation' just as much as a 'union,' there is no European 'nation' in the making let alone an Atlantic one."

He maintains that there are basic historical differences between the United States and Europe which cannot be glossed over. One reason he has advocated European federation is to provide sufficient inner autonomy for its member nations so as to assure the continuity of Europe's pluralistic nature, arising from its culturally distinct fatherlands. Therefore the federal institutions that will unite Europe must be "extremely different from those of the American type. . . . It would therefore be wholly unrealistic to put the European 'states' on the same footing as those that formed their 'more perfect union' in North America around 1780, or to merge both types into one federation, 'The United States of the Atlantic.' In fact, the building materials of an Atlantic Union are not fifty odd states on the one side, and six or sixteen on the other. The material has to be twofold: Europe and America, both 'united.' "[14]

One finds a similar theme in the writings of Maurice Allais, who has been an outspoken advocate of a full-fledged Atlantic Union. As a Frenchman and as a European he has likewise reflected the reservations of the "good Europeans" about the potentially dominant role of the United States. The first necessary step toward constructing "an effective Atlantic Community" is to build Europe. This would involve not only making Britain part of Europe, but transforming the economic European Community into a political European Community. "Only a solidly structured Europe could constitute a desirable and acceptable partner for the United States, and only such a solidly structured Europe could discard the fear of losing its own personality in a closer association with the United States."[15] Even so, an Atlantic Community that included both the United States and Britain would likely only be acceptable to the Continental Europeans if it included, in addition to the original Six of the European Community, the Scandanavians, Ireland, and perhaps even Spain and Austria. French public opinion, he conjectured, would certainly oppose an Atlantic Union in which the political combination of the United States, Britain, and Canada would prevail. The unhappy minority experience of the French Canadians and the Turkish community on Cyprus would indicate the need for adequate ethnic balances within a federal system, if it is to work well. "The Latin countries, France and Italy in particular, would surely hesitate decisively at entering an Atlantic system where both the United States and Britain figured strongly, since it is beyond doubt that there would be a very powerful tendency towards the predominance of the English language and Anglo-American culture. A cultural equilibrium must be realized within an Atlantic system so that it may become viable and the danger of excessive Anglo-American predominance may be eliminated."[16]

Allais judged that "Europe's apprehensions regarding an eventual Atlantic Community are no less great than those of the United States; *they are probably even greater.* Paralyzed by a kind of inferiority complex and subjected, throughout Europe, to a skillful and tenacious anti-American propaganda which is by no means the work of the Communists alone, Europeans are anxious not to be dominated by the United States." The Gaullists have joined the Communists both in questioning America's good faith in defending Europe and in accusing the United States of seeking to exploit and control Europe. However little a basis in fact there may be for these charges, they have made their impact on European opinion and account must be taken of them. Allais's own appraisal is that "viewed realistically on the political as well as on the economic level, these apprehensions about United States domination of an Atlantic Community appear to be unjustified. In terms of population, material resources, and culture, as well as technical know-how, the United States could certainly not dominate the countries associated in such a Community."[17] To quiet unreasonable fears and provide adequate psychological safeguards, however, the eventual Atlantic Community should be an extended and ethnically balanced one.

CANADA AND AMERICAN POWER

Canadian spokesmen often reflect similar hesitations about coming into a closer embrace with the United States. John W. Holmes, a former high official in the Canadian Foreign Office, has frequently spoken with candor about the fears of the smaller powers, should a country like Canada be included in an Atlantic Union. "The largest powers . . . far from submerging their identity in a broader political organism, could confidently expect to dominate it politically and culturally." Such domination, he readily admits, would not be due to malice on the part of the United States. "It would be grossly unfair to accuse the United States of calculating aggrandizement or even of hypocrisy when Americans call upon allies to surrender their sovereignty to common institutions, and yet lesser countries cannot fail to foresee that such institutions would in practice lead to no real dimunition of American sovereignty but rather to an extension of the area in which the American writ would, in fact, run." In short, "the incompatibility stems not from American arrogance, but from American power." The disparity in power is especially striking in the Atlantic nuclear arsenal, and this alone, he feels, would render an Atlantic Union impossible. "Neither the United States nor any other ally could accept North Atlantic institutions in which decisions were made by simple majority or even by a weighted majority because the United States, which has a near monopoly of the crucial weapons, could not permit a veto on its freedom of movement and the rest of us could not in such an unequal situation give up our right to dissent and contract out."[18]

All these considerations comprise a formidable set of obstacles to Atlantic Union. American leadership lacked the vision to lead toward this goal when leadership might have been easy. Neither, for that matter, was there a potential followership with an unprepared American public. While the United States was held captive by the illusion of its self-sufficient omnipotence, its partners on both sides of the Atlantic reasserted their historical distinctions and were fearful of formalizing the preponderant power of the United States through any constitutional bonds.

THE ATLANTIC UNION OF CLARENCE STREIT

Throughout these years and despite all obstacles, Clarence Streit, seemingly incapable of discouragement, had never ceased to raise his voice in favor of Atlantic Union. Ever since the publication of *Union Now* in 1939 he has worked as a tireless proponent of the federation of Western democracies, adapting details of his basic plan from time to time so as to take account of political developments. If nothing else, Streit served the continuously useful function of bringing discussion back to first principles by insisting upon the obsolescence of the nation-state system for the West in which leagues, alliances, and even confederations will, in the long run, be unable to provide reliable conditions for security and progress.

Streit's patron saints were Hamilton, Madison, and Jay, as authors of *The Federalist*, while his image of an Atlantic federation was largely molded by the American experiment of 1787. This provided him with a successful example of the federation of separate states which had endured for nearly 200 years. But heavy reliance upon the American experience also locked him into a number of difficulties.

Standing in awe of the supreme achievement of the American federal union, Streit occasionally remarked that its creation bordered on a miracle. If one recalls the difficulties in convening the Constitutional Convention, the moments of despair during its proceedings recorded by Washington and others, and the perilously close votes for its ratification in several of the important states, then the events of 1787 were, indeed, good fortune bordering on a miracle.*

By analogy, Streit called for a supermiracle today. Comparing the 13 American states before federation with the NATO alliance, Streit acknowledged that the bond "formed by the Articles of Confederation was structurally much stronger than NATO, and its members were not nations of widely varied languages and institutions who had long warred with one another. They were states of the same language and basic institutions, with a common history devoid of war among themselves, living in the days of ox-carts and sailing ships—not in jet atomic times." From this Streit concluded that "since the alliance system failed, even in these most favorable conditions, how can one reasonably hope to escape through NATO the fate of 'all alliances in all times' " (the phrase Washington used in his Farewell Address when he warned of the inevitable instabilities of any alliance system)?[20]

Unfortunately this is a nonsequitur. If the Articles of Confederation proved a failure for the 13 states, it would not be easier, but infinitely more difficult, to create a federation among the historically and culturally diverse states of the Atlantic that are

---

*Consider the slim margins for ratification, which were in Massachusetts 187 to 168, in New Hampshire 57 to 47, in Virginia 89 to 79, and especially in New York where there was only a three vote margin of 30 to 27. North Carolina postponed ratification in July 1788 by a vote of 184 to 83 and did not join the union until November 1789, while Rhode Island did not ratify the constitution until May 1790.[19]

bound together by the admittedly more fragile ties of NATO. Streit also confused desirability with possibility. Because something is demonstrably desirable and necessary, it does not follow that it is possible. In any event, if an Atlantic federation should someday become possible, it would not likely come into existence through a single grand constitutional act such as the one that transformed the Articles of Confederation into the Constitution of the United States.

By way of reply, Streit argued that each period of history had different obstacles to overcome. In the days of oxcarts and sailing ships, it seemed inconceivable to many to be able to federate an extensive geographic area only loosely held together by primitive conditions of transportation and communication. While one must grant the merit of this argument, it would still seem necessary to conclude that in human affairs it is much easier to overcome the obstacles of transportation and communication than to dismantle the barriers of a separately formed historical consciousness. And the states of the Atlantic Community are not simply unformed societies that can readily be molded into a new, larger entity. For better or for worse, and it is probably for worse, they are still acutely aware of their separate historical legacies that tend to keep them separate.

Again, reasoning from the U.S. model, Streit adamantly insisted upon federating the existing NATO states, large and small, instead of first encouraging a political union in Europe with which the United States could associate itself. Reduced to a slogan, Streit advocated "a European Community within an Atlantic federation, rather than a European federation within an Atlantic Community." He welcomed functional entities such as the European Economic Community, so long as they were confined to economic functions. But he was "against the idea of federating Europe into a *political* union *before* federating Atlantica as a whole."[21]

If there were a European Union roughly equal in power to that of the United States, Streit reasoned, the prospect would not be one of cooperation and eventual Atlantic Union, but of contention between two great powers, each of which could serve to veto the actions of the other. The result would most likely be discord and stalemate that could only benefit the enemies of the West. Streit repeatedly cited as an analogy the policy stalemate that prevailed in the 1920s and 1930s between equally strong Britain and France, which helped bring Hitler to power, and the possibility today of an Atlantic Community divided and checkmated between two equally strong powers in the face of Communist designs and turmoil in the underdeveloped world.

Experience has shown that "reducing the parties involved to two equally powerful sovereign unions would result, not in easing argument, but in prolonging deadlock."[22] And the greater the sovereign power, the prouder it is apt to be, the more difficult it would be for each to back down and seek accommodation, and hence the greater the possibility of frequent deadlock. As to the long-term prospect, Streit saw "nothing in history to make one believe that two fairly equal democracies or two fairly equal powers, democratic or otherwise, are likely to federate or form a confederation. I know of no such case, certainly among the democracies."[23] The logic of this argument cannot easily be dismissed.

The only reliable guide, in his view, was the Connecticut Compromise formula, successfully worked out in 1787, whereby a number of states of varying sizes could all be joined together in a single political union. This was done by means of a bicameral legislature in which the power of the large states was represented on the basis of population in one house, while the small states found protection behind equal representation for the contracting state units in the second chamber. When applied to the present Atlantic Community, the instant and instinctive response of many Europeans and Canadians would be that this is an intolerable formula, since it would combine the U.S. superpower with a collection of medium and smaller powers and so inevitably would lead to American domination. But, Streit maintained, this would not be so. If the other nations entered an Atlantic Union as direct members in a federation with the United States, they "would have, together, more voting power than the American people in *both* Houses of its Congress or Parliament." Since the combined populations of the non-American states would exceed that of the United States, their representation in the lower house would be greater, while in the upper house the sheer number of other states would naturally outnumber the voting power of the United States. Even if an adjustment were made in the second chamber, such as Streit had suggested in *Union Now*, whereby each nation would have two Senators, plus two more for every 25 million people above the first 25 million—an idea that to some degree follows the Canadian precedent—this would still give the United States 14 Senators, Canada 2, and the European nations on the eastern shore of the Atlantic at least 30.[24]

In somewhat the same vein, Livingston Hartley has devised an illustrative formula of weighted voting for the 15 individual member nations of NATO. According to his proposal, the United States would have 22 out of 80 votes, or less than one-third of the total. He would seek to protect the American minority position, however, by requiring decisions of the NATO Council to be passed by a two-thirds vote. In this case any decision could be blocked by a combination of the United States and any one medium power, such as Canada, Britain, France, Germany, or Italy. As Hartley admits, "the real difficulties to be overcome in order to establish such a voting system within the North Atlantic Council are not mechanical but political."[25] The concept of protecting the American minority position in this fashion is an interesting one, but when viewed as a proposal to reorganize the workings of the NATO Council, the U.S. Congress would most likely focus upon the figure of 22 votes out of 80 and go no further. The difficulty, indeed, is political, in the sense that the United States exerts political power out of all proportion to its population or size when compared with the rest of the Atlantic Community.

The disparity in the realities of political power among the individual states is reflected most sharply in Streit's demand for a full-blown Atlantic federation deciding matters by simple majority votes in a bicameral legislature, in which the United States would be in a minority position in both houses. Instead of Europe and Canada fearing U.S. control, the question would rather be: What possible incentive would the United States have to submit its enormously disproportionate power to such a minority status?

This question would occur not only to Americans, but to some Europeans as well. Pierre Uri, a prominent European federalist associated with Jean Monnet, has asserted: "Looking at the share of the United States in total population, production, contribution to defense, etc., no democratic rule could force it to accept minority status." On the other hand, "it is also a political fact that it would be inconceivable to give only one country [i.e., the United States] a veto, while other nations which consider themselves great powers could be overruled. It is this very nature of things which commends the creation of a large European bloc, and the organization of the Atlantic Community as a continuing process of closer relationships and joint action. In this respect, there is no other procedure than agreement between two parties."[26]

As one who helped draft the Treaty of Rome, Uri emphasizes the need for constant inventiveness in building new institutions to meet new problems. It is always easy to copy the past, but then, he insists, you are sure to be wrong. It is necessary to meet fresh problems step by step, always inventing anew at each stage to devise solutions for a concrete set of circumstances. The method of building a European federation will obviously differ greatly from the way the United States came into being, and the forms for creating joint institutions on an Atlantic scale will differ again both from the American and from the European federating experiences. In rejecting Streit's formula for an Atlantic federation, based on the Connecticut Compromise of 1787, Uri is chary of analogies taken from what he considers to be an irrelevant past.

In the view of most European federalists, then, Streit's plan for the direct federation of existing Atlantic nations suffers from one of two fates. It is either misunderstood as a scheme for institutionalizing American domination of the Atlantic Community and therefore rejected, or if his proposal is properly understood, it is rejected as incredible, since Europeans cannot believe that the United States would voluntarily submerge its superior power in this kind of an arrangement. Many European federalists are kindly disposed toward closer trans-Atlantic ties, and some specify Atlantic Union as the ultimate goal. Yet they argue that the United States will find little reason to restrict its freedom of action in carrying out its worldwide commitments so as to accommodate the more parochial views of the separate European states, or to risk constitutional union with the individually weak and, in many cases, unstable nations of Europe that have had poor records of political democracy. Only if Europe itself first unites, and through union is given the undergirding for erecting strong and stable democratic institutions, capable of matching American power and of assuming global responsibilities, can the United States have any real incentive to form a larger union. The very fact of great power status would make Europe feel safe in negotiating for some sort of intimate and permanent bond with the United States, including the Atlantic Union itself.

There remains, of course, an irreconcilable conflict in assumptions: The European federalists believe that great power status for a united Europe is the sole path toward closer union with the United States, while Streit insisted that this is the sure design for disaster. One should not be dogmatic about the merits of each argument. Time and particular circumstances could conceivably validate either view.

Streit nevertheless asserted with unflagging optimism that his proposal, if genuinely understood, would be acceptable both to the Americans and Europeans. A major difficulty in gaining European acceptance, he claimed, is that most Europeans are not well informed about the workings of the federal system, but are better acquainted with the practices of traditional diplomacy among states. In diplomacy people think primarily in terms of the equality of sovereign states, whereas in the federal system one thinks primarily in terms of the equality of the sovereign citizen, who is the ultimate source of all authority both on the state and federal level. As a consequence, the exact arithmetic of the votes allocated to the various constituent states is not nearly as important as it might at first seem. The American federal experience, in his view, has shown that voting follows party lines far more than state lines. Or if voting does not follow party lines, it is influenced by economic, moral, and other considerations that equally do not conform to voting by state blocs. Echoing the arguments of Madison in *The Federalist*, Streit maintained that the guarantee for escaping the domination of any one group is the creation of an extended republic, in which there are so many interest groups, so many crosscurrents of opinion, and so much shifting of alliances on different issues that no one bloc can permanently dominate the others. This principle would not merely "assure Europeans that the United States colossus would not dominate them, but also assure Americans that the Europeans would not use the majority they would have in both Atlantic houses to dominate us."[27]

All this assumes that an Atlantic federation would duplicate the experience of the American federation, so that an Atlantic Union would, in effect, be the United States writ large. It is precisely this assumption to which the European federalists vigorously object. Admittedly, if an Atlantic federation on the U.S. model had worked successfully for several generations, one could say that the voting formula had not raised any obstacle to the functioning of a trans-Atlantic Euro-American society. But the problem is how to get from here to there, how to convince the nations on both sides of the Atlantic, each formed by its historic peculiarities, that they could, in fact, amalgamate so that the arithmetic of votes allotted to the constituent states would not really matter.

It is again an American concept to think in terms of two major political parties, each spanning the entire federal union, but each with such weak central discipline that temporary majorities in the

Congress can constantly arise from coalitions of different interest groups. How untypical this is of the Atlantic Community as a whole becomes obvious when one considers the various parliamentary systems, where parties exercise a much stricter discipline over their members, and where there are frequently multiparty systems in which some of the splinter parties are of a very limited appeal, even in a geographical sense. Despite his American-centered concept of Atlantic Union, Streit made an effort to incorporate the operation of the various parliamentary systems into his plan. He proposed that there be a supreme executive lodged in a five-man executive board, which would delegate substantial powers to a premier, who would exercise his powers with help of a cabinet of his choice until he lost the confidence of the House or Senate. As one scholar has observed, "the whole scheme constitutes an obviously unworkable mixture of the parliamentary and the presidential system, compounded by all of the evils of plural executive."[28]

THE DIALECTICS OF ATLANTIC UNIFICATION

If one may doubt the feasibility of creating an Atlantic Union along the Streitist pattern, what prospect might seem more realistic for moving toward the same general goal? Amitai Etzioni's interesting study on "the dialectics of supranational unification" suggests that "the process of forming consensus in international systems seems to be quite similar to the national one." Individuals participate in national political life not as individual units but through a series of intermediary bodies or groups operating at different levels, which vary in nature from one national society to another. A national consensus is finally attained by means of what he calls "a multi-level consensus formation structure." So too, in the life of nations, the most promising approach for achieving political integration is to build supranational institutions upon several levels of consensus. "First, the lower level of consensus is attained by grouping a few states at a time; once the union of such groups solidifies, a more encompassing union—and a higher level of consensus—is produced." The dialectical character appears in the process whereby a smaller union of states joins with another group of states to become a larger union. "In the initial stage of the formation of this multi-level structure there are seldom harmonious relations between two groups of nations (or unions). In fact, intense rivalry among them is more frequent. Such rivalry seems to help the integration of each group, preparing it for the next step, i.e., the formation of higher level, more encompassing unions." The final synthesis comes about only after a transitional period of antagonism between the two subgroups or smaller unions, which may be viewed as the thesis and antithesis.[29]

It is, of course, dangerous to press historical data into a conceptual mold in order to "prove" one's point. There is, nevertheless, a good deal of factual basis for substantiating this conception. Etzioni cites the development of Benelux as an example of multilevel consensus formation moving dialectically from a lower to a higher level. During the period of 1795 to 1814 under a republic, and again from 1814 to 1830 under a kingdom, efforts were made to integrate the Low Countries into a single political entity by uniting individually all the separate provinces. These efforts did not produce a lasting success, since in 1830 the southern provinces, as a subgroup, rebelled and formed Belgium. This was followed by a war between Belgium in the south and the Netherlands in the north, which helped consolidate each set of provinces into distinct nations. After a period of time it was found possible to have both nations mesh their policies so that eventually the economic union of Benelux resulted. (As early as 1921 Luxembourg had created a customs union with Belgium, as another subunion or level of consensus formation.) Then Benelux in turn became a subunion within the larger European Economic Community, which was composed of various other national building blocks of consensus formation.

The history of the United States, Etzioni feels, also supports this general thesis. The 13 colonies each formed separate units of consensus formation and their federation did not abolish state governments, which continued to carry on many functions and find expression on the federal level by state representation in the Senate. Building on these state units, regional groupings of interests emerged as intermediary levels of consensus formation, and before long the principal regional antagonisms between the South and the North became so sharp that civil war broke out. This might be compared roughly to the war between Belgium and the Netherlands, which previously had been joined together in one country. Again the American union was reconstituted, just as within a differing time span Benelux was created, but the subgroups of South and North still functioned as intermediary levels of consensus formation in American politics. Similarly, the present Swiss federation was not achieved until the conservative Catholic cantons of the Sonderbund were crushed by a group of liberal cantons in the Sonderbund War of 1847.

Turning to current Atlantic relationships, Etzioni notes that the strains between the United States and Europe, particularly over the question of controlling nuclear deterrents, may "advance rather than retard the political unification of France and West Germany," and in the long run this "will not necessarily, as often claimed, undermine the proposed Atlantic Union."[30]

This note of optimism about the possibility of attaining an ultimate Atlantic Union must certainly be tempered by the more immediate probability of conflict between Europe and the United States. Indeed, if one is to follow faithfully the historical examples cited, it would seem necessary for Europe and the United States, as subgroups of the future trans-Atlantic federation, to go to war with each other before they could complete the dialectical process of forming a greater union! This horrendous prospect would more than confirm Streit's worst fears about an Atlantic Community that was divided between the two great powers of the United States of America and the United States of Europe.

In short, if there is a dialectical pattern of supranational integration, one must do everything possible to keep the antagonisms between the American thesis and the European antithesis within reasonable bounds. Otherwise, in today's world, there would be no point even of speculating about the synthesis of an Atlantic Union. And how is it to be done? No one can prescribe an exact course for developing the relationships among the nations within the Atlantic Community. In general, however, it would seem necessary to encourage the growth of a European Union, but always within the broader framework of a constantly strengthened Atlantic Community. If, as seems likely, it will not be possible to federate the existing, individual nations in one step into an Atlantic Union, neither should one encourage the formation of a European Union that will break all Atlantic ties. Wherever, in special circumstances, it may be possible to skip over the intermediate level and create Atlantic institutions directly, this would be highly desirable. In most cases where this will not be possible, Atlantic ties should serve to reinforce those already created on lower levels, even though the Atlantic relationships would at first be less well integrated and less supranational than those bonds established among the state units on either side of the Atlantic. Above all, one must be constantly aware that there is nothing inevitable about the hoped-for harmony between a growing European Union and a strengthened Atlantic Community. In fact, if nature were allowed to take its course, the most likely result might be a condition of antagonism between these two integrative processes.

Assuming that some sort of Atlantic Union might someday be consummated, the time span involved will obviously be very great. By way of contrast, Streit's concept of *Union Now* emphasized the "now" and looked upon the federating process as a single apocalyptic act. He insistently opposed the functional, pragmatic approach that seeks to take each area of common Atlantic concern and work for common programs and institutions on a piecemeal basis, moving from one field to another separately and successively as opportunities for progress become apparent in different functional areas. Streit's approach "would deal with these functions together, as forming an organic whole."

STREIT'S ATTEMPT TO ACCOMMODATE REALITY

The increasing unreality of awaiting a single, all-encompassing constitutional miracle, plus the successful example of the "Monnet method" in moving toward the integration of Europe by stages on an empirical, functional basis, caused Streit to modify his original concepts somewhat. During the 1960s he arrived at the proposition of a single organic union achieved gradually. Whereas the functional approach would envision common political institutions forming the capstone after the processes of separate functional integration had been completed, "Federal Union would start by crossing the political Rubicon and constituting an Atlantic federal government, whose first task would be to create *gradually* an Atlantic market, currency and defense force."[31] If taken literally this would seem to be a contradiction in terms; one cannot presumably constitute a government without first reaching agreement upon what concretely is to be governed. This blank-check approach to Atlantic Union was seemingly inspired by those clauses in the Treaty of Rome that left blank spots, such as the provisions for the creation of a European common market in agriculture, that were to be filled in on a certain timetable after the other parts of the treaty had been put into operation. But if one reads the Treaty of Rome, one is overwhelmed by the explicit detailed arrangements that the original contracting parties insisted upon inserting before they agreed to its signing. It was assumed that if these extremely concrete arrangements would succeed in working, the contracting parties would be so locked in that it would then be feasible to fill in the selective blank spots that seemed too difficult to negotiate in the first instance. Then, too, the Treaty of Rome was still confined to the objective of an economic union; none of the blank spots referred to such vast areas as defense or foreign affairs.

If the blank-check approach is taken figuratively, then what might be forthcoming is not an Atlantic federal government, but rather a declaration of intent to create one. This would seem to be the essence of the Streit-inspired concurrent resolution first introduced into the Congress in October 1965. It proposed that the Congress authorize an Atlantic Union delegation to participate in a convention with similar delegations from the other NATO countries in order to explore the possibility of agreement on "a declaration that the eventual goal of their peoples is to transform the present alliance into a federal union." In addition, they would seek agreement on "a tentative time table for the transition to this goal," as well as decide upon the interim "democratic institutions to expedite the necessary stages" in moving toward this objective. Should agreement be found possible, "the convention's recommendations shall be submitted to the Congress for action by constitutional procedure."[32] If all went well up to this point, presumably this would still not mean that they had, in fact, created a skeletal Atlantic federation. Rather it would still seem necessary for the states involved to call another convention, this time to work out specific constitutional provisions for a sort of Atlantic Treaty of Rome, which would, in turn, have to be ratified by the appropriate procedures within the contracting states. To digest such vast transformations all in one gulp, as Streit's literal blank-check theory had implied, would surely exceed the capacity of the constitutions of the various political bodies involved.

The difficulty of getting all 15 NATO members to participate in such a constitution-making endeavor was also recognized. "Perhaps it is too much to hope," Streit acknowledged, "that all the NATO nations are now ready to agree on a common objective, however distant."[33] He would therefore use the device of partial agreement, beginning with those who are willing to begin, and leave an open-ended agreement for others to follow as they saw fit. There is surely good sense in this approach, since the trouble with NATO as a basis for an Atlantic federation is that it is both too big and too small. Before 1974, when Portugal was a quasi-clerical Fascist regime it was inconceivable that it could have had any interest in federating with its NATO partners that were Atlantic democracies. Other NATO nations—such as Greece, with its military dictatorship from 1967 to 1974, and Turkey, with its propensity for intermittent military dictatorship—could scarcely qualify as stable democratic societies. On the other hand, it is well to recall the fears expressed by Allais of an Atlantic federation dominated by an English-speaking culture and his plea for including a sufficiently strong makeweight of Latin peoples. Should Spain someday break the mold of its dictatorship it might well be capable of being brought within such a federation. This would be more likely of attainment if, in the meantime, some sort of supranational core had taken form, to which others might later adhere.

ATLANTIC UNION AND PRACTICAL POLITICS

One of the great shortcomings of any movement that seeks to transcend the existing relations among nations is the tendency to rely heavily upon public pronouncements and the mechanistic devices of constitution making while ignoring the need to penetrate and transform the attitudes of the various national societies that are to be merged. The International Movement for Atlantic Union, of which Streit was the principal founder and moving force, has been a typical example of this approach. One must be charitable in rendering judgments, of course, since he always worked with untiring personal devotion and with slender financial resources, and he did succeed in associating a great number of eminent figures on both sides of the Atlantic with his enterprise. Yet the International Movement for Atlantic Union has been composed of a heterogeneous group of people who may agree vaguely upon the ultimate goal of Atlantic

Union, but otherwise lack a common philosophy or an effective action program.*

A more successful model might be Jean Monnet's Action Committee for the United States of Europe. Rather than collecting a large number of prominent people who would do little in the way of concrete activity, Monnet concentrated upon gathering together a small group who shared his ideas in depth and who were willing to pursue specific action programs each within his own field of endeavor. This involved mobilizing carefully selected leaders of various groups, such as political parties, trade unions, and farm organizations in all the countries of the European Community. Instead of tossing slogans in the air, they concentrated on proposals for a series of specific problems which they wished to solve in common, and which each member carried back to his constituent organization so as to persuade it to come along in the common cause. This appraoch, which has been called one of "open conspiracy," tested the readiness of public opinion, spotted specific obstacles to be overcome in each area, and then drew up carefully worded recommendations for action.[35]

Such a technique could conceivably be applied to an Atlantic Community as well. Properly selected representatives of different interest groups could themselves take part in, or at least directly sponsor, international commissions that could meet, make well-prepared studies, and draw up specific proposals on problems of common concern. By exchanging opinions and circulating them within the various constituent groups it would be possible to test what might be acceptable to public opinion in the different countries and then come forward with a concrete and politically defensible action program for the countries of the Atlantic Community.

More fundamentally, the success for any such international political organization depends upon the depth and scope of the

---

*In conversations this writer had with Dr. Kurt Birrenbach and Lord Boothby, respectively vice-president and vice-chairman of the International Movement for Atlantic Union, it became evident that neither shared Streit's concept of Atlantic Union. Birrenbach insisted that the federal pattern of the United States could not be extended across the Atlantic, as Streit advocated. Only if Europe first federates can there be some type of transAtlantic union, in his view. Lord Boothby, in the typical British tradition, has no faith in federal constitutional blueprints, but prefers to work empirically and gradually toward this goal.[34]

network of personal associations that exist across national borders. Where these do not exist they must be built up patiently and carefully so as to support concerted international activities.

THE MODEL OF FRANCO-GERMAN RECONCILIATION

A recent successful example of creating this "human infrastructure" can be found in the organizations that supported the postwar Franco-German reconciliation. Alfred Grosser, who was the first secretary general for the French Committee for Exchanges with the New Germany, recalls that "beginning in 1945, a certain number of men, most of whom came out of the Resistance Movement and the German concentration camps, began to create what has become in the following years the infrastructure of Franco-German relations." Widespread exchanges were arranged, especially among the youth and others who would be moving into leadership positions within a decade. The most useful way found to destroy prejudices and foster sympathetic communications was to have mixed groups discuss the concrete problems in the political life of each country so that the vital interests of one country were understood by those of the other. Genuine personal engagement, emotionally and intellectually, resulted from programs of reciprocal exchanges among groups of student leaders, trade union officials, and the like, each gaining first-hand experience in the life of the other people. When they went back home, they radiated the effects of their contacts among their colleagues within the specific groups from which they came and whose policies, whether in a political party, labor union, church organization, or whatever, would thereby be influenced and changed. This was a modest and concrete approach, but it had the lasting merit of a feedback that generated further action. As a consequence, Grosser explains, "there exists today, independently of whether there are good or bad governmental relations between France and Germany, in the embassies, in the ministries, as well as in the leadership of trade union, of political parties, and in various other diverse groups in the two countries, men who have known each other for years, who have acquired the habit of working together and who, whatever the political circumstances, examine the same problems in the same manner."[36]

It is obviously necessary to implement this technique of community building across the Atlantic so as to form the human infrastructure which can support closer political ties and common institutions. Here, Grosser suggests, is a vast unexplored area which American foundations, among others, have not yet discovered. While it is true that individual students are subsidized for work abroad, this is not specifically directed at this type of community building and it is a long-term investment that pays off slowly. Instead, widespread exchanges should be arranged that concentrate on the potential elites of the different countries in all fields, and, most important to remember, the programs must be reciprocal, so that delegations of European trade union leaders, mayors, journalists, professors, etc., would visit their counterparts in the United States, and vice versa. If such a program should be instituted, as it could, given the political foresight and resources, very substantial changes in the relationships of the nations of the Atlantic Community could be brought about within a generation. Lacking this, it will be much more difficult to outride the ups and downs of official policies pursued by the various governments, let alone influence them toward weaving tighter political bonds.

The link between a greatly increased mutual responsiveness among peoples and supranational institution building was pointed up in the classic study, *Political Community and the North Atlantic Area*, by Karl Deutsch and others. Their findings showed that some of the most important attributes that were, at the same time, the farthest from being achieved in the Atlantic Community concerned the building of "unbroken links of social communication between the participating countries." It is necessary, they emphasized, to extend both the range and volume of communication and personal dealings, including a greatly expanded program of mobility of persons throughout the Atlantic area. Such a strengthened network of human associations would, in turn, require that there be established political habits and functioning political institutions favoring mutual communications and consultations. These are necessary in order "to insure that messages from other governments would not merely be received, but that this would happen speedily, that they would be understood, and that they would be given real weight in the process of decision-making."[37] Or, put another way, more and better communication involves "not only a greater exchange of goods, persons, and ideas, but also more institutions for carrying on consultations between governments and, where possible, for making joint decisions. It would also involve providing appropriate legal and institutional safeguards, such as those needed when the mobility of persons is increased. These safeguards, however, should not prevent imaginative experimentation with hybrid political institutions."[38]

There is obviously much to be done before Atlantic Union becomes practical politics. And yet many who work at the art of practical politics on both sides of the Atlantic have not hesitated to raise this issue publicly. Particularly in the early 1960s, when momentum was gathering for the integration of broader groups of nations in the Atlantic Community, the idea of Atlantic Union did not seem extravagantly fanciful, although admittedly it was not widely understood.

ROCKEFELLER AND NIXON

The issue was cast headlong into the contest for the Republican presidential nomination in 1960 by Nelson Rockefeller. On June 21 Rockefeller issued a major policy pronouncement in which he called upon the free nations of the West to "join together in a truly grand design." This involved American initiatives that would "encourage the free nations to develop and deepen their bonds with one another so that regional alliances can grow into working confederations." Looking coldly at the political needs of the day, he insisted, "this is neither a dream nor an abstraction. It simply suggests the logical and inevitable next step in the history of free nations. We must face the fact that we have reached a point in history at which the nation-state, standing alone, is becoming as obsolete as the city-state of ancient Greece or medieval Europe."[39]

Rockefeller elaborated these ideas in a personal presentation to the Republican Platform Committee on July 19:

> The truly urgent challenge to America today is to act with a vision and a faith and a courage worthy of our own forefathers, who did create a political structure to meet the needs and hopes of free men in their age. We must, therefore, take the lead with other free men in developing political concepts and political institutions that can serve

the hopes of free peoples everywhere as boldly and realistically as the men who founded America served the hopes of their generation. The free world, in short, must have a grand design. This grand design can take shape with regional confederations of nations. Such political groupings of nations on a regional basis would serve to define common purposes and common actions.[40]

Specifically Rockefeller foresaw the emergence of a group of such nations in the North Atlantic Community and in the Western Hemisphere.

In the maneuvering for the nomination, Vice President Richard Nixon felt compelled to take account of this challenging statement of intent. As a result, a Rockefeller-Nixon meeting of July 23 produced a 14-point accord on a number of issues, of which one specified: "The vital need of our foreign policy is new political creativity—leading and inspiring the formation, in all great regions of the free world, of confederations, large enough and strong enough to meet modern problems and challenges. We should promptly lead toward the formation of such confederations in the North Atlantic Community and in the Western Hemisphere."[41]

KENNEDY AND JOHNSON

There was no comparable stir within the Democratic Party on this issue. Candidate John Kennedy revealed in an interview, however, that "we are going to try and put a great deal more emphasis on NATO . . . above all on its economic and political potentials."[42] The first vigorous endorsement of this theme came from Vice President Lyndon Johnson at a NATO commerative ceremony on April 6, 1961. Upon this occasion he pledged that "the United States is resolved to do everything within its power—and I emphasize the word 'everything'—to enhance the strength and unity of the North Atlantic Community." Progress in integrating the European Community was embraced as a welcome component "within a developing Atlantic Community." The existing condition of interstate relations was not good enough, since "the essentially national and loosely coordinated efforts of the past will no longer suffice. Our end goal . . . should be a true Atlantic Community in which common institutions will increasingly be developed to meet common problems." The nature of these new common Atlantic institutions remained undefined. Yet apparently Johnson envisioned fundamental changes in the Western state system because he perceived "the basis for a new and even closer relation between North American and Europe. . . . A genuine political—as well as economic—community might appear increasingly feasible as our long run goal."[43]

THE RESPONSE FROM MONNET AND EDEN

The concept of new Atlantic institutions was quickly echoed by Jean Monnet on June 11, 1961. Crossing the Atlantic to speak to an American audience, the words of the chief architect of a united Europe seemed especially responsive. While great cooperative steps have been made on an Atlantic level, he said, "it is evident that we must soon go a good deal further towards an Atlantic Community. The creation of a United Europe brings this nearer by making it possible for America and Europe to act as partners on an equal footing. I am convinced that ultimately, the United States too will delegate powers of effective action to common institutions, even on political questions. Just as the United States in their own day found it necessary to unite, just as Europe is now in the process of uniting, so the West must move towards some kind of union."[44]

Speaking from England literally on the eve of Monnet's address, Sir Anthony Eden suggested how one could make a start toward such a union. The West as a whole could learn lessons from the intimate Anglo-American military collaboration perfected during World War II. The joint chiefs of staff proved to be an indispensable factor in coordinating combined operations and in facilitating the cooperation between their heads of government. "Without them, all would have been confusion and disarray, each ally playing its own hand in its own part of the world, often without an understanding of another ally's interests, sometimes regardless of them. This," Eden reflected, "is exactly what has been happening between the politically free nations in the postwar world. We need joint chiefs of a political general staff."[45]

FULBRIGHT JOINS THE DISCUSSION

Eden's suggestion was promptly picked up on the other side of the Atlantic and developed by Senator J. William Fulbright, Chairman of the Senate's Committee on Foreign Relations. "While I fully agree with Sir Anthony's contention," Fulbright noted, "I think that we must carry the analysis farther bearing in mind that while common peril may be the measure of our *need*, the existence or absence of a positive sense of community must be the measure of our *capacity*." Admitting that "it is hazardous to project the trend of history, it seems clear that a genuine community is painfully emerging in the Western world, particularly among the countries of Western Europe." Beyond that, however, "it may well be that the unification of Europe will prove inadequate, that the survival of free society will require nothing less than the confederation of the entire Western world."[46] In the summer of 1961 Fulbright was most explicit in his language: "Our proper objective must be the development of a broader community, a concert of free nations transcending the limits of national frontiers and national perspectives.... As an almost existing community, the North Atlantic nations, with their common values as well as common enemies, must surrender far more of their jealously guarded sovereignty than they have already done and press forward with the development of supranational institutions." Specifically, both NATO and the recently formed Organization for Economic Cooperation and Development (OECD) could be organs for increasingly intimate political and economic ties, and in addition, Fulbright looked forward to "the expansion of existing organs of European unification with Great Britain, Canada, and the United States moving toward full participation."[47]

GERMAN POLITICAL LEADERSHIP
FAVORS ATLANTIC UNION

This trans-Atlantic dialogue was augmented early in 1961 by the Defense Minister of the German Federal Republic, Franz-Josef Strauss. How should Europe see its future in relation to the new world, he queried? Viewed realistically, Europe's own union was still far off, and even if it were achieved, its role as an independent world power would be over before it had begun. "Europe in the future can be nothing more than the European component of an Atlantic system which embraces North America and Western Europe. This Atlantic system must be developed into an Atlantic Community—perhaps even into an Atlantic federation."[48]

The leadership of the Social Democratic opposition agreed with the German government on this issue. In the spring of 1961, Willy Brandt, then Mayor of West Berlin, declared before an American audience: "We must realize the Atlantic Community politically. . . . We should envisage political measures bringing us step by step closer to the political Atlantic Community. Some sort of an Atlantic confederation will always remain the natural goal, as long as we are confronted by the differences between East and West. The final victory of freedom and democracy will not be attained unless we work out together a Western policy, a rallying of our forces and a concentration on our common aim." Brandt cautioned that progress would likely only occur slowly. Nevertheless, "in the long run, a further reduction of national sovereignty is inevitable" within the Atlantic Community.[49]

In November 1961 Strauss came to Washington and delivered a speech that, it was later revealed, was made at the direction of Chancellor Konrad Adenauer.[50] "I advocate the establishment of an Atlantic Union," Strauss bluntly declared. NATO must be turned "into a truly political institution. We cannot do anything else than voluntarily give up some of our rights of sovereignty and thereby provide to our Alliance a superiority which not only neutralizes, but surpasses the technical advantages of the Communist bloc." OECD, he suggested, might serve as an initial approach toward the gradual creation of an Atlantic Common Market. A necessary part of this institutional development would include the creation of some sort of Atlantic parliamentary assembly, to which the other organs could be made responsible. In his view, these developments should not stand in contradiction to the process of uniting Europe. "It is rather a continuation of the road to European integration. For some European nations," Strauss speculated, "a decision to go along in this direction might even be an easier one, and one they would make more quickly, than the decision to join a 'United States of Europe.' "[51]

A systematic interview project conducted at that time revealed that these pronouncements were broadly representative of the entire German leadership. "In 1961 a survey of European elites found that nearly every German interviewed considered the nation-state obsolete and looked forward to its final disappearance. Supranationalism as an ideal," the survey noted, was "accepted by practically all contemporary West German leaders." As regards the application of supranationalism to the Atlantic Community, "ideally, many German leaders would apparently like NATO to become the framework for a North Atlantic supranational political association. In 1961 six out of ten German leaders interviewed believed that an Atlantic Community that would include North America would be the most effective form of association."[52]

But the Atlantic Community could not be given a supranational, federal character without U.S. concurrence and, indeed, without its active leadership. A fortnight after the Strauss speech of November 1961, an official of the Kennedy administration provided the American rejoinder. Speaking in Chicago on December 6, 1961, presidential adviser McGeorge Bundy held that "a full-blown Atlantic Union . . . is still constitutionally and psychologically out of range for the people of the United States."[53] Instead, he suggested a partnership between the United States and the European Community, then hopefully in the process of enlargement. This date might be considered the formal American launching of the partnership theme, since on the same day President Kennedy was elaborating the same idea in New York.[54]

Strauss later remarked to this writer that he recognized that he had been rebuffed, and that there was nothing to do but go along with the partnership concept and concentrate upon building Europe politically. However, "the creation of a European Union," he continued to insist in 1962, "must not be considered to be contradictory to the creation of an Atlantic Community. The objective cannot possibly be to set up Europe as a third independent power between, or beside, the United States and the Soviet Union."[55] This might appear to be a rather curious remark in view of his subsequent political fortunes. When Strauss was forced out of the Bonn cabinet, it was frequently held that he gravitated toward the faction of his party that seemed to flirt with Gaullist ideas. Perhaps Strauss came to see de Gaulle as a rallying point for building Europe, but if so it is clear that their conceptions of Europe diverged drastically. Both could agree that Europe should be capable of sustaining its own political and military policies. Yet in a political manifesto of 1965, Strauss nevertheless insisted upon creating a fully supranational European federation that would maintain close ties with the United States. He held to "the concept of a common Atlantic culture," which on the other side of the water "requires a European-minded and European-oriented United States." In this tract Strauss also reaffirmed his earlier belief that in the long run even the creation of a federal Europe "does not mean that we should give up entirely the idea of an Atlantic Union."[56]

THE ATLANTIC CONVENTION OF NATO NATIONS

Strands of Clarence Streit's Atlantic Union movement and President Kennedy's program for economic partnership with the Common Market were intermingled at the Atlantic Convention of NATO nations, which was convened in Paris, January 8-20, 1962. After a decade of lobbying, Streit finally obtained the necessary support for this idea during 1960 from the newly appointed Secretary of State, Christian Herter. This, in turn, led to an act of Congress authorizing the appointment, with appropriate financial aid, of a U.S. delegation of leading representative citizens who were to meet with their counterparts from the other NATO nations in order to consider proposals for strengthening the Atlantic Community. With the U.S. initiative assured, the other nations followed suit, and the Convention as actually assembled gathered 90 representatives from the various NATO nations on both sides of the Atlantic speaking nine different national languages. The U.S. delegation was headed by two cochairmen, the then former secretary of state, Christian Herter, and former Under Secretary of State, Will Clayton.

Both Herter and Clayton had been instrumental in sparking the movement in Congress that ultimately resulted in the passage of the Trade Expansion Act of 1962, which was to permit the United States sufficient freedom of action to become a worthy trading partner in the Kennedy partnership program.[57] Following successful congressional action on the Trade Expansion Act, President Kennedy appointed Herter as the chief U.S. negotiator for the "Kennedy Round" of trade talks.

The involvement of these two prominent American figures must be viewed in a wider context than a desire merely to expand trade with the Common Market. Both were thoroughly familiar with the federalist concept of Atlantic Union. The trade partnership established between the United States and the European Community, Clayton confided to this writer in the fall of 1962, should form the basis for a close working arrangement between the two sides, which should be extended into as many other areas as it was possible to go. He agreed with Jean Monnet's belief that the object of the Common Market was political, not economic, and with Monnet's expressed hope that from this nucleus of an economic partnership, common political institutions for the West would, in time, arise. He also recalled how he had for years given substantial financial support to Streit's federalist activities, although he realized full well that it was not an immediately practical political proposition. He declined to speculate on just how these political institutions of the West might arise, or on what their shape might be. Clayton, however, was firmly committed to the idea that it was absolutely essential for the industrial nations of the West to integrate their activities and institutions, not only for their own survival, but also so that through their joint efforts they could ensure the future prosperity of the underdeveloped countries as well.

Herter's views at this time are a matter of public record, expressed with particular clarity in the proceedings of the Atlantic Convention in January 1962, of which he was elected Chairman. His keynote address posited as the central purpose of their business the need to generate a public awareness, with the resulting demand for change, so as to "foreshadow new political arrangements. How can we accelerate the historic process of Atlantic unity; how engineer a political breakthrough; how project the institutions to succeed the breakthrough; how produce an act of multiple national wills?" Hopefully, it might be possible to overcome the inertia of national selfishness through enlightened leadership. Then again, "perhaps a galvanic shock will be needed. . . . But must we wait for some great catastrophe to produce the necessary compression of our sovereignties, the critical mass from which great new political energies should emerge?"

The call for boldness was moderated by a counsel of caution. "Integrative measures now in train should be fostered." At the same time, "counter productive would be undue political anticipations which would have a delaying effect on economic and military functional cooperation." Herter was fearful, for one thing, that the historic restructuring of Europe, which then seemed to be in process, might be overturned by too-insistent pressures for an Atlantic Union. On the Atlantic level, "as we push for political ties to crown our economic and military coordinative efforts, let us not try to outrun the maturation process lest our political product die stillborn."[58] This attitude fell far short of the aspirations that Streit held out for what the Convention might accomplish. The Convention was, in large measure, his brainchild, and the model for these proceedings as he conceived them was Philadelphia in 1787. He had hoped for nothing less than prolonged deliberations that would bring forth full blown a constitution for an Atlantic federal government, which could then be submitted for ratification by its participating states.

As Herter elaborated elsewhere, "neither military alliances nor trade partnerships can of themselves be enduring without the essential cement of political institutions." Yet the way to proceed in building political institutions was by gaining successful experience through various functional organizations concerned with military and economic cooperation. He acknowledged that there are those who feel that "we should be working to assure political unity at once, on the theory that the military and economic problems are more likely to fall into place if a federal mechanism is first set up. With these views I disagree." Despite this apparent conservatism of the gradualist approach, Herter enthusiastically endorsed the proposals that emerged from the Atlantic Convention, and he continued thereafter to speak out publicly in their behalf. The recommendations that he specifically advocated included the appointment of a special governmental commission of various NATO nations, charged with the task of formulating plans for the creation "of a true Atlantic Community, suitably organized to meet the challenge of this era"; the formation of a permanent High Council at the highest political level "to concert and plan, and in agreed cases to decide policy on matters of concern to the Community as a whole" (the Declaration of Paris of the Atlantic Convention added "by a weighted, qualified majority vote"), and capable of exercising its political decision making on such sensitive problems as those associated with "the sharing or usage of nuclear military capabilities"; the transformation of the unofficial NATO Parliamentarians' Conference into some sort of an official Atlantic Assembly with additional, consultative functions; and the establishment of an Atlantic High Court of Justice to decide legal controversies that might arise as a result of the growing network of contractual ties in the Atlantic Community.[59] These "moderate" proposals, in fact, contained a rather heady wine, and if they had been fully implemented, the Atlantic Community would have taken spectacular steps toward its political integration.

IN THE AFTERMATH OF THE
ATLANTIC CONVENTION

Immediately following the Atlantic Convention, in early February 1962, Rockefeller returned to the idea that he had raised during the 1960 campaign. In a series of three Harvard lectures he repeated many of the phrases he had used earlier about the obsolescence of the nation-state and the need for a grand design for integrating groupings of free nations. There was one significant variation, however. Instead of advocating "confederation," he explicitly shifted to the more ambitious goal of "federation," which, in the American experience, denoted a higher form of political integration. "The answer to the historic problems the free world confronts," he said, "can be found in the federal idea." Or again, he advocated that the United States take the leadership among all free peoples so as to make the underlying concepts and aspirations which were vainly sought in national sovereignty "truly meaningful through the federal approach."[60]

Given a measure of momentum and bipartisan support for the idea of strengthening the Atlantic Community, President Kennedy made his historic "declaration of interdependence" on the steps of Independence Hall at Philadelphia on July 4, 1962. This was not, to be sure, a plea for federation or Atlantic Union, but neither was it an outright rejection of this as an ultimate concept. Kennedy's words were framed in terms of the partnership idea. When he first launched this theme, on December 6, 1961, he carefully tailored his approach to the conservative nature of his audience, which happened to be a gathering of the National Association of Manufacturers. On that occasion, he specifically stressed that "I am *not* proposing—nor is it either necessary or desirable—that we join the Common Market." Neither was it envisioned that we "alter our concepts of political sovereignty."[61] But on the Fourth of July of the following year, Kennedy felt in a more expansive mood and spoke more boldly. He looked to a Europe that was hopefully merging into a new union and which could become "a partner with whom we could deal on a basis of full equality in all the great and burdensome tasks of building and defending a community of free nations." Such an Atlantic partnership, the President added, "would serve as a nucleus for the eventual union of all free men."[62] Nearly a year later Kennedy reaffirmed and refined his long-range vision while speaking before a European audience. "Let us go on," he urged, "from words to action, to intensify our efforts for still greater unity among us, to build new associations and institutions on those already established." He warned that "the Atlantic Community will not soon become a single overarching superstate. But practical steps toward stronger common purpose are well within our means." Political ties would "inevitably" be strengthened as the Atlantic nations widened their common efforts in defense and economics. "In the far future," Kennedy concluded, "there may be a new great union for us all."[63]

DE GAULLE AND VIETNAM

Between these two Kennedy speeches fell the long shadow of Charles de Gaulle. In January 1963 he abruptly halted the effort to enlarge the European Community by vetoing Britain's entry. Thereafter he increasingly sought to put sharp restrictions on the integrative process within the European Community itself. The prospects for the development of a vigorous European partner in Kennedy's Atlantic partnership scheme seemed very dim, and Kennedy's ultimate vision of Atlantic partnership evolving into "a new great union for us all" seemed hopelessly remote. In the Atlantic Alliance, de Gaulle scornfully rejected an American offer to create an Atlantic nuclear force, and French cooperation and participation in NATO, already greatly reduced, became largely symbolic in character until they ceased altogether.

On the other side of the Atlantic, American attention became increasingly preoccupied with the hopeless undertaking in Vietnam. The beginning measures of large-scale U.S. involvement under Kennedy mushroomed under Johnson, and with them came a growing estrangement of Europe from the United States. There were few in Europe who shared Johnson's zeal to solve the Vietnam problem by armed force, and so Europe was forced to search out its separate path of development. With the attention of U.S. officialdom consumed by the events in Southeast Asis, there was little propensity to give serious thought to Europe and the European-American relationship. Johnson's pledge, given in the halcyon days of 1961, that "the United States is resolved to do everything within its power—and I emphasize the word 'everything'—to enhance the strength and unity of the North Atlantic Community" had a hollow ring to it.

ATLANTIC UNIONISTS PERSIST IN THEIR EFFORTS

Despite the discouragement and apparent stagnation in the evolution of the Atlantic Community, a few voices continued to be heard reaffirming their belief in the goal of Atlantic Union. Both Nelson Rockefeller and Anthony Eden (who became the Earl of Avon in July 1961) reiterated their faith in the soundness of the federalist solution. Lord Avon made explicit that his earlier suggestion for a political general staff for the West was intended as an interim measure designed to lead to full political integration. In a trans-Atlantic television interview of July 1963, he said that for those nations that edge the Atlantic, "the only future really deserving of our efforts and our idealism is some form of Atlantic Union."[64] He repeated this sentiment in a declaration of November 1964.[65] On this same occasion Governor Rockefeller delivered an address devoted exclusively to Atlantic federation. He held that "the need for a viable political structure for the nations of the North Atlantic is no longer an issue that upsets or frightens the American people," and that with determined American initiatives aimed at "the goal of federal union, the orientation of national leaders here and abroad will change to such an extent that we will make progress toward the goal much faster than people generally think possible."[66]

In April 1965 Lord Avon again publicly endorsed Rockefeller's federalist proposals,[67] and in the beginning of 1966 he sought to relate the idea of Atlantic Union to U.S. global commitments. It was profoundly disquieting, Lord Avon held, for the United States to undertake far-flung burdens on its own. Nor was it healthy for America's allies, since once worldwide decisions taken in isolation had become a habit, the Western alliance would soon lose all vitality. It was therefore in the interests of all the leading Western powers to assume a proper share of the burden and global policy making. "Many of the free nations would, I believe, like to see Atlantic Union become something more than a pious aspiration. A federal political structure could be our declared objective. . . . For any country which refuses, I would leave an empty chair, always at its disposal, but I would not wait upon it."[68] In the following year Lord Avon urged the NATO powers "to accept federal union as their long-term political objective."[69]

Christian Herter also continued to affirm the validity of the goals and institutions elaborated in the Declaration of Paris. Testifying at a Senate hearing in the spring of 1966, Herter restated as his "conviction that in the long-run neither military alliances nor customs unions will survive without the cement of political institutions. This does not mean necessarily the exact type of union which we created here in the United States. It may well be something new based upon the needs of today's world, but it would likewise have to be based on some form of federal principles. The ties might well be looser and more flexible as between the different nations. They might well have to grow by degrees rather than by any single blueprint, but they should be part of our objective." Taking stock of the prospects for regaining a forward momentum, Herter registered his fear that "if the leadership does not come from us it will not come at all, and that the question will be too frequently asked in the future as to why we did not exercise a leadership which could well retrieve the hopeful beginning made toward Atlantic unity from drifting or being pushed by one nation [that is, France] into hopeless disunity."[70]

The proposal introduced into the Congress in October 1965 to establish a citizens' commission authorized to explore the question of Atlantic Union provided a means of focusing the opinions of American political leaders on this topic. In one sense this was an effort to resume the trans-Atlantic dialogue tentatively begun at the level of a citizens' commission in the Atlantic Convention of 1962. In another sense, however, the aim of the later resolution went beyond the earlier experiment. The 1962 Atlantic Convention was only authorized "to explore means by which greater cooperation and unity of purpose may be developed" among the NATO nations. The 1965 resolution explicitly directed the participants to explore the possibility of agreement on a declaration that the eventual goal of the NATO states would be to transform the Atlantic Alliance "into a federal union." Subsequent variations of the proposal held that the parliamentary democracies in NATO should explore the possibility of transforming "their present relationship into a more effective unity based on federal principles."[71] In all its forms, however, the various resolutions that were introduced in succeeding years all retained specific reference to federal union or federalism as the organizing principle.

Among the many endorsements the Atlantic Union resolution received, perhaps the most interesting, from the perspective of hindsight, was that of Richard Nixon. Testifying as a private citizen on September 1, 1966, Nixon asserted: "It is fitting that the United States, the world's first truly federal government, should be a main force behind the effort to find a basis for a broad federation of free Atlantic nations." He acknowledged that while "the accomplishment of the ultimate goal of the resolution may well be impossible to attain for many years, recent events of history and the numerous scientific and technological advances of the last twenty years point the way in this direction. It would be foolish for us to ignore the fact that science and history are even now fatefully combining to accomplish the same goal." Therefore the trans-Atlantic dialogue that the resolution anticipated would provide a resourceful tool for coping with the problems that lie ahead in a continually shrinking world. Nixon expressed regret at the renewed outburst of nationalism from Gaullist France that impeded the adoption of the federal principle among European states. But "by adopting a measure such as the Atlantic Union resolution, we could give new impetus to the spirit of federalism in Western Europe." Its effects would also spill over into the Atlantic Community. "To be sure," Nixon concluded, "the concept of an 'Atlantica' is at present only a dream, but in the age of rockets, dreams become reality with a speed which is difficult to imagine. The Atlantic Union resolution is a forward-looking proposal which acknowledges the depth and breadth of incredible change which is going on in the world around us. I urge its adoption."[72]

Among those who also gave their support to the Atlantic Union resolution and became prominent presidential candidates in the 1968 election were Senator Hubert Humphrey, Senator Eugene

McCarthy, and the late Senator Robert Kennedy among the Democrats, while Governor Rockefeller again joined Nixon among the Republicans.[73]

Nixon's election as President in 1968 would seem to have portended active presidential support for the passage of the Atlantic Union resolution. However, during Nixon's first term in office those who waited for a welcome word from the White House waited in vain. In 1970 Streit's Federal Union movement sought to elicit a positive response from Nixon by conferring an award upon him for his past work for the cause of Atlantic Union which, the award noted, went back as far as 1951 when as a Senator, Nixon had cosponsored the original Atlantic Union resolution in Congress. Nixon sent White House aide Robert Finch to the ceremony, bearing the President's words of support for "improving the relationships of the peoples of the Atlantic Community," and for exploring "new channels of constructive cooperation." Finch meticulously confined the President's sentiments to these generalities, while avoiding the mention of the goal of Atlantic Union or of federalism in the Atlantic Community. Finch then proceeded to give a speech on problems of the environment, which he also carefully did not relate to the idea of federal union.[74] Even the State Department continued to voice its opposition in congressional hearings to the Atlantic Union resolution during the first three years of Nixon's administration. Finally this came to an end in 1972.[75]

Perhaps in part because of the new State Department position, the 1972 congressional session saw the Atlantic Union resolution pass the Senate and the House Foreign Affairs Committee. However a tie vote in the House Rules Committee prevented it from being considered on the House floor.[76] In preparing for the reintroduction of the resolution in 1973, its chief advocate, Representative Paul Findley, at last succeeded in obtaining a somewhat ambiguous response from President Nixon, who supported the "concept" of Atlantic Union, while not endorsing the resolution itself. In a letter to Findley of March 10, 1973, Nixon stated: "As a goal and a concept I have favored Atlantic Union for many years, dating back to my service in the Congress. As President I have made it a policy not to give specific endorsement to resolutions of this kind, but I want you to know that my long-standing position on the concept and the goal which you are seeking to achieve through this resolution has not changed."[77] In short order the resolution again passed the Senate and the House Foreign Affairs Committee. Once again the resolution was not brought before the full House, which instead blocked its consideration on a procedural question by a vote of 210 to 197, with 26 votes paired.[78] And so the process had to begin all over again. Presumably the Congress might someday pass the Atlantic Union resolution. However, it is a long distance between the appointment of a citizens' commission to ponder the goal of Atlantic Union and the achievement of the goal itself.

President Nixon's resignation brought to power Gerald Ford, who had never recorded any views on the subject of Atlantic Union. However, President Ford's choice of Nelson Rockefeller as Vice-President put a long-time, articulate advocate of Atlantic federalism in the nation's second highest office. It will be interesting to observe whether Rockefeller will attempt to raise this issue in an official capacity or whether it will be neglected and overwhelmed by the day-to-day pressures and recurrent crises in foreign affairs.

Can one any more realistically think in terms of Atlantic federalism? A foremost exponent of the "realist" school of politics, Hans Morgenthau, could still declare at the height of Gaullist power, when the prospect seemed gloomiest: "Political 'Atlantic Union' . . . impossible to achieve at present," should nevertheless "be sought for a not too distant future."[79]

Taken on its merits as an abstract concept, there is much to be said for the idea of Atlantic Union. Yet perhaps it is an idea that came both too soon to be widely appreciated and accepted and too late to be implemented once it had been widely understood. Only the future can tell if it can ever be realized.

NOTES

1. Text of the Report of the Committee of Three, "Non-Military Cooperation in NATO," *NATO Letter*, Special Supplement, January 1, 1957, p. 5. The "Three Wise Men" consisted of Halvard Lange (Norway), Gaetano Martino (Italy), and Lester B. Pearson (Canada).

2. Henry A. Kissinger, *The Troubled Partnership* (New York, 1965), pp. 117-18.

3. Ibid., pp. 124-25.

4. Ibid, pp. 162-63. Similarly, in the judgment of Hans Morganthau, "a traditional alliance armed with nuclear weapons is politically obsolete." Hans J. Morganthau, "The Four Paradoxes of Nuclear Strategy," *American Political Science Review*, March 1964, p. 35. Also note Klaus Knorr's essay in Knorr, ed., *NATO and American Security* (Princeton, 1959), pp. 304-05, in which he recognizes that NATO is in need of a more centralized alliance, and that such a "high degree of interdependence is impossible without federation." This, however, he acknowledges is not now a practical proposition. George Stambuck's study, *American Military Forces Abroad* (Columbus, Ohio, 1963), pp. 172-81, likewise demonstrates that NATO's "jurisdiction is far too narrow to provide the necessary political foundation for its military machinery," and urges that the outmoded concept of national sovereignty give way to political federation.

5. Address by Under Secretary of State George W. Ball at Washington, D.C., April 26, 1963, Department of State Press Release No. 224, pp. 5, 8.

6. Text of the Report of the Committee of Three, op. cit., p. 5.

7. Ibid., p. 3.

8. The confusion of terms associated with the movement toward political union in Europe is examined in N. Schumacher, "A Lexicographer's Guide to Political Europe," *Journal of Common Market Studies*, June 1972, pp. 297-313.

9. Hans J. Morganthau, *The New Atlantic Community* (Bologna, 1961), pp. 7-9.

10. Robert Strausz-Hupé, "The Crisis of Political Leadership," in *NATO in Quest of Cohesion*, eds. Karl H. Cerny and Henry W. Briefs (New York, 1965), p. 145.

11. Address by Secretary of State Dean Rusk at Brussels, May 8, 1964, Department of State *Bulletin* 50, no. 1300: 811.

12. Quote is from a conversation with this writer on November 16, 1965.

13. "The Political Future of NATO" Michael de Grailly, rapporteur, Document 324, November 27, 1964, Assembly, WEU, *Proceedings*, December 1964, III, p. 191.

14. Hendrik Brugmans, "From Political Defense to World Leadership," *Atlantic Community Quarterly*, Summer 1964, p. 203.

15. Maurice Allais, "Toward an Integrated Atlantic Community," in Cerny and Briefs, op. cit., pp. 376-77.

16. Letters from Professor Allais of August 30 and September 22, 1965 to this writer, quoted with permission.

17. Allais, "Toward an Integrated Atlantic Community," in Cerny and Briefs, op. cit., p. 379.

18. John W. Holmes, "The Advantages of Diversity in NATO," in Cerny and Briefs, op. cit., p. 296.

19. See A. T. Mason and R. H. Leach, *In Quest of Freedom* (Englewood Cliffs, N.J., 1959), p. 131.

20. Clarence K. Streit, *Freedom & Union*, February 1964, pp. 4-5. Streit elaborated the greater strength of the Articles of Confederation, compared with the structure of NATO, in *Freedom's Frontier: Atlantic Union Now* (Washington, 1961), pp. 63-69.

21. Clarence K. Streit, "Atlantic Union," *NATO's Fifteen Nations*, October-November 1962, p. 18.

22. Clarence K. Streit, *Freedom & Union*, January 1965, p. 13.

23. *Freedom & Union*, February 1963, p. 29.

24. *Freedom & Union*, November 1962, pp. 3-4. Another variant of the idea of unequal votes in the second chamber is that "such a weighting of national representation might take into account certain factors other than population, such as relative contributions to the Community's budget." This formula would have to be "agreed upon when the Community was established," and "the representation to be accorded any new member in this house could then be determined in the negotiations leading to its accession." (*Strengthening the Free World Through Steps Toward Atlantic Unification*, Joint Statement by the National Planning Association Board of Trustees and Standing Committees, Special Report, No. 63 [Washington, D.C., 1966], pp. 9-10.) Such a formula might prove difficult to arrive at and then to maintain in view of the constant fluctuations in national budgets.

25. Livingston Hartley, *Atlantic Challenge* (New York, 1965), pp. 83-85.

26. Pierre Uri, "Economic Dimensions of Atlantic Partnership," in Cerny and Briefs, op. cit., p. 347. See also the exchange between Uri, Streit et al., pp. 112-122.

27. Clarence K. Streit, *Freedom & Union*, November 1966, p. 4.

28. Klaus Epstein's review of Streit's *Freedom's Frontier: Atlantic Union Now* in *The New Leader*, July 3, 1961, p. 24.

29. Amitai Etzioni, "The Dialectics of Supranational Unification," *American Political Science Review*, December 1962, pp. 928-29.

30. Ibid, p. 930. See also Amitai Etzioni, "European Unification: A Strategy of Change," *World Politics*, October 1963, pp. 32-51, where he demonstrates that the strategy for a limited, not an overly ambitious, plan for supranational integration has brought greater success.

31. Clarence K. Streit, *Freedom & Union*, April-May 1963, p. 3 (italics added). See also *Freedom & Union*, November 1963, p. 16, where Streit called for a constitutional convention to create an Atlantic federal government and then to assign "to this government the task of working out, as a whole, the gradual transition to complete Union in the various inter-related fields to be given it, and fixing a definite time-table for the attainment of each of these objectives."

32. Senate Concurrent Resolution 64, 89th Cong., 1st sess., October 18, 1965, reprinted in *Freedom & Union*, November 1965, pp. 12-13. On the subsequent versions of this Atlantic Union resolution that were introduced into the Congress, see *Freedom & Union*, March 1967, pp. 12-17; April 1967, pp. 3-4; April-May 1968, p. 5; June-July 1969, p. 6; May 1970, p. 15; March 1971, p. 4; August 1971, p. 3; October 1971, p. 2; August-September 1972, p. 4; January-February 1973, p. 18.

33. Clarence K. Streit, *Freedom & Union*, December 1964, p. 26.

34. For an account of the divisions of opinion within the American organizations working for Atlantic Union, see Istvan Szent-Miklosy, *The Atlantic Union Movement* (New York, 1965).

35. For a detailed history and an evaluation of its operations, see Walter Yondorf, "Monnet and the Action Committee," *International Organization*, Autumn 1965, pp. 885-912.

36. Alfred Grosser, "Bilan Politique des relations Franco-Allemandes," *Allemagne* (Bulletin bimestriel d'information du Comite Francais d'echanges avec l'Allemagne nouvelle), August-September 1962, p. 1. See also Alfred Grosser, *The Colossus Again: Western Germany from Defeat to Rearmament* (New York, 1955), pp. 232-36.

37. Karl W. Deutsch et al., *Political Community and the North Atlantic Area* (Princeton, N.J., 1957), p. 166.

38. Ibid., p. 201.

39. Address by Governor Nelson Rockefeller at Binghamton, N.Y., June 21, 1960, in *Freedom & Union*, July-August 1960, p. 6.

40. Statement by Governor Nelson Rockefeller prepared for delivery before the Platform Committee of the Republican National

Committee at Chicago, July 19, 1960 (mimeo), p. 3. See also the New York *Times*, July 10, 1960, for a preliminary memorandum on the same subject.

41. Rockefeller-Nixon Accord of July 23, 1960, New York *Times*, July 24, 1960. For a perceptive appraisal, see the comments by James Reston, New York *Times*, July 25, 1960.

42. C. L. Sulzberger, New York *Times*, October 22, 1960.

43. Address by Vice President Lyndon Johnson at Paris, April 6, 1961, Department of State *Bulletin* 44, no. 1139: 581-83.

44. Address by Jean Monnet at Dartmouth College, Hanover, N.H., June 11, 1961, p. 8 (mimeo). This passage is reprinted in Jean Monnet, "A Ferment of Change," *Journal of Common Market Studies* 1, no. 3 (1962): 209.

45. Address by Sir Anthony Eden at Yorkshire, June 10, 1961, p. 3 (mimeo).

46. J. W Fulbright, "For a Concert of Free Nations," *Foreign Affairs*, October 1961, p. 12.

47. Address of Senator J. William Fulbright at Stanford University, July 28, 1961, p. 6 (mimeo). The same idea, somewhat revised, appears in Fulbright's October 1961 *Foreign Affairs* article, p. 17.

48. Federal Defense Minister Franz-Josef Strauss, "Towards an 'Atlantic Federation' "? *The Bulletin*, Press and Information Office of the German Federal Government, February 14, 1961; reprinted from *Aussenpolitik*, February 1961.

49. Address by Willy Brandt at New York, March 17, 1961, *Columbia University Graduate Faculties Newsletter*, May 1961, p. 4.

50. Testimony of Congressman Paul Findley, *Freedom & Union*, August 1971, p. 8.

51. Address by Federal Defense Minister Franz-Josef Strauss at Georgetown University, November 27, 1961, pp. 19-20 (mimeo). The same passage, translated somewhat differently, is reprinted in *Survival*, January-February 1962, p. 8.

52. Karl W. Deutsch, Lewis J. Edinger, Roy C. Macrides, and Richard L. Merritt, *France, Germany and the Western Alliance* (New York, 1967), pp. 160-61.

53. Address by McGeorge Bundy at Chicago, December 6, 1961, in *Freedom & Union*, January 1962, pp. 10-11.

54. Address by President John F. Kennedy at New York, December 6, 1961, Department of State *Bulletin* 45, no. 1174: 1039-47.

55. Federal Defense Minister Franz-Josef Strauss, "How East and West Can Meet in Europe," *The Bulletin*, Press and Information Office of the German Federal Government, June 26, 1962, p. 4.

56. Franz-Josef Strauss, *The Grand Design* (London, 1965), pp. 103-04.

57. See the Clayton-Herter Report, *A New Look at Foreign Economic Policy*, transmitted on October 23, 1961 to the Subcommittee on Foreign Economic Policy of the Joint Economic Committee of the Congress of the United States, (Washington, D.C.: U.S. Government Printing Office, 1961).

58. Address by Christian A. Herter at the Atlantic Convention, Paris, January 8, 1962, in *Freedom & Union*, February-March 1962, pp. 21-22. This issue of *Freedom & Union* contains the most complete printed record of the Convention's proceedings. See also the report, *United States Citizens Commission on NATO*, referred June 18, 1962 to the House Committee on Foreign Affairs, House Document, No. 433, 87th Cong. 2d sess., (Washington, D.C.: U.S. Government Printing Office, 1962).

59. Christian A. Herter, "Atlantica," *Foreign Affairs*, January 1963, pp. 305-08.

60. Nelson A. Rockefeller, *The Future of Federalism* (Cambridge, Mass., 1962), pp. 69, 74. See also Nelson A. Rockefeller, *Unity, Freedom and Peace* (New York, 1968), pp. 133-36, 143-48, for a somewhat muted restatement of these ideas.

61. Address by President John F. Kennedy at New York, December 6, 1961, Department of State *Bulletin* 45, no. 1174: 1046.

62. Address by President John F. Kennedy at Philadelphia, July 4, 1962, Department of State *Bulletin* 47, no. 1204: 132-33.

63. Address by President John F. Kennedy at Frankfurt, June 25, 1963, Department of State *Bulletin* 49, no. 1256: 122-23.

64. Transcript of Telstar interview, July 10, 1963, in *Freedom & Union*, September 1963, p. 6.

65. Message of the Earl of Avon, sent to a convocation of Federal Union, Inc., Philadelphia, November 20, 1964, in *Freedom & Union*, December 1964, pp. 7-8.

66. Address by Governor Nelson A. Rockefeller at Philadelphia, November 20, 1964, in *Freedom & Union*, December 1964, pp. 22.

67. Address by the Earl of Avon at Boston, April 20, 1965, in *Freedom & Union*, June 1965, pp. 17-18.

68. Anthony Eden, Earl of Avon, "The Burden of Leadership," *Foreign Affairs*, January 1966, pp. 235-38.

69. Anthony Eden, Earl of Avon, " 'Prize is Enormous' If NATO Adopts Federal Goal," *Freedom & Union*, June 1967, p. 16.

70. Testimony of Christian A. Herter, May 5, 1966, *Hearings before the Subcommittee on National Security and International Operations*, U.S. Senate, 89th Cong., 2d sess., Part 2 (Washington, D.C., 1966), p. 40.

71. For the different texts of the Atlantic Union resolutions, see note 32 supra.

72. Statement of Richard M. Nixon, September 1, 1966, *Hearings before the Committee on Foreign Affairs*, House of Representatives, 89th Cong., 2d sess., on Pending Resolutions to Establish an Atlantic Union Delegation (Washington, D.C., 1966), p. 161.

73. *Freedom & Union*, April-May 1968, pp. 3-6.

74. *Freedom & Union*, November-December 1970, pp. 8-14.

75. *Freedom & Union*, January-February 1972, p. 2.

76. *Freedom & Union*, August-September 1972, pp. 3-8.

77. *Congressional Record*, March 15, 1973, p. E1613.

78. *Congressional Record*, April 10, 1973, p. H2563.

79. Hans J. Morgenthau, "The Crisis of the Alliance," in Cerny and Briefs, op. cit., p. 134.

CHAPTER
2

THE POLITICS OF
FRAGMENTATION:
DE GAULLE
THE DISINTEGRATOR

While many voices have been raised in the cause of greater cohesion in the Atlantic Community, the actual policies pursued by the various nations tend to reflect the inescapable fact that the Atlantic Community is still composed of independent states, each giving priority to their individual concerns. No nation has been free of the politics of fragmentation. It is inevitable that the diverse forces of nationalism remain strong despite the obvious need to tame them for the common good, since all of modern history has conspired to entrench national interests above those of a wider community of nations.

It would be a mistake, however, to equate the nationalistic strivings of the policy-making elites in the various countries of the Atlantic Community.

There is no doubt that Britain too long lived in the dream world of the past, hoping to continue playing a lone hand as a great world power. As a result it passed up numerous opportunities to take the leadership in creating a European federation in which it would have merged many of its sovereign prerogatives. It is true that the arguments advanced by the Conservative government of the early 1960s to justify the British nuclear deterrent had a Gaullist ring to them. Yet Britain did apply for membership in the European Community, however belatedly, and it did commit its national nuclear force to NATO. De Gaulle, on the other hand, not only kept Britain out of the European Community, but he tried to strip its institutions of their unique communitarian or federalizing attributes.

And de Gaulle hardly assigned his *force de frappe* to NATO. Instead, he sought to disrupt the functioning of NATO and drove NATO headquarters out of France.

The United States has been generous in supporting and urging the European states to merge their sovereignties in a European Union, but it has been noticeably lacking in enthusiasm toward suggestions that American sovereignty be merged in some larger political entity. At the height of Gaullist power in 1965, Alastair Buchan asked: "After a decade and a half in which European governments have been regularly told that this or that measure of Atlantic integration or U.S. self-restraint cannot be contemplated because the Congress or the Middle West or the U.S. aircraft industry or the farmers wouldn't stand for it, is it really surprising, that European governments should be disillusioned with the prospects of an Atlantic Community and be considering alternatives?"[1] The revival of nationalism in the different European countries and the general search for European self-assertion unquestionably feed on expressions of American nationalism. Conversely, the surest way to undercut the dangers of nationalism in Europe is by reducing the American inclination to go it alone. In sum, the integration of the Atlantic Community depends, in great measure, upon the willingness of the United States to share its political power, as well as its burdens.

THE UNIQUE QUALITY OF GAULLIST NATIONALISM

Recognizing the shortcomings in U.S. policy, can one say that the nationalism of Gaullist France was merely reactive in nature? Or was there not a qualitative difference between American and French nationalism? Did the nationalist manifestations of American policy spring from a strident, consciously chauvinistic search for the mystique of national glory and grandeur, or did they arise largely out of the possession of enormous power and the capacity to act independently, supported by the illusion that such independent, unilateral acts enhanced the security of the United States? The hallmark of Gaullist France has certainly been the independent, unilateral act, although it must surely appear less convincing than similar American behavior, since the much smaller power base of France limited de Gaulle's credibility in conducting a meaningful independent policy. But beyond this, de Gaulle's nationalism systematically glorified the nation-state in theory, as well as in practice. This raised a formidable ideological barrier against the gradual erosion of national sovereignty, which concrete collaboration among allies might otherwise quietly encourage.

Although in many practical respects the United States has yet been unwilling to merge its sovereignty in Atlantic Community institutions, responsible American spokesmen have tried to mitigate the effects of nationalism by repeatedly pointing out that for the mature states of the West the age of the nation-state is over. It is true that U.S. policy makers have applied this concept in the first instance and with greater force to the nations of Western Europe, but President Kennedy did talk in terms of partnership with Europe and held out the long-range prospect that "there may be a new great union for us all." It would be a misreading of an important part of high-level U.S. policy to ignore the genuinely creative impulses in some of the theorizing about the development of the Atlantic Community. "While Atlantic language can be used to rationalize American hegemonial tendencies," an Oxford scholar noted, "it can also be used to restrain them: the concept of partnership, in particular, is a double-edged sword. . . . Many of the American 'Atlanticists' are best viewed, not as rationalizers of special American interests, but as innovators groping toward a concept of a new form of an international association."[2]

De Gaulle, of course, was not the sole cause of disunity in the West, but during his ascendence in the Elyseé he nonetheless presented the principal obstacle to the development of the Atlantic Community. While he did not have the capability for undertaking great constructive action, he undeniably achieved sufficient power to arrest progress toward further integrative measures. In 1964, for example, a high NATO official was cited as saying that of the 27 urgent, unresolved problems in NATO planning, 22 related directly to the obstructionist policies of de Gaulle.[3] This might perhaps serve as a rough index to the dimensions of the problem de Gaulle posed for his partners in the Atlantic Alliance.

DeGaulle cared not at all for the Atlantic Community. He cared only for France, and for bringing France into the "front rank" of world powers. Lyricizing about France in the typical romantic tradition of nineteenth-century nationalism, the opening lines of de Gaulle's memoirs revealed that his image of France was "inspired by sentiment as much as by reason. The emotional side of me tends to imagine France, like the princess in the fairy stories or the Madonna in the frescoes as dedicated to an exalted and exceptional destiny. . . . France is not really herself unless she is in the front rank. . . . In short, to my mind, France cannot be France without greatness."[4]

These much-quoted words could indeed serve as an accurate guide to all of de Gaulle's thought and action. From them flowed his unalterable commitment to the nation-state as the only valid building block in world politics and to the dominant role he thought the French nation was destined to play in organizing and leading lesser nations that happen to be grouped around her.

De Gaulle's words bear close scrutiny on several accounts. His rule was so intensely personal in nature that the clues to French policies were, in fact, found in his utterances. In his autocratic style of rule, even his most senior ministers very often were kept in ignorance of a Gaullist policy declaration until the moment before it was made public. His texts also provide an impressive continuity of recurrent political themes that remained essentially unchanged over a period of many decades, beginning perhaps most conspicuously with the publication of *The Edge of the Sword* in 1932.

A "EUROPEAN EUROPE"—THE ARBITER IN WORLD POLITICS

Two of these themes directly affected Gaullist policy toward the Atlantic Community. One consisted of de Gaulle's image of a small continental Western European bloc of states maneuvering its way between the United States and the United Kingdom on the one hand and the Soviet empire on the other. The second was the longer-range Gaullist vision of the organization of a greater European bloc extending across Eastern Europe and into the heart of Russia, which would presumably become possible with the withering away of Communist rule. Significantly, the United States and Britain were also excluded from this grand design. "When all is said and done," de Gaulle remarked in 1940, "Great Britain is an island; France the cape of a continent; American another world."[5] In effect, there was no image of an emergent Atlantic Community reaching from the continent across the English Channel and across the Atlantic Ocean.

Whatever collaboration France had undertaken in this direction, in the Gaullist view, was forced upon it because of the temporary military threat arising from the East. De Gaulle consistently aimed to release France from its Atlantic ties and turn it toward his concept of Europe, both small and large, at the earliest moment he judged expedient.

De Gaulle's striving to formulate an independent continental European bloc was evident from the moment Hitler invaded the Soviet Union in June 1941. Even though France was languishing in defeat and occupation, de Gaulle recorded his hopes for the future. He acknowledged that "a victory in which the Soviets would have taken a major share might well, *ipso facto*, face the world with other perils later. . . . At the same time her presence in the allied camp brought Fighting France a balancing element over against the Anglo-Saxons of which I was determined to make use."[6] Here in capsule form was de Gaulle's frank statement of intentions, which he hoped to implement once France had regained the power to play a prime role in world politics: France was to lead a grouping of European states that could pursue independent policies by playing off the Soviets against what, in his simplistic terminology, he called "the Anglo-Saxons."*

Speaking in Algiers in March 1944, prior to the allied invasion of the continent, de Gaulle outlined his view of his French-led European coalition, which he called "a sort of Western group." This would constitute a major world center for production, trade, and security.

---

*"In his references to Britons and Americans, de Gaulle termed them 'the Anglo-Saxons' which, curiously enough, was Hitler's terminology." Among the inhabitants of the United Kingdom, one wonders how de Gaulle accounted for the Normans, originally French-speaking, who conquered the Anglo-Saxons in 1066, or for the non-Anglo-Saxon Scots, Welsh, Irish, and others. When one considers the melting pot of national strains in the United States, the Gaullist designation was even more absurd. Ambassador Murphy, who worked closely with de Gaulle in Algiers in 1943, provided an interesting first-hand assessment of de Gaulle's basic attitude toward the United States. "I formed an opinion of de Gaulle as an ardent French patriot, but I never regarded him as a close friend of my country. I did not find that he then was a great admirer of American military or political sagacity. He knew little of the United States or of Americans and it seemed to me that he was cynical in his appraisal of how the United States could be 'played' vis-a-vis the Soviet Union and Europe for the benefit of France."[7]

Its arteries would be the Channel, the Rhine, and the Mediterranean, although its influence would be extended throughout Africa and the Orient.[8] Following the liberation of France, de Gaulle used the occasion of Churchill's visit to Paris in November 1944 to propose a Western grouping of nations built around an Anglo-French core. De Gaulle acknowledged that France would "not regain her former power all at once," and therefore, it was in need of allies, while British power would be diminished because of war losses "and, particularly the rise of America and Russia, not to mention China!" If France and Britain could act together they could establish "the equilibrium of Europe" and guarantee peace along the Rhine as well as uphold the independence of the Vistula, Danube, and Balkan states. This would be "an organization of nations which will be something more than an arena for disputes between America and Russia." De Gaulle implored Churchill to "come to an agreement in order to uphold these interests. If you are willing to do so, I am ready. Our two nations will follow us. America and Russia, hobbled by their rivalry, will not raise any objection." Churchill refused to abandon the British connection with the United States, and so de Gaulle's project did not materialize. "In politics as in strategy," Churchill replied, "it is better to persuade the stronger than to pit yourself against him. That is what I am trying to do. . . . I have formed a close personal tie with Roosevelt. With him I proceed by suggestion in order to influence matters in the right direction."[9]

Rebuffed in his effort to separate Britain from the United States, de Gaulle immediately sought to find a counterweight against what he imagined were the pretentions of "Anglo-American hegemony." In December 1944 he flew to Moscow to conclude a Franco-Soviet Treaty. "Perhaps it would be possible," de Gaulle speculated, "to renew old Franco-Russian solidarity which, though repeatedly betrayed and repudiated, remained no less a part of the natural order of things, as much in relation to the German menace as to endeavors of Anglo-American hegemony." It was his hope that "the signing of a Franco-Russian Treaty could help us to participate at once in the elaboration of European settlements."[10]

Immediately following the allied military victory in 1945, de Gaulle considered that "the hour for settling accounts had come." Now "it seemed likely that the new period would allow me to achieve the great plans I had conceived for my country. . . . I intended," de Gaulle explained with explicit candor, "to cooperate with East and

West and if need be contract the necessary alliances on one side or the other without ever accepting any kind of dependency." He further intended "to persuade the states along the Rhine, the Alps, and the Pyrenees to form a political, economic and strategic bloc; to establish this organization as one of the three world powers and, should it become necessary, as the arbiter between the Soviet and Anglo-American camps. Since 1940 my every word and act had been dictated to establishing these possibilities; now that France was on her feet again, I tried to realize them"[11] This justly famous statement of intentions represented perhaps the sharpest formulation of the Gaullist ambition: To lead a continental European bloc that could become the arbiter between the Soviet and the Anglo-American camps. Needless to say, there was no hint of any interest in the concept of the Atlantic Community.

Even after France had joined NATO, and de Gaulle periodically affirmed the need for allied solidarity against Soviet military threats, he nevertheless maintained his vision of a separate continental European bloc whose existence might be endangered by the rivalry between the Soviet and Anglo-American camps. In 1958 he conjured up the spectacle of the sinister interplay between the "Anglo-Saxons and the Soviets" that could obliterate Europe. He asked himself: "What was to prevent them [the United States and the Soviet Union] from dropping their bombs in between their two countries, in other words on Central and Western Europe?" And so de Gaulle concluded, "for the Western Europeans, NATO had thus ceased to guarantee their survival."[12] When de Gaulle met with President Eisenhower in September 1959 he asserted: "For Russia and America the deterrent is real. But it does not exist for their respective allies. What, after all, is there to prevent Russia and America from wiping out what lies between their own vitals, in other words the European battlefield?" De Gaulle then asked a totally incredulous Eisenhower, "is this not, in fact, what NATO is preparing for?"[13]

De Gaulle proceeded to air this fantasy that bordered on paranoia in public when at a press conference in November 1959 he asked:

Who can say whether, in the future, if basic political facts should change completely, as has already occurred on the earth, the two powers that would have a monopoly on nuclear weapons might not make a deal with each other to divide the world between them. Who can say whether, should the occasion arise, while each side might follow a policy of not hurling its devices at the principal adversary, so as not to be threatened by them itself—who can say whether the two rivals might not crush others. One can well imagine, for example, that on such a terrible occasion, Western Europe might be destroyed from Moscow, and Central Europe from Washington. And who even can say whether the two rivals, as a result of some unforeseeable political and social upheaval, will not come to the point of uniting?[14]

De Gaulle publicly raised the spectre of this unholy alliance again in 1963,[15] and once again in 1967.[16] Even though France was legally a member of the Atlantic Alliance, de Gaulle thus repeatedly found it possible to consider France as standing apart equally from both camps. The prospect of superpower collusion not only envisaged the complete faithlessness of the United States to its European allies, but also conceivably implied the abandonment of several hundred thousand American soldiers who were deployed along forward positions of the Central European front in Germany. One could perhaps argue that de Gaulle had assumed that America's disinterest in its European allies would have prompted Washington to have removed its troops from the continent, so that the United States would only be guilty of betraying its partners in NATO Europe. However these Gaullist prophecies might be deciphered, one idea stood forth: In de Gaulle's view there was no firm and unbreakable bond holding Europe and the United States together; or conversely, Europe must always be prepared to maneuver on its own between two hostile camps and seek to insure its own survival with its own completely independent means.

The extent to which official French pronouncements equated American and Soviet behavior and ambitions was really quite startling. Gaullist Premier Michel Debré drew such a comparison before the National Assembly in October 1960: "It will undoubtedly be said that the destiny of the world is in the hands of the greatest powers—the United States and Russia. But what is notable is their inability to impose their will universally. In the East as in the West, we are witnessing the development of the phase in which the greatest empires see their power confronted by limitations." In this view both the United States and the Soviet Union were equally credited with seeking great empires. However, their failure to realize their designs "is what gives the second-ranking powers—to which we belong, but which are aware of their past role and of their future responsibilities—the opportunity to exercise their influence in the direction of progress and of peace."[17] De Gaulle reiterated this theme in his press conference of July 23, 1964 when he held that "the division of the world into two camps led by Washington and Moscow respectively corresponds less and less to the real situation. . . . It appears that Europe, provided that it wishes it, is henceforth called upon to play a role which is its own." For France "it is a question of Europe's being made in order for it to be European. A European Europe means that it exists by itself for itself."[18]

The impact of de Gaulle's "European Europe" was not to be confined to Europe. By disassociating France from what he called "the two hegemonies" of the United States and the Soviet Union, de Gaulle hoped to appeal to the wide-spread neutralist sentiment in the "third world." He repeatedly held up France as the model showing the way to a new global balance of power that was especially applicable to the countries of Latin America, Asia, and Africa.[19] In third world countries where U.S. and Communist policies came into conflict, de Gaulle offered himself, to use his own words, as "a free arbiter."[20]

DE GAULLE AND ATLANTIC UNION

The idea of acting as an arbiter in the global struggle between "the two hegemonies," in which Europe would exist "by itself for itself," implicitly rejected the concept of a strengthened Atlantic Community or an Atlantic federation. This might appear to labor the obvious, were it not for the quaint interpretation of Gaullist thought by Clarence Streit, who persistently saw de Gaulle as a potential supporter of Atlantic Union. Such wishful thinking was based upon reported private expressions of support of Atlantic Union from several anonymous but highly placed Gaullists, as well as upon one passage in de Gaulle's press conference of May 15, 1962.[21] Upon that occasion de Gaulle rejected the proposal to transform the Six of the European Community into a supranational entity. "Such an entity cannot be found without their being in Europe today a federator with sufficient power, authority and skill." Such an integrated Europe would drain the national will of each state so that there would be "no France and no Europe," since in his view such a Europe would be incapable of "making any policies at all. But then, perhaps, this world would follow the lead of some outsider who did have a policy. There would perhaps be a federator, but the federator would not be European. And it would not be an integrated Europe, it would be something quite different, much broader and much more extensive with, I repeat, a federator."[22]

This Delphic pronouncement, to be sure, was open to various interpretations. From it Streit concluded that "in his press conference of May 15, 1962, President de Gaulle indicated that he considered Atlantic federation more realistic than a European one" if only the United States, as the outside "federator," would take the initiative in proposing an Atlantic Union.[23] A more likely interpretation was that, to an ardent nationalist like de Gaulle, the idea of federation was totally abhorrent, and an outside "federator" was synonomous with an external conqueror. Such a suspicion was confirmed in a subsequent press conference when de Gaulle returned to this theme. He decried the "concept of a European federation in which, according to the dreams of those who conceived it, the countries would lose their national personalities, and in which, furthermore, for want of a federator—such as in the West, Caesar and his successors, Charlemagne, Otto I, Charles V, Napoleon and Hitler tried to be, each in his fashion, and such as, in the East, Stalin tried to be—would be ruled by some technocratic, stateless and irresponsible Areopagus. We also know that France is opposing this project."[24] That is, de Gaulle rejected rule by the "stateless technocrats" in Brussels, while he equated Streit's image of the United States as an outside "federator" with intervention by a Hitler or a Stalin.

There was, in fact, ample explicit evidence about how de Gaulle viewed the Atlantic Community. One of the reasons he gave for rejecting the British application to the Common Market was that British entry would open the way for the accession of other states in the Atlantic Community.

We would then have to envisage the construction of another Common Market. But the 11-member, then 13-member, then perhaps 18-member Common Market that would be built would, without any doubt, hardly resemble the one the Six have built. Moreover, this Community, growing in that way, would be confronted with all the problems of its economic relations with a crowd of other states, and first of all with the United States. It is foreseeable that the cohesion of all its members, who would be very numerous and very diverse, would not hold for long and that in the end there would appear a colossal Atlantic Community under American dependence and leadership which would soon completely swallow up the European Community.

Such an outcome, de Gaulle concluded, "is not at all what France wanted," which was to build "a strictly European construction."[25]

On a later occasion de Gaulle echoed that France "cannot and does not wish to see either the nascent economy of Europe or its own dissolved in a system of a type of Atlantic Community which would only be a new form of that famous integration."[26] He also returned to an attack upon the advocates of a supranational Europe, whom he continued to identify as partisans of an Atlantic Community. De Gaulle claimed that they argued: "No European Union, without its being incorporated into an Atlantic Community. Yet it is clear," he protested, "that not one of the peoples of Europe would allow its destiny to be handed over to an assembly composed mainly of foreigners. In any case this is true for France." The result of such a course would be "to merge the policy of Europe in a multilateral Atlantic policy" and this "would be tantamount to Europe's having no policy itself."[27]

To leave no doubt about the issue, de Gaulle's Ambassador in Washington explained that "what we do not believe desirable or possible . . . is that either in the military, economic or political field, the Atlantic Alliance should lead to a fusion of Euorpe and of America, in which we would lose our individuality little by little. An 'Atlantic Community' or an 'Atlantic federation' would necessitate giving up part of our sovereignty. And I believe that none of our nations would accept that for many years to come."[28]

DE GAULLE'S SINGULAR ATLANTIC POLICY

It would not be wholly true to say that de Gaulle had no Atlantic policy, since in one special case he tried to cultivate an intimate trans-

Atlantic tie. De Gaulle used the occasion of his visit to the French-speaking Canadian province of Quebec in July 1967 to cry out: *"Vive le Quebec libre! Vive le Canada francais! Vive la France!"* Exciting the Quebec separatist sentiment that sought to recognize Quebec as a separate and distinct nation, de Gaulle repeatedly used the favorite separatist slogan *"maître chez nous"*—"to become masters in our own house."[29] The astonishment and outrage of the Canadian government caused de Gaulle to cancel his scheduled visit to Ottawa and to beat a hasty retreat to Paris. Upon returning home the French government issued a communique that stated: "General de Gaulle told the French Canadians and their government clearly that France intended to help them to reach the objectives of liberation that they themselves have set."[30] The official Canadian reply came from Prime Minister Lester Pearson: "The people of Canada are free. Every province of Canada is free. Canadians do not need to be liberated. Indeed, many thousands of Canadians gave their lives in two World Wars in the liberation of France and other European countries."[31]

Not content to leave matters there, de Gaulle elaborated his singular Atlantic policy in a press conference of November 27, 1967. Reciting his version of the history of the French Canadians, de Gaulle asserted: "The fact is that a French nation, a piece of our people, is appearing today in Canada and wishing to be recognized and treated as such. . . . They aspire to become masters of their destiny. . . . All this makes the movement of emancipation that has seized the French people from across the Atlantic perfectly understandable and also shows that nothing is more natural than the impetus that at the same time makes it turn toward France." De Gaulle then made explicit the elements in his trans-Atlantic policy: French assistance in the dismemberment of Canada and the organization of a French trans-Atlantic bond. "That Quebec be free is indeed what is at issue." In order to liberate Quebec, "two conditions are necessary: the first entails a complete change regarding the Canadian structure . . . which created the federation. In my opinion, this will necessarily result in the advent of Quebec to the rank of a sovereign state. . . . The second condition, on which depends the solution to these great problems, is that the solidarity of the French community on both sides of the Atlantic become organized."[32] Prime Minister Pearson promptly arose in the House of Commons in rebuttal. De Gaulle's "statement distorted some Canadian history, misrepresented developments and wrongly predicted the future." Consequently, de Gaulle's intervention was "intolerable," and Canada was in no need of outside instruction. "Self-determination is no new discovery for us. We do not need to have it offered to us."[33]

These Gaullist initiatives were all the more extraordinary in view of the second theme de Gaulle repeatedly enunciated in his dealings with the Canadians, namely, fight the danger of American intervention in Canadian affairs. According to this double standard, de Gaulle was telling the Canadians: Resist American, but welcome French inroads on Canadian sovereignty. In a series of acts that followed, Paris sought to treat Quebec as a sovereign power by dealing directly with French Canadian spokesmen without first going through Ottawa.[34] The sum total of these efforts was to aggravate a Canadian domestic problem and embitter the foreign relations between Ottawa and Paris.

DE GAULLE THE ARCHITECT OF WESTERN EUROPE

Aside from this aberrant case of Atlanticism that, in essence, was another instance of the glorification of French nationalism, de Gaulle concentrated his efforts upon reshaping Europe in his own image. How did he appriase the prospects for organizing a totally independent Europe? De Gaulle early recognized the formidable obstacles to the creation of a lasting and cohesive grouping of sovereign states. Writing in 1932, he depicted states in a condition of perpetual conflict. "Is it really likely that the present balance of power will remain unchanged so long as the small want to become great, the strong to dominate the weak, the old to live on?" To him "the root cause of armed conflict in men and in nations" is "passion and self-interest," and who could imagine that "human nature will ever become something other than it is?" There could be temporary truces and solemn pledges to abide by a common code, but such arrangements would be built on foundations of sand. "Even supposing that nations should agree, for a time, to conduct their mutual relations in accordance with a sovereign code, how effective could such a code be?" he asked. " 'Laws unsupported by force soon fall into contempt,' said Cardinal de Retz. International agreements will be of little value unless there are troops to prevent their infringement."[35]

Such a Machiavellian assessment of man's nature and the behavior of states might have given excessive weight to the role of force, but there was at least a clear recognition of the difficulties standing in the way of forming an enduring and effective organization among sovereign states. Logically one might conclude that the only way to escape from this basic condition of anarchy was by creating a new and a larger community of nations that would be based upon enforceable law, capable of transcending the old parochial sovereignties. But this was not de Gaulle's answer.

From his earliest days de Gaulle imbibed the assumptions of nationalism as if they were tenets of religious dogma. It is precisely here that de Gaulle entrapped himself. On the one hand he declared: "To build Europe, that is to say, to unite it, is evidently something essential." On the other hand he asked: "Now what are the realities of Europe? What are the pillars on which it can be built? The States are, in truth, certainly very different from one another, each of which has its own spirit, its own history, its own language, its misfortunes, glories and ambitions; but these States are the only entities that have a right to order and the authority to act. To imagine that something can be built that would be effective for action and that would be approved by the peoples outside and above the States—this is a dream"[36] Ridiculing those who would wish to build some sort of a supranational or federal Europe, de Gaulle announced that "there cannot be any other Europe than a Europe of States, apart, of course, from myths, stories and parades."[37]

One was entitled to ask: Who was immersed in dreams and myths? How exactly could a "Europe" be built that would assume complete responsibility for its own destiny, and play the role of arbiter between the "two hegemonies," when the only real political entities in Europe were the separate national states? What in fact would this "Europe" amount to, except a repetition of the classic nationalist strivings in which "the small want to become great, the strong to dominate the weak, the old to live on"? What magic, automatic harmony of interest would bind together a conglomeration of separate states that were caught up in their traditional power rivalries and instabilities? As a strident nationalist de Gaulle demonstrated his ability to activate nationalist ambitions that have been destructive of efforts to build broader communities of nations both in Europe and the Atlantic area. By the same token, as a strident nationalist de Gaulle demonstrated his total inability to construct a "European Europe," or, indeed, any kind of Europe.

Within France de Gaulle's authoritarian nationalism found fertile ground upon which it could blossom. From its position as a first-rate power in 1939, France suffered a series of unmitigated disasters: defeat, occupation, humiliation, and finally emergence on the side of the winners in World War II without itself really being a winner, and then the frustrations of losing an empire in Southeast Asia and Africa, which debilitated the country and brought it to the brink of civil war. It was not difficult to grasp the nature of de Gaulle's appeal when he returned to power in 1958. The mystique of his nationalism, emphasizing the traditional sources of French prestige, made the retreat from empire seem like a triumph of French grandeur and the restoration of national glory. His self-proclaimed image as the living incarnation and the symbol of the French nation brought a welcome feeling of unity and relief from the apparently impotent, bickering politicians of the Fourth Republic. His high-handed arbitrary style of rule could be overlooked or forgiven.

THE MACHIAVELLIAN STYLE AND
THE EUROPEAN COMMUNITY

It was, however, precisely this "style" that added another impediment to his effort to build "Europe." How could de Gaulle establish a feeling of confidence and intimate ties with other European leaders, given his blatantly Machiavellian concept of rulership?

These principles of personal style and rulership were clearly set forth as early as 1932, and he faithfully demonstrated his adherence to them ever afterward. A true leader must remain aloof and be self-reliant, he recorded. "This passion for self-reliance is obviously accompanied by some roughness in method." He complained of those who did not realize "that asperity is, more often than not, the reverse side of a strong character."[38] The essence of "the plan on which the leader has concentrated all his faculties," he said, is that it "shall bear the mark of grandeur." In this enterprise, "the question of virtue does not arise. The perfection preached in the Gospels never yet built up an empire. Every man of action has a strong dose of egotism, pride, hardness and cunning. All these things will be forgiven him, indeed they will be regarded as high qualities, if he can make them the means to achieve great ends."[39] The true statesman must be able to captivate men's minds. "He must know how to dissemble, when to be frank. He must pose as the servant of the public in order to become its master. He must outbid his rivals in self-confidence and only after a thousand intrigues and solemn undertakings will he find himself entrusted with full power. Even when he has it in his grasp, he can never be completely open in his dealings." The statesman, aware that realities are complex, "sets himself to master them by trickery and calculation."[40]

De Gaulle's personal brand of statesmanship, as he conceived it, had tragic consequences for the European Community. At the moment he assumed power the Community of Six was the only existing nucleus for a future Europe, which de Gaulle professed a desire to mold. It was also quite clear that France would never have accepted the Treaty of Rome had de Gaulle been in power at the time of its ratification. (The Gaullist members of the National Assembly voted against it.) However, from 1958 through 1962 de Gaulle was so preoccupied with the Algerian problem that the Six could proceed with their own unique experiments.

It was generally recognized among those working in the Community institutions that only by progressively transferring national loyalties to supranational bodies could a new entity called "Europe" ever come into existence. These new forms of association were necessarily delicate and tenuous, and had to be nurtured with care if they were to prosper. As the institutions of the Six increasingly became the object of joint expectations and rewards, it became possible to speak of "the Community spirit." National negotiators were inclined to take account of the long-term common good and upgrade the common interest, even if it meant making short-term national concessions that were not strictly on a quid pro quo basis. This novel and exciting experiment among European states held out the promise that the selfish national concerns of the past might somehow recede as the various peoples became caught up with their concern for a common European future.

When the parliamentary election of November 1962 gave de Gaulle an absolute majority in the National Assembly, he felt that there were no longer any effective domestic restraints on his policies, so that he could safely turn his attention to foreign affairs. In January 1963 came de Gaulle's brutal and unilateral veto of Britain's attempt to enter the Common Market, and then a series of threats, ultimata, and boycotts of the Community institutions, all designed to restructure them along the lines of traditional intergovernmental organizations that would be compatible with Gaullist nationalist concepts. The first casualty of these assaults was the fragile Community spirit. This was a devastating blow, since without it there can be no prospect for building a European Union that will transcend the tragic, historic divisions among the separate nations of Europe.

De Gaulle, at times, acknowledged that the institutions of the Six made a positive contribution to Europe. "Of course it is true," he noted, "that while waiting to come to grips with Europe's problem and tackle it as a whole, it has been possible to institute certain organs that are more or less extranational." Their role must be strictly limited, however. "These organs have their technical value, but they do not have, they cannot have authority and, consequently, political effectiveness."[41]

In the eyes of the "good Europeans" of the Monnet school, such institutions embodied a philosophy that made them highly political in nature. There was the novel concept of an independent Commission, detached from the separate national interests, entrusted with the responsibility of transcending them by consciously seeking out the common interests of the Community, endowed with considerable powers of initiative and capable of carrying on a dialogue with the Council of Ministers, who represented the constituent countries. There was the European Parliament, at first given limited powers and elected only indirectly. But there were provisions for the direct election of its members and the intention gradually to augment its scope of authority. Such beginnings were viewed as the nucleus for the future political transformation of the separate states into a United States of Europe. The essence of this community approach was to replace the old patterns of national domination and rivalries by a new concept that accorded all partners legal equality and equal respect and which arrived at solutions that would benefit the broader community of nations.

De Gaulle condemned the idea of European "integration as not being able to lead to anything other than an American protectorate."[42] This rather curious conclusion stemmed from his commitment to nationalism, which precluded the possibility of any entity other than the national state having political significance. To him, the Community institutions constituted an arid technocracy without the possibility of developing political roots, and hence they would be susceptible to easy manipulation by the far-reaching schemes drawn up in Washington. "Instead of participating, as in normal, in organized cooperation among the free nations of the Old Continent," de Gaulle castigated those who wanted "to be literally dissolved in a Europe described as integrated which, lacking the incentives of sovereignty of the peoples and responsibility of the States, would automatically be subordinate to the protector across the ocean."[43]

There was genuine irony in the Gaullist position. De Gaulle rejected any hegemony over Europe except his own. Yet his own imperious, high-handed methods and arrogant mentality made the Gaullist image of Europe unattractive to all of his prospective partners. Short of conquest, a Gaullist "European Europe" could not be had. The only possible basis for creating a powerful Europe, truly independent of the United States, fully capable of pursuing independent action, was to renounce the nationalist and imperialist molds of the past and integrate the separate states in a new supranational community. That is, the Monnet school, which he openly scorned, provided the only answer for the kind of institutional strength that would make a truly independent Europe possible. Monnet contended, of course, that he wanted to form a partnership with the United States to tackle the great common problems of the West. What in fact might happen cannot yet be fully foreseen, since such a supranational Europe does not yet exist, but it must be acknowledged that the *capacity* for implementing independent, Gaullist-type policy would best exist in precisely the kind of Europe that de Gaulle totally rejected.

Max Kohnstamm, Vice-President of Monnet's Action Committee for the United States of Europe, placed the issue of American "hegemony" in a different perspective. After World War II the United States saw that it could only return to its prewar isolation at the price of accepting Soviet domination over Europe. Reluctantly the United States concluded that it had no choice but to remain in Europe.

> From 1945 on, the United States consented to be, and was, Europe's protector. Economically it made European reconstruction possible through generously given aid; militarily it took care of Europe's defense through NATO. . . . Such an alliance, whereby one very strong

nation protects and leads others is usually called a
hegemony, but from the beginning there was something
very unusual about this relationship. In the first place, the
United States was in Europe without really wanting to be
there. . . . But secondly—and this is even more unusual in
history—from the beginning the United States spurred
Europe to unite. I do not know any example in history of a
hegemonial power urging its clients to unite.[44]

As Europe regained its strength, gradually "political leaders in
America and Europe stopped thinking in terms of protector and
protege and began thinking in terms of partnership. But such a
partnership, to be effective and real, could only be a partnership with
the Community as a whole, not a partnership with any of the
relatively small European powers separately, not even with America's
old ally, the United Kingdom."[45] De Gaulle, however, continued to
complain of American "hegemony" at a time when the United States
was seeking ways of creating a more equal relationship between the
two sides of the Atlantic. He rejected the partnership offer, vetoed
Britain's entry into the European Community, and attempted to
undermine the Community institutions that might permit a strong
European partner to emerge. In short, de Gaulle raised the loudest
protests against American "hegemony," and yet did everything
possible to perpetuate the conditions that would make this unequal
relationship inevitable. In a very real sense de Gaulle had a vested
interest in perpetuating the image of American "hegemony," since
without it he would have lost his own role as the "liberator" of
Europe.

THE FRANCO-GERMAN NUCLEUS
FOR LITTLE EUROPE

Since de Gaulle's principles for organizing a "Europe of States"
were totally incompatible with the aims of the Community
institutions, he was forced to try another tack. The Germans seemed
particularly vulnerable to Gaullist manipulation, since their recent
Nazi past made them anxious for international rehabilitation and
political respectability. Following de Gaulle's sedulous campaign of
wooing German public opinion that was especially calculated to
flatter the aging Chancellor Adenauer, the two leaders signed a

Franco-German Friendship Treaty in January 1963. This came, significantly, only a fortnight after de Gaulle's rebuff to Britain's Common Market bid. The formal reconciliation of France and Germany was, of course, wholly praiseworthy. But de Gaulle's motives went beyond that. As he explained in 1963, "the French-German Treaty provides an example which may be followed and a framework which may be enlarged." The treaty was to provide a model for the nations of Europe "to organize themselves in order to conduct together a policy which is European." Referring to the negotiations for a partial nuclear test ban then under way, he warned that "the direct contacts which are being reestablished between the Anglo-Saxons and the Soviets and which once again may commit Europe's fate, should convince it that it is time for it to be itself, or that it run the risk of never being it."[46]

What became of the Franco-German Treaty which, in de Gaulle's mind, was to be the opening wedge for organizing a "European Europe" that could be directed equally against "the Anglo-Saxons and the Soviets"? In 1964, almost exactly one year after the above pronouncement, de Gaulle complained of German behavior. "One could not say that Germany and France have yet agreed to make together a policy and one could not dispute that this results from the fact that Bonn has not believed, up to now, that this policy should be European and independent." De Gaulle was thus reduced to the position of claiming that France alone represented Europe, and would be forced to chart a "European" course, even if no other Europeans went along. "In waiting for the sky to clear, France is pursuing, by her own means, that which a European and independent policy can and should be."[47]

De Gaulle's recognition of his limitations in organizing any kind of Europe, even one restricted to a Franco-German core area, turned upon the question of Europe's trans-Atlantic relations. In the negotiations for the Franco-German Treaty, the Germans originally proposed a clause stipulating that the treaty would be consonant with the parties' NATO obligations. This provision, however, was deleted at de Gaulle's insistence.[48] However, the Bundestag inserted a preamble to the treaty before ratification which stated that the treaty was also intended to preserve "a close partnership between Europe and the United States of America" and to insure "collective defense within the framework of the North Atlantic Alliance, and the integration of the armed forces of the States bound together in that Alliance."[49] The extraordinary act of inserting such a preamble amounted to a pointed rejection of de Gaulle's concept of a European defense and foreign policy on the part of his newly embraced German ally. As de Gaulle later complained, the Germans were "applying not our bilateral treaty, but the unilateral preamble that changed all its meaning and that they themselves had added."[50]

Nor did de Gaulle fare any better with his other partners in the Six. As France was withdrawing from NATO in 1966, Foreign Minister Couve de Murville complained of the repeated French failures "to give our countries all together the means for better affirming their personality and independence" by formulating their positions on a variety of issues in a purely European rather than an Atlantic context.

> This means that those European countries must strive to build in common their economy, their foreign policy and their defense. If this is indeed what is involved, then I am obliged to note that none of our partners shares our views. Shall I give corroboration of this? Every time, for the past six years, that we have together discussed measures to take toward what is generally called the political Europe, everyone has always taken the stand that defense was a taboo subject: That is NATO's business. As for international policy, doubtless one could be bold enough to discuss it a little, but the really appropriate forum was, nevertheless, that of NATO.[51]

There could scarcely be a clearer statement of the total bankruptcy of de Gaulle's effort to create a "political Europe."

His European partners, and especially the Germans, were quick to realize that if de Gaulle's formula of a "European Europe" existing "by itself for itself" were taken seriously, this would involve a withdrawal of support from Western Europe of "the Anglo-Saxons," so that Europe's future existence would be dependent upon the sufferance of Soviet power. With such a disequilibrium of power arising on the continent, it would be difficult to imagine any "European Europe" other than a Soviet-dictated Europe. These fears were explicitly confirmed when de Gaulle publicly declared in February 1965 that the settlement of the German problem was purely a matter of concern for the European states, thereby simultaneously excluding an American role while including one for the Soviet

Union.[52] The Soviet and other European Communist leaders naturally received this statement with delight.

DE GAULLE TURNS EAST

A gradual rapprochement of Gaullist and Communist positions had been underway for some time. When de Gaulle discovered that he could not organize Western Europe on his terms, and that even his special German protege did not turn out to be a pliable junior client, he had nowhere to turn except to the East. Beginning in late 1963 there was a marked expansion of French diplomatic contacts with various East European Communist states. Thereafter, in July 1964, de Gaulle received Rumanian Premier Maurer in Paris; in late November the Czechoslovak and Bulgarian Foreign Ministers and the Rumanian Vice Premier visited the French capital; while the Hungarian Foreign Minister came to Paris at the beginning of 1965.

On the occasion of a reception for Soviet Ambassador Vinogradov, in March 1965, de Gaulle and Vinogradov exchanged congratulations on the French adoption of Soviet color television. (Germany and the other European states had meanwhile adopted the American process for color television, with the result that an all-European system became impossible.) De Gaulle then listened calmly as Vinogradov expounded this rather remarkable thesis: "The national interests of our two great European powers are nowhere in conflict."[53] The Soviet Ambassador had already gone on record as endorsing de Gaulle's concept of an exclusively continental European settlement for the future of Germany by mentioning the European states he thought should be involved while specifically omitting any role for the United States and Britain.[54] Subsequent U.S. and British protests brought a reluctant French admission that the United States and the United Kingdom also had a stake in Germany's future, by virtue of their positions as original occupying powers.

Soviet Foreign Minister Gromyko's widely hailed visit to Paris in April 1965 opened the way for a renewal of Polish-French contacts in the summer of 1965. During the course of an interview with Polish journalists, Gaullist Minister of Information Alain Peyrefitte persisted in maintaining: "A 'European Europe' should depend on no one.... The European countries alone should take care of their security."[55] The Poles had many reasons to be happy with de Gaulle. Among them, in particular, was the fact that France was, at the time, the only Western power to give formal recognition to the Oder-Neisse line.

In the fall of 1965 French Foreign Minister Couve de Murville journeyed Eastward to be received by the Soviet leaders. Soviet Premier Kosygin warmly welcomed the French emissary with the message that further Soviet-French consultations "need to be regular, because they help solve many questions. They should not be casual or temporary."[56] All this served as preparation for de Gaulle's Moscow visit during the summer of 1966. There, further provisions were made for regular Franco-Soviet Foreign Ministers' meetings and the installation of a "hot line" between the Elysée and the Kremlin. These arrangements were buttressed by consular, scientific, cultural, and economic agreements of varying importance. On the central issue of a European settlement, a jointly sponsored declaration stated: "Both governments agree that the problems of Europe should be first of all discussed within European limits. They believe that the states of the continent should exert efforts to create conditions necessary for the establishment of an atmosphere of detente between all countries of the West and East."[57] This declaration, which was in line with past Gaullist policy as well as Soviet aims, significantly omitted mention of the United States, as though these grand objectives could be reached without the participation of one of the two superpowers. The role of the United States was not ignored, however, since French spokesmen accompanying the General revealed that in his talks with Brezhnev, de Gaulle "welcomed the fact that the existence of the Soviet Union counterbalanced the United States tendencies toward hegemony," while he equally welcomed "the fact that the existence of the United States counterbalances similar Soviet tendencies."[58] The Soviet leaders at least received the benefit of an authoritative, first-hand statement of the image de Gaulle created for himself as the balance wheel in world politics.

RUSSIA AND DE GAULLE'S EUROPE
TO THE URALS

What aspects of de Gaulle's dream world made him believe that he could deal successfully with the Soviet leaders and arrive at a satisfactory rearrangement of Europe without American power? What caused de Gaulle to believe that a badly divided West could encourage the Communists to arrive at an accommodation with Paris, and with the French concept of Europe? Why did he not perceive that a divided West would only confirm Moscow's belief in the validity of its ideological tenets about the inevitability of conflict among capitalist states, which invite not accommodation with the West but increased Communist exploitation of these conflicts, an intensification of its political warfare, and the return to intransigent policies that seek to restructure Europe according to the Soviet concept? The answers would seem to lie in de Gaulle's understanding of communism and in his vision of a greater Europe.

It was significant that de Gaulle always referred to the Soviet Union as "Russia." Seen from the perspective of this nineteenth-century nationalist, the Russian empire was never fully transformed into the Soviet Union, on two accounts. First, the basic and determining fact about this state entity, he believed, was the continued existence of the Russian nation and Russian national interests, not the transitory and rather insubstantial abberation of Communist ideology that might appear to overlay these fundamental national concerns. Second, "Russia" remained part of Europe, and it was destined to rejoin the other states of Europe in a grand all-European political construction. De Gaulle viewed such an all-European arrangement as the ultimate goal lying beyond the attainment of his "European Europe." Its achievement would, in fact, mean the latter's demise, since a "European Europe" was intended to maneuver as an independent force between "the Anglo-Saxons" and the Soviets. The long-run Gaullist vision of a greater Europe assumed the dissolution of the Soviet camp and the incorporation of the nations of East Europe and a reborn, traditional Russia into an all-European concert of nations.

As with the rest of de Gaulle's concepts, these views can be traced back long before the time he achieved power in France. Following Hitler's attack of June 1941, which brought the Soviet Union into the war on the side of the Allies, de Gaulle considered what role the French Communists might play in the resistance. His answer clearly illustrated the relative weight he assigned to Communist ideology and French nationalism. "In the ceaseless movement of the world," he recorded, "all doctrines, all schools, all rebellions have one moment only. Communism will pass. But France will not pass."[59]

Then in 1944 de Gaulle outlined his ultimate goal for a postwar European settlement. "After the terrible lacerations she had undergone in the last thirty years, and the vast changes which had occurred the world over, Europe could find equilibrium and peace only by an association among Slavs, Germans, Gauls, and Latins." It is significant that de Gaulle specifically did not include "the Anglo-Saxons," who were, at the time, otherwise constantly on his mind. He expressed the hope that "the unity of Europe could be established in the form of an association including its peoples from Iceland to Istanbul, from Gibraltar to the Urals." Here the future position of Britain was open to question, although there was no doubt about the exclusion of the United States from his scheme. The thrust of de Gaulle's grand ambitions was clearly Eastward "to the Urals" and the Slavs, not Westward across the Atlantic.

He acknowledged that the Slavs would be difficult to accommodate in this greater Europe while they were ruled by an aggressive communism. Europe "must take into account what was momentarily tyrannical and aggrandizing in the Russian regime." The "momentary" nature of Communist rule was underscored when he said that "communism was apparently trying to gain control of the Vistula, the Danube and the Balkans" by using a combination of totalitarian oppression and invoking the solidarity of the peoples of East Central Europe against the German peril. "But once Germany ceased to be a threat, this subjection, for lack of a *raison d'etre*, would sooner or later prove unacceptable to the vassal states, while the Russians themselves would lose all desire to exceed their own boundaries." The mainspring of Soviet expansionism was thus explained in terms of traditional balance-of-power considerations and conflicting national interests, instead of the commitment by a regime to a universal revolutionary ideology that did not aim to perpeturate the nineteenth-century nation-state system. Even "if the Kremlin persisted in its desire for domination," de Gaulle speculated, "it would be against the will of the nations subject to its government." Such a regime could not last, since "in the long run there is no regime that can hold out against the will of nations."[60]

Following his return to power, de Gaulle's first press conference in March 1959 revived the image of a greater Europe, which was now defined as lying "between the Atlantic and the Urals."[61] It was this terminology that de Gaulle continued to employ. He also continued to make the emergence of this greater Europe dependent upon the breakup of the Soviet empire in Eastern Europe and the mellowing, if not the disappearance, of communism. Just how much of a transformation in the Communist regimes would, in fact, be required or how soon this might be expected was not very clear. In part this imprecision stemmed from de Gaulle's persistent refusal to take Communist ideology seriously.

THE ROLE OF COMMUNIST IDEOLOGY

When asked in July 1963, for example, about the ideological conflict between Moscow and Peking, de Gaulle shot back: "Over what ideology? During my lifetime, Communist ideology has been personified by many people. . . . I know as many holders of the Communist ideology as there are fathers of Europe. And that makes quite a few." Communist ideology was simply not worthy of discussion as a topic of serious inquiry. The whole question of Communist doctrine could be reduced, in his view, to a figleaf hiding personal and national rivalries. "I refuse to enter into a valid discussion on the subject of the ideological quarrel between Moscow and Peking. What I want to consider, are the deep-rooted realities which are human, national and consequently international. The banner of ideology in reality covers only ambitions. And I believe that it has been thus since the world was born."[62] Returning somewhat later to the question of ideological rivalry in the Communist world, de Gaulle reaffirmed his belief that "under a cloak that is torn a little more every day, appears the inevitable difference in national policies."[63]

If the Communist system of thought and government could be dismissed as a cloak disguising the inevitable differences in national policies, why need one be concerned about communism at all? Why would any transformations in it be required before the nations of Eastern Europe would be eligible to join with their Western brothers in building a Europe from the Atlantic to the Urals? De Gaulle showed considerable indecision on this point and wavered in his answers.

Thus in February 1965, de Gaulle reaffirmed that "the success of such a vast and difficult undertaking implied many conditions. Russia must evolve in such a way that it sees its future, not through totalitarian constraint imposed on its own land and on others, but through progress accomplished in common by free men and peoples. The nations which it has satellized must be able to play their role in a renewed Europe."[64] This would seem to imply that communism was, indeed, a relevant factor and that intimate ties with the East could not be arranged until there was a certain evolution in the totalitarian constraints found there.

Two months later, however, on April 10, 1965, de Gaulle struck quite a different note in his effusive, public welcome to Valerian Zorin, the new Soviet Ambassador to Paris. "Over and above all, and even above ideologies," de Gaulle declared, "there are two necessities in the world of today, namely peace and progress. I am sure that Russia and France today fundamentally agree on attaining these two objectives and also agree, as far as they can, to attain them together."[65] Here ideology posed no barrier to the warmest relations between states. For his part, Zorin tailored his pronouncements to fit de Gaulle's prejudices. "The Soviet Union and France, the great continental European powers, are called upon by their very location to play an important role in guaranteeing European security. The improvement in Franco-Soviet relations is a natural process; I should venture to say it is an unavoidable historical process."[66] The status of France was compared with that of a superpower, while the role of the United States in a European security system was studiously omitted. Ideology was also carefully ignored in projecting future relations between Paris and Moscow.

As Gaullist policy intensified its Eastward course in 1965, ideology seemed to disappear entirely as a consideration. In September, de Gaulle could report: "Our contacts and our exchanges are multiplying with the countries of the East, each of them, of course, being treated *only* in consideration of its *national* personality. In this respect," de Gaulle continued, "we attach great importance to the new trend of our relations with Russia." He was also pleased to note the results achieved by the visit to Paris of the Rumanian Premier, and he looked forward to the visit of the Polish Premier in the hopes that "his presence here will serve the practical rapprochement of the French and Polish peoples, friends and allies at all times in their history." Again, it was only the historic association among nations that counted. Then, without pausing, de Gaulle projected the culmination of these renewed ties between East and West. "We do not hesitate to envisage that the day will come when, in order to achieve a constructive entente to the Urals, all of Europe will wish to settle its own problems and, above all, that of Germany, by the only means that will make it possible to do so—that of a general agreement. On that day, our continent could once again assume in the world, for the good of all men, the role that is worthy of its resources and its capacities."[67]

De Gaulle was on a state visit to Rumania in May 1968 when he was obliged to hurry home to a France seized by widespread riots and paralyzed by a general strike. These massive disorders were not begun by the French Communist Party, which, in the initial phases, Party Chief Waldeck Rochet denounced as anarchist adventurism. The French Communists under Rochet had been trying to make themselves acceptable to French political life, and in March 1967 had, in fact, broken out of 20 years of isolation by forming working coalitions with other leftist groups in the elections for the National Assembly in the spring of 1967. This newly found respectability had, in great measure, been aided by de Gaulle who had systematically been wooing the Communists in Moscow and Eastern Europe. The Gaullist view that these leaders were really just good Russians, Poles, or Rumanians lent credence to the French Communist claim that they were really good Frenchmen who should be accepted into the governing circles of French politics. But when de Gaulle was plunged into the chaos of the "May events," as these riots and strikes were euphemistically called, whom could he blame for such an upheaval? Certainly not his own paternalistic policies that had largely ignored popular claims for social improvement. For a decade de Gaulle had been obsessed with the quest for prestige abroad, while he took little interest in domestic reforms that were urgently needed to adapt the archaic aspects of French life to modern conditions. And so, suddenly, on May 30, 1968, de Gaulle broadcast to the nation that "France is indeed threatened by a dictatorship . . . of totalitarian communism."[68] Communism was thus conveniently rediscovered, and then systematically used in an anti-Communist crusade to frighten the French people into returning a Gaullist majority in the subsequent elections to the National Assembly. Gaullist spokesmen emphasized, however, that communism was only an important factor in domestic politics, and that de Gaulle's search for friendly contacts with the East would continue uninterrupted, since communism, they held, had no bearing on the conduct of foreign policy.

This thesis was quickly put to the test in August 1968, when the Soviet Union invaded Czechoslovakia. The dispute that led to the invasion was in essence ideological, since the Soviet leaders were alarmed by the elements of liberalization and democratization that had been introduced by the Dubcek regime, and which, if they had developed successfully in Czechoslovakia, would have threatened

Communist rule not only in the rest of Eastern Europe, but ultimately in Moscow as well.

De Gaulle acknowledged that the forcible imposition of Soviet control over Czechoslovakia had revealed "the persistence of the Eastern bloc and consequently that of the Western bloc." This did not cause de Gaulle to reconsider his hostility toward NATO, however, nor to cease in his efforts to end the system of blocs. "Our policy," he said, "even if it appears to have been momentarily thwarted, is consistent with the fundamental European realities." Soviet behavior represented an "absurd," temporary lapse. "All of Europe expects from it [Russia] something quite different and much better than seeing it shut itself in and chain its satellites behind the walls of a crushing totalitarianism." Dismissing all evidence to the contrary, the Czech affair had demonstrated that "it is too late for any ideology, notably communism, to prevail over national sentiment. . . . It is too late to succeed in dividing Europe forever into two opposed blocs." Instead, events were pushing toward a single Europe from the Atlantic to the Urals, and such "evolution will inevitably continue."[69] To almost every other observer, Czechoslovakia represented a forcible reminder that Europe was divided into two blocs, which did not seem likely to merge into some greater Europe.

THE THREE STEPS IN ORGANIZING
ALL OF EUROPE

Let us suppose that sooner or later an attempt would be made to form this association of nations from the Atlantic to the Urals. Upon what principles would it be organized? The model was found in the "Europe of States" that de Gaulle sought to create in Western Europe, beginning with the Franco-German ties. Even before the conclusion of the Franco-German Treaty, de Gaulle explained: "There is a solidarity between Germany and France. On this solidarity depends the immediate security of the two peoples. . . . On this solidarity depend all hopes of uniting Europe on the political and defense levels as on the economic level. On this solidarity depends, in consequence, the destiny of the whole of Europe, from the Atlantic to the Ural Mountains."[70]

De Gaulle explicitly reiterated this three-step sequence on several occasions: First, a political entente with West Germany, then with the Western Europe of the Six, and then with all of Europe. "We must," de Gaulle entreated in 1965, "behave like the Europeans we are and, in that capacity, attempt to re-establish, from one end of our continent to the other, an equilibrium based on understanding and cooperation among all the peoples who live on it as we do. This is exactly what we are doing by reconciling ourselves with Germany; by proposing a real solidarity of the Six to our neighbors on both sides of the Rhine and the Alps; by resuming with the Eastern countries, as they emerge from their crushing constraint, the relations of active understanding which formerly linked us to them."[71] There would emerge from such an active understanding "a Europe in a state of equilibrium, peace and cooperation from one end to the other of the territory which nature has given it."[72]

Step three, the achievement of an idyllic state of equilibrium, peace, and cooperation from the Atlantic to the Urals, was to follow the successful attainment of these conditions in steps one and two in Western Europe. What might be the prospects for realizing this grandiose goal? Here one must recall all of the Gaullist illusions about the possibility of organizing a grouping of sovereign nation-states that somehow would be able to shed their traditional power rivalries and instabilities so as to live with each other in peace and harmony. What, in fact, would result from an attempt to organize Europe from the Atlantic to the Urals on the Gaullist pattern? As former Under Secretary of State George Ball had noted, one would find

> a Europe in which each of the middle-sized states would seek to make its own deal with one or the other of the "great hegemonies" in the hope of establishing for itself a first-class power position while keeping the others in an inferior role. Such a Europe—a continent of shifting coalitions and changing alliances—is not the hope of the future. [Rather it would mean] a reversion to the tragic and discredited pattern of the past—a return to 1914, as though that were not good enough, and with the same guarantee of instability—yet made more dangerous, not less, by the ideological drive of the Soviet Union and the existence of nuclear weapons.[73]

Experience had proved beyond doubt that de Gaulle failed to organize consistently harmonious, cooperative relations between the Two of the French-German Treaty and was even less successful in reorganizing the Six along Gaullist lines. Within the Six, in fact, de Gaulle most often found himself arrayed against the other five. If

Gaullist principles could not be made to work between the Two or among the Six, then how could they ever be expected to work among the 20 or more nations lying between the Atlantic and the Urals? It would be necessary not only to accommodate all of the revived sovereignties of Eastern Europe, each bringing with it its traditional national squabbles that never produced peace or an equilibrium in the past, but one would also be faced with the divergent ideological heritages of this conglomeration of states. Simply to list the ingredients that would go into making this supposed entente was to reveal that the Gaullist conception of a Europe from the Atlantic to the Urals was pure fantasy.

But the fantasy hardly stopped here. The very phrase of Europe "to the Urals" implied drastic alterations in the easternmost partner of the entente. The Urals were not only a geographical expression marking the end of Europe, but a political expression marking the end of Russian power. This partition of Russia would be the result of the growing intensity of the Sino-Soviet rivalry. "Russia," de Gaulle predicted in 1959, was "a white European nation which has conquered part of Asia," and "nothing can happen to prevent her from having to reckon with the yellow multitude which is China— numberless and wretchedly poor, indestructible and ambitious, building by dint of violent efforts a power which cannot be kept within limits and looking around her at the expanses over which she must one day spread."[74] That the reckoning with China would, in fact, mean the partition of Russia was confirmed by de Gaulle's Minister of Information, Alain Peyrefitte. In an interview he was asked: "What of General de Gaulle's mention of the Urals? Does he look forward to the division of Russia in two, or has it escaped his attention that nearly half the Russian nation is now to be found beyond the Urals, in Siberia?" Peyrefitte retorted that "in Siberia, after all, the Russians are occupying what is Chinese soil. Will the Chinese forever tolerate this intrusion?"[75]*

---

*"The General does not loosely use this conventional geographical definition of 'Europe.' He is quite aware that such a 'Europe,' terminating in the heart of the Soviet Union, politically implies some future partition of the USSR. This inference is deliberate. De Gaulle conjectures that the mighty China whose rise he foresees will some day pre-empt Russia's Siberian and Central Asian territories, which he considers artificially administered by Moscow since they result from 'colonial' conquests. The fact that this displeases Russia does not bother de Gaulle. He holds 'that is their affair, not mine.' " (C. L. Sulzberger, New York Times, August 22, 1965.)

De Gaulle, in effect, was telling the Kremlin: Join with me in rediscovering your European vocation, and together we can lead the nations of Europe in building a continental equilibrium. Perhaps this vision was rooted in the Treaty of Tilsit, whereby Napoleon and Alexander I divided Europe, for a time, between them. But what incentives did the Russian leaders have to enter seriously into the Gaullist framework of a Europe from the Atlantic to the Urals? Was Moscow going to allow de Gaulle to demote it from its position as a world power to that of a merely European one, and one that de Gaulle had gratuitously dissected at the Urals? Could this maimed Russia then be expected to extend a friendly hand to France?

Even assuming that such obstacles could somehow be surmounted and a Europe from the Atlantic to the Urals had come into existence, what assurance would there be that this Europe could be run from Paris and Moscow? Such a Europe would presumably have dissolved the Europe of opposing blocs, and with it the division of Germany into two parts. Was it not still more fantasy to suppose that a populous and powerful reunified Germany could be contained by a weaker France on the West and a truncated Russia on the East? And if a reunified Germany should emerge in a Gaullist Europe, what if it would be stimulated by the toxin of Gaullist nationalism and, no longer feeling the stigma of the Nazi past, reassert German power by emulating the imperious, nationalist behavior of de Gaulle? When viewed from this perspective, the Gaullist dream became a nightmare.

Taken together, all of the dangers and difficulties of de Gaulle's concept of a Europe from the Atlantic to the Urals amounted, as Zbigniew Brzezinski put it, to a vision but not a policy. In terms of its practical effect, "his insistence on a Europe detached from America disunited the West without causing any substantial change in the East. Indeed, his attitude could have the effect of driving America out of West Europe . . . without driving Russia out of East Europe."[76] Thus the concrete impact of de Gaulle's grandiose scheme was not manifest in any constructive European political structure, but rather in his destructive assault upon the trans-Atlantic bond holding Europe and America together. NATO was the clearest symbol of this bond, and it was against NATO that de Gaulle turned his energies.

DE GAULLE'S NATO POLICIES IN PERSPECTIVE

Even before returning to power in 1958, de Gaulle had clearly formulated his policy toward NATO. In an interview with C. L. Sulzberger on February 20, 1958, but only published eight years later, de Gaulle declared: "I would quit NATO if I were running France. NATO is against our independence and our interests. Our membership in NATO is said to be for the reason of protecting France against a Russian attack. But I don't believe the Russians will attack at this time. . . . NATO is no longer an alliance. It is a subordination."[77] De Gaulle confirmed this assessment in his memoirs, which appeared shortly before his death in 1970, when he wrote that upon resuming the reins of power in 1958 his aim was "to disengage France, not from the Atlantic Alliance, which I intended to maintain by way of ultimate precaution, but from the integration realized by NATO under American command."[78] Had these views been known and believed in 1958, Western statesmen could have been spared the endless agonies of trying to discern de Gaulle's true intentions and placate his essentially implacable demand for the restructuring of NATO.

De Gaulle found NATO repugnant because it placed France merely on a par with the other European countries, all of which looked to the overwhelming power of the United States for leadership. And among the European states Britain still stood out as a world power, even though this role had been somewhat tarnished. In addition, Britain maintained a special relationship with the United States, inherited from their wartime collaboration, in the development of atomic weapons. This rankled de Gaulle and made him vow that France would at least receive a status equal to that of Britain. But as events were to demonstrate, even equality with Britain inside NATO would not suffice, since his ambitions for the role of France went far beyond that.

DE GAULLE'S SECRET TRIUMVIRATE PROPOSALS

The issues of rank and prestige were first brought to a head in July 1958 as a result of the American and British military landings in Lebanon and Jordan in response to the call of these governments for help against Nasser-inspired rebellions. France played no part in these events, but de Gaulle was fully prepared for the possibility of such troop landings, which occurred on July 15-17, since Secretary of

State John Foster Dulles flew to Paris and discussed this contingency with him on July 5-6. The French government, however, circulated the complaint that it had not been consulted, but a subsequent interview with Dulles revealed that this was simply not so. The spurious French complaint was perhaps rooted in the unsatisfactory nature of the exchange that took place. De Gaulle insisted that the French people must "be made to believe again that France is a great power," and this took the form of a demand that France be recognized as a world power instead of being treated as just another continental European state. Dulles paid tribute to the French contribution to Western civilization and agreed that a strong France should emerge again, but he warned that in reviving its strength there would be serious strains in NATO if France should set itself apart from and above the positions of Germany and Italy. To this de Gaulle retorted that the Germans and Italians did not seem upset by the special position of Britain as a world power. Dulles also reaffirmed the need for the "integration" of NATO forces, while de Gaulle spoke only of "cooperation" among allied states.[79]

In this exchange of views was found the seeds of the demands that de Gaulle formally submitted in a document to President Eisenhower, with a copy to Prime Minister Macmillan, dated September 17, 1958. This communication, consisting of a memorandum with an attached cover letter, has not been made public, although its contents have been widely, and sometimes inaccurately, reported. The most useful published account of it is found in David Schoenbrun's masterful biography of de Gaulle.[80] It can be stated with assurance that he accurately described this famous secret document, since the present writer was also privileged to read it in full. This account was likewise confirmed by the brief summary of de Gaulle's letter that the State Department subsequently made public.

The Anglo-American landings in the Levant, de Gaulle noted, might have precipitated events that could have quickly developed into a general war, in which France and the other members of the Atlantic Alliance might have become involved. The scope of the Atlantic Alliance was therefore unsatisfactory if it was confined to the defense of Europe, since the need to concert policies was worldwide. De Gaulle later explained this aspect of his secret proposal in a public press conference. It had become obvious, de Gaulle said, "that the possibilities of conflict and consequently of military operations were spreading far beyond Europe, were spreading all over the world. It became evident that the Middle East and Africa, in particular, were danger spots quite as much as Europe, and that there existed, between the principal members of the Atlantic Alliance, political differences concerning them which, if the occasion arose, might turn into disagreements on strategy." Consequently it was necessary for the NATO states with global responsibilities, which in de Gaulle's view were the United States, Britain, and France, to make some special arrangements among themselves. "We feel that, at least among the world powers of the West, there must be something organized— where the Alliance is concerned—as to their political conduct and, should the occasion arise, their strategic conduct outside Europe, specially in the Middle East, and in Africa, where these three powers are constantly involved."[81]

De Gaulle's memorandum of September 1958 had been more specific about how the three powers should be organized. They should "create a tripartite organization to take joint decisions on global problems." The Atlantic Alliance should be revised so as to become worldwide in scope, with subregions or subcommands set up within it. One of the special functions assigned to the Big Three would be the making of "joint decisions" on the use of nuclear weapons. This tripartite organization of the Atlantic Alliance (the word "directorate" was not used) should be entrusted with drawing up "strategic plans" and be empowered to "put them into effect," thereby governing "the use of nuclear weapons anywhere in the world."

At first glance, these proposals seemed eminently sensible. What was more needed than the global coordination of Western policies? One might, of course, object that it was somewhat immodest of de Gaulle to consider France a great world power (although de Gaulle had never been bothered by the requirements of modesty), since at the time he first advanced his proposal France was extremely weak. At home, it had just come from the brink of civil war and domestic strife had by no means been quelled, while abroad France had lost its empire in the Middle East and Southeast Asia and was in the process of losing what was left of it in Africa. But even so, would it not have been extremely beneficial for the West to have a concerted global policy?

Only a closer look at de Gaulle's proposal and the subsequent exchange of notes and diplomatic activity that sought to clarify it revealed the true meaning of this initiative. All indications point to the conclusion that de Gaulle was not really concerned with achieving a common Western global policy but with elevating the status and prestige of France to the publicly recognized position of a great world power.

By attempting to become a member of the Big Three within NATO's 15 member states, de Gaulle obviously sought to arrogate to himself the role of speaking for continental Europe. The first time de Gaulle broached this subject, Dulles warned of the difficulties such a pretention would create with the other NATO nations on the continent, especially with Italy and Germany. In order to surmount this objection and before dispatching his memorandum to Eisenhower and Macmillan, de Gaulle sent his Foreign Minister to Rome and Bonn in order to gauge the depths of the anticipated resistance. De Gaulle then personally courted Chancellor Adenauer. Through a carefully staged reception at de Gaulle's home at Colombey, which cultivated and flattered Adenauer's sensitivities, and by de Gaulle skillfully playing upon the character of a "Europe" that France shared with Germany, but that might be betrayed by the "Anglo-Saxons," de Gaulle succeeded in winning over the aging German leader. A highly amicable communique noted the results of the de Gaulle-Adenauer talks of September 14, 1958. Adenauer was soon shocked to learn, however, that de Gaulle had completely withheld information about his celebrated memorandum, which, at the time, was in its final drafting stage, since it was completed and dated September 17. De Gaulle's deviousness only succeeded in enraging Adenauer.[82] Nor did the idea sit well with lesser German figures. This writer clearly remembers discussions with highly placed members of the German Foreign Office during Adenauer's reign who bitterly denounced the Gaullist triumvirate proposal. They resented the idea of two classes of membership in NATO and insisted that since Germany had contributed by far the greatest number of troops to NATO of all the European member states, it should at least be given an equal voice in NATO affairs. The thought was sometimes expressed that a more limited group of states might be useful in the management of allied nuclear policy and related strategic questions. However, three was too restricted a number, and if membership was expanded to five or seven, room should be left in this group for other states to participate on a rotating basis.

The idea of a closed, exclusive inner club had, in fact, already been tried in NATO, and had been proven a failure. Former NATO

Secretary General Dirk Stikker recalled that when the North Atlantic Treaty went into effect in 1949, the United States, Britain, and France, as the occupying powers in Germany, consulted closely and regularly among themselves to the exclusion of their other NATO partners. Their mode of operation in handling the German problem spilled over into other areas. "Tripartite dominance was underscored by the custom of the Big Three to meet privately before each meeting of the NATO Council for an exchange of views on the agenda." Stikker recounted the resentment this aroused and the countermove in which he participated in his capacity at that time as Dutch Ambassador to NATO. "These arrangments finally led to the creation of a 'Little Three.' Pearson of Canada, Lange of Norway and I adopted the habit of meeting purely as friends, before each Council session for an exchange of views." From 1950 on they were able to exercise considerable influence in shaping important NATO decisions. "It has been my experience," Stikker concluded, "that when the big powers, be they three or five, try too much to dominate an organization, counterforces inevitably arise to restore the balance. If the balance cannot be restored in this manner, the organization is doomed to failure."[83]

In one respect, NATO had a formal triumvirate in existence from its beginning. The highest military representatives of the United States, Britain, and France together formed the Standing Group, which in theory was the executive arm of the larger NATO Military Committee. Since the members of the Standing Group received their political and military instructions from their separate capitals, and since these directives were usually in disagreement, Stikker pointed out that the Standing Group frequently found "itself unable to formulate decisions." As a consequence, "the Standing Group had, because of disagreement in this tripartite body, been unable to give any advice on the vital problem of strategy. It has proved already on other occasions to be impossible to arrive at an agreed opinion on military questions within NATO for lack of agreement in the Standing Group. If ever proof was needed that in an organization like NATO a triumvirate does not work, then the Standing Group provides a glaring example."[84] Following the French withdrawal from NATO, the Standing Group went out of existence.

President Eisenhower replied to de Gaulle's triumvirate proposal in a letter of October 20, 1958. For a number of years even the existence of this letter was kept secret, so that rumors repeatedly charged Washington with ignoring or snubbing de Gaulle.[85] Eisenhower agreed that the threat to the free world was global in nature and noted that the United States had sponsored a network of regional defense pacts covering Europe and North America, the Middle East, and Southeast Asia. Furthermore, France was a member of NATO and SEATO and could already participate with other allies in planning a global defense. This, of course, rejected the exclusive tripartite arrangement advocated by de Gaulle. The NATO Council in particular, Eisenhower argued, offered a forum for broadening still further the invaluable habit of consultation among the Western powers not only on events inside the NATO Treaty area but also about the threats facing the free world in the Far East and the Middle East. Such consultation was imperative, since "we cannot afford to adopt any system which would give to our allies, or other free world countries, the impression that basic decisions affecting their own vital interests are being made without their participation." This position ran contrary to the Gaullist scheme of an exclusive tripartite organization, which necessarily would have to take decisions affecting the vital interests of other allies without their participation. Eisenhower's letter ended with the invitation to explore the subject further.[86]

In an effort to satisfy de Gaulle, Eisenhower instructed Dulles to set up a "tripartite committee" at the subcabinet level in order to discuss de Gaulle's proposal. Dulles appointed Deputy Under Secretary of State Robert Murphy, who twice met with the French and British Ambassadors in Washington in December 1958. The French Ambassador echoed de Gaulle's demand for upgrading and extending this arrangement to include joint strategic nuclear planning on a global scale. On December 15 Dulles was received by de Gaulle in Paris and was told that the world situation was too critical for "playing political games with committees." Dulles again offered to exchange views on any subject in any part of the world, but he held fast to the position that it was not possible to establish an official tripartite organ either over NATO or over the rest of the free world. However, in an effort to accommodate French demands, Dulles proposed tripartite consultations on the situation in the Far East. Two such meetings were held in February 1959 at the same level as the tripartite talks in December 1958, with the addition of general staff officers who would contribute to a discussion of the strategic aspects of the question. In April 1959 four days of tripartite talks took place on African problems, and the United States and Britain indicated that they were willing to hold further tripartite discussions among military experts on Africa, but the French did not respond to this initiative. When Dulles first raised the possibility of tripartite planning on Africa in his December 1958 interview with de Gaulle, the French President retorted sharply that France might have been spared needless difficulties in North Africa had a common policy existed there before. Then de Gaulle added: "Of course a common policy in North Africa would necessarily be a French policy."[87]

In a second exchange of secret letters between de Gaulle and Eisenhower, in March 1959, de Gaulle continued to press for an exclusive tripartite organization, while Eisenhower spoke in terms of maintaining the fullest, closest cooperation among all allies in NATO. Then on June 10, 1960 de Gaulle repeated his demand in still another secret letter for a "high level planning group" among the Big Three which would give France "an equal voice in joint decisions on the use of nuclear weapons."[88] This now fully confirmed what had been properly assumed up to this point: De Gaulle, in effect, wanted a veto right on the global use of the total Anglo-American nuclear arsenals. This demand de Gaulle repeated in a public statement in October 1960 when he said: "France intends that if, by misfortune, atomic bombs were to be dropped in the world, none should be dropped by the free world's side unless she should have accepted it."[89]

To appreciate the scope of this demand, one need only consider the nature of the "special relationship" that existed between the United States and Britain. Under the "two-key system" of control, British agreement was required to fire American nuclear weapons deployed in Britain. In this limited sense only did Britain hold a veto over the use of U.S. nuclear weapons. But de Gaulle, to repeat, wanted a veto on the use of all American and British nuclear weapons whenever deployed on a global scale! When Dulles met de Gaulle for the last time at the beginning of 1959, Dulles reportedly "held out the possibility of a French veto on American nuclear weapons deployed in continental Europe"[90] in return for French cooperation inside NATO. But de Gaulle failed to respond to this offer. De Gaulle's demands were both extreme and nonnegotiable. It served his purpose better not to meet his prospective triumvirate partners halfway, since the failure of these probings would provide him with the rationale to go his own way with "free hands" (to use a favorite Gaullist phrase).

Viewed in retrospect, it seems clear that de Gaulle was not really serious about his own proposals, except in the most unlikely event that they would be totally accepted and completely implemented as he saw fit.

Eisenhower resumed the secret correspondence on August 2, 1960 by asking de Gaulle why he continually made proposals for joint planning on a global scale but then took no action to implement suggestions in this direction, such as, for example, the U.S. offer of joint planning with regard to Africa. Although de Gaulle had finally agreed to appoint a French delegate, Eisenhower noted, a year and a half had gone by and the French chair remained vacant. Eisenhower then proposed a broader type of consultation, within a high-level three-power military committee, to consider de Gaulle's demands for a global strategy. This stopped short of the Gaullist requirement for a formal tripartite "organization" that could take "joint decisions," but it seemed to be a big step in that direction. It was, in fact, as far as Eisenhower could go without impinging upon the interests of the other excluded NATO partners and disrupting NATO itself.

De Gaulle shot back in his last secret letter to Eisenhower that a three-power summit meeting of the West would be preferable to a high-level committee to consider global strategy. This summit meeting, de Gaulle added, could undertake joint planning of global strategy, and, in addition, it could "reorganize the Alliance." In his final reply of August 31, Eisenhower tried to keep his anger under control. He reminded his French counterpart that twice before de Gaulle had promised to send a detailed memorandum about suggestions for reorganizing the Allinace, but that he had never done so. Without such a document in hand, no useful discussion could be conducted.[91]

Surveying the history of the de Gaulle-Eisenhower exchanges, Schoenbrun made a useful distinction between the form and substance of allied collaboration and concluded that de Gaulle was more interested in the form. "Since an 'organization' is a formal institution, General de Gaulle was not only insisting upon the right to *participate* in *decisions*, he wanted this right to be *recognized officially* and *publicly* by creation of a formal institution. De Gaulle would not have been satisfied even if Eisenhower had granted him all his extraordinary demands, including a full French voice in American strategy and a French veto over the Anglo-Saxons' decisive power implied in 'joint decisions' on the use of nuclear weapons. Nothing less than the public formalization of these arrangements would satisfy General de Gaulle."[92]

After retiring from office, Eisenhower read Schoenbrun's manuscript account of these events. Eisenhower confirmed that "our biggest arguments as presidents came out of this idea . . . to have a publicly proclaimed triumvirate. You've got that right in your book, that tripartite business and public recognition of France as a great power. That is exactly what he wanted."[93] He then related additional details to show how far he went in trying to satisfy de Gaulle. Eisenhower proposed that London become the center for triumvirate planning, since France maintained a big embassy there.

> I'll make special appointments [Eisenhower recalled telling de Gaulle], I'll strengthen the embassy with special people, high-ranking people, both in the political and military world, and you can do the same. Britain can do it, of course, because they're right there in London. We will have all these top people there and we will put them, if you want, under a director, or some such title, and they will be authorized to take current plans, current problems, emerging problems— and we will give them authority and plenty of time to coordinate our view so we can plan to be in a position to operate in unison, anywhere in the world, on any problem, or at least not to act in disunion. We can map out broad areas of agreement for there are many, and can identify and contain the disagreements.

Eisenhower summed up his efforts with the affirmation: "I tell you I was offering him everything it was possible to offer and very far toward his requests. But he wouldn't have it. It was all or nothing with him. He wanted it at the top, all the way like Cicero* and Pompey and Caesar."[94]

Since President Kennedy was convinced that the issue of the tripartite organization was at the heart of all the difficulties in Franco-American relations, when he visited Paris on June 2, 1961 he

---

*Eisenhower's reference to Cicero was an obvious slip. The famous Roman triumvirate consisted of Crassus, Pompey, and Caesar.

personnally reviewed with de Gaulle the entire history of the exchanges conducted with Eisenhower. In another effort to placate de Gaulle, Kennedy suggested the creation of a tripartite group of senior military officers to draft joint plans for Berlin, the Congo, and Laos, which at the time were troubled areas threatening world peace. Kennedy hoped that by tackling specific crisis situations, experience could be gained and confidence built up that would dissolve the past impasse. De Gaulle once again agreed to nominate top-level officials to participate in these working groups, and once again he failed to carry out his pledge. Later Kennedy showed dismay at de Gaulle's unwillingness to implement plans that were drawn up for his benefit. In response to the President's questions, the explanation was again offered that de Gaulle was really not interested in such talks, even at a senior military level, because they were too restricted in scope and were to be conducted in secret. What de Gaulle wanted was public recognition of a formally organized tripartite group, meeting at the highest level at regular intervals, thereby openly acknowledging the great power status of France. In short, de Gaulle was not searching for agreed policies for the West, but for an institutionalized way of proclaiming French grandeur. Kennedy admitted the logic of this explanation, but still found it hard to believe.[95] And for anyone not viewing the world through de Gaulle's eyes, it was, indeed, hard to believe.

This was not quite the end of this remarkable triumvirate story. In January 1962 de Gaulle sent Kennedy another letter again proposing a permanent, high-level political planning group along with a combined military staff that would prepare "common decisions and common actions," this time beginning with policies toward the nonaligned countries of the underdeveloped would. "Kennedy marveled at de Gaulle's unabashed presentation of new proposals after failing to act on any of the old ones." As before, de Gaulle promised to dispatch a following memorandum providing the details as to how this plan might be implemented. And as before, no such memorandum was ever sent. Thus ended the fruitless and frustrating exchange of views on the triumvirate idea.[96]

When NATO Secretary General Stikker visited Kennedy, the President returned to the subject of de Gaulle, probing for answers about his behavior. He asked what would have happened if the United States had helped de Gaulle with the development of his force de frappe. Stikker replied: "If de Gaulle had had atomic weapons it would have made no difference; he would not have been more helpful in NATO. He would have wanted the veto for himself, but he would not have wanted anyone else to have it. His motivation is French nationalism, pure and simple."[97]

If this stark fact is accepted, then all the contradictions disappear. His idea of a common nuclear strategy was to have a French veto over the Anglo-American deterrents, even before France had an operational deterrent of its own, but once the force de frappe came into existence no one would have a veto over it. He asked for a common global policy among the Big Three of the West, and yet as he remarked about North Africa, "of course, a common policy in North Africa would necessarily be a French policy." One wonders if de Gaulle did not also expect a common global policy to be a French policy. It is at least certain that he would have used the tripartite forum as a way of projecting himself into the world arena as a world statesman and asserting French interests and views on the world stage, but without abandoning his right to decide policies for France. In effect, de Gaulle's notion of formulating global policies was to influence the course of allied decisions, while insulating French policies from allied pressures designed to influence France.

Experience also informs us that de Gaulle's style of leadership never made him an accommodating type of statesman and that he had had a consistently poor record as an ally, beginning with his rise to prominence during World War II. In view of this, how could he have cooperated constructively in forming joint policies? Even in European matters where the West has many vital common interests that are highly apparent, de Gaulle had been extremely negative. But then consider the difficulty of implementing a common policy with de Gaulle beyond Europe, where, for example, France had joined with the Soviet Union against the United States and Britain by refusing to pay for the U.N. peacekeeping activities in the Middle East or in the Congo. There are great obstacles preventing the formulation of common policies around the world among any group of Western powers, but of all partners with whom one could have tried to achieve it, surely the most difficult would have been Gaullist France.

Essentially de Gaulle's nationalist philosophy was incompatible with his professions of a common allied cause. While still actively negotiating with Eisenhower about his triumvirate proposal in March 1959, de Gaulle withdrew the French Mediterranean fleet from NATO. His rationale was that NATO did not extend to the Middle East or Africa and that France might be obliged to act in these areas. "She would therefore have to act independently of NATO. But how could she do so if her fleet were not available?"[98] In effect, de Gaulle was beginning to implement the threat posed at the conclusion of his September 1958 memorandum. If his demands were not met, he had then warned, henceforth France would "subordinate" participation in NATO to the "recognition of French world-wide interests."[99]

FRENCH DEFENSE VS. NATO INTEGRATION

On November 3, 1959 de Gaulle proceeded to declare war on the principle of NATO integrated commands in an address to the *Ecole Militaire*. "If one would allow for a long period of time the defense of France to be in something other than the national framework, or for it to be fused or confused with something else, it would no longer be possible for us to maintain the idea of the State." He then openly vowed to begin the process of disentangling France from NATO. "The system known as 'integration,' which was introduced and even put into practice to some extent after we had undergone great trials, and when we had not yet recovered our national entity, and at a time when it was thought that the free world was confronted by an imminent and unbounded danger—such a system of integration has had its day." As part of the reassertion of independence from NATO, he added, France would proceed to build its force de frappe as a strictly French national nuclear force. Moreover, it would be endowed with a global mission: "Since one will be able eventually to destroy France from any point in the world, our force must have the capability of being able to act against every part of the world."[100]

Logically there was an inconsistency in demanding a single global strategy for NATO while withdrawing national forces from NATO for independent action on a global scale and in denouncing NATO integration as incompatible with upholding the glory of the national state. De Gaulle claimed to have sought a coordinated global policy for the West, but he also always insisted on maximum freedom for independent national action. Again, these two demands could be reconciled only if the global NATO policy also happened to be French policy.

The impulse behind de Gaulle's memorandum and his subsequent behavior toward NATO can perhaps best be summed up in the phrase of a former Minister in de Gaulle's cabinet who remarked to this writer: "De Gaulle wants to be bound by nothing." De Gaulle himself acknowledged this when he declared: "To have allies and to have the allies we have goes without saying for us in the period we are in. But it is also a categorical imperative for a great people to have the free disposition of itself, for alliances have no absolute virtue, whatever the sentiments on which they may be based. And if one spontaneously loses, even for a while, the disposition of oneself, there is a strong risk of never regaining it."[101] Alliances were therefore necessarily uncongenial to him, while the idea of frank and intimate collaboration with allies for the common good was simply not a part of his character.

The North Atlantic Council has frequently been used to exchange views and align policies of the member states, not only within the NATO area, but throughout the world. This process was consciously stepped up as a result of the "Three Wise Men's Report" of December 1956, which followed closely upon the debacle of Suez. To what extent did de Gaulle avail himself of this diplomatic forum? When I asked this question of one of the senior members of the Council who had served as his country's permanent representative to NATO all during de Gaulle's tenure in office, the Ambassador retorted: "De Gaulle consulted about nothing." De Gaulle's offer of consultation was confined to the exclusive context of the Big Three. If the others would not play the game according to his rules, he would not play at all.

Stikker contrasted the treatment he received from France and from the other allies when he was NATO Secretary General. "During these years every morning I received a briefing on U.S. foreign policy in different areas. Every year, I went to Washington several times for meetings with the State Department, Pentagon and White House. All these discussions were carefully prepared and when, at the end of my visit, the President received me, he had been briefed on the issues which would have to be submitted to him. Similar arrangements were always made in other capitals, but nothing of the kind ever happened in France. On the contrary, on taking office, my initial request to pay my respects to President de Gaulle went unanswered for three months." It was only through the intervention of Chancellor Adenauer, who was concerned about the fate of the Alliance, that

Stikker's one and only interview with de Gaulle was brought about. "I was summoned, after three months, to the Elysée at short notice," he related, "just when I was about to take a plane for London." In the blunt exchange that followed, de Gaulle touched on several topics. Did Stikker believe in integration, de Gaulle asked. The Secretary General replied: " 'Undoubtedly modern war or defense is no longer possible without integration.' " De Gaulle disagreed. " 'But we are fighting for our joint freedom,' I replied, 'we can only remain free if we all join our forces. Separate efforts of the small countries, or of Germany, have no meaning.' . . . De Gaulle disagreed: he wanted to be 'independent.' "[102]

Other prominent French leaders who considered de Gaulle's proposed reform of the Alliance came to different conclusions. Maurice Faure, for example, noted that it would be difficult not to subscribe to the idea of a single strategy for the West, especially if "strategy" went beyond military considerations to include those of psychological warfare, diplomacy, and economics. "But," he asked, "how is one to devise a 'global strategy' without alienating sovereignty, without transferring responsibilities and competences to common authorities? The question is self-evident, and can only be given one response. This answer is the political strengthening of NATO."[103] Indeed, the way to arrive at common answers to common problems is by strengthening common institutions like NATO that increasingly become supranational in character.

De Gaulle's nationalist approach to the solution of common world problems was no more possible than his attempt to create a cohesive Europe out of self-consciously sovereign national states. When applied to NATO, de Gaulle's nationalist approach consisted of two alternate plans: Either downgrade NATO by creating an exclusive triumvirate within it, or if that failed, destroy NATO by other means. When it became apparent that the Gaullist concept of a triumvirate would never be adopted, those statesmen and officials associated with NATO recognized what was in store for them. The debate shifted, Stikker recalled, to the question of "how far it was feasible for France to be 'less and less in NATO' [de Gaulle's words to Macmillan at Rambouillet in December 1962] and how much harm the new French attitude might do."[104]

For a while it appeared that de Gaulle's assault on NATO would take the form of proposals to "reform" the Alliance in accordance with his nationalist principles. In a joint communique issued following a de Gaulle-Adenauer meeting in July 1960, the two statesmen said that it was their judgment "that without haste but at an appropriate time a reform of the Atlantic organization would serve a useful purpose."[105] Subsequent developments soon showed that each had a very different idea of what "reform" meant.

De Gaulle's interpretation, elaborated at a press conference of September 5, 1960, consisted of two points. First, he reiterated his demand made in his triumvirate proposal that the scope of the Alliance be extended from Europe to the whole world, "at least among the world powers of the West." Second, he repeated his attack on the principle of integration. "The defense of a country, while being of course combined with that of other countries, must have a national character." He cited the withdrawal of the French Mediterranean fleet from NATO command as an example of what such a reorganization should entail. Another example was French refusal to permit the stockpiling of U.S. nuclear weapons under American custodianship on French soil for use by aircraft assigned to NATO. "France feels that if atomic weapons are to be stockpiled on her territory, these weapons should be in her own hands. Given the nature of these weapons and the possible consequences of their use, France obviously cannot leave her own destiny and even her own life to the discretion of others." In sum, "this is what France understands by the reform of the Atlantic organization."[106]

Secretary of State Christian Herter promptly replied with arguments that were to be heard continually as de Gaulle pushed NATO toward its crisis. Herter took issue with the Gaullist political premise by holding that "integration in defense is possible without detracting from the sovereignty of independent yet interdependent members of the alliance." In military terms, modern weapons technology "substantially reduces the margins of time and space available for military defense. This means that a collective security effort, to be capable of fulfilling its purpose in the present age, requires a far greater degree of integration in planning, command and logistic support than has been the case in the past."[107] The experience in two world wars of mobilizing and creating combined commands after the start of hostilities would no longer be possible. Adenauer soon reinforced Herter's position, thereby renouncing his own joint communique with de Gaulle, when he declared: "It is impossible that NATO be permitted to dissolve into national armies that will have to be called together in the moment of danger. I believe that integration cannot be strong enough."[108]

What Herter and Adenauer neglected to mention was the anomaly of de Gaulle's willingness to continue to accept U.S. nuclear weapons under American custodianship for French aircraft stationed in Germany. Doubtless they purposely avoided raising this issue publicly so as not to aggravate an already tense relationship. It is significant that de Gaulle continued to accept U.S. nuclear weapons for French aircraft in Germany for another six years, until they were withdrawn on American initiative as a result of de Gaulle's decision to pull out of NATO. How could one explain the illogic of de Gaulle's policy of rejecting U.S. nuclear weapons for France while accepting them for French forces in Germany? Surely this could not be ascribed to military considerations, since supersonic aircraft and missiles have, in effect, obliterated national boundaries on the crowded beachhead of Western Europe. Only if one viewed the world through the eyes of a nineteenth-century nationalist who held uppermost considerations of political prestige and national pride could this illogic be understood.

De Gaulle's determination to pursue his own unique nuclear policy was emphasized by his unwillingness to accept the Athens guidelines for the use of nuclear weapons, which were adopted by all the other NATO partners at the NATO Ministerial meeting in May 1962. His commitment to pursue a solitary French nuclear policy was also reaffirmed in the aftermath of the Kennedy-Macmillan conference at Nassau in December 1962.

The decision taken at Nassau to offer Britain the Polaris missile in place of the cancelled Skybolt was a piece of hasty improvisation that had unfortunate consequences for Anglo-American relations with de Gaulle. This appeared to be another instance of U.S. aid to its "privileged" British ally at the expense of similar aid to France. For the sake of protocol, it was a blunder not to have de Gaulle present, although the Americans had come to Nassau not expecting to have to make such an offer and therefore there had seemed to be no reason to invite de Gaulle. Nevertheless, before issuing the Nassau communique, both Kennedy and Macmillan agreed that France would be eligible for the same arrangements agreed upon for Britain and so notified de Gaulle. Even so, the Polaris offer presented difficulties for France, since unlike Britain, the French had neither the nuclear warheads for the Polaris missiles nor the needed submarine technology to make them operational. Both Kennedy and Macmillan realized that prolonged negotiations would be required to bring the French up to the British level of nuclear sophistication, yet both were prepared to see such a deal as an opportunity to move de Gaulle back toward NATO. Consequently the American and British Ambassadors in Paris, Charles Bohlen and Sir Pierson Dixon, were instructed to see de Gaulle at once and enter into the detailed examination of the full scope of nuclear assistance that France would require. The offer of aid that Bohlen and Dixon presented to de Gaulle would have given France a small but modern nuclear submarine force, which France would not otherwise have achieved on its own for another decade.

The only condition was that France "assign" this nuclear force to NATO so that it could be targeted for NATO purposes. Even this requirement had a loophole, since Britain was entitled under the Nassau accord to withdraw its force from NATO whenever it judged that "supreme national interests" were at stake. Since such a crisis was clearly the only time that these weapons might be used, for all practical purposes Nassau asked very little of the British. Similarly, its extension to France asked very little of de Gaulle. Part of the Nassau agreement did mention the idea, otherwise poorly explained, of a multilateral nuclear force, but in their discussions with de Gaulle the American and British Ambassadors both made it clear that they were talking only about assigning to NATO a French nuclear force that would otherwise remain fully under French control.

What de Gaulle was offered amounted, in effect, to a nuclear triumvirate inside NATO, and this seemed to go a good way toward meeting de Gaulle's various tripartite proposals. Yet de Gaulle turned the offer down. A nuclear triumvirate was only one element in his scheme, and if he could not have it all he would have none of it. Furthermore the consequences of accepting this offer would only have made France the equal of Britain and would have kept both at least nominally within NATO. De Gaulle's aim was that France should be both bigger than Britain and be so outside of NATO.[109]

And so de Gaulle proceeded undeterred to disengage from NATO. In June 1963 he withdrew the remaining elements of the French fleet under NATO command; first those assigned to the Channel Command and then those in the North Atlantic under the SACLANT. Neither of these moves could be rationalized by the possible need to use these fleets outside the NATO Treaty area in the Middle East or Africa, which was de Gaulle's explanation for withdrawing his Mediterranean fleet from NATO. The blow at the Channel and Atlantic Commands was clearly aimed at weakening NATO naval forces in the heart of the treaty area itself.

These moves were followed by a statement in July 1963 in which de Gaulle again voiced his dissatisfaction with NATO: "As far as the French government is concerned, important modifications are necessary with regard to the terms and conditions of our participation in the Alliance, since this organization has been built on the basis of integration, which today is no longer valid for us."[110] Whether this was a renewed invitation to examine NATO reform or a veiled threat to quit NATO was, at the time, not clear. But as one NATO diplomat then remarked to this writer: "If de Gaulle wants a greater share in running the Alliance or if he has some specific ideas on reforming the Alliance, then he has to *talk* in the Alliance." De Gaulle continued periodically to issue Delphic public pronouncements, but did nothing in the way of private political consultation aimed at evolving concrete plans for Alliance reform.

By the time Stikker retired as NATO Secretary General in the summer of 1964, French participation in NATO was almost nominal in character. As a private citizen, Stikker was then free to describe the political guerilla warfare de Gaulle had waged all during his tenure as Secretary General.

> France, for instance, vetoed for many months a long overdue increase in salaries for the international staff; it vetoed the appointment of one man who should be the responsible officer, under the Secretary General, for a work of $300 million for a new communications system for modern airplanes; it vetoed for a long time the appointment of a Science Advisor; it tried to prevent the Secretary General from asking personal advice on a military problem from SACEUR; it refused for a long time to explain to me or my staff its policy on strategy, and only once or twice in more than three years was I permitted to read a French political report.[111]

To this might be added a long list of obstructionist tactics, such as de Gaulle's *demarche* to prevent Stikker from mediating the Cyprus dispute between Greece and Turkey,[112] French adoption of its own rifle bore, which broke the hard-won Alliance agreement for weapons standardization;[113] and the persistent French refusal to permit the repair of SHAPE Headquarters, which were hastily erected in temporary buildings.[114] These moves, to be sure, were not crippling, and the North Atlantic Council was somehow able to proceed with its business, but as Stikker concluded, "the waste of time and energy, which could have been spent on so many other important questions, but which was required to deal with the French attitude, was a high price to have to pay."[115]

THE FRENCH WITHDRAWAL FROM NATO

In the fall of 1965 de Gaulle finally gave clear warning of his intention to withdraw French forces from NATO and, it would seem, to denounce the North Atlantic Treaty itself. "Upon the expiration of the commitments formerly undertaken—that is, in 1969 by the latest—the subordination known as 'integration' which is provided for by NATO and which hands our fate over to foreign authority shall cease as far as we are concerned."[116] This statement was not only ambiguous, but inaccurate. From it one might conclude that the commitments undertaken by the North Atlantic Treaty would expire in 1969. Not so, since there was no time limit placed on the duration of the treaty. However, Article 13 provided that "after the treaty has been in force for 20 years" a state could give one year's notice of denunciation, after which it would cease to be a member. The treaty came into force on August 24, 1949; 20 years later, or August 24, 1969, would have been the first date upon which the treaty could have been properly denounced, and a member would only be entitled to withdraw one year later, or August 24, 1970.[117] But de Gaulle was apparently not talking about denouncing the treaty. Rather, he was objecting to what he called "the subordination known as 'integration' which is provided for by NATO." He had previously drawn a distinction between the treaty and NATO,[118] and in his view it was possible to disengage from NATO while remaining a treaty signatory.

It was this solution that de Gaulle fixed upon in his declaration of February 21, 1966. "Without going back on her adherence to the Atlantic Alliance, France is going, between now and the final date set for her obligations, which is April 4, 1969, to continue to modify successively the measures currently practiced, insofar as they concern her." Again de Gaulle misrepresented the treaty. April 4, 1969 would have been 20 years after the treaty was signed, not 20 years after it had come into force, and as already noted the earliest date a state could cease to be a treaty member would be in August 1970. Moreover, these dates referred to the denunciation of the treaty, and de Gaulle was talking about leaving NATO, for which there were no legal provisions. As for his intentions regarding NATO, he said that he aimed to restore what he called "a normal situation of sovereignty," in which all French forces, on the ground, in the air, and on the seas would be withdrawn from NATO commands, and every foreign element stationed in France, if it chose to remain there, would also have to come under sole French control.[119]

Having so decreed, de Gaulle then reportedly disconcerted his ministers by instructing them to prepare memoranda "dealing with the implications and modalities of extricating France not just from NATO but from the Alliance itself."[120] It was judged that French interests in Germany and perhaps French rights in a German settlement might be jeopardized by withdrawing from the Atlantic Alliance. Moreover, French leverage with Moscow would probably be greater if de Gaulle remained inside the Alliance where he could pursue his obstructionist policies than outside it where he could have little influence over allied affairs. While de Gaulle decided to adhere to his previously stated position of disengaging only from NATO, his willingness to contemplate withdrawing from the Alliance, to which he publicly professed to remain loyal, provided a clue about the earnestness of his intentions to be a reliable partner.

Subsequent official French delcarations only served to arouse further anxiety. In de Gaulle's handwritten note to President Johnson of March 7, 1966, a curious phrase appeared when de Gaulle asserted that although France would cease participation in the integrated commands and no longer place French forces at the disposal of NATO, France would continue to be ready "to fight on the side of her Allies in the event that one of them should be the object of an unprovoked aggression."[121] The words "unprovoked aggression" were obviously not a meaningless slip, since they were quickly picked up and repeated in a variety of official statements and speeches by Gaullist spokesmen. While this qualification was meant to apply to all of the NATO states, the Germans instantly understood that it was especially directed at them. Since they lived along a tense and exposed frontier, conceivably some border incident might occur in which Paris would only support Bonn if the French decided that the incident was provoked by the East. An "unprovoked" attack, as Dean Acheson observed, "is a slippery term, because an attack is usually the result of a quarrel and nobody knows who provoked whom. . . . Suspicion always arises when someone introduces a new and slippery phrase to loosen up their obligations."[122]

Similar evidence of the attempt to loosen up the French obligations under the North Atlantic Treaty was found in the declaration of then Premier Georges Pompidou. In an interview on French television on March 28, 1966, Pompidou said: "Do not pretend that we are leaving NATO because we do not wish to send a few battalions to Vietnam. . . . It is not there that we risk being dragged into war." Asked about the position of France "in the case of a war between the Soviet Union and the United States," the French Premier responded: "I believe that if we are not integrated into the American system, we have a better chance of keeping out of such a war."[123] Pompidou repeated the substance of this remark in his speech before the National Assembly on April 20.[124] This was not just an argument directed against the organization of NATO, but against the essential purpose of collective Western defense of the North Atlantic Treaty itself, to which France presumably remained faithful. Such a statement stood in bold opposition to the heart of the treaty, found in Article 5, which held: "The Parties agree that an armed attack against one or more of them in Europe or North America shall be considered an attack against them all." This article clearly could not be reconciled with French neutrality in the event of a war between the Soviet Union and the United States.

De Gaulle thus sought to draw several exceedingly fine lines. He distinguished between the North Atlantic Treaty and the political and military organism that placed forces in being under a common political authority and an integrated military command, which alone made credible the paper commitments of the treaty. He then repudiated the spirit and substance of the treaty itself, and while misrepresenting its withdrawal provisions, claimed to cling to its letter and to remain a signatory in good standing. He drew the distinction between aggression and unprovoked aggression as a qualification for bringing the treaty into force, with himself as the sole judge as to which type of action had occurred. Finally he attempted to retain the guarantee of NATO protection, while doing nothing himself to contribute to the strength of NATO.

It is frequently held that de Gaulle carried French opinion behind his foreign policy ventures. In many instances this may have been the case, but it was clearly not so with respect to his NATO policies. A poll taken just after de Gaulle's demarches of March 1966 asked the question: "Do you believe it is desirable for France to withdraw from NATO?" Of those polled, 40 percent offered no opinion, but of the 60 percent who did, 38 percent said "no," while only 22 percent agreed with de Gaulle by saying "yes."[125] That is, of those who expressed an opinion, the sentiment ran against de Gaulle nearly two to one. This could hardly be considered an overwhelming mandate for the Gaullist campaign against NATO.

Lack of popular support, however, was not to deter de Gaulle from moving toward his long-sought objective of maneuvering France with "free hands" in an effort to become "the arbiter between the Soviet and Anglo-American camps." In effect, de Gaulle had opted for neutralism under the protective cover of one of the two antagonists. It is true, of course, that in defending Europe, NATO would be obliged to defend France as an unavoidable consequence of its geographical position. But perhaps another way of viewing this prospect would be to say that France, whether integrated into NATO or not, would be engulfed by the same hostilities that swept over NATO Europe. However, without the benefit of participating in the integrated military activities of NATO, French forces, including their nuclear forces, might lack the crucial information needed to make a timely and effective response. As Dirk Stikker noted, "one of the principal technical functions of NATO has been to prepare in advance the commitments to be undertaken by its members under the terms of Article 5." But once de Gaulle had asserted his full freedom of action, France could not expect "that it may now receive the same automatic support in extreme circumstances on which the Fourteen can rely between themselves."[126]

One of the consequences of the French withdrawal from NATO was the brusk eviction notice for the U.S. forces and equipment located in France. Here de Gaulle did not even pretend to abide by the letter of the treaties involved. He simply declared that April 1, 1967 would be the terminal date for the removal of all allied troops and installations.[127] The United States responded by pointing out that four bilateral U.S.-French agreements relating to a U.S. depot, air bases, military headquarters, and pipeline provided "that they shall remain in force for the duration of the North Atlantic Treaty, unless the two governments by mutual consent decide before hand to terminate them." Despite these provisions for mutual consent and with no other mention of a cut-off date, de Gaulle unilaterally declared that all such U.S. installations must be out of France within one year. In addition, another bilateral treaty on communications systems provided "that if one party should wish to modify its terms, the parties will consult and that, if they are unable to come to agreement within one year, the agreement may be terminated effective after a period of one additional year."[128] While this treaty did have provisions for unilateral denunciation, at least two years should have elapsed under its terms before it could be terminated. Clearly de Gaulle violated all five bilateral treaties.

In denouncing the integrated, multilateral NATO command structure what would de Gaulle have put in its place? Presumably he would have had the West revert to a classic nineteenth-century military type of alliance, that is, a series of bilateral military agreements. And how much confidence would any NATO member be entitled to put in a new series of bilateral agreements, in view of de Gaulle's blatant disregard of those that he had just torn up? All this, of course was quite aside from the political and military dangers of trying to unscramble the NATO omelet and to replace a defense system designed to face the risks of the missile age with an archaic alliance system that has already proven to be disastrous under less exacting conditions.

THE REASONS FOR THE ASSAULT ON NATO

De Gaulle had given clear warning in his secret triumvirate proposal of September 1958 that unless his demands were met he would henceforth subordinate French participation in NATO to the pursuit of French national interests on a global scale. But did that mean that de Gaulle not only was prepared to leave NATO, but to destroy it as well? Paul-Henri Spaak, who dealt with de Gaulle as NATO Secretary General during the period when the secret memorandum was under consideration, thought that de Gaulle sought both objectives. "Since his views on how the world should be run had been rejected, he was determined to destroy the organization which was the chief obstacle to his schemes. From that time on, NATO was under sentence of death so far as de Gaulle was concerned."[129] It was simply a matter of awaiting the right time to strike.

At the beginning of 1966, when de Gaulle had judged that the decisive moment had come, he gave various reasons for opening his grand assault on NATO. In his declaration of February 21, 1966 he cited several "new conditions" that he claimed justified his initiative. It was "quite clear," he said, "that owing to the internal and external evolution of the countries of the East, the Western world is no longer threatened today as it was at the time when the U.S. protectorate was set up in Europe under the cover of NATO."[130] Or, as de Gaulle stated at the end of 1966: "In Europe the cold war that lasted for twenty years is in the process of disappearing."[131] Since de Gaulle preferred to ignore the factor of Communist ideology in Soviet behavior, it is quite likely that he genuinely regarded the Kremlin as a benign power.

At the same time that Soviet hostile intentions toward Europe could be substantially dismissed, he thought that the U.S. nuclear guarantee for the defense of Europe had lost credibility because Soviet ICBMs could now directly strike the United States, thereby introducing great caution in an American nuclear strike at the Soviet Union in the event that NATO Europe was attacked. The first generation of the force de frappe had just become operational, and this permitted de Gaulle to claim that France, "having become for its part and by its own means an atomic power, is led to assume itself the very extensive strategic and political responsibilities that this capacity involves."[132] Here one's credulity is stretched if one is asked to believe that the first-generation force de frappe, which lacked an invulnerable second-strike capability, could on its own protect France from a Soviet nuclear attack without the aid of the U.S. nuclear force. Perhaps de Gaulle thought these military factors were irrelevant, since Soviet intentions were so benign that the military realities might be safely disregarded. If this explanation is accepted, then there would also be no reason to call the credibility of the U.S. nuclear deterrent into question. It would appear that de Gaulle did not really consider the force de frappe the serious military instrument he professed it to be; rather it was to be a serious political instrument in the pursuit of French grandeur.

A third reason advanced in his February 1966 statement justifying French withdrawal from NATO related to the prospects of a world war breaking out as a result of U.S. involvement in Vietnam. "In that case Europe—whose strategy is, within NATO, that of America—would be automatically involved in the struggle."[133] This argument is also suspect since the commitments undertaken through the North Atlantic Treaty were confined to the European-North American treaty area and did not extend to Asia. Moreover, as already noted, Premier Pompidou had declared in March 1966: "Do not pretend that we are leaving NATO because we do not wish to send a few battalions to Vietnam. . . . It is not there that we risk being dragged into war."[134]

A final factor related to de Gaulle's assessment of the overall global balance of power, which he thought had shifted in America's favor. If France was to assume the position of arbiter between the two camps, it was accordingly necessary to act as if the United States, not the Soviet Union, was the principal enemy, in order to restore the global balance. This reasoning undoubtedly was an important factor in the decision to withdraw from NATO in 1966, but it became explicit in 1967. During the Six-Day War in June, de Gaulle's diplomacy concerning the Middle East coincided almost entirely with Soviet policy.

> Those who approve the French President's policy and those who criticize it [an editor of *L'Express* commented] are agreed on one point: General de Gaulle no longer believes that the United States and Soviet blocs represent powers of the same magnitude. He believes that from now on there is but one superpower in the world—namely, the United States. . . . The General's conclusion is that any American success, whatever it may be, wherever it occurs, can only increase the world's imbalance. He believes that it is in France's best interests to constitute the kernel of a little nucleus capable of offering public opposition to the designs of American policy. "When faced with the power of the United States, only two options are open to you, yes or no," so General de Gaulle recently told a visitor. The General has elected to say no.[135]

De Gaulle personally confirmed this appraisal in his remarks to the press in Bonn, following his meetings with Chancellor Kiesinger on July 12 and 13, 1967. "At the bottom of everything," de Gaulle commented, "lies one fact that appears to dominate reality: America's enormous power. . . . The United States has become the greatest power, and it is automatically moved to extend its power." It is naturally inclined "to exercise preponderant action, that is to say, a hegemony over the others." Under these circumstances, "one can accept things as they are. That is the easiest alternative . . . to be part of the whole in which American power will dominate." De Gaulle rejected this in favor of safeguarding "our national personality." In order to do this France and Germany must remain firmly tied together. "Otherwise it will not be possible to avoid American preponderance." Moreover, the Six of the European Community must ward off American influence, for if they would not do so, "then we would become merged in a different system . . . one under American preponderance."[136]

If de Gaulle genuinely believed that Europe was threatened by American, not Soviet, designs, then it would follow that his purpose in attacking NATO was really to destroy it. That his moves did not bring about this result must have been counted as a bitter disappointment.

This premise has been challenged by Harlan Cleveland, the U.S. Ambassador to NATO during the tumultuous days of de Gaulle's onslaught. In his view, "the whole highly publicized affair was an elaborate charade designed for domestic political effect." According to this interpretation, de Gaulle wanted NATO to remain essentially intact, so as to profit from its continued protection. Cleveland approvingly cited the views of one of his NATO colleagues: "French 'withdrawal' was a cheap, anti-American gesture, which changed almost nothing militarily, certainly did not harm French security, yet enabled the General to crow that he had 'withdrawn from NATO'— for home consumption."[137] This is an appealing and clever explanation. De Gaulle's diplomacy was always theatrical, frequently with greater attention to appearances than to substance. And de Gaulle, according to his own rule book of diplomacy, was capable of deception on a grand scale. Yet Cleveland's interpretation may be too clever to be true. It is difficult to dispel the hunch that de Gaulle's appraisal of the Russians, combined with his anti-American animus, led him to hope that he could really make the whole NATO structure come tumbling down.

De Gaulle certainly showed no inclination to take up the offer of his allies to present ideas on the reform of NATO, which might have made the organization more acceptable to Paris. Instead, acting in his typically independent, unilateral fashion, de Gaulle simply presented his allies with the fait accompli of his decision to withdraw. His failure to consult with his allies was explained by "the fact that no discussion on an effective reform of NATO could be usefully undertaken."[138] A chorus of allied diplomats responded with the query of how it was possible to foreclose successful negotiations unless they had been tried. And Christian Herter complained that "time after time we have inquired of the French government as to what specific changes in the NATO structure it would find desirable, with never an affirmative answer of any kind. This makes all the more incomprehensible the argument that unilateral action by France was in any way justified."[139]* But Spaak, now in the capacity of Belgian Foreign Minister, conjectured that de Gaulle deliberately advanced no proposals for NATO reform, since "he was afraid that any proposals he might make might be accepted. His aim was not to convince but to destroy."[140]

However, de Gaulle did not destroy NATO. The irony in de Gaulle's action was that unwittingly he doubtless did NATO a favor. If de Gaulle had moved ambiguously, hinting that some accommodation might have been possible, while privately holding to

---

*Secretary of State Dean Rusk similarly confirmed that de Gaulle had made the "fundamental announcements of decisions taken without consultation with other members of NATO in March. We have been in touch with France for the last four years asking them for their views about what steps could be taken by NATO to take account of what France has been referring to as changed conditions. We have never heard anything from France on that subject." (Testimony of June 16, 1966, in *Hearings before the Subcommittee on National Security and International Operations of the Committee on Government Operations, United States Senate,* p. 173). Belgian Foreign Minister Spaak added: "The French government has never tried to convince its allies of the validity of its arguments. I testify to that categorically. Of course we knew that changes were desired, but they have never been explained to us, not even in broad lines; I would add that each time that we have tried to examine the problem the French government has evaded the issue. During NATO's spring session at The Hague in 1964 I attempted to open such a discussion. But in vain. At that time M. Couve de Murville, the French Foreign Minister, replied that a discussion was useless because he was convinced that we would never reach agreement. But how could he have known that? How could we ourselves have known that? We had not been able to hear the reasons for what was demanded of us or the extent of the changes thought necessary." Following the French withdrawal from NATO, one of the reasons offered by French spokesmen was their disagreement over NATO nuclear strategy. To this, Spaak observed: "Here I assert with even greater force that not only has France never raised this problem within NATO but that it is she who, in one way or another, has opposed the examination, discussion and clarification of the Alliance's strategy, as the Ottawa meeting in 1963 decided should be done." (Paul-Henri Spaak, "Chaos in Europe," *Atlantic Community Quarterly,* Summer 1966, pp. 212-13.)

his determination to reject NATO integration in any form, he could have embroiled the Alliance in an endless and paralyzing debate. Many of France's European neighbors who had shown themselves to be easily intimidated, and perhaps because of this had been caught up in wishful thinking, would have refused to believe that de Gaulle really was an intransigent nationalist with whom cooperation on any terms except his own was next to impossible. But the brutal manner of de Gaulle's withdrawal from NATO and the expulsion of his allies from France cleared the air and made it possible for the Fourteen to join in a declaration in which they reaffirmed their faith in the basic principles of "an integrated and interdependent military organization" to which "no system of bilateral arrangements can be a substitute." They also rejected as specious the distinction between the treaty and the organization of NATO. "The North Atlantic Treaty and the organization established under it are both alike essential to the security of our countries."[141] By raising the fundamental issue of NATO's survival, de Gaulle forced the other allies to reevaluate NATO and to realize afresh what they had come to take for granted, namely that NATO was an imperative necessity.

As Raymond Aron commented, the Gaullist concept of an alliance was totally out of joint with the nuclear era.

> Those who would like to see the Atlantic Alliance replaced by an alliance of the traditional type, each member free to use atomic weapons as it sees fit and able to rely on automatic support from its allies, has simply failed to grasp the most elementary facts of the new diplomacy shaped by nuclear explosives. What thermonuclear weapons have rendered obsolete is not alliances as such but alliances of the traditional type. The big nations are still able to protect the small ones but will not consent to do so if the latter claim the prerogative of initiating thermonuclear disaster. Alliances will either evolve toward communities or else dissolve altogether: They will certainly not revert to their pre-atomic prototypes.[142]

Aside from maintaining a credible deterrent that was committed to the defense of the Alliance, NATO developed a number of other important functions that contributed to the well-being of its members in peacetime. After surveying some of these functions, one observer concluded: "The range of the organization's activities is immense. It can, of course, be argued that some of its essential work could be done without the machinery provided by NATO. Yet it certainly would not be done efficiently and effectively and some of it would not be done at all." Among the benefits of the organization is the often neglected fact that it is only through the multilateral context of NATO that the smaller powers manage to exert their influence. On the other hand, "in a system of bilateral treaties, only the big countries would really count and the lesser powers would be left to fend for themselves."[143]

NATO INTEGRATION AND GERMANY

It is not only the smaller states that find NATO of value. An official German spokesman explained the commitment of his government to the principle of integration. "The integration of the staff structure is a prerequisite for well-balanced common planning. What is to the advantage of the Alliance as a whole can more easily be worked out by an integrated body than by a number of individual national general staffs." Experience has shown that the various NATO integrated commands tend to develop their own esprit and their own thinking that transcends that of the individual members. In arriving at a truly well-balanced Alliance strategy, "the higher the degree of integration on the staff level, the easier the task will be. The more integration is impeded or cut back, the greater grows the danger of paralyzing if not divisive conflicts." Directly facing the Gaullist argument that "our insistence on the indispensability of Atlantic defense integration is dangerous because of a possible curtailment of the independence of individual nations to the advantage of the United States, and that furthermore, it is even unnecessary because the United States would have to defend Europe anyway," the German spokesman responded that "neither argument is justifiable, at least from the German point of view." The Germans participating in NATO "have learned from experience that teamwork between America and Germany is not a one-way street. It has frequently also led to American understanding and even acceptance of German opinions and practices." One must also face up to a stark fact of U.S. nuclear predominance and the enormous contribution of U.S. forces stationed in Europe. Under these conditions, "it is preferable that the nations to be defended have a seat in the cockpit rather than wait and guess whether and when support will come." Finally, "by strengthening the Alliance and fostering integration within, we hope to develop an institution more durable and reliable than that provided by the classical type of alliance."[144]

The widely shared hope that NATO might develop into a durable institution for uninterrupted military planning as well as continuous and effective interchange of political information, analysis, and consultation is of especial importance in the case of Germany. It was only through the medium of NATO that German rearmament occurred, and all the German armed forces that came into being were assigned to NATO commands. "By seeking to disintegrate NATO," the London *Times* commented, de Gaulle risked "destroying the reassuring political and military framework within which West Germany's leaders have so far been content to make their contribution to West Europe's defense. It is hard to think of a greater disservice the French leader could render his fellow-Europeans, whether in the West or in the East."[145] The disintegration of NATO would necessarily cause the formation of a purely national German army, and with it perhaps a growing demand for the national possession of nuclear weapons. This Germany, set adrift in the midst of Europe, would be faced with the unpalatable choice de Gaulle tried to force upon it: align itself either with Paris or Washington, whereas both should remain firm allies.

Such a Germany might also be gripped by the historical fear of being caught in Franco-Russian pincers and would be tempted to shift its ties and accommodate itself to Moscow. Without NATO, Western Europe, including West Germany, would become much more exposed to all sorts of Soviet pressure tactics that could not be adequately resisted by the small and medium-sized European states all running off to Moscow to strike bargains for their own survival. Instead of stability and detente in Europe, there would be chaos and renewed opportunities for Moscow to shape Europe in line with its own ambitions that had been so successfully frustrated since NATO came into existence. A Western Europe under various degrees of Soviet influence and control would, of course, also be an intolerable threat to the security of the United States.

FRENCH-NATO RELATIONS WHEN THE DUST HAD SETTLED

French defection was not imitated by any other ally, so that Germany remained firmly embedded in NATO, which continued to function substantially intact. De Gaulle's actions, however, did pose a series of special problems between France and NATO that required solution.

The most potentially damaging blow against NATO would have been denial to NATO aircraft of the right to fly over French territory. Without such overflight permission, France, together with neighboring Switzerland and Austria, would have formed a neutral belt splitting NATO Europe in two. The need to fly around instead of over France would have greatly reduced the flexibility of troop dispositions as well as the timely dispatch of reinforcements at moments of crisis. In May 1966, de Gaulle canceled all of the bilateral overflight rights that France had with its former NATO allies, which had been subject to virtually automatic annual renewal. The United States alone had standing authorization for 39 different categories of overflights.[146] Instead, these rights were subjected to monthly review, and then in October 1966 de Gaulle announced that "airplanes that will want to enter our country will do so by virtue of the authorizations that we will grant them *for each separate case* and for the specific period of time that they will be in France or in our skies."[147]

In practice, these regulations produced a mountain of red tape but did not significantly affect overflight patterns. De Gaulle came to realize that denial of these rights would have so embittered relations with his European partners in the Six, especially with Italy and Germany, that it would have had a profound and lasting effect in all other aspects of their relations. Moreover, the Americans surprised de Gaulle by meeting his April 1, 1967 deadline for the evacuation of all French bases and facilities. The French were reportedly convinced that the deadline could not be met and that de Gaulle was ready to invoke cancellation of overflight rights as a penalty. But following the speedy U.S. evacuation, the French announced that starting January 1968 overflight rights would be restored to an annual basis.[148]

From the French point of view, the most dangerous result of the rupture with NATO would have been exclusion from the NATO air defense system. The professional French military was alarmed at this prospect, but the Gaullist political leaders at first gave the impression of being unconcerned. A prominent member of the National Assembly who also had close ties with the military told this writer that the French Chief of Staff, General Ailleret, sent an urgent note to Premier Pompidou, stressing French dependence upon NATO air defense and pleading for a cooperative attitude. Instead, Pompidou's speech to the National Assembly of April 20, 1966, evidently drafted under direct instructions from de Gaulle, said just the opposite: namely, that France found the NATO air alert system of little use, while "our own network—more important than you seem to think— is also useful to the armies of NATO and of the United States itself, do not doubt this."[149]

It seems likely that Pompidou and de Gaulle could not really have believed such an assertion; at least their subsequent action showed that they did not. The unanimous judgment of the French military held that unless France were hooked into the NATO air intelligence and air defense system, the force de frappe would be flying completely deaf and blind. This would have removed whatever shred of credibility that might still have clung to the force de frappe. Consequently, when NATO asked de Gaulle if he wanted to participate in the construction of NADGE, the improved, integrated NATO air defense system, in which, incidentally, a French company shared in the construction contract, de Gaulle replied in the affirmative. Such French participation was mute but explicit recognition of the fact that the realities of twentieth-century interdependence had triumphed over the nineteenth-century Gaullist concept of untrammeled independence.[150]

The NADGE decision served as a test case for establishing the relationship between France and NATO. De Gaulle, in effect, remained both in and out, since he was given the right to pick and choose on an a la carte basis which NATO projects he wished to participate in. Spaak thought the Fourteen made a "mistake; they have been much too generous in conceding some of the French demands. The French government is bold, if nothing else. It rejects all obligations which flow from its membership in NATO, but is quite ready to take part in any joint projects from which it stands to gain." It was strange, Spaak held, that "France's partners have consented to this odd bargain." He asked "what would become of the Alliance if all its members accepted its advantages but rejected any obligations that might benefit their partners? It is mistaken decisions such as this that encouraged General de Gaulle to think he could afford to indulge his every whim."[151]

There is no doubt that de Gaulle had intimidated many of his allies, and in so doing achieved a unique, privileged position. But the Fourteen also wished to keep the breach as narrow as possible. Not only did they fear Gaullist retaliation on issues such as overflight rights, but they wished to prevent de Gaulle from denouncing the Atlantic Alliance itself. This would have made it much more difficult for any post-Gaullist government to move back toward NATO and the whole Western Alliance system.

For his part, de Gaulle showed a willingness to permit the continued use of a American pipeline crossing France from the Atlantic coast at Donges to Metz, which had been constructed to supply U.S. forces in Europe. The French inserted two provisions, however. The pipeline must be operated by a French company, and there could be no assurances that it would be kept in operation in time of emergency or war.[152] These terms were accepted since they appeared preferable to shutting off the peacetime oil flow.

The status of French troops stationed in Germany was also resolved by pragmatic arrangements that provided something less than full satisfaction to all concerned.

General Johannes Steinhoff, who until the summer of 1966 had been Chief of Staff, Allied Air Forces Central Europe, explained why it was impossible to keep French forces with a nuclear mission on German soil. "The introduction of tactical nuclear weapons into SACEUR's arsenal in the mid-1950s," he recalled, "was accompanied by the development of the 'automatic response,' the integration of planning, the standardization of weapons, the unification of intelligence services and codes and the agreement of degrees of combat-readiness to be enforced simultaneously, all of which made collective response to an aggressive act appear credible." When the French authorities were asked in June 1966 how the force de frappe could be related to these agreed procedures, they simply refused to discuss what its status might be "in the event of an emergency." It was clear that "France was unwilling to submit to the type of automatic action that characterizes, for example, air defense and offensive operations." This contrasted with SACEUR's "squadrons of fighter-bombers carrying nuclear weapons" for which "automatic contingency planning has reached a peak of perfection. . . . All assigned units and particularly air units are, in fact, fitted into a common operational plan as has never before been the case in military history." The conclusion was obvious: "A contingent like the French, which will not permit itself to be directed or inspected, for this reason drops out of the air defense system."[153] French insistence upon "coordination" instead of "integration" for its air squadrons in

Germany presented insurmountable obstacles for their continued operation, and so Paris announced that it would withdraw them, effective October 1966.[154]

Those air units that had tactical nuclear missions would have become useless in any event, since the United States removed the nuclear weapons that had been made available to them under the two-key system. For the same reason, de Gaulle was obliged to withdraw his ground-launching rocket and missile forces from Germany, since they too had been armed with U.S. nuclear warheads. The United States had originally provided these nuclear components upon the clearly stipulated understanding that they would only be assigned to an integrated NATO mission. The firepower of the U.S. nuclear warheads formerly allocated to the French forces in Germany, incidentially, amounted to several times that of the entire force de frappe.

The status of conventional French ground troops in Germany did not pose quite the same difficulties as those raised by the air squadrons. Here there was a certain superficial plausibility in opting for cooperation over certain air-defense forces, which must be able to respond to an instant alert. In the case of ground troops, the Supreme Allied Commander had no direct peacetime control over the various national forces. Instead, they would only come under his command at various agreed levels of alert, which differed somewhat from country to country. Therefore, peacetime integration for ground forces has largely been limited to the various NATO command headquarters engaged in planning operations conducted by integrated staffs, and certain other elements of logistic support such as the NATO infrastructure, which has also been a collective, integrated enterprise. As Under Secretary of State Ball pointedly remarked in an interview with *Le Monde* in March 1966, with the exception of the air-defense units, "no French soldier can be given an order to make the slightest move by anyone but the French command. Even in case of war, troops would be placed under the operational command of SHAPE only if the French government 'deemed it necessary,' under Article 5 of the North Atlantic Treaty. Consequently, for the NATO command to be able to dispose of French forces, a national decision, made by the French government, would be necessary."[155] If this is understood, then de Gaulle's violent objection to the principle of integration for ground forces largely came down to an unwillingness to make adequate peacetime arrangements for coordination, which he claimed to support. The provisions of Article 3 of the North Atlantic Treaty regarding continuous individual and collective preparations to resist armed attack had been given substance over the years by the preassigned arrangements, drawn up prior to hostilities, for the joint use of allied ground troops planned by the integrated commands, reinforced by agreements to submit these troops to integrated controls at predefined stages of alert. With French ground troops removed from these arrangements, how useful would their role be in Germany, either as a dependable ally or as a credible foe?

The Germans would have preferred the two French divisions in Germany to be under an integrated NATO command, as were all other foreign troops in Germany. But de Gaulle offered Bonn the choice either of total troop withdrawal or of their remaining in West Germany solely under French control, outside of the NATO framework. Given these alternatives, the German leaders chose the latter course. The continued presence of French troops on German soil, even though there on unsatisfactory terms, at least provided a tangible commitment on the part of France to help defend Germany, since any Soviet aggression against the Federal Republic would also immediately have involved French forces. SACEUR and the French Chief of Staff entered into negotiations "regarding the role of the French forces in Germany and their coordination with NATO in the event of crisis or war," but the French offered "no assurances on which SACEUR could count for planning purposes."[156] It was this relationship of a privileged bilateral arrangement that was given a legal basis when the French and German Foreign Ministers exchanged notes on December 21, 1966, stating in effect that the French troops could remain with no defined NATO role.[157]

"TOUS AZIMUTS": THE LOGICAL END
OF GAULLIST STRATEGY

Official Gaullist doctrine moved even farther away from NATO during 1967-68. The Chief of Staff of the French Armed Forces, General Charles Ailleret, elaborated a new function for the future French strategic nuclear force, which would have profound military and political implications. In the past, the force de frappe had been pointed at the Soviet Union. But "today an analysis of the world situation shows that we should not allow ourselves to be obsessed by the contemplation of this one danger." He attributed peaceful intentions to the Soviet leaders. "Busy as they are in rapidly developing their economy, in striving to raise the people's standard of living, they realize that to do this they need peace and also a certain amount of technical cooperation with the West." Therefore the hypothesis of Soviet aggression "is certainly not to be considered the only or even the primary hypothesis."[158]

From where must one fear aggression in the future, and what doctrine is required to meet it? The answers were that threats could arise from anywhere and this called for a *tous azimuts* response. "It is justifiable to fear that almost anywhere, in the future, large-scale wars may break out, which would probably tend to spread very quickly and take in the greater part of our planet. . . . Since we cannot anticipate from which part of the world the threat to future generations will come," the force de frappe should "not be oriented in only one direction, that of the *a priori* enemy, but be capable of intervening everywhere, or as we say in our military jargon [*à tous azimuts*], at every point of the compass."[159]

The military requirements of such a strategy were clearly the development of ICBMs, which to that time France had not an announced intention of creating. Beyond the first-generation Mirage IV airplanes, there were plans for building an intermediate-range, second-generation, land-based missile force with a reach of about 1,800 miles, and a third-generation, submarine-based missile force of about 1,500-mile range. But, General Ailleret noted, the tous azimuts doctrine would be realized "by developing our present strategic nuclear force to become a thermonuclear force with a worldwide range." That was not all. It would be constructed so that it could "expand further, when this becomes necessary and possible, into a spacial force in an age when the military use of space will have become a reality."[160]

The political implications were equally far-reaching. The Atlantic Alliance was deficient since it was based on deterring aggression by an a priori enemy, the Soviet Union. In the future, however, France would have to face "serious threats other than that of the possible Soviet aggression anticipated by the Atlantic Alliance."[161] "An a priori alliance could not give us a general guarantee of safety, since it is almost impossible to foresee what could one day be the cause of a serious conflict."[162] Here was an official pronouncement that could not only justify the French rupture with NATO, but the denunciation of the Atlantic Alliance and the North Atlantic Treaty itself.

There could be no question that this was official Gaullist doctrine. De Gaulle himself had outlined the tous azimuts theory in his famous speech to the *Ecole Militaire* of November 3, 1959, although apparently few people had then fully grasped its implications. At that time he predicted that "during the coming years we must achieve a force capable of acting exclusively on our behalf— what one might suitably call a 'force de frappe'—susceptible to deployment at any moment anywhere. . . . Since one will be able eventually to destroy France from any point in the world, our force must have the capability of being able to act against every part of the world."[163]

Following the publication of Ailleret's article in December 1967, de Gaulle again appeared before an audience at the *Ecole Militaire*, this time on January 27, 1968, to give the doctrine his personal endorsement. "Our strategy must be all azimuths," he told the assembled officers. "You must know it, you must see it and your studies and your state of mind must get used to it. It is a new system destined to last for a very long period of time."[164]

The long-term prospect was for France, a medium-sized power, to invest heavily and continually in a force de frappe on a scale that could only be realized by the neglect of its conventional forces. As Raymond Aron observed: "France, from the moment when she disavows permanent alliances and asserts a worldwide role, will require a complete military panoply which is clearly beyond her resources." De Gaulle was opting for global neutrality, somewhat like Switzerland, except that "there is a difference between Swiss neutrality and the French version of neutrality. Switzerland does not intervene, by word or deed, in any of the world conflicts. She has no allies because she has no enemies. Gaullist France intervenes, at least with words, in every conflict in the world. If she keeps allies without having enemies, it is because she irritates each in turn. . . . The turn of the others will come again."[165]

Not only would French military resources be inadequate for a policy of active global neutrality, but what of the sacrifices that would have to be imposed on the resources devoted to domestic social welfare programs? Alastair Buchan pointed out the "fraud" in the Gaullist budget figures, which systematically tried to hide the expenditures on the force de frappe, compared with other needs.[166]

But de Gaulle's attention was not turned toward alleviating domestic social needs, only toward glorifying French nationalism. The tous azimuts doctrine represented de Gaulle's megalomania in its purest form: France, independent, standing alone, would achieve grandeur by maneuvering on a global scale with completely "free hands," unfettered by a priori alliances. France, in short, would take on the world.

There were other practical difficulties involved in this doctrine beside the overextension of resources. Every state, however great, if it is to undertake meaningful planning, has "to decide who [its] most probable enemies are, and to this extent," Buchan commented, "a strategy of tous azimuts is nonsense. It is, indeed, the very abnegation of planning." Moreover, by viewing all states as potential enemies, even if the contingency is a distant one, all states would necessarily engage France in an adversary relationship. "The position of a small nuclear power with small counterforce capability and many potential adversaries is not a happy or secure one. . . . The rest of the international community may treat you as we treat porcupines—with respect, but with neither deference, affection nor confidence."[167] Buchan aptly summed up the tous azimuts concept as the "*folie de grandeur.*" "The idea of a global French system of deterrence seems as fantastic as the General's policy for the liberation of Quebec."[168]

De Gaulle was to discover that this doctrine, which was "destined to last for a very long period of time," was destined to last for but a few months. The May-June "events" of 1968 that convulsed France required, among other things, a serious diversion of funds from the force de frappe to pressing social problems. The month-long general strike undermined the strength of the French economy and led to a crisis of the French franc in November and to its devaluation in 1969. The resulting austerity budgets cut deeply into the ambitious plans for the force de frappe, which were both scaled down and implemented at a slower pace. It was subsequently decided that of the 27 second-generation, land-based IRBM launchers planned, only 18 would be built. Five ballistic missile submarines were still planned for the third-generation force, although their completion dates were pushed back a number of years. As to the much-heralded fourth-generation ICBM force, the keystone of the *tous azimuts* strategy, plans for its construction were simply abandoned.[169]

The turmoil in France had scarcely subsided when the Soviet Union invaded Czechoslovakia in August 1968. Now all of the Gaullist premises about the evolution of European politics in general, and Soviet behavior in particular, were contradicted by events. Europe was not moving toward a cooperative entente from the Atlantic to the Urals. The Soviet invasion simply reaffirmed the division of Europe into hostile blocs. Neither was Soviet conduct testimony to its willingness to release the states of Eastern Europe from its grip, as de Gaulle had sought to encourage by his trips to Poland and Rumania. The Soviet leaders, whom de Gaulle and Ailleret had credited with peaceful intentions, again demonstrated that they were willing to employ massive armed force if they felt their interests threatened. In Czechoslovakia their interests revolved about the ideological questions of how a Communist dictatorship might be modified in a more humane direction. The Leninist tenets about the nature of dictatorship remained very much alive, despite de Gaulle's willingness to dismiss ideological questions as irrelevant. Meanwhile France, weakened by disorders at home and with its prestige damaged abroad, could do very little to enhance its security by pursuing its policy of "free hands."

THE GAULLIST RETREAT TO REALITY AND IMPROVED RELATIONS WITH NATO

De Gaulle did not publicly eat his own words. He did not have to; his ministers did it for him. They now took significant steps back toward NATO and the Atlantic Alliance.

In November 1968 Foreign Minister Michel Debré associated France with the NATO Ministerial warning to the Soviet Union that any further "Soviet intervention directly or indirectly affecting the situation in Europe or in the Mediterranean would create an international crisis with grave consequences." Gone were the illusions of the tous azimuts doctrine about the United States being an equal, if not greater, threat to France than the Soviet Union. Further, the NATO Ministers took note of a declaration by Debré that, "for its part, unless events in the years to come were to bring about a radical change in East-West relations, the French Government considers that the Alliance must continue as long as it appears to be necessary."[170] When Defense Minister Pierre Messmer appeared before the National Assembly on December 5, 1968, he affirmed simply: "We are in the Atlantic Alliance, and there we shall remain."[171]

French strategic doctrine also underwent a radical revision. In a lecture on March 3, 1969 to the Institute of Advanced National Defense Studies, the new Chief of Staff, General Michel Fourquet, unveiled a nuclear strategy that substantially repudiated the views of his predecessor, General Ailleret (who was killed in a plane crash on March 9, 1968). Instead of anticipating hostilities equally from all directions, Fourquet expected that French forces would be engaged "against an enemy coming from the East," and that such French units would "normally act in close coordination with the forces of our allies."[172] Moreover, Fourquet spoke of a "graduated response" in the use of force to repel aggression. While this doctrine was not identical to the accepted NATO doctrine of a flexible response, it represented a significant evolution of French strategic thought toward that of NATO, in contrast to the "all or nothing" doctrine of General Ailleret which had totally contradicted the NATO strategy.[173]

Fourquet's doctrine provided the theoretical basis for the marked increase in French cooperation with NATO, which had obviously been undertaken with de Gaulle's personal approval, commencing in the fall of 1968. The public discussion of the new doctrine in the spring of 1969 coincided with de Gaulle's political retirement. In April 1969 de Gaulle put his personal prestige on the line one time too many when submitting a referendum to the electorate, and when on this occasion the people disapproved, he stumbled out of power. However, the movement back toward NATO could not be interpreted as a "betrayal" on the part of de Gaulle's successors, since, however quietly, de Gaulle himself had recognized the failure of his tous azimuts strategy and found it necessary to abandon it in favor of strengthened ties with NATO and the Atlantic Alliance. "Integration," of course, remained forbidden, but there were a number of activities in which France could participate without reentering the NATO integrated military command structure.

Even before the jolt of Czechoslovakia, French units had joined in various NATO military and naval exercises that were designed to improve common action in the face of an enemy threat.[174] Such activity was always discreet and unpublicized, since the French officers did not want to present an open challenge to Gaullist theory, while the NATO commanders were pleased to get French cooperation on any terms that, in practice, were often surprisingly good.

When French relations with NATO could be regarded as more respectable from the fall of 1968 onward, such activity became both more intense and less clandestine. The liaison between the French army, in particular the two French divisions in Germany, and the NATO forces in Central Europe increased considerably. When MARAIRMED, a NATO command to improve air surveillance of Soviet activity in the Mediterranean, was activated in November 1968, French air reconnaissance squadrons informed NATO of their flight plans and of results obtained.[175] Subsequently, Vice Admiral Isaac Kidd, commander of the U.S. Sixth Fleet, remarked that aside from the fact that French vessels were no longer committed to an integrated NATO command in time of war, the result of the French withdrawal from such commands "had brought little change in close cooperation between French and NATO naval operations in the Mediterranean."[176]

The French have also maintained a high-level liaison mission with NATO's Military Committee, even though France was no longer formally a member of it. Over time France began to participate in military discussions of the Alliance through liaison arrangements with a member state on the various military groups, which was charged with the mission of keeping the French informed and even of reporting back French views for consideration.[177]

France also retained membership in a number of NATO organizations and especially held a keen interest in those that undertook research and development on the frontiers of military technology that the French thought useful for themselves. French participation in NADGE, the air defense warning system, has already been noted. In addition, France has continued to participate in the following NATO agencies: the Central Europe Operating Agency, which controls a NATO oil pipeline and storage system, with headquarters in Versailles; the NATO Maintenance and Spare Parts Agency in Luxembourg; the NATO Hawk Production and Logistics Organization, established for the Hawk antiaircraft missile, located at Rueil-Malmaison, France; the Military Agency for Standardization in Brussels; the Advisory Group for Aerospace Research and Development in Neuilly, outside of Paris; the Allied Naval Communications Agency in London; the SACLANT Anti-Submarine Warfare Research Center in La Spezia, Italy; the Conference of National Armament Directors in Brussels; and three small organizations, the Allied Radio Frequency Agency, the Allied Long Lines Agency, and the Allied Communications Security Agency, whose personnel are drawn from the NATO International Military Staff in Brussels.[178] France also displayed great interest in the NATO

Integrated Communications System, but finally did not accept membership.

France never relinquished its seat on NATO's highest political body, the North Atlantic Council, although it does not consider military questions that relate to the integrated military commands. The latter questions are discussed by the Council through the simple device of having the same individuals from the same countries, minus France, convene as the Defense Planning Committee.

When the Eurogroup was formed in 1969, it included all the European members of the Atlantic Alliance except France, Portugal, and Iceland. Here again France employed its a la carte technique by sending observers to some of the Eurogroup's working parties that were of special interest to it.[179] One of the principal purposes of the Eurogroup is to rationalize European arms procurement programs so as to meet the equipment needs of its members at lower costs than are possible through the small, redundant, and conflicting national arms programs. Since France is a major European armaments producer, it would appear to be in French interests to become a full member of the Eurogroup so as to prevent it from being excluded from any future international procurement arrangements. The Eurogroup was not established as part of the integrated military structure of NATO, and thus France could play its full part in the Eurogroup without raising any doctrinal questions about military integration.

It would not be quite so easy to solve the problem that must arise as France makes available the pluton tactical nuclear weapon for use by its two divisions in Germany. Here the logic of geography and weapons systems calls for the reentry of French forces in Germany into the integrated NATO Central European commands. Since these French tactical nuclear weapons would be deployed on German territory, the Federal Republic and more broadly NATO, into which all German forces are integrated, would have the right to demand some control over their use so as to avoid conflicts with the planned uses of tactical nuclear weapons on the part of NATO-assigned troops. From the Soviet point of view, the existence of French nuclear weapons on German soil "integrates" France into German and NATO defenses, regardless of what French intentions might be. It would therefore be far better for Paris to acknowledge this and to resume its former intimate collaboration, not only in the field in Central Europe, but also by joining the work of the Nuclear Planning Group where overall Alliance nuclear doctrine is evolved.

Such a step would be difficult for those who still cling to Gaullist dogma about the supremacy of the nation-state. However, the leadership groups in France cannot be expected to adhere to this position forever. Even at the height of de Gaulle's power in 1965, a survey of French elite opinion revealed the limited basis from which de Gaulle operated. When asked, "do you think that present trends are making the nation-state obsolete as a political form?" 64 percent of the respondents answered "yes." And when asked, "do you consider this to be a good thing?," 62 percent replied in the affirmative.[180] Since that time, the countries in the Atlantic Community have obviously become increasingly interdependent. It is now a matter of awaiting the time until new French leaders discard those remaining aspects of Gaullism that prevent France from fully coming back into the twentieth century.

NOTES

1. Alastair Buchan, review of Drew Middleton's *The Atlantic Community*, in the New York *Times Book Review*, October 31, 1965.

2. James Richardson, "The Concept of Atlantic Community," *Journal of Common Market Studies*, October 1964, p. 2. The creative concept of an Atlantic Community, on both sides of the ocean, "would include a wide range of policy tendencies: Those interested in pragmatic solutions to specific Atlantic problems as well as those seeking to establish new Atlantic institutions; Europeans interested in an independent Europe closely related to the United States, as well as those who give priority to Atlantic over European ties; Americans prepared to move toward European nuclear partnership in the future as well as those prepared to work for it in the present" (p. 6).

3. William Henry Chamberlin, "NATO's Future," *New Leader*, April 13, 1964, p. 20.

4. Charles de Gaulle, *The Call to Honour, 1940-1942* (New York, 1955), p. 9.

5. Ibid., p. 109.

6. Ibid., p. 228.

7. Robert Murphy, *Diplomat Among Warriors* (New York, 1964), p. 182.

8. Charles de Gaulle, *Unity, 1942-1944, Documents* (New York, 1959), pp. 259-60.

9. Charles de Gaulle, *Salvation, 1944-1946* (London, 1960), pp. 55-56.

10. Ibid., p. 58.

11. Ibid., pp. 178-79.

12. Charles de Gaulle, *Memoirs of Hope* (London, 1971), p. 201.

13. Ibid., p. 214.

14. President de Gaulle's second press conference, November 10, 1959, Ambassade de France, New York, Speeches and Press Conferences, No. 145, pp. 4-5.

15. Speech by President de Gaulle, April 19, 1963, Ambassade de France, New York, French Affairs, No. 154, p. 4.

16. Speech by President de Gaulle, August 10, 1967, Ambassade de France, New York, Speeches and Press Conferences, No. 268, p. 4.

17. Speech by Premier Michel Debré, October 13, 1960, Ambassade de France, New York, Speeches and Press Conferences, No. 156, p. 8.

18. President de Gaulle's tenth press conference, July 23, 1964, Ambassade de France, New York, Speeches and Press Conferences, No. 208, p. 5.

19. See, for example, speech by President de Gaulle, May 19, 1965, New York *Times*, May 20, 1965.

20. Speech by President de Gaulle, September 28, 1963, New York *Times*, September 29, 1963.

21. See the articles by Clarence K. Streit in the following issues of *Freedom & Union*: April 1960, pp. 1-5; February 1963, pp. 3-4; March 1963, pp. 7-12; July-August 1963, pp. 22-23; June 1965, p. 5; September 1965, pp. 2-6; April 1966, pp. 11-12, 16.

22. President de Gaulle's sixth press conference, May 15, 1962, Ambassade de France, New York, Speeches and Press Conferences, No. 175, pp. 5-6.

23. Clarence K. Streit, *Freedom & Union*, July-August 1963, pp. 22-23.

24. President de Gaulle's twelfth press conference, September 9, 1965, Ambassade de France, New York, Speeches and Press Conferences, No. 228, p. 4.

25. President de Gaulle's seventh press conference, January 14, 1963, Ambassade de France, New York, Speeches and Press Conferences, No. 185, p. 7. When de Gaulle rejected Britain's renewed entry bid in 1967, he conjured up the same fear that Britain's

Atlantic orientation would deprive the Six of their European personality. See President de Gaulle's fifteenth press conference, May 16, 1967, Ambassade de France, New York, Speeches and Press Conferences, No. 260A, p. 11. See also ibid., pp. 6-7.

26. President de Gaulle's eighth press conference, July 29, 1963, Ambassade de France, New York, Speeches and Press Conferences, No. 192, p. 9.

27. President de Gaulle's ninth press conference, January 31, 1964, Ambassade de France, New York, Speeches and Press Conferences, No. 201, pp. 11-12.

28. Speech by Ambassador Herve Alphand, October 22, 1963, Ambassade de France, New York, Speeches and Press Conferences, No. 195, p. 5.

29. Jay Walz, " 'Vive Quebec Libre!' de Gaulle Cries Out to Montreal Crowd," New York Times, July 25, 1967.

30. "Text of Statement of French Government," July 31, 1967, New York Times, August 1, 1967.

31. Jay Walz, "Pearson Rebukes de Gaulle on Call for 'Free Quebec,' " New York Times, July 26, 1967.

32. President de Gaulle's sixteenth press conference, November 27, 1967, Ambassade de France, New York, Speeches and Press Conferences, No. 276, pp. 7-9.

33. "Text of Pearson's Reply to de Gaulle on Quebec," November 28, 1967, New York Times, November 29, 1967.

34. See, for example, the events reported in the New York Times, August 24, 1967, April 28, 1968, May 5 and 10, 1968, September 12, 1968, October 17, 1969.

35. Charles de Gaulle, The Edge of the Sword (London, 1960), translated from the French edition, 1932, p. 13.

36. President de Gaulle's third press conference, September 5, 1960, Ambassade de France, New York, Speeches and Press Conferences, No. 152, p. 8.

37. President de Gaulle's sixth press conference, May 15, 1962, p. 5.

38. De Gaulle, The Edge of the Sword, pp. 41-42.

39. Ibid., pp. 60-61.

40. Ibid., pp. 96, 98.

41. President de Gaulle's third press conference, September 5, 1960, p. 8.

42. President de Gaulle's tenth press conference, July 23, 1964, p. 6.

43. Speech by President de Gaulle, April 27, 1965, Ambassade de France, New York, French Affairs, No. 175, p. 2. See also President de Gaulle's tenth press conference, July 23, 1964, p. 5.

44. Max Kohnstamm, *The European Community and Its Role in the World* (Columbia, Mo., 1964), pp. 37-38.

45. Ibid., p. 41.

46. President de Gaulle's eighth press conference, July 29, 1963, pp. 12-13.

47. President de Gaulle's tenth press conference, July 23, 1964, p. 7.

48. Conversation of May 30, 1963 with Arthur J. Olsen, then Bonn correspondent for the New York *Times*.

49. *The Bulletin*, Press and Information Office of the German Federal Government, May 21, 1963, p. 2.

50. President de Gaulle's fourteenth press conference, October 28, 1966, Ambassade de France, New York, Speeches and Press Conferences, No. 253A, p. 4.

51. Speech by Foreign Minister Maurice Couve de Murville, April 14, 1966, Ambassade de France, New York, Speeches and Press Conferences, No. 244A, p. 7.

52. President de Gaulle's eleventh press conference, February 4, 1965, Ambassade de France, New York, Speeches and Press Conferences, No. 216, p. 12. See also Drew Middleton, "U.S. Refuses to Abandon German Unity Settlement to France and Soviet," New York *Times*, May 11, 1965.

53. New York *Times*, March 24, 1965.

54. New York *Times*, March 12, 1965.

55. Quoted in Adam Bromke, "Poland and France: The Sentimental Friendship," *East Europe*, February 1966, p. 13.

56. New York *Times*, November 1, 1965.

57. "Text of Franco-Soviet Declaration of June 30, 1966," New York *Times*, July 1, 1966.

58. New York *Times*, June 23, 1966.

59. De Gaulle, *The Call to Honour*, p. 271.

60. De Gaulle, *Salvation*, p. 51.

61. President de Gaulle's first press conference, March 25, 1959, Ambassade de France, New York, Speeches and Press Conferences, No. 128, p. 4.

62. President de Gaulle's eighth press conference, July 29, 1963, pp. 9-10.

63. President de Gaulle's ninth press conference, January 31, 1964, p. 13.

64. President de Gaulle's eleventh press conference, February 4, 1965, p. 12.

65. New York *Times*, April 11, 1965.

66. *Le Monde*, June 23, 1965.

67. President de Gaulle's twelfth press conference, September 9, 1965, p. 9. (Italics added.)

68. "Text of Address by General de Gaulle to the French People," May 30, 1968, New York *Times*, May 31, 1968.

69. President de Gaulle's seventeenth press conference, September 9, 1968, Ambassade de France, New York, Speeches and Press Conference, No. 1128, pp. 2-3.

70. President de Gaulle's sixth press conference, May 15, 1962, p. 8.

71. Speech by President de Gaulle, April 27, 1965, p. 2.

72. President de Gaulle's eleventh press conference, February 4, 1965, p. 12.

73. Address by Under Secretary of State George Ball at Washington, April 29, 1966, Department of State *Bulletin*, 54, no. 1403: 767.

74. President de Gaulle's second press conference, November 10, 1959, p. 2.

75. Joseph Alsop, New York *Herald Tribune*, European edition, March 29, 1963.

76. Zbigniew Brzezinski, *Alternative to Partition* (New York, 1965), p. 115.

77. C. L. Sulzberger, New York *Times*, February 23, 1966.

78. De Gaulle, *Memoirs of Hope*, p. 202.

79. David Schoenbrun, *The Three Lives of Charles de Gaulle*, (New York, 1966), pp. 291-94.

80. Ibid., pp. 295-300. See also John Newhouse, *De Gaulle and the Anglo-Saxons* (New York, 1970), pp. 69-84; Dirk U. Stikker, *Men of Responsibility* (New York, 1965), p. 360; Paul-Henri Spaak, *The Continuing Battle* (Boston, 1971), pp. 312-19.

81. President de Gaulle's third press conference, September 5, 1960, p. 11.

82. Newhouse, op. cit., pp. 69-70, 74.

83. Stikker, op. cit., pp. 290-91.

84. Ibid., pp. 384, 386.

85. Schoenbrun, op. cit., p. 300, notes that Eisenhower's response of October 1958 was first leaked to the press in May 1964, in order to set the record straight. In correspondence with this writer, Schoenbrun made the distinction between the deliberate, officially inspired State Department leak that was first mentioned by James Reston in the New York *Times*, May 1, 1964 and was then elaborated by Schoenbrun in a series of articles in *Le Figaro*, July 9-17, 1964, and the earlier private discoveries published by C. L. Sulzberger in the New York *Times*, March 18, 1963, as well as broadcast over CBS by Schoenbrun in the spring of 1963. Finally, so that all misunderstanding might forever be laid to rest, the State Department released the text of the Eisenhower letter of October 20, 1958 on August 11, 1966 through the office of Senator Henry M. Jackson, chairman, Subcommittee on National Security and International Operations, and Senator J. William Fulbright, chairman, Committee on Foreign Relations.

86. *Text of Letter from President Eisenhower to General de Gaulle of October 20, 1958 and Department of State Statement Recording the Events Surrounding the French Proposal and Later Developments Regarding It* (mimeo), Annex, pp. 1-2.

87. Ibid., pp. 2-3; Schoenbrun, op. cit., p. 303.

88. *Text of Letter*, op. cit., p. 3; Schoenbrun, op. cit., pp. 305, 309.

89. New York *Times*, October 8, 1960.

90. Newhouse, op. cit., p. 82.

91. *Text of Letter*, op. cit., p. 3; Schoenbrun, op. cit., pp. 309-10; James Reston, New York *Times*, May 3, 1964.

92. Schoenbrun, op. cit., p. 299.

93. Quoted in ibid., pp. 335-36.

94. Quoted in ibid., p. 339.

95. Ibid., pp. 314-15; *Text of Letter*, op. cit., pp. 3-4; Newhouse, op. cit., pp. 132-33.

96. Schoenbrun, op. cit., pp. 316-17.

97. Stikker, op. cit., pp. 367-68.

98. President de Gaulle's first press conference, March 25, 1959, p. 8.

99. Schoenbrun, op. cit., p. 299.

100. Address by President de Gaulle to the *Ecole Militaire*, November 3, 1959, in Charles de Gaulle, *Discours et Messages* (Paris, 1970), vol. III, pp. 126-27.

101. President de Gaulle's seventh press conference, January 14, 1963, *Le Figaro*, January 15, 1963.

102. Dirk U. Stikker, "The Role of the Secretary General of NATO," *Internationale Spectator*, April 8, 1965, pp. 675, 677, 679. See also, Stikker, *Men of Responsibility*, pp. 364-65.

103. Maurice Faure, "Politique et défense," in *L'avenir de l'Alliance Atlantique*, ed. Claude Delmas et al. (Paris, 1961), p. 215.

104. Stikker, *Men of Responsibility*, p. 361.

105. New York *Times*, August 3, 1960. The de Gaulle-Adenauer meeting occurred at Rambouillet on July 30-31, 1960.

106. President de Gaulle's third press conference, September 5, 1960, pp. 11-12.

107. New York *Times*, September 9, 1960.

108. New York *Times*, November 12, 1960.

109. Newhouse, op. cit., pp. 222-26.

110. President de Gaulle's eighth press conference, July 29, 1963, p. 9.

111. Stikker, "The Role of the Secretary General," op. cit., p. 676.

112. C. L. Sulzberger, New York *Times*, May 6, 1964.

113. New York *Times*, June 10, 1964.

114. New York *Times*, October 18, 1965.

115. Stikker, "The Role of the Secretary General," op. cit., p. 677.

116. President de Gaulle's twelfth press conference, September 9, 1965, p. 7.

117. For an authoritative interpretation, see Secretary General Manlio Brosio, "NATO and East-West Detente," *NATO Letter*, December 1967, p. 8. See also interpretation in *NATO Facts and Figures* (Brussels, 1971), p. 24.

118. For example, in a 1964 New Year's Eve interview de Gaulle stated: "One must not confuse the pact—that is, the Alliance—with its organisms. I think the present form of the Alliance organism is not destined to last indefinitely. No one thinks it should. But the Atlantic Alliance is another matter. The Alliance exists and should last, while its organisms will develop according to circumstances." Providence *Journal*, January 1, 1965.

119. President de Gaulle's thirteenth press conference, February 21, 1966, Ambassade de France, New York, Speeches and Press Conferences, No. 239, p. 9.

120. Newhouse, op. cit., pp. 285-86.

121. President de Gaulle's Letter to President Johnson, March 7, 1966, *NATO Letter*, May 1966, p. 22.

122. *Hearings before the Subcommittee on National Security and International Operations of the Committee on Government Operations, United States Senate*, April 27, 1966 (Washington, D.C.: 1966), pp. 32-33.

123. "Face a face" on O.R.T.F., March 28, 1966; transcript printed in *Le Monde*, March 30, 1966.

124. Speech by Premier Georges Pompidou, April 20, 1966, Ambassade de France, New York, Speeches and Press Conference, Nos. 243A and 245A, pp. 16-17.

125. Poll conducted by the Institut Francais d'Opinion Publique from March 25 to April 4, 1966, *Sondages*, No. 2 (1966), p. 41.

126. Dirk U. Stikker, "The Fourteen and France," May 1966, (mimeo), p. 7.

127. French Aide Memoire of March 29, 1966, Department of State *Bulletin* 54 no. 1401: 702-03.

128. U.S. Aide Memoire of April 12, 1966, in ibid., p. 701.

129. Spaak, op. cit., p. 318.

130. President de Gaulle's thirteenth press conference, February 21, 1966, p. 8.

131. President de Gaulle's New Year message, December 31, 1966, Ambassade de France, New York, Speeches and Press Conferences, No. 255, p. 2.

132. President de Gaulle's thirteenth press conference, February 21, 1966, p. 9.

133. Ibid., pp. 8-9.

134. *Le Monde*, March 30, 1966.

135. Marc Ullmann, "De Gaulle's Secret Diplomacy," *Interplay*, August-September 1967, pp. 38-39.

136. Quoted in Roland Delcour, " 'Pour éviter la preponderance Américaine,' " *Le Monde*, July 15, 1967.

137. Harlan Cleveland, *NATO: The Transatlantic Bargain* (New York, 1970), p. 104.

138. Text of French statement of March 9, 1966, New York

Times, March 10, 1966. See also French Aide Memoire of March 10, 1966, Department of State *Bulletin*, 54, no. 1399: 617.

139. *Hearings before the Subcommittee on National Security and International Operations of the Committee on Government Operations, United States Senate*, May 5, 1966 (Washington, 1966), p. 36.

140. Spaak, *The Continuing Battle*, p. 466.

141. Declaration of Fourteen NATO Nations, March 18, 1966, Department of State *Bulletin*, 54, no. 1397: 536.

142. Raymond Aron, "The Spread of Nuclear Weapons," *Atlantic Monthly*, January 1965, p. 50.

143. Otto Pick, "The 'O' in NATO," *NATO Letter*, December 1965, p. 20.

144. Horst Blomeyer, "Germany in NATO," in *The Western Alliance*, ed. Edgar S. Furniss, Jr. (Columbia, Ohio, 1965), pp. 95, 99-100.

145. London *Times* editorial, March 13, 1966.

146. New York *Times*, May 5, 1966.

147. President de Gaulle's fourteenth press conference, October 28, 1966, p. 5. (Italics added.)

148. Ronald Koven, "France Eases Flight Rules for U.S. Military Planes," *International Herald Tribune*, September 15, 1967.

149. Speech by Premier Georges Pompidou, April 20, 1966, p. 14.

150. Anne Sington, "NATO's Air Defenses—A Child's Guide to NADGE," *NATO Letter*, April 1967, pp. 8-16.

151. Spaak, *The Continuing Battle*, p. 469.

152. For the Franco-American accord of March 24, 1967, see *France and NATO*, brief by Lucien Radoux, rapporteur, Committee on Defense Questions and Armaments, Assembly, WEU, June 1967, pp. 90-93.

153. General Johannes Steinhoff, "NATO Crisis: A Military View," *Europe-Archiv*, August 10, 1966; reprinted in *Survival* November 1966, pp. 367-68.

154. New York *Times*, July 2, 1966.

155. Interview with Under Secretary of State George Ball, Paris, March 30, 1966, Department of State *Bulletin*, 54, no. 1399: 615.

156. Institute for Strategic Studies, *Strategic Survey, 1967* (London, 1968), p. 14.

157. "Paris and Bonn Set Troop Accord," New York *Times*, December 22, 1966; *Survival*, February 1967, pp. 50-51; *France and NATO*, Assembly, WEU, June 1967, pp. 90-91.

158. General Charles Ailleret, " 'Directed' Défense or an 'All Azimuths' Defense," *Revue de défense nationale*, December 1967; reprinted in *Survival*, February 1968, p. 40.

159. Ibid., pp. 41-42.

160. Ibid., p. 42.

161. Ibid., p. 40.

162. Ibid., p. 42.

163. De Gaulle, *Discours et Messages* (Paris, 1970) vol. III, p. 127.

164. Quoted in John L. Hess, "France Stresses Atom Deterrent," New York *Times*, January 30, 1968. See also the account in *Le Monde*, January 30, 1968.

165. Raymond Aron, "From Independence to Neutrality," *Atlantic Community Quarterly*, Summer 1968, p. 269.

166. Alastair Buchan, "Battening Down Vauban's Hatches," *Interplay*, May 1968, p. 6.

167. Ibid., p. 7.

168. Ibid., p. 6.

169. Institute for Strategic Studies, *Strategic Survey, 1970* (London, 1971), pp. 22-24.

170. NATO Ministerial Meeting Final Communique, Brussels, November 1968, *NATO Letter*, December 1968, pp. 18-19.

171. Quoted in Guy de Carmoy, "The Last Years of de Gaulle's Foreign Policy," *Studies for a New Central Europe*, No. 4 (1968/1969), p. 198.

172. General Michel Fourquet, "The Use of Different Systems of Force within the Framework of the Strategy of Deterrence," *Revue de défense nationale*, May 1969; reprinted in *Survival*, July 1969, p. 208.

173. For the military implications of the Fourquet doctrine, see Jacques Isnard, "Revamping French Military Strategy," *Atlantic Community Quarterly*, Summer 1969, pp. 241-44; Michael J. Brenner, "France's New Defense Strategy and the Atlantic Puzzle," *Bulletin of the Atomic Scientists*, November 1969, pp. 4-7.

174. See, for example, William Beecher, "French Join U.S. in Fleet Exercise," New York *Times*, May 6, 1967.

175. Drew Middleton, "France Moving to Cooperation with

NATO Again," New York *Times*, November 21, 1968. See also Middleton's subsequent reports, New York *Times*, March 29, 1970 and December 26, 1971.

176. *Atlantic News*, April 15, 1971, p. 3.

177. *Atlantic News*, January 19, 1972, p. 3.

178. "The Future Organization of Western Defense," James Boyden, rapporteur, Document 557, November 16, 1971, Assembly, WEU, *Proceedings*, December 1971, III, pp. 139-41; "The Structure of NATO Following the Withdrawal of France from the Military Organization," NATO Information Service, March 1968, p. 2.

179. "The Future Organization of Western Defense," op. cit., pp. 120-21.

180. Daniel Lerner and Morton Gorden, *Euratlantica* (Cambridge, Mass., 1969), p. 197.

3

ATLANTIC PARTNERSHIP:
SLOGAN OR SOLUTION?

"The future of the West lies in Atlantic partnership," President John F. Kennedy confidently declared. He envisioned "a system of cooperation, interdependence and harmony" in which the peoples on both sides of the Atlantic "can jointly meet their burdens and opportunities throughout the world."[1] Atlantic Union was not excluded as a dimly perceived, distant objective, but it was not considered within the realm of practical politics. Neither was the Gaullist glorification of the independent nation-state accepted as practical politics, since the problems that faced the West could only be met successfully by joint programs that expressed the inescapable interdependence of the nations of the Atlantic Community.

The prerequisite for forming a consensus of European-American policies was the creation of a united Europe. The origin of the partnership idea lay as much with Jean Monnet and the members of his Action Committee for the United States of Europe as it did with the State Department and President Kennedy. Both groups agreed upon the need for reaffirming American support for a united Europe, which had been official U.S. policy ever since the Marshall Plan. The failure of Europe to achieve effective union, both argued, frequently left the impression that the Atlantic Community was an American imperium, since willingly or not, the massive power of the United States tended to overwhelm the individual medium- and small-sized European states. Only if a united Europe could deal with the United States as an equal could this harmful disequilibrium be eliminated, and only a united Europe could muster the resources to share equitably with the United States the many burdens and responsibilities of maintaining the viability of the non-Communist world. It was necessary to create an important European center of decision making, a "second America in the West," to use Monnet's phrase, to stand alongside Washington, because it was both psychologically unhealthy and physically impossible for America to attempt to manage all the problems of the free world by itself. Looking forward to the union of Europe, President Kennedy articulated the belief that "a united Europe will be capable of playing a greater role in the common defense, of responding more generously to the needs of poorer nations, of joining with the United States and others in lowering trade barriers, resolving problems of currency and commodities, and developing coordinated policies in all other economic, diplomatic, and political areas. We see in such a Europe a partner with whom we can deal on a basis of full equality in all the great and burdensome tasks of building and defending a community of free nations."[2] "Partnership," Monnet responded, "is the expression of willingness to tackle in common and as equals whatever concrete problems present themselves. It is the willingness to develop rules to govern relations between the two partners and policies to associate them in their dealings with the rest of the world."[3]

It was with these broad aims in mind that the Kennedy administration launched the Trade Expansion Act of 1962. The most promising beginning in trans-Atlantic collaboration appeared to be the formation of a trade partnership with the Common Market, which at the time seemed on the point of negotiating the entry of Britain and some of the other member of the EFTA Seven. However, in short order de Gaulle obstructed the accession of Britain to the Common Market and thereby perpetuated the division of Europe between the Six and the Seven. Even among the Six his opposition to supranationalism hobbled the development of a strong and cohesive European Community. De Gaulle effectively blocked any movement toward creating a political union of the Six, he stubbornly fought strengthening the Common Market Commission in Brussels and the European Parliament in Strasbourg, he waged a bitter battle against majority voting in the Common Market Council of Ministers, and he boycotted meetings of various Common Market bodies for nearly eight months in 1965-66, with the result that the Common Market spokesmen at Geneva were forced to waste precious time in conducting their trade negotiations at the Kennedy Round.

This delay compounded the difficult substantive problems that arose out of the tough bargaining, so that the qualified success finally attained by the Kennedy Round had all the drama of a cliffhanger. An intense last-minute effort was required to conclude the negotiations that had dragged on for over four years, before the Trade Expansion Act expired in June 1967. While important overall results were obtained, with an average tariff reduction of about 35 percent, this still fell considerably short of the original hopes. The first major blow to the Kennedy Round came with Britain's exclusion from the Common Market. A provision in the Trade Expansion Act that was especially tailored for British entry into an enlarged European Community authorized tariff cuts up to 80 percent in those items in which the United States and the Common Market were dominant suppliers to the world. This clause became virtually meaningless following de Gaulle's veto. But even without Britain, there was still room for linear tariff cuts of up to 50 percent with the Six. In view of the enormous difficulties encountered, the final results must be regarded as a considerable achievement.

Despite the prolonged frustrations involved in beginning a trade partnership and the difficulty in forming a partnership with Europe in other areas—since "Europe" still did not exist—the concept of an Atlantic partnership has remained in the official rhetoric of Washington. In Europe it has also been upheld as the unswerving aim of Monnet's Action Committee, as well as of other influential European groups. Given this sense of commitment, one is entitled to ask several basic questions: Does this represent attachment to an idea that only has a certain antiquarian interest, or is it still a valid aim that may, over time, increasingly become a reality? And looking beyond that, should it ever fully become a reality, what are some of the likely implications of this power configuration for the functioning of the Western community of nations?

The partisans of partnership have adopted a number of well-defined tenets, each of which deserves careful examination. One of the fundamental premises is that the West will operate on the basis of bilateral relations between something called "Europe" and the United States. The metaphors usually employed to depict this concept are two pillars presumably supporting some sort of common structure, or an exercise dumbbell in which equally balanced spheres at either end are connected by a rod. In either case, the Atlantic Community is invariably reduced to two parts.

As we know it, the Atlantic Community is essentially multilateral, not bilateral, in nature. NATO and OECD, for example, as the principal organs of Atlantic military and econimic cooperation, are composed of a cluster of many states, not just one on either side of the Atlantic. In the future it is conceivable that Europe, or at least a major part of Europe, could function as a unit, so that multilateral organizations could be reduced essentially to bilateral ones. While this would seem to be a purely academic question, experience has shown that this was not so. Up until the spring of 1962, the State Department was actively talking about reorganizing and reforming NATO as a multilateral organ.[4] But as this writer learned from sources involved in this planning, with the adoption of the partnership theme, as officially proclaimed in President Kennedy's Declaration of Interdependence at Philadelphia on July 4, 1962, such talk of NATO reform virtually stopped. That is, the bilateral partnership concept had the effect of being viewed as an alternative to NATO, instead of as a complement to it.

WHO IS A MEMBER OF "EUROPE"?

Even when Britain, Denmark, and Ireland finally became full members of the European Community, the question of membership was not fully resolved. Neutral Ireland has not become a member of NATO. Norway, Iceland, and Portugal remained in NATO, but did not enter the European Community, although they negotiated special ties with it. Greece and Turkey have still another status. Both were NATO members that negotiated association agreements with the Common Market. Greece became an associated member in November 1962, and Turkey in December 1964, with prolonged and different transition periods in each case before either could attain full membership in EEC. Then with the military coup in Greece in April 1967, the Greek relationship became frozen. The return to parliamentary democracy in Greece in July 1974 has permitted the resumption of progress toward closer association.

The European Community has also entered into preferential association agreements with Austria, Sweden, and Switzerland, all of which are neutrals like Ireland, although not full Community members like the Irish. In short, the European Community has not come to resemble NATO Europe. And during the prolonged period when Britain and its two EFTA partners were excluded from the European Community, the Europe of the Six had even less claim to being identified with NATO Europe. In retrospect, one could say that if NATO could have been reformed and strengthened, such plans should have been pursued independently of developments in establishing an Atlantic partnership.

The rationale of these officials who were pushing partnership was doubtless that nothing should be done in the way of a meaningful and dramatic strengthening of a multilateral organ like NATO, since this would distract attention from the bilateral partnership arrangements. While these relations were at first to be conducted on an economic plane, the supporters of European unity, both in Europe and in Washington, anticipated a spillover effect from economic union to a political and military one. Consequently, moves toward economic union in the Common Market, functioning in partnership with the United States, were viewed as having political and military implications.

Even in the purely economic field in which the Common Market began to operate, its impact has often been to confound and delay the functioning of a multilateral organization. One of the main difficulties in conducting the business of the Kennedy Round under GATT at Geneva was that in negotiating with the Common Market one was "dealing with an it that is a they."[5] As the late Christian Herter, the chief American trade representative, had testified: "My experience in negotiating with the Common Market Commission, which has been charged by the six governments with speaking as their sole voice, has been that this voice is highly uncertain and frequently inaudible."[6] Progress in the Kennedy Round had been slow for many reasons, but one of the chief problems was the difficulty the Six had in reaching agreement on a common position among themselves. Toward the end of the negotiations the EEC Commission was finally granted greater authority to speak for the Six, and this was an important factor in the negotiations reaching a satisfactory conclusion.

However, as the European Community moved into new areas,

the same problems reappeared. In November 1971, when the United States sought to negotiate new currency exchange rates with members of the European Community so as to resolve an international monetary crisis, Treasury Secretary John Connally went to Rome with a presidential mandate to reach an agreement. There he found that the Finance Ministers of the European Community caucused as a bloc, but were totally unable to arrive at a common position, and so no decisions were possible. "It was exasperating and Mr. Connally said so." Paul Volcker, Connally's deputy, also showed his irritation. Finally, in December, as the monetary crisis deepened and the threat of a world economic recession became real, the parties were pressured to produce the Smithsonian agreement in Washington.

When the next monetary crisis erupted in February 1973, Volcker, now the principal American negotiator, carefully avoided talking to the European Community Finance Ministers as a bloc, nor did he have any dealings with Community spokesmen in the Commission. He turned, rather, to the separate Finance Ministers in Bonn, Paris, and London, and then as an afterthought in Rome. In a brief period of intensive negotiation an agreement was reached, and after consultation with the Japanese, a revised parity arrangement was announced. Volcker acted under the rubric: "If you have to deal with the Common Market, don't. Go where the power lies instead."[7] A month later, in March 1973, another adjustment of currency values took place, this time in collaboration with officials of the European Community. It was only possible to reach agreement, however, by closing down all official foreign exchange markets for a period of 18 days. Even then, agreement for common action among members of European Community was not complete, since only six of the nine agreed on a joint currency float. Hopefully this performance can be improved over time. The members of the European Community have committed themselves to create a monetary union by 1980, and should this ambitious goal in fact be realized, it would then be easier to negotiate meaningfully directly with Community officials in Brussels.

Eventually, the members of the European Community "will have great bargaining power when they can agree to act collectively, but it will be a long time before they can function smoothly, flexibly, and effectively as a unit." Meanwhile, as Miriam Camps observed, "the Community will be difficult to deal with collectively," while the separate member "countries will be difficult to deal with individually, for there will be few issues on which they are either fully united or wholly free to act individually."[8] Even after the Community has surmounted the considerable obstacles that stand in the way of achieving a full economic and monetary union, it will be faced with the still greater difficulties of arriving at common agreement in foreign policy and defense affairs, which is essential for a genuine political union. One can only speculate about when, if ever, these more ambitious aims will be achieved. The only certainty is that the European Community will long remain, in various ways, "an it that is a they."

ATLANTIC PARTNERSHIP AND CANADA

While there would seem to be some obstacles and inconveniences in organizing the European side of the Atlantic into a bilateral partnership, both in terms of the membership and functioning of the European Community, there are also some problems in organizing the partnership on the other side of the Atlantic. Here we come to the anomalous position of Canada. A former high Canadian official in the Department of External Affairs, John W. Holmes, put the matter bluntly:

The whole dumbbell idea was highly offensive to Canada— or had you noticed? Perhaps it put us in our place, because the advocates of "the Grandiose Design" gave us the impression that they had either misplaced or quite forgotten us. Dumbbellists on both sides of the Atlantic, if queried about the Canadian role, have the habit of suggesting that we should run off and find happiness also in our regional bundle. Sometimes this means simple "union" with one nation ten times our size; sometimes on a grander scale it wrapped us up with our neighbors in Paraguay in accordance with prevalent myths about the naturalness of hemispheric ties. Canada was clearly a nuisance to these designers.

Canada, in short, simply would not fit into a bilateral pattern of Atlantic partnership. On the other hand, the multilateral concept of an Atlantic Community would be meaningful for Canadians. "I would prefer an Atlantic Community," Holmes concluded, "in which the Atlantic has less significance as a divider. I do not believe in looking upon NATO as composed of a European wing with a fixed point of view and a North American wing with a point of view."[9] In 1965 the Canadian Secretary of State for External Affairs, Paul Martin, likewise affirmed: "We do not believe . . . that continentalism, whether European or North American, is compatible with the Canadian interests."[10]

Prime Minister Lester Pearson also rejected the bilateral partnership principle on several occasions. "The Atlantic nations must come together in one Atlantic Community," he told the NATO Ministerial meeting in May 1963. "The West cannot afford two such communities, a European one and a North American one, each controlling its own policies and perhaps moving away from the other as the common menace recedes."[11] In June 1966 Pearson elaborated these views. For Canada, "continentalism either of the European or North American variety is not the answer." Instead of separating the nations that border the Atlantic into two distinct parts, "we must move forward with new resolve toward a more closely knit international community with common political institutions, which covers more than a single continent, and spans the Atlantic. . . . We must develop common, unifying political institutions which would provide for collective foreign and economic policies, as well as genuinely collective defense." Pearson readily acknowledged that the nations of the Atlantic Community were not likely to form a federal union at this moment of history. "If we are realistic," he said, "we may have to accept at this time the more practical immediate objective of a United Europe." However it must not be viewed "as an obstacle to, but as a stage on the way to, Atlantic Union. If we cannot at the present achieve a pattern of Atlantic federalism, it may be necessary to acknowledge the realities of the situation, and, as North Americans, work with Europeans in the hope that, in the longer sweep of history, both Europe and North America will come to realize that their respective affairs can best be harmonized in a wider union. If an intervening European stage is necessary, however, it must take place not in continental isolation, but in close Atlantic cooperation and understanding."[12]

It is strange that the role of Canada could have been so overlooked by the theorists of partnership, since the destinies of

Canada and the United States are bound closely together in every respect. Strategically, Canada lies athwart the shortest route between the United States and the Soviet Union. Canadian-American wartime collaboration was therefore continued in 1947 in the form of a Permanent Joint Board of Defense, which still continues to operate. During the 1950s a joint air defense system for North America was created, including a continentwide radar warning network. In 1958 both countries integrated their defense systems under one command, the North American Air Defense Command (NORAD), with headquarters in Colorado. Canada keeps a permanent military liaison staff in Washington, while the United States maintains a permanent Air Force coordination staff in Ottawa. Canada has access to the latest military equipment under the terms of a joint defense production program, while U.S. nuclear weapons have been stationed in Canada since 1963 under the dual-key arrangement. This network of ties provides, in fact, what logic demands: the indivisibility of Canadian-American defense.

But Canada is also an important Atlantic power. It was not only a charter member of NATO, but has been credited with writing Article 2 of the North Atlantic Treaty which deals with the prospect of building nonmilitary cooperation among the NATO states. From time to time Canadian spokesmen renewed their plea to give greater reality to Article 2, and in 1956 Pearson was one of the three so-called "Wise Men" who drew up the basic document on political consultation and cooperation among the NATO countries, which remains, despite frequent lapses, the standard of conduct to which the NATO allies aspire. Canada was also a founding member of OECD.

The Atlantic orientation of Canadian foreign policy shifted markedly when Pierre Trudeau became Prime Minister in 1968. Although of Pearson's Liberal Party, Trudeau moved in a quasi-Gaullist direction by emphasizing issues involving Canadian sovereignty and significantly reducing the strength of the Canadian military commitment to NATO Europe.* Yet Canada would remain in NATO, Trudeau explained, because it "provides us with an opportunity for discussing military questions and the defense of the Atlantic Community without talking exclusively to Washington.

---

*As Trudeau put it himself: "I think our slight easing out from NATO corresponds somewhat to certain French initiatives in the past."[13]

NATO enables us to address a wider audience."[14] Even though Canada under Trudeau had pulled somewhat away from NATO Europe, it was evident that he showed no more desire than his predecessors to engage in continentalism. Canada still did not wish to have Washington speak for it or be swallowed up by its southern neighbor, whose population is ten times that of Canada's with a gross national product 14 times as large. Canada's long-term future still depended upon a constructive Atlantic solution whereby it could take its place in the broader context of like-minded nations of a multilateral Atlantic Community, which could not be reduced to two simple parts, as the proponents of partnership would have it.

This writer recalls the irony of a discussion about the place of Canada with one of Monnet's personal aides in Paris. This European federalist was explaining at great length that good relations between Europe and the United States could only be founded on a feeling of equality that would result from the unification of Europe and the creation of a European partner. At this point I asked what was his solution for the future of Canada and how it might be assured a feeling of equality, which was admittedly of such great importance. With a shrug, he replied that Canada must recognize facts. Militarily it was part of North American defense plans and economically it was overwhelmingly dependent upon the United States. The logical solution, therefore, would be to have the United States represent the interests of Canada in the trans-Atlantic dialogue. Furthermore, as Britain would be part of Europe it would help represent Commonwealth interests inside a European Union. Looked at realistically, he explained, the position of Canada would not be worse than today and it would probably be better, since the context of discussing and deciding issues would be broadened once an Atlantic partnership began to function. But in all this, good relations based on a feeling of equality, which was vital for the Europeans, simply disappeared as a consideration for Canada. Another close associate of Monnet went further. He declared to this writer that "facing facts" for Canada meant consummating Canada's close bonds with the United States in the form of political federation, just as the European states must acknowledge their common interests by federating. This would then provide the basis for a neat dialogue of continents. U.S. officials, however, have been sufficiently acute to Canadian sensitivities to disclaim such a prospect. Thus Under Secretary of State George Ball declared with regard to Canadian-American relations in 1964: "Given the desire on both sides to preserve the freedom of political decision, neither nation is pressing for any experiments in supranationality."[15]

The authors of the Trade Expansion Act of 1962, who had their eyes exclusively on the European Economic Community, likewise ignored the position of Canada. This, despite the fact that at the time Canada was the most valuable trading partner of the United States. More trade has flowed across the Canadian-American border than any other national border in the world. Over a period of years about 70 percent of Canada's foreign trade, both in terms of imports and exports, has been conducted with the United States. From the American point of view, as a trade official noted in 1964 when the Kennedy Round negotiations were getting under way, "taking exports and imports together, total United States trade with Canada added up to almost eight billion dollars a year as compared with six and a half billion dollars with the Common Market."[16] U.S. economic involvement in Canada was further demonstrated by the high degree of American ownership of Canadian industries: Americans control nearly 100 percent of Canada's auto industry, about 90 percent of its rubber industry, 75 percent of its chemical industry, over 60 percent of its petroleum industry, more than half of its mining, smelting, electrical, and farm machine industries, and good proportions of other enterprises.[17] This economic intertwining would make Canada unusually sensitive to any major American economic program. Yet the Trade Expansion Act was not framed with these Canadian interests in mind. All reductions under the Act that were consummated between the United States and the Common Market were automatically extended to third parties under the "most-favored-nation" clause, but since Canada was not an important producer of many of the goods affected, these reductions had a limited effect on Canada. Moreover, the method of linear tariff reductions of the Trade Expansion Act, as a privately sponsored Canadian-American Committee explained, "seemed poorly tailored to Canada's peculiar circumstances." As a result, Canada applied to GATT so that it might bargain for tariff reductions with the United States on a different basis, by "making specific offers by commodity groups rather than adhering to the linear principle." A Canadian-American agreement for "qualified free trade" in automobile products was subsequently concluded, and similar arrangements for other industries were contemplated in Ottawa.[18] As Pierre Uri, one of

Monnet's closest advisors, was candid enough to remark about the Trade Expansion Act: "Incidentally, Canada had been forgotten as one of the possible partners in computing the Atlantic share of world exports."[19] All this belatedly testified to the one-sided interest of the advocates of Atlantic partnership in the exclusive relationship they envisioned between the United States and the European Community.

THE ORIGIN OF THE PARTNERSHIP
IDEA: ITS BROADER BASIS

The problem raised by Canada on one side of the Atlantic and by nonmembers of the European Community on the other side demonstrates the difficulty in conceiving of these nations within the narrow framework of a bilateral Atlantic partnership, rather than within a larger multilateral Atlantic Community. In view of the subsequent evolution of the partnership idea, it is interesting to recall that the theorists of partnership themselves initially spoke in terms of a broadly based Atlantic Community. In 1953, after the Six had created the European Coal and Steel Community, Jean Monnet said: "The countries of the Schuman Plan are free nations sharing a common way of life, and all belong to the Atlantic Community." It would be a mistake, he insisted, to think that "a united Europe would simply create a new fixed frontier. That's quite wrong. European unity is above all a growing concept. The only limit of the new community is the limit of the number of free peoples who wish to join our common enterprise."[20] In a like manner, Monnet's Action Committee adopted a Joint Declaration in November 1959, which spoke in terms of "the West as a whole." "We cannot solve the problems of the Six and the Seven as if we were alone with our European problems," the Declaration stated, "nor can America solve her problems alone or contribute alone to the solution of those of the West as a whole. In the present situation, it is their responsibility to solve them together." The Delcaration proposed that the Common Market states join with Britain and selected non-Community countries of Europe as well as with the United States in seeking a "joint solution to what are from now on joint problems." In order to facilitate such joint action, these states should "examine the permanent forms to be given to these consultations."[21]

When a group of governmental experts recommended in May 1960 that the OECD be set up, with the United States and Canada as full members, in addition to 18 European members of the old OEEC, the Action Committee applauded this move as an important step that would give permanent form to the economic consultations among the nations of the West. The Action Committee recalled its pledge that the Common Market countries, Britain and some of its EFTA associates, and the United States must together seek ways of acting as the driving force of the world's economy. "It is with this in mind that the Organization for Economic Cooperation and Development should be launched as quickly as possible and practical content be given to the new association with the United States."[22] In July 1961 an Action Committee Joint Declaration was again conceived in the broad-gauged terms of the future unity (the word "union" was also used) of the nations of the West. "European unity is taking shape and, with the United Kingdom, will lead to the United States of Europe. It was already made possible the association with America which will culminate in the unity of the West. Only through this union can the West gradually solve its problem and help to reduce the political, economic and social tensions in the world which are liable to spark off conflicts capable of destroying civilization."[23]

Meanwhile, in May 1961, Walter Hallstein, President of the Commission of the EEC, anticipated the birth of all-encompassing economic organs for the West. "What we need in the Western alliance is a kind of Ministry of Economics which not only looks after free trade but stimulates the development of harmonized short-term and long-term economic policy."[24] Such a ministry would span the Atlantic, while taking within its purview the activities of the smaller, but more tightly integrated, European Community. "The same political challenge that is leading us to unite in Europe makes it all the more necessary for us to cement our European Community within the larger and perforce looser community that is the Atlantic Community." In this conception the nations of the Atlantic were not divided into two distinct parts, but the European Community would be cemented within the larger though more loosely bound Atlantic Community. Whatever the nature of the problem, be it aid to developing countries, agricultural surpluses, currency reserves, or whatever, "we must rally the forces of the Atlantic Community," Hallstein concluded, "to tackle these problems together, and to create a new economic order in the free world."[25]

In June 1961, Monnet gave his celebrated Dartmouth speech with its sweeping demands for common institutions in the West. "What is necessary is to move towards a true Atlantic Community in which common institutions will be increasingly developed to meet common problems. . . . Just as the United States in their own day found it necessary to unite, just as Europe is now in the process of uniting, so the West must move towards some kind of union." This speech was also noteworthy, however, for its public introduction of the word "partnership." Intermingled with phrases about the "Atlantic Community" were others proclaiming that an emerging European Union held to the belief that "a partnership between Europe and the United States is necessary and possible. . . . The partnership of Europe and the United States should create a new force for peace. . . . A partnership of Europe and America would also make it possible ultimately to overcome the difficulties between East and West." Partnership, as first conceived in Monnet's words, was in no way contradictory to the concept of an Atlantic Community. "It is evident," Monnet proclaimed, "that we must soon go a good deal further towards an Atlantic Community. The creation of a united Europe brings us nearer by making it possible for America and Europe to act as partners on an equal footing."[26] Here a partnership was viewed as the means for fulfilling the aims of the Atlantic Community. At the same time, the Atlantic Community began to be defined in the bilateral terms of a two-sided partnership between Europe and the United States.

PARTISANS OF PARTNERSHIP REDEFINE ATLANTIC COMMUNITY

The effect of Monnet's redefinition of the Atlantic Community into a bilateral partnership was not at first fully appreciated, since he seemed to be using partnership and Atlantic Community almost interchangeably. By the end of 1961, however, the dialogue between Monnet and leading U.S. officials had resulted in the conclusion that henceforth the idea of an Atlantic Community would be compressed into strictly bilateral terms. Presidential advisor McGeorge Bundy, launching the partnership theme for the Kennedy administration in a speech of December 6, 1961, stated that "the most productive way of conceiving the political future of the Atlantic Community is to think in terms of a partnership between the United States on the one hand and a great European power on the other."[27]

From this it was but a short step to think exclusively in terms of an Atlantic partnership while dropping the concept of an Atlantic Community as a discredited idea. Speaking in April 1962, Hallstein protested against continued references to the "so-called Atlantic Community."

> Many people, it is true, have chosen to call this partnership the formation of an "Atlantic Community"; but for myself I prefer the formulation proposed by President Kennedy. In fact, when I hear the words "Atlantic Community" I am sometimes reminded of Voltaire's remark about the Holy Roman Empire—that it was neither Holy, nor Roman, nor an Empire. The so-called "Atlantic Community," that is, cannot be confined to the Atlantic area, for it must embrace our other friends and partners in the Pacific and elsewhere. Nor, on the other hand, is it a "Community" in the same sense that this word applied to the European Community— that is, a full economic union with strong political implications. [In Hallstein's view, what seemed] much more likely to emerge, in fact, is a close partnership between the European Community and the United States, open to the participation of other countries in the free world as and when their own interests are more particularly involved. Already, we have at our disposal the instruments of such a partnership in the GATT and the OECD. The GATT is working well, both as a code of good conduct and as a broad negotiating forum. [As for OECD,] which the United States and Canada helped the European countries to establish as the successor body to the OEEC, [its creation] marks both the completion of European recovery and the recognition that what is needed now is economic cooperation and development on a much wider scale.[28]

In this passage, Hallstein clearly used "partnership" in two different senses: an exclusive bilateral relationship between the United States and the European Community, and a broader multilateral one involving Canada and non-Community states in

GATT and OECD. When he said that what seems likely to emerge "is a close partnership between the [European] Community and the United States, open to the participation of other countries in the free world" where their interests were involved, this larger grouping might with justice be called an Atlantic Community. As for Hallstein's confusing use of the term partnership, one might also with justice call it "the so-called partnership," which was no purer than the Holy Roman Empire.

Undaunted, Hallstein continued his attack before an assemblage of NATO parliamentarians in November 1962. "I have spoken exclusively of an Atlantic partnership, never of 'an Atlantic Community.' ... My reason for rejecting the term 'Atlantic Community,'" he explained, "is to avoid misunderstanding. In the sense that we are now accustomed to use it, the word 'Community' is an innovation, adopted to describe the fundamentally new organism established by the Treaties of Paris and Rome. If that organism is not fully either a federation or a confederation—I leave to constitutional lawyers the distinction between the two—it is nevertheless very different from even such an international organization as NATO." Here Hallstein, as chief spokesman for the Common Market, exhibited his vested interest in seeking to restrict the idea of Community to the institutions peculiar to his own European Community. From this, however, it certainly need not follow that the word "Community" was a recent European innovation. Nor was it self-evident that NATO, though admittedly different in structure, scope, and purpose from the Common Market, could not continue to be viewed as a key instrument of the Atlantic Community.

As Hallstein pursued his explanation, it became clear that there was more involved than simple semantics. He rejected the idea of an Atlantic Community not only because he wanted to reserve "Community" for the European institutions of the Six, but also because he wanted to keep the European Community exclusively European. It would not be reasonable to expect the United States to adhere to such a thoroughgoing venture, he held, since American public opinion would not support the idea of a merger with the Common Market. Beyond that, however, was another proposition that did not concern the United States alone. "Even if American public opinion were by some miracle to accept the idea of America's 'joining the European Community,' thus transforming it into 'an Atlantic Community,' I have very grave doubts as to whether it would be feasible in practice. So vast a geographical extension of the Community, I am convinced, would wreck the whole operation." Thus an Atlantic Community taken in Hallstein's terms, even if it were possible, would not be desirable. The prospect of an Atlanticwide institution was therefore dismissed as dangerous and ill conceived. "I am not tempted by the notion," Hallstein elaborated, "that we should straightaway set up some central Atlantic body to direct our efforts." This would have the effect of reducing the sense of separate identity between Europe and the United States and of moderating the competition between them. "A major part of those efforts, paradoxical as it may seem, must continue to be competitive." It would also be unwise to speculate on the nature of Atlantic institutions, since this "would involve us all in the sterile discussion of constitutional principles and the meaningless dispute of as yet non-existent powers."[29]

This was the same Hallstein who, a year and a half before, had called for "a kind of Ministry of Economics" for the Western alliance that would be Atlanticwide in scope. At that time he had also found it necessary for the Europeans "to cement our European Community within the larger and perforce looser Community that is the Atlantic Community." Between these two expressions of views came the birth of the Atlantic partnership idea. Its implications were clear: the Atlantic Community became the "so-called Atlantic Community," and the goal of common institutions spanning the Atlantic, binding Europe and America together, was replaced by the aim of dividing the Atlantic into two distinct parts, each functioning in friendly competition with the other.

Hallstein proceeded to step up his attack in ever sharper terms. "Given a fully united Europe," he asked rhetorically in 1963, "should it be integrated—some would say 'dissolved'—into a so-called 'Atlantic Community'?"[30] Respectable language of the "good Europeans" had always referred to the dangers of the individual small- and medium-sized European countries being "dissolved" or "swallowed up" in an American-dominated Atlantic Community. Now, however, Hallstein went beyond this by imagining that a presumably powerful united Europe would still risk being dissolved in an Atlantic Community if it aimed at integration of any sort on an Atlantic scale. Here again was a marked change from his previously stated goal of integrating, or at least "cementing," the European Community within the larger though looser Atlantic Community.

While Hallstein certainly could not be considered a Gaullist, the evolution in the thought of this authoritative European interpreter of partnership began to acquire Gaullist overtones.

In 1964, Hallstein went so far as to borrow the Stalinist term "monolithic," to which de Gaulle himself could hardly object, in order to characterize the Atlantic Community idea. "Partnership means the opposite of a monolithic Atlantic Community in which the European states would play the part of a bridgehead towards the East, as were the Hellenic settlements in Asia Minor. It is not this maritime attitude but the continental approach which fits President Kennedy's Grand Design." At this point Hallstein introduced a new element into the partnership concept. By emphasizing the "continental" character of the European partner, he adumbrated a variation of the Gaullist appeal for a Europe from the Atlantic to the Urals. "Free Europe," Hallstein demanded, "must develop its own personality in order to become a partner for America and to serve as a magnet for the countries of Eastern Europe."[31] This assumed that a powerful, united Atlantic Community of free nations could devise no effective policies toward the Communist states of Eastern Europe so as to attract them toward the West. Only the free states of Europe could serve to attract the East Europeans, since there was something special about the European personality that precluded American participation in a joint venture of this nature. Such manifestations of what might be called unconscious Gaullism increasingly permeated the Hallstein brand of Europeans. Significant differences, of course, remained: the goal for Hallstein was still a federal Europe linked to America in an Atlantic partnership, while de Gaulle's Europe would consist of a collection of sovereign nation-states that would essentially sever their Atlantic ties. Nevertheless, the more de Gaulle insisted upon the special mystical quality of a "European Europe" that set it apart from the rest of the world, the more the non-Gaullists took up the theme of Europe's unique personality that must not be "dissolved" in a "so-called Atlantic Community."

The perceptive Dutch commentator J. H. Huizinga made explicit the connection between the "good Europeans" and Gaullism. "There is hardly a leading statesmen anywhere in the Europe of the Six," he remarked in 1965, "who does not feel compelled at any rate to pay lip service to the ideal of a Europe that can stand on its own feet as an 'equal partner' of the United States. It is an ideal that can, of course, only be realized if Europe finds the way to organic union, federation." While de Gaulle opposed European federation, he had excited European ambitions that would outlast him and "which can achieve satisfaction only through the creation of what he ceaselessly reviles." Thus de Gaulle would be the *"federateur malgre lui"* (the federator in spite of himself). "In his role as the first rabble-rouser the Six ever had—though a very stylish one—he has done a good deal to stimulate the will to self-assertion. He more than anyone else, has given voice to a new self-confidence born of impressive achievement."[32]

Hallstein's quasi Gaullism was reflected in the policies of the EEC Commission that he directed. The process of European economic integration had the effect of magnifying Europe's newfound assertiveness. It was therefore not accidental that in most economic negotiations, "the position of the Common Market Commission has been close to that of France despite profound differences about the political organization of Europe. The economic interests of the Common Market often coincide with the political goal of France to assert a more independent role for Europe."[33]

Many European leaders increasingly caught some form of the Gaullist fever of Europeanism that rejected the idea of an Atlantic Community, although this reaction was not universal. A Belgian Ambassador holding a prominent post in Europe, for example, confided to this writer that he was deeply concerned about the brand of nationalism that the European Community was creating. "The Atlantic Community exists," he insisted, "and the soul of the Atlantic Community is greater than the smaller bodies within it, like the EEC." He readily acknowledged that it was difficult to articulate this soul with precision, but it was nonetheless founded upon commonly accepted values that "transcended Hallstein's juridical mind in which 'Community' was identified exclusively with an entity built up by a group of technicians and technocrats." Other prominent Europeans were quick to point out the difficulty in defining "Europe." Political and cultural facts belied Hallstein's desiccated, legalistic approach. Culturally, there is a sharp demarcation in the mentality of the continental Europeans between the Latin peoples of the South and the Europeans of the North. Beyond the continent, psychologically the distance between Britain and the United States is often closer than between Britain and France. The United States is itself infused with such a high degree of kinship for peoples of European stock that this creates a sense of belonging to one large community, in which Europe is not something distant and apart. The result is that the peoples of the Atlantic Community can talk a common political language and share basic assumptions, such as are simply not present in a Soviet-American dialogue. Those Europeans who have been most insistent upon drawing a sharp distinction between the United States and Europe are frequently those who have, in effect, intellectualized an anti-American bias in order to preserve and enhance their separate positions of power in Europe.

It was appropriately at a ceremony honoring Jean Monnet in January 1963 that Christian Herter voiced his doubts about the wisdom of abandoning the larger concept of an Atlantic Community for the more narrowly conceived goal of Atlantic partnership. "Partnership," he said, "good as it is, can never remain the ultimate and final objective of Europe and America. The forces of history are working toward a broader and deeper relationship than that." Both Europeans and Americans are heirs to the same cultural heritage that imparts similar views about man's destiny and the character of his society. "In other words, we already belong to each other. Our task in the years ahead is to find out how to express the reality of this fact in institutional terms." For this reason, many Americans "prefer to talk about the future in terms of an Atlantic Community. I know that our European friends shy away from this phrase because for them the word 'Community' has already acquired a clear and precise meaning—technical, economic and political—as the emerging structure of their continent. In short, they feel that the use of the word has already been preempted by Europe and that its use here to describe our ultimate goal merely produced confusion of thought and intention. At the same time, for many Americans, 'Community' is such a good word to describe relationships between peoples that I suspect some of us will continue to use it."[34]

Many Europeans associated with NATO also found continuing validity in the term "Atlantic Community." As NATO Secretary General Brosio explained to the North Atlantic Assembly in 1967, belief in an Atlantic Community was "the basic principle inspiring the Alliance. Preexistent to the Treaty, the idea of this Community is clearly expressed in the preamble and in Article 2." In some remote future the Atlantic Community might be embodied in the "form of an interstate union which could one day succeed the present Alliance." But one need not wait for that; rather, "the Atlantic Community is already something real, indeed tangible, since it is in essence the expression of the common roots, history, culture, religion and way of life which, for better or worse, link the peoples of European origin and those associated with them, on both sides of the Atlantic Ocean." Such ties have been "present and active for centuries and they have had major practical consequences. The intervention of North America in two European wars in this century—an intervention which on both occasions guaranteed victory—is the most convincing proof that such a community of origins and interests exists."[35]

Thus, despite the wishes of the partnership patriots, "Atlantic Community" did not disappear entirely from the mentality or speech of all Americans and Europeans. Indeed, in the decade following de Gaulle's January 1963 veto of Britain into the European Community, "Atlantic partnership," as a concept of bilateral relations, was particularly deficient as a way of describing trans-Atlantic transactions. What developed in practice during this period was that public figures both in Europe and America began using Atlantic Community and Atlantic partnership interchangeably, so that the latter came to be identified with the multilateral network of ties that already existed in the form of the association of free nations clustered about NATO and OECD.[36] All through this gloomy period, however, Monnet stubbornly insisted upon speaking solely about an Atlantic partnership as a bilateral arrangement between America and a united Europe, more no doubt as an expression of hope than a description of reality.

PARTNERS, SEPARATE BUT NOT RIVALS: EARLY ASSUMPTIONS

Since Monnet and his proponents of partnership continued to adhere rigidly to the aim of creating "two separate but equally powerful entities,"[37] it is necessary to explore some of the further implications of what might be called "the separate but equal doctrine." (Though the phrase is the same, the separate but equal doctrine of European integrationists had no relation to the old separate but equal doctrine of American segregationists.)

Underlying this doctrine was the simple, optimistic assumption that President Kennedy enunciated in his famous Fourth of July Declaration of Interdependence: "We do not regard a strong and united Europe as a rival, but as a partner."[38] J. Robert Schaetzel, speaking as Deputy Assistant Secretary of State for Atlantic Affairs, elaborated the rationale behind this bald assertion. The belief that Europe would be a partner and not a rival was founded on a novel policy, since it represented the "conscious encouragement by a major world power of the development of a coequal power. We do this with full awareness that while Europe and the United States may differ on tactics, there can be no disagreement on fundamental objectives."[39] In the fall of 1962 Schaetzel further explained that this optimism was supported by a web of trans-Atlantic human ties. "Practically without exception these present-day leaders of the new Europe are well disposed toward the United States. We have a special advantage in dealing with the European integration movement. A number of our key officials have had close, long-term professional and personal relationships with the leading officials of the integration movement."[40]

This rosy assessment had barely been made when it was shattered by the first of de Gaulle's many blows aimed at halting the European integration movement. The "good Europeans," of course, were not only frustrated by de Gaulle, but were influenced by him as well, especially with his insistence upon a "European Europe." Writing in the spring of 1966, now as U.S. Ambassador to the organs of the European Community in Brussels, Schaetzel took note of the Gaullist elements that had crept into America's European partner when he acknowledged that "a degree of 'European nationalism' is also inevitable. . . . Nor can we expect that European attitudes will be wholly free of anti-Americanism." He professed to minimize these difficulties, however, since European nationalism would presumably not be aggressive in nature, but would arise from the preoccupation of Europeans with their own affairs as they created a united Europe. Nevertheless, one must recognize that just as a "giant America is one stimulus toward forming a united Europe, so the evolution of Atlantic relations will be colored by envy, resentment and, on occasion, policies that self-consciously set Europe apart from the United States." Despite these qualifications, Schaetzel's belief in the long-run feasibility of two separate partners collaborating successfully remained unshaken. "Seen from any distance and in any perspective, the basic interests of the United States and Europe appear to converge rather than conflict."[41] This would be so, he held, because there were no real doctrinal differences between the two partners, while their complex industrial societies were so interconnected that they would have to realize that they faced largely identical problems that would dictate common solutions.

The partnership concept also sought to recognize that the immediate post-World War II relationship between Europe and the United States was a historical anomaly that was not, nor should it have been, destined to endure. During this period the United States, perhaps of necessity, made decisions almost alone that affected Europe directly or indirectly, without adequate participation of a European voice. The devastation of war had reduced Europe from its traditional position of occupying the center of world politics to that of dire dependence on the military protection and economic largesse of a United States that was suddenly thrust into a predominant and protective role for which it was psychologically unaccustomed. But a generation after the end of the war brought economic recovery and political reinvigoration to the life of the European states and the launching of the irrevocable idea of a united Europe, which has yet to find its fulfillment. In short, the postwar period had come to an end.

With its close, a "new" balance of forces and responsibilities necessarily restored many of the old European capabilities and the desire of Europe to manage its own destiny. Essentially this was a healthy transformation, since Europe needed to regain its self-respect. Moreover, a Europe that would continue to rely unduly upon the United States for its defense would tend to lose interest in its defense and might easily drift toward neutralism. A Europe that was economically withdrawn into itself would not be inclined toward Atlantic economic cooperation, nor would it help to meet the needs of the underdeveloped world.

Once Europe had regained its vigor, it was neither wise nor proper for the United States to assume unneeded military and economic burdens. Nor should it be the butt of endless political frustrations for which it would be held responsible so long as it perpetuated the dominant position that was so necessary, indeed that was so eagerly sought by the Europeans, in the postwar period. The partnership idea therefore embodied the truth that Europe must participate fully in the decisions that would shape its future. The absence of such full discussion could only produce resentment and lead to a continuing crisis in European-American relations. Partnership thus sought to recognize differences and to organize a continuing dialogue so as to produce an institutionalized exchange of each other's views and intentions with the aim of arriving at common decisions. This view of partnership assumed mutual goodwill. As a prominent official of the European Community remarked to this writer soon after the partnership idea was launched: "Responsible people on both sides of the Atlantic want to work together."

Those who held this cooperative attitude felt that the destructive impact of de Gaulle's policies could be minimized and contained. De Gaulle could afford to be irresponsible precisely because he was weak. He knew that regardless of what he did the United States could not abandon its commitment to defend Europe, and therefore behind this protective cover he was free to pursue blatantly anti-American policies. But a powerful, united, federal Europe that could presumably stand on its own, it was argued, would have to be responsible. Moreover, a European federation could only be created by the free votes of the constituent states and it would therefore be formed on a democratic basis. In such a European Union, the Gaullist tendencies of particular areas, it was held, would be offset by other sources of opinion that would seek close cooperation with the United States and which would support an Atlantic partnership. Whatever European nationalism might arise would not, as a consequence, be as strong as the nationalism of the individual nations, since a federal Europe would be comprised of too many cultures, languages, and diverse national traditions to coalesce into virulent European chauvinism.

There was, finally, the expectation that the solution of the German problem would bind Europe to the United States. In response to my question about the danger of Europe and America becoming self-sufficient entities pursuing separate policies, instead of acting as partners in concert, Monnet was emphatic: The solution to the problem of a divided Germany could never be found if either entity behaved as if it were a self-sufficient unit in world politics. Only by creating an Atlantic partnership could the West marshal the unity and strength that would make an approach to the Soviet leaders meaningful, since Soviet consent was needed to overcome Germany's division.

MONNET'S EUROPE NOT ANOTHER GREAT POWER?

Monnet went further in his conception of a future federal Europe that would join forces with the United States in creating conditions of peace. Such a Europe, he contended, would bear no similarity to a traditional great power. "Unity in Europe does not create a new kind of great power," Monnet said in 1961. The European Community is not "a potential 19th century state with all the overtones of power this implies."[42] "The Common Market has not been created just to build a better system of exchanging goods, or to create a new power," Monnet repeated in 1963. "We have had and have as our objectives essentially the creation of a united Europe and the elimination between nations and their peoples of the spirit of domination that has brought the world close to destruction many times."[43] While Monnet admirably sought to abolish the spirit of domination in the world, and while this might occur among the nations within a viable European Union, still what assurance might there be that Europe, as a collective entity, might not continue to act as a traditional great power in its foreign policy? This thought does not seem to have troubled Monnet, for in 1966 he could reiterate that "the establishment of an equal partnership between the United States and a united Europe does not mean making a new world power, but is an essential element in the organization of peace, in particular with the U.S.S.R."[44]

Interwoven with these assertions, however, one found another strand of thought that might not be entirely reconcilable. Monnet noted that "our world is a world of vast units. We have reached the scale of continents, and it is in a partnership of continents that we must act."[45] Upon this same occasion, Monnet demanded that a Europe that would be a "vast unit" of continental scope should also assume responsibility for defending itself with nuclear weapons.[46] Hallstein was more explicit. "Brutal political facts," he said, present "a challenge of scale, a challenge of size. In a world of giants, we cannot afford to be midgets. Here, then, is a further political motive of seeking real unity—political unity—in Europe."[47] And so while in Monnet's words, the creation of "a united Europe does not mean making a new world power," the new Europe would, at the same time, become a political unit of vast scale, a giant in a world of giants.

Some authors of the partnership plan recognized that it would be fatuous to disguise the fact that a European Union would be a new, great world power. The then Under Secretary of State George Ball cast the prospect plainly: "A united Europe will not need to seek first-power status; it will have it. . . . There will be a third large center of power and purpose." In his view, "because it is strong" it would be capable of bringing about a European settlement and dismantling the iron curtain. "As this develops, and only as it develops, will we Atlantic peoples be able to give full meaning to the concept of equal partnership."[48]

Whether or not the sponsors of partnership admitted that a European Union would, in fact, be a third great power center, they all insisted that it would not be a "third force" politically. Ball candidly acknowledged that "to be sure, it will be an independent voice, not always agreeing with us—but then the United States has no monopoly of wisdom." Underlying this attitude was the commitment of faith that the two paths could not seriously diverge. "We are prepared to take our chances," Ball concluded, on "a Europe with a common voice."[49]

One associate of Monnet, Francois Duchene, was also straightforward in assessing the possible perils of a bilateral Atlantic partnership. A political union of Europe, especially one that included Britain, "would have the power to carry out the policy it chose to pursue. . . . If the United States proved, against all expectations, unwilling to pursue the same route, nothing could prevent such a Europe from also going its own way." Touching the essence of the matter, which Monnet himself tended to disregard, Duchene said that "where one provides the means one can also provide the ends."[50] Given these separate massive capabilities, what then was to prevent them from being used separately? Duchene recognized that "by its very nature a bilateral relationship could not be binding: There is no way of binding two partners who fundamentally disagree." Here, indeed, was the danger of reducing Atlantic relations to a purely bilateral pattern, instead of enmeshing or integrating the various entities of the Atlantic Community directly into bodies that were Atlanticwide in scope from the beginning. Having faced up to the dangers of a bilateral partnership, Duchene proposed a dialectical resolution of them. "Paradoxical though it sounds, recognition of the potential bipolarity of the West is essential to its cohesion. Mutual persuasion demands a genuinely reciprocal relation in which each feels his position is an honorable one. The Europeans cannot be drawn into permanent association with the United States (and vice versa) unless Europe's autonomy is accepted. . . . The equality of Europe with America must be encouraged, the right to go separate ways be allowed for, if separation is ever to seem irrelevant, as it ought to become. Only those who feel free to make their own choices can chose not to assert their freedom."[51] Duchene admitted that these assumptions underlying partnership were risky. However, he was convinced that emphasizing the autonomy of each partner, and of its right to go its separate way, would not produce the result of increased autonomy and of each side actually going its own separate way. Only experience in operating a bilateral partnership could prove whether this clever formula would be, in fact, too clever to work.

BRITAIN AS A MODERATING INFLUENCE?

Conventional wisdom held that the impulse of an independent European partner to pursue separatist, Gaullist policies would be significantly modified by British entry into the European Community. It was widely assumed that the ancient British ties of culture and sentiment with the United States would turn Europe outward toward the seas and insure the healthy development of Europe's policies in tandem with America.

This reassuring image was quickly challenged by Lionel Gelber, an articulate critic of British entry. By becoming part of Europe, he argued upon the first British application, the United Kingdom would be "converted into a mere outer island province of a European Union," with the consequence that "the Commonwealth will dissolve automatically, and so will an Anglo-American factor that has been another overseas source of British strength."[52] An enlarged European Union, endowed with the immense capabilities for pursuing separate policies, in Gelber's view, would be a third force both in fact and in political intent. "Is it anticipated that Britain could operate within the European fold as a check on any larger third force isolationism? She is as likely, after the means for independent action have been jettisoned, to be swayed by it."[53] "The British people," Gelber warned "must beware of a tight integration within restricted European confines that could split NATO and paralyze the West."[54]

While Gelber assumed that British accession to a European federation would confine the scope of British ties to Europe, the reverse could also be argued: namely, that the European Community would inevitably have to widen the range of its interests so as to become a genuine world power. This, at least, was the explicit intent of Prime Minister Harold Macmillan when he was negotiating for British entry into the Common Market. The new Europe of which he hoped to be a part would be a great, independent world power. "We have to consider the state of the world as it is today and will be tomorrow," he said in October 1962, "and not in outdated terms of a vanished past. There remain only two national units which can claim to be world powers in their own right, namely the United States and Soviet Russia. To these may soon be added what Napoleon once called the 'sleeping giant' of China." Faced with this prospect, "a divided Europe would stand no chance of competing with these great concentrations of power. But in this new European Community, bringing together the manpower, the material resources and the inventive skills of some of the most advanced countries in the world, a new organization is rapidly developing with the ability to stand on an equal footing with the great power groupings in the world." And what policies might this greater Europe pursue? "As Prime Minister, I have done my best to promote personal contacts between the Communist and Western worlds and seek a better understanding. This is one of Britian's main functions, and I am sure it is a task which we can fulfill much more effectively as active members of the European Community than by remaining outside."[55] Macmillan's theme of playing the "honest broker" between Moscow and Washington was, in effect, a moderate form of Gaullism, since the Europe that would be a world power in its own right would have the satisfaction of great power status and would pursue its own interests, primary among which would be the preservation of its independence by balancing the other great powers off against each other.

When Labor Prime Minister Harold Wilson renewed Britain's bid for entry into the EEC toward the end of 1966, his arguments for economic integration with the Six contained a distinctly Gaullist flavor. "However much we welcome new American investment," he said in a policy statement of November 30, 1966, "there is no one on either side of the Channel who wants to see capital investment in Europe involve domination or, in the last resort, subjugation."[56] Britain could make an important contribution to Europe's industrial strength, Wilson suggested, by making available its considerable advances in technology to a European Technological Community. By pooling Europe's indigenous technological resources, Europe could become more self-reliant and be neither dependent on imports nor dominated from the outside.[57]

Wilson reaffirmed his European credentials before the Consultative Assembly of the Council of Europe in January 1967 when he envisioned a Europe that could "speak from strength to our Atlantic partners." Trans-Atlantic industrial development, he warned, "must never mean subservience. Still less must it mean an industrial helotry under which we in Europe produce only the conventional apparatus of a modern economy, while becoming increasingly dependent on American business for the sophisticated apparatus which will call the industrial tune in the '70s and '80s."[58] Later in 1967 Wilson reiterated his warning that "there is no future for Europe, or for Britain, if we allow American business and American industry so to dominate the strategic growth-industries of our individual countries, that they, and not we, are able to determine the pace and direction of Europe's industrial advance, that we are left in industrial terms as the hewers of wood and the drawers of water while they, because of the scale of research, development and production which they can deploy . . . come to enjoy a growing monopoly in the production of the technological instruments of industrial advance." With this in mind, he renewed his offer of intensive British technological cooperation with the European Community. In addition, he pledged British support for the speedy enactment of a European company law that would help Europeans compete with the Americans in Europe. "It is a telling reflection on all of us in Europe that apart from a handful of established organizations," Wilson lamented, "the only companies which transcend Europe's national frontiers on an integrated basis are the American-owned corporations in Europe."[59] Despite these colorful expressions of Europeanism, which were cast in anti-American overtones so pleasing to the Gaullists, de Gaulle once again vetoed Britain's attempt to enter the European Community.

It was only when Georges Pompidou replaced de Gaulle as President that a breakthrough became possible. As Franco-British conversations in May 1971 approached the critical stage that led to a reversal in the French position, Pompidou stated the nub of the problem in an interview over British television: "There exists a concept of Europe, and we must find out if Britain's concept really is European." He further explained that "a European Europe is a Europe in which decisions concerning it are made within it. . . . If decisions are taken under the influence and under the guidance of a non-European country, even if they are taken by the Community, then they are not European decisions."[60]

Pompidou was apparently satisfied that his subsequent discussions with Prime Minister Edward Heath had produced agreement on this key Gaullist concept of a "European Europe." The communique issued following the Pompidou-Heath talks of May 20-

21, 1971 noted that as regards the role of Europe following British accession to the European Community, the two leaders "had a thorough exchange which showed that their views were very close. They expressed in particular their determination to contribute through the enlarged and deepened Community to increasing European cooperation and to the development of distinctively European policies, in the first instance principally in economic matters and progressively in other fields."[61] When Heath was asked in the House of Commons if he had "simply accepted the French view of Europe," and in particular the one that Pompidou had just expounded over British television, Heath replied: "We reached agreements about the sort of Europe we want to see. . . . It is a Europe which, by its unity, will be of a size and nature and in an equal position with the United States, Japan or the Soviet Union, to enter into international trading arrangements and international financial arrangements and to use its influence in the world. On this the French and British Governments find themselves in agreement."[62]

Pompidou also obtained Heath's agreement that the nature of the European Community should develop along Gaullist lines. "We agreed in particular," Heath continued, "that the identity of national states should be maintained in the framework of the developing Community." This meant that while the Commission would continue to make a valuable contribution, "the Council of Ministers should continue to be the forum in which important decisions are taken, and that the processes of harmonization should not override essential national interests. We were in agreement that the maintenance and strengthening of the fabric of cooperation in such a Community requires that decisions should in practice be taken by unanimous agreement where vital national interests of any one or more members are at stake." Heath added that "this is indeed entirely in accordance with the views which I have long held. It provides a clear assurance, just as the history of the Community provides clear evidence, that joining the Community does not entail a loss of national identity or an erosion of essential national sovereignty."[63]

THE GAULLIST LEGACY

Altogether, the Gaullists could rest assured that their concept of Europe and the further development of the European Community would not be endangered by British entry. When calling for approval of a referendum on the enlargement of the Community, Pompidou said that an affirmative vote would demonstrate "our faith in the grandeur of France within a Europe that is mistress of her destiny." He acknowledged that "nobody in the world sees without concern the birth of a great new economic, monetary and political power." But he added that the new, enlarged Community must be determined "to assert its independence and character."[64]

It can be readily demonstrated that there is a wide basis of support for such assertions, particularly in France. There is no blinking the fact that de Gaulle's version of a completely independent Europe has made a deep impression on French opinion. A poll of the French Institute of Public Opinion, conducted in June 1962, asked whether a unified Western Europe would be able to have its own policies, independent of those of the United States. Of the respondents, 59 percent said "yes," 15 percent said "no," and 26 percent had no opinion. A breakdown of the affirmative 59 percent showed that 51 percent wished Europe to secure such independence, 2 percent opposed this goal, while the remaining 6 percent had no opinion as to its desirability. In December 1969 perferences were surveyed concerning two different conceptions of a future Europe. "The creation of a united Europe that would be a partner of the United States within the framework of the Atlantic Alliance," was approved by only 22 percent, while "the creation of a united Europe constituting a third force between the two great powers," significantly was supported by 51 percent, while 27 percent gave no opinion. Similarly, in April 1972, in response to the question, "Do you think that Europe can be really independent of the United States," 54 percent answered "yes," 24 percent said "no," and 22 percent had no opinion.[65] When the results of those polls are read together, the meaning of a Europe that "can be really independent of the United States," means, more often than not, a third force Europe.

It would be folly to underestimate the effect de Gaulle has had upon Europeans by raising into their consciousness the image of absolute independence for a "European Europe." Even after his death, the Atlantic Community will never be the same again. The easy assumption of a basic identity of interests in pursuing common tasks and sharing common burdens, which underlay Kennedy's partnership proposal, could well prove to be wistfully naive. Even if one may be kindly disposed toward the United States, it is quite clear that the pervasive mentality of Gaullism has made it impossible for any French political figure to declare publicly that he is pro-American. While such sentiment is obviously not as strong in Britain, neither is it, as we have seen, entirely absent there either.

In Germany, which is the third great source of power in the European Community, the Gaullist concept of an independent Europe has been formulated less clearly. This has been largely due, no doubt, to the German need to rely upon U.S. military protection through NATO. Even so, Chancellor Kurt Kiesinger tended to lapse into Gaullist language. "I have no satellite complex in regard to the United States," he told the Bundestag in June 1967. The most important problem that faced Europeans, he added, was to unify European economic and political strength "in such a fashion that Europe may enter into the history of the remaining years of this century as an entity capable of unilateral action."[66] In March 1968 Kiesinger likewise stated before the Bundestag that "we should not seek our own future and, we believe, that of a united Western Europe within the firm framework of a North Atlantic imperium." Instead of a Europe that was tied in partnership with North America, he spoke of "an independent Europe" that "could help to build a bridge between West and East."[67] Here was a German echo of the Gaullist call for a European third force.

Even Willy Brandt who, as German Chancellor, had been most favorably disposed toward the United States, increasingly made clear that his advocacy of partnership arose primarily out of security considerations. As to the future character of the European Community, Brandt commented after his consultations with Pompidou in Paris in January 1973: "It became apparent, after we talked candidly, that both want an independent Europe. . . . Let me reiterate, we both believe that we must closely cooperate with America, but that we must develop into an independent factor in world affairs."[68]

All of the above assertions about the need for an independent Europe should not, of course, be equated with one another, since there are frequently significant gradations in meaning. Yet a common thread has emerged: The separate European partner in an Atlantic partnership must be truly independent, and to ensure its independence it must become a truly great power capable of undertaking unilateral action. That is, many Europeans have seized upon the partnership offer largely as a way of legitimating the resurgence of Europe. They have been more interested in restoring the strength and prestige of Europe than in cooperating with the United States; at least the aim of a strong Europe as an independent center of power has frequently taken priority over the goal of creating a strongly unified West. With the passage of time this tendency has strengthened perceptibly. As a result, the most important motivation for "building Europe," it would seem, is to supply the power base for those who continue to think in terms of a great power, but who have lost its substance so long as they have remained within the confines of their separate nation-states. This is a decided shift in emphasis from the original vision of Monnet. His federalist dream was founded on the motivation of international cooperation: Through such political union Europe would combine its resources for the common good in a way that would be denied the various European states if they remained disunited, while the concerted power of Europe could be added to that of the United States in a constructive effort to solve common problems. But with the slow progress made by the federalist movement, popular enthusiasm for these positive aims waned. What has remained as the most persistent and pressing reason for creating a united Europe is the stark compulsion to become a great power for its own sake.

PARTNERSHIP AS A FORMULA FOR STALEMATE

With ever-greater frequency the arguments heard for a united Europe are not phrased in terms of possessing great power so as to be able to work harmoniously with the United States. Rather, the acquisition of great power is sought so as to be able to stand up to the United States. The sense of a separate European identity is increasingly formed by a common antagonism to America, since intimacy is always achieved by discrimination against outsiders. Some political commentators state the prospect candidly: "The necessary basis of European political union is a European nationalism whose content is autonomy, power and status for Europe as ends in themselves."[69] Add to this the astute observation that "institutional autonomy encourages political intractability,"[70] and the partnership idea appears not as a prescription for harmonious cooperation, but as a recipe for conflict and stalemate.

It is curious to follow the logic of some of the most ardent of Monnet's admirers. John Pinder, for example, has convincingly described the advantages of the Community method for organizing relations among states over the practices used in traditional intergovernmental organizations. The functioning of the independent European Commission, articulating the Communitywide interest, the Court of Justice, the European Parliament, and the progressive introduction of qualified majority voting into the Council of Ministers are all appropriately praised for their capacity to take effective action while safeguarding the integrity of the constituent states.[71] When he considered the logic of applying institutions patterned on those of a European Community onto a trans-Atlantic scale, however, he found this idea unsuitable, despite the admitted similarity of background between Europe and the United States. If the separate European states were joined with the United States under some Community-type institutions, the result, in his view, would be an American "hegemony within supranational institutions, which would resemble an empire more closely than a democracy. If, on the other hand, domination is mitigated or avoided because Europe is united, it is hard to see how a Community or federal system consisting of two very powerful members and a few much smaller ones could work. Either America, with its greater economic strength and political cohesion, would dominate the European side despite its new unity; or there would be the danger of a deadlock with each side vetoing any clear and constructive policies."[72] Rather than work toward any type of trans-Atlantic supranational institutions, therefore, Pinder enthusiastically advocated the formation of an Atlantic partnership between an independent United States and an independent but united Europe.

As noted, the logic is curious: When applied to an Atlantic scale, if all the devices and innovations of the Community institutions, such as an impartial Commission and weighted majority voting, would produce either domination by one side or the other, or deadlock between the two, how then could one ever expect an Atlantic partnership to work? In the latter there would be none of the catalysts for Communitywide action or safeguards for the participating nations found in the European Community. Logically, the tendency toward domination or stalemate would be infintely stronger in a partnership arrangement between two separate and sovereign powers. Moreover, given the fact that each side would be sovereign and capable of taking independent action, the likely outcome would be not so much domination but stalemate. As Monnet's associate, Pierre Uri, has aptly remarked, "in a partnership of two equals there is no alternative to agreement by both if any effective action is to be taken."[73] Or put another way, if there is no agreement by both sides, the alternative is stalemate, or, perhaps worse, a destructive working at cross purposes. If Pinder has been hung by his own logic, one might conclude that his advocacy of partnership hides other motives. Lurking behind the arguments of many European federalists for the partnership scheme there is less a desire for evolving workable trans-Atlantic institutions than the consuming aim of federating Europe and of maintaining a separate European identity at any price.

In short, the divisive potential of an Atlantic partnership can only be kept in check if the process of European unification is accompanied by a movement toward strengthening existing Atlantic institutions, as well as creating new ones where possible. It would be simplistic to ask for a mechanical application of the institutions of the European Community across the Atlantic, and one must recognize that in all probability the intra-European ties will develop more rapidly and more solidly than the trans-Atlantic ones. Nevertheless, the crucial element in a viable partnership scheme will be found in the strength of the tie connecting the two pillars, rather than in developing the separateness of the pillars themselves. As a German critic of partnership correctly observed, "everything would depend on the stability of the one single connection, i.e., that between the United States and the European federation. If there once were a breach, it would be extraordinarily hard to heal it. Nobody would really have the power to coordinate the policies of these two strong 'partners.' " It is simply impossible to obtain a majority view between two entities, since a majority decision has no meaning in this context. While both partners would share a general commitment to common values and a democratic way of life, at the same time, "the policy of states is determined not only by common ideals, but also by conflicting interests and policies." It is predictable that such interests and policies would not always run parallel with each other. "Nobody can foretell whether in an individual case the bond of freedom or the divisive power interests of the two partners would prove stronger."[74] Therefore, the advocates of partnership must be constantly concerned, if not preoccupied, with reinforcing the structure of the Atlantic Community as Europe moves toward unity. To say, as some do, that the two processes are antithetical, is to acknowledge that the partnership idea is bankrupt, indeed that it is dangerous.

TRANSFORMATIONS IN AMERICA'S SELF-IMAGE

While the European conception of partnership progressively emphasized the independent nature of the European partner, significant changes occurred in America's self-image that also have had an important influence on the viability of the partnership scheme.

In the generation that followed World War II, the United States was perceived, both by others and by itself, as an overwhelming power when compared to the separate European states. This was true whether power was measured in collective terms of size or in individual terms of per capita income. The United States also appeared invulnerable to outside threats, while it seemed to be capable of undertaking an effective foreign policy, which most Europeans welcomed as protective of their interests.

The first disillusioning blow doubtless came with the Suez crisis of 1956, which found the United States ranged with the Soviet Union against Britain and France. The Soviet launching of Sputnik also jolted many who had assumed an American monopoly of advanced technology. The Bay of Pigs fiasco and the questionable American intervention in the Dominican Republic raised further serious doubts about the use of force in the pursuit of American foreign policy. But it was America's long and agonizing involvement in Vietnam that finally undermined the belief in America's ability to conduct a rational and effective foreign policy. The result was widespread alienation of Europeans from an America that was badly torn by its own internal dissensions. The United States was no longer viewed as a benign giant, but as a great but frustrated power, angered by its inability to shape events as it wished abroad.

Meanwhile the seemingly unchallengable position of the dollar showed increasing signs of weakness when, beginning in 1958, the United States developed ever-larger balance-of-payments deficits that eventually reached crisis proportions. As an overvalued dollar finally caused American products to lose their competitive position abroad, the United States even developed a balance-of-trade deficit for the first time since the end of the nineteenth century.

The American position had changed, but as Raymond Vernon persuasively argued, it was by no means desperate.[75] A trade deficit could only have limited domestic effects, since barely five percent of America's gross national product was involved in foreign trade. Despite all the trouble the dollar had encountered, the sheer size of the U.S. economy and of the huge volume of American assets abroad guaranteed that the dollar would remain the dominant currency in world commerce. While the United States had become more reliant on imported raw materials than in the past, Europe was infinitely more dependent on vital imports, especially of oil, than the United States. In the area of high technology, Europe began closing the technological gap during the 1960s, but the U.S. command over the industrial heights in advanced technology remained and the U.S. lead will probably widen again. In short, there was enormous residual strength in the U.S. economy. While the United States increasingly tended to perceive itself as weak, in fact it remained strong—surely strong enough to conduct itself as a responsible partner in its relations with its European allies.

It was not facts, however, but the perception of facts that mattered. As the perception changed, so did the official American pronouncements that gave Europeans a clear warning that the United States could no longer be counted upon as a benign partner.

In his foreign policy report to the Congress in February 1970, President Nixon restated the American position that had been maintained ever since the days of the Marshall Plan: "We recognize that our interests will necessarily be affected by Europe's evolution, and we may have to make sacrifices in the common interest. We consider that the possible economic price of a truly unified Europe is outweighed by the gain in the political vitality of the West as a whole."[76] This assertion was probably out of date when it was made. In any event, later in 1970 Deputy Under Secretary for Economic Affairs Nathaniel Samuels, who had become a principal American spokesman in dealings with the European Community, could declare: "I don't think it is a question any more of trading short-term economic costs for long-term political advantages. . . . We even question the *need*," he added, for the United States to pay any further short-term economic costs for this end. "Europe is an economic giant and can stand on its own competitive feet. . . . Henceforth the U.S. government will be very alert to damage done by one or another Community policy. We will follow a policy of more vigorous protection of U.S. trade interests than has sometimes been the case."[77] In view of this shift in attitude, it was not surprising to find Nixon's February 1971 report to the Congress assert: "For years . . . it was believed uncritically that a unified Western Europe would automatically lift burdens from the shoulders of the United States. The truth is not so simple. European unity will also pose problems for American policy, which it would be idle to ignore."[78]

In July 1971 the President enunciated what might be called another Nixon Doctrine on the future relations of the United States with the outside world. "Instead of just America being number one in the world from an economic standpoint, the preeminent world power, and instead of there being just two superpowers, when we think in economic terms and economic potentialities there are five great power centers in the world today." This pentagonal world would remain for the foreseeable future. "What we see as we look ahead five, ten and perhaps fifteen years, we see five great economic superpowers: the United States, Western Europe, the Soviet Union, mainland China and, of course, Japan." As regards the two non-Communist powers with which the United States would have to deal, Nixon noted that "both Western Europe and Japan are very potent competitors of the United States; friends, yes; allies, yes; but competing and competing very hard with us throughout the world for economic leadership."[79]

An immediately apparent feature of this analysis is that the European Community was not at all regarded as a partner, nor was there any mention made of Atlantic partnership. Rather, Europe was put on a par with the other power centers that would compete with the United States in a world in which America's presumed "allies" would henceforth be regarded as potential rivals and antagonists, quite as much as the Russians and Chinese.

This philosophy was promptly implemented on August 15, 1971, when Nixon abruptly announced unilateral American economic and monetary restrictions that vitally affected Europe and Japan. America's allies had long complained that American preoccupation with Vietnam had produced a policy toward them of benign neglect. Now apparently this had given way to a policy of malign attention. The new foreign economic policy was cast in nationalist rhetoric that emphasized the unfair treatment the United States had presumably sustained at the hands of its non-Communist allies. Treasury Secretary John Connally's abrasive behavior was particularly offensive to the Europeans and Japanese, who perceived the situation quite differently. They resented taking the entire blame for the deterioration of America's economic position, which in their view was closely related to inflationary pressures arising from financing the Vietnam war and for which they thought the United States was responsible. We need not be detained by the exchange of all the accusations and an evaluation of the differing perceptions. The Americans especially objected to the inequities in the European Community's common agricultural policy and the discriminatory nature of its preferential trade arrangements. For their part, the Europeans drew up their own catalog of complaints. Above the din of the verbal battles it became clear that America's "partners" were regarded as rivals who had to be cut down to size.

Nixon's subsequent diplomatic initiatives in 1971-72, which led to his visits to Peking and Moscow, only served to aggravate the situation. In Japan, in particular, Nixon's China trip, which was undertaken without any consultation with the Japanese leaders, badly shook the Japanese government and together with the economic measures of 1971 became known in Japan as "the Nixon shocks." It indeed appeared as Nixon had claimed that the United States was moving from confrontation to negotiation with its enemies. But it also appeared as though the United States was moving from negotiation to confrontation with its allies.

Even before these developments had occurred, Ambassador Schaetzel, from his Brussels vantage point as U.S. envoy to the organs of the European Community, articulated the changing American mood at the beginning of 1970. "The wide enthusiasm for the Community in America of the Eisenhower and Kennedy periods, the rosy expectations of rapid and brilliant progress toward unity, [have] largely evaporated and been replaced by irritation, frustration and a brooding sense of apprehension."[80] This was discouraging commentary, in startling contrast to his own optimistic assertions of the early 1960s about the promising prospects for partnership.

When Schaetzel resigned his post in 1972 he spoke freely about what he called "a slow deterioration of understanding and the onset of actue mutual deafness." Both sides had been conducting themselves badly. "What has been happening to U.S.-E.C. relations is a kind of common death wish. America and Europe are cursed by a preoccupation with their own affairs and an inclination to deal with domestic problems in ways that ignore their impact on the other side of the Atlantic." The drift toward mutual hostility in economic and monetary affairs could have unfortunate consequences for trade and the search for a viable international monetary system. "Most important of all, it could weaken the common cultural, economic and defense interests that link the nations of the Atlantic Community." He admonished both sides to acknowledge that they had each sinned against the other. Beyond this they needed to raise their sights from the dangerous adversary roles into which they had fallen in order to resume a constructive dialogue of partnership. He urged that they return to the "assumption tested by time: at bottom, European-American affairs involve common interests, not inevitable conflict." But, he warned, "we have only a brief moment in history when the U.S. and the Europeans together can recover a clear view of our deep common interests."[81]

The extent to which a commitment to partnership can attenuate the perception of rivalry will determine what kind of trans-Atlantic arrangements can be arrived at in the future. The prospect would seem to be one of tough bargaining between two parties, each absorbed in the search for narrow, short-range advantage, which will generate bitter feelings and produce thin, brittle agreements. Perhaps this is an unduly pessimistic assessment. At least one would hope so.

THE CALL FOR A NEW ATLANTIC CHARTER

Sober second thoughts about where the deteriorating relationship with Europe would lead finally prompted the Nixon administration to pledge that it would draw back from its combative attitude toward Europe and seek to infuse the idea of an Atlantic partnership with new life. In a major policy statement of April 23, 1973, Henry Kissinger first frankly acknowledged the extent to which rivalry had displaced cooperation. "We knew that a united Europe would be a more independent partner. But we assumed, perhaps too uncritically, that our common interests would be assured by our long history of cooperation. We expected that political unity would follow economic integration, and that unified Europe working cooperatively with us in an Atlantic partnership would ease many of our international burdens. It is clear that many of these expectations are not being fulfilled. . . . We cannot ignore the fact that Europe's economic success and its transformation from a recipient of our aid to a strong competitor has produced a certain amount of friction. There has been turbulence and a sense of rivalry" both in international monetary relations and in trade with the European Community.

Kissinger then entered a plea for a reversal of the destructive trends in trans-Atlantic relationships. "The gradual accumulation of sometimes petty, sometimes major economic disputes must be ended and be replaced by a determined commitment on both sides of the Atlantic to find cooperative solutions." He quite properly pointed out that economic questions are too important to be left to the economists. The ensuing trade and monetary negotiations "must engage the top political leaders for they require above all a commitment of political will. If they are left solely to the experts, the inevitable competitiveness of economic interests will dominate the debate." It would therefore be the "responsibility of national leaders to insure that economic negotiations serve larger political purposes." If economic rivalry is not put within the restraints of a broader political framework, it will in the end damage other political and security relationships that should bind Europe and the United States together. In short, "a revitalized Atlantic partnership is indispensable."[82] To this end, Kissinger suggested that the member countries of the Atlantic Alliance draw up a new comprehensive Atlantic Charter that would reflect their determination to resolve the increasingly dangerous Atlantic rivalry in the spirit of accommodation and partnership.

Kissinger had anticipated a quick, stirring debate that would produce a single declaration, in which all of the interrelated issues of Atlantic partnership would be placed in their proper relationship. If he had foreseen that it would only open up a prolonged, acrimonious controversy, Kissinger later admitted, he would not have launched the project in the first place.[83]

The first disappointment arose when the Nine of the European Community insisted upon segregating economic issues from the other concerns and making them the subject of a separate E.C.-U.S. declaration. The European Community wanted not only to assert its separate identity, but also to avoid any linkage between security and economic issues. The Europeans, and particularly the French, feared that a linkage would create pressure upon the Europeans to make economic concessions in order to keep U.S. troops in Europe.

The second and more disappointing development involved the substance of the E.C. draft declaration, which, at French insistence, carefully made no mention either of "partnership" or of "interdependence."[84] "Some Europeans," Kissinger complained, "have come to believe that their identity should be measured by Europe's distance from the United States." The United States strongly supports European strides toward unity. "But as an old friend we are also sensitive to what this process does to traditional ties that, in our view, remain essential to the common interest. Europe's unity," he warned, "must not be at the expense of Atlantic Community, or both sides of the Atlantic will suffer."[85]

Ultimately the whole contentious project of an E.C.-U.S. declaration was left to die; only a NATO declaration dealing largely with security and political affairs was eventually forthcoming. Nearly a year after Kissinger's ill-starred "Year of Europe" speech it was decided the better part of wisdom to divert attention from formulating an E.C.-U.S. declaration to the pragmatic problems of improving E.C.-U.S. consultations.

Traditionally it was the Europeans who had complained of inadequate consultation on the part of the United States. But the Nine's groping to speak with a single voice now raised problems of trans-Atlantic consultation from the European side. Kissinger acknowledged that the United States had, in the past, "not consulted enough or adequately, especially in rapidly moving situations." However, this was not done out of preference. Rather, it represented "a deviation from official policy and established practice." Kissinger found a different rationale behind European behavior. "The attitude of the unifying Europe, by contrast, seems to attempt to elevate refusal to consult into a principle defining European identity. To judge from recent experience," he said in December 1973, "consultation with us before a decision is precluded, and consultation after the fact has been drained of content. For then Europe appoints a spokesman who is empowered to inform us of the decisions taken, but who has no authority to negotiate."

The United States did not object to Europe having a single spokesman; this was to be encouraged as part of the process of European unification. The issue was rather that "the United States should be given an opportunity to express its concerns before final decisions affecting its interests are taken." The United States understood the "difficulty of the first hesitant steps of political coordination. But we cannot be indifferent to the tendency to justify European identity as facilitating separateness from the United States: European unity, in our view, is not contradictory to Atlantic unity."[86]

This, indeed, is the central issue: Can Europe only find its identity by becoming a separate and rival force and by measuring the growth of a European entity in terms of its political distance from the United States? To this question France has steadily answered "yes." Milder echoes of this view were also heard from Britain's Conservative government of Edward Heath. When Labor came to power in the spring of 1974, British Foreign Secretary James Callaghan pointedly disassociated his government from the position of his predecessor. "We repudiate the view," Callaghan asserted, "that Europe will emerge only after a process of struggle against America."[87]

Bonn has consistently tried to play the role of an intermediary by advancing conciliatory proposals. German Foreign Minister Walter Scheel suggested that the E.C.'s Political Cooperation Committee and Commission discuss policy papers affecting American interests with American officials before forwarding them to the Council of Ministers. France countered with the suggestion of a highly restricted form of consultations with the United States only when the Nine had agreed a particular case warranted them, and then if raised only at the ministerial level.[88] An interim, informal agreement among the Nine was reached in June 1974 to the effect that any member state may suggest consultations with the United States, but they will proceed through the country holding the chairmanship of the Council of Ministers only if all Nine agree.[89] Thus the French veto on closer consultations with Washington, at least for the moment, has been substantially upheld.

THE DOCTRINE OF EQUALITY: ATLANTIC DECISION MAKING

The "separate but equal doctrine," designed to create a separate European partner, obviously contains elements both of hope and of danger, and time alone will determine which factor will prevail. However, what are the implications of the other half of this doctrine, demanding equality? To recall the formulation of Monnet's Action Committee: "The partnership between America and a united Europe must be a relationship of two separate but *equally powerful* entities."[90]

The demand for two equally powerful entities has frequently been justified on the pragmatic grounds that it would facilitate agreement between Europe and the United States. A typical State Department pronouncement explained that as a politically integrated "European Community developed, the United States could anticipate an even more fruitful consultative relationship than now exists, for the divergencies which inevitably arise because of the difference in size and strength among the Atlantic partners would be greatly diminished."[91] Or as Under Secretary of State Ball put the matter in 1966: "So long as there remains the great disparity in size and resources between the United States and the nations of Europe acting individually, there will be an awkwardness in any Atlantic arrangement."[92]

Undeniably, there is a good measure of truth in these assertions. As several members of the international staff of NATO explained to this writer, for example, the task of NATOwide military planning would be made immeasurably easier if the separate European states would merge into a single political entity, and so be able to participate more meaningfully in the planning processes. As it is, the separate European states do not have the resources in terms of planning staffs as well as research and development facilities to match those of the United States. Moreover, the smaller, individual European states have more narrowly defined interests and so do not see the overall Alliance needs as easily as the United States. As a result, the European states always seem to be overwhelmed by American proposals, since the United States has both a broader world view and a vast governmental machine at its disposal that can engage in comprehensive and sophisticated planning that is beyond the capabilities of the separate European states. NATO plans therefore inevitably tend to be American plans. This creates resentment in Europe, but it can only be rectified by Europe becoming a political entity of roughly comparable capabilities. "The real cause of European resentment," one NATO official remarked, "is not American 'dictation' or poor American planning, but rather that the Europeans cannot match the competent American staff work by their own, and so are placed in a position of dependence and inferiority." He also emphasized that "the need to consult each individual European state enormously complicates the planning processes."

While it would doubtless be easier to deal with a single, more technically competent European entity, would it necessarily be easier to arrive at agreed policies? The answer to this would depend, in the first instance, upon how differently Europe and America perceived their own interests. As Europe developed its own sources of power, its dissatisfaction with some aspects of American policies might *not* lend more support for Atlantic unity or assure a strengthened NATO. The mere existence of a strong European partner of itself would provide no such guarantees. The combined power of a European entity, however, would be certain to restrict America's accustomed freedom of action. This would either force a compromise in the policies of one or both partners or else result in policy stalemates. Given a European Union and real differences of interest between Europe and the United States, Laurence Martin argued that these differences "would be compounded by synthesis into a single center of responsibility disposing of the resources [that would permit it] to attempt an independent course. The arguments that only equals can cooperate can thus be countered with the thesis that divergent interests become irresistible when the parties concerned have pretensions to self-sufficiency."[93] Similarly, Timothy Stanley, an experienced NATO hand, observed that "it is not necessarily true that a partnership is impossible without equality of size and power or that it is easier to negotiate a satisfactory arrangement with two major parties than it is with a large number. On the contrary, bilateral confrontations sometimes make it harder to compromise than with negotiations where there are many and each knows it must yield in some measure."[94]

Those who advocate a bilateral confrontation of equals must also be prepared to mitigate its dangers. This can only be done by assuring that the confrontation takes place within the context of common Atlantic agencies that are capable of coordinating and mediating differences and suggesting terms of settlement based on the highest degree of common interest. To take the example of NATO planning again, such activity between two entities of roughly equal competence and resources would require a strengthening of NATO's international civil-military staff so that it could successfully gear together the planning of both partners. Perhaps it would be necessary to endow the office of the Secretary General with a mandate somewhat analogous to that of the Commission in the EEC, so that both sides could begin negotiations upon a set of proposals advanced by this impartial third party, who could upgrade the common concern and help break policy deadlocks when they occur. This example is intended to illustrate once again the fundamental thesis that the movement toward European Union must be accompanied by a strengthening of the Atlantic organs of joint planning and decision making, since it is dangerous to speak only of the need for European Union without thinking simultaneously of commensurate steps toward firmer trans-Atlantic ties. It is not enough to assume that both sides of the Atlantic are bound by a common civilization and by sharing a general sense of purpose. To be held together by a long-term goal is necessary but insufficient; there must also be adequate means immediately available to pursue these goals.

THE PSYCHOLOGICAL ASPECTS OF EQUALITY

The discussion thus far has accepted at face value Monnet's assertion that the Atlantic relationship should be between two "equally powerful" entities. To what extent does a closer examination reveal that this phrase has been inflated rhetoric? At the time the partnership concept was first popularized, the population of the United States was slightly larger than that of the Six, although in terms of economic power, the GNP and per capita income of the United States was more than twice as great as that of the Six. With the enlargement of the European Community, the population of the United States became only about 80 percent as large as the Nine, although the GNP of the Nine was only two-thirds that of the United States. This disparity of living standards seems likely to continue, despite the greater population resources of the European Community. Even before enlargement, the European Community was the world's largest trading unit, and it has become even more so with the accession of a great trading nation like Britain. The significance of this should be viewed in light of the fact, however, that the United States is infinitely less dependent upon foreign trade than the Nine for its economic well-being. In terms of expenditure for military items, the American lead over the Six was overwhelming, although this imbalance was corrected somewhat when the Six became the Nine. In the nuclear field, however, the United States continued to possess somewhat over 96 percent of the nuclear power of the West. In view of these data, what meaning should be attributed to the concept of Europe and the United States as two "equally powerful" entities?

In the mid-1960s Francois Duchene sought to reinterpret "equality" so as to make Monnet sound reasonable. It is true, he acknowledged, that "Europe's collective power, even now, is much inferior in material terms to that of the United States. But, in the modern world, 'equality,' illusive concept that it is, does not always depend on material factors." While there was admittedly a great gap between the productive and military power of the United States and Europe, on the other hand, "in many ways, the diplomatic position of the Common Market countries, based on trade and finance (in monetary policy and the Kennedy Round), has proved to be the stronger." He concluded, therefore, that "the problem is not statistical equality, but equality in the political process of mutual persuasion." Thus, strictly speaking, equality was a mirage. Yet by trading off European elements of strength against American material superiority, "equality" was nevertheless achieved. Some aspects of European strength were quite intangible. "America depends on the European connections in the world balance of power," Duchene contended, "almost as much as Europe on American military power. If some of the material factors of equality are likely to be lacking for a long time, Europe as a region seems to have more than sufficient political and economic assets to make its weight felt."[95]

The image of "equally powerful" entities might therefore be conceived of in terms of a marriage, in which the partners would be grossly unequal in some respects, each bringing different assets to the common partnership, and in which each is equal in rights. This metaphor breaks down, of course, inasmuch as each partner is to remain a distinct entity and not consummate the "marriage" in a political union. Partnership, in fact, is an attempt to gain the benefits of political union without actually creating one. To this extent partnership has always contained an element of legerdemain.

Despite these qualifications, the existence of a European Union would undeniably make a considerable difference in trans-Atlantic arrangements. While still not creating equal partners, it would mark a significant step away from the extreme inequality that has so long haunted the relationship between the United States and the separate European states. A united Europe, in which the sum would be greater than the existing parts, could assume more responsibility in its own defense and could even construct its own respectable nuclear deterrent, for example, if Europe should opt for this choice. The capacity for more effective collaboration with the United States would also be present in economic and political matters, whether it be trade, aid, and monetary policies, or negotiations with the East over a European settlement. The increased capacity for effective action, to reiterate, would not guarantee greater trans-Atlantic collaboration, since the exercise of this capacity is a function of political will.

The "good Europeans" insist that the necessary political will could be mobilized for common Atlantic purposes, in large measure because of an improved psychological atmosphere. A united Europe would be a sufficiently important entity so as to be treated as a respected partner, whose views would have to be earnestly consulted before decisions were taken. This would dispel the pervasive feeling of inferiority with which the Europeans have been afflicted ever since the end of the war, and which has continuously bedeviled Atlantic relations.

The psychological dimension is, indeed, basic to the demand for equal partnership. Monnet earnestly impressed this writer with this thought. "Europe," he said, "has an inferiority complex and America is in danger of developing a superiority complex." The sense of superiority did not arise, he added, from arrogance or the desire to dominate, but from the desire to get things done. American power was so great that it had the capability of acting alone in many areas, and in his view the danger is that this would become the habitual way of doing things, unless the power of a united Europe could be brought to bear in an effective way upon the joint problems that faced the West.

The image of an all-powerful United States was doubtless more widely accepted by Americans and Europeans alike before the frustration of American aims in Vietnam in the late 1960s, when the massive application of U.S. power proved to be of little avail. Nevertheless Monnet could comment in 1968: "I am said to be an optimist, but today I must confess that I am not." In terms of economic power, Europe remained vastly inferior to the United States. Monnet asked what the Europeans had done "to organize our Community technologically? Where are the computers, the telecommunications satellites, the scientific transformation of production coming from? They are coming less and less from us, and more and more from America." This phenomenon has been a central Gaullist complaint as well, with the important difference that de Gaulle had imputed evil, or at least imperialist, motives to the Americans who presumably sought to dominate Europe. Monnet put the blame elsewhere—upon European disunity. Only a European Union could correct the Atlantic imbalance. "Unless it pools its resources in a single whole, Europe in ten years time will be an underdeveloped continent using as a client what others—the United States, the USSR and perhaps Japan—produce."[96]

Erasing the European sense of inferiority would also be the most effective way of undercutting the lingering appeal of Gaullism. The incessant Gaullist theme of American "domination" or American "hegemony" has responded to the European striving for self-assertion, which the Gaullists turned into anti-American channels. The exploitation of anti-American feelings would appear to be inevitable so long as the gigantic power of the United States tends to overwhelm the collection of individual small and medium-sized European states. The resentment generated in this relationship is unavoidable until "Europe" exists. It is among the ironies of Gaullism, of course, that de Gaulle's insistence upon the nation-state as the sole legitimate repository of sovereignty made it impossible to build a European federation, and thereby to mitigate the bitter feelings that de Gaulle so persistently incited.

All this presents a problem. The Europeans who are aware of their proud political past and present economic well-being insist on treatment as equals now, even though a European political entity does not yet exist. If they are not treated as equals, then one reinforces the appeal of Gaullism; if they are treated as equals, then one fosters illusions about where power really resides. Realism would also suggest that the abuse that the United States receives for "dominating Europe" at least be divided with the Europeans, who cannot agree among themselves on the creation of a "Europe" to which equal treatment could be extended.

But such realism rarely operates in politics. Rather, man is moved by myths that accord with his emotional needs, even though these myths are articulated in intellectual terms. Unfounded beliefs thus become real social forces that must be taken into account in formulating policy. In this instance, it would seem that the psychological requirements of European self-esteem would call for the United States to discount to a considerable extent the actual disparities in power and where possible to treat Europe almost as if it were a single entity and equal counterweight to the United States. This would be much easier to do in some areas than in others. In matters relating to trade and monetary policy the European

Community could genuinely be considered an equal partner, although as long as the Nine have not truly become one there will be the continuing problem, as already noted, of "dealing with an it that is a they." However the disparities in military, and especially strategic, power will make the illusions of equality much more difficult to sustain. Moving through the world of illusions, necessary though it may be, can still prove to be dangerous if it breeds false expectations between the "equal partners." At some point, the world of "as if" will have limits set by the realities of power. In short, the psychological dimensions of partnership cannot be satisfactorily resolved until an equal European partner, in fact, exists.

EQUALITY AND BURDEN SHARING

One of the principal incentives for encouraging Europe to unite, especially from the U.S. point of view, was the expectation that a united Europe would be capable of sharing more equitably the defense burdens of the West, as well as contributing more effectively to the growth and stability of the underdeveloped world. State Department spokesmen have therefore professed confidence in the movement toward a European Union that would share global responsibilities with the United States. Speaking of the future of Europe, Under Secretary of State Ball, for example, asserted in 1966: "There is a compelling logic that underlies the movement toward unity today." The emergence of the superpowers and the consequences of technology have transformed the structure of world politics, thereby creating "a new requirement of size for nations that are to play a significant role in world affairs. European states that a quarter of a century ago occupied the center of the stage now find themselves only medium powers, with a limited capacity to influence world events." In Ball's view, the creation of a new, great European power would automatically kindle the desire to shape the course of events on a global scale. Given union, "I do not think that the European peoples will be content for long to stand aside from a major participation in world affairs."[97]

Similarly, J. Robert Schaetzel, long an authoritative State Department spokesman on Atlantic affairs, connected the size of the European states with the range of their activities. "Given the limited size and capacity of the individual European nations, they are neither willing nor able to play more than supporting roles. And the United States, carrying a large share of the burdens and costs, cannot realistically share responsibility for policy decisions with reluctant junior associates. . . . We want European participation, but cannot fully share decisions in the absence of a European contribution commensurate with our own; the Europeans are neither organized to make this contribution nor much interested in doing so."[98]

Historically it is not true, of course, that modest-sized European nations had only limited interests. Before Europe divested itself of its colonies, a small nation like Holland had extensive interests and considered itself a world power of sorts. The correlation that State Department spokesmen made was therefore a postcolonial phenomenon. It was their hope that European Union would be the surrogate for colonies in relaunching Europe back into the world. If the separate European countries now tend to be limited in outlook, having been cut off from their former foreign basis of power, the combined strength of a united Europe would hopefully raise their sights and desires to be a world power again. As Walt W. Rostow put it, when he was a State Department policy planner: "Europe must generate a global vision, and that global vision is only likely to emerge as Europe moves toward integration."[99]

The Dutch critic, J. L. Heldring, did not find this entirely convincing. "It seems more likely," he protested, "that a united Europe would, in the first period of its existence, be so inward-looking, so concentrated on the task of keeping the precarious union together and creating an identity of its own, that it would have little time and energy left for acquiring a global vision and tackling global tasks."[100] This might be especially so, one might add, because many of the global burdens carried by the United States were precisely those inherited as a result of being forced to fill in the power vacuums left by the former European colonial powers. Since the United States had been a most vigorous advocate of decolonization, the Europeans generally felt little compulsion to rush back to aid the Americans in the areas from which they had so recently been expelled with American encouragement. This feeling was, for a long time, reinforced by the expectation that American power was so enormous that the United States would somehow manage to carry these burdens alone, or at best that the Europeans can get by with little more than token support.

In the longer range, the prospect may be somewhat different. A tested, viable European Union would be a big power and would doubtless begin to act like a big power. Europe is still too much of a world power in mentality and has too many intellectual and economic ties throughout the world to draw in upon itself permanently. But again the question arises: Would a great power Europe play the kind of global role that the United States would find compatible? At this point mutual adjustments of interest between Europe and the United States would be required, and increasingly intimate institutional ties across the Atlantic would be necessary, so as to formulate common approaches toward global problems. Again, unless European Union is accompanied by the strengthening of the Atlantic Community, the difficulties of the West will surely be compounded. The combined resources and political dynamism of a united Europe would provide the possibility for effective burden sharing, but the extent to which this will be realized would depend upon the achievement of an Atlantic consensus that would emerge from the organized power of the Western world. That is, burdens will not likely be shared in a meaningful way unless there is more sharing in the decision-making processes of the West.

NOTES

1. Address by President John F. Kennedy at Frankfurt, June 25, 1963, Department of State *Bulletin*, 44, no. 1256: 119.

2. Address by President John F. Kennedy at Philadelphia, July 4, 1962, Department of State *Bulletin*, 47, no. 1204: 132.

3. Address by Jean Monnet at Bad Godesberg, February 25, 1964, p. 7.

4. For the type of proposals then under consideration, see Alastair Buchan, "The Reform of NATO," *Foreign Affairs*, January 1962, pp. 165-82.

5. The phrase is that of Edwin L. Dale, Jr., the economic specialist of the New York *Times*, who watched the GATT negotiations at close quarters.

6. *Hearings before the Subcommittee on National Security and International Operations of the Committee on Government Operations, United States Senate*, May 5, 1966 (Washington, D.C., 1966), p. 39.

7. Clyde H. Farnsworth, "U.S. Avoided Common Market in Recent Money Crisis Talks," New York *Times*, February 18, 1973.

8. Miriam Camps, *What Kind of Europe? The Community since de Gaulle's Veto* (London, 1965), pp. 138-39.

9. Address by John W. Holmes at Ottawa, September 15, 1964, *Atlantic Community Quarterly*, Winter 1964-65, pp. 528-29.

10. Paul Martin, "The State of the Atlantic Alliance," *NATO Letter*, February 1965, p. 15.

11. Quoted in ibid.

12. Address by Prime Minister Lester B. Pearson at Springfield, Ill., June 11, 1966, *Freedom & Union*, July-August 1966, pp. 16-17. See similar arguments developed in Pearson's 1968 Reith Lectures over the BBC printed in *Saturday Review*, February 15 and 22, 1969.

13. Claude Julien, "Interview with Prime Minister Trudeau," *Le Monde Weekly Selection*, February 25, 1970. On Trudeau's NATO policy, see Harlan Cleveland, *NATO: The Transatlantic Bargain* (New York, 1970), pp. 125-26.

14. Julien, op. cit.

15. Address by Under Secretary of State George Ball at Harriman, N.Y., April 28, 1964, Department of State *Bulletin*, 50, no. 1299: 774.

16. Ambassador W. Michael Blumethal, Deputy U.S. Representative for Trade Negotiations, *EFTA Reporter*, No. 104 (September 18, 1964), p. 5.

17. *Foreign Ownership and the Structure of Canadian Industry*, Privy Council Office (Ottawa, 1968), p. 11; C. W. Gonick, New York *Times*, January 26, 1970; Edward Cowan, New York *Times*, February 7, 1971.

18. "A New Trade Strategy for Canada and the United States," *Atlantic Community Quarterly*, Summer 1966, pp. 254-55.

19. Pierre Uri, "Economic Dimensions of Atlantic Partnership," in *NATO in Quest of Cohesion*, eds. Karl H. Cerny and Henry W. Briefs (New York, 1965), p. 349.

20. "Jean Monnet on European Union," *Freedom & Union*, April 1953, p. 25.

21. Action Committee for the United States of Europe, Joint Declaration, adopted November 19-20, 1959, Paris, p. 10.

22. Action Committee for the United States of Europe, Joint Declaration, adopted July 11, 1960, Paris, pp. 6-7.

23. Action Committee for the United States of Europe, Joint Declaration, adopted July 10-11, 1961, Paris, p. 2.

24. Address by Walter Hallstein at New York, May 18, 1961, p. 4.

25. Address by Walter Hallstein at Cambridge, Mass., May 22, 1961, p. 8.

26. Address by Jean Monnet at Hanover, N.H., June 11, 1961, pp. 7-9.

27. Address by McGeorge Bundy at Chicago, December 6, 1961, in *Freedom & Union*, January 1962, p. 10.

28. Address by Walter Hallstein at Medford, Mass., April 18, 1962, pp. 72-73.

29. Address by Walter Hallstein at Paris, November 12, 1962, in *Addresses by Speakers at the Eighth Annual Conference of NATO Parliamentarians* (Paris, 1962), pp. 35-36, 38-39. See also address by Walter Hallstein at Paris, June 22, 1962, p. 14: "Partnership means constant close and systematic cooperation, no more and no less. It is not a 'Community' in our European sense, nor can it be. . . . This kind of partnership calls for no new institutions. Nothing of the sort is needed between two friends."

30. Address by Walter Hallstein at New York, March 2, 1963, p. 18.

31. Walter Hallstein, *Some of Our "faux problemes"* (December 4, 1964, London), p. 14.

32. J. H. Huizinga, "Which Way Europe?" *Foreign Affairs*, April 1965, pp. 490-491.

33. Henry A. Kissinger, *The Troubled Partnership* (New York, 1965), pp. 7-8.

34. Address by Christian Herter at New York, January 23, 1963, *Freedom & Union*, February 1963, p. 14.

35. Address by NATO Secretary General Manlio Brosio, November 20, 1967, to the Thirteenth Annual Session of the North Atlantic Assembly, Brussels, in *Addresses by Speakers, NAA, 1967*, p. 18.

36. Livingston Hartley, *Atlantic Challenge* (New York, 1965), pp. 45-48. To confound the confusion, by the fall of 1966 President Johnson found it possible to discuss Atlantic relations without using the phrase "Atlantic partnership." However, he mentioned the idea of a European partner in two senses: first the collective concept in which "a united Western Europe can be our equal partner," and then he spoke of "the bonds between the United States and its Atlantic partners," implying that the United States had multiple partners in

Europe. Johnson laid great stress on NATO and specifically referred to the "Atlantic Community." "The Atlantic Alliance is the central instrument of the entire Atlantic Community but is not the only one." The economic tasks of the Atlantic nations could be confronted in other multilateral organizations, presumably OECD and GATT. (Address of President Lyndon B. Johnson, New York, October 7, 1966, Department of State *Bulletin*, 55, no. 1426: 623-25.)

37. Address by Jean Monnet at New York, January 23, 1963, p. 6.

38. Address by President John F. Kennedy at Philadelphia, July 4, 1962, Department of State *Bulletin*, 47, no. 1204: 132.

39. Address by Deputy Assistant Secretary of State J. Robert Schaetzel at Sackville, New Brunswick, Canada, August 18, 1962, Department of State *Bulletin*, 47, no. 1210: 353.

40. J. Robert Schaetzel, "Better Preparation for the Conduct of Atlantic Community Affairs," Department of State *News Letter*, December 1962, p. 14.

41. J. Robert Schaetzel, "The Necessary Partnership," *Foreign Affairs*, April 1966, pp. 428-29.

42. Jean Monnet, "A Ferment of Change," *Journal of Common Market Studies* 1, no. 3 (1962): 210.

43. Address by Jean Monnet at New York, January 23, 1963, pp. 4-5.

44. Jean Monnet, "America and Ourselves," *La Nef*, February 17, 1966, p. 2.

45. Address by Jean Monnet at Bad Godesberg, February 25, 1964, p. 5.

46. Ibid., pp. 8-9.

47. Address by Walter Hallstein at Cambridge, Mass., May 22, 1961, p. 8. Hallstein, however, also continued to insist "that we must not regard the European Community as just a new power bloc or a new coalition. It is not, in my view, just the magnification of 19th century nationalism to a more than national scale. It is the embodiment of a new method and a new approach to the relations between states." (Address by Walter Hallstein at New York, March 2, 1963, p. 10.)

48. Address by Under Secretary of State George Ball at Washington, D.C., April 29, 1966, Department of State *Bulletin*, 54, no. 1403: 767.

49. Ibid., p. 768.

50. Francois Duchene, *Beyond Alliance* (Boulogne-sur-Seine, 1965), p. 27.

51. Ibid., p. 34.

52. Lionel Gelber, "A Marriage of Inconvenience," *Foreign Affairs*, January 1963, p. 321.

53. Lionel Gelber, *Beyond the New Europe* (London, 1963), p. 45.

54. Ibid., p. 53.

55. Harold Macmillan, *Britain, the Commonwealth, and Europe* (London, 1962), pp. 5-6.

56. Address by Prime Minister Harold Wilson at London, November 30, 1966, Policy Statements, British Information Services, New York, p. 2.

57. Address by Prime Minister Harold Wilson at London, November 14, 1966, *British Record*, British Information Services, New York, Supplement to No. 18, November 30, 1966, pp. 1-2.

58. Address by Prime Minister Harold Wilson at Strasbourg, January 23, 1967, *British Record*, British Information Services, New York, No. 2, February 8, 1967, p. 1.

59. Address by Prime Minister Harold Wilson at London, November 13, 1967, Policy Statements, British Information Services, New York, pp. 5-8.

60. Interview of President Georges Pompidou over BBC Television, May 17, 1971, Ambassade de France, New York, pp. 2-3.

61. Joint French-British Communique, May 21, 1971, quoted in *Parliamentary Debates (Hansard), House of Commons, Official Report*, May 24, 1971, pp. 48-49.

62. Ibid., pp. 38-39.

63. Ibid., pp. 32-33.

64. Quoted in Henry Giniger, "Pompidou, Explaining Vote, Sees Market as a Great New Force," New York *Times*, April 6, 1972.

65. *Sondages*, No. 1-2, 1972, pp. 125-28.

66. Address by Chancellor Kurt Kiesinger at Bonn, June 14, 1967, *News from the German Embassy*, Washington, D.C., June 30, 1967, p. 2.

67. Address by Chancellor Kurt Kiesinger at Bonn, March 11, 1968, *News from the German Embassy*, Washington, D.C., March 1968, pp. 2-3.

68. Television Interview with Chancellor Willy Brandt at Paris, January 22, 1973, *Relay from Bonn*, German Information Center, New York, January 23, 1973.

69. Harold van B. Cleveland and Joan B. Cleveland, *The Atlantic Alliance: Problems and Prospects* (New York, 1966), p. 45.

70. Zbigniew Brzezinski and Samuel P. Huntington, *Political Power: USA/USSR* (New York, 1964), p. 199.

71. John Pinder, *Europe Against de Gaulle* (London, 1963), pp. 11-17.

72. Ibid., p. 130.

73. Pierre Uri, *Partnership for Progress* (New York, 1963), p. 102.

74. Rudolph Wagner, "Atlantic Federation or Partnership— Which?" *Freedom & Union*, March 1966, p. 22. Dr. Wagner, as president of the Union Atlantischer Federalisten, Munich, was arguing for an Atlantic Union. The fact that this is not in the realm of the possible should not, however, invalidate his perceptive critique of the partnership idea.

75. Raymond Vernon, "Rogue Elephant in the Forest: An Appraisal of Transatlantic Relations," *Foreign Affairs*, April 1973, pp. 573-85.

76. Report of President Richard M. Nixon to the Congress, February 18, 1970, Department of State *Bulletin*, 62, no. 1602: 285.

77. "Washington Spells Out a Tougher Attitude Toward the EEC," *Vision*, November 1970, p. 29.

78. Report of President Richard M. Nixon to the Congress, February 25, 1971, Department of State *Bulletin*, 64, no. 1656: 351.

79. Remarks by President Richard M. Nixon at Kansas City, Mo., July 6, 1971, Department of State *Bulletin*, 65, no. 1674: 94, 96.

80. J. Robert Schaetzel, "America's View of Europe Now," excerpts from an address of February 12, 1970, *European Review*, Spring 1970, p. 42.

81. J. Robert Schaetzel, "A Dialogue of the Deaf Across the Atlantic," *Fortune*, November 1972, pp. 148-49, 154.

82. Address by Henry A. Kissinger, Assistant to the President for National Security Affairs, at New York, April 23, 1973, Department of State *Bulletin*, 68, no. 1768: 595-98.

83. David Binder, "U.S. Cancels Meeting with Europeans," New York *Times*, March 9, 1974.

84. "Text of The Modified Draft of a U.S.-Common Market Statement," and Paul Kemezis, "Common Market Said to Resist U.S. on Joint Statements," New York *Times*, November 9, 1973.

85. Address by Secretary of State Henry A. Kissinger at

London, December 12, 1973, Department of State *Bulletin*, 69, no. 1801: 778-79.

86. Ibid., p. 779.

87. Quoted in Alvin Shuster, "New Government in Britain Urges Closer U.S. Ties," New York *Times*, March 20, 1974.

88. Craig R. Whitney, "Bonn Bids Europe Give U.S. Access to Policy-Making," New York *Times*, March 21, 1974; Robert Kleiman, "The Atlantic Connection," ibid., April 2, 1974; "Paris Again Balks a Europe Accord," ibid., April 3, 1974; *Relay from Bonn*, March 20 and 25, 1974.

89. Craig R. Whitney, "New Bid to Arabs Made by Market," New York *Times*, June 11, 1974; Craig R. Whitney, "Kissinger Cool to European Bid to Arabs," ibid., June 12, 1974; *Relay from Bonn*, June 11, 1974.

90. Action Committee for the United States of Europe, Joint Declaration, adopted June 26, 1962, Paris, p. 3. (Italics added.)

91. David H. Popper, "NATO after Sixteen Years: An American Assessment," April 12, 1965, Department of State *Bulletin*, 52, no. 1346: 527.

92. Under Secretary of State George Ball, testimony before the Senate Committee on Foreign Relations, June 30, 1966, Department of State *Bulletin*, 55, no. 1413: 145.

93. Laurence W. Martin, "The Future of the Alliance," in *Changing East-West Relations and the Unity of the West*, ed. Arnold Wolfers, (Baltimore, 1964), p. 233.

94. Timothy W. Stanley, *NATO in Transition* (New York, 1965), pp. 71, 73.

95. Duchene, op. cit., p. 28.

96. Address by Jean Monnet at Saarbrucken, January 25, 1968, pp. 3-4.

97. Address by Under Secretary of State George Ball at Philadelphia, July 4, 1966, Department of State *Bulletin*, 55, no. 1415: 196.

98. J. Robert Schaetzel, "The Necessary Partnership," *Foreign Affairs*, April 1966, p. 426.

99. Quoted in J. L. Heldring, "Europe a 'Greater Holland?' " *Internationale Spectator*, April 8, 1965, p. 545.

100. Ibid.

4

ATLANTIC PARTNERSHIP: ITS FURTHER INSTITUTIONAL DEVELOPMENT

The initial experiments in partnership have been largely confined to the realm of economics. However, Jean Monnet consistently held that the trans-Atlantic sharing of burdens and decision making must be extended across the board. "The partnership between Europe and America must not be merely economic," stated the Joint Declaration of his Action Committee on June 26, 1962. "It is necessary that it should rapidly extend to the military and political spheres. Both are faced with common risks, the chief of which stems from the conflict with the East." Only a united West could disabuse the Soviet leaders of their intentions to play on the divisions of their adversaries and only when the West can demonstrate that "it is consolidating its unity on a long-term basis, then the conditions will be created for a lasting peaceful settlement between East and West."[1]

PARTNERSHIP IN NUCLEAR WEAPONS: PROBLEMS OF A EUROPEAN DETERRENT

Partnership in the military and political spheres soon focused upon the concrete possibility of creating a European nuclear deterrent. Speaking for the Kennedy administration on September 27, 1962, McGeorge Bundy told a gathering of the Atlantic Treaty Association that it would "be wrong to suppose that the reluctance which we feel with respect to individual ineffective and unintegrated forces would be extended automatically to a European force, genuinely unified and multilateral, and effectively integrated with our own necessarily predominant strength in the whole nuclear defense of the Alliance."[2] Under Secretary of State George Ball renewed this proposal when addressing the NATO parliamentarians in November 1962. He foresaw the formation of a European nuclear force as the European component of an Atlantic partnership, "employing NATO as the military expression of that partnership to achieve the indivisibility of response—the indivisibility of command and direction—that is the indispensable element of an effective defense in this nuclear age."[3] Or as Ball later formulated the prospect: "If Europe were sufficiently far advanced toward political unity that it could by itself manage and control an atomic deterrent, we could hopefully look forward to an effective and integrated Atlantic defense founded on a true nuclear partnership."[4]

The idea of a European nuclear deterrent, as expressed in these statements, attempted to harness two horses that may have been pulling in opposite directions. On the one side, these American spokesmen attempted to fulfill the aspirations of the European federalists, who sought to replace the old nationalisms of their continent with a broader but equally satisfying frame of reference for all major functions of government. "Europe" could not exist, in their view, unless it had all the trappings of state power and possessed the whole spectrum of capabilities, including its own powerful nuclear deterrent. The dangers of the nuclear age could never be faced, so the reasoning went, unless Europe had a feeling of self-reliance and self-confidence that would arise when Europe "could by itself manage and control an atomic deterrent," to recall Ball's phrase.

The other side of this unwieldy tandem revealed that the Europeans might achieve the illusion of self-reliance, but little else. They would manage and control their deterrent, but it would be "effectively integrated with our own necessarily predominant strength in the whole nuclear defense of the alliance," as Bundy put it. NATO would be the instrument for "the indivisibility of response— the indivisibility of command and direction," so that, as Ball informed us, nuclear partnership could produce "an effective and integrated Atlantic defense." If independent European management and control is to have substance, however, surely the option must always remain for the Europeans to respond independently. But this would necessarily threaten the indivisibility of command and direction and disintegrate an effective Atlantic defense structure. In the American view, then, a European deterrent would be designed to reinforce an indivisible NATOwide response, rather than be a purely European force that was autonomous in its operation.

The opinion of the "good Europeans" was far from unanimous on the subject of a European deterrent. Some, like Pierre Uri, argued that Europe must, indeed, be able to undertake independent action if need be, since the use of the U.S. deterrent might be held in check by Soviet ICBMs capable of striking directly at the United States. "If the credibility of atomic defense by America is not entirely satisfactory, while the credibility of a national deterrent force is practically nonexistent," Uri observed, "it is necessary to find another solution. The only way open is a European force de frappe that would be capable of use without an American veto."[5]

Other French advocates of European Union displayed considerable caution about the effects of a European nuclear force, precisely because of the question of its deterrent value and credibility. A report by the Club Jean Moulin, an influential group of non-Gaullist intellectuals, warned against overestimating the value of such a force. In the first place, "its 'autonomous' character will be limited for many years, since its planning would have to take place within the confines of NATO, and its will for a separate status will lead to a useless duplication of effort. During the whole long period of its construction, the political credibility of a European force will be limited. Its credibility will be that of a minor nuclear power." During this phase, the principal value of a European force would be to play "a supporting role for the American deterrent, within the framework of the Atlantic Alliance," and "to influence the American strategic decision." But after a European deterrent had beent built and had taken on the pretensions of a self-sufficient force, other equally serious problems would arise. "Paradoxically, the security of Europe would be weakened: The construction of an autonomous European force would have been interpreted in the United States as a European desire finally to eliminate the American guarantee. The indisputable character of this guarantee would then have been rendered uncertain."[6]

Europe would indeed be dependent upon the American nuclear guarantee for a very considerable time, even after it had begun the construction of its own deterrent. This caused some observers, like

Theodore Geiger, to wonder if, under these circumstances, the Europeans would ever really begin to construct their own separate force. It would only be in the absence of the American guarantee that "the European sense of the adequacy of the nation-state might again decline sufficiently to provide a significant impetus toward unification in the military and political fields." But at this point a dilemma would arise that would not likely foster the development of a supranational European nuclear force. "On the one hand, the United States cannot take the risk of explicitly removing its nuclear protection before the Europeans have developed a credible nuclear deterrent of their own. On the other hand, the Europeans need not divert substantial resources to this purpose and risk the political uncertainties of who would control the European nuclear force so long as the United States maintains its nuclear 'umbrella' over them."[7]

Similar ambivalence greeted the American-sponsored project for a Multilateral Force (MLF). Purists of the dumbbell theory unequivocally embraced the "European clause" in the proposed MLF treaty, which would have permitted a European nuclear force to emerge out of a trans-Atlantic one. It was anticipated that this might be done either by having the European members buy out the American share, so that the MLF would become purely European, or by the United States remaining within the force but abandoning its veto, so that the force could come under European control. In the spring of 1963 the lure of the European clause prompted Monnet to declare that a proper trans-Atlantic relationship "requires, among other things, the organization of a European atomic force, including England, and in partnership with the United States."[8] State Department spokesman J. Robert Schaetzel soon afterward elaborated on the value of the European clause as a method for encouraging European Union. "An integrated European nuclear force," Schaetzel concluded, "would strengthen and not divide Europe *and the Atlantic*."[9]

Not all members of Monnet's Action Committee were persuaded of this logic, however. A number of them felt that a European deterrent might, in fact, divide the Atlantic and thereby jeopardize or remove American military protection that was so essential to their security. In its Joint Declaration of June 1, 1964, which recorded rare disagreement, the Action Committee considered the prospect of the European clause in the MLF. Among its conclusions was the recommendation that a united Europe should join with the United States "to organize their joint action as regards nuclear weapons, including the scientific and industrial resources at their disposal." This rather vague prescription was not made more precise by this sentence: "Europe must contribute not only to the conventional resources, but also to the nuclear resources of the West."[10] The idea of a European contribution to the nuclear resources of the West did not disavow a separate European deterrent, nor did it confirm it. Henry Owen, speaking as Deputy Chairman of the State Department's Policy Planning Council, was probably correct when he interpreted this statement to mean that "responsible European opinion about MLF evolution seems to be moving more and more toward the concept of Atlantic *interdependence* in nuclear affairs, rather than toward the concept of European nuclear *independence*. . . . The concept that a nuclear partnership of equals can be sought by uniting Europe within a force which will remain trans-Atlantic in character, management and control seems to be an increasingly interesting one to the Europeans."[11] The subsequent Joint Declaration of the Action Committee of May 1965 was content to maintain that "on nuclear questions . . . Europe and the United States should as soon as possible seek together ways of arriving, by collective action and successive phases, at a situation in which the major decisions are taken jointly and the burdens are shared."[12]

PROBLEMS OF THE DOUBLE VETO PROPOSALS

Upon closer examination, it was not easy to determine what such joint decision making would mean. The late Fritz Erler, a defense spokesman for the German Social Democrats and a member of Monnet's Action Committee, offered one explanation: "What would a joint control solution be? It would consist of preventing either of the two partners from imposing its will upon the other, and insisting on agreement between the two. Neither of the two partners could act alone. Act where? In Europe, or in the world? In the world!" Even though undertaking global responsibilities, Erler acknowledged that the European contribution would be very modest in size. Europe, he estimated, "could not itself, even if it included Great Britain, assemble more than two percent of the American potential."[13]

Erler's intent was to make the nuclear defense of the West indivisible. "Everyone should recognize that his fate is bound up with everyone else's," he told this writer, "and consequently there should be one strategy and, in effect, one deterrent." With both partners locked into a single system, the United States would have no fear of being triggered into war by the smaller European force, while a weaker Europe would not be susceptible to Soviet nuclear blackmail tactics.

Granted these advantages, the double veto system seems highly unrealistic. From the American point of view, it is scarcely conceivable that the United States would accept a European lock on its own vastly preponderant force. This would doubtless apply in the NATO theater, and would be even more difficult to envision on a global scale. Europe could presumably mount a great effort and so create a force that would equal more than 2 percent of the American one, but even so the great imbalance of nuclear strength would surely continue for many years. To get around the imbalance of nuclear power, a joint force could conceivably be created in which the American share would equal the total European contribution. But from the European point of view, what motivation would Europe have to exert great efforts on behalf of a force that would be put under an American lock, especially when the bulk of the U.S. deterrent would remain outside the joint force? Finally, from the point of view of a potential aggressor, a joint force that operated under a double veto would be less credible as a deterrent than a force that had a single decision-making center. Once again, partnership between Europe and the United States means a one-to-one relationship in which there is either agreement or stalemate, since no majority view can emerge between the two sides. This inflexible arrangement could permit separate positions to crystalize and make a timely response unlikely. Over time the joint force might so diminish in credibility that it would split apart. This possibility would always be present so long as each side could demonstrate that it retained physical control over its contingent in the joint force. The independent capability to implement conflicting policies increases the probability that conflicting policies will be implemented. One would have to rely, in the last analysis, on the declared political intent of sovereign governments to abide by the double veto system, which would tie the European and American forces together. In times of great stress, this might be a weak reed to lean on.

This difficulty could be overcome, of course, with mixed-manning of a thoroughly integrated "joint" force that would deny each partner possession of its separate capabilities. But here the distinctive character of the European fish would be swallowed up by the American sea. Europe needs its own force to which it can point, many European federalists have insisted, because Europe must possess all the symbols and attributes of great power status. Perhaps the complexity of the strategic problem might allow the "good European" to settle for something short of this requirement, which is advanced primarily for reasons of prestige. It is conceivable that "Europe" could exist politically and economically, without having to acquire its own nuclear force. If nuclear strategy imposes thought in intercontinental terms, the logical arena for satisfying the European need for nuclear sharing would be in a single Atlanticwide context.

Many of the objections raised against Erler's proposal for a double veto over a joint deterrent would hold in similar schemes advanced by other European federalists. Kurt Birrenbach, a leading German Christian Democrat and also a member of Monnet's Action Committee, for example, has been so concerned about keeping the American military guarantee for Europe that Europe's "independence would have to be installed into a system of joint agreements which would ensure that America and the united Europe would follow a common path."[14] A European deterrent, Birrenbach told this writer, must be placed inside NATO under the command of an American SACEUR and operated with a double-key system, which, in effect, would mean a joint force under a double lock. In a like manner, the Club Jean Moulin, which had warned of the dangers of a purely separate or autonomous European deterrent, advocated forming a European component for a common Atlantic force. "This would involve creating an Atlantic association with two heads, one European, the other American. Such bipolarity established between two equal partners, and no longer between a protector and a protected, will permit Europe both to escape from the shadow of Soviet constraint and from a unilateral American decision." The complete realization of this proposal would require considerable time, since Europe must first form federal institutions competent in matters of defense and foreign policy. Then on an Atlantic scale, "the existence of a common bipolar force demands an intimate political association and a common organ of decision-making. It is possible to proceed by parallel steps. The creation of a federal European organ and the construction of a common Atlantic force, entrusting ever-increasing nuclear responsibility to the Europeans, could go hand in hand."[15] However, the attractiveness and plausibility of this plan for a bipolar force soon fade since, depending on the details of its implementation, it is also vulnerable to most of the criticisms directed against Erler's proposal for associating two vastly unequal partners.

THE ANALOGY OF THE U.S.-U.K. RELATIONSHIP

One way to avoid the problems involved in a joint or an integrated Atlantic deterrent controlled through the codetermination of European and American partners is to have purely European control over a European force that is operationally meshed with the American deterrent. Such a solution has been recommended by Robert Bowie, who was intimately associated with American military planning for a considerable period both as a State Department and White House advisor. Actually, Bowie was willing to see the evolution of an integrated NATO force in which the United States would participate without a veto, but he viewed as equally, if not more promising the prospect of "an integrated European force (without the United States as a member), closely coordinated with United States forces, but under ultimate European control." The close coordination of the European and American forces would be modeled essentially upon the past "special relationship" that has existed in the nuclear field between Britain and the United States. This would include the right granted Britain under the Nassau agreements to withdraw its Polaris force from NATO command for separate use in an extreme national emergency. "We should be ready to concede to a multilateral force the same degree of ultimate autonomy as has already been granted the British national force."[16] One advantage of a European deterrent is that it could absorb the existing British and French forces as well as discourage others from being created. Separate European national deterrents, Bowie continued, should be considered harmful, if not dangerous, because they needlessly duplicate effort, perpetuate discrimination against the nonnuclear European states, are not really credible as deterrents, while in terms of political impact they threaten Western unity and render impossible responsible political control over the nuclear weapons in the NATO area. An additional danger of national deterrents is that "the national components can always be pulled out of the NATO commitment."[17]

This argument causes some puzzlement: National European deterrents are held undesirable and dangerous, among other reasons, because they can be pulled out of the NATO commitment, while a more powerful collective European deterrent, which would surely be more capable of undertaking independent action, would not threaten Western unity and should be given the ultimate autonomy to pull out of the NATO commitment. When questioned about this inconsistency, Bowie explained that national forces are dangerous precisely because they are small and weak, and this weakness lends itself to irresponsibility. Small forces are so obviously unfit for separate use that national leaders might think it possible to make political capital of them by threatening to use them to trigger off the American deterrent, but without ever seriously meaning to do so. Such gestures might be misunderstood by Moscow or Peking, however, and lead to an unwanted war. A collective European deterrent, he held, would be of sufficient magnitude so that it would not be toyed with, but treated responsibly by its political leaders. Nor would the right of withdrawal be a menace, since the facts of a military crisis, when it arose, would necessarily shape a common response on the part of Europe and the United States. Those who controlled the European deterrent would recognize the folly of setting it in motion unless fully supported by the American force. The importance of a European deterrent, therefore, would be primarily political: to provide Europe in peacetime with a feeling of self-respect, prestige, and equality with the United States that is presently lacking and that consequently embitters trans-Atlantic relations.

Some of these propositions are not entirely self-evident. Is it not perilous to assume that a crisis would shape a common response? It might, but then it might not. If the nuclear diplomacy of Europe and the United States had taken separate lines leading up to the crisis, might not the Kremlin play upon these differences and, under the threat of destruction, force one or the other of the Western "partners" to opt out of an ensuing conflict in the hope of saving itself? A West thus divided would be poorly equipped to resist Soviet pressure for political concessions, or if the worst came, to conduct a nuclear conflict.

As to the relation between the size and responsibility of nuclear forces in Europe, can it be said that small forces tend to be irresponsible, while big ones can always be relied upon to be responsible? History is strewn with examples of great power used irresponsibly, while the United States has not felt that the British have managed their small deterrent irresponsibly. Bowie objected to the British deterrent because its continued existence has provided an obstacle to the unification of Europe, has helped to justify de Gaulle's force de frappe, and might serve as a possible incentive for the development of a German force at some unspecified time in the future. The problem, therefore, is not one of size, but of how a European force could be intertwined with the American deterrent and of how the political aims motivating the use of such a force might mesh with American political objectives. Those who have reasoned like Bowie assume that a collective European deterrent would form the same type of close working arrangement that has characterized British-American nuclear collaboration in the past.

What is the basis for this analogy? The effective integration of British and American nuclear forces came as an outgrowth of the United States integrating its own weapons systems held by the different American services. At first, each service had its own war plans for the use of atomic weapons, which were then coordinated ex post facto. But it soon became apparent that this cumbersome process might result in the planes or missiles of one service blowing those of another out of the sky. The Joint Chiefs of Staff concluded that efforts at coordination were insufficient and that only a continuously functioning integrated plan would work. They therefore organized the Joint Strategic Target Planning Staff under the direction of the Commander of the Strategic Air Command. SAC was the only organization that had sufficient knowledge of how to lay down a comprehensive global plan, and thus Omaha was made the center of the new integrated planning process. Under this arrangement a Single Integrated Operations Plan (SIOP) was worked out and has been revised periodically. SIOP, though built on the foundation of common target planning, also involves detailed arrangements for command and control of the forces it covers, as well as the flexible use of these forces through the elaboration of options on how they might be employed in different circumstances.

From the beginning the British RAF worked smoothly with their U.S. counterparts at SAC, fitting the missions of the V-bombers into

SIOP. For reasons of security, however, the overall SIOP design has remained privy to the United States. The British have accepted this in good faith and have been willing to participate in the part of SIOP alloted to them. De Gaulle, with his insistence upon complete independence, never cooperated in this way. The force de frappe could have been included in SIOP, but the French excluded themselves. In a like manner, a collective European nuclear force could be included in SIOP, but what would the likelihood of this be? If France would not cooperate as the British have, would a proud and powerful European Union with a strong political will of its own be satisfied to follow the British example? Those who look to Anglo-American nuclear collaboration as a model for a future nuclear partnership between an American and a European deterrent will most likely look in vain. On the other hand, those who call for the mere coordination of two forces, instead of their thorough integration into a single operations plan, underestimate the elemental requirements for centralized control imposed by the complexity and dangers of the nuclear age. Ideally, of course, the formulation of the overall integrated plan should be shared by all its participants, but realistically this is only likely to occur as the participants move toward their *political* integration.

Short of this, it might be possible to devise ways of allowing some latitude in the control of a European deterrent without disrupting an integrated operations plan. "What most worries some Europeans," Malcolm Hoad noted, "is that there might be no American nuclear response after a Soviet attack on Europe that had overwhelmed its non-nuclear defenses." Perhaps these fears could be relieved if Europe and the United States together built a force that would be "designed to ensure European control over some nuclear response," so that "we give them a trigger for the case where we already expect to respond. Consequently we give nothing away *if* the nature of their response fits our global operations."[18] Specifically, the guidance system of the European deterrent would be under a joint European-American lock, although the Europeans could detonate their nuclear force independently. But by ensuring that the European force would be aimed only at key Soviet military installations instead of population centers, for example, it might still be possible to maintain the option of a flexible, centrally controlled response in a nuclear exchange. This would be unlike the situation that has long obtained between the U.S. deterrent and the force de frappe, where the French have targeted their initial strikes at population centers and, if so used, would conflict with NATO guidelines for a graduated and flexible response under a centrally controlled plan.

Again the question arises whether an independent, united Europe would be willing to mesh the operation of its deterrent with the United States so as to ensure that the two would not work at cross purposes. Perhaps the logic of nuclear life would dictate this, especially if satisfactory ways were found for arriving at a commonly agreed strategic plan that would be supported by a whole network of other ties, such as joint intelligence, coordinated research, development, and production of weapons systems, joint use of bases, combined logistical support, etc. In essence, if a European deterrent were to come into existence, the optimum prospect would be one that minimized the independent nature of both the European and American deterrents and caused both of them to form links that would move them toward political integration.

THE COSTS AND POSSIBLE CONSEQUENCES
OF A EUROPEAN DETERRENT

Would Europe have a sufficiently strong incentive to build this type of force? The cost of a respectable European deterrent might be prohibitive. Up through the middle 1960s, for example, the United States spent more each year on its nuclear force alone than the Six plus Britain spent for both their conventional and nuclear forces. Even if an independent European strategic force were built upon the basis of the existing British and French forces, as Alastair Buchan pointed out, "it would have to fulfill a more ambitious range of functions than would the two national forces. Since it would have to protect the integrity of more countries than Britain and France, it would have to be considerably larger than an Anglo-French force. The force would have to have many of the characteristics of the American strategic force," that is, an assured destruction capability for purposes of deterrence and a damage-limiting capability for the conduct of nuclear war by means of a graduated, controlled response. A conservative estimate of the cost of providing a European nuclear force with these capabilities "suggests an increase in European defense expenditure of between an eighth and a quarter."[19]

There would be a strong temptation to sacrifice the credibility of all nonnuclear defenses in the effort to muster resources for a European deterrent. James Richardson, who is otherwise an advocate of a European force, has warned: "Those who would make Europe a great power are on difficult ground in asserting that this can be achieved without significant increases in defense expenditure, by diverting resources from conventional forces into European nuclear weapons. The choice of European nuclear weapons at the expense of ground defense is a gamble when the political adversary is superior in both kinds of force. And a policy which opts for deterrence to the neglect of defense is not that of a great power, but that of an impoverished or a reckless one."[20]

It is not simply a question of spending money, however. The "technological gap," about which Europe complains, is especially marked in the whole field of developing highly sophisticated nuclear devices and their associated delivery systems. There is also the consideration of creating some sort of an antimissile defense, so as to permit the deterrent force to remain effective. The lead in all such endeavors that the United States and the Soviet Union now have over the British and French forces is considerable and it would not quickly be made up by a united Europe. Although the SALT agreements appear to have brought some stability into the Soviet-American balance of terror, it is still possible that significant technological breakthroughs could inject new elements into the equation and threaten to destabilize the nuclear confrontation. The dynamic character of this process with its spiraling costs is constantly widening the gap between the superpowers and what would be required of Europe, if it would create a meaningful deterrent. European opinion might recoil at the size of the effort in manpower and other resources and conclude that it could not justify the effort. This would be especially so if Europe already felt sufficiently sheltered under the American nuclear umbrella and had worked out reasonably satisfactory ways of helping influence and manage the American force in the defense of the entire Atlantic Community. For their part, the Americans recognized, admittedly belatedly, the need for opening up Alliance channels for the interchange of views that shape nuclear policy through the Nuclear Planning Group, and the success of this venture has diminished the desire among many Europeans to create a European nuclear force. Moreover, if efforts to normalize political relations in the center of Europe produce the basis for a lasting detente, the Europeans will continue to find further justification for cutting defense spending. The impulse to make the sacrifices needed to build a European deterrent might be very weak indeed.

All these difficulties have been compounded by the obstacle placed in the way of constructing a European deterrent by a Non-Proliferation Treaty (NPT). As adopted in 1968, the NPT prohibited the transfer of nuclear weapons or explosive devices "to any recipient whatsoever." However, Secretary of State Dean Rusk interpreted this prohibition to mean that the British and French national nuclear forces could be transferred to a federal European state, which would absorb the nuclear status of its former components. While such a successor state would not have to assume all the functions of government, "a new federated European state would have to control all of its external security functions, including defense and all foreign policy matters relating to external security." Short of a European state containing these powers, the NPT would prohibit the transfer of nuclear weapons to any lesser European body, "including a multilateral entity."[21]

The NPT aroused bitter reactions among many European federalists who had looked forward to the gradual extension of a European competence into the defense field, including that of nuclear weapons. As one European observer complained: "There is no provision in the treaty permitting any federation of states or federated state to acquire the nuclear power of its members. The argument is entirely based on interpretation, and negative interpretations at that, based not on what the treaty says but on what it does not say." There could be no certainty that in the future other signatories, and particularly the Soviet Union, would "accept that interpretation and commit themselves to it." Furthermore, even Rusk's interpretation had foreclosed "the only road to unification of European defense that can be realistically foreseen," that is, some sort of a multilateral entity that would not, in the first instance, be a fully developed European federation as Rusk had defined it. "Integration of European defence," it was argued, "is a stage, and a very important stage, in the road toward federation, not vice versa. To say that Europe as a 'federated state' could have a nuclear role, at the same time making it impossible for Europeans to establish an integrated defense community, is like offering a man a prize if he reaches the tenth step of a ladder while putting barbed wire around the sixth step."[22] In any event, it became clear that under the NPT the United States would not help any interim European arrangement for the gradual development of a European strategic nuclear force. That is, not only would the Europeans have to create it entirely on their own, but it could only emerge from a full-blown European federal state.

Advocates of nuclear partnership also surely underestimate the degree of political cohesion that must exist before it will be possible to create a European deterrent. The Action Committee's Joint Declaration of June 1964 anticipated that "when the time comes, a new treaty on foreign policy and defense, applying the institutional system of the Common Market must be negotiated by the States and ratified by the Parliaments, as was done in the case of the Treaty of Rome." The methods followed by Euratom "in organizing such joint efforts are applicable to the other fields in which nuclear energy is used."[23] The institutional system of the EEC and Euratom, which disperses executive power over a Commission and Council of Ministers, has proved largely successful for dealing with the economic problems of the Common Market, while it has been much less successful in the case of Euratom. But this is a most improbable way to manage nuclear weapons. To be effective, responsibility would have to be concentrated in a President of the United States of Europe, and this implies a much more intimate degree of political integration than exists under the institutional system of the Common Market.

Experience has already shown that defense has been very difficult to bring under common control. Even before de Gaulle's return to power the French prevented the formation of a conventionally armed European Defense Community in 1954. The question of creating a nuclear EDC would be even more sensitive and less likely to succeed. Extensive interviews conducted in 1964 with a cross section of the French elite revealed little propensity on the part of the French for any sort of nuclear sharing with the Germans, despite the special Franco-German Treaty that had been concluded the year before. "Virtually no one," the survey showed, wanted to grant West Germany nuclear capabilities outright, or even to allow "effective West German participation in deciding over-all nuclear strategy for a European atomic force (if and when such a force is established)."[24] It was the Gaullists who raised the loudest cries against the American attitude toward nuclear sharing and derided the modest American gestures in this direction, such as the MLF. But French willingness to share with their fellow Europeans could hardly be described as generous. Thus the French opposition to creating an Atlantic Multilateral Force would be carried over to a purely European one, and the same problems of sharing decision making would have been raised on a smaller scale. (Moreover, as noted above, the NPT subsequently prohibited any attempt to create a European MLF.) In some respects the French elite respondents showed a willingness to move beyond the nation-state to some form of supranationalism, but the areas mentioned were economic, social, and political, with a common defense authority approved only by a minority of the respondents.[25] This would suggest that a European deterrent, if it were ever built, would be one of the last elements to come into existence in a united Europe.

A European nuclear force could still be built, of course, despite this rather formidable list of economic and political obstacles. The conditions under which this would most likely happen, however, would be the emergence of a Europe obsessed with the quest for great power status and driven by an exceptionally strong political will. Only such a Europe could exact the sacrifices in economic resources and political traditions that would be required to shape a powerful new entity in the world. Such a Europe would be motivated by a search for maximum independence and would doubtless be conceived more as an instrument to expel American influence from Europe than to forge new close links with the United States. In effect, this Europe would be Gaullism writ large. Under these circumstances, it would be most improbable, as Buchan commented, that the United States "would give assistance or encouragement to a European strategic system intended to express Western Europe's ability to disassociate itself from American policy."[26]

The response of the United States would be entirely predictable. A European deterrent that would not be integrated in some trans-Atlantic arrangement, but only coordinated in the Gaullist concept of a classical alliance, would remove the automatic character of the American guarantee for the protection of Europe. The United States would find it intolerable to be committed to support Europe in the event of hostilities resulting from acts undertaken by Europe against American wishes and interests. The consequences of European unilateralism, or even its reasonable possibility, would result in American unilateralism: withdrawal of American troops in Europe, a disengagement from the defense of European interests everywhere, and the destruction of NATO. A European nuclear deterrent conceived in these terms would not produce the nuclear partnership of Monnet and Bowie, but the political and military divorce of Europe from the United States.

The specter of a European deterrent having these consequences has been widely recognized by European leaders. In November 1964, Prime Minister Harold Wilson declared bluntly: "We reject categorically any idea of a separate European deterrent," giving as reasons the fear that it would divide NATO and prompt the United States to reappraise its attitude toward Europe.[27] In January 1965, German Defense Minister von Hassel warned that "a European nuclear force could have a disintegrating effect on the Atlantic Alliance and would be bound to whittle down the United States engagement in Europe, to Europe's severe disadvantage." Should a united Europe ever succeed in producing its deterrent, this must never divert attention from the trans-Atlantic ties. "Europe must not allow herself to be isolated by the fact of possessing her own nuclear force, but must rather strengthen her standing by playing an active part in the strategy and in the nuclear weapons systems of the Atlantic Community."[28] This view seemed to be a typical expression of German opinion. Those who conducted a survey among German leaders in 1964 reported: "An independent European force is seen as inviting reduced American commitments, a possibility which few of the German leaders we interviewed care to contemplate. Even a united Europe could not dispense with American deterrent power in the view of nine out of ten Bundestag defense experts."[29] Subsequent German leadership has consistently upheld the importance of the American nuclear guarantee for Europe and has warned against anything that might seem to jeopardize it.

In the Netherlands, the prospect of a European nuclear force was treated even more gingerly. In the spring of 1965, 38 leading representatives of various Dutch parties and sectors of opinion issued a manifesto in which they rejected further efforts to define a common European position on questions of foreign policy and defense. By then the Gaullist theme of a "European Europe" had become sufficiently strong so that a European policy in these areas might be understood as directed against the United States. "Fresh discussions by the Six," they feared, "would lead to further concessions to France and to a continuing cleavage of the Atlantic world." The very thought of a European deterrent would therefore be harmful. "The attempt to detach defense policy from NATO and to bring it over into a continental European context would eventually cause the splitting up of the Western world, with all the resulting dangers both for our national and personal survival." They declared themselves "in favor of a further development of military integration—also in the field of nuclear weapons—in an Atlantic context."[30] By the spring of 1967, one of the organizers of this statement, E. H. van der Beugel, went so far as to say that "in the present circumstances, to talk about a European foreign and defense policy is dangerous, absurd and irresponsible."[31]

Following de Gaulle's retirement, the European Community summit meeting in the Hague in December 1969 relaunched the European idea and with it the vision of a European political union and a European foreign policy. However, the differences remaining between France and its European associates over cooperation in NATO made it very difficult to approach the question of a common European defense policy. So long as there are continuing differences of conception about trans-Atlantic ties among Europeans, no European consensus can be reached in the area of defense policy. That is, the construction of a European partner in this area is as much a matter of Atlantic relations as it is purely intra-European ones. Until all the members of the European Community come to a common understanding about the role of the United States in Europe, the prospects for creating a European defense community are dim, while the realization of a European nuclear deterrent arising from the defense community is infinitely more remote.

THE EURATOM-AEC RELATIONSHIP AS AN INSTITUTIONAL MODEL OF PARTNERSHIP

In one sense, nuclear partnership has already taken shape. While nothing has come of the proposed partnership in nuclear weapons, in the area of peaceful uses of atomic energy the United States has consistently encouraged the development of Euratom, with which it has worked out a variety of joint programs. The collaboration between Euratom officials and their American colleagues in the Atomic Energy Commission had been hailed by Secretary of State Rusk as a "concrete example of Atlantic partnership at work,"[32] while Monnet's Action Committee pointed to the Euratom-AEC relationship as a prototype for other joint Atlantic enterprises.[33]

Monnet's functional approach to politics and a piecemeal method of institution building were presumably expressed in this experiment. As the Action Committee's Joint Declaration of December 1962 explained, partnership does not demand that one must "aim at solving all problems at once." Rather, "Europe and America must together seek to deal with the concrete and immediate problems which neither the one nor the other can settle alone and for which the resources of both must be used or developed in common. For this, joint ad hoc institutions should be created when the occasion arises."[34]

To what extent might the Euratom-AEC relationship prove instructive about the possible future growth of ad hoc institutions on a trans-Atlantic scale?

The first fact that strikes one in reviewing this history is that there were elements present that are not likely to be duplicated. In 1958, soon after the creation of Euratom, two joint Euratom-AEC boards were set up: a Joint Reactor Board that was entrusted with constructing U.S. proven reactors in Europe, and a Joint Research and Development Board that allocated research projects that were associated with these American reactors. In all, three European reactor plants were finally built with American equipment, and each partner spent about $37 million over the ten-year operating life of the R and D Board on proposals advanced by one side or the other, or that were formulated jointly.

These two joint boards are past history, however, since they were set up under circumstances that will not be repeated. At the time, this partnership seemed mutually beneficial, since no one in Europe was engaged in operating nuclear reactors and this program facilitated the rapid transfer of America's new technology to Europe. In addition, the adoption of American nuclear technology gave the United States a significant foothold in Europe and tended to make European utilities dependent upon American reactor types and fuel supplies. Politically, both sides were anxious to give Euratom some substance and status so as to bolster the movement toward European Union. As part of this effort the United States abandoned its practice of insisting upon retaining control rights for AEC inspectors, thereby helping to create an important Euratom inspection and safeguard system.

In practice, the joint boards encountered considerable difficulties, in part because Euratom never acquired the authority to speak effectively for Europe in these matters. The constituent states, and especially Gaullist France, frequently refused cooperation or set up competing national programs that made joint management awkward, while the joint boards lacked flexibility in adapting budgets to changing needs. As a result, when the Additional Agreement was signed in 1960, and subsequently amended several times, the pattern of joint boards and joint management was abandoned in favor of a more straightforward business-like arrangement for mutual advantage, which provided for the exchange of scientific information and technical cooperation, as well as the lease or sale of fissionable material by the AEC to Euratom.[35]

Within this more limited context, fruitful exchanges of information and sharing of experiences did take place. For example, Euratom promoted a heavy-water reactor, ORGEL, as a second-generation development in nuclear power reactors in order to produce electricity, while the AEC found it particularly adaptable for the desalinization of sea water. The concentration of Euratom's resources on ORGEL was widely criticized, however, since it seemed uncertain that it could provide commercially exploitable energy at competitive prices. In the phrase of one commentator, ORGEL was either, "Euratom's own white elephant, or white hope."[36]

Euratom-AEC collaboration also extended to the third generation of reactor types, the fast breeder reactor, which has the extraordinary ability to produce, or "breed," more fissionable fuel than it consumes. Joint Euratom-AEC committees have administered detailed exchanges of information on such fast reactor research facilities both in the United States and in the Euratom countries, as well as supervising exchanges of personnel and associated technical consultations. Euratom helped to finance the SEFOR fast breeder reactor, constructed in the United States in collaboration with the AEC and several private industrial firms from Europe and America. SEFOR represented a fuel test reactor that could provide important information about preventing a reactor from overheating and getting out of control, which was one of the key problems of fast breeders.

The programs for developing fast breeder reactors within Euratom and in the United States have differed drastically, however, as a result of the structural differences between the two partners. As the Commission of the European Community complained in 1969, "there are three separate and practically self-sufficient fast reactor programs going on in the Community." France, Germany in association with the Benelux countries, and Italy each "has its own immediate objective in the form of a representative plant, with a parallel longer-term R and D program." Unfortunately, "these three programs overlap at many points and are neither complementary nor based on planned diversification."[37] The result has been to spread, or more accurately to squander, Europe's limited resources in triplicate, instead of developing a coherent Euratom fast breeder program. This stood in contrast to the AEC policy of "systematically building up a capability in industry, by placing contracts for components, tutoring, monitoring, exploring crucial weak spots (like fuel testing), which will ensure that once the program takes off, it will succeed." Europe will doubtless "find that any lead it has had in fast breeders will vanish when the time comes for commercial exploitation."[38]

The pattern of developing fast breeder reactors in Europe has, in fact, been characteristic of all nuclear programs within the Euratom countries. An official Euratom survey frankly admitted that "on the whole the Community has not managed to coordinate the efforts of the member countries, even less to weld them into a coherent whole." The shortcomings of Europe's programs could not be attributed to "some hypothetical European inferiority in a sector which is well within the capabilities of European scientists." Moreover, "in the nuclear sectors, it cannot be arugued that the Community has not made adequate sums available to research." On the contrary, "the effort of the Six, on both the national and Community levels, as regards public spendings on civilian research, has been only marginally lower than in the USA, which means that it has been higher in proportion to the gross national product." Nevertheless, the industrial and commercial return on Europe's outlay has been disappointing. As of 1968, for example, "the number of nuclear power stations under construction, on order or planned in the Community is only 16, representing some 6,500 MWe, in comparison with 87 units in the United States, representing some 70,000 MWe." Significantly, the 87 U.S. nuclear power plants were being constructed by four or five contracting firms, while the 16 units in Europe were dispersed among some dozen firms. As a result, the total value of the orders within the Euratom countries was "less than that of the order placed with each of the American firms." The poor showing in Europe, the Euratom report concluded, "has been caused by fragmentation of efforts, the bulk of which has been pursued at the national level and with national objectives in view."[39]

The Euratom-AEC "partnership" has therefore consisted of relations between two asymetrical partners. When the collaboration commenced with the creation of the two joint boards in 1958, for the construction of proven reactors in Europe and for accompanying research on them, they were not founded upon a balance in technical competence between the United States and Europe. Rather, these joint ad hoc institutions were essentially arrangements for American tutelage. As Europe acquired competence in nuclear affairs and became increasingly independent of the United States, the joint boards were superseded by other, looser ties. A more mature relationship therefore ironically caused a close institutional partnership to decline. This development would seem to run contrary to the doctrinaire assumptions held by partisans of partnership on both sides of the Atlantic.

This apparently bizarre conclusion about the Euratom-AEC experiment in partnership might be explained by the fact that Euratom, as previously noted, did not evolve into an adequate counterpart to its American partner. If Euratom had acquired substantial supranational qualities, it would have been easier to operate jointly administered programs, because the Euratom partner would have been more of an "it" than a "they," and it could have spoken with authority to its trans-Atlantic associate. And had such collaboration proved successful because it would have been based on solid building blocks, it might have led to further development of joint programs and further advances in new, joint ad hoc institutions.

As it was, Euratom was only given dynamic leadership when Etienne Hirsch was President of the Commission and made a bid to fulfill its supranational potential. His reappointment was blocked by de Gaulle, precisely because the prospect of supranationalism had been forcefully raised. In 1966 Commission President Pierre Chatenet could review Euratom's history and conclude that it was "a disappointing, apparently sterile but very promising experiment."[40] Somewhat less ambiguously, Lawrence Scheinman judged: "Euratom has withered rather than blossomed into an influential regional nuclear organization." "Euratom bears the indelible imprint of failure."[41] Ernst Haas concurred that "despite the wide planning and control powers written into the treaty, Euratom has remained a technical and research agency."[42] By 1970 a WEU report could state categorically! "Now . . . Euratom is moribund."[43]

British accession to the European Community provided for a more intimate association between Euratom and the substantial

British achievements in the peaceful uses of atomic energy. However, Euratom had previously been associated with a number of British projects before formal British membership through the operation of a Continuing Committee for Euratom-United Kingdom Cooperation. Thus the British contribution did not promise to be decisive in reviving the fortunes of Euratom, since Euratom's fundamental deficiency was not technological but political.

Given this kind of a European partner with whom partnership can be practiced, one might conclude, to be charitable, that the Euratom experience to date has proven indecisive as an example of ad hoc trans-Atlantic institutional cooperation.

THE COMMITTEE OF ENTENTE IDEA

During 1962, which marked the floodtide of hopes for rapid progress toward integration both in Europe and the Atlantic Community, Lord Franks proposed that the agencies of partnership be given trans-Atlantic institutional forms similar to those operating within the European Community. "The partnership of the Atlantic group of nations," he insisted, "cannot get where it wants simply by the established processes of cooperation and negotiation: conferences with the unanimity rule and the compromising out of agreement between national interests." He identified the areas in which new methods transcending traditional diplomatic practices were especially called for as aid and trade policies with the underdeveloped countries, the rational disposal of agricultural surpluses from the temperate zone, and the improvement of the international monetary system, which is essentially the creation of the Atlantic nations. The scale and urgency of these problems made the old methods inadequate for seeking common solutions to common problems. "A new way has to be found: a new organization, institution or commission, which will have sufficient standing, independence and initiative to formulate common solutions and put them forward to the governments of the several nations of the group, so that they will have to face in argument not merely each other but also and at the same time the solution proposed for the partnership as a whole as best realizing its common good."[44]

De Gaulle's subsequent assaults on the EEC and the very idea of an Atlantic Community soon put this proposal beyond reach.

Nevertheless, Monnet's Action Committee continued to uphold the general aim that Lord Franks had advanced. In its Joint Declaration of June 1964 the Action Committee elaborated a proposal for "the establishment of a Committee of Entente between Europe and the United States in those fields where Europe has begun to exist." Initially this would be in the realm of economic relations, and it could logically deal with such topics as the liberalization of trade, international monetary organization, balance-of-payment problems, and American investments in Europe. "The task of the Committee of Entente would be to prepare joint positions on problems as they call for action, thus making easier the decisions to be taken by the European institutions and the American government both in their mutual economic relations and in their respective negotiations with the rest of the world. The Community would be represented on a basis of parity with the United States." As Europe took shape in other areas, the competence of the Committee of Entente could be correspondly expanded. "The institutional forms of equal partnership with the United States will necessarily evolve as Europe strengthens its unity and extends it to new fields."[45]

As Monnet explained in 1966, "the relationship between ourselves and America has *not yet* developed to the point where it would be possible to entrust to common institutions the task of making common proposals." This would indicate that when the appropriate time came, it should be possible to establish on an Atlantic scale a body somewhat like the EEC Commission, which would be given the initiative in launching proposals aimed at upgrading the common interests of all parties. Until that time ripened, the Committee of Entente could undertake the more modest functions of encouraging an agreed appraisal so that the parties might attack a problem in common, instead of attacking each other. At least, Monnet added, "we have reached the point where we should have the assurance that we are seeking to solve a problem we have in common and not merely bargaining for a diplomatic solution."[46]

Despite the prolonged and at times extremely bitter bargaining that accompanied the Kennedy Round of GATT trade negotiations, Monnet's Action Committee pointed to the final outcome as the successful practice of partnership. The Action Committee's Resolution of June 1967 welcomed "the success of the Kennedy Round, which has shown that united Europe can negotiate as an equal with the United States," and it again urged that "there now be negotiated between the United States and the European Community the establishment of a 'Committee of Entente,' in which the common institutions and the American government are represented on a footing of equality. The task of this Committee would be to enable the Community and the United States to expound and if necessary to debate the European view and the American view before taking decisions on major questions of common concern,"[47] once more citing as appropriate topics for discussion the development of the international monetary system, the problems of balance of payments, the impact of American investments and technological innovations in Europe, as well as the strengthening of joint Western aid efforts to developing countries. In November 1967, Monnet broadened the prospect for such collaboration by holding that "as European unification progresses, the United States and a united Europe can and should build common institutions based on real equality that will enable them to discuss not merely economic problems, but defense and international policies." This concept, he insisted, would be qualitatively different from present institutional procedures. "Today we have a number of institutions for the discussion of a wide range of problems that face us on both sides of the Atlantic. But all are based on the notion of separate national interests. Each individual state speaks in terms of its own interests and not of the common problems that must be solved."[48]

The logic of the Committee of Entente idea was especially appealing to Chancellor Willy Brandt and Foreign Minister Walter Scheel, both of whom incidentally had long been members of Monnet's Action Committee. At the Hague summit meeting of the European Community in December 1969 the German leaders proposed the establishment of a "High-Level Contact Committee" between the United States and the European Community that would meet at least twice a year to examine the whole range of economic, and particularly trade, policies that threatened to disrupt trans-Atlantic relations. Erik Blumenfeld, a leading member of the Christian Democratic opposition in Germany, vigorously endorsed this initiative in his report to the 1970 session of the North Atlantic Assembly.[49]

In March 1970, Scheel broached the idea at a meeting of the EEC Council of Ministers, emphasizing that the existing multilateral forums of the OECD and GATT were not adequate to deal with the special trans-Atlantic economic transactions, which also had profound political and security implications.[50]*

A modest gesture in this direction was begun in October 1970 when the first of a series of informal, regular consultations among a small group of senior American and European officials took place. The American delegation was initially led by Deputy Under Secretary for Economic Affairs Nathaniel Samuels, while Ralf Dahrendorf, the member of the European Commission responsible for external relations, first chaired the European side.[51]

At the beginning of 1971 Belgian Foreign Minister Pierre Harmel judged that this arrangement was insufficient and called for "structures providing for permanent and adequate consultation between the EEC and the U.S. in order to define a common and open approach to our common problems. This is already done in the realm of defense, and must now be done in the realms of the economy, money and aid to the third world."[52] Similarly, Monnet's Action Committee renewed its demand in a resolution of February 1971 for "the establishment of a permanent organ for reciprocal consultation in which the European Communities and the United States are represented at a high level."[53]

A response from the American side was forthcoming in President Nixon's February 1971 report to Congress, in which he welcomed the implementation of any suggestions from the European Community for expanding consultations, including the possibility of higher-level Community representation in the United States.[54] In April the European Community announced that the Commission would upgrade its permanent delegation in Washington with the

---

*Rolf Pauls, speaking as German Ambassador to the United States, emphasized the political and security implications of trans-Atlantic economic relations. The importance of resolving trade and monetary problems, he said, "by far exceeds the framework of mere trade policy, because overcoming present difficulties in European-American trade relations will greatly influence the attitude of the American public and of Congress towards the [Atlantic] Alliance and thereby affect its very cohesion and strength. It is for this reason that the German government has long been stressing the importance of an organized, constructive, high-level dialogue between the U.S. and the EEC." (Rolf Pauls, "On German-American Relations," *Aussenpolitik,* English edition, No. 1 [1973], p. 10.)

appointment of Ambassador Aldo Mazio. Subsequently he was replaced by the former Danish Prime Minister, Jens Otto Krag.[55]

Scheel continued to press his European colleagues for the formal institutionalization of a European-American dialogue when, for example, he submitted a proposal to that effect to the EEC Foreign Ministers conference in November 1971.[56] And Brandt pressed his counterparts at the summit conference of the nine members and prospective members of the European Community in October 1972 to "decide here to initiate an organized dialogue, beginning with our most important partner, the United States."[57]

These German proposals were not adopted, however, for as Brandt was forced to admit, "in Europe, not least of all in Paris, there was concern lest an organized dialogue, meaning one that was held on a high level and with a certain regularity, might lead to a kind of American 'co-regency' in the Common Market."[58] At the October 1972 summit conference, Prime Minister Heath also identified himself with the French position by opposing any formal arrangement for such an organized dialogue.[59]

Scheel subsequently responded that an organized Atlantic dialogue need not infringe on European independence. On the contrary, "especially in economics, we are not only partners on the world market but also competitors. The Americans must reconcile themselves to that fact." Nevertheless, the exercise of such independence by one Atlantic partner could prove dangerous to all concerned if it were pursued without sufficient information about the needs and consequences for the other side. Adequate mutual understanding requires an intensive trans-Atlantic dialogue, and therefore "we must create agencies within which this dialogue can take place. But," Scheel lamented, "like everything in Europe, a good idea takes time to take hold."[60]

Looking beyond the time when such agencies might have come into existence, it is possible to speculate upon what they might bring in their wake. Conversations with Common Market officials revealed a number of ideas about the gradual development of Atlantic bodies that could conduct the varied business of partnership. One could begin modestly with joint, consultative, fact-finding bodies in the different functional areas of contact. From there it might be possible to negotiate treaties providing for arbitration of disputes growing out of the contractual arrangements that arose from such contacts. In some cases, as alluded to in the Euratom-AEC experiment with joint boards, joint management of trans-Atlantic industrial enterprises might be feasible. These could be expanded into various areas, especially of advanced technology, where European firms need not always compete with American ones, but rather joint European-American ventures might pool their skills so that different trans-Atlantic enterprises would compete with each other. The approach increasingly favored by the Commission of the European Community, however, has been that of concentrating upon the growth of technologically sophisticated industries within Europe itself, before attempting to reach out for technological cooperation on a trans-Atlantic scale. The Commission has held that trans-Atlantic assocation will have a better chance of succeeding by beginning with concrete European collaboration in the Community.[61] Whichever approach is used, or perhaps both approaches could be used in varying degrees simultaneously, the terms and forms of trans-Atlantic competition could appropriately be encouraged and supervised by some partnership body.

The idea, in effect, would be to build up piecemeal an Atlantic Treaty of Rome. In the beginning, common Atlantic institutions could be called upon for their help, without making binding legal commitments. As specific problems ripened for a common approach, powers could be transferred de facto to Atlantic bodies, and as confidence was built up in the new methods of common action, the incremental powers assumed could later be ratified de jure. At some point the momentum gathered could be given legal form in a treaty that would provide for still further areas of common action.

Here the example of Article 235 of the Treaty of Rome might prove a useful device.[62] It sanctions Community action in cases where the treaty did not previously provide for the requisite powers, if such action appears necessary to achieve the aims of the Community. This grant of authority could be exercised on a proposal of the Commission that had received unanimous approval of the Council of Ministers. The approach hoped to make it possible to act in new circumstances without having to go back to the parliaments of the constituent countries on each occasion for specific consent to move into fresh territory. This was not a blank check, however, since such action could be blocked by a dissenting government through the Council of Ministers. This provision was characteristic of the spirit of the Treaty of Rome, which assumed that one should not try to provide for everything from the beginning, but that with goodwill it would be possible to move ahead and fill in the specifics within a general frame of reference. The unique quality of the Treaty of Rome is that it combined precise goals and specific deadlines in some areas with procedures and principles by which further detailed agreements could be evolved in other areas. Many knotty problems were jumped over initially, leaving exact settlements to be worked out after the treaty had entered into force. This same approach could be envisioned for the dynamic evolution of Atlanticwide bodies. By studying problems in common that faced the Atlantic Community, common solutions would appear and common institutions would evolve.

THE LIMITS OF FUNCTIONALISM

Ernst Haas described the momentum of this process as "the expansive logic of functionalism," when he examined its operation in his 1958 groundbreaking study, *The Uniting of Europe*.[63] Reviewing the validity of his assumptions nearly a decade later, he admitted that "something is missing in the exploration of the integrative process. . . . The phenomenon of a de Gaulle is omitted."[64]

The Monnet method of community building that Haas described purposely sought to make progress in small steps, so as not to confront at once a head-on political decision to jump directly from national to European sovereignty. It was feared that an all-or-nothing political approach would generate needless sources of opposition and prove counterproductive. Hence during the initial period, "high politics" was assiduously side stepped. There was a fundamental political commitment to European Union on the part of the major politicians in the Six, but they "had simply decided to leave the game of high politics" and build Europe by more modest and indirect methods. "Thus the economic technician could play his role within the shelter of the politicians' support."[65] The theory of gradual functional integration that operated within this setting was grounded upon the concrete, specific, economic advantage that accrued differently to the different partners, but whose general benefits enhanced the well-being of all. "Each of the Six, for individual national reasons, and *not* because of a clear common purpose, found it possible and desirable to embark on the road of economic integration using supranational institutions."[66] The technocratic approach that played down politics could succeed because of the political conditions at the time the Common Market was formed. The war had sufficiently discredited the old nationalist ideologies and undermined the national power positions of the Six so that the inhabitants of the various states were receptive to the idea of a gradual transfer of loyalties to a wider framework. The process of the gradual accretion of strength in European institutions could conceivably have continued apace, even after the economic and political revival of Europe. Prosperity, an improved power position for the national state and the increased tendency of the citizen to reaffirm his traditional feeling of national identity need not, in themselves, have disrupted progress toward supranationalism, although perhaps movement toward this goal might have become more difficult. What proved genuinely disruptive in these new circumstances was the explicit reintroduction of a nationalist ideology by de Gaulle, and his blunt challenge of "high politics," which the technocrats had so carefully sought to avoid.

In this conflict the adversaries were not evenly matched. "Pragmatic interest politics, concerned with economic welfare, has its own built-in limits. . . . Pragmatic interests, simply because they are pragmatic and not reinforced with deep ideological or philosophical commitment, are ephemeral. Just because they are weakly held they can be readily scrapped." It used to be fashionable to speak of the "automaticity" of engagement toward a higher form of supranationalism, and of the "spillover" from economic to political union. The object lesson de Gaulle taught is that "a political process which is built and projected from pragmatic interests . . . is bound to be a frail process, susceptible to reversal." Similarly, "incremental processes, because they rest on pragmatic interests, are always subject to reversal. Just as pragmatic interest politics is its own worst enemy, so is the incremental decision-making style." The technocratic bias of the functionalists relied heavily upon the expertise of a body of international civil servants, but lacked the mass appeal of popular involvement. Ideally, decisions were to be arrived at impartially, by a rational examination of the merits of each case, and in an atmosphere insulated from the welling up of popular emotions and vulgar slogans. Life would be administered, not governed, by the prejudices of mass politics. The only trouble with this theory is that when put to the test, it did not work. "High politics may not have taken the place of pragmatic economic calculation for all the players in the game; but if one of them so defines the situation, the others seem compelled to follow suit."[67]

Even if the personality of de Gaulle had not intervened, there might well be a grave flaw in the functionalist approach to integration. Most often overlooked in this theory is the role of positive political leadership and the growth of political institutions, which express an awareness that creating a supranational union is an essentially political undertaking. A close student of the operation of the Commission of the European Community, David Coombes, concluded that this body, which was perhaps the most "supranational" of the Community's institutions, has not been capable of providing the required political impulse toward political federation, despite the good intentions and dedicated nature of its past leadership. The difficulty rested in the circumscribed political base of the Commission, which could not carry through major decisions at the Community level. "On every major issue the final authority to make Community decisions rests with the ministers of the member states' governments sitting in the Council and these men are responsible only to their own national governments and parliaments. The governments also appoint the members of the Commission, provide its financial resources, and approve the Community budget. The 'supranational' element is confined to a body whose constitutional relationship to the national governments is parallel to that of a bureaucracy to the executive leadership of a state."[68]

Coombes did not deny the ever-increasing web of social and economic interdependence and interpenetration crossing national boundaries. What his evidence suggested, rather, "is that this process is not sufficient by itself to bring the benefits expected from integration. There must be separate provision for a legitimate, autonomous political authority at the federal level before integration can be regarded as worthwhile. This authority will be ineffective if it is bureaucratically organized like the present Commission. Instead it must be directly based on some kind of political support which is at the same time independent of the national governments."

How precisely to create such federal institutions is a matter of debate. It would seem to require the mobilization of public opinion for the attainment of political ends, such as the direct election of members of the federal executive, as well as members of the European

Parliament (which was envisioned in the Treaty of Rome) and then granting the European Parliament substantial powers over the Community budget. "Such a federal government is necessary because it is simply not practicable, however much the national governments concerned declare themselves to be committed to European unity in the long run, to entrust integration of social and economic policy in the short term to a set of institutions which rely for guidance and support on a number of different governments. Such a situation must turn the Executive part of the Community institutions into bureaucracy. This is not only inefficient as a means of making decisions, but also prevents the growth of political commitment and dynamism at a Community level."[69]

ONWARD TO EUROPEAN UNION?

All this raises very disturbing questions both about the future of Europe and the Atlantic Community. As for Europe, does it, indeed, have a future? By 1967 Paul-Henri Spaak, who for a generation had been a leading statesman seeking to build Europe, despaired publicly: "I confess that, as a European, it is not without melancholy that I view the situation. The Europe that we wanted, the Europe whose position in the world we intended to restore, the Europe that we hoped to make the equal of the United States and of the Soviet Union, is no longer realizable. It is dead for ever. Phrases from speeches I made in the 1950s come back to mind. My earlier enthusiasms, I can now appreciate, were illusions."[70] Some scholars tend to confirm this view. A team of investigators using criteria on community building drawn up under the direction of Karl Deutsch found that "European integration has slowed since the mid-1950s, and it has stopped or reached a plateau since 1957-58."[71]

Other scholars using different criteria and indices of European integration have come to different conclusions. All agree that Gaullism dramatically slowed down the tempo of movement toward supranationalism, but they would take issue with those who would prematurely issue Europe's death certificate. Leon Lindberg contends that Deutsch's concept of international integration is more "a theory of social or moral community," with the result that "it ignored too much that is politically relevant." Lindberg, who has been closely associated with the work of Haas, states that on the contrary, "Haas and I have argued that it is since 1957 that integration has made its greatest strides."[72] This finding was supported by the investigations of Ronald Inglehart. His study of political socialization in Western Europe also led him to radically different conclusions from those reached by the Deutsch team. "Far from finding a stagnation of integrative processes since 1958, I would argue that, in some respects European integration may have moved into full gear only *since* 1958."[73] Deutsch's pessimism "may have been unduly influenced by a study of top-level decision-making," where admittedly movement has been most severely restricted. However, de Gaulle's successors will be faced with broadly based pressure to resume integration at all levels.[74] Inglehart discerned a stable commitment to European integration that persisted in the face of discouragement, especially among the younger age groups that will likely prove decisive in the future. "Despite an apparent realization that European unification had bogged down," he wrote in 1967, "the youth in our samples gave a relatively strong measure of support for 'European' proposals."[75] Inglehart's subsequent research conducted following de Gaulle's death substantiated his earlier findings that nationalism was a declining force among Europe's youth, who were notably inclined to approve the surrender of some national sovereignty to European political institutions.[76]

Results of subsequent inquiries have demonstrated the steady growth of attitudes favorable to European integration. Carl Friedrich sharply attacked the methodology used by the Deutsch team, which he claimed had led to false conclusions about the evolution of Europe.[77] The data he collected showed, on the contrary, that a "growing consensus is molding all those who live within the boundaries of the Common Market into a community possessing legitimate authorities engaged in governing and defending it."[78] Friedrich views Europe as an emergent nation, not yet in the sense of the traditional, close-knit political and cultural entities of the modern European nation-states, but in the sense that these building blocks can form a cohesive group in international politics that can produce an effective government. Europe is therefore launched upon a federalizing process that is admittedly slow, but may nonetheless achieve lasting results. Federalism should be perceived as "an ongoing process" instead of a single, dramatic constitutional act.[79] Similarly, the extensive interview data collected from European elites by a team headed by Daniel Lerner and Morton Gorden challenged the Deutsch findings. "While the strength of nationalism [in the separate nations of Europe] is asserted to be strong by Deutsch et al., we find it to be diminishing."[80] A principal conclusion of the Lerner-Gorden researchers was that "Europe—a more or less integrated, and even unified, set of European nations acting as a single transnational body—is very likely to grow and prosper."[81]

It would seem prudent to say that there are grounds for hope of a European Union, but that the returns are not yet in. As Europe recaptures its forward momentum, it would also be well to remember Haas' observation about the built-in limits of functional, pragmatic politics. Ultimately, Europe is only likely to be built if a vigorous political leadership makes an open and unqualified commitment to weld the separate nationalisms into a new, larger entity. But it is precisely the emergence of a strong European nationalism that could make Europe a rival instead of a partner, and render Atlantic partnership difficult, if not impossible.

The only remedy for this malady is the concomitant growth of trans-Atlantic ties while Europe itself is taking shape. Inglehart's research on the nature of the commitment West European youth holds toward European unification suggested "that Europeanness tends to go *with* a broader internationalism: The predominant tendency is for those who support European integration to also support measures favorable to Atlantic ties or even global political integration."[82] If this proves to be true, a healthy, outward-looking European nationalism would be compatible with further integration on an Atlantic scale. But such a forecast is laden with uncertainties. The whole network of trans-Atlantic ties, which in its initial phases would likely be based on functional, pragmatic interests, would, at bottom, be a frail set of connections that could come unstuck as a result of a strong political challenge from either partner. Just as the technocratic bias of the Brussels officials has tended to overestimate what can be done in Europe by skirting around "high politics," so one must be aware of the limitations on an Atlantic scale of trying to solve highly political problems on the basis of the technical and rational expertise of a Committee of Entente. Hopefully, if such a Committee of Entente could begin to function, it could perform a considerable amount of useful work. But at some point fundamental political issues involving supranationalism would have to be faced. What might ultimately happen in shaping the body politic of the Atlantic

Community, then, would depend upon such factors as the popular acceptance of new loyalties, the depth of commitment and the political vision of the leadership groups, as well as the pure luck of the prevailing circumstances.

THE VISION BEYOND PARTNERSHIP

It is reasonably clear that the theorists of partnership have shared long-range political conceptions that anticipate continuing transformations in the nation-state system, and with it transformations going beyond the partnership arrangement. This was even true of the original views of Walter Hallstein, who at one time talked of unity for the entire West, although he later made partnership between the separate entities of Europe and the United States a fixed end in itself. Hallstein's official role as head of the Common Market Commission, however, came to an end on July 1, 1967, when as a result of de Gaulle's personal objection, Hallstein was prevented from becoming the President of the merged executive bodies of the three Communities (ECSC, EEC, and Euratom). Unofficially, views like Hallstein's will obviously continue to exert influence, and should they come to prevail, the goal beyond partnership might be lost sight of.

There is no doubt that originally many prominent European federalists looked upon the attainment of a European Union as part of the larger process of uniting the West. Robert Schuman, who as French Foreign Minister gave practical implementation to Monnet's scheme for a European Coal and Steel Community, also applauded efforts in behalf of Atlantic Union. In 1955 he looked hopefully for action by the U.S. Congress to explore ways of reaching this broader objective. "I have long been an ardent partisan of a European federation, itself to be integrated in the Atlantic Community. But certain European nations have hesitated to advance far in this direction so long as the United States, Canada and Great Britain were not disposed to explore in common with them an eventual political, economic and military union." Should delegates from the Atlantic nations be able to produce "the outline of an acceptable plan of union, in which each of the member nations would be attributed an equitable voting right protecting it from any eventual domination by a single nation," Schuman concluded, "we would then certainly have made a great step toward world peace and general prosperity."[83]

The argument that union, both in Europe and across the Atlantic, would be a powerful factor for international stability and world peace has been a recurrent theme. Max Kohnstamm, Vice-President of Monnet's Action Committee, has viewed the movement toward union in the West as part of "the process of civilization, which is the process of law and institutions penetrating into ever wider circles." As common institutions are developed, anarchy among nations is reduced and freedom is protected. "But the free nations of the West will only remain united if they succeed in setting up between themselves the necessary mechanism of collective action, if they succeed in replacing, between themselves to begin with, the laws of the jungle by the rule of law." Therefore, "whatever the present difficulties," Kohnstamm warned us never to lose sight of the need for community building both in Europe and on an Atlantic scale. "We must continue to build up our European institutions and, eventually, institutions to serve the Atlantic partnership, institutions to which Europe and America both will have to delegate powers."[84]

Kohnstamm subsequently elaborated upon the connection between common institutions in the West and the search for a peaceful world order. "European integration cannot be an objective in itself," since its larger aim is to change the structure and content of international relations. "We have come to a point from which European integration can only move forward if it proves to be the beginning of a process pushing beyond itself." In answer to the question of how this can be done, Kohnstamm related the existence of common Atlantic institutions to the resolution of the East-West struggle. It is first necessary to establish "organic relations—rules and institutions—between uniting Europe and the United States of America. Our challenges, however, involve East and West. Consequently, integration plus partnership, in order to constitute a valid model, must push forward—towards organic relations with the East. What we need with the East is not just a settlement; we need continuing institutions, capable of peacefully adapting the situation to a constantly changing reality."[85]

It is worth recalling that Monnet himself, in his famous Dartmouth speech of June 1961, held out a similar vision. "What is necessary is to move towards a true Atlantic Community in which common institutions will be increasingly developed to meet common problems." It was in this speech that Monnet first coined the partnership idea, and yet he also went beyond the call for two separate but equal partners. Both partners, the United States included, would some day be bound together in a common union. "I am convinced that ultimately, the United States, too, will delegate powers of effective action in common institutions, even on political questions. Just as the United States in their day found it necessary to unite, just as Europe is now in the process of uniting, so the West must move towards some kind of union." His motivation, like Kohnstamm's, was to attain the still more elusive goal of world peace. "This is not an end in itself. It is the beginning on the road to the more orderly world we must have if we are to escape destruction."[86]

Curious about what "some kind of union" for the West meant, this writer pressed Monnet, totally without success, to be more explicit. Monnet absolutely refused to speculate on what these institutions might be like, turning away questions with a catalog of explanations. Discussion of future theoretical blueprints, he held, only distracts attention from practical steps that might be undertaken now. In moving toward common institutions one must go pragmatically, letting life unfold the concrete form of collaboration step-by-step. New circumstances would bring forth new institutions. Just as the U.S. federation was novel, just as the institutions of the European Community are novel, so will the joint Atlantic institutions growing out of partnership be unique. Monnet, however, did explicitly deny that he had ever endorsed Clarence Streit's concept of Atlantic Union.* "We do not seek integration with the United States," Monnet explained in 1967. "While relying upon the fundamental element of equality, the forms of organization of our relations with it will necessarily be different from the form which our common European institutions have taken."[87]

One reason that it is idle to tie oneself down in advance, Monnet insisted, is that institutional forms would be contingent upon the greater aims of policy. The larger purpose of institution building is the organization of peace, and one cannot foretell exactly how far it

---

*When this writer showed Monnet Streit's claim in *Freedom & Union* (April 1966, p. 16) to the effect that Monnet had been a partisan of Streit's ideas on Atlantic federation during the 1940s, Monnet emphatically denied it.

will be necessary to go in consolidating the strength of the West in common institutions before it will be possible to arrive at an understanding with the East, in the form of a durable detente with Soviet power.

Glimmerings of the ultimate vision of partnership moving to union have also been found in statements by U.S. spokesmen. President Kennedy's original offer of partnership was coupled with the hope that Atlantic partnership "would serve as a nucleus for the eventual union of all free men."[88] Despite the difficulties in implementing partnership, officials of the State Department continued to keep alive the long-range prospect. In 1966, for example, Under Secretary of State George Ball expressed the belief that as Europe united, Atlantic Union would become more likely. "I think it would become more realistic because I think that once you have created units which are of comparable size and resources, that they will tend over time to have comparable interests given the kind of common heritage and civilization from which Western Europe and North America spring. Thus, as a result, they would find it very much easier to combine their interests in some political arrangement than is now the case. . . . I certainly don't rule out the possibility that somewhere down the road we can move toward much closer political arrangements with Europe, and they may even take a federal form ultimately."[89] Similarly, J. Robert Schaetzel, as State Department specialist on Atlantic affairs, could foresee that "at some point in time interest in Atlantic partnership and in the goal of Atlantic Union may very well converge. There is nothing in the concept of Atlantic partnership that precludes an eventual fusing of a united Europe and the United States."[90]

Whatever the distant image of trans-Atlantic fusion might be, all advocates of partnership have agreed that it can only be brought into the arena of practical politics by first uniting Europe and perfecting the instruments of partnership. Paul-Henri Spaak, who was widely known as an advocate of European Union, was also a supporter of the cause of Atlantic Union. But the federation of Europe was a necessary prerequisite for a trans-Atlantic merger. "I think that an Atlantic Union is only possible if opposite the American partner there is a European partner who can be valid. I think that opposite the United States of America equilibrium demands the presence of the United States of Europe." Given this qualification, Spaak concluded that "those who are in favor—must one say the dreamers?—of an Atlantic federation are beyond all question indubitably right."[91]

The requirement of a valid European partner for the achievement of Atlantic Union rests on the assumption that it is only when the United States will be faced with problems it cannot solve alone and with a European power it cannot dominate that it will be inclined to accommodate itself to a new situation by merging sovereignty in some new joint Atlantic organs. So long as the United States is under the illusion that it can act alone, or for lack of a European partner is obliged to act on its own, it will have little incentive to delegate power to a wider political body. American willingness to forego its freedom of action, Schaetzel speculated, could come as a result of a crisis or when "Europe is so organized as to make such changes, or restraints attractive, necessary or inevitable." He cited the fact that the United States had responded to increased European economic strength with concessions in the trade and monetary fields as evidence that a powerful European Union could erode more American independence of action and stimulate further American moves toward Atlantic integration.[92]

It is in this sense that Robert Bowie has complained: "Atlantic Community is a complete non-starter." An overpowering United States amidst a collection of smaller powers does not inspire Americans to concert action in a common cause. An independent Europe, defining its own interests will, according to this view, come up with basically parallel interests to the United States. However, the threat that this power might be used in a contrary manner would force the American hand and cause a devolution of sovereignty in order to meet the challenge of a more assertive Europe. The largest states always find it more difficult to place restraints on their actions, but this will become politically more acceptable as the dangers of independent action become more apparent. At this point the advantages of merging sovereign powers would seem to outweigh the benefits of "going it alone."

Much the same conclusion was reached from the European point of view by a leader of the European Movement like Maurice Faure. Europe, he told this writer, would be willing to go as far as the United States toward integration, including an Atlantic political federation, but so long as the United States showed no willingness to subject itself to a common authority, Europe would not either. The ultimate problem of Atlantic Union, then, rests with the United States.

Admittedly, there is logic in using partnership as a device to spur the United States on. Yet it would seem hasty to abandon the idea of a multilateral Atlantic Community. The formation of a supranational

Europe is still in the future. To the extent that a full-fledged European partner remains unrealized, partnership is a nonstarter. Meanwhile, multilateral trans-Atlantic organs like NATO and OECD do exist and perform valuable functions, and their operations can be improved simply by building on what is at hand. In some respects it may be easier to move ahead by perfecting existing Atlantic institutions, and where possible creating new ones, than by waiting upon Europe to take shape. "It is senseless to wait for the Europeans to unite among themselves," a Dutch journal remarked in 1966, "before institutionalizing the Atlantic relationship. . . . Waiting for the Europeans to unite first themselves means in practice further disintegration of Atlantic unity."[93]

At the same time, trans-Atlantic arrangements need not prejudice the future internal organization of Europe. In 1967 Secretary of State Dean Rusk explicitly restated an American willingness to reshape NATO, for example, to meet evolving European needs and desires: "We would welcome now, as before, a European caucus, if they want to call it that, in NATO, something like a European defense community, as a full partner in a reconstituted alliance. They should not feel sensitive about constituting their own European defense community, because it was not the United States which blocked earlier efforts to do just that."[94]

The European members of NATO (with the exception of France, Iceland, and Portugal) did, in fact, respond to the initiatives of British Defense Minister Denis Healy to form the Eurogroup, which first met in November 1968. It has since worked effectively toward the dual aims of rationalizing European defense efforts, so as to make optimum use of the limited European defense resources, and of consolidating the trans-Atlantic bond with America inside NATO. Thus the various Eurogroup defense improvement programs have both upgraded the European defense contribution and have sought thereby to prove to the Congress that the Europeans were pulling their weight in the Alliance so as to ensure the continued American military commitment to Europe. The Eurogroup members are keenly aware of the danger that they might pursue some policies that could be interpreted as anti-American, but they have carefully avoided doing anything that might result in a weakening of NATO.[95]

Looking toward the future, the Eurogroup might well be modified and adapted to the needs of an emergent European Union by becoming the military body that could take its place alongside the strengthened political and economic institutions of the European Community. Among the various modifications required, there would have to be a change in the attitude of France toward both the Eurogroup and NATO, and this might occur within the context of a reconstituted Alliance that would take account of the changed needs among Europeans as well as between Europe and the United States.

Just as the Eurogroup might exhibit greater European cohesion in the military field, so somewhat analgous developments might unfold in the areas of economic or monetary policy. In each case the European component of the Atlantic Community might undergo transformation, but without breaking the essential trans-Atlantic ties. If movement is considered in this manner, progress could be made both on a European and Atlantic scale when and where possible, without assuming rigid priority in one area as a prerequisite for creative acts in the other.

Strengthening the existing framework of multilateral trans-Atlantic ties is also essential precisely because of the strategy by which partnership hopes to proceed to some higher form of integration. The more the negative or threatening aspects of partnership become apparent, so goes the theory, the more apparent it will be that common action will be required and the more willing each partner will be to delegate power to some new common institution so as to avoid the impending dangers of conflict. But there are obvious risks in this dialectical strategy for a unity of opposites. The greater the possibility of conflict, the more important is the existence of common Atlantic forums in which common interests may be perceived, discussed, and hopefully acted upon. The leavening and mediating functions of third parties might also prove useful to prevent a purely bilateral confrontation between the European Community and the United States.

Finally, the multilateral organs of the Atlantic Community are essential and require reinforcement because partnership is too narrow to encompass the nations that share the common Western heritage and that are capable of contributing to its preservation and enrichment. Both NATO and OECD, for example, provide room for Canada on one side of the Atlantic, and for various European nations that are not members of the European Community on the other side. Partnership may eventually prove to be a valuable inner core of the larger Western society of nations, but the institutions of the Atlantic Community must be sufficiently flexible and broad in scope to contain the smaller, more coherent groupings within it, while giving full expression to the varied needs of the West.

NOTES

1. Action Committee for the United States of Europe, Joint Declaration, adopted June 26, 1962, Paris, pp. 3-4.

2. Address by McGeorge Bundy at Copenhagen, September 27, 1962, Department of State *Bulletin*, 47, no. 1217: 604-05.

3. Address by Under Secretary of State George Ball at Paris, November 16, 1962, Department of State *Bulletin*, 47, no. 1223: 835.

4. Address by Under Secretary of State George Ball at Washington, D.C., May 7, 1964, Department of State *Bulletin*, 50, no. 1300: 825.

5. Pierre Uri, "Comment sortir de la querelle nucleaire?" *Le Monde*, February 26, 1963.

6. Club Jean Moulin, *La force de frappe et le citoyen* (Paris, 1963), p. 117.

7. Theodore Geiger, *Transatlantic Relations in Prospect of an Enlarged European Community* (London, 1970), p. 31.

8. New York *Times*, April 8, 1963. See also Monnet's statement in the New York *Times*, February 26, 1964.

9. Address by Deputy Assistant Secretary of State for Atlantic Affairs J. Robert Schaetzel at Enstone, England, September 27, 1963, p. 5. (Italics added.)

10. Action Committee for the United States of Europe, Joint Declaration, adopted June 1, 1964, Bonn, pp. 11-13.

11. Henry Owen, "What the Multilateral Force Could Achieve," *European Review*, Autumn 1964, p. 14.

12. Action Committee for the United States of Europe, Joint Declaration, adopted May 8 and 9, 1965, Berlin, p. 6.

13. Fritz Erler, "Partners in Strategy," *Atlantic Community Quarterly*, Summer 1964, p. 300.

14. Kurt Birrenbach, "The Federal Republic and America: Problems of the Alliance," *Aussenpolitik*, No. 2 (1966); reprinted in *German Tribune*, April 30, 1966, p. 3.

15. Club Jean Moulin, op. cit., pp. 119-20. The British Conservative, Duncan Sandys, acting as rapporteur of the Defense

Committee of the Assembly of Western European Union, likewise viewed with favor the prospect of "a joint nuclear force on a NATO basis," at some future time when the Europeans could "constitute a unified European component of a joint force, controlled by the two partners on equal terms." (Assembly, WEU, *Proceedings,* November 1965, IV, p. 82.)

16. Robert R. Bowie, "Strategy and the Atlantic Alliance," *International Organization,* Summer 1963, p. 728.

17. Ibid., p. 726. See pp. 720-21, where Bowie argued the advantages of centralized NATO-wide political controls over nuclear weapons.

18. Malcolm W. Hoag, "Nuclear Policy and French Intransigence," *Foreign Affairs,* January 1963, p. 297. Hoag spoke in terms of European control of some component of a multilateral NATO force, but conceivably the same arrangement could be devised for a European deterrent linked to the U.S. one.

19. Alastair Buchan, "The Future of NATO," *International Conciliation,* November 1967, p. 48.

20. James L. Richardson, *Germany and the Atlantic Alliance* (Cambridge, Mass., 1966), p. 223.

21. Testimony of Secretary of State Dean Rusk before the Senate Committee on Foreign Relations, July 10, 1968, Department of State *Bulletin,* 59, no. 1518: 133.

22. Sergio Fenoaltea, "Non-Proliferation and Europe," *Interplay,* November 1968, pp. 13-14.

23. Action Committee for the United States of Europe, Joint Declaration, adopted June 1, 1964, Bonn, pp. 6, 12. See also Action Committee for the United States of Europe, Joint Declaration, adopted May 8 and 9, 1965, Berlin, p. 4.

24. Karl W. Deutsch, Lewis J. Edinger, Roy C. Macridis, and Richard L. Merritt, *France, Germany and the Western Alliance* (New York, 1967), p. 67.

25. Ibid., pp. 74-77.

26. Buchan, op. cit., p. 45.

27. New York *Times,* November 17, 1964.

28. Kai-Uwe von Hassel, "Organizing Western Defense," *Foreign Affairs,* January 1965, pp. 213-14.

29. Deutsch et al., op. cit., p. 192.

30. "Open Letter to the Netherlands Minister for Foreign Affairs," March 2, 1965, *Atlantic Community Quarterly,* Spring

1965, pp. 120-25. Foreign Minister Luns replied: "We believe it highly desirable that the slow process of European unification should take place within the framework of Atlantic cooperation. . . . As the late President Kennedy stated, there is nothing to prevent a United Europe from taking part in an Atlantic Community." (*European Community,* No. 80 [April 1965], p. 15.)

31. E. .H. van der Beugel, "Relations Between Europe and the United States," *Knickerbocker International,* April 1967, p. 29.

32. *European Community,* No. 72 (June 1964), p. 1.

33. Action Committee for the United States of Europe, Joint Declaration, adopted June 1, 1964, Bonn, p. 10.

34. Action Committee for the United States of Europe, Joint Declaration, adopted December 17 and 18, 1962, Paris, p. 3.

35. Rene Foch, "An Example of Atlantic Partnership: Euratom," *Atlantic Community Quarterly,* Spring 1964, pp. 75-78; Warren H. Donnelly, *Commercial Nuclear Power in Europe: The Interaction of American Diplomacy with a New Technology,* prepared for the Subcommittee on National Security Policy and Scientific Developments, Committee on Foreign Affairs, U.S. House of Representatives (Washington, D.C., 1972), pp. 96-108.

36. Christopher Layton, *European Advanced Technology* (London, 1969), p. 125.

37. Secretariat General of the Commission, *Euratom's Future Activities,* Supplement to Bulletin No. 6 (1969) of the European Communities, Brussels, p. 26.

38. Layton, op. cit., p. 112.

39. Secretariat General of the Commission, *Survey of the Nuclear Policy of the European Communities,* Supplement to Bulletin Nos. 9/10 (1968) of the European Communities, Brussels, pp. 5-6.

40. *Le Figaro,* April 28, 1966, quoted in Lawrence Scheinman, "Euratom: Nuclear Integration in Europe," *International Conciliation,* May 1967, p. 26.

41. Ibid., pp. 35, 54.

42. Ernst B. Haas, "*The Uniting of Europe* and the Uniting of Latin America," *Journal of Common Market Studies,* June 1967, p. 323.

43. "Political Decision-Making and Advanced Technology," Paul Elvinger, rapporteur, Document 522, October 7, 1970, Assembly, WEU, *Proceedings,* November 1970, III, p. 86.

44. Lord Franks, "Cooperation Is Not Enough," *Foreign Affairs,* October 1962, p. 33.

45. Action Committee for the United States of Europe, Joint Declaration, adopted June 1, 1964, Bonn, p. 10. See also Action Committee for the United States of Europe, Joint Declaration, adopted May 8 and 9, 1965, Berlin, pp. 5-6.

46. Jean Monnet, "America and Ourselves," *La Nef,* February 17, 1966, p. 14. (Italics added.) See also Jean Monnet, "The Future of the Atlantic World," *Diplomat,* June 1966, p. 22.

47. Action Committee for the United States of Europe, Resolutions, adopted June 15, 1967, Brussels, p. 5.

48. Address by Jean Monnet at New York, November 29, 1967, p. 7.

49. Report of the Political Committee, Erik Blumenfeld, rapporteur, adopted by the Sixteenth Annual Session of the North Atlantic Assembly, November 1970, The Hague, in *Addresses, Reports and Texts Adopted, NAA, 1970,* pp. 102-3.

50. Clyde H. Farnsworth, "End to Wrangling Sought for U.S. and Market Bloc," New York *Times,* March 17, 1970.

51. Address by Deputy Under Secretary for Economic Affairs Nathaniel Samuels at New York, November 15, 1971, Department of State *Bulletin,* 45, no. 1694: 671.

52. *Atlantic News,* No. 298 (January 12, 1971), p. 2.

53. Action Committee for the United States of Europe, Resolutions, adopted at Bonn, February 23 and 24, 1971, p. 7.

54. President Richard M. Nixon, Report to the Congress, February 25, 1971, Department of State *Bulletin,* 44, no. 1656: 351.

55. *European Community,* No. 145 (May 1971), p. 9; No. 174 (March 1974), p. 3.

56. Proposal by Foreign Minister Walter Scheel to the Ministerial Conference of the EEC at Rome, February 5, 1971, *Relay from Bonn,* November 8, 1971.

57. Proposal by Chancellor Willy Brandt to the Summit Conference of the EEC at Paris, October 19, 1972, *Relay from Bonn,* October 20, 1972.

58. Willy Brandt, "Germany's 'Westpolitik,' " *Foreign Affairs,* April 1972, pp. 421-22.

59. "Market Countries Set Goal of Uniting Policies by '80," New York *Times,* October 21, 1972.

60. Interview with Foreign Minister Walter Scheel over ZDF-TV, March 18, 1973, *Relay from Bonn,* March 19, 1973.

61. "Political Decision-Making and Advanced Technology," op. cit., p. 86.

62. Article 235 of the Treaty of Rome was, in turn, inspired by certain provisions in Article 95 of the European Coal and Steel Community Treaty.

63. His understanding of "functionalism" differs considerably from the earlier functional theorists. For a full explanation, see Ernst B. Haas, *Beyond the Nation-State* (Stanford, Calif., 1964), pp. 3-85. A brief, useful comparison between the functionalist David Mitrany and the "neofunctionalist" Haas is provided by Paul Taylor, "The Concept of Community and the European Integration Process," *Journal of Common Market Studies,* December 1968, pp. 83-101.

64. Haas, *"The Uniting of Europe,"* op. cit., p. 327.

65. Ibid., p. 323.

66. Ibid., p. 322.

67. Ibid., pp. 327-29. See, however, the very useful warning about the absence of a clear line of distinction between "low" and "high" politics, and the complicated way in which they interact. Karl Kaiser, "The U.S. and the EEC in the Atlantic System: The Problem of Theory," *Journal of Common Market Studies,* June 1967, pp. 389-95.

68. David Coombes, *Politics and Bureaucracy in the European Community* (London, 1970), p. 296.

69. Ibid., pp. 322-23.

70. Paul-Henri Spaak, "Europe, Defend Yourself," *Spectator,* April 18, 1967, p. 482.

71. Deutsch et al., op. cit., p. 218. See also pp. 223, 229-30, 237, 245, 298-301.

72. Leon N. Lindberg, "The European Community as a Political System," *Journal of Common Market Studies,* June 1967, pp. 344-45. See also Lindberg, *The Political Dynamics of European Economic Integration* (Stanford, 1963), and "Integration as a Source of Stress on the European Community System," *International Organization,* Spring 1966, pp. 233-66.

73. Ronald Inglehart, "An End to European Integration?" *American Political Science Review,* March 1967, p. 91.

74. Ibid., p. 105.

75. Ibid., p. 99.

76. Ronald Inglehart, "Changing Value Priorities and European Integration," *Journal of Common Market Studies,* September 1971, pp. 1-36.

77. Carl J. Friedrich, *Europe: An Emergent Nation?* (New York, 1969), pp. 35-43, 211-12. For further studies that challenge Deutsch's methodology and conclusions, see William E. Fisher, "An Analysis of the Deutsch Sociocausal Paradigm of Political Integration," *International Organization,* Spring 1969, pp. 254-90; Robert Weissberg, "Nationalism, Integration, and French and German Elites," in ibid., pp. 337-47. On attempts to perfect tools measuring integration, see James A. Caporaso, "Fisher's Test of Deutsch's Sociocausal Paradigm of Political Integration," in ibid., Winter 1971, pp. 120-31; James A. Caporaso, "Theory and Method in the Study of International Integration," in ibid., Spring 1971, pp. 228-53; James A. Caporaso and Alan L. Pelowski, "Economic and Political Integration in Europe," *American Political Science Review,* June 1971, pp. 418-33.

78. Friedrich, op. cit., p. 46.

79. Ibid., pp. 213-15. Friedrich elaborated the "federalism as process" thesis in his *Trends of Federalism in Theory and Practice* (New York, 1968), pp. 3-10, 173-85.

80. Daniel Lerner and Morton Gorden, *Euratlantica: Changing Perspectives of the European Elites* (Cambridge, Mass., 1969), p. 69.

81. Ibid., p. 308. See also "Europeans Vote for Europe," *European Community,* No. 134 (May 1970), p. 15; "Unity: A Probe of European Attitudes," ibid., No. 139 (October 1970), pp. 16-17.

82. Ronald Inglehart, "The New Europeans: Inward or Outward-Looking? *International Organization,* Winter 1970, p. 139.

83. "Ex-Premier Schuman's Statement," *Freedom & Union,* June 1955, p. 14.

84. Max Kohnstamm, *The European Community and Its Role in the World* (Columbia, Mo., 1963), pp. 64-66.

85. Max Kohnstamm, "The Future Shape of Europe," in *The Atlantic Community and Eastern Europe: Perspective and Policy* (Boulogne-sur-Seine, 1967), p. 103.

86. Address by Jean Monnet at Hanover, N.H., June 11, 1961, pp. 7-8.

87. "Jean Monnet répond aux questions de *Réalités,*" *Réalités,* July 1967, p. 25.

88. Address by President John F. Kennedy at Philadelphia, July 4, 1962, Department of State *Bulletin,* 47, no. 1204: 133.

89. *Hearings before the Committee on Foreign Affairs, House of Representatives,* 89th Cong., 2d sess., on Pending Resolutions to

Establish an Atlantic Union Delegation, September 20, 1966 (Washington, D.C., 1966), pp. 176-77.

90. J. Robert Schaetzel, "The Necessary Partnership," *Foreign Affairs,* April 1966, p. 431.

91. Paul-Henri Spaak, "I Could Not But Feel a Great Anxiety," *Atlantic Community Quarterly,* Spring 1969, pp. 44-46.

92. Schaetzel, "The Necessary Partnership," op. cit., pp. 429-30.

Freedom & Union, May 1966, p. 17.

94. Address by Secretary of State Dean Rusk at New York, December 2, 1967, Department of State *Bulletin,* 57, no. 1487: 858.

95. For a good analysis of its origin and development, see "The Eurogroup: An Experiment in European Defense Cooperation," Carl Damm and Philip Goodhart, rapporteurs, Military Committee, North Atlantic Assembly, October 1972, P 147, MC (72) 8.

5

NATO AND DETENTE: THE GAULLIST AND SOVIET VIEWS

NATO has provided the principal multilateral forum for the consideration of Atlantic political and security affairs. Yet according to a significant segment of public opinion, an improvement in East-West relations has rendered NATO obsolete.

De Gaulle specifically linked detente with the dissolution of NATO. According to his view, the Soviet threat to the West had all but disappeared, thereby rendering unnecessary the military and political association of Western Europe with the United States through NATO. In any event, de Gaulle argued, the American guarantee of Western Europe's safety became unreliable the moment American cities were directly exposed to Soviet intercontinental missiles. The states of Western Europe must, therefore, disassociate themselves from the United States, and look to themselves for new political arrangements by exploiting opportunities both to establish closer ties with the states of Eastern Europe, which were increasingly restive of Soviet controls, and with the Soviet Union itself, which was basically transforming its character.

DE GAULLE "DISCOVERS" DETENTE

"In 1958," de Gaulle recalled in his memoirs, "I considered that the world situation was very different from what it had been at the time of the creation of NATO." The Soviet military threat to Europe could be discounted, and communism had little chance of taking root in the countries of the West, short of "some national calamity." Moreover, "it was towards Asia rather than towards Europe that the Russians must now turn their attention on account of the ambitions of China." It would be "madness" for any state to launch a nuclear war because of the certainty of wholesale destruction. Therefore, "if one does not make war, one must sooner or later make peace. No regime on earth, however oppressive, is capable of maintaining indefinitely in a state of war-like tension peoples who believe they will not have to fight. Everything, therefore, led me to believe that the East would feel more and more strongly the need and the attractions of a detente." Given these assumptions, de Gaulle said that his aim was "to disengage France, not from the Atlantic Alliance, which I intended to maintain by way of ultimate precaution, but from the integration realized by NATO under American command; to establish relations with each of the states of the Eastern bloc, first and foremost Russia, with the object of bringing about a detente followed by understanding and cooperation."[1]

While de Gaulle is widely credited with "discovering detente," it is frequently forgotten that for a long time his actions were sharply at odds with the above sentiments. Rather than initiating measures to limit the East-West confrontation, for years he bitterly resisted moves in this direction. De Gaulle opposed British arms control proposals advanced to Moscow in 1959 and greeted with suspicion the Eisenhower-Khrushchev meeting at Camp David in September 1959, which, on the American side, was an attempt to defuse the Berlin crisis by means of summit diplomacy. French reservations then succeeded in delaying by several months the convocation of the 1960 summit conference. From 1961 onward, de Gaulle withdrew entirely from the Anglo-American talks that were held with Soviet spokesmen over Berlin. Nor did de Gaulle ever permit a French representative to take his seat at the meetings of the Eighteen Nation Disarmament Committee in Geneva, whose deliberations on issues affecting East-West tensions continued for a number of years.

What was the Gaullist rationale for this behavior? In October 1961 de Gaulle explained that the Soviet Union was so threatening that one could not even take the risk of conducting discussions with it over a question like Berlin. "It is our duty to stand firm and erect in the face of demands from the totalitarian bloc and to urge our allies to do the same. For nothing would be more dangerous to our cause, our safety, our alliance and our peace than to retreat step by step before those who are menacing us."[2] This hard-line public stance was accompanied by a private soft-line position adumbrated to the Soviet leaders, by which de Gaulle signalled the Kremlin that he had no interest in German reunification, and that if only the Russians would stop issuing threats and ultimatums it would be possible to sign a treaty with Moscow based on the division of Germany and the recognition of the G.D.R.[3]

By his intransigent public policy de Gaulle sought to win the allegiance of the West Germans, who were fearful of Western concessions over Berlin at the expense of German interests. Exciting German suspicions against the "Anglo-Saxons" also served his larger aim of creating a Franco-German alignment as the core of a "European Europe." British and American diplomacy over Berlin during this period often did not sufficiently take German sensitivities into account, thereby giving de Gaulle openings to exploit, although in fact the Western powers made no concessions of substance. In the end it was Khrushchev who was forced to withdraw his ultimatum on Berlin and to leave unfulfilled his promise of signing a separate peace treaty with East Germany, which supposedly would have exercised sovereign rights over Berlin.[4]

In October 1962 the focus of East-West crisis shifted from Berlin to Cuba. To many, the successful resolution of the Cuban missile crisis opened the prospect for a new era in Western relations with the Soviet Union. The superpowers had faced each other at the rim of a nuclear abyss and had drawn back, resolving in the process never again to let events take them so far down the path toward mutual destruction. Hence, a measure of detente was introduced into Soviet-American relations in late 1962 and 1963 by acts such as the installation of the "hot line" and the signing of the limited nuclear test ban treaty. But in a press conference of July 1963 de Gaulle warned that conditions for detente had not yet matured. "France, in effect, has for a long time believed that the day might come when a real detente, and even a sincere detente, will enable the relations between East and West in Europe to be completely changed and it intends, if this day comes . . . to make constructive proposals with regard to the peace, balance and destiny of Europe." Unfortunately, it remains "true that the Soviet bloc holds to its totalitarian and threatening ideology and again recently the Berlin wall, the scandal of the Berlin wall, or the installation of nuclear arms in Cuba have shown that, because of the Soviet bloc, peace remains precarious." He noted that the "human evolution" in the Soviet bloc, the economic and social difficulties in those countries, and the emerging Sino-Soviet dispute might, in time, require the Kremlin "to insert a note of sincerity" in its talk of peaceful coexistence. But that was a matter for future evolution.

As for the just-signed Moscow agreement banning nuclear testing, de Gaulle saw only the specter of a new Yalta, which he interpreted to mean making Europe the victim of a deal between "the Anglo-Saxons and the Soviets." "Thus, the United States which, since Yalta and Potsdam, has nothing, after all, to ask from the Soviets, the United States sees tempting prospects opening up before it. Hence, for instance, all the separate negotiations between the Anglo-Saxons and the Soviets, which, starting with the limited agreement on nuclear testing, seem likely to be extended to other questions, notably European ones, until now in the absence of the Europeans, which clearly goes against the views of France."[5] Here again were the two Gaullist themes denouncing detente: the Soviet threat remained undiminished, and a "European Europe" must organize itself against the schemes of "the Anglo-Saxons," who, together with Moscow, were ready to sacrifice European interests under the guise of detente.

Unfortunately, this latter charge seemed to have the coloration of truth in Bonn, since the Americans negotiated the test ban in Moscow without adequate prior consultation with officials of the Federal Republic, whose rights seemed to be endangered. The accession to the treaty of the G.D.R. raised the prospect, if only by implication, of official recognition of the East German regime on the part of the other signatories. This difficulty was overcome by inventing the ingenious device of triple depositories, so that each state could sign only in association with other states it wished to recognize. Subsequently, the United States supplied the further assurance that even this circumscribed form of East German accession did not amount to legal recognition of the G.D.R.[6] This incident proved not that the Americans neglected the interests of Bonn; on the contrary, they fought tenaciously for them in Moscow. Nonetheless, hard feelings arose because the Americans presented Bonn with a fait accompli: The West Germans were obliged to accept a treaty that was formulated without their participation. This method of negotiation raised the prospect that perhaps on another occasion West German interests might not be adequately protected. De Gaulle's insistent harping upon his concept of Yalta therefore inevitably struck a responsive chord among the West Germans. However, these seeds of suspicion did not succeed in disrupting the basic German orientation toward NATO, which de Gaulle was then actively seeking to sabotage.

De Gaulle did effectively immobilize NATO initiatives toward the East, for in all the political deliberations of the North Atlantic Council, Gaullist policy assumed a persistently negative attitude toward every aspect of detente. "Between 1961 and 1966," Belgian Foreign Minister Paul-Henri Spaak recalled, "France's consistent refusal to agree with her partners in what area of international relations the concept of peaceful coexistence between the West and the Communist camp should be applied." Spaak repeatedly advanced ideas at the ministerial meetings of the Council to explore emerging possibilities for an improved relationship with the East. "It was [French Foreign Minister] Couve de Murville who opposed my arguments most strongly." While there were others who also resisted moves toward detente, Spaak was convinced that if there had been French cooperation instead of obstructionism "there would have been some progress, for neither the Americans nor the British were opposed to these efforts." Thus, "for a number of years it was de Gaulle who prevented the Atlantic Alliance from taking this particular course."[7]

While de Gaulle could exert considerable negative influence in preventing the Atlantic Alliance from moving toward detente, he could exhibit scant positive influence over his allies to construct a "European Europe," which would have entailed a break between the European Community and the "Anglo-Saxons." And so persistent frustration to make headway with his design in the West inevitably caused de Gaulle to turn Eastward, in search of other European partners that might be willing to collaborate with him in his attempt to restructure the existing power balance in the world and especially in Europe. During 1964-65 French diplomacy intensified its activity in Eastern Europe and openly developed warm relations with the Soviet leaders themselves.

New themes now appeared in de Gaulle's pronouncements. It was no longer forbidden to deal directly with the Russians on the German problem. Quite the opposite, it was necessary for all responsible statesmen to discuss the conditions for a settlement of

East-West tensions. In February 1965 de Gaulle found remote the possibility of "a general conflagration, since the reciprocal nuclear deterrence is succeeding in preventing the worst. But it is clear that real peace and, even more, fruitful relations between East and West, will not be established so long as the German anomalies, the concern they cause and the suffering they entail continue."[8] Somewhat belatedly and indirectly de Gaulle found respectability in the hope that lay behind the Anglo-American effort to conclude the test ban treaty, namely, that conditions of nuclear standoff might be stabilized as a first tentative step toward approaching the fundamental, unsolved political issues dividing Europe.

THE GAULLIST SOLUTION FOR AN EAST-WEST SETTLEMENT

What was de Gaulle's long-range solution for the German problem and an East-West settlement? "What must be done will not be done, one day, except by the understanding and combined action of the peoples who have always been, who are and who will remain principally concerned by the fate of the German neighbor—in short, the European peoples." It was a matter for the Europeans "to envisage first examining together, then settling in common, and lastly guaranteeing conjointly the solution to a question which is essentially that of their continent—this is the only way that can make reappear . . . a Europe in a state of equilibrium, peace and cooperation."[9] Though late in acting upon the idea of detente, de Gaulle left his own distinctive imprint upon it. The seemingly innocuous view that a European settlement will be devised by the peoples of Europe pointedly excluded the United States from this process. In effect, de Gaulle grasped the standard of detente as an anti-American weapon. More precisely, perhaps, his version of this idea was directed against "the Anglo-Saxons," since de Gaulle's persistent refusal to admit Britain to the European Community was justified on the ground that the British did not qualify as Europeans. Detente thus became an additional facet, although an attractive and powerful one, in the Gaullist campaign, to break Europe's trans-Atlantic ties and create a "European Europe." As de Gaulle had earlier explained, "a European Europe means that it exists by itself for itself."[10]

One of the most important trans-Atlantic bonds with "the Anglo-Saxons" was in the form of NATO. The political motivations that once led de Gaulle to assume an intransigent stand against the Kremlin as a great menace now led him to deal freely and intimately with the Russians, who, as it turned, out, were no longer a menace. NATO, which had always stood in the way of de Gaulle's political ambitions, could now be shattered. In short order he withdrew France from NATO and expelled all NATO forces and facilities from French soil. Movement toward detente and disengagement from NATO were part of the same process; in the Gaullist view, NATO was an obstacle to detente and the building of a "European Europe." France was now moving as de Gaulle had always said it should, as "a nation with free hands, whose policy is not being determined by any pressure from without."[11]

De Gaulle's war on NATO was in both the military and political realms. Technically, the French distinguished between a withdrawal from NATO, the military organization that was set up following the signing of the North Atlantic Treaty, and their continual adherence to the treaty itself, which under Article 9 provided for membership in the political body of the North Atlantic Council. This legal nicety was ignored by the substance of Gaullist policy, however. As the Gaullist deputy Michel Boscher explained to a meeting of the North Atlantic Assembly in November 1967: "It would be nonsense to wish, at the moment when a detente which is desired by all is coming into being, to make the Alliance play a political role that it does not possess."[12] The proper manner of pursuing detente, in the French view, was made explicit following the Kiesinger-de Gaulle consultations in Paris in February 1968. According to West German and French sources, "the French government has invited West Germany to develop a joint approach to European Communist countries, independent of the United States and Britain."[13] In short, de Gaulle hoped to lead the Germans toward detente, and presumably even achieve the reunification of Germany, without the assistance of the Atlantic Alliance, and in particular without "the Anglo-Saxons."

TESTING THE GAULLIST THESIS IN EASTERN EUROPE

This theory was given several practical tests. On his state visit to Poland in September 1967, de Gaulle urged his vision of Europe on Gomulka: French-Polish solidarity, de Gaulle held, was "comparable to no other in Europe"; like France, Poland "must be in the front ranks" of nations, therefore neither must be absorbed by "an enormous foreign mechanism"; the "center" of Europe was distinct from the "East," implying that Poland should liberate itself from Soviet hegemony and the Warsaw Pact as France had liberated itself from American hegemony and NATO; finally, Poland should join with France in agreeing upon a solution for the German problem. Gomulka answered point by point. French-Polish solidarity in the past was "unable to protect either Poland or France from the catastrophe of defeat and Hitlerian occupation." From these historic experiences, Gomulka said, Poland has drawn the "fundamental conclusion expressed in the adoption of the path of friendship and alliance with its greater neighbor of the East—the Soviet Union." The Warsaw Pact is "Poland's principal guarantee of security." As for the German problem, Gomulka insisted upon "acceptance of the existence of two equal German states," involving among other things, legal recognition of the G.D.R.[14]

There was one aspect of de Gaulle's concept of Europe, however, that Warsaw fully embraced: "Poland and France hold basically similar views concerning the solution of the problem of European security; it can be reached only with the agreement of the countries involved. This coincides with Polish theory and is compatible with de Gaulle's political line: The security of Europe is primarily the affair of Europeans—from the Atlantic to the Urals."[15] The solution of European problems should, indeed, be left to the Europeans, by excluding the United States and including the East Europeans and the Soviet Union, so that the terms of the settlement would be heavily influenced by Communist ambitions. Gomulka thus refused "to do a de Gaulle" with respect to the Warsaw Pact, but he was delighted with de Gaulle's attempted disruption of NATO and his effort to expel American power from Europe. Jean Lecanuet, a leader of the Democratic Center in France, aptly summed up de Gaulle's Polish mission in search of detente. It demonstrated, he said, "two fallacies: that France alone could guarantee the freedom of other countries or her own, and that the disintegration of the West would bring about the disintegration of the East."[16]

Rumania presented a more logical target for de Gaulle, because of the greater independence Bucharest had demonstrated toward Moscow. Yet de Gaulle's state visit to Rumania in May 1968 produced meager results. When there, de Gaulle again projected his familiar vision of a "European Europe" of the sovereign national states that could live beyond the influence of "outside hegemonies." He invited Rumania to seek national fulfillment by breaking out of the Eastern bloc, holding out the model of France, which, he said, was "disengaging herself, if not from her friendships with the West, from her Atlantic subordination, be it political, military or monetary." Rumanian sources, however, were quoted as saying that "Bucharest has no interest in deepening the split with the Soviet Union for the sake of vague general principles." Instead, it was maintained that Soviet-Rumanian relations would be examined pragmatically, as separate issues arose. And when the French Communist paper, *L'Humanité*, sought to embarrass de Gaulle by writing that he had come to Bucharest for the purpose of trying to detach Rumania from the Soviet Union, the Rumanian party chief, Ceausescu, denounced this story as "utterly untrue." The final joint communique, significantly, contained no mention of the division of Europe into two blocs, which de Gaulle had wished the Rumanian leaders to denounce, in concert with him. Ironically, the effect of de Gaulle's Rumanian trip was not to show how identical the two countries were, but rather how much farther France had broken with the West than Rumania had with the East.[17]

Even the dramatic Soviet invasion of Czechoslovakia in August 1968 did not budge de Gaulle from his position on detente, although it obviously shook the basic premises of his detente policy. To be meaningful to the Gaullist scheme, the Soviet-bloc nations of East Central Europe would have to emerge as independent actors, permitting the nations of Western Europe, under French leadership, to contract them out of the "double hegemonies" of the two blocs that divided Europe. At the same time, the Soviet Union itself would have to become less totalitarian and increasingly amenable to cooperation with France in building a "European Europe." The events in Czechoslovakia obviously undercut both of these preconditions. Following the invasion, de Gaulle was forced to admit that the Soviet-bloc states had not moved toward greater independence, nor had the Soviet Union basically transformed its character. He complained that the Soviet regime had chained "its satellites behind the walls of a crushing totalitarianism." He also acknowledged that the events in Czechoslovakia "are absurd when viewed in the perspective of European detente."

Upon further reflection it became obvious that de Gaulle had been pursuing two irreconcilable objectives. On the one hand he advocated the dissolution of military blocs and the reassertion of the independence of the satellite states in Eastern Europe, while on the other hand he sought to foster good relations with Moscow, which felt threatened by any increased freedom for the states in the Warsaw Pact.

With his detente policy in shambles and the Warsaw Pact very much intact, one might have reasoned that NATO still had useful functions to perform. However, de Gaulle simply bemoaned "the persistence of the Eastern bloc and consequently that of the Western bloc," and reaffirmed the wisdom of detaching France "from the military organization of NATO which subordinates the Europeans to the Americans." His own policy of national self-reliance, combined with bilateral contacts with the East that had sought to wish NATO and the Warsaw Pact out of existence, appeared "to have been momentarily thwarted," although it was still "consistent with the fundamental European realities."[18] The phantoms that de Gaulle called "realities" consisted of his own peculiar vision of what the future *should* become.

BUILDING A NEW EUROPE WITH OLD AND INADEQUATE MEANS

A Gaullist might argue that the rebuffs and setbacks to de Gaulle's policy toward Eastern Europe were only temporary, and that at some future time it would be possible to find Communist leaders who would share de Gaulle's image for remaking Europe. In order to pursue the analysis let us grant this seemingly remote premise so as to examine the validity of the Gaullist scheme, quite apart from the question of Communist ambitions.

Having, for the sake of argument, disposed of communism, the basic difficulty with the remainder of the Gaullist design for refashioning Europe is the one of relating the means available to the end sought. The Gaullist end, we are told, is "Europe in a state of equilibrium, peace and cooperation." This is to be achieved by means of a completely free-wheeling French diplomacy, by France as a "nation with free hands, whose policy is not being determined by any pressures from without." France must have maximum flexibility in maneuvering among power combinations that become increasingly possible as a bipolar power structure recedes. However, as the French political scientist, Pierre Hassner, observed, de Gaulle had reservations about extending his own code of detente behavior to others. "If it is good for the whole world that France should have free hands, it is not necessarily good for France that the whole world should have free hands." Equality in freedom of action for all would endanger French hegemonial designs. "By this standard detente must be limited and selective. Certain ties must be cut but others must be maintained or restored in place of the severed ones, if need be by a renewal of tensions. Thus France encourages Germany to imitate her in recovering her freedom from the United States, but not to imitate her all the way, to the point of 'not denying herself any kind of possibility' [as de Gaulle would say], including nuclear arms, 'the prerequisite of national independence.' "[19]

In another respect, the goals of a European settlement and a reunified Germany simply outran the French means available to bring them within reach. Ultimately, it is the Soviet Union that must release its hold on East Germany if the division of Germany is to be overcome on any terms other than those set by the Kremlin. And it is only by a continued engagement of American power, or perhaps more precisely of "the Anglo-Saxons," on the European continent that any prospect for a satisfactory European settlement can remain alive, except again unless it be on Soviet terms. The Soviet leaders knew very well that de Gaulle did not have it within his power to offer them a settlement, but they were happy to cultivate de Gaulle in the hope that he would so weaken Western cohesion that they might improve their chances of obtaining a favorable settlement from the United States, which in despair or disgust would abandon Europe to its own devices. But this is not how de Gaulle envisaged the bargaining power of France. Hassner describes the fantasy world of Gaullist France: "She suggests to Germany that she herself is in a better position than the United States to facilitate German reunification, and to the USSR that she is better placed to keep Germany from becoming dangerous. In fact, she can neither bring about the reunification of Germany nor guarantee Germany's continued denuclearization." It is here that one finds "a basic flaw in the French concept of detente. It lies in the double contradiction of trying to cast a player without trump cards in the central role, while coupling mobility for that player with minimum mobility for all the rest."

Beyond these difficulties was an even more profound contradiction. Detente will supposedly bring about international reconciliation and a new, stable international order. Yet, as Hassner pointed out, "in order to rebuild a stable and acceptable order, and thus establish a detente on bases which do not immediately produce fresh conflicts, it is indispensable to accept at least a minimum of permanence in one's obligations and hence limits to one's freedom of action."[20] Yet it was precisely de Gaulle's insistence upon keeping his hands free that rendered the prospect of a meaningful and lasting detente impossible. "One of the chief obstacles to the realization of the grand design is its author's inability to pass from detente to genuine entente and cooperation with anyone, through his refusal to relinquish his freedom of action, not only in the form of sovereignty, as an integrated alliance and community demand, but even in that of secrecy and surprise, which are demanded, at least to some degree, by an alliance of the classic type."[21] In short, the Gaullist concept of a detente moving toward a cohesive European entente was flawed by the basic premise of Gaullism, which is unbounded nationalism. No satisfactory international order ever was or ever will be founded upon this concept.

SOVIET MANIPULATION OF GAULLIST DETENTE THEMES

The Soviet leadership, particularly in the post-Khrushchev period, has been adept at popularizing and manipulating a variety of Gaullist detente themes: The Soviet threat to Europe has disappeared; nationalism in the West is a positive good to be glorified, except, of course, in the case of West Germany where the opposite is true; movement toward greater cohesion in the West is bad and must be opposed, as in the case of supranationalism in the European Community or integration in NATO; NATO is obsolete and an obstacle to detente and should therefore be disbanded; a European settlement is a matter for the Europeans, which means excluding, or at least attempting to exclude, "the Anglo-Saxons" from any future political and security arrangements for the European continent. This coincidence of views did not, of course, make the Kremlin Gaullist, nor de Gaulle a Communist, since each sought to exploit these ideas for different ends. Yet the practical effect had often been for one to reinforce the appeal of the other.*

The Kremlin embraced with special vigor, and even refined, the Gaullist image of NATO that flowed from his detente policy: Eliminate NATO and one will create conditions for a peaceful settlement of Europe's problems. As an inducement toward this end, the Soviet leaders proposed mutual pactocide. The dissolution of NATO, they promised, would be accompanied by the disbanding of the Warsaw Pact.

This promise had, in fact, been incorporated in the text of the treaty that created the Warsaw Pact. Article 11 had stipulated: "Should a system of collective security be established in Europe, and a General European Treaty of Collective Security concluded for this purpose . . . the present Treaty shall cease to be operative. . . ."[22] The Russians first advanced the idea of a general European collective security system at the Berlin conference of the Big Four Foreign Ministers in February 1954, when their aim was to prevent the Federal Republic from rearming and joining NATO. Having failed in these objectives, they devised the Warsaw Pact in May 1955 as a response to the West German accession to NATO and as a means of offsetting its political impact. But beyond that they conceived of the Warsaw Pact as a bargaining counter to be traded away in the mutual dissolution of military blocs, which would presumably be superseded by a new European security system. The Soviet leaders set out a detailed proposal for the creation of this security system and the dissolution of the two military blocs at the Geneva summit conference of July 1955.

The Soviet military position in Eastern Europe would not have suffered with the disbandment of the Warsaw Pact, since Moscow already had a system of bilateral military treaties with its European

---

*Soviet and Gaullist policies not only coincided on significant foreign policy issues, but as noted in Chapter 3 the French Communist Party made important gains in French domestic politics in 1967. The Communists' newlyfound respectability in French public life was in large measure an inevitable, though perhaps inadvertent, byproduct of de Gaulle's pursuit of detente, which often cast him as an uncritical associate of the Kremlin. This relationship might have continued if de Gaulle had not found it necessary to make the French Communists the scapegoat for the May-June "events" of 1968.

satellites, which also had military alliances with each other. All this made the multilateral ties of the Warsaw Pact unnecessary. Moreover, East European Communist leaders have explicitly stated that their network of alliances anchored in Moscow would continue to exist, even after the dissolution of NATO and the Warsaw Pact.[23]

The original Soviet ploy in the mid 1950s was made from the essentially defensive posture of attempting to prevent the expansion and strengthening of NATO. When it was revived about a decade later, it was fashioned as an offensive weapon that could be used to capitalize on the controversy and disarray into which de Gaulle had thrust the Atlantic Alliance. The timing of the second major anti-NATO campaign was significant: De Gaulle's final assault against NATO, launched in February 1966, had by summer led to a full and acrimonious dispute with the Alliance. On July 4-5 the Political Consultative Committee of the Warsaw Pact met in Bucharest and issued a lengthy declaration that systematically attempted to maximize the fissures in the West. "The United States aggressive circles," the declaration asserted, "are, with the help of the North Atlantic military bloc and the military machine created by it, trying further to deepen the division of Europe, to keep up the arms race, to increase international tensions and to impede the establishment and development of normal ties between the West European and East European states."[24] The reconciliation of European states, East and West, was allegedly obstructed by the continued existence of NATO. Therefore, "the need has matured for steps to be taken towards the relaxation, above all, of military tension in Europe." This could be achieved by "the simultaneous dissolution of the existing military alliances." Recognizing that this ambitious proposal might not be implemented in a single step, a less-far-reaching alternative was also advanced: "If, however, the member states of the North Atlantic Treaty are still not ready to accept the complete dissolution of both alignments, the states that have signed this declaration consider that it is already now expedient to reach an understanding on the abolition of the military organizations, both of the North Atlantic Pact and the Warsaw Treaty." Here the Communists picked up precisely the distinction de Gaulle had earlier drawn between the military instrumentality of NATO and the North Atlantic Treaty and indicated that they would be satisfied, as an initial measure, if the other NATO states imitated de Gaulle's behavior by abandoning the NATO military organization. And in the absence of military alliances, how would security be provided for? "Their place ought to be taken by a European security system."[25]

"A European security system" turned out to be a Communist reworking of de Gaulle's "European Europe." "The problem of European security can be solved by the joint efforts of the *European states*." The declaration left no doubt about the need for Europe to break all trans-Atlantic ties. "The European states are capable of solving the questions of relations between them without outside interference."[26] The irrelevance of the United States, and other NATO members beyond the European continent, to the construction of the security system was pointed up by a Soviet commentator who hailed "the establishment of friendly contacts and extensive cooperation between the two largest powers on the continent—the Soviet Union and France—who bear special responsibility for European peace and security."[27] This was, in part, meant to flatter de Gaulle and feed his animus against "the Anglo-Saxons," but it also reflected the permanently subservient position intended for Germany. The Bucharest declaration called for recognition of all existing frontiers, including the Oder-Neisse, and of "the fact of the existence of two German states." Sanctifying the status quo would foreclose the presumably revanchist demands of West Germany, which, in addition, should be denied entry into any international scheme for nuclear sharing, such as the then proposed multilateral nuclear force. In the very distant future, the German people were offered the prospect of reunification "through a gradual rapprochement between the two sovereign German states." Just how the future fusion of two sovereign German states could be accomplished was left vague, while the immediate aim of recognizing two separate Germanies was stressed repeatedly. Taken together, this program would bring about "the normalization of the situation in Europe" and foster detente.[28]

A conference of European Communist parties at Karlovy Vary in April 1967 substantially reaffirmed these positions, and added a few flourishes. West Germany must be precluded from any opportunity "to gain access to nuclear arms in any form, either European, multilateral or Atlantic," while relations must be normalized between two sovereign German states and "West Berlin as a separate entity." In this document, the distant prospect of German reunification was not even mentioned. The central proposal remained the demand for "a simultaneous liquidation of both military alliances" for "the purpose of achieving a detente and strengthening the security of the peoples of our continent."[29]

The issues raised by the Bucharest and Karlovy Vary declarations became the subject of prolonged, complex East-West negotiations involving many parties, although the Bonn-Moscow tie formed the central core of these relationships. With the entry of the Social Democrats into the grand coalition government of Chancellor Kiesinger in December 1966, a cautious, muted dialogue was begun with the Kremlin. This quickly developed into an open and active *Ostpolitik* when Willy Brandt became Chancellor in October 1969. In short order Bonn signed the Moscow Treaty of August 1970 with the Soviet Union and the Warsaw Treaty of December 1970 with Poland. The status of Berlin was clarified in an agreement of the four occupying powers signed in September 1971. These accords cleared the way for agreements between the Federal Republic and the G.D.R., first on regulating intra-German traffic and then in December 1972 to the so-called Basic Treaty between the two German states.

In the process of reaching these agreements both sides made concessions. The Federal Republic recognized the existing political frontiers, including the Oder-Neisse border of Poland. Bonn also recognized the existence of the G.D.R. as the second, independent German state, although not in the same manner as it would recognize a foreign country. Thus the two German states exchanged "representatives," not ambassadors, and acknowledged the special nature of their inter-German relations in such matters as trade and post and telephone arrangements. The future option of German national unity was retained, and the rights and responsibilities of the Four Powers were reaffirmed, with the result that the solution of the "national question" remained open.

By coming to terms with the existing situation in Eastern Europe, Moscow dropped its claim that the Warsaw Pact states were threatened by an aggressive West German nationalism, and so it ceased calling the Federal Republic "revanchist." Moreover, since West German ratification of the Moscow Treaty was made contingent upon an improvement in the position of West Berlin, the Communists abandoned their demand for the recognition of West Berlin as a separate political entity. Instead, a Four Power agreement affirmed the existing ties between West Germany and West Berlin and provided for West Germany to represent the interests of West Berlin abroad.

Finally, the Communist leaders were forced to abandon their effort to confine the consideration of a future European security system to a "European Europe," a la de Gaulle. It soon became painfully evident that, France aside, no West European country would attend a European Security Conference at which such a security system might be examined, except on the condition that the United States and Canada be explicitly invited as full participants. In June 1970 the Foreign Ministers of the Warsaw Pact accordingly extended such an invitation to the trans-Atlantic partners of NATO Europe.[30]

Left unchanged was the demand for a new all-European security system, in which both military blocs would be dissolved. Following the Soviet invasion of Czechoslovakia in 1968, the Warsaw Pact appeared to have been a useful instrument in bringing a wayward state back into the fold of the "socialist commonweath," and so the call for its disappearance was temporarily muted. The declaration of the Warsaw Pact states in Budapest on March 17, 1969, for example, called only for the Soviet version of a European collective security system, without mentioning the need to end military blocs.[31] However, a month later *Pravda* published a "Declaration of the Soviet Government," which tied the Budapest statement to the earlier, more explicit declarations of Bucharest in 1966 and Karlovy Vary in 1967 and then went on to condemn "the continued existence of the aggressive NATO bloc."[32]

It became apparent that the earlier demand was still fully upheld when an international conclave of Communist parties meeting in Moscow in June 1969 declared: "The interests of world peace call for the disbandment of military blocs. . . . A genuine guarantee of the security and one of the conditions for the progress of each European country must be the establishment in Europe of an effective system of security founded on relations of equality and mutual respect among all the states in the continent, on the combined efforts of all European peoples. In this light the socialist countries have already declared for the simultaneous dissolution of NATO and the Warsaw Treaty."[33] Similarly, Soviet Party chief Leonid Brezhnev told the 24th Congress of the CPSU in March 1971: "We reaffirm our readiness, which has been jointly expressed by the member-countries of the defensive

Warsaw Treaty, for the simultaneous abrogation of this Treaty and of the North Atlantic Alliance, or—as a first step—for the dismantling of their military organizations."[34] This sentiment was again echoed by the Political Consultative Committee of the Warsaw Pact in April 1974.[35]

EUROPE WITHOUT NATO

What would be some of the consequences of the proposed mutual pactocide? One function of NATO has been to keep the German problem in bounds and make it more manageable by incorporating German armed strength within the larger multilateral NATO entity. The West German armed forces, the most powerful in existence among the European members of NATO, have been completely integrated into the NATO command structure. The disbandment of NATO would necessarily cast these powerful forces into a purely national mold and require the creation of a German General Staff that would direct their use for nationally conceived ends. Since the dissolution of NATO would almost certainly also mean the end of an American military presence in Europe, the West Germans would remain unchallenged as the dominant conventional military force in Western Europe. Would not the Soviet leadership and de Gaulle, both of whom sought to control the development of German military power, have found that the success of their attacks upon NATO would have brought about precisely what they professed to abhor?

The departure of American troops from Europe would also drastically alter the East-West equation in both conventional and nuclear forces in Central Europe. The West Europeans have always wanted Americans on hand both to help deter or defend against conventional attack, as well as to keep hold of a friendly hostage, so that the instant involvement of American troops would insure American nuclear retaliation against a Soviet nuclear strike. The dissolution of the Warsaw Pact, on the other hand, would bring no such dramatic shifts in the power structure of the East. As NATO Secretary General Brosio properly recalled, at the time the Soviet pactocide offer was made: "A veil is drawn over the fact that the Soviet Union has already concluded a network of bilateral pacts with its allies, such as to render the Warsaw Pact superfluous and make the dependence of the Eastern countries upon the Soviet Union even more entire."[36] Soviet troops would doubtless remain in East Germany, since it is supported by Soviet bayonets. But even if Soviet troops were thinned out in Eastern Europe, in exchange for a withdrawal of U.S. and other forces from Western Europe, units of the Soviet Army could be easily and quickly reintroduced with little fanfare, while the reentry of American and other allied troops into Western Europe would be a major undertaking both in terms of reversing a political commitment and as a logistical military enterprise. Furthermore, the open way in which the recommitment of troops to Western Europe would have to be carried out would not serve to avoid a crisis, but rather to precipitate one. Foreknowledge that Western troop reentry would stimulate a major crisis would further inhibit their reintroduction, thereby leaving the separate countries of Western Europe increasingly exposed to Soviet political influence, which would be backed by a disequilibrium of military power.

This imbalance would be especially marked in the case of nuclear weapons. The 700-odd medium-range ballistic missiles stationed along the Western border of the Soviet Union and in Eastern Europe would still be aimed at all the major targets of Western Europe. Meanwhile, American forces in Europe that had been an earnest pledge of the American nuclear guarantee would have gone home and taken with them the tactical nuclear weapons stationed in Western Europe under the two-key system. The remaining French and British national nuclear forces would not provide credible deterrents if used alone, since the price of such use would be certain national suicide. Despite the questionable worth of such a small national nuclear deterrent, the West Germans might feel compelled to strike out for one, given their exposed and defenseless position. This would involve breaking West German treaty commitments to abstain from creating a national nuclear force and would certainly set off violent reactions with unforeseeable consequences. Thus the only certainty is that detente and peaceful accommodation would not ensue from the dissolution of NATO and the Warsaw Pact.

The West Germans, on the other hand, might well be persuaded of the dangers and futility of building a national deterrent, but this need not create stability in Europe. In these circumstances, the Kremlin might find the temptation of nuclear blackmail too great to resist. With overwhelming Soviet force arrayed against them, the West Germans might succumb to Soviet threats, while hoping, in the bargain, to salvage the reunification of their nation, even if achieved on Soviet terms. The shock waves of this realignment would spread over the remainder of the European continent and, in one fashion or another, subordinate it to Soviet control. Mutual pactocide, it would seem, is a matter of form but not substance for the Warsaw Pact, while for NATO it involves both form and the essence of power.

The replacement of the confrontation of military blocs by a pan-European collective security system appears to be an alluring idea that has, in fact, aroused widespread interest and appeal. The difficulty with this general theoretical proposition lies not in the idea of collective security, but in how it should be implemented. Collective security, as an abstract principle, was incorporated into the Covenant of the League of Nations and the United Nations Charter. It only became an effective force, however, when it was given embodiment in some specific alliance that was formed to counter a particular threat to the peace. Nor, in the nuclear age, is it sufficient to say that everyone shares an interest in avoiding nuclear war, so that military alliances have become superfluous. As one commentator has noted,

> the trouble is that this common interest in avoiding nuclear war can be made into a force for peace only by creating a situation in which any hostile act creates, or seems to create, an unacceptable risk of escalation to nuclear war. This . . . is precisely the function of the Atlantic Alliance and its military dispositions, which the advocates of European collective security would dismantle. A collective security guarantee directed only against an unnamed "aggressor," and without the support of an American military presence, would not make peace in Europe more stable. Nor would it serve the cause of "world peace" or "reduction of tensions" which its advocates profess. On the contrary, it would weaken deterrence by weakening the seriousness of the guarantee and making the risk of nuclear escalation more doubtful.[37]

Even if the Soviet version of a collective security system for Europe did not lead to war, its political effects would be profound. Manlio Brosio observed as NATO Secretary General: "A system of collective security, where every country is supposed to guarantee the security of every other country, risks leading to a situation where no country guarantees any other any more. In Europe, such a system, without a united Western Europe and without the guarantee of the United States, would lead to the inevitable predominance of the Soviet Union over all the continent."[38]

This new configuration of power would at least lead to a Soviet "solution" for the German problem. Brezhnev had envisioned it when he said in October 1969: "Looking back on the glorious path travelled by the G.D.R. in the past twenty years, one can see very clearly that it is here that the prototype of the future is being created for all Germans."[39] Such a united Germany would be the core around which a united Europe could emerge, once Europe had been freed of antagonistic blocs. A Soviet political commentator candidly acknowledged that

> the socialist states have never regarded the establishment, existence and confrontation of coalitions as the last word in political wisdom, or the "balance of forces" between them as a genuine guarantee of peace and security for any European state or the whole of Europe. [On the contrary,] Marxist-Leninists believe that in the long term . . . the different state systems can and will be overcome, and not through "convergence," but on a socialist basis, and then there will be true grounds to speak of a united Europe in the broadest and fullest sense of the word. Lenin repeatedly pointed to this socialist prospect for the whole of Europe, to this solution of the question of its genuine unity."[40]

In the Soviet view, the ultimate objective of a European detente is a united Soviet Europe.

DETENTE AND COMPETITION IN NUCLEAR ARMS

Soviet detente policy regarding the political future of Europe has tried to exclude, or at least minimize, American involvement. The Soviet leaders thus found it expedient to magnify the status of de Gaulle and manipulate the Gaullist concept of a "European

Europe." On the other hand, Soviet detente policy arising out of the global strategic relationship with the United States has been almost totally confined to the nuclear confrontation between the two superpowers, to the neglect of a role for Europe. This aspect of Soviet detente policy has been conducted with little regard for Gaullist pretensions of grandeur, since it has been based on a realistic assessment of power. Instead, a bilateral relationship on strategic questions evolved between Moscow and Washington, leaving all of Europe, including Paris, on the sidelines. The striking dichotomy between these Soviet detente policies nevertheless served a common purpose, since the successful execution of each approach would have divorced the United States from its European allies.

It would appear necessary to ask whether some misconceptions have grown up regarding the nature of the strategic detente that the United States thought it had reached with the Soviet Union. It was the terrifying experience of the Cuban missile crisis of October 1962 that generated the initial impulse toward mutual restraint and introduced an element of detente between the nuclear superpowers. In the aftermath of the missile crisis, President Kennedy called for a reexamination of the traditional attitudes of East-West hostility, which he held must be made subordinate to the common interest humanity shares in avoiding nuclear war. "Both the United States and its allies, and the Soviet Union and its allies, have a mutually deep interest in a just and genuine peace and in halting the arms race. . . . Let us not be blind to our differences, but let us also direct attention to our common interests and to the means by which those differences can be resolved."[41] To say that the United States and the Soviet Union "have a mutually deep interest in a just and genuine peace" implied that they shared common political goals. This fed hopes for a far-reaching accommodation on the gamut of issues that divided East and West. Agreement on the test ban treaty, for example, touched off a wave of wishful thinking throughout the West, which in some places has since become permanent, about the presumed transformation in the Soviet regime and in Soviet aims.

The post-Stalinist leaders undeniably introduced significant changes in the style of life at home, while losing control of a once monolithic Communist movement abroad. They have also explicitly recognized the dangers of nuclear war and have therefore introduced a measure of caution into aspects of their foreign policy. Taken together these innovations have fostered the comfortable illusion that the Soviet Union has become just another nation-state maneuvering amidst the anarchy of international politics, willing to accept political compromises as the price for a stable world order. The reality is somewhat harsher. The Stalinist tyranny has been modified, but Soviet political life remains conspiratorial in nature, with political power lodged in a self-perpetuating elite that continuously seeks to repress the expression of unapproved ideas and innovations bubbling up in Soviet society. The Soviet leaders are also surely convinced that they must remain true to the principles of Communist internationalism, as they interpret those principles. At the bedrock of these tenets is the belief in the irreconcilability of the Communist and non-Communist political systems and in the inevitable, though perhaps long-delayed, demise of the non-Communist world. For the West, the fact that there are now many communisms does not eliminate the Communist challenge, but rather calls for a more differentiated and complicated response.

An accurate reading of experience with detente would reveal that two different processes have been going on simultaneously. There is mutual recognition of an interest in preventing nuclear war by seeking agreement upon measures of crisis management and arms control. This community of interest between the superpowers, however, is essentially negative; it has had little effect upon reaching agreement on common programs of a positive nature for a political detente. Alongside the pursuit of overlapping negative interests in avoiding nuclear catastrophe, there has continued a very sharp and very real global power conflict between two adversaries that hold incompatible images of a desirable international order. Kennedy did, in fact, try to guard against undue conclusions being drawn from his detente efforts. "A pause in the cold war," he warned, "is not a lasting peace, and a detente does not equal disarmament. The United States must continue to seek a relaxation of tensions, but we have no cause to relax our vigilance." As Kennedy properly pointed out, "there are still major areas of tension and conflict, from Berlin to Cuba to Southeast Asia. The United States and the Soviet Union still have wholly different concepts of the world, its freedom, its future."[42] These qualifications, however, tended to be drowned in the welling floodtide of hopes that peace had finally broken out.

There was one illusion that the Kennedy administration itself apparently entertained about the nature of its detente with the Soviet Union. President Kennedy declared that both sides not only had a mutual interest in a just and genuine peace, but also that both sides were interested "in halting the arms race." The main point of the test ban treaty, in Kennedy's view, was that it represented a move toward his goal of stabilizing the international equilibrium of power. Kennedy looked upon the test ban, Arthur Schlesinger informs us, as an indication of "a mutual willingness to halt the weapons race more or less where it was. In the Soviet case this meant acquiescence in American nuclear superiority. . . . The Russian willingness to accept such margins showed not only a post-Cuba confidence in American restraint, but a new understanding of the theories of stable nuclear deterrence."[43] The United States doubtless wished to believe that detente meant stopping, or at least greatly slowing down, the arms race and reaching a stable deterrence, based on American nuclear superiority. The only difficulty with this attractive prospect is that the Kremlin never accepted it.

The Berlin crisis in the spring of 1961 had already dramatically raised the possibility of a nuclear conflict mushrooming from the confrontation of Soviet and American tanks at "Checkpoint Charlie" on the sector border in Berlin. Here the Soviet advantage in ground troops was offset by the decisive superiority of American strategic weapons that could have been called upon if a local clash had escalated to nuclear proportions. Faced with this disparity of forces, Marshall Shulman speculated that "in the forefront of the consciousness of the Soviet leaders . . . was the conviction that the strategic military superiority of the United States must be overcome as soon as possible." In September 1961 the Kremlin began a series of nuclear weapons tests that continued through 1962, during which time efforts were apparently made to increase the meager Soviet stockpile of ICBMs. "The most daring effort to find a short-cut toward strategic parity was, of course, the abortive emplacement of medium and intermediate range missiles (of which the Soviet Union had an abundance) in Cuba. The targeting of the United States from Cuba would have enabled the Soviets to perform a strategic function, substituting for their deficiency in in intercontinental missiles."[44]

The withdrawal of Soviet missiles from Cuba only reinforced the Kremlin's determination to attain strategic parity in ICBMs. As their production run hit full stride, from October 1966 to October 1967, they more than doubled the operational Soviet ICBM force, turning out more than one new missile a day.[45] During the same period, the Kremlin started building an antiballistic missile system (ABM). This represented a significant push upward in the spiraling nuclear arms race, which Washington was eager to tamp down.

Secretary of Defense Robert McNamara's announcement on September 18, 1967 of the intention to build a "thin" ABM system[46] was made with the hope of minimizing, if not abandoning, this project, if only agreement could be reached with the Kremlin about the futility of both sides constructing ballistic missile defenses. McNamara's arguments had persuaded President Johnson to approach the Soviet leaders in December 1966 with a bid for talks aimed at limiting ABM systems. In March 1967 Moscow approved the idea in principle, adding that offensive missiles should also be included in these discussions—a provision that President Johnson promptly accepted. As time passed and the talks did not begin, McNamara seized upon the occasion of the Johnson-Kosygin summit conference at Glassboro, N.J. in June 1967 to appeal directly to the Soviet Premier to take action that could stop the dangerous and enormously costly missile race from getting out of hand.[47] The Soviet bureaucratic machine ground exceedingly slowly, but finally at the end of June 1968 Foreign Minister Gromyko publicly indicated that the Soviet government was prepared to enter into discussions with the United States about the limitation of offensive and defensive missile systems.[48] President Johnson responded on July 1, at the signing of the nuclear Non-Proliferation Treaty (NPT) by declaring a willingness to commence "in the nearest future" Soviet-U.S. discussions about the limitation and reduction of both offensive and defensive missiles.[49]

President Johnson hailed the agreement to talk about missile limitations as another significant contribution to a growing pattern of Soviet-American understanding that could have far-reaching political implications. Just prior to this announcement, he had returned to Glassboro to dramatize the importance he attached to his meeting with Kosygin of the previous year. He pointed with pride to various commitments recently undertaken or that were about to be concluded: the treaty prohibiting nuclear weapons in outer space, the NPT, an astronaut rescue agreement, a Soviet-U.S. consular convention, a Soviet-U.S. air agreement, as well as a renewal of the Soviet-U.S. cultural exchange agreement. "We believe genuinely," the President said, "that every one of those steps is a step toward peace." He noted that areas of disagreement lingered on, "but in the last year we have made some progress. We have proved that we can agree, can agree in part, on some occasions at least on some issues. We have proved that our two countries can behave as responsible members of the family of nations." Still addressing his Glassboro audience, Johnson exuded optimism: "I believe that the two great powers who met here . . . last year have begun—however haltingly— to bridge the gulf that has separated them for a quarter of a century."

This appraisal of the detente process went far beyond the negative community of interest that both states had recognized in their efforts to avoid nuclear war through crisis management and arms control measures. It staked out the hope for agreement on positive programs that would result in a political rapprochement between the superpowers. "There are many other fields in which we should begin to build new programs of cooperation." Johnson specifically suggested as points of departure: joint ventures in an international biological program on the human environment, joint participation in a global satellite communications system, cooperation in exploring natural resources on the ocean floor and in the great rain forests of the tropics, as well as extending the existing Soviet-U.S. cooperative efforts in the Antartic to the Artic.[50]* In short, the superpowers should collaborate wherever possible for the benefit of all mankind. This vision of the future assumed that both powers would share a fund of common values and hold a common interest in promoting world order.

The plea for extensive East-West cooperation found an unexpected response from a highly unofficial source in Moscow. The

---

*President Johnson made a number of statements at this time in which he read general political implications into limited agreements. For example, on the Consular Convention: "We can hope that this treaty between the Soviet Union and the United States will be a sign for the future. It could help to establish a pattern of progress: in disarmament, in space, in science, in the arts, and —I hope—in a broadening area of politics." (White House Press Release on the Occasion of the Ratification of the Soviet-American Consular Convention, June 13, 1968, Department of State *Bulletin*, 59, no. 1515: 40.) On the Non-Proliferation Treaty: "I consider this treaty to be the most important international agreement limiting nuclear arms since the nuclear age began. . . . There is hope that the treaty will mark the beginning of a new phase in the quest for order and moderation in international affairs." (The President's Message to the Senate of the United States, July 9, 1968, Department of State *Bulletin*, 59, no. 1518: 126-27.)

prominent Soviet nuclear physicist, Andrei Sakharov, had privately circulated a bold essay on the urgent need for Soviet-American collaboration, and during July 1968 managed to have its text smuggled out of the Soviet Union and published in the United States. All issues, he insisted, must be judged from the perspective of how mankind can preserve its civilization, which is imperiled by nuclear war arising from nationalism, racism, militarism, and intolerant ideologies. Man is also threatened by overpopulation and catastrophic hunger, as well as by environmental pollution that will have unforeseeable consequences for the conditions of life on our planet. Man's creative thought everywhere must be mobilized for the mastery of these immense common challenges, and every impediment to such thought must be eliminated. The world can no longer afford "stupefaction from the narcotic of 'mass culture' and bureaucratized dogmatism, nor a spreading of mass myths that put entire peoples and continents under the power of cruel and treacherous demagogues." Therefore, "any action increasing the division of mankind, and preaching of the incompatibility of world ideologies and nations is madness and a crime. Only universal cooperation under conditions of intellectual freedom ... will preserve civilization." Sakharov called for an "ever increasing coexistence and collaboration between the two systems and the two superpowers" that would result in their convergence upon the principles of democratic socialism, and by the year 2000 would lead to the creation of a world government. While this would require important modifications in American society, they would be minor compared to Sakharov's forthright demand for the total extirpation of the Stalinist legacy in the Soviet Union. Writing with an extraordinary display of personal courage, he pictured, among various remedies, the demise of the dictatorship of the Communist Party and its replacement by a pluralistic democracy.[51]

The Soviet leadership responded promptly to this threat to its existence. Though not mentioning Sakharov by name, his arguments were taken up and answered one by one. An *Izvestia* article on the issues facing the world during the remainder of the twentieth century attributed the threat of nuclear war overhanging mankind exclusively to the forces of Western imperialism. Overpopulation and hunger could only be conquered when the people of the underdeveloped world followed the example of the Soviet Union and adopted its social and political system. Conservation and renewal of natural resources on a global scale would have to be based on "a scientifically planned regulation of resource extraction and production throughout the world. All this requires changes in the social climate of the entire nonsocialist part of the world." As to the increasing convergence of the superpowers, *Izvestia* reaffirmed that "socialism and capitalism, the two fundamentally different world systems, are developing in diametrically opposed directions. . . . The struggle between two basic tendencies, two opposing world forces— capitalism and socialism—permeates the course of history in the last third of the century." Sakharov's vision of a world government by the year 2000 was therefore totally rejected. Instead, the "revolutionary currents, whose guiding force is found in the socialist countries, led by Marxist-Leninist parties, comprise the mighty power that will bring all countries into the orbit of socialism and open the way for harmonious socialist action on a global scale."[52] As if to dramatize the determination of the Kremlin to brook no challenge to the Communist Party's monopoly of power, or to efforts to subvert or compromise its ideology, this pronouncement was followed ten days later by the Soviet invasion of Czechoslovakia.

Since the democratization program in Czechoslovakia was seeking to lift the heavy hand of Party controls over broad areas of life, the invasion forced many people to reconsider their easy assumptions about the willingness of the Soviet regime to move in the direction of a pluralistic, liberal democracy. Such a move, as Sakharov rightly understood, was a necessary precondition for a Soviet-American political rapprochement and for the broadly based collaboration between East and West that would be required to save mankind for disaster.

The shock of the Soviet invasion even placed in jeopardy the delicate arrangements that had so laboriously been pieced together on issues relating to the negative community of interest that the superpowers had evolved in trying to avoid nuclear war. The opening of Soviet-American talks on limiting offensive and defensive missiles was scheduled to be announced on August 21, but the Soviet action against Czechoslovakia, begun the preceding night, caused its postponement. Along with this, plans for another Johnson-Kosygin summit conference went down the drain.

Soon thereafter Foreign Minister Gromyko defended Soviet action in Czechoslovakia before the United Nations, and at the same time he renewed the Soviet offer to talk about the limitation of missiles. Secretary of State Rusk, however, struck a different note in his address to the United Nations General Assembly: "Let us say very plainly to the Soviet Union: The road to detente is the road to the Charter," which had been so callously ignored by the massive Soviet armed intervention.[53]

It was not until November 1969 that the Strategic Arms Limitations Talks (SALT) were finally convened. The complexity of the issues dictated a cautious pace, and by early 1971 the inability to make progress toward a comprehensive agreement on both offensive and defensive weapons systems threatened to stalemate the negotiations. At that point direct intervention by President Nixon with the Soviet leaders produced the understanding of May 20, 1971, which recognized that agreement on regulating all offensive strategic missiles was not within reach, and that consequently they would seek an interim agreement on offensive weapons that would freeze only selected categories at agreed levels. Defensive weapons proved easier to negotiate, so that the understanding anticipated a permanent solution for ABMs.[54] This was the form the SALT agreements took when they were concluded the following year, on May 26, 1972, on the occasion of Nixon's summit meeting with the Soviet leaders in Moscow.[55]

The fact that the ABM agreement limited each side to no more than 200 launchers at two locations meant that both parties had abandoned the hope of trying to defend their populations against a nuclear attack. This institutionalized the condition of mutual assured destruction. The likelihood of a first strike attempt by either side was also rendered improbable, since both sides acknowledged the ability to destroy each other even after absorbing a first strike. Accordingly the offensive missile package froze the land- and sea-based strategic missiles of both sides, with the Soviet Union having a lead in both categories.

Such a gap would have existed even without an agreement, since the United States had completed deployment of its Minuteman ICBMs and Polaris submarines in 1967, while the Soviet Union was engaged in the rapid build up of strategic weapons on land and sea right up to the signing of the SALT I agreement in 1972. Without an agreement the numerical gap would have become steadily worse for the United States.

There were other disparities as well. The megatonnage of some Soviet missiles vastly exceeded anything in the American nuclear arsenal, while the American possession of multiple independently targetable reentry vehicles (MIRVs) gave the United States a large lead in deliverable warheads. In addition, the agreements did not deal with manned bombers, in which the United States had a substantial lead.

The overall balance struck by the agreements was one of relative parity. However, the agreements allowed for qualitative improvements in both nuclear arsenals. Thus it was recognized that it would only be a matter of time until the Soviet missiles would be fitted with MIRVs, thereby offsetting the American advantage in deliverable warheads. In fact, slightly more than a year later, in August 1973, the Pentagon announced that the Soviet Union had successfully flight-tested MIRVed missiles. Given the greater number of Soviet strategic missiles allowed, the SALT I agreements appeared to guarantee that at some future point there would be a permanent Soviet advantage both in strategic missiles and in warheads.

The Nixon-Brezhnev meeting in Washington in June 1973 produced a joint statement of intentions to accelerate the negotiations on a permanent treaty on offensive strategic weapons with the aim of reaching a conclusion some time during 1974.[56] When the two leaders met a year later in Moscow they were obliged to admit that this had been an unrealistic expectation. Instead of a permanent treaty limiting offensive nuclear arms, the best they could agree upon was an extension of the life of the interim agreement from 1977 to 1985.

The only nuclear weapons accords signed were more a matter of form than substance. Both parties decided to limit themselves to one instead of two ABM sites. But then both had already concluded that they would not build a second ABM site in any event. They also agreed to prohibit underground nuclear tests exceeding 150 kilotons after March 31, 1976. At this point, presumably both sides would have carried out all the tests needed for the family of weapons then under development. While it would not affect the current generation of MIRVs, it might, however, affect the next.[57]

The possibility of reaching a comprehensive agreement controlling offensive nuclear weapons seemed to be beyond reach until President Ford met Brezhnev at Vladivostok in November 1974. There a conceptual breakthrough was achieved when both sides accepted in principle that they would each agree to a limit of 2400 strategic delivery vehicles (ICBMs, SLBMs, and bombers) and that within this armory 1320 missiles could be MIRVed. This would negate the prospect left by SALT I of an eventual, permanent Soviet advantage in both missiles and warheads, although the United States would have to resume its missile building program in order to reach the agreed limit. In the short run this agreement, which was advertised as "putting a cap on the arms race," therefore sanctioned a new strategic buildup, although over the long run it would, if adhered to, limit further production of strategic weapons after 1985.*

Under this agreement the Soviet Union would still retain its advantage in the greater megatonnage or throw weight of many of its missiles. Thus while both sides agreed that they would only MIRV 1320 missiles, the larger Soviet missiles could be fitted with a greater number of multiple warheads than was the case with smaller American missiles. Exactly how great this Soviet advantage will be can only be a matter of speculation. The American negotiators had long sought in vain to get Soviet agreement for on-site inspection for MIRVed missiles. There is simply no way to verify the number of multiple warheads deployed on a MIRVed missile through the means sanctioned by the SALT agreements, namely through nationally operated satellite reconnaissance. Unless one is actually able to go around and open missile nose cones so as to count the number of warheads they contain, the count of missile sites by satellite reconnaissance is inadequate and misleading.

Furthermore, it would remain extremely difficult to monitor research and development efforts of the various weapons systems, which the SALT agreements freely sanction. There is always the possibility of a technological breakthrough in the qualitative improvement of nuclear weapons, which could upset the seeming stability of a condition of parity. Thus detente, even when reduced to its strictly negative aspect of trying to avoid nuclear catastrophe, can prove to have a very fragile nature.

The way in which arms control arrangements may be in danger of being overturned by the dynamics of technological breakthroughs in weapons development is perhaps best illustrated by the efforts to ban nuclear weapons from outer space.

In October 1963, soon after the signing of the partial test ban

---

*In response to widespread criticism, the Vladivostok accord was amended to allow for the possibility of nuclear arms reductions before 1985.

treaty, American and Soviet representatives vigorously supported a U.N. resolution that called on all states to refrain from placing in orbit around the earth any objects carrying nuclear weapons or other weapons of mass destruction. This principle was elaborated in a treaty regulating the use of outer space, signed in January 1967, again with Soviet and American sponsorship and adherence.

While the treaty represented an effort to control competition in arms between the superpowers, its restricted scope could not offer the basis for extravagant hopes. Article 4 did not prohibit deployment in space of weapons not capable of mass destruction, such as antisatellite or antimissile weapons that did not contain nuclear warheads, nor did it ban military support activities in space, such as command and control stations, manned orbiting laboratories, weather modifying devices, and the like. Finally, it did not restrict the testing or use of nuclear missiles that would pass through space on route to their targets, so long as these missiles were not placed in full orbit.

At the moment the treaty was signed, American intelligence discovered that the Soviet Union was testing a delivery vehicle for nuclear weapons with a trajectory that took it into outer space, from where it was targeted, before striking the earth. This fractional orbital bombardment system (FOBS) provided a shorter flight time for its nuclear missile than an ICBM and therefore made defense against it more difficult. At the end of 1967 the United States revealed the development of its counterpart weapon, which John S. Foster, Jr., Defense Department Director of Research, called a "space bus." Like the Soviet FOBS, it traveled a partial orbit in space. However, it could carry a number of individually maneuverable nuclear warheads that could be separated and dropped off, target by target, as it reentered the earth's atmosphere and passed over enemy territory. Again, technically this did not violate the space treaty, since it did not go into full orbit; yet the refreshing candor that prompted it to be called a space bus clearly indicated that this type of nuclear missile was considered a space weapon.

The last shred of credibility for a meaningful space treaty had been worn thin before the treaty was even written. As early as May 1965, the Russians had displayed a large three-stage rocket that they claimed would be a multiple orbital bombardment system (MOBS) that would permit a nuclear warhead to be placed in repeated, full orbit for prolonged periods, before being recalled to earth. In deference to the space treaty, the Soviet government has maintained that this global rocket has not been tested, although Washington has reported monitoring secret flight tests of Soviet rockets that could be used to guide nuclear weapons down from full orbit. In any event, a MOBS capability would simply be an extension of the proven FOBS, as well as the techniques already mastered in the numerous Soviet manned and unmanned orbital systems. The same logic would apply, of course, to the United States.[58] Therefore it must surely tax the imagination to believe that detente between the superpowers has been extended to effect restraints on the use of nuclear weapons in space.

Efforts to regulate the disposition of nuclear weapons in outer space were subsequently extended to the ocean floor. The treaty as signed in February 1971 by the United States and the Soviet Union, together with other nations, prohibited fixed installations for nuclear armaments and other weapons of mass destruction on the seabed beyond the 12-mile coastal limit of the signatories.[59] Presumably no state had yet deployed such weapons on the ocean floor, so that the treaty did not affect existing practices. Moreover, the treaty did not extend to nuclear-armed submarines that might rest on the seabed, nor did it forbid the emplacement there of submarine detection devices. In all these respects the agreement was less substantial than it at first appeared.

The extent to which SALT I and the accords that might issue from SALT II can provide effective restraints upon nuclear weapons designed for use in the earth's atmosphere remains to be seen. One should at least be aware of the limits within which efforts to control competition in nuclear weapons has been able to operate and the ease with which such understandings might be shattered.

The contacts established at SALT produced two ancillary agreements, signed in September 1971. One dealt with the obligation of each party to notify the other in the event of an unauthorized or accidental detonation of a nuclear weapon that might risk the outbreak of a nuclear war. Under its provisions each party pledged to render harmless or destroy such a weapon before it could damage the other. Both sides also pledged to alert each other regarding the detection of unidentified objects on their missile warning systems and to notify each other in advance of planned missile launches beyond their national territories that were in general aimed at the other party.

The second agreement dealt with an improvement in the existing Moscow-Washington hot line by making use of orbiting satellites instead of a cable as a means of transmitting urgent messages.[60]

These measures were reinforced by an agreement, signed at the summit conference in Moscow in May 1972, which was designed to avoid hostile incidents on the high seas between the naval and air units of the two countries. At the Washington summit meeting the following year both parties agreed to a general declaration of principles on the prevention of nuclear war that would presumably guide their behavior in international relations.[61] All of these accords served to elaborate the earlier Soviet-American arrangements for crisis management and arms control that sought in various ways to eliminate practices that could lead to nuclear conflict. As previously noted, this aspect of detente rests upon an essentially negative community of interest, namely, upon efforts to prevent nuclear catastrophe.

EXPANDING THE RANGE OF SUPERPOWER ACCORDS

The Moscow summit of May 1972 also produced a number of agreements that committed the two parties to collaborate for positive purposes. Detailed accords were signed that were designed to prevent environmental pollution, to conduct joint studies of meteorology and of outer space, including joint missions by American and Soviet astronauts, to undertake cooperative research in medical science and public health, and to establish regular ties between Soviet and American scientific and technological institutions that might lead to joint projects in both abstract and applied sciences.[62] The two governments also agreed upon a joint commission that would facilitate trade and economic relations between the two countries, and several large-scale Soviet-American trade agreements were subsequently concluded. When Brezhnev paid Nixon a return visit to Washington in June 1973, further agreements were signed pledging Soviet-American cooperation in oceanography, agricultural research, transportation, income tax accommodation, cultural exchange, and research in the peaceful uses of atomic energy.[63] These were supplemented by agreements on housing and other construction, on artificial heart research, and on cooperation in the field of energy, which Nixon and Brezhnev signed at their third summit meeting in the summer of 1974.[64]

The sum total of these agreements went considerably beyond what the Soviet leaders previously had been prepared to do in undertaking collaborative efforts with the non-Communist world for the purpose of improving the human condition. What significance could be read into these moves? Did they signal a Soviet desire for open, wide-ranging contacts that could lead to a political accord between East and West?

A careful reading of the evidence would compel one to conclude that all such agreements were not in any manner intended to produce political accommodation with the West. Rather it appeared as though the Soviet leaders thought they could successfully compartmentalize detente. Almost unlimited cooperation in the areas of science, technology, and trade could be insulated from alien and unwanted political influences and so prevent ideological subversion and infection from abroad.

At home, the screws in the political system were tightened precisely at the moment of greater Soviet-American contacts. Peter Reddaway, who is perhaps the outstanding authority on the *samizdat* (or political underground) press in the Soviet Union, noted that the conclusion of the various agreements with the United States in 1972 was accompanied by an intensification of domestic political repression. "The Soviet regime felt: as soon as these agreements are settled, we can, so to speak, do what we like at home and there will not be too much noise from abroad, there will not be too many protests. It will be much easier to embark on a campaign against the democratic movement." As a result, the Soviet regime launched "a whole wave of arrests, searches, interrogations and political trials, which clearly demonstrate the desire of the regime to suppress all dissidents and all democratic trends."[65] Similarly, Theodore Shabad reported from Moscow a year after the Moscow summit: "The general view among Western residents is that internal security is being tightened as the controlled press proclaims its desire for closer relations with the West."[66]* The conclusion to be drawn from this paradox was well put

---

*Shabad subsequently reported (August 10, 1973) the open letter from the Soviet dissident writer Vladimir Maksimov to the German Novelist Heinrich Boll complaining of the Soviet domestic repression that accompanied Brandt's *Ostpolitik*. "The letter, circulating among Western

by Sidney Ploss: "The inner oppression serves to deprive a U.S.-Soviet detente of any moral content whatever."[67]

The importance of this basic fact has often been lost upon large segments of Western opinion, which mistakenly held that intensified Soviet contacts with the West involved an accommodation on the fundamental political aims of the two systems. This illusion was fostered by the agreement on basic principles of relations between the United States and the Soviet Union which was signed at the Moscow summit in May 1972. In it both parties pledged to "proceed from the common determination that in the nuclear age there is no alternative to conducting their mutual relations on the basis of peaceful coexistence."[68]

Any misunderstanding that might have arisen from this declaration was the result of wishful thinking in the West, since the Soviet leaders made no effort to conceal the meaning they attached to it. "We approached the Soviet-American summit talks," Brezhnev remarked on June 27, 1972, "from positions affirming the principle of peaceful coexistence of states. . . . In striving for the affirmation of the principle of peaceful coexistence, we recognize that successes in this important matter in no way signify the possibility of weakening the ideological struggle. On the contrary, it is necessary to be prepared that this struggle will intensify, will become a still sharper form of the antagonism between the two social systems. We have no doubts about the outcome of this confrontation, since the truth of history and the objective laws of social development are on our side!"[69]

At the end of 1972 Brezhnev elaborated upon the nature of the unbridgeable chasm that separated the United States and the Soviet Union. "The CPSU has always held and now holds that the class struggle between the two systems—the capitalist and the socialist—in the economic, political and also of course in the ideological spheres will continue. It cannot be otherwise, because the world outlook and

---

newsmen, appeared to reflect growing concern among the Soviet Union's shrinking community of dissidents that they were rapidly becoming the principal losers in the present relaxation of tensions between East and West. . . . The increasingly close relations with Western countries have not been accompanied by any significant changes for the average Soviet citizen, who remains largely isolated from the mainstream of world events. If anything, domestic restrictions are being tightened in what the Kremlin says will be continuing ideological warfare against Western influence."

class aims of socialism and capitalism are opposed and irreconcilable." Conducting relations on the basis of peaceful coexistence in the nuclear age means that "we will strive to shift this historically inevitable struggle onto a path which will not threaten wars, dangerous conflicts and an unrestricted arms race."[70]

Soviet spokesmen do leave room for misunderstanding, however, when they declare that it is now possible "to end the cold war." What they mean by this assertion is that the cold war arose purely at American or Western instigation, for which the Soviet Union bore no responsibility. Therefore, in order to end it the West simply has to cease anti-Communist activities and abandon policies aimed at shoring up lost causes and adjust to the new realities of the world balance of power that has shifted in favor of Moscow. At the same time, since their concept of peaceful coexistence sanctions a continuation and even an intensification of ideological and political warfare on the part of the Soviet Union, the Soviet definition of peaceful coexistence fits almost exactly what the West has traditionally understood by "cold war." Thus ending the cold war and conducting relations on the basis of peaceful coexistence both demand unilateral concessions on the part of the West. Both concepts are conceived of as one-way streets, on which the Soviet Union alone has full freedom of movement. Moreover, it is inadmissable that increased exchanges and contacts with the West should encourage "bridge building" between the two systems, nor bring about any "convergence" in their mutual development.[71] It is precisely because increased contact with the West threatens to undermine, or at least modify, the Soviet system that Soviet ideological struggle must be intensified.

The activities subsumed under ideological struggle go considerably beyond what the West thinks of as "the struggle for men's minds." Soviet ideology not only helps to determine Soviet goals, but also influences the various methods of struggle used in pursuing those goals. As a Soviet theorist commented: "The specific objectives of ideological struggle, its intensity and the choice of the methods, depend at every stage mainly on the rivalry between the two systems in the economic, political and other fields. As a form of confrontation between socialism and capitalism, the ideological struggle is organically linked with all its other forms."[72] Moreover, the scope of the confrontation between the two irreconcilable systems is global in nature. In the words of a Soviet ideologue: "Marxist-Leninists have consistently associated peaceful coexistence with the prospect of further deepening and extending the inevitable development of the world revolutionary process."[73]

How does such comprehensive and unyielding struggle square with the Soviet pursuit of detente policies? Again, in the Soviet view there need be no contradiction between the two, since the Soviet leadership finds it possible to seek an element of truce with the West during a given period, while simultaneously fighting foreign influences and tightening the dictatorship inside the Soviet Union. The Kremlin firmly rebuffs Western proposals that would extend detente to the free circulation of ideas and persons between East and West.

In the Western view, a genuine and meaningful detente must rest upon the foundation of increased understanding among all peoples, and such understanding can only grow with the free flow of people and ideas across political borders. However, Soviet policies, including detente policies, require the exclusion of all Western influences that could threaten the regime's continued control over its captive population, which the Soviet leaders seek to keep in a state of permanent ideological hostility to the West. Therefore, only when the Soviet principle of irreconcilable and fundamental hostility to all other forms of political life is eroded away will it be possible to entertain the prospect for a genuine and lasting detente between East and West. When the Soviet Union can freely allow the circulation of all sorts of ideas, it will have lost its totalitarian pretensions and its pervasive enmity to the non-Soviet world. Until that day, the Soviet understanding of detente, like its view of peaceful coexistence, will remain a conditional and highly qualified concept.

DETENTE AND THE IMPACT OF FOREIGN TRADE

It is commonly held that one of the best ways to liberalize the Soviet regime and the Soviet bloc generally is to expand greatly their foreign trade and other economic relations with the West. It is often uncritically assumed that such increased trade will have a benign effect upon the nature of the Communist elites, since the increased flow of goods from the West will presumably make the East more receptive to Western ideas that are somehow thought to be attached to Western material imports. But as a Polish journal warned in 1972:

"The advantageous exchange of goods and technical know-how in the world can by no means be interpreted as a free exchange of ideas, as our political-ideological Western opponents put it."[74] The Soviet regime is more firmly committed to orthodox ideological tenets than the various Communist states in Eastern Europe, and so this warning should be applied with even greater force to the Soviet Union.

Those who argue that increased economic contacts will modify the political structure of Communist states have fallen victim, perhaps unwittingly, to a simplistic type of economic determinism. Paradoxically it is the Communists, who as Marxists are supposed to be economic determinists, who have proven precisely the opposite. Lenin always insisted upon the primacy of the political struggle. Accordingly when he created a Party that seized political power in an economically backward country, he did not hesitate to decree that he would at once start building socialism even though Russia lacked the solid proletarian base that was presumably required for socialist rule. This task was carried through by Stalin, who quite accurately said that he had launched "a revolution from above," in which the commands issued by the political leadership remolded the economic foundations of society. In Marxist terms, the political "super-structure" created a new economic "base," and not the other way around as Marx would have it.

From the beginning of the Soviet regime, Lenin's insistence upon the primacy of politics over economics prompted him to make foreign trade a state monopoly, so that all economic relations with the outside world would serve his political aims. The importance of economic transactions with the West during the early years of the Soviet regime is frequently forgotten, but as one careful study concluded, "Soviet economic development for 1917-1930 was essentially dependent on Western technological aid."[75] Yet this dependence did not bring about the *embourgeoisment* of the Soviet Union. During the early 1930s Stalin imported large numbers of industrial plants and technicians from the West, but this did not hamper his exercise of political terror over a subject population and the creation of thoroughgoing totalitarianism.

In the late 1960s and early 1970s the Kremlin resumed the large-scale importation of industrial plants and technicians. The equipment for the Togliatti automobile factory on the Volga, for example, came entirely from Italy. One of the basic decisions taken by the 24th Congress of the CPSU in 1971 recognized that the Soviet Union would require a massive infusion of capital and technology from the United States, Western Europe, and Japan well into the 1980s, and that efforts should be intensified to attract foreign economic assistance. Once again the refrain was heard in the non-Soviet world that such extensive commercial contact would mellow the Soviet political system.

A closer inquiry should give pause to such optimism. Imports of foreign economic aid on a grand scale essentially reflect the failure of the Soviet domestic economy to produce the things needed for a fully modern, developed society. In part the fault lay with the continuously huge Soviet outlays for military purposes, well beyond the percentage of the GNP the United States devoted to military expenditures, for example.

Another equally important reason is the failure of the Soviet domestic economy in the nonmilitary realm. The increasing technology gap between the United States and the Soviet Union is traceable in large part to the management weaknesses that are linked to traditional methods of Communist Party control that impede innovation and efficiency. Over the years there have been repeated attempts to reform the Soviet economic system in the hope of making its operation more rational and more productive by introducing decentralization of economic decision making and by using other devices involving market mechanisms familiar to the West. And repeatedly any meaningful implementation of these reforms has been sabotaged by the *apparatchiki*, who wanted all decisions to hang on the will of the centrally directed Party. They correctly saw in such reforms the seeds of a liberalization not only of economic, but also of political, controls. It was more important for the Party to retain firm political controls than make the Soviet economy more productive, if the latter could only be done at the expense of its own political power.

It is at this point that the crucial nature of large-scale economic aid from the outside world becomes understandable. The Soviet Union needs such massive external help in order to compensate for the structural weaknesses of its economy, which it dare not subject to bold reforms. The importation of capital and advanced technology have therefore become the surrogate for Soviet domestic liberalization, which might revive a lagging economy. The Soviet leaders could now have the best of both worlds: both a substantial, external stimulus to their failing economy *and* the retention of their rigid domestic political controls. The Kremlin eagerly seeks access to

foreign scientific and technological developments and increased
foreign trade, but it has repeatedly indicated that it will closely
monitor these foreign contacts so as to avoid the spread of unwanted,
alien political influences.

The Soviet pursuit of detente and peaceful coexistence can thus
be summed up in a series of propositions that are frequently at odds
with the views popularly held in the West. The Soviet Union wants to
extract maximum benefits from the expansion of scientific-
technological and economic relations with the West, while screening
out Western political ideas that could conceivably liberalize the
Soviet political structure. The West is implored to "end the cold war"
by ceasing to oppose Soviet policies in the political, economic,
military, or ideological spheres. The Kremlin, on the other hand, is
not to be put under similar constraints, but is to be left free to
promote its interests and support its allies and clients abroad by
whatever means it chooses, so long as the form of struggle does not
threaten to escalate into nuclear war. And in its relations with other
Communist states, the Soviet Union reserves the right under the
Brezhnev doctrine to intervene into their internal affairs in any way it
sees fit, including the use of armed force.

DETENTE AND THE ROLE OF THE
SOVIET ARMED FORCES

Intermingled with Soviet professions about detente and about
the necessity of avoiding conflicts that could escalate to nuclear war
are other Soviet pronouncements sanctioning Soviet military aid and
even Soviet armed intervention in conflicts far beyond its borders.
Wars of national liberation and other "just" and "progressive" wars
are worthy of Soviet support, and it is apparently a matter of
judgment in individual cases of what form Soviet military assistance
can take and how far it can proceed before such intervention risks
undesirable escalation.

An editorial in the Soviet military newspaper, *Red Star,* of
September 19, 1970 pledged: "We love peace, but the measure of our
love for it has always been and will be readiness at any time and in any
place to give a crushing rebuff to any aggressor if he dares to encroach
on the security of our great motherland *and its allies and friends.* . . .

Our international friendship and cooperation with revolutionary, liberation and antiimperialist forces throughout the world are developing."[76] In a similar vein Marshall A. A. Grechko told the 24th Congress of the CPSU in April 1971: "We can state boldly that the Soviet Army is an army of proletarian internationalism rendering aid to all those struggling against imperialism and for freedom and socialism."[77] In June 1971 General of the Army A. A. Yepishev affirmed that "under modern conditions, the defense of socialism is closely associated with furnishing comprehensive assistance to national liberation movements and to young states struggling to achieve their freedom and independence."[78]

The rapid expansion of the Soviet deep-water fleet has given the Soviet Union a flexible instrument for overseas intervention. In February 1972 Admiral of the Soviet Fleet S. G. Gorshkov emphasized "the special features of the Navy as a military factor which can be used in peacetime for purposes of demonstrating the economic and military might of states beyond their borders," and which is "capable of protecting the interests of a country beyond its borders."[79] Following the Moscow summit of May 1972 two Soviet military writers summed up in general terms the Soviet commitment. "The Soviet Union, firmly faithful to the principles of proletarian internationalism, supported and supports the struggle of peoples for social and national liberation. The forms of this aid can be most varied, depending upon circumstances." Since some circumstances could involve armed force, "the intensification and expansion of the international tasks of the Soviet armed forces also objectively condition the need for their further strengthening. The situation requires unceasing attention to questions of Soviet military construction, which is carried on while taking account of the foreign political situation."[80]

One should not neglect the fact that while the Kremlin has been engaged in detente diplomacy, the Soviet Union has also continued to build up and deploy its armed forces at a considerably faster pace than the United States and the other NATO countries. Thus the missile crisis of October 1962, which is generally credited with launching the superpowers on the course of detente, was a landmark of sorts, but not the kind that it was often thought to be. While it caused Moscow to back down in a nuclear confrontation with the United States, it also demonstrated that the Soviet leaders were prepared to gamble for high stakes, even from a position of nuclear inferiority. One of the principal consequences of the Cuban showdown was the Soviet decision to remedy this condition of strategic inferiority by greatly increasing its ICBM force. With it went a continuing willingness to contemplate military risks for political gains, this time from a greatly strengthened strategic posture.

The most likely impact of a larger and more versatile Soviet nuclear arsenal would be to widen the possible range of political conflicts with the West. In the judgment of the strategic analyst, Thomas W. Wolfe, the Kremlin will be tempted "to test the new strategic relationship, seeking such political gains as the traffic might bear. This in itself may be no more than a replaying of past Soviet performance. But operating from a more favorable correlation of forces, the Soviet leaders would probably attempt to reopen various stalemated issues and to seek fresh advances in the third world, thus introducing new elements of turbulence into international relations."[81] The Soviet attainment of nuclear parity, therefore, will not necessarily enhance detente and the reasonable settlement of conflicts. "In past Soviet probings," Senator Henry Jackson recalled, "the strategic inferiority of Soviet power has set limits to the extent of the risks that Moscow was willing to run. It is disquieting to contemplate the risks the Kremlin might consider taking in the future if it was confident of being closer to an equality or a superiority of overall deterrent strength, and also possessed a local superiority of forces."[82]

Andrew Pierre usefully pointed up the role of momentum in the changing superpower relationship: "There is a wide psychological canyon between a nation that is catching up and achieving general parity in conventional as well as nuclear arms, and another that has or is losing its superiority. A newly acquired confidence on the part of the Soviet leadership could well produce a more assertive foreign policy. . . . The Soviet leadership may now come to believe that their recently acquired rough equality in strategic nuclear forces places them in a position of new strength for the extraction of political gains."[83]

What the Kremlin will do depends upon the intentions of the Soviet leadership as they are revealed over time. What the Kremlin can do, however, is already clear from the direction of the development of Soviet military capabilities. Beginning in the Khrushchev era, and continuing at a rapid pace ever since, the Kremlin has significantly extended the reach of its conventional military power by investing in long-range airlift transport, in addition to the helicopter carriers, amphibious landing vessels, and the overall expansion of the Soviet Navy. The effect of these measures, a military expert notes, is "to improve the maritime-air-logistic elements of power needed to project Soviet military influence into distant areas without having to invoke the threat of immediate nuclear holocaust. . . . At the very least, the Soviet leadership is providing itself with wider options for global intervention than it has hitherto possessed."[84]

It is inherently impossible to provide an accurate reading of Soviet intentions simply by assessing their capabilities at any given moment, since there are so many variables involved. A variety of factors must always be considered, such as the personal relationship among the Soviet leaders at the summit of power within the Kremlin, their need to establish priorities between solving domestic problems and undertaking foreign adventures, their need to assert leadership within the world Communist movement by supporting foreign commitments that involve risk, their judgment of the risks involved, which, in turn, rest on assumptions concerning the anticipated response of their opponents, both in the Communist and non-Communist worlds, their assessment of how events, once set rolling, can be kept from getting out of control, etc. Despite these qualifications, several fundamental observations can nevertheless be made. One can be put in the form of a question: Why should the Soviet regime divert scarce and extremely costly resources to create a growing capability for global intervention if there was never any intention of making political capital out of them, should targets of opportunity arise? Another concerns the basic nature of the Soviet regime. A dictatorship, even one that is no longer completely totalitarian, is still relatively immune from the pressures of public opinion and can change its professed intentions overnight. And one must still take account of the long-term, fundamental commitment of the Soviet leaders to an ideology, however modified, that seeks to reshape the world in its own image, and whose authoritative interpretation continues to serve as the justification for the Soviet leaders' monopoly of power. Intentions, then, are related to capabilities, although not in any self-evident manner, and the hard fact that there has been a significant increase in Soviet capabilities must be taken seriously.

All this in no way contradicts the fact that the Soviet leaders have sought detente, as they have understood detente. In the Soviet view, detente is entirely compatible with encouraging or engaging in political struggle and even in military adventures on a wide-ranging scale, so long as they remain below the nuclear threshold and do not endanger the existence of the Soviet Union.

TESTING THE SUMMIT AGREEMENTS: THE YOM KIPPUR WAR

The Middle East war of October 1973 quickly tested the nature of the superpower detente, which had presumably been enshrined in the summit agreements of 1972 and 1973. Here was a classic case where the extension of Soviet political influence through military assistance to allies, and even the threat of direct Soviet military intervention, had to be weighed against the possibility of a superpower confrontation that might get out of hand. Soviet behavior in the Yom Kippur war clearly demonstrated that the Soviet leadership did not feel unduly inhibited by its pledges of good behavior made to President Nixon.

It is instructive to recall the commitments undertaken in 1972 and 1973. Article 2 of the Soviet-American Declaration of Principles of Relations of May 29, 1972 held that both parties "will do their utmost to avoid military confrontations." Furthermore, both "will always exercise restraint in their mutual relations and will be prepared to negotiate and settle differences by peaceful means." This avowal held not only for superpower relations, but also for the relations between each party's allies or client states: "Both sides recognize that efforts to obtain unilateral advantage at the expense of the other, directly or indirectly, are inconsistent with these objectives." Article 3 asserted that the superpowers have a special responsibility "to do everything in their power so that conflicts or situations will not arise which would serve to increase international tensions."[85]

These general undertakings were expanded in the Agreement on Prevention of Nuclear War of June 22, 1973. The Preamble contained the significant phrase that both parties sought to reduce and ultimately eliminate the danger of the outbreak of such war "anywhere in the world." Given this global mandate, Article 1 reiterated the pledge that both parties will act so "as to prevent the development of situations capable of causing a dangerous exacerbation of their relations, [and so] as to avoid military confrontations." Article 2 provided that "each party will refrain from the threat or the use of force against the other party, against the allies of the other party and against other countries, in circumstances which may endanger international peace and security." In order to implement these provisions, both parties agreed in Article 4 that if relations between them, or between either party and other countries, or even between other countries not party to this agreement, appeared to involve the risk of nuclear war, then "the United States and the Soviet Union, acting in accordance with the provisions of this Agreement, shall immediately enter into urgent consultations with each other and make every effort to avert this risk."[86]

At the beginning of October 1973 those who placed their trust in these agreements assumed that the Soviet leaders would promptly notify Washington about an impending war, if they had any prior knowledge of it. Further, the superpowers would be expected to join forces in order to prevent war, or if that were no longer possible, then to limit the conflict and bring it to an end as quickly as possible.

The reality was rather different. Following the Yom Kippur war the Soviet Ambassador in Cairo, Vladimir Vinogradov, revealed that "on 4 October," that is, two days before Egypt launched its surprise attack on Israel, "President Sadat informed me of Egypt's decision that it had no course before it now except war." Vinogradov further told Sadat of a Soviet message he had received from Syria via Moscow. It reported that "a few days before the outbreak of the fighting" Syrian President Assad "had informed the Soviet leadership that Syria and Egypt were about to enter on all-out military confrontation with Israel."[87] Vinogradov assured Sadat that while Moscow held that the decision to go to war was an Egyptian decision, "the Soviet Union would fulfill its commitments and would support the Arab right with all military, political and economic means."[88]

The mass evacuation of Soviet civilian personnel from the potential war zone in the days prior to October 6 also provided confirmation of the Kremlin's knowledge of the impending events. Soviet forewarning of the Arab attack may well have been more than a few days, however, for as Marvin and Bernard Kalb pointed out, the Russians "contributed directly to the initial Arab successes by shipping massive quantities of ammunition to Cairo and Damascus in the two or three weeks immediately preceding the outbreak of hostilities."[89] Needless to say, all throughout this period Moscow did not transmit one word of warning to Washington, nor did it activate its undertaking to enter into urgent consultations.

On the third day of the war the Israelis stopped the Arab advance on the Golan Heights. "On the fourth day the Soviets began a massive air lift of arms to Egypt and Syria and even arranged for the dispatch of North Korean and North Vietnamese pilots to serve with the Arab air forces."[90] This huge, rapid operation stood in contrast to the 1967 war, when the Russians only resupplied the Arabs after the end of hostilities. For its part, the United States held off resupplying Israel until three days after the Russian arms flow began, and even then the initial American effort was extremely timid.[91]

From the outset Secretary of State Kissinger tried to draw the Russians into a joint effort to achieve a prompt cease-fire. Brezhnev responded on October 9 with a message to President Boumediene of Algeria, urging him to send all possible aid to Egypt and Syria. Moscow then appealed to other Arab noncombatants to join the battle. For some time the Russians had also been coaching the Arabs in the use of oil as a political weapon against the West. It was only after Israel took the offensive and seriously threatened Arab positions that the Russians, in Bernard Lewis' apt phrase, turned "from arsonists to firemen."[92]

On October 16 Soviet Premier Kosygin flew to Cairo to work out a peace proposal with Sadat. Two days later Soviet Ambassador Dobrynin in Washington gave Secretary Kissinger the draft of a Soviet proposal for a U.N.-sponsored cease-fire, which Kissinger quickly rejected as a "nonstarter" because of the extreme demands it made upon Israel. Kissinger then responded to Brezhnev's request that he come to Moscow for urgent consultations on the war. Closeted in the Kremlin the two worked out the details of a cease-fire arrangement, which was subsequently adopted by the U.N. Security Council on October 22. The cease-fire quickly broke down when the commander of the Egyptian Third Corps, which was trapped on the East bank of the Suez Canal, tried to break out of the Israeli encirclement. Israeli forces took full advantage of this violation to extend their lines on both sides of the Canal and to move toward the strategic prize of Suez. On October 23 U.S. intelligence detected a sudden drop-off of Soviet planes carrying supplies to Egypt and Syria. The suspicion that these planes were being diverted for the possible transport of Soviet troops to the Middle East were confirmed by other signals that a number of Soviet divisions had been placed on alert. The following day Washington reported that more Soviet air-transport troops had been alerted, bringing the total to seven divisions, or about 50,000 men. Soviet naval presence in the Mediterranean also rose to an unprecedented number.

At this point the Russians pressed for a proposal that would have introduced a big-power police force into the Middle East. Nixon and Kissinger vigorously rejected this idea. On October 24 Brezhnev sent Nixon an urgent message in which he declared that if the United States would not act jointly with the Soviet Union on the dispatch of troops, the Soviet Union would act unilaterally.[93] The unilateral introduction of Soviet troops into the Middle East against violent American objections—this was scarcely Soviet-American detente in action!

American verbal protests had been ineffective. Apparently the only way to send Brezhnev the message was to put U.S. troops on a worldwide strategic alert, which is what Nixon ordered in the early hours of October 25. In a press conference the next day Nixon described what had transpired. "A very significant and potentially explosive crisis developed," he said, when "we obtained information which led us to believe that the Soviet Union was planning to send a very substantial force in the Mideast, a military force." Upon receipt of this information Nixon recalled how he had ordered "an alert for all American forces around the world. This was a precautionary alert. The purpose of that was to indicate to the Soviet Union that we could not accept any unilateral move on their part to move military forces into the Mideast." Nixon had characterized his exchange of messages with Brezhnev: "I would say that it [Brezhnev's note] was very firm and it left very little to the imagination as to what he intended. And my response was also very firm and left little to the imagination of how we would react." In this respect, superpower cooperation had turned into a genuine confrontation. "It was a real crisis. It was the most difficult crisis we've had since the Cuban confrontation of 1962."[94]

What then had become of the detente with the Soviet Union? Nixon maintained that despite this very severe conflict, both sides still had an overriding interest in larger issues, such as continuing a detente in Europe and in joining forces to control the nuclear arms race. These efforts would proceed as before.

The experience of the Yom Kippur war nevertheless placed the Soviet-American detente in a sharper perspective. It was evident that it still rests on a fragile and artificial basis. Perhaps NATO Secretary General Joseph Luns best characterized the meaning of detente in light of the Middle East experience when he observed that "the Soviet Union will not hesitate to use its power to advance its interests and damage those of the West whenever and wherever it sees the opportunity to do so without running unacceptable risks."[95]

NOTES

1. Charles de Gaulle, *Memoirs of Hope* (London, 1971), pp. 200-02.

2. President de Gaulle's radio and television broadcast, October 2, 1961, *Major Addresses, Statements and Press Conferences of General Charles de Gaulle, May 19, 1958-January 31, 1964* (New York, 1965), p. 152. See also de Gaulle's statement of September 5, 1961, in ibid., pp. 140-42.

3. John Newhouse, *De Gaulle and the Anglo-Saxons* (New York, 1970), pp. 102-03, 106, 143-44.

4. For an even-handed evaluation of Western diplomacy on the Berlin issue, see James L. Richardson, *Germany and the Atlantic Alliance* (Cambridge, Mass., 1966).

5. President de Gaulle's eighth press conference, July 29, 1963, Ambassade de France, Speeches and Press Conferences, No. 192, p. 8.

6. On the problem of the accession of the G.D.R. to the nuclear test ban treaty, see Department of State *Bulletin* 44, no. 1262: 353-55.

7. Paul-Henri Spaak, *The Continuing Battle* (Boston, 1971), pp. 457-58.

8. President de Gaulle's eleventh press conference, February 4, 1965, Ambassade de France, Speeches and Press Conferences, No. 216, p. 11.

9. Ibid, p. 12.

10. President de Gaulle's tenth press conference, July 23, 1964, Ambassade de France, Speeches and Press Conferences, No. 208, p. 5.

11. President de Gaulle's twelfth press conference, September 9, 1965, Ambassade de France, Speeches and Press Conferences, No. 228, p. 8.

12. Address of Michel Boscher to the Plenary Session of the North Atlantic Assembly, Brussels, November 23, 1967, verbatim record, p. 110.

13. "Paris Bids Bonn Join East Europe Approach," *Providence Journal,* February 18, 1968.

14. "Gomulka Rebuffs de Gaulle's Call for More Independent Poland," New York *Times,* September 12, 1967; A. Ross Johnson, "Franco-Polish Relations," *Survival,* December 1967, pp. 390-91.

15. *Polityka,* Warsaw, September 16, 1967; quoted in *East Europe,* November, 1967, p. 23.

16. New York *Times,* September 14, 1967.

17. Henry Kamm, in the New York *Times,* May 15, 16, 18, 19, 1968.

18. President de Gaulle's seventeenth press conference, September 9, 1968, Ambassade de France, Speeches and Press Conferences, No. 1128, pp. 2-3. De Gaulle again raised the Yalta agreement as basis for the 1968 Soviet invasion of Czechoslovakia. Yalta, he said, was "a calculated understanding between Washington and Moscow," and "whatever were the vague formulas of principle that covered up that usurpation," the two powers divided Europe between them, thereby "inevitably delivering the central and eastern parts of our continent to Soviet domination" (ibid., p. 1). This time de Gaulle's widely accepted distortion of Yalta was promptly challenged by Ambassador W. Averell Harriman, who happened to be in Paris as the chief U.S. negotiator for the Vietnam peace talks. Harriman recalled how "both President Roosevelt and Prime Minister Churchill [whom de Gaulle had ignored] wanted to have an agreement that the people of these countries . . . would have the right to pick their own governments, and not to come under the domination of the Soviet Union." Going back to his wartime experience as U.S. Ambassador to the Soviet Union, Harriman recounted his efforts to safeguard the future of Eastern Europe. "I suppose I talked to Stalin more about Poland while I was Ambassador than about any other subject. And there was a final agreement at Yalta, which unfortunately was broken." Similarly, "I remember I was sent to Rumania in January 1945, and helped establish a coalition government at that time. Unfortunately, it didn't last," again as a result of broken Soviet promises. "There is an interesting aspect of the Yalta agreement that I ask to be considered by those people who say the agreement favored the Soviet Union:

Why did Stalin go to such extreme lengths in breaking these agreements if they were favorable to him?" (Excerpts from the text of Ambassador Harriman's broadcast over Radio Luxembourg, September 11, 1968, Providence *Sunday Journal,* September 15, 1968). See also the rebuttal of the "myth of Yalta" in Address by Secretary of State Dean Rusk at New Haven, Conn., September 12, 1968, Department of State *Bulletin* 59, no. 1528: 350-51; for a French rebuke, see Andre Fontaine, "End of Detente," *Le Monde,* August 24, 1968: reprinted in *Survival,* November 1968, pp. 368-69.

19. Pierre Hassner, "From Napoleon III to de Gaulle," *Interplay,* February 1968, pp. 15-16.

20. Ibid., p. 19.

21. Ibid., p. 16.

22. *The Atlantic Alliance and the Warsaw Pact, a Comparative Study,* NATO Information Service (Brussels, n.d.), p. 24.

23. Charles Andras, "The Evoluation of the Warsaw Pact's Approach to European Security," Radio Free Europe research paper, August 1968, pp. 57-58.

24. "Declaration on Strengthening Peace and Security in Europe," issued by the Political Consultative Committee of the Warsaw Treaty at Bucharest, July 4 and 5, 1966, Appendix III, Document 387, Assembly, WEU, *Proceedings,* December 1966, III, p. 136.

25. Ibid., p. 140.

26. Ibid., p. 138. (Italics added.)

27. Y. Rakhmaninov, "For European Security," *International Affairs* (Moscow), November 1967, p. 85. See also Y. Shvedkov, "West European Political Forces and European Security," *International Affairs,* March 1968, pp. 8-13.

28. Assembly, WEU, *Proceedings,* December 1966, III, p. 141.

29. The Karlovy Vary Statement of European Communist Parties, April 26, 1967, in *The Soviet View of NATO,* Subcommittee on National Security and International Operations of the Committee on Government Operations, U.S. Senate (Washington, D.C., 1967), pp. 19-20.

30. Memorandum of the Warsaw Pact Foreign Ministers Meeting, Budapest, June 21-22, 1970, *NATO Letter,* September 1970, p. 24.

31. *Pravda,* March 18, 1969.

32. *Pravda,* April 10, 1969.

33. *International Meeting of Communist and Workers' Parties,* Moscow, June 17, 1969 (Prague, 1969), p. 32.

34. *Pravda,* March 31, 1971.

35. Communique of Political Consultative Committee of the Warsaw Treaty at Warsaw, April 18, 1974, *Atlantic News,* April 20, 1974, p. 3.

36. Secretary General Manlio Brosio, "NATO and East-West Detente," *NATO Letter,* December 1967, p. 6. U.S. Ambassador to NATO, Harlan Cleveland, similarly remarked: "The Soviets are testing Allied endurance with their proposal to abolish both NATO and the Warsaw Pact. I can see why they would want to exercise their military command over other Communist forces directly, without a structure that implies their allies should have something to say about how and when the forces are used, against whom and for what purpose." (Ambassador Harlan Cleveland, "The Transformation of NATO," *NATO Letter,* November 1967, pp. 5-6.)

37. Harold van B. Cleveland, *The Atlantic Idea and Its European Rivals* (New York, 1966), p. 169.

38. Address by NATO Secretary General Manlio Brosio at Rome, February 19, 1971, *NATO Letter,* March-April 1971, p. 33.

39. *Pravda,* October 7, 1969.

40. E. Novoseltsev, "Europe Twenty-Five Years Later," *International Affairs* (Moscow), July 1970, p. 21.

41. Address by President John F. Kennedy at Washington, D.C., June 10, 1963, Department of State *Bulletin* 49, no. 1253: 4.

42. Address by President John F. Kennedy at Orono, Maine, October 19, 1963, Department of State *Bulletin* 49, no. 1271: 695.

43. Arthur M. Schlesinger, Jr., *A Thousand Days* (New York, 1967), p. 831.

44. Marshall D. Shulman, "Recent Soviet Foreign Policy: Some Patterns in Retrospect," *Journal of International Affairs,* No. 1 (1968), pp. 30-31.

45. William Beecher, "U.S. Sees Soviet Closing Gap on Strategic Missiles," New York *Times,* February 19, 1968.

46. Address by Secretary of Defense Robert S. McNamara at San Francisco, September 18, 1967, Department of State *Bulletin* 57, no. 1476: 443-51.

47. Information supplied by the late Assistant Secretary of Defense John McNaughton to Robert Kleiman, as reported by Kleiman, New York *Times Book Review,* September 8, 1968, in his review of McNamara's book, *The Essence of Security.*

48. Address by Minister of Foreign Affairs Andrei A. Gromyko to the Supreme Soviet of the USSR, June 27, 1968, *Pravda,* June 28, 1968.

49. Remarks by President Lyndon B. Johnson at the Signing of the Nonproliferation Treaty, Washington, D.C., July 1, 1968, Department of State *Bulletin* 59, no. 1517: 86.

50. Address by President Lyndon B. Johnson at Glassboro, N.J., June 4, 1968, Department of State *Bulletin* 58, no. 1513: 813-17.

51. Text of the essay by Academician Andrei D. Sakharov, "Thoughts on Progress, Peaceful Coexistence and Intellectual Freedom," New York *Times,* July 22, 1968.

52. Viktor A. Cheprakov, "Problems of the Last Third of the Century," *Izvestia,* August 11, 1968.

53. Address by Secretary of State Dean Rusk to the United Nations General Assembly, New York, October 2, 1968, Department of State *Bulletin* 59, no. 1530: 407. Foreign Minister Andrei A. Gromyko addressed the same body on October 3, 1968, *Pravda,* October 4, 1968. Secretary Rusk reportedly told Soviet Ambassador Dobrynin on November 25, just before his departure for consultations in Moscow, that the United States was willing to reopen missile talks. (Bernard Gwertzman, New York *Times,* December 7, 1968.) However, the Kremlin by then preferred to wait for the incoming Nixon administration.

54. Briefing to Congressional Leaders on SALT Agreements by Henry A. Kissinger, Assistant to the President for National Security Affairs, at the White House, June 15, 1972, Department of State *Bulletin* 67, no. 1724: 44.

55. "Strategic Arms Limitation Agreements," signed May 26, 1972, Department of State *Bulletin* 66, no. 1722: 918-21.

56. "Basic Principles of Negotiations on Strategic Arms Limitations," signed June 21, 1973, Department of State *Bulletin* 69, no. 1778: 158.

57. For the Protocol to the ABM Treaty and the Treaty Limiting Underground Nuclear Testing, both signed July 3, 1974, see Department of State *Bulletin* 71, no. 1831: 216-18.

58. Reports by Evert Clark on both Soviet and U.S. nuclear space weapons, New York *Times,* December 14 and 26, 1967, April 2 and 25, 1968. See also *The Soviet Military Technological Challenge,* Center for Strategic Studies, Georgetown University (Washington, D.C., 1967), pp. 52-53, 86; Institute for Strategic Studies, *The Military Balance, 1968-1969* (London, 1968), p. 5.

59. On the signing of the Seabed Arms Control Treaty, February 11, 1971, Department of State *Bulletin* 64, no. 1660: 535. For an extended analysis of the Treaty by Secretary of State William Rogers on forwarding it to the Senate for ratification, July 21, 1971, see ibid. 65, no. 1677: 185-87.

60. "U.S. and U.S.S.R. Sign Agreements to Reduce Risk of Nuclear War," September 30, 1971, Department of State *Bulletin* 65, no. 1686: 399-403.

61. "Agreement on Prevention of Incidents at Sea," signed May 25, 1972, Department of State *Bulletin* 66, no. 1722: 926-27; "Agreement on Prevention of Nuclear War," signed June 22, 1973; ibid. 69, no. 1778: 160-61.

62. For the texts of these agreements signed May 23 and 24, 1972, see Department of State *Bulletin* 66, no. 1722: 921-26. These understandings were elaborated by the "Announcement of the U.S.-Soviet Commission on Scientific and Technical Cooperation," signed July 28, 1972, ibid. 67, no. 1730: 214-16 and the "Memorandum on the Environmental Agreement," signed September 21, 1972, ibid. 67, no. 1738: 451-55.

63. For the texts of these agreements, signed June 19-22, 1973, see Department of State *Bulletin* 69, no. 1778: 159-73.

64. For the texts of these agreements, signed June 28, 1974, see Department of State *Bulletin* 71, no. 1831: 219-23.

65. "A Talk with Peter Reddaway about the 'Chronicle of Current Events,' " Radio Liberty Dispatch, April 26, 1973, p. 3.

66. Theodore Shabad, "Soviet Called Confident on U.S. Benefits," New York *Times,* May 23, 1973.

67. Sidney I. Ploss, "Soviet-American Relations: Hope and Anxiety," *Russian Review,* July 1972, p. 222.

68. "Text of Basic Principles," signed May 29, 1972, Department of State *Bulletin* 67, no. 1722: 898.

69. Speech by Leonid I. Brezhnev at Dinner in Honor of Fidel Castro, June 27, 1972, *Pravda,* June 28, 1972.

70. Leonid I. Brezhnev, "Speech at Celebration of the 50th Anniversary of the Formation of the U.S.S.R.," December 21, 1972, *Pravda,* December 22, 1972.

71. Foy D. Kohler, Mose L. Harvey, Leon Gouré, and Richard Soll, *Soviet Strategy for the Seventies: From Cold War to Peaceful Coexistence,* Center for Advanced International Studies, University of Miami (Miami, Fla., 1973), pp. 8-9.

72. Y. Zakharov, "The Present State of the Ideological Struggle between Socialism and Capitalism," *International Affairs* (Moscow), March 1972, p. 78; quoted in Kohler et al., op. cit., p. 61.

73. A. Sovetov, "Peaceful Coexistence—A Real Factor in International Relations," *International Affairs* (Moscow), September 1972, p. 13.

74. *Glos Pracy,* December 1972; quoted in the Warsaw dispatch by James Feron, "Soviet Bloc Bars Freer Exchange," New York *Times,* December 17, 1972.

75. Antony C. Sutton, *Western Technology and Soviet Economic Development, 1917-1930* (Stanford, Calif., 1968), p. 283.

76. Editorial, "Imperialism—Mankind's Bitterest Enemy," *Krasnaia Zvezda,* September 19, 1970 (italics added); quoted in Kohler et al., op. cit., pp. 229-30.

77. Speech of Marshall A. A. Grechko to the 24th Congress of the CPSU, *Pravda,* April 3, 1971; quoted in Kohler et al., op. cit., p. 230.

78. General of the Army A. A. Yepishev, *Sovetskii Patriot,* June 9, 1971; quoted in Kohler et al., op. cit., p. 230.

79. Admiral S. G. Gorshkov, "Navies in Wars and in Peace," *Morskoi Sbornik,* February 1972; quoted in Kohler et al., op. cit., p. 232.

80. Colonels V. Serebriannikov and M. Iasiukov, "Peaceful Coexistence and Defense of the Socialist Fatherland," *Kommunist Vooruzhennykh Sil,* August 1972; quoted in Kohler et al., op. cit., p. 234.

81. Testimony of Colonel Thomas W. Wolfe, November 7, 1967, *Hearings before the Subcommittee on Military Applications of the Joint Committee on Atomic Energy,* 90th Cong., 1st sess. (Washington, D.C., 1967), p. 73. See also the testimony of Philip E. Mosely, who came to the same conclusion, ibid., pp. 52-63.

82. Address by Senator Henry M. Jackson at Chicago, March 24, 1968, p. 3.

83. Andrew J. Pierre, "American Down, Russia Up: The Changing Political Role of Military Power," *Foreign Policy,* Fall 1971, pp. 182-83.

84. Wolfe, op. cit., p. 71. See also Thomas W. Wolfe, "Russia's Forces Go Mobile," *Interplay,* March 1968, pp. 28-37; "The Soviet Maritime Threat," Patrick Wall, rapporteur, Military Committee, North Atlantic Assembly, November 1972, P 119, MC (72) 5.

85. "Text of Basic Principles," signed May 29, 1972, Department of State *Bulletin* 66, no. 1722: 898.

86. "Agreement on Prevention of Nuclear War," signed June 22, 1973, Department of State *Bulletin* 69, no. 1778: 160-61.

87. The Beirut (anti-West) newspaper, *As Safir,* quoted in Murray Marder, "Press Reporting '73 Soviet Alert," Washington *Post,* May 2, 1974.

88. *As Safir,* quoted in *Near East Report* (Washington, D.C.), May 8, 1974.

89. Marvin and Bernard Kalb, "Twenty Days in October," New York *Times Magazine,* June 23, 1974.

90. Testimony of Bernard Lewis, March 8, 1974, in *Negotiations and Statecraft: Hearings before the Permanent Subcommittee on Investigations of the Committee on Government Operations,* U.S. Senate, 93rd Cong., 2d sess. (Washington, D.C., 1974), p. 129.

91. On the American resupply of Israel, see the Kalbs, op. cit.

92. Lewis, op. cit., p. 129.

93. Kalbs, op. cit.

94. Press Conference of President Richard M. Nixon at the White House, October 26, 1973, Department of State *Bulletin* 69, no. 1794: 581-84.

95. *Atlantic News,* February 6, 1974, p. 4.

6

NATO AND DETENTE MANAGEMENT

NATO'S FUTURE IN A CHANGING EUROPE

The Gaullist and Soviet concepts of detente and an eventual East-West settlement, which have been premised upon breaking the trans-Atlantic tie between Europe and America, stand in sharp contrast to the view that an easing of tensions and an ultimate reconciliation between the parts of a divided Europe can only materialize if Europe and America work in a close and continuing partnership. Monnet's Action Committee declared in June 1962:

> The conflict between East and West cannot be resolved without a change by both sides in their conception of the future. While the West gives the impression that it can be divided, the USSR will not be disposed to come to agreements in the belief that it can always upset the world balance of power. But when America and Europe have made it clear to everyone that the West is changing by its own will from within, but cannot be changed by outside pressure, that it is consolidating its unity on a long-term basis, then the conditions will be created for a lasting peaceful settlement between East and West.[1]

Subsequent Action Committee declarations focused on the solution of the German problem, which would be inconceivable "if

297

Europe did not seek it together with the United States."[2] The security system arising from a German settlement must rest on broad agreement between the superpowers, as well as among peoples of Europe. Otherwise, "how could any settlement be made reuniting the East and West Germans if it lacked the assurance of security which the USSR, Europe and the United States all need?"[3] While awaiting the solution of these admittedly intractable problems, the Action Committee declared itself "in favor of enlarging, by means of realistic projects, the bases of relations with the nations of Eastern Europe." This would supplement the evolution of improved relations between the West and the Soviet Union. Again, the West could only be in a position to negotiate a lasting settlement if it had established a firm partnership between united Europe and the United States.[4]

These European sentiments were reciprocated on the part of the United States by President Kennedy. Speaking, significantly, at a NATO headquarters in Naples in July 1963, Kennedy cited the words of Mazzini: " 'We are here . . . to build up the unity of the human family.' " The prerequisite for this is the achievement of effective unity of the West. "In time," Kennedy added, "the unity of the West can lead to the unity of East and West."[5]

Both parties to the partnership scheme assumed that NATO would necessarily remain the principal security arrangement within the West that must evolve with the changing demands of the East-West confrontation in Europe. In this view, there was nothing irreconcilable between continued reliance upon NATO and the search for detente. In 1966 President Johnson related the two themes by saying that it was necessary "to modernize NATO and strengthen other Atlantic institutions," as well as "to quicken progress in East-West relations." The Atlantic Alliance must be viewed as "a living organism. It must adapt to changing conditions." Our proper concern is both "to keep NATO strong and abreast of the times. . . . The Alliance must become a forum for increasingly close consultations. These should cover the full range of joint concerns—from East-West relations to crisis management." NATO could thus become an important instrument for associating the United States with its European partners in the common effort "to heal the wound in Europe which now cuts East from West and brother from brother."[6]

At the same time, NATO would not be an obstacle to forming a better balanced relationship between the United States and a gradually uniting European component within the Atlantic Alliance, if that should become possible. On the same occasion, President Johnson reaffirmed the long-standing American commitment "to further the integration of the Western European community."[7] This reassurance might be seen as a response to the European desire, most frequently expressed by Belgian Foreign Minister Pierre Harmel, for "representing and expressing the coherent ideas of the peoples of the European continent within the context of the Atlantic Alliance."[8] Subsequently, Secretary of State Dean Rusk was explicit about the American willingness to reshape NATO to meet European needs when he noted that the United States would welcome a European grouping "in NATO, something like a European defense community, as a full partner in a reconstituted alliance."[9]

NATO was thus seen as a flexible institution, capable of adjusting to changing demands in both Western and Eastern Europe. It was also viewed as having both military and political dimensions; deterrence and defense were the necessary prerequisites for an enduring and meaningful detente.

NATO AND THE EUPHORIA OF DETENTE

The nexus between the military and political functions of the Atlantic Alliance have been frequently overlooked by enthusiasts of detente. The ready armed strength of the NATO defense system will continue to be needed, as Ambassador Harlan Cleveland had properly noted, "to persuade the Soviets and their allies to talk sense about the future of Europe. We will need it to keep them talking when the going gets rough, as it assuredly will. And we will need an effective Western system to keep the deal honest, whenever a bargain can be struck for a durable peace in Europe."[10] During the initial stages of detente, conditions of military stability had to be preserved so as to prevent the Soviet bloc forces from undertaking any moves that could destroy the possibility of detente itself. Once engaged in negotiations about the future shape of Europe, NATO would still be required as a stand-by military organization for use both as a bargaining counter in arriving at the political settlement and as an assurance of continued security until such time as some new European security system could take its place. Unilateral or premature withdrawal of NATO forces would have removed the Soviet incentive to make the necessary concessions for a mutually satisfactory European settlement. Even worse, it might have invited military adventures, based on a miscalculation of a Western response, which in turn could escalate an incident into a general war.

The Germans, who feel most acutely exposed, have been ever fearful of this type of scenario unfolding before them. In the aftermath of the Arab-Israeli war of June 1967, Georg Kliesing, the Christian Democratic defense expert, warned his fellow European parliamentarians of the dangers of being carried away by the illusions of detente. "We are being told that, after Cuba, Israel is the second example of the Soviet Union making a mistake in her calculations. This may be true. But for us the crucial question is, who can guarantee that the Soviet Union will not miscalculate a third time, with Western Europe as the area concerned? This could happen through a Western policy of detente, which can no longer recognize the boundary between policy and euphoria. . . . I do not want to see a policy of detente—or, perhaps better, a euphoria of detente—result in disaster for Europe."[11]

It was not necessary to wait long for a third Soviet miscalculation involving armed force; this time the scene was Czechoslovakia in August 1968. This action precipitated a massive deployment of battle-ready Soviet troops to the Czech-West German border and a threatening campaign of political vituperation aimed at West Germany. The jolt of these events momentarily reintroduced a measure of realism into Western security calculations by dispelling some of the euphoria that had surrounded the talk about detente. Moscow seemed to have little interest in thinning out its troops in Central Europe, for example, nor did the reunification of Germany appear to be any nearer.

There were also wider implications that the NATO states were forced to consider. The Soviet operation in Czechoslovakia was a bizarre combination of a flawlessly executed military mobilization and invasion by Warsaw Pact troops with an unanticipated and unmanageable political reaction on the part of the people and Communist Party leaders of Czechoslovakia. As Ambassador Cleveland observed, "a government that can move troops so efficiently behind so sloppy a political plan might be capable of misreading Western determination too."[12] Preinvasion hopes for detente, based on benign estimates of Soviet political intentions, were now thrown in doubt. Instead of attributing mature, rational judgment to the Soviet leaders, who were presumably weighed down by a cautious, bureaucratic mentality, it was necessary to recognize that they could launch unpredictable, adventurist policies. The previously popular theory of "the victory of intentions over capabilities" appeared hollow, since it was demonstrated how intentions could suddenly take on a menacing appearance to match the huge military capabilities of the Soviet bloc.

The political consensus that emerged in the West was that the Soviet leadership would confine its military activity to controlling countries in the Soviet bloc that seemed to be getting out of hand. But even here there was reason for apprehension that Soviet moves might spill across the military confrontation in Central Europe into West Germany. As part of the drumfire of Soviet accusations aimed at the West Germans, which sought to distract attention from the Soviet-led invasion of Czechoslovakia as well as give it justification, the Kremlin pointed to a presumed military threat arising from the Federal Republic. Moscow claimed that under articles 53 and 107 of the U.N. Charter it had the right, as a victor in World War II, to intervene unilaterally and by force if necessary to repress aggressive acts by the former enemy state of West Germany.[13] Washington promptly reassured Bonn that these outdated articles could not justify Soviet or other Warsaw Pact intervention in the affairs of the Federal Republic, and that if it should be attempted it would lead to an immediate response on the part of NATO.[14]

This pretext for Soviet armed intervention in West Germany was presumably nullified by the 1970 German-Soviet renunciation of force treaty that Chancellor Brandt negotiated with the Kremlin in 1970. According to the secret protocols of the negotiations prior to the treaty's signing which were later revealed in Bonn, the Soviet Union undertook not to apply the enemy states clauses of the U.N. Charter against the Federal Republic.[15] Pledges to renounce the use of force among sovereign states necessarily flourish in an Alice-in-Wonderland atmosphere. It should be recalled that Moscow had also formally promised not to threaten to use force or actually to employ it in connection with its partners in the Warsaw Pact,* yet not only

---

*Article 1 of the Warsaw Treaty states: "The Contracting Parties undertake . . . to refrain in their international relations from the threat or use of force."

was force used, but it was ideologically legitimated by the Brezhnev Doctrine. Brandt was surely enough of a realist not to believe that a renunciation of force agreement would restrain the Kremlin if in Soviet judgment it appeared necessary for force to be used. Yet Brandt's *Ostpolitik* was premised upon creating a web of relations with the Soviet bloc in which both sides would derive sufficient advantages so that threats to West German security would become improbable.

This reciprocity of interests was illustrated by the fact that Bonn refused to ratify the 1970 Soviet-German Treaty until the Soviet Union satisfactorily clarified the status of West Berlin, which it did in the Quadripartite Agreement of 1971. Resolution of the Berlin problem was also made a precondition by the NATO partners for the convocation of the Conference on Cooperation and Security in Europe (CSCE), which the Soviet Union had so ardently sought for a number of years.

Soviet enthusiasm for CSCE was presumably based on its desire to legitimate its post-World War II conquests in Eastern Europe, as well as perhaps to set up some permanent pan-European body that could facilitate Soviet intervention in the affairs of Western Europe. Such contacts could also accelerate East-West trade and the access to Western capital and technology which the Kremlin had determined it badly needed.

The CSCE also provided an admirable opportunity for a renewed wave of detente euphoria. As the London *Economist* commented during the conference's preparatory stages, "The likely outcome of the political part of the negotiations is a very general and carefully qualified declaration of unenforceable principles that will not improve the conditions under which people live in Eastern Europe, but will reinforce the belief of many people in Western Europe that they can afford to spend less money on their defense." Eventually movement in the direction of unilateral Western disarmament would have serious consequences. "If the West European countries feel they are militarily weaker than they were before, and that their once high hopes of creating a more liberal Eastern Europe have been frustrated, they will be that much less resistant to the next set of proposals from Russia. It is, of course, very unlikely that the Russians are thinking of an invasion of Western Europe. But it should be all too evident that the Russians' ability to invade, made manifest by a probably growing superiority of armed force, will change the way Western Europe behaves towards them."[16]

DETENTE AND THE EROSION OF THE
NATO MILITARY POSITION

It was this subtle but indispensible connection between military strength and a viable diplomatic bargaining position that permitted Chancellor Brandt to pursue his *Ostpolitik*. While negotiating the 1970 Soviet-German Treaty, Brandt never lost sight of the fact that a credible NATO defense system was the prerequisite for proceeding to the dismantling of East-West tensions. "A peace arrangement for Europe can only be achieved," Brandt asserted, "if the relative balance of forces is maintained. Otherwise not only would our security be threatened, but the prospects for an East-West accord would vanish."[17] Similarly, Helmut Schmidt, speaking as the West German Defense Minister, reflected on the process of "improving the relations between East and West. . . . We fully know what the limitations of our actions are: the limits are defined by the fact that the balance of forces between East and West must be maintained. This cannot be accomplished without NATO and coherence and solidarity within this Alliance."[18]

Unilateral Western disarmament would provide the Soviet leaders with the opportunity to exert pressure in areas where the West had rendered itself incapable of taking countermeasures, and this could only toughen the Soviet bargaining position and raise the cost of detente. At this point the effective choice would be either increased East-West tension that would imperil movement toward detente, or "detente" on Soviet terms. Inescapably, we return to the fact that NATO must be an essential element in moving toward a political settlement, and that only a respectable Alliance posture will demonstrate to the Soviet leaders that there is no profit in a militant policy, nor are there Western military weaknesses that can be exploited for political ends.

The maintenance of a stable military environment will continue to depend heavily upon the presence of an adequate U.S. military force in NATO Europe. "The deterrent effect emanating from the

U.S. forces in Europe," Schmidt explained, "is incomparably greater than that which European armies could ever have." In European eyes, U.S. conventional forces in Europe provide a credible linkage with the U.S. strategic forces, and as this linkage is weakened, NATO Europe becomes more vulnerable to Soviet military and political pressures. Moreover, the United States would risk losing influence over the evolution of events in Europe, which after the superpowers still remained the greatest source of economic and latent political power in the world. "Any unilateral American withdrawal without a simultaneous and comparable reduction of Soviet forces" Schmidt continued, "would be bound to lead to a shift in the psychological-political equilibrium in Europe with long-term and far-reaching consequences which would later be recognized also in the United States as a serious blow to the American position as a world power. At that time, however, it might be too late."[19]

Much would be clearer, as Kurt Gasteyger correctly observed, if we realized that the crux of the problem is "our being unaware of the changing nature of our insecurity. It is thus not the all-too-visible presence of a potentially aggressive military giant that we have to worry about, but the elusive and invisible political weight of a reasonably peaceful superpower. In a situation like this the reaction is not so much the organization of military defense against an unlikely aggressor, but rather political accommodation with a power whose superiority, indefinite in duration and still growing in size, is casting its shadow over the whole of Europe." Therefore, "without overstretching our imagination we could then conceive of situations in which Western Europe sees its interests better served by refraining from actions which it otherwise would take, or agrees to proposals which it otherwise would reject."[20]* This is the familiar, but still essentially valid, image of the Finlandization of Western Europe, which would not be beyond the realm of possibility, given the deterioration of NATO in the face of a still formidable Warsaw Pact.

---

*In a like manner, Josef Korbel warned that the presence of U.S. troops in Europe is, in essence, the problem of confidence. Any one-sided "reduction of American forces would create a psychosis of uncertainty in which the West European countries may in their quest for security seek an accommodation with the Soviet Union at the expense of others and open the doors to Soviet pressures, supported by its military power."[21]

Under these circumstances, the behavior of the West could easily degenerate into efforts to appease the East. And appeasement does not ensure peace and detente, but instability and danger.

U.S. FORCE LEVELS IN EUROPE

Dismissing the perils of such a prospect, Senator Mike Mansfield has since August 1966 repeatedly proposed legislation to bring about an immediate, unilateral, and substantial reduction of U.S. force levels in Europe. An effort to mollify the Mansfield bloc in Congress took the form of a decision in May 1967 to redeploy up to 35,000 American troops from West Germany. Though stationed in the United States, they remained committed to NATO on a rotation plan with other U.S. forces and they were to be transported back to Germany for annual military exercises.

This scheme was based on assumptions that cast doubt upon the American security guarantee for NATO Europe. Contingency planning assumed that there would be a warning period of several weeks while Soviet mobilization would be under way, and that this would provide the time for the prompt return of the NATO-assigned troops to Europe. However, the experience with the Soviet invasion of Czechoslovakia in 1968 demonstrated the difficulties of trying to act upon this premise. There was ample political warning time while Warsaw Pact troops massed near the Czech borders, and yet very few responsible figures in the West predicted the Soviet-led invasion. In retrospect, as one commentator noted, "we now know that 'political warnings' might be ambiguous at best, that mobilization and plans for an invasion of West Germany could be hidden under the cloak of Warsaw Pact maneuvers, that the availability of reliable intelligence does not guarantee accurate evaluation of its meanings, and that Western governments, like all humans, might be inclined not to believe what they do not wish to hear."[22]

Kenneth Rush, U.S. Ambassador to the Federal Republic during this period, candidly reported that the "German leaders were shaken by what they considered the failures of the United States government to take rapid action in August 1968 to support and reassure them. . . . One byproduct was that already limited German confidence in the concept of dual basing of American forces vanished.

For the Germans, what happened showed that political considerations would inevitably intervene in a situation of increased tension in Europe, placing the return of American forces to Europe for emergencies in serious question."[23] Any American President would indeed be placed before a difficult choice: A massive, sudden airlift could needlessly aggravate a tense situation, while an inadequate response might encourage and embolden the enemy. If the American troops were already positioned in Europe, neither of these painful choices would have to be hazarded.

General Lyman Lemnitzer, speaking as SACEUR, sounded a further alarm about the inadequacy of the airlift concept. Especially in the wake of Czechoslovakia, which stationed several divisions of the Soviet Army near the Czech-West German border for an indefinite period and established the supply and communication lines that would facilitate the rapid deployment to forward positions of huge forces held in reserve, General Lemnitzer said that the proper disposition of NATO ground troops must be viewed "in terms of hours and days, not weeks and months." Consequently, "there can be no major reliance placed on a Big Lift type of operation to ensure the prompt return of U.S. troops to Europe in a time of crisis."[24] There are other important qualifications as well. What if massive troop movements by air were hampered by bad weather? And what assurance would there be that the landing fields and prepositioned arms stockpiles would not be overrun prior to the time of return? All these considerations argued for the proposition, in military parlance, that strategic mobility is not a substitute for forward deployment.

Some have supported the return of American troops to the United States in the belief this would reduce the cost of the defense budget. There are undoubtedly some savings that could be made by a careful pruning of American headquarters and other support units in Europe, which have become overstaffed.[25] However, any further budgetary savings from stationing NATO-committed troops in the United States are illusory.[26] It would be necessary to duplicate heavy equipment and arms that could not be readily airlifted by maintaining large supplies in European depots. This type of dual basing would involve a heavy and continuous expense. Further, in order to make dual basing seem credible, it would be necessary to have available at all times an expensive fleet of huge transport planes in order to redeploy these troops to Europe in times of emergency. But even paying the extra costs for these facilities would not assure that they would be used when needed, since the crucial element in their use would still depend upon the vagaries of a correct political decision for which, as we have noted, there can be no guarantee.

There are significant balance-of-payments costs, as distinguished from budgetary costs, arising out of keeping American troops in Europe. Ever since 1961 the Federal Republic has concluded a series of offset payment agreements with the United States, which sought to compensate for the balance-of-payments losses in stationing American troops in Germany. These agreements have provided an inadequate solution to this problem, both because of the terms of some of the agreements and also because they were arrived at through a series of bilateral arm-twisting encounters. The American troops in Germany serve to defend all of NATO Europe, not just the Federal Republic and this fact should be recognized through a multilateral arrangement that could effectively neutralize the balance-of-payments issue.

One proposal that would permit the United States to keep its troops in Europe with no different financial effects than if they were stationed at home rests upon sharing the title and use of foreign base facilities with the host country, which would assume the major part of the local operating expenses.[27] Another more far-reaching proposal would create a NATO International Security Fund, a multilateral foreign exchange scheme, to which all NATO members in a surplus balance-of-payments position on military account would contribute, although the host country (Germany) would still pay the largest share. Such funds would not come from defense budgets, but rather from the general-purpose budgets of each country, thereby permitting the United States to draw upon the large number of U.S. dollars that had glutted the Bundesbank in Germany, for example, without curtailing normal German expenditures for defense.[28]

NATO was slow in moving toward a solution along these lines, which undoubtedly required an exercise of political will. The Ministerial meeting of the Defense Planning Committee of June 1973 set up a special study group to examine ways to resolve the balance-of-payments problem by either bilateral or multilateral arrangements.[29] Though a multilateral scheme would have theoretically been preferable, subsequent experience showed that, for the moment at least, it was too difficult to negotiate.

In the fall of 1973 the Congress enacted the Jackson-Nunn amendment to the defense appropriations bill, which gave new urgency to the balance-of-payments problem. According to its provisions, NATO Europe was required to offset entirely the dollar outflow resulting from the stationing of U.S. troops in Europe, and it made mandatory a U.S. troop withdrawl in proportion to the failure of the Europeans to meet this offset requirement. The sponsors of this bill hoped in this way to neutralize the balance-of-payments issue and so head off the more sweeping demands of Senator Mansfield. Laboring under the threat of this legislation, the Federal Republic agreed to provide $2.22 billion covering fiscal years 1974 and 1975, which would completely offset the balance-of-payments cost for keeping American troops in Germany. Lesser bilateral arrangements with other allies satisfied a similar requirement for other U.S. troops stataioned elsewhere in Europe.[30]* NATO Europe had only passed the initial test posed by the Jackson-Nunn amendment, however, which will remain a recurrent threat to the maintenance of U.S. force levels in Europe.

The American commitment to continue stationing troops in Europe was thus related to the willingness of the European members of NATO to assume an increasing share of the financial burden. It is difficult to calculate what a "fair share" of the burden is, since there are different criteria that can be used. NATO expenditures by the United States have represented a higher percentage of its GNP than that of the European members, but when these expenditures are related to per capita income, which in NATO Europe is approximately half that of the United States, it is evident that the Americans have a greater capacity to bear a somewhat higher defense burden. That is, when defense expenditures are related to the ability to pay, the burden has been shared almost equally between the United States and NATO Europe. This fact has not been understood by Americans, who have continued to press Europe for greater budgetary contributions to NATO.

In December 1970 President Nixon pledged that, "given a similar approach by the other allies, the United States would maintain and improve its own forces in Europe and would not reduce

---

*Ironically this effort to help the U.S. balance of payments was legislated just as the oil embargo and the quadrupling of the price of oil sent the balance of payments of the states of European NATO, with the possible exception of West Germany, into serious deficits of their own.

them except in the context of reciprocal East-West action." This was accompanied by the announcement of a European Defense Improvement Program, by which the Eurogroup (the European members of NATO, minus France, Portugal, and Iceland) undertook to spend an additional $1 billion over a five-year period in order to improve the European forces as well as the NATO infrastructure.[31] This commitment was followed by a series of increased defense spending on the part of the Eurogroup. In December 1971 it announced that their combined defense budgets for 1972 would be $1 billion higher than for 1971, and the final figure of the increase was actually $1.3 billion.[32] This momentum was maintained when the Eurogroup pledged in December 1972 to increase its expenditures for 1973 by $1.5 billion.[33] Again the actual increase exceeded the estimate, with the Eurogroup spending an additional $2.9 billion. In 1974 they pledged to spend $2 billion more than in the preceding year, and they actually spent $4.5 billion more.[34]

Such European initiatives were welcomed by the American public, which had in any event become accustomed to underestimating Europe's defense efforts. It therefore came as a surprise to many when the U.S. Department of Defense estimated in 1971 that of the troops on duty in NATO Europe, the Europeans provided 90 percent of the ground forces, 80 percent of the naval forces, and 75 percent of the air forces.[35]*

The maintenance of an adequate military posture in Europe is a formidable undertaking, since there are relentless pressures both in Western Europe and North America pushing toward unilateral disarmament. There is, first of all, a strong tendency in Western public opinion to confuse the prospect of a stable detente with its realization as an accomplished fact. Beyond that, the propensity for wishful thinking has been aggravated by the economics of the new defense technology, which involves enormous and mounting

---

*Senator Nunn points out that these figures are somewhat misleading since almost half the allied manpower in this count is found in Southern Europe (Italy, Greece, and Turkey), where there are no significant U.S. ground forces. The U.S. contribution in Central Europe is accordingly more important. Moreover the quality of U.S. ground and air forces tends to be better than that of most allies. As far as naval forces are concerned, the allies have nothing to compare with the U.S. carriers.[36]

expenses in developing and deploying increasingly sophisticated weapons systems. Under these circumstances NATO has needed all the help it could get, including an occasional piece of good fortune, in order to sustain it.

One such stroke of luck occurred in May 1971 when Senator Mansfield proposed that the U.S. force levels in Europe be cut in half by the end of 1971. NATO had waited in vain for any clear response to its Reykjavik Ministerial offer of June 1968 to the Warsaw Pact to enter into negotiations on mutual and balanced force reductions.[37] Mansfield introduced his resolution on May 11, and in what can only be counted a Soviet political blunder, Brezhnev made a speech in Tiflis three days later in which he offered to begin exploratory talks on mutual troops reductions in Europe.[38] It may well be that Brezhnev's speech had been prepared long before Mansfield's May initiative, and the inertial momentum of the Soviet bureaucracy could not prevent its delivery. In any event, Brezhnev appeared to reply by raising the prospect for the first time that negotiations on mutual reductions might be possible. Mansfield's proposal for unilateral American troop withdrawals therefore seemed especially untimely and this contributed to its defeat.* For the moment the argument seemed persuasive that the Kremlin would have no reason to negotiate seriously on mutual reductions if the United States unilaterally gave away the game before the starting whistle.

In September 1973 Mansfield resumed the offensive with a proposal for a 40 percent unilateral reduction of U.S. troop strength abroad over the next three years. This measure actually passed the Senate by a 49 to 46 vote, although it was rescinded a few hours later by a vote of 55 to 41. While Mansfield did not specify Europe, it was apparent that U.S. troop levels in Europe would have been affected by such a large withdrawal. Subsequently the Senate adopted the proposal of Senator Hubert Humphrey for a 23 percent reduction of U.S. troops overseas, leaving it to the President to decide where to

---

*In May 1971 Mansfield's proposal to cut U.S. troop strength in Europe by half was defeated by a Senate vote of 61 to 36. In November 1971 Mansfield returned with a more modest proposal to reduce U.S. troops by 60,000 (from 310,000 to 250,000) by June 1972. This was also defeated by a vote of 54 to 39, again in part because the prospect of mutual reductions seemed to be in the offing.

make the withdrawals. It was the intent of this proposal to draw down troop strength from Asia and the Pacific, without disturbing the U.S. position in NATO or upsetting the negotiations with the Russians on mutual troop reductions in Europe. Even this watered-down compromise failed to pass the House of Representatives. In June 1974 Mansfield again sponsored two proposals that were also defeated, which would have required sharp cutbacks in U.S. forces abroad. While U.S. troops had not actually been withdrawn as a result of Mansfield's initiatives, the display of continuing and mounting congressional pressure for unilateral reductions could not help but undermine the U.S. bargaining position. Such a state of affairs might well be enough to remove any genuine incentive for the Russians to respond with concessions on their part, since they could calculate upon successfully playing a waiting game until they painlessly won their objective.

Perhaps for this reason the Soviet leaders subsequently displayed the greatest reluctance to implement Brezhnev's pledge. It was only by tying the convocation of the Conference on Security and Cooperation in Europe, which the Russians wanted, to negotiations on mutual force reductions, which the NATO states wanted, that it was possible to enter exploratory talks at the beginning of 1973 and to commence actual bargaining on mutual reductions of troops and armaments in Central Europe in October 1973.*

In entering these negotiations the deck was unavoidably stacked in favor of the Kremlin. As the two alliances faced each other in Central Europe, the Warsaw Pact was superior both in troop strength and in armaments. Moreover, the Soviet bloc states are in large measure immune to the pressures of public opinion that can restrict defense spending in the West. Due to the differences in the social systems in East and West, the funds actually spent on defense in the NATO countries buy much less defense potential, since the costs of military pay in the West have nearly doubled the rate of inflation,

---

*At the exploratory talks on Mutual Balanced Force Reductions in 1973, the Russians insisted upon deleting the "B" from MBFR. The official title became "Negotiations on Mutual Reduction of Forces and Armaments and Associated Measures in Central Europe." The U.S. claimed it salvaged the idea of balanced reductions by incorporating into the agreement "the principle of undiminished security for each party." (*Atlantic News,* June 29, 1973, p. 3.)

while the personnel costs of the Warsaw Pact countries have stayed roughly level. In addition, the Soviet bloc has maintained conscription, while it has been abolished in several major NATO states, and the terms of service have worsened in others. In terms of equipment, Soviet models have been largely imposed on the Warsaw Pact, giving it widespread standardization and interoperability of parts, unlike NATO which has never attained significant standardization.

Geographically, the Warsaw Pact forms a contiguous land bloc that is not reliant of sea power for its internal lines of supply and communications. NATO is dependent upon control of the Atlantic and Mediterranean for its survival, but these lifelines have become increasingly vulnerable to a Soviet submarine force, which is nearly five times the size of the German U-boat force at the outbreak of World War II. The mission of interdicting NATO shipping is infinitely easier than assuring its protection.

There is another geographic asymmetry in the forces facing each other in Central Europe. A withdrawal of U.S. forces across the Atlantic does not equal the withdrawal of Soviet forces behind the Bug. The return of the Soviet forces would be by a secure overland route of slightly more than 300 miles, while the U.S. forces would have to rely upon a complicated land-sea-air line of communication of more than 3,000 miles. Politically there would also be fewer inhibitions to the return of Soviet troops to Central Europe. Moreover, the advantage in returning these forces would lie with the attacker who would wish to seize the initiative. The easier Soviet reinforcement ability would permit the Kremlin to decide the time, place, and mode of attack by concentrating its forces at critical points that would not likely be adequately defended, since a NATO defense must prepare plans and dispose forces against many possibilities. In order to forestall the rapid return of forces, verification and early warning systems must be built into any accord on force reductions. Without these safeguards the existing disparities would be greatly magnified. However, the different political and social systems in East and West make the implementation of verification schemes much more difficult in a closed than in an open society.[39]

Despite all of these qualifications, there is no doubt that a less-than-perfect formula for mutual troop reductions is infinitely preferable to unilateral Western ones. This is especially true of the withdrawal of U.S. forces. "Reciprocal troop withdrawals," Theo

Sommer accurately judged, "are the best way for the Americans to leave Europe without losing it. On the basis of mutuality, U.S. troop withdrawals would not appear as a retreat but rather as a contribution towards the evolution of a more cooperative relationship in Europe."[40]

To oppose unilateral U.S. troop withdrawals from Europe is not necessarily to defend the military status quo. A growing number of military observers have concluded that the U.S. forces in Europe are costing more than necessary while providing less than the necessary war-fighting capabilities. These defects can be overcome, it is argued, by restructuring the U.S. forces and reshaping NATO's military posture. NATO and particularly U.S. forces are modeled too closely on the requirements of an all-purpose, expeditionary-type force capable of indefinite and sustained offensive operations that were appropriate to World War II, but that are largely irrelevant to the needs of contemporary Europe.

Soviet troops are structured for a *blitzkreig*, that is, they possess great shock power for a short, intensive campaign. The U.S. forces, by comparison, are prepared for an improbable long war that requires them to drag behind a long logistical tail while skimping on front-line combat troops. Thus less than 30 percent of U.S. costs for NATO are directly related to the assignment of fighting a short war in the crucial central region. Priority attention must be given to improving the U.S. "teeth-to-tail ratio" so that its forces will be tailored to provide an effective initial defense in depth against the kind of assault for which the Warsaw Pact forces seem designed. The restructuring of U.S. forces, and to a lesser extent those of the other NATO allies, could free enough resources to generate the combat forces that could make the NATO strategy of flexible response and forward defense a reality.

The disparity in war-fighting ability is readily apparent when one considers that the nearly 200,000 U.S. troops in Europe have only generated 4-1/3 large divisions, while the Russians have managed to squeeze out 20 divisions from their 300,000 Soviet Army personnel in East Germany. Admittedly the Soviet divisions are smaller, but by virtue of their emphasis on combat troops, in the aggregate they represent much greater shock power than the U.S. forces. The argument here is that there is no reason why NATO has to spend huge sums for its forces and still come up with conventional combat inferiority.

A small step in the right direction was taken when Secretary of Defense James Schlesinger, acting in response to persistent congressional pressure, announced in November 1974 that the United States would establish two new combat brigades in Germany. The creation of these new combat units would not, however, alter the total number of U.S. troops abroad since there would be a reduction in a comparable number of support troops.

In addition to a more rational design of the force structure, there are a number of technological innovations that could greatly contribute to better defense at lower costs. The Yom Kippur war demonstrated the extraordinary effectiveness of modern antitank and antiaircraft weapons, particularly the use of "smart" bombs and artillery (those either with television or laser beam guidance).* The lesson from this experience is apparently that defense can overwhelm offense. Since "smart" bombs have a very high probability of "one shot/one kill," there would be a greatly reduced need for various kinds of ordinary ammunition. Moreover, their ability to stop invading tanks and planes would mean that NATO forces adequately supplied with "smart" weapons could nullify the numerical superiority of Warsaw Pact armor and aircraft. It should also be possible, for example, to reduce the need for extremely expensive aircraft that are now held for use in close tactical air support missions.

Through these and other related measures NATO could effectively offset the offensive threat of the Warsaw Pact and achieve parity in conventional forces. Politically, in conditions of a nuclear standoff, the attainment of conventional parity would eliminate the Kremlin's ability to make Western Europe hostage to the overwhelming power of Soviet conventional strength. Deprived of the political advantage from the deployment of its conventional forces, the Kremlin might be better motivated to arrive at some negotiated solutions for Europe's outstanding problems. At a minimum it should be more feasible to arrive at reciprocal force reductions once both sides had achieved comparable military strengths than it is at present, where great disparities exist both in effective troop strength and weapons systems.[41]

---

*In per unit cost, the "smart" bombs are ten times more expensive than conventional, gravity, or "dumb" bombs. However, the "smart" bombs are a hundred times more accurate. Therefore in terms of cost-effectiveness, the "smart" bombs are ten times cheaper than the "dumb" ones.

Over a prolonged period of time the military confrontation in the center of Europe might give way to the reconciliation of opposing forces and the creation of some new system of security and cooperation. In the meanwhile, maintaining reduced but still adequate NATO, and in particular U.S., force levels is required in order to provide the basis from which such a future political settlement in Europe might proceed. NATO must be viewed as an instrument both for performing the military function of peace keeping and the political function of peace making. Both tasks are interdependent, and neither one can succeed without the other. Western unity cannot be maintained on the limited basis of a purely defensive alliance, while the pursuit of detente makes it essential to infuse the military aspect of NATO with a meaningful political goal. But success in moving toward the political goal will be impossible unless it is firmly rooted in a strong Atlantic Alliance.

In pursuing the long-term political objective, difficulties commonly arise from a confusion in priorities and time scale. As Marshall Shulman has wisely counseled, "the essential point is to keep our priorities clear. Above all, the Soviet political challenge requires primary concern for the vitality and integrity of the Western Alliance."[42] Admittedly, Western cohesion may be more difficult to maintain than it was in the Stalinist era when a military threat to the West appeared imminent. Though still supported by a menacing military posture, the post-Stalinist leadership became adept at a more indirect thrust that was essentially political in nature by taking full advantage of the divisive nationalist tendencies that have come to the surface as the immediate military danger seemed to recede.

The most exaggerated form of Western nationalism was found in Gaullist doctrine, which held that the trans-Atlantic NATO bond was obsolete and should be replaced by intra-European ties aimed at creating a "European Europe." Faced with this challenge, it is necessary to stress "the order of priorities," as Shulman explained, since "the revival of Western Europe and trends toward greater autonomy in Eastern Europe have raised the question whether the effort to integrate Eastern and Western Europe should now take precedence over the effort to maintain and develop the association between Western Europe and the United States." In order to answer this question, it is necessary to recognize that each relationship presents "quite different time perspectives: The prospects for a union of East and West depend upon the dissolution of fundamental characteristics in the Soviet Union and its relations with Eastern

Europe which do not appear to be likely for many years, probably many decades; while the association of Western Europe and the United States is now the heart of the power of the West, the main bulwark against Soviet pressures, and an important factor in encouraging a long-term trend toward moderation in Soviet policies."[43]

The ultimate aim of a strong Western Alliance is to liquidate the division of Europe, resulting from World War II, and to negotiate a peaceful reconciliation with the East. The question of priorities, however, cannot be neglected. Europe will not likely be made whole by the efforts of Europe alone. If NATO were dissolved, so that the United States became estranged from Western Europe, while the European countries imitated the Gaullist pursuit of individual nationalist causes, is there any doubt that the Soviet Union could succeed in preserving and deepening these divisions until such time as it would be in a position to dictate its own all-European settlement? Soviet willingness to come to terms with the West on terms the West could find acceptable will only evolve over a considerable period of time, during which Western power and a general consensus on political purpose must be maintained. There will be the constant temptation for individual Western nations to short-circuit this prolonged process by giving priority to their relations with the East, rather than upholding their sense of community in the West. While the separate Western countries might gain some short-run tactical advantages, this reversion of priorities is a certain formula for long-term disaster.

NATO'S POLITICAL ROLE IN THE SEARCH FOR DETENTE

To what extent has NATO developed the capacity to help formulate Western political aims? And as NATO has become involved in the politics of detente, what mechanics are appropriate for pursuing this goal?

Staking a maximum claim for its future scope of activity, Lord Avon suggested in 1967 that NATO's "new tasks should be mainly diplomatic as well as military. It should be the negotiating body with the Warsaw powers to see whether agreements can be reached which will benefit Europe as a whole."[44] During the same period Belgian Foreign Minister Pierre Harmel also proposed that selected aspects of detente, such as disarmament by agreed stages, be negotiated between the two alliances as such, instead of between individual countries.[45] Viewed as a means for avoiding different Western policy initiatives that could work at cross-purposes and for endowing the West with the strongest bargaining position, there is much to be said for this approach. Its implementation, however, involves a cumbersome process. NATO has certain elements of integration in the military realm, and in this respect it represents an effort to transcend a traditional military alliance. Politically, however, NATO is not a sovereign entity and its highest organ, the North Atlantic Council, remains a permanent diplomatic conference, however elaborately it may be organized with a supporting network of agencies, committees, and subcommittees. Therefore, any "NATO" position is dependent upon continuous, intensive, and the always fragile process of multilateral consultations.

There was sufficient cohesion among the NATO members on the question of mutual and balanced force reductions to permit the NATO Ministerial meeting of June 1971 to announce its willingness to appoint "a representative or representatives who would be responsible to the Council for conducting further exploratory talks" with the Soviet bloc states about force reductions.[46] In October 1971 the North Atlantic Council duly appointed retiring Secretary General Manlio Brosio as NATO "explorer" for this purpose.[47] As it turned out, nothing came of this initiative, since the Soviet leaders studiously ignored Brosio's request for an audience. The fact that an individual could be empowered to deal with the Warsaw Pact on behalf of NATO was nevertheless a considerable step forward, since it assumed a high degree of allied solidarity and an ability to work out agreed positions that the NATO emissary could transmit to the opposing side.

France, reflecting the Gaullist abhorrence about "subservience" to military blocs, did not participate in these or other NATO proceedings that related to negotiations on force reductions. But this proved to be a happy solution since it removed an obstructionist and discordant voice from the allied forum and permitted the others to get on with the business at hand. If there are difficulties associated with bloc-to-bloc negotiations, the Gaullist alternative of purely bilateral relations is surely worse. For each Western country to emulate de Gaulle's policy of moving with "free hands" would be to institutionalize chaos and weakness, which the Kremlin would certainly exploit.

Under the most favorable circumstances this danger would always exist, because of the growing number of East-West contacts that would be conducted on a bilateral basis over a wide range of topics, whether they dealt with cultural, scientific, or economic arrangements, or with political and military issues. "But precisely because we will all be negotiating about improvements of East-West relations," Ambassador Cleveland properly pointed out, "there is a growing problem of political management and diplomatic coordination."[48] When moving into a period of detente, therefore, use of the Alliance forum for concerting policies on matters that have a significant impact on the concerns of each other must become increasingly important. The more the West negotiates with the East, the more it is necessary to perfect the structure of the relations within the West. This will remain true despite the fact that it might also become increasingly difficult, since a period of lower international tensions sorely tempts each nation to go its own way, under the illusion that it can do so in safety.

A forum for multilateral diplomacy, like the North Atlantic Council, can, if properly used, overcome many of the drawbacks inherent in bilateral negotiations. It can save an enormous amount of time and energy; instead of having to write diplomatic notes to 15 governments and receive 15 disparate replies, it is possible, in one setting, to raise an issue and work out a common approach through joint consultation and discussion. It is also easier at times to get agreement on individual topics, since a sort of quid pro quo expectation develops in a group setting; agreement by one national representative today might bring support for his country's special interests elsewhere tomorrow. Moreover, multilateral diplomacy often makes it easier to apply pressure upon individual recalcitrant members so as to achieve a greater consensus. The Council's ability to meet continuously and privately also provides an opportunity for quiet diplomacy quite unlike deliberations in the United Nations, for example, where a good share of the effort is consumed by the need to produce propaganda both for foreign and domestic audiences.

Ambassador Cleveland plainly stated the American attitude toward using the NATO forum in 1967, as the politics of detente was becoming increasingly prominent: "Our NATO allies want us to push for detente with the Soviets; but they also want to be cut in, early and often, on any discussions which affect their interests. The proposition which we are putting to our allies is very simple. Each East-West negotiation by any ally touches the interests of all. We should certainly keep each other closely informed, as we mostly do already through political consultation in NATO." Moreover, when negotiations get under way, "we should try to get to each stage of agreement together, not making little deals piecemeal and hand the Soviets the enormous negotiating advantage of setting national self-interest against the common interest of the West." In his view, "the Atlantic Alliance is of course the framework for organizing the politics of detente, and this function falls naturally to the North Atlantic Council."[49] The discharge of this function was conceived both as long-termed and low-keyed. "We tend to look upon the role of the Council as a kind of standing diplomatic conference on East-West relations, as a place for study and analysis, a clearinghouse for exchange of experience; as a forum in which the allies try out their ideas on each other; as a mechanism for coordinating and guiding, but not usually for conducting, a range of West-to-East initiatives which together add up to a coherent whole."[50]

NATO Ministerial meetings since May 1965 have regularly dealt with the possibility of achieving improvements in East-West relations, and since then both the Council and its Committee of Political Advisors have carried standing East-West items on the agendas of their weekly meetings. The Committee of Political Advisors, consisting of the political specialists in each NATO delegation, customarily examines in some detail the first stages of policy considerations. It sorts out ideas and policy positions on key issues that will be brought before the Council and seeks to discover areas of consensus or fresh approaches that might transcend different national positions. When discussing East-West affairs, it has frequently called in for consultation officials from the different member countries who are directly concerned with formulating policies that bear upon contacts with the East.[51] Following the 1967 Harmel study on the future tasks of the Alliance, a second "senior" Committee of Political Advisors, consisting of the deputy permanent representatives, was set up in order to provide intensive study of specific topics on projects that had been requested by the North

Atlantic Council. This little-noted but valuable committee has met often and has undertaken comprehensive studies on the most challenging issues involved in East-West negotiations.[52]

The political stock-taking involved in the Harmel study emphasized the importance of the political functions the Alliance must perform in the search for a European settlement. "The way to peace and stability in Europe rests in particular on the use of the Alliance constructively in the interest of detente." It was recognized that discussion of complex East-West questions might be conducted "bilaterally, or multilaterally," and that while "currently the development of contacts between the countries of Western and Eastern Europe is mainly on a bilateral basis," nevertheless, "certain subjects, of course, require by their very nature a multilateral solution." In any event, "the chances of success will clearly be greatest if the allies remain on parallel courses." This report, which the NATO Ministerial meeting of December 1967 adopted unanimously, directed "the Council in permanent session to carry out, in the years ahead, the detailed follow-up resulting from this study.* This will be done either by intensifying work already in hand or by activating highly specialized studies by more systematic use of experts and officials sent from capitals." On the basis of these studies of East-West problems, further reports would be made available for the consideration of future NATO Ministerial meetings.[53] The political resources of NATO were thus pledged to dealing with the problems of detente management for an indefinite future.

---

*The unanimous adoption of this report was a diplomatic success of sorts, although the importance of French agreement should not be exaggerated. After threatening to dissent, France finally went along, most likely out of consideration for the sensitivities of the Germans, who are so immediately affected by any East-West contacts or arrangements. French adherence, however, was bought at the price of watering down sections of the report that called for a stronger commitment to the Alliance and its machinery. In any event, the French fully protected themselves by the sentence in the report: "As sovereign states the allies are not obliged to subordinate their policies to collective decision." De Gaulle never consulted the North Atlantic Council about any of his policies, including East-West relations. The Pompidou presidency did produce more accommodating behavior, particularly in coordinating policies toward CSCE, and while Pompidou continued de Gaulle's campaign against military blocs conducting negotiations about mutual troop reductions, from 1970 on he affirmed the importance of maintaining U.S. troops in Europe.

The Council and its various committees, supported by the work of the NATO Secretariat, proceeded to examine on a continuing basis all the issues on East-West relations that finally came before both the CSCE and the negotiations on mutual reduction of forces and armaments in Central Europe. The CSCE began preparatory meetings in Helsinki in November 1972 and later reconvened in Geneva in September 1973 for its substantive deliberations. Preliminary meetings on the troop reductions issue opened in Vienna at the end of January 1973, while the negotiating phase was launched in Vienna at the end of October 1973.

Each forum presented a somewhat different picture, both with regard to the topics discussed and the states represented. The CSCE talks covered a variety of subjects, ranging from confidence-building measures for military security to the free flow of ideas and people to cooperation in economic, scientific, and environmental fields. In all there were 33 European states of every political persuasion, including neutrals, plus the United States and Canada. In the midst of this diversity the members of the European Community and of NATO sought systematically to align their policy positions through prior consultations. The Vienna talks were restricted to the single but immensely complex topic of mutual troop reductions. This was an assemblage of 19 states. Those with troops on the Central European front were cast as the principal negotiators, while their allies on the flanks were given observer status. Although not officially billed as bloc-to-bloc negotiations, this in effect is what they were, since those who represented the West were all members of NATO, while all the participants from the East were members of the Warsaw Pact.

Early in 1973 NATO Secretary General Joseph Luns reviewed the intensive preparation that had taken place at NATO, especially since 1970, in anticipation of these conferences. "A number of allied bodies have devoted most of their energies to harmonizing the position of member countries on all matters likely to be discussed" at both multilateral conferences. "The number and size of the dossiers compiled for this purpose reflect diplomatic activity on a quite unprecedented scale. Members of the Council and of the various committees have made a point of dealing in the fullest possible detail with all the issues which could come up during these first multilateral contacts between East and West. Allied countries have agreed that consultation on the harmonization of their positions should take place within the framework of the Alliance." Since in-depth consultations on such a range of topics exceeded any previous experience in NATO, Luns found cause for considerable satisfaction. "We can, it seems to me, be legitimately proud of what it has done, working from existing bilateral or regional arrangements, to help achieve a general discussion on all the problems relating to security and cooperation between East and West, the importance of which escapes no one."[54]

This positive appraisal was confirmed by West German Foreign Minister Walter Scheel in June 1973, when he asserted that "during the talks in Helsinki and Vienna NATO has proven that it can handle such negotiations, that its internal ties are not loosened by such talks but rather that they are strengthened. We were able to prevail with the goals we set for our negotiations, due to the effective mechanism of consultations among each other."[55]

Similarly, Deputy Secretary of State Kenneth Rush declared in the spring of 1973: "NATO is playing a central role in the formulation of Western positions for both of this year's major multilateral negotiations with the East." He acknowledged that "when the Alliance began to prepare for those conferences several years ago, there were disagreements on a number of important issues. Starting from this point, NATO is moving toward agreement on basic issues and is strengthening itself considerably in the process. At no time in its history has political consultation been more successful nor more important. The Alliance has grown as it faced new challenges." The mechanism for concerting policies begins in NATO, where "overall Alliance policy is being established in NATO's North Atlantic Council. After intensive study of the issues within NATO, our representatives in the Council reached coordinated positions which serve as general guidelines for negotiators from allied countries in Helsinki and Vienna. . . . This consultation, both in NATO and at the talks themselves, demonstrates the allies' willingness and ability to compromise and reach consensus on specific issues in the interest of continuing allied unity."

Rush also looked ahead to the conclusion of CSCE, which some have anticipated might result in some sort of a permanent Standing Commission on East-West Relations. "Whether or not this conference establishes permanent East-West machinery, it is clear that NATO will have a considerable role to play after the conference. NATO logically should be the forum for allied consultations on East-West military security issues." If East-West negotiations succeed in a liberalization of the movement of people and ideas, a NATO role would also be appropriate here. "And there undoubtedly will need to be a framework for coordinating allied views in connections with other East-West initiatives."[56] In short, NATO has established itself as a principal diplomatic forum for the management of East-West relations both for the present and the future.

The gravity of the issues to be faced and the potential for the disruption of allied solidarity should not be underestimated. The negotiations on force reductions, in particular, will raise divisive issues about how to measure the widely differing military capabilities of the participants and how to decide whose forces should be reduced and under what circumstances. All of the fundamental and long-debated questions of the Alliance will be revived in a new context: What should be the allied force posture and strategic doctrine? What meaning should be attributed to the American nuclear guarantee for Europe under the changed conditions of a new alignment of forces? What of the future rules for the British and French nuclear deterrents? How can the interests shared by the superpowers be reconciled with Alliance commitments? These and other questions cannot be avoided as the allies proceed to deal with the complexities of the problems that are inherent in far-reaching East-West negotiations. The most severe challenge to the Alliance still lies ahead.

AMERICAN POLICY MAKING AND NATO'S POLITICAL FUNCTIONS

In order to maximize the usefulness of NATO as a political forum, policy making in the largest and strongest partner must proceed more or less simultaneously with the consideration of the same issues in the Council. Otherwise, if prior policy determinations have been made in Washington, experience has shown that it is exceedingly difficult to modify them in a Council discussion, and political consultation is reduced to a rather sterile exchange of formal diplomatic positions. The same maxim of intertwining national and NATO policy making holds for all member states, of course, but the United States presents a special problem. "It is simply the size of the American bureaucracy which makes a qualitative difference," Alastair Buchan contends. "The United States government itself has the characteristics of an alliance and the process of evolving decisions on high policy is probably more difficult for it than in that of any other government in the world." The crucial factor is one of timing, rather than the impenetrability of the American governmental apparatus. "American public servants," Buchan holds, "are perhaps the most open-minded in the world, are less hampered by traditional conceptions than their European counterparts, and are closely linked to a system of academic discussion and research on public policy of great vitality. This means that in the preliminary stages of the evolution of a new policy or strategy, or reaction to an external challenge, the discussion is a relatively free one and in which the views of allies are welcome. But so difficult is the process of reconciling the views of different departments, agencies and branches of the government that the further it moves up the chain of authority the more inflexible positions become."[57]

Proposals for reaching into the American political apparatus so as to interweave it with NATO, as well as efforts to strengthen significantly the political functions of NATO itself, could predictably be expected to generate resistance from the United States. In one respect it is all too easy for a superpower to act unilaterally, since it feels fewer restraints upon its capabilities than its less powerful allies. The late Italian Foreign Minister Gaetano Martino testified to the difficulties he encountered in this regard. Several times at NATO Ministerial meetings he recalled urging measures "to transform the Alliance into a true Community." Martino was also a member of the committee of the "Three Wise Men," whose report of December 1956 on political cooperation in NATO recommended procedures to attain greater allied political solidarity. "Unfortunately the suggestions made by this committee," he noted with regret a decade later, "have not been rightly implemented; and we must not forget that this is partly due to the resistance opposed at that time by the American government to the concept of transfer of sovereignty."[58]

In another respect it is already too difficult for the U.S. government, given its complexity, to arrive at a policy decision even when left strictly to itself. Infusing foreign ingredients into the policy mix before reaching an agreed position would only make the process more complicated and time consuming, so that such a procedure might understandably be resisted by American officialdom. The easy and superficial argument therefore appears to be clearly in favor of going it alone. But the price for this is certainly high, and in the long run it is bound to complicate, not simplify, the American policy-making problem. By injecting allied ideas and getting their reactions to American policy planning in the formative stages, it should be possible to avoid the emergence of radically different national approaches, which would otherwise have to be argued out largely in public after the different national positions had hardened and were not readily amenable to negotiation. American unilateralism either isolates the United States from its allies and creates needless and corrosive controversy, or at best it produces superficial support that gives way at the first test of a crisis. In either case, the American ability to deal with Alliance problems is gravely weakened, European confidence in American policies is undermined, and the West's capacity to act effectively is complicated by discord within the Alliance. The North Atlantic Council is also obviously drained of its potential for creating a common way of looking at problems of mutual concern and becomes an empty shell.

Harlan Cleveland, speaking as U.S. Ambassador to NATO, conveyed the earnest intent of his government to take allied views into account and make the Council a meaningful center of allied political discourse. "We should practice in the Alliance," he said with reference to his colleagues, "a Golden Rule of Consultation: you should consult with us as early, as frankly, and as often as you would want to be consulted by us."[59] This was a commendable pledge, but to be meaningful the consultative process cannot be confined to the Council forum. Taken as part of a broadly conceived method of allied consultation conducted simultaneously on both sides of the Atlantic, however, this American commitment could acquire genuine importance. Former Ambassador Theodore Achilles put the case well when he said that "the jealously manned ramparts of national sovereignty will not yield to bold frontal attacks," but rather to "the gradual development of common policy and common action in the common interest. This is where we need joint formulation of policy" which would require "common or agreed intelligence, integrated staff work serving the common rather than the national interest, and full participation in the process by senior officials responsible for policy formation within their own governments." Rudimentary progress in these directions had been made in NATO, but "given the political will on the part of the U.S. government to grant its allies a share in the *formulation* of its policies, results could be spectacular. Policies formulated in common raise few decision-making problems when the time comes to implement them."[60]

In practice, efforts have been made to observe the two basic rules of meshing the American and NATO political processes by cranking allied policy preferences into the American governmental machine in the early stages of policy consideration and of coordinating planning studies in Washington with those undertaken at NATO headquarters. For some time there has existed in Washington an informal club, consisting of officers in the embassies of the NATO countries at the subambassadorial level who are assigned to make regular rounds of their colleagues as well as keep in close contact with the U.S. State Department and the International Security Affairs office of the Department of Defense.* Also those engaged in policy planning on both sides of the Atlantic find themselves frequently on a jet shuttle between Brussels and Washington.

In order to make such contacts more dependable and fruitful, Buchan suggested formalizing and upgrading these arrangements. "A good case can be made for developing subsidiary NATO political machinery in Washington, perhaps in the form of a consultative council of the ambassadors of the NATO countries, meeting regularly with the Secretaries of State and of Defense, and with a small permanent staff. Its essential purpose would be to provide a multilateral setting in which American ideas and proposals could be raised before they solidified into official policy."[61] Similarly, in the case of NATO contingency planning and crisis management, he proposed that the NATO Treaty area possibly be subdivided into three areas, with the United States a member of each region and Washington the site for the permanent deliberations of the diplomatic and military representatives of each group. These would function on the model of the high-level quadripartite consultative group that was developed following the 1958 Soviet threat to Berlin. Meeting on an ambassadorial level at first in Washington, and then

---

*The usefulness of these contacts declined under the Nixon administration, especially in the period before Henry Kissinger became Secretary of State, since the concentration of power in the White House over foreign policy decisions frequently left the State and Defense Departments in the dark.

also in Bonn, much valuable work was accomplished in arriving at common approaches, or at least in narrowing the divergent viewpoints of the powers responsible for the safety of Berlin.[62] While this particular arrangement might be more appropriate for crisis management in a situation of East-West conflict, the basic principle of involving high-level American policy makers with their European counterparts is equally valid for East-West relations that are concerned with detente management.

Eugene Rostow, who served as Under Secretary of State for Political Affairs from 1966 to 1969, likewise recommended making Washington the site of additional NATO political machinery, especially as it might relate to crisis management. "On the basis of my experience," Rostow related, "I have concluded that Washington is the only possible base for the management of political crises, because of the pressure of time." Therefore he recommended that "improved arrangements for crisis management, which are an urgent task for the Alliance, should consider the feasibility of dual basing, to borrow a military term, or other devices to assure the possibility of a stronger, more regular, and more considered allied voice in Washington. Such tasks are beyond the reach of ambassadors alone, however expert and experienced. They cannot take the place of experts and of ministers responsible for policy in the particular area which is the subject of the crisis." This could be a flexible arrangement with consultations limited to those allies that were willing, in principle, to assume responsibility for the decisions taken. Such dual basing, however, was not intended to undercut the operation of NATO in Brussels. "This is not in any way to suggest a diminution in the functions and responsibilities of the Council or the Secretariat. On the contrary, my thought is to extend and enlarge those responsibilities, by involving the Council more directly in the task of making decisions. The Council meets regularly in all our capitals. My suggestion is that we build informally and inflexibly on that practice, as circumstance may make such developments desirable and feasible."[63]

Thoughtful suggestions have also been advanced for improving NATO long-term policy planning. Buchan specifically conceived of a NATO Policy Planning Council in permanent session, to which member states would be expected to assign senior, first-rate officers. In order to give continuity to long-range planning, it was suggested that they serve in their posts for at least three or four years, and since they would be obliged to make frequent trans-Atlantic trips between

NATO headquarters and Washington, as well as between other allied capitals, they should be relieved of distracting diplomatic duties of a routine nature.[64]*

NATO'S EFFORTS AT LONG-TERM POLICY PLANNING

Over the years, NATO has taken hesitant steps toward fulfilling the need for long-term policy planning. A decision of the NATO Ministerial meeting in the spring of 1961 created the Atlantic Policy Advisory Group (APAG), which began to function in July 1962. Composed of senior policy planners in the various NATO foreign offices, APAG has generally met twice a year for a total of five or six days and has devoted its sessions to problems of mutual concern which do not usually have an immediate operational character.[65] The basic conception behind these deliberations is sound, since the NATO ambassadors in the Council tend to be overwhelmed with a continuous stream of day-to-day operational problems, sometimes of crisis proportions, which make it impossible to devote the time to a more detached evaluation of long-range policy projections.

Another limited effort to establish high-level, systematic political consultations came at the end of 1964, out of American concern for Europe's misunderstanding of the growing American involvement in Vietnam. Under Secretary of State George Ball proposed adding four annual meetings at the level of foreign ministers or deputy foreign ministers to consider any problem beyond the geographic limits of the NATO Treaty area. The NATO Ministerial meeting in December 1964 agreed, with France dissenting, to hold a few such meetings on an ad hoc trial basis, and three such special sessions were assembled in 1965. Ball reported that

---

*As to the seat of the Planning Council, Buchan admits that "it is a nice question whether it should be based in Washington or Europe: the argument of Washington is a very strong one, for locating it there would provide the proper relationship to the world-wide policy of the United States. To locate it in Europe would, on the other hand, preserve the balance between the European and the North American halves of the Alliance."

Belgian Foreign Minister Paul-Henri Spaak and Dutch Foreign Minister Joseph Luns were "enthusiastic participants," although no agreement was reached on what to do about Vietnam—which was scarcely surprising. This limited-purpose experiment then lapsed.[66]

The need still remained to provide more effective consideration of all sorts of important political issues that would continue to arise in the coming decades, both within and beyond the NATO Treaty area, and preferably to discuss them thoroughly and frankly before a crisis had blossomed. In an effort to develop better methods for assessing basic political concerns, President Nixon seized the occasion of NATO's twentieth anniversary celebration in April 1969 to propose the creation of "new machinery for Western political consultation, as well as to make greater use of the process that already exists." He suggested that "deputy foreign ministers meet periodically for a high-level review of major, long-range problems before the Alliance." In addition, Nixon advocated the "creation of a special political planning group, not to duplicate the work now being done by the Council or by the senior political advisers, but to address itself specifically and continually to the longer range problems we face."[67] It was also made clear that the intensified political consultations on an Atlanticwide basis that might arise from such arrangements would not, in the American view, be intended to inhibit efforts to form a European identity, but rather that movement toward European unity could proceed within the larger trans-Atlantic community of interest.

After these proposals had been thoroughly considered by the North Atlantic Council, it was determined that it would be better to build upon the existing Atlantic Policy Advisory Group than to create a new high-level political planning body. Starting with an initial two-year trial period beginning in the fall of 1969, APAG functions were reformulated and enlarged. Policy planners were to meet once a year at some quiet retreat away from NATO headquarters, as under the old format, to discuss long-range issues. The Council was to keep in close touch with these deliberations by making certain that the topics were relevant to the mainstream of Alliance concerns, and instead of simply noting an APAG report as in the past, the Council would be confronted with specific recommendations, that it would be obliged to review and discuss.

A second type of APAG session was designed to take place at NATO headquarters, and this effort at political planning would be directed more toward middle-term policies. It would be attended by operational officials and representatives from within the NATO delegations at Brussels, as well as by high-level foreign office personnel and policy planners from the various capitals. This type of session would, in effect, be an enriched or reinforced Council meeting that would deal with more than day-to-day problems and yet be essentially oriented toward operational objectives of a chronic nature. It was agreed that these meetings would be held at least once a year, although probably more often, but that they would be convened as needed. President Nixon had suggested periodic meetings at the level of deputy foreign ministers, but it was found that this was impractical since some NATO foreign offices did not have an official designated at this rank and, in addition, it was too restrictive, since these meetings might wish to be attended by the foreign ministers themselves.

Among those present at the first reinforced Council policy planning meeting, which convened in November 1969, the high-level representation varied from the Belgian Foreign Minister, the British Minister for European Affairs, the U.S. Under Secretary of State, the German State Secretary of Foreign Affairs, down to the level of the French Permanent Representative on the North Atlantic Council.[68] The Permanent Representatives and their senior political advisors were entrusted with supervising the agenda for this type of APAG meetings, as well as following up the reports that would issue from them. Another indication of the use to which such an enriched or reinforced Council meeting might be put was found in the decision of the Ministerial meeting of the North Atlantic Council in June 1971, which commissioned a high-level Council meeting, to be attended by deputy foreign ministers and other high officials, to examine the issues relating to mutual and balanced force reductions in Central Europe.[69] It was this high-level Council meeting in October 1971 that designated Manlio Brosio at the NATO "explorer" on the issue of troop reductions.[70]

Another variant of a reinforced Council meeting was suggested by Secretary Kissinger in December 1973, following the breakdown in Alliance consultations that was associated with the events of the Yom Kippur war. He proposed that the political directors of the Foreign Ministries of the NATO countries meet regularly, somewhat similar to the practices for political consultation that had been worked out by the Davignon Committee in the European Community. As might be expected, the French objected.

Nevertheless the other NATO countries proceeded to implement this idea in March 1974 when special high-level representatives of the various foreign offices met with the Permanent Representatives of the North Atlantic Council. (France was only represented by its Ambassador to the Council.) In time this might become a regular practice that would supplement other forms of NATO political consultation.[71]

These efforts to expand and remodel APAG have doubtless been useful, although they might have their limitations. By attempting to make the planning apparatus more relevant to operational concerns, it risks becoming bogged down in operational problems and in losing its policy-planning functions. It is not always easy to distinguish between long-range and middle-run problems, nor to prevent either from being reduced to short-term considerations. Moreover, these meetings may not be sufficiently frequent or long so as to provide a continuity of high-level dialogue about policy planning for the Alliance as a whole. Such a revamped APAG falls considerably short of the suggestion advanced by Buchan, for example, for a NATO Policy Planning Council in permanent session, composed of national representatives of exceptional ability and political grasp who could devote their full time to planning functions.

In one respect the proposals that Buchan formulated in the early and middle 1960s seem to have been partially satisfied by the creation of the senior Committee of Political Advisors, which was set up as a result of impetus given to detente management, by the Harmel report of 1967. This committee, meeting frequently just under the ambassadorial level (at the level of deputy permanent representatives), was entrusted with studying all the issues that would affect the long-term future of European security and cooperation. This committee, together with the other previously existing committees and the Council itself, was obliged to undertake intensive consultations and formulate acceptable allied positions on a gamut of topics that were to be subjected to East-West negotiations at Helsinki and Vienna. The prospect of these conferences therefore acted as a forcing house for the articulation of policy positions that were all embedded in some long-range vision of what Europe, and East-West relations generally, should look like in the coming decades. While the deliberations of these various NATO bodies also involved examination of current operational problems, the very scope and extent of the implications of the issues raised by these negotiations demanded that the short-term problems be placed in some meaningful, long-term frame of reference. To the extent that NATO has succeeded in concerting policies for such multilateral negotiations, it may have also taken an important step toward long-range policy planning. Furthermore, to the extent that the United States has shown itself willing to gear its thinking into the Alliance planning mechanisms, it may have succeeded in avoiding the dangers of unilateral behavior, which many observers had long foreseen.

NATO AND THE "THIRD DIMENSION"

President Nixon also used the occasion of NATO's twentieth anniversary to urge upon the Alliance an initiative designed to "explore ways in which the experience and resources of the Western nations could most effectively be marshaled toward improving the quality of life of our peoples." Such an innovation could be inferred from Article 2 of the North Atlantic Treaty dealing with social and economic cooperation, but past efforts to activate it had always proven barren. The time nevertheless had arrived, Nixon concluded, to add to NATO's military and political activities "a third dimension" in the social sphere. One could scarcely dispute Nixon's assertion that the NATO nations comprised advanced technological societies that all faced the urgent challenge of "bringing the 20th century man and his environment to terms with one another—of making the world fit for man and helping man to learn how to remain in harmony with the rapidly changing world."[72]

In effect, the Alliance had the opportunity and obligation to make more livable the quality of life that it was defending. In so doing, it could strengthen the fabric of political solidarity among its members and by adding a valuable dimension to its other activities, gain support that could help sustain its basic military and political functions. Furthermore, the benefits of such a NATO program, which would deal entirely in unclassified documents, would be made available to the rest of the world. Even though the concern with environmental control was universal in nature, there was some logic in having NATO specifically concern itself with these tasks, since its membership represented the most developed countries of the West where the problems of environmental pollution, urban blight, and in general the adverse effects of technology on human existence have already reached the most acute stages.

At first this American proposal met with a mixed reception. While some welcomed the expansion of Alliance interest into areas of positive and constructive programs that transcended its more restricted, traditional activities, others worried that it might distract attention from what they considered were NATO's basic military and political functions. There was also widespread skepticism about the way in which a NATO committee could effectively tackle such a comprehensive catalog of problems posed by this "third dimension." The Belgian parliamentarian, Georges Mundeleer, in a report on this topic to the North Atlantic Assembly in October 1969, pointed out that Europeans were already involved in four international organizations that had for several years been studying the problem of water pollution, but "that has not prevented this calamity from spreading." NATO must avoid adding still another sterile committee and more confusion. To avoid a similar fate, Mundeleer suggested that NATO discussions on different projects take place, at least in their final stages, at an important political level, and that the results of such programs be pursued actively by the NATO parliamentarians within their own national assemblies.[73]

There is little doubt that a routine bureaucratic approach to the vast environmental problems of modern life would make no dent on the public consciousness nor produce tangible results. Success for such a bold venture would obviously require sponsorship at the highest level of the participating governments and a constant determination to enlist the talents of personalities of considerable repute and prestige. President Nixon appointed as the first U.S. representative to NATO to deal with this task his advisor on urban affairs, Daniel Moynihan, who was soon thereafter raised to cabinet rank. The initial American reaction was clearly to give this new NATO undertaking a significant political thrust. In the fall of 1969 the North Atlantic Council formally established a Committee on the Challenges of Modern Society (CCMS), which began functioning in December 1969.[74]

On the eve of its creation, Moynihan explained the rationale for NATO assuming this new function to the parliamentarians of the North Atlantic Assembly. "NATO is unique. For almost two decades now it has carried on, at ever-increasing levels of complexity, a massive system of technology transfer. There has been no such sustained experience in the history of the world. If technology is the issue, NATO is uniquely the forum in which to raise it." There was also reason to turn to NATO because of its political status. "If the issue is one of pressing urgency which somehow does not seem to command the attention it deserves, NATO is doubly appropriate: for here is an institution which year in and year out has been able to command attention and response at the highest levels of government."[75]

In its operation, CCMS has fostered the exchange of national research efforts and sponsored programs undertaken in common by several or all allies in areas that affected them jointly. As projects have been defined, one or two NATO nations have offered to be pilot countries for the study of a specific problem and have assumed the responsibility for preparing reports and for making recommendations for action. Since the pilot countries supply the funds and the personnel for the various studies, it has been possible to avoid the creation of a large bureaucracy for this purpose at NATO headquarters. Hence the NATO International Secretariat and the NATO budget have not been greatly affected by the operating method of CCMS. Furthermore, since a country assumes the role of pilot voluntarily, it might be assumed that it is seriously committed to its chosen project and that it could be relied upon to pursue it vigorously.

CCMS also has been designed to draw upon and add to the work of outside bodies, such as OECD, the Council of Europe, and various U.N. programs concerned with the control of the environment. CCMS has thus become a catalyst, stimulating action by NATO nations either individually, jointly, or through various international organizations, as seemed most appropriate in each case. The risk of duplicating projects in different international organizations may not be entirely avoided, but this difficulty has at least been foreseen and some steps have been taken to minimize the problem. When the Secretaries General of NATO, the Council of Europe, and OECD met in April 1970, NATO Secretary General Brosio stressed the firm determination of CCMS to coordinate its work with that of the other organizations, and as a step in this direction he affirmed that CCMS documents would be circulated widely and freely so as to facilitate a broad exchange of information.[76]

CCMS was not conceived as a research organization, however. As Brosio told the first CCMS meeting, "our efforts will not be directed towards research, but towards questions of government policy formulation and legislation."[77] Or as his successor, Joseph Luns, put it: "CCMS has chosen a specific task: to take existing knowledge and, over a relatively short term, turn that knowledge into action recommendations which can lead to their early implementation and thus to amelioration of selected urgent proglems."[78]

The crucial difficulty indeed becomes one of obtaining effective implementation of CCMS studies on the part of national governments. Here we find that all developed states are poorly organized to deal with the problems of modern society, and so there is an urgent need for each to learn from the other how to gain the necessary competence to make their environment livable. The basic difficulty, as Moynihan suggested, is simple. "Modern governments fail because they are not modern. They face the problems created by technology with the mentality and the organization of a pretechnological society." As the most technologically developed societies, NATO nations must provide their governments with the managerial skills needed to cope with technology. "The task of government is to keep abreast of such new realities, which is to say that government has got to learn to respond to new knowledge at at least something like the rate at which technology does. Otherwise technology is always ahead on creating problems, and government is always behind on resolving them."[79] The functioning of CCMS in fact stimulated the reorganization of the governmental structures in a number of NATO states, including the creation of new bureaus or departments competent to handle environmental matters.

From the beginning CCMS has conceived of the "environment" in broad terms so as to include not only technological problems but also issues with broad social implications. Thus projects have been undertaken in technical matters like water and air pollution, road safety, the disposal of hazardous substances, and the development of solar and geothermal energy, while other projects have dealt with sociological issues such as the quality of life and individual fulfillment in a modern industrial society, the relationship between regional planning and the environment, and the transmission of scientific knowledge to the decision-making processes in government.

The work of CCMS represents in many respects a new type of commitment for the member governments, both nationally and internationally. In order to enhance the international status and acceptability of CCMS recommendations and endow them with the force of law, the German parliamentarian, Erik Blumenfeld, elaborated in several reports to the North Atlantic Assembly procedures for establishing Atlantic legal conventions that would reduce CCMS recommendations to specific treaty commitments. The international convention technique has been used successfully for some time by the Council of Europe to apply legal sanctions among the signatory states to questions relating to human rights, as well as to a number of other social and economic matters. This concept might logically and usefully be adapted to the concerns of CCMS on an Atlantic scale.[80]

FRENCH DEFECTION AND THE ADAPTATION OF NATO TO THE TASKS AHEAD

Ironically, French defection from NATO provided a welcome opportunity to tighten up and modernize the Alliance apparatus so that it might better manage its varied tasks. While NATO presents the anomaly of trying to defend Western Europe without France, it has also made use of its departure from French soil to rid itself of several anomalies of long standing. Previously the Council, as the supreme political body, was located in Paris, while the Military Committee and its executive arm, the Standing Group, were located in Washington. The principal political and military organs of NATO were thus separated from each other, although the Military Committee maintained a representative in Paris, who was assisted by an allied staff, to act as liaison with the Council.

In practice, this arrangement proved highly unsatisfactory. Working in isolation, the Council was unable to get adequate military information or advice on vital questions of strategy and planning, with the result that the political body of NATO had little influence on the shaping of basic military decisions, even though such policies were also highly political in nature. The situation was worse in the case of the Secretary General and the International Secretariat. Dirk Stikker recalled that as NATO Secretary General he was without any official military advisor, and he had to resort to informal assistance wherever he could find some kindly disposed General who would furnish advice on a strictly private basis. Moreover, the military authorities refused to permit the presence of civilians, either as representatives of the Council or of the Secretariat, at any of their meetings, nor did they permit the civil authorities access to any of their records or working papers.[81]

The Standing Group, consisting of representatives of the American, British, and French Chiefs of Staff, was presumably a select executive agency of the Military Committee, but in fact it became totally useless. In the early days of NATO when the three governments worked in considerable harmony, it assisted in providing guidance to military policies. In the Gaullist period, however, the French constantly interposed a dissenting voice and prevented the issuance of any advice or recommendation, which had to be unanimous before transmittal. The Standing Group was thus doubly defective: It excluded other allies, such as Germany which subsequently provided the largest European military contribution to NATO, and it was a multinational not an integrated, international body, and so was unable to transcend narrow national viewpoints. Stikker sought to remedy these difficulties as best he could, and in June 1964 he managed to have appointed a German General as the head of a new integrated, international strategic planning staff consisting of other smaller powers that could service the Standing Group.[82]

Since the Council and the Secretary General needed to conduct a dialogue with a military spokesman who could look at problems in a NATO wide context, the practice developed of relying upon the advice of the Supreme Allied Commander Europe (SACEUR). On the organizational chart, SACEUR was only a regional allied commander, although obviously an important one, but at least here was an authoritative individual who could speak from an allied, international point of view as formulated by an integrated staff. As a result, SACEUR acquired a position of influence and a quasi-diplomatic role never intended for him.

French withdrawal from NATO permitted a number of useful steps to be taken. The Standing Group was abolished and its integrated, international planning staff was put at the service of the Military Committee, which, in turn, moved to Brussels along with the North Atlantic Council. The demise of the Standing Group was certainly no loss, while the co-location of the Council and the Military Committee ended the artificial separation between NATO's highest political and military organs. This permitted the cultivation of personal contacts between the political and military authorities on a daily, casual basis, which was necessary in order to break down the previously existing barriers. The Military Committee remained a multinational group, although helpfully without the paralyzing influence of Gaullist France. Yet it still retained the difficulty of counterposing and reconciling purely national policies, even though it was supported by an expanded international, integrated staff that could help evolve a common NATO military assessment of problems.

The logical extension of these developments would be to make the work of the international planning staff fully available to the Secretary General and the International Secretariat, channeled perhaps through the appointment of a civilian of high standing, who might become the rough equivalent of a NATO Minister of Defense. He would not have the power of Defense Ministers in NATO's member states, since NATO is not a supranational government. Yet here would be a single individual who could serve as a focal point for NATO defense problems. Since he would be fully briefed on matters of military policy by an international staff, he could deal directly with the various Defense Ministers in the constituent states and thereby aid in the formation of an allied military consensus. He would also naturally be placed at the service of the Council, providing a formal link between the military and civilian authorities, which in the past has been missing. In this event, it would no longer be necessary to continue the expedient of turning for advice to SACEUR, who after all reflected the views of a regional allied commander, although by force of circumstances he was called to speak upon matters beyond his immediate realm of competence. In addition, the NATO Defense Minister would be a civilian and would strengthen the democratic tradition of civilian control over the military, which until recently was not the case, since NATO from the beginning tended to be dominated by the military element.

The co-location of the Council and Military Committee in Brussels noticeably improved the coordination of the diplomatic and military functions within many of the national delegations to NATO by permitting an ambassador to understand more fully the technical implications of military discussions conducted in the Council. Moreover, in those cases where the NATO ambassador was a forceful political figure, his nation's senior military representative could more easily be brought under civilian control by becoming in effect the national military advisor to his country's chief political spokesmen.

This long-sought strengthening of civilian control in NATO, both at the national and international levels, will become increasingly relevant as NATO moves forward into the coming political phase of detente management.

The meshing of political aims with military requirements was also advanced significantly by a plan, initiated by Secretary General Stikker, which was adopted in principle by the NATO Ministerial meeting in Ottawa in May 1963. The so-called Stikker Exercise committed the Council to undertake "studies of the interrelated questions of strategy, force requirements and the resources available to meet them."[83] The previous unsatisfactory practice consisted of the military authorities first stating their "minimum force requirements," which in turn were considered but never fulfilled by NATO's political representatives. As Stikker remarked to this writer, if the military had its way, NATO would have spent $25 billion a year more on defense than it actually did. The problem, familiar to any democratic government, was to temper the military demands with civilian judgments and to coordinate the two into a workable plan that had some chance of acceptance and implementation. Underlying this process was the need for consensus on allied strategy that could serve as a basis upon which civil-military agreement could be reached.

This eminently sensible plan quickly ran into French delaying tactics that seized upon every opportunity to impose procedural difficulties. Nearly a year of work was occupied, or rather wasted, by responding to such Gaullist harassment. Finally serious work began on the attempt to reconcile force requirements and resources, although there was no possibility of reaching accord on an up-to-date allied strategy so long as France remained in NATO.

When de Gaulle announced the French withdrawal from NATO in the spring of 1966, work that had long been in process soon began to take form. The procedures introduced by the Stikker Exercise succeeded in creating a better dialogue between the military and civil authorities and in collecting and integrating information from the national military establishments to a much greater extent from before. By July 1966 the NATO Defense Ministers had approved guidelines for the development of force goals beyond 1970. They also adopted measures, which had been accepted in principle by the NATO Ministerial meeting of December 1965, to project allied force goals and country plans five years ahead each year beginning in 1967.[84] This long-range planning represented a considerable advance over the inefficient and cumbersome annual reviews, initiated in 1952 and expanded to triennial reviews in 1962. Although five-year planning papers had been produced as early as 1958, they were static in nature, whereas the new method was that of a rolling five-year projection, based in large part upon sophisticated Pentagon planning techniques. This called for five-year plans that would be reformulated each year so as to take account of rapidly changing technological advances. The NATO Ministerial meeting of December 1967 adopted for the first time a rolling five-year-force plan that began in 1968 and ran through 1972.[85] Meanwhile, the NATO Defense Ministers (minus France), meeting in the spring of 1967, finally abandoned NATO's 11-year-old strategic doctrine of massive retaliation, which could only continue to justify the strategy for the force de frappe. Instead, they agreed upon a new allied strategy of a flexible and balanced range of appropriate responses that provided multiple options for meeting aggression at many levels of violence.[86] The new strategic doctrine, designated MC-14-3, was confirmed by a decision of the NATO Ministers in December 1967.[87]

Other innovations were also pressed with vigor. A conventional communications system that relied upon facilities in France was quickly revamped, and in September 1966 the United States submitted a formal proposal in the Council for the construction of a NATO satellite communications system. Here was a means by which technology could overcome the obstacles of geography, since this system could not only bypass France, but it could provide an almost instantaneous, clear communications network among the NATO capitals and military headquarters, which was virtually invulnerable to enemy action. It could also facilitate simultaneous consultation by the NATO heads of government during a time of crisis. This initiative was enthusiastically embraced by the NATO member states. The construction of a two-phased program for satellite communications was begun in 1968 and completed at the beginning of 1971.[88]

In a related move, the new NATO headquarters in Belgium included the construction of two allied intelligence centers that for the first time could furnish a prompt, day-by-day pooling of military and political intelligence on an alliedwide basis. A SHAPE Operations Center at Casteaux contains an electronic and computerized data bank, linked with subsidiary data banks at far-flung lower-echelon commands, which can constantly gather and evaluate information necessary for military decision making. Attached to the North Atlantic Council in Brussels is its political counterpart, the Situation

Center, which not only collects military data, but more especially political and diplomatic information that would be essential for crisis consultation by allied political authorities. These new facilities, which are great improvements over the accommodations that NATO had available in France, should also provide the NATO civil-military international staff with a more timely and adequate information base for its work.[89]

Ambassador Cleveland recounted how the Brussels facilities were promptly put to use at the time of the Soviet invasion of Czechoslovakia in August 1968. "When the Russians struck, NATO was readier for round-the-clock crisis management than it had ever been before." The new headquarters had "a modern Situation Room, complete with up-to-date visual aids and serviced by a new NATO-wide communications system. And the Council's Committee of Political Advisors . . . had been converted to an every-day 'watch committee' producing overnight political assessments to guide NATO's military commanders. These facilities proved their value as the allies turned immediately to consulting together about what had happened and what it meant for Western security."[90]

Allied nuclear policy making was also given institutional form. At the initiative of Defense Secretary Robert McNamara, the North Atlantic Council created a special committee of ten Defense Ministers in November 1965 to examine means of increasing allied participation in various aspects of nuclear planning and consultation. The evolution of this group led to the creation of two permanent bodies as a result of a decision of the NATO Ministerial meeting of December 1966. A parent group, the Nuclear Defense Affairs Committee, was opened to the participation of any interested NATO nation, while detailed studies and policy proposals were entrusted to a Nuclear Planning Group, consisting in the beginning of seven Defense Ministers drawn from the full committee.[91] While far from solving NATO's nuclear dilemmas, there was general agreement among the participating European states that Europeans were getting meaningful access to American nuclear thinking and obtaining the kinds of information relating to nuclear weapons in which they have been interested. Conversely, American nuclear policies might be more easily influenced by an intimate and continuing contact with European defense officials.

Since the French withdrawal, one might also mention the decision of December 1967 to create a multinational NATO destroyer fleet, the Standing Naval Force, Atlantic, which could be rushed to any trouble spot in the Atlantic in order to demonstrate the concern and power of the whole Alliance.[92] This was a rough equivalent to the previously established Mobile Force, Allied Command Europe, which was composed of ground and air units of a number of member countries. Its mission was likewise to stand ready, at short notice, so as to be rushed to any threatened area, particularly on Europe's thinly defended extreme northern and southern flanks, and to demonstrate allied solidarity in time of crisis.

In response to the sharply increased Soviet naval activity in the Mediterranean following the June 1967 Middle East war, NATO also took several measures to strengthen its position there. In November 1968 it activated a new command, Maritime Airforces Mediterranean, which headquarters at Naples, which could operate an integrated NATO maritime air surveillance over the activities of the sizable Soviet flotilla in the Mediterranean.[93] In January 1969 NATO approved the creation of an allied naval force in the Mediterranean, which could be assembled "on call." While not regarded as a permanent standing naval force, as in the Atlantic, the NATO Mediterranean fleet was designed to come together periodically for exercises and visits and to be available for special missions in times of international tension or crisis.[94] Finally, in May 1973 NATO commissioned a second naval standing force, this one designed to operate under the Channel Command.[95]

This brief review of NATO developments in the period following French defection indicates that NATO did not collapse from trauma, as de Gaulle had doubtless anticipated. The French action was psychologically unsettling, caused enormous inconveniences and sizable, needless expense, and yet among its side effects were a number of fresh allied advances that were clearly impossible so long as France remained within NATO. Given the continuing political will of its remaining members, NATO was in a position to fulfill its traditional political and military functions effectively. The real test for the future lies, however, in the area of detente management, in which NATO has only recently gained some experience.

Rapid progress in adapting NATO's military structure to current requirements was made possible by the French withdrawal from the integrated NATO military commands and the principal associated agencies. French obstructionism was likewise removed from the highest civilian body dealing with military affairs by the simple expedient of convening the North Atlantic Council minus France and calling it the Defense Planning Committee.

Since France remained a signatory to the North Atlantic Treaty, it retained a voice in the political deliberations of the Council, and here the possibility of mischief making continued. In practice, when de Gaulle personally retired from the scene, French policy became noticeably more cooperative. This was even true for stepped-up military collaboration with NATO, although this was undertaken unobtrusively and stopped short of formal reentry into NATO military organs. Thus France remained outside of a number of bodies, such as the Eurogroup and the Nuclear Planning Group, which logically called for active French participation. President Pompidou also continued to draw the distinction between military and nonmilitary subjects by refusing to participate in negotiations between military blocs about mutual troop reductions while usefully taking part in prior NATO consultations on the gamut of issues that were later considered at the multilateral forum of CSCE. France also assumed a role in some of the CCMS projects, which were launched after de Gaulle had relinquished power.

But what if France had remained obdurately uncooperative in all of the Alliance activities in which it continued to participate? Would this have condemned the North Atlantic Council, for example, to political paralysis? Such behavior could cause delays and difficulties, but not necessarily total paralysis. There are firmly established precedents for the Council to take action without unanimous consent by means of partial agreement among the remaining Council members that exhibit the political will to act.

Dirk Stikker recalled instances of moving ahead by partial agreement when he was Secretary General. In 1959, for example, all the Council members except France agreed that only an integrated European air defense system would be feasible. The Council then proceeded to establish such a system since, as Stikker explained, "it was now time for a deliberate application of the principle that no single member of NATO can prevent the others from taking a collective action they deem necessary."[96] Stikker argued persuasively that unanimous agreement is required for the accession of new members to the treaty, but in other respects, the "parties, separately and jointly," as Article 3 puts it, will develop their individual and collective defense capacities, while Article 5 also speaks of resisting aggression by aiding the state attacked "individually and in concert with the other Parties." The leeway allowed in these questions, Stikker contended, provides the treaty basis for implementing policies by those "members of NATO who wish to proceed to a joint

plan of action in which one or more members do not wish to join."
Therefore, Stikker's "answer to the question of whether the rule of
unanimity exists in NATO has always been, and remains, 'Certainly
not.'" After citing a number of joint ventures from which individual
member states had abstained, he formulated what he called "the
doctrine of flexibility," which "implies that no single member of the
Alliance can impose its course of action on the others; that several
members can together take such action as they consider necessary;
and finally, that the right of any one member to prevent the others
from taking an action they deem vital to their interests is excluded."[97]
Furthermore, the Council had entrusted the Secretary General with
the right of initiative in raising questions for Council consideration.
"This means that he is not obliged to wait until all members of the
Alliance are in agreement to propose action, or to watch passively
while thorny issues destroy the cohesion and effectiveness of the
Alliance."[98]

This view was fully supported by the testimony of Thomas
Finletter, who served as U.S. Ambassador to NATO from 1961 to
1965. It was not sufficiently well understood, he affirmed, that
"thanks to the skillful handling of Secretary Generals Stikker and
Brosio, among others, the principle has been well established in
Alliance practice that unanimity is not needed for consultation, and
that unanimity is not even necessary for various kinds of decisions
which can be taken within the Alliance framework." Finletter
likewise noted that "the record is full of cases where a certain number
of the allies have gone ahead in activities of their own, always
reporting back to the Atlantic Council on what they have done. In
short, the rule of unanimity, which would necessarily destroy any
organization such as the Alliance if it were enforced, does not exist.
There is a kind of rule of reason and moderation which has been
substituted for it and has worked very well in practice for these many
years."[99] It was this tradition of partial agreement that prompted
President Johnson to declare about NATO in May 1965: "We will go
all together, if we can. But if one of us cannot join in a common
venture it will not stand in the way of the rest."[100]

Finletter's successor, Harlan Cleveland, described the workings
of the Council, which made such flexible behavior possible. "The
North Atlantic Council has no written rules of procedure, never takes
a vote, and seldom passes a resolution." Instead of taking votes, the
Council "operates 'by consensus,' which means the Council's

Chairman draws from the discussion a summary which, if no Representative objects, becomes the Council's decision. The process is therefore something like a jury or a Quaker meeting: until there is general agreement there is nothing." He acknowledged that such an "arrangement does give a strong-willed nation or even a strong-minded Representative a considerable advantage—up to a point. But it does not seem to operate in such a way that the term 'veto' applies. If one nation objects too much, or for too long, the others usually find some way to go ahead together anyway." The result has been that "in its naked form, the veto question has never been sharply posed or tested."[101] The institutional practices that have developed in NATO have given it a unique capacity to adapt to changing circumstances and survive where other intergovernmental organizations might well have failed.

NATO'S FUTURE INSTITUTIONAL EVOLUTION

Presumably at some point in the future there will be sufficient progress toward European Union to permit the emergence of a distinctively European organ dealing with defense. This could conceivably grow out of a refashioned Eurogroup, which France would be obliged to join, or it might come from some entirely new body to which France would adhere. In either case it would be necessary to remold the network of NATO ties so as to ensure that the vital trans-Atlantic bond will remain firm and unbroken.

As European institutions take form, the process of arriving at a trans-Atlantic consensus will necessarily change. Just as special provisions should be made to gear in the huge governmental machinery of the United States at an early stage of policy making, so new devices will have to be established to take account of the unwieldy institutions of a European Union. If anything, the problems involved in dealing with the European side may be more severe, because of the difficulties of assimilating the separate national identities and traditions and welding them into a single European political entity. In any event, whatever the new arrangements, it is quite clear that stronger European institutions will also require stronger Atlantic institutions. Those who are captivated by the slogan of equal partnership between Europe and America are more likely to be preoccupied with building Europe than with working out the mechanism of partnership. Yet both must proceed hand in hand, for otherwise the present obstacles to coordinating American policies and plans with those of NATO would be duplicated on the other side of the Atlantic. If such neglect for building a general NATO consensus were to prevail, the conflict in military and political policies could jeopardize the existence of the West.

Making the structural changes necessary to take account of the growth of the organs of a European Union while preserving an Atlantic consensus is a problem of the future internal organization of NATO which will arise only as European institutions take shape. There is, however, a problem relating to NATO's external relations which clearly demands action in the near future.

The capability and willingness of Alliance members to fulfill their commitments to NATO depend upon more than the military and political issues discussed in NATO. U.S. troop levels in Europe, for example, are related to the issue of equitable burden sharing, and this in turn is dependent upon a number of economic and monetary issues, such as the economic health of the American and European economies, the balance of trade between Europe and the United States, the strength or weakness of the dollar compared to European currencies, the U.S. balance-of-payments deficit, and efforts to reform the international monetary system. It is highly artificial and unrealistic to compartmentalize each of these issues and seek to solve military, political, economic, and monetary problems in separated, isolated forums.

This realization was forcefully articulated at the beginning of 1973 by Helmut Schmidt, who had the advantage of viewing trans-Atlantic relations first from the viewpoint of the German Federal Minister of Defense and then as Minister of Finance, before he became Chancellor. When he was in charge of defense he recalled how he was able to keep in almost daily contact with the other NATO Defense Ministers so that each could know what interests the others were preparing to defend. Thus "we knew exactly how we could arrive at joint decisions." However, when he shifted to economic and monetary concerns, he became acutely aware of the lack of satisfactory contacts at the Ministerial level on these problems among members of the Atlantic Alliance. "There exist no institutional means for constructive exchange of views. It is not just a question of technical experts meeting. What is necessary is regular contacts between the people who really matter."

He suggested that a body along the lines of the Group of Ten in the monetary field be set up among Economic Ministers of the Atlantic Alliance and that it meet at least every quarter or possibly eight or ten times a year. The functioning of such a body could help, for example, avert a trade war between the United States and the European Community. "It must really be understood that you cannot have a foreign policy or an Alliance policy apart from monetary and trade policies."[102] Members of the Atlantic Alliance have demonstrated how closely they are capable of cooperating in dealing with difficult and controversial security policies. "The same degree of cooperation must now be achieved in further fields and the necessary machinery must be provided."[103]

Schmidt made these personal pronouncements into official recommendations when he introduced the budget of the Brandt government to the Bundestag in April 1973. He warned against the fateful consequences of a "continental drift" between the United States and Europe and called for "a broadening of the defense and foreign policy base of the North Atlantic Alliance to include economic cooperation, particularly on questions dealing with currency, credit, trade and development aid policies."[104]

The Economic Committee of the North Atlantic Assembly had partially anticipated these views in its recommendations of November 1972. It had proposed, among other things, that the Ministerial meetings of the North Atlantic Council be attended by Finance and Economic Ministers, as well as by Defense and Foreign Affairs Ministers; the Council in permanent session should devote at least one meeting a month exclusively to economic matters; and the authority and activity of NATO's Economic Committee be increased, and national representation on it be maintained at the highest possible level.[105] When NATO Secretary General Luns reviewed these recommendations in the spring of 1973, in the process of bringing them before the Council, he indicated his warm approval of these efforts to have NATO deliberations take greater account of economic and monetary questions.[106] "My main concern," Luns stated in a public comment at this time, "is that many of those involved, both in Europe and in the United States, do not seem to be fully aware of the essential and vital interaction between the defense component and the monetary and economic components of the Atlantic relationship."[107]

It was in this setting that Henry Kissinger made his "Year of Europe" speech of April 23, 1973, in which the Nixon administration called for a new Atlantic Charter that would reflect all the interrelated needs and goals of the Atlantic Community. It was President Nixon's approach, Kissinger said, "to deal with Atlantic problems comprehensively. The political, military and economic issues in Atlantic relations are linked by reality, not by our choice nor for the tactical purpose of trading one off against the other." Moreover, it would be a fatal mistake to leave the problems in each area solely to the experts, who would examine the issues in isolation from each other. All future negotiations must be infused with a broad commitment of political will on the part of the top political leaders. "The solutions will not be worthy of the opportunity if left to technicians. They must be addressed at the highest level." The comprehensive approach to Atlantic problems would also reveal the inadequacy of institutional arrangements in the Atlantic Community. "We deal with each other regionally and even competitively in economic matters, on an integrated basis in defense, and as nation-states in diplomacy. . . . The various parts of the construction are not always in harmony and sometimes obstruct each other. If we want to foster unity, we can no longer ignore these problems."[108]

European reaction was mixed, but generally cautious. The Dutch responded favorably and promptly, while the French, as usual, viewed the Kissinger initiative with suspicion, intimating that a new Atlantic Charter was merely a covert attempt to bring Europe once again under American hegemony. Many Europeans recognized the logic in emphasizing the interrelatedness of security, economic, and monetary problems. However, there was also a widespread fear that the Europeans would be required to agree to excessive sacrifices in the trade and monetary fields in return for the continued U.S. military protection of NATO Europe.[109] Some European circles spoke openly of a presumed plot to "blackmail" Europe into making such economic concessions. Kissinger responded that "the affirmation of the pervasive nature of our interdependence is not a device for blackmail. On the contrary, it is the justification for conciliatory solutions." Since the specialized concerns of experts and technicians in each area necessarily involve a narrow, sectarian bias, the

American proposal aimed "to override these divisive attitudes by committing the highest authority in each country to the principle that our common and paramount interest is in broadly conceived cooperation."[110]

NATO accepted the challenge to formulate a response that would take account of the complex web of European-American relationships. Its attempt, however, to deal comprehensively with all trans-Atlantic problems was at once opposed by the Nine of the European Community, who insisted on separating out the economic issues and those political factors relating to them. These concerns, it was proposed, should be the subject for a separate E.C.-U.S. declaration, while a NATO declaration should deal only with security and political affairs. Thus the European Community unlinked what Kissinger had sought to tie together. Moreover, controversy among the Nine on the form of their response, created in large measure by the French refusal to include the words "partnership" and "interdependence," as well as to approve more intimate European consultation procedures with the United States, resulted in the abandonment of the attempt to draw up an E.C.-U.S. declaration.

Meanwhile, the NATO declaration, which was finally concluded in June 1974, had only a brief and general mention of Atlantic economic relations. The allies, it asserted, "wish also to ensure that their essential security relationship is supported by harmonious political and economic relations. In particular they will work to remove sources of conflict between their economic policies and to encourage economic cooperation with one another." These phrases were inserted both in deference to the wishes of Alliance members who were not members of the European Community and to give some minimal recognition that NATO necessarily had broader concerns than military affairs. The bulk of the NATO declaration nevertheless dealt with security and political questions. The principal thrust of the declaration was a renewed promise of "frank and timely consultations," including a specific reference to the fact that the common interests of the allies "can be affected by events in other areas of the world."[111] In practice, the North Atlantic Council had long discussed events outside the NATO Treaty area, but as the 1973 Middle East war had demonstrated so spectacularly, these consultations were often inadequate. The declaration therefore stated for the first time in an official Alliance document that the allies were committed to consult on a global scale.

The Atlantic Community was obviously still not organized to deal in a comprehensive manner with all of the interrelated matters that affected its destiny. Some observers, like Johan Holst, have continued to focus attention on this problem. Fearful that escalation of conflicts in trade and monetary affairs would sooner or later endanger security arrangements, he warned that problems in one sector could easily spill over into the others. "The problems are endemic and can probably only be remedied by institutional reconstruction. There is an obvious need for a trans-Atlantic institutional framework which will facilitate joint management and conflict resolution through the construction of cross-sectoral package solutions and compromises. As long as trans-Atlantic relations are channelled through single-sector institutions there can be little bargaining and the institutional incentives for evolving overall policies are missing."

Holst suggested that "the Atlantic states need to establish joint E.C.-U.S. institutions to handle the broad spectrum of interstate and intersocietal relations. NATO would be but one element of a larger structure in the institutionalization of the trans-Atlantic order." At the pinnacle of these restructured relationships "an Atlantic Ministerial Council should be vested with the competence and authority to deal with the issues across functional frontiers, and at the level of permanent representatives serve as a forum for continuous consultation and bargaining."[112]

It is difficult to envision exactly how such an Atlantic Ministerial Council would function, both in dealing with problems across the spectrum of trans-Atlantic affairs and in its relations to the subsidiary bodies such as NATO. Holst also recognized the difficulties in reconciling the memberships of the different constituent bodies. By building the institutions around a joint E.C.-U.S. relationship, how does one take account of the fact that a "subsidiary" body like NATO would have as members Canada and the states in NATO Europe that are not members of the European Community, while Ireland is a member of the latter, but not of NATO? For all its shortcomings, the proposal has the merit of probing in the right direction and hopefully might stimulate further consideration of this knotty problem.

A final, but by no means incidental, point is how to relate Japan to the institutional reshaping of the Atlantic Community. As Kissinger properly emphasized, "Japan has emerged as a major power center. In many fields, 'Atlantic' solutions to be viable must include Japan. . . . Just as Europe's autonomy is not an end in itself, so the Atlantic Community cannot be an exclusive club. Japan must be a principal partner in our common enterprise."[113]

Japan would not, of course, be expected to join NATO, but it is already a member of the otherwise essentially Western institutions dealing with trade, economic, and monetary policies, as well as with development aid. It would appear that flexible, pragmatic arrangements to gear Japan more intimately into these various mechanisms would eventually show what further institutional steps might be appropriate and possible.

NOTES

1. Action Committee for the United States of Europe, Joint Declaration, adopted June 26, 1962, Paris, pp. 3-4. See also Action Committee for the United States of Europe, Joint Declaration, adopted December 17 and 18, 1962, Paris, p. 1. Again note that these pronouncements long preceded de Gaulle's pursuit of detente.

2. Action Committee for the United States of Europe, Joint Declaration, adopted June 1, 1964, Bonn, p. 13.

3. Action Committee for the United States of Europe, Joint Declaration, adopted May 8 and 9, 1965, Berlin, p. 5.

4. Action Committee, Joint Declaration, June 1, 1964, p. 14. See also, Action Committee for the United States of Europe, Resolutions, adopted June 15, 1967, Brussels, p. 5, where the institutions of the EEC were requested "to take the necessary initiatives with the Soviet Union and the countries of Eastern Europe with a view to establishing a Committee of Cooperation, whose task would be to ensure permanent consultation on economic and cultural questions of common concern." This would function alongside the suggested "Committee of Entente" between the European Community and America, where policies could be concerted on a wide range of issues.

5. Address by President John F. Kennedy at Naples, July 2, 1963, Department of State *Bulletin* 44, no. 1256: 135-36.

6. Address by President Lyndon B. Johnson at New York, October 7, 1966, Department of State *Bulletin* 55, no. 1426: 623-24.

7. Ibid., p. 623.

8. Address by Minister of Foreign Affairs Pierre Harmel at Paris, June 15, 1966, Assembly, WEU, *Proceedings*, June 1966, II, p. 120.

9. Address by Secretary of State Dean Rusk at New York, December 2, 1967, Department of State *Bulletin* 57, no. 1487: 858.

10. Ambassador Harlan Cleveland, "The Transformation of NATO," *NATO Letter*, November 1967, p. 6.

11. Assembly, WEU, *Proceedings*, June 1967, II, p. 206.

12. Quoted by Anthony Lewis, New York *Times*, September 8, 1968.

13. *Pravda*, September 18, 1968; *Izvestia*, September 20, 1968.

14. "Bonn Reassured of NATO Response in Event of Soviet Intervention," U.S. Statement, September 17, 1968, Department of State *Bulletin* 59, no. 1528: 365. Britain and France, as former occupying powers, also rejected the Soviet contention. The French reply, however, upheld the validity of articles 53 and 107 of the U.N. Charter, and naturally omitted mention of NATO. See *The Bulletin*, Press and Information Office of the German Federal Government, Bonn, September 24, 1968, pp. 265-66.

15. "Bonn Reveals Secret USSR Paper in Enemy States Clause," *Relay from Bonn*, German Information Center, New York, April 15, 1971. See also ibid., March 23, 1971.

16. "It's Mostly Bubbles," *The Economist*, April 14, 1973.

17. "Bonn's Defense Policy," *The Bulletin*, Press and Information Office of the German Federal Government, June 9, 1970, pp. 137-38.

18. Address by Minister of Defense Helmut Schmidt at Princeton University, April 21, 1971, p. 5.

19. Interview with Minister of Defense Helmut Schmidt in *Die Welt*, February 16, 1970; quoted in *The Bulletin*, Press and Information Office of the German Federal Government, February 25, 1970, p. 40.

20. Curt Gasteyger, "The Fragile Balance," *Interplay*, March 1971, p. 29.

21. New York *Times*, October 28, 1972.

22. Andrew J. Pierre, "Implications of the Western Response to the Soviet Invasion of Czechoslovakia," *Atlantic Community Quarterly*, Spring 1969, p. 66.

23. Testimony of Ambassador Kenneth Rush, April 18, 1970, in *United States Relations with Europe in the Decade of the 1970s*,

Hearings before the Subcommittee on Europe, Committee on Foreign Affairs, House of Representatives, 91st Cong., 2d sess. (Washington, D.C., 1970), p. 391.

24. Address by General Lyman L. Lemnitzer at Washington, D.C., October 28, 1968; quoted in *The Bulletin*, Press and Information Office of the German Federal Government, November 5, 1968, p. 313.

25. Roland A. Paul, *American Military Commitments Abroad* (New Brunswick, N.J., 1973), pp. 138-42.

26. Address by Under Secretary of State Elliot L. Richardson at Chicago, January 20, 1970, Department of State *Bulletin* 62, no. 1598: 156-57.

27. Edward R. Fried, "The Financial Cost of the Alliance," in *U.S. Troops in Europe*, ed. John Newhouse, (Washington, D.C., 1971), pp. 110-13, 126-35.

28. Timothy W. Stanley, "The Political Economics of Defense: Burden-Sharing," *Atlantic Community Quarterly*, Winter 1971-72, pp. 442-50; "Proposal for a NATO International Security Fund," *NATO Review*, November-December 1971, pp. 29-30.

29. Communique of the Defense Planning Committee of NATO, Ministerial Session, June 7, 1973, paragraph 12, *NATO Review*, No. 4 (1973), p. 22.

30. "President Reports on NATO's Effect on Balance of Payments," Message to the Congress of May 16, 1974, Department of State *Bulletin* 70, no. 1824: 626-27.

31. Final Communique, NATO Ministerial Meeting, December 3-4, 1970, *NATO Letter*, December 1970, pp. 21-22; "Alliance Defense for the Seventies," ibid., pp. 6-8.

32. "The Eurogroup," *NATO Review*, November-December 1972, p. 9.

33. Eurogroup Communique, December 5, 1972, ibid., November-December 1972, p. 26.

34. Eurogroup Communique, December 6, 1973, *NATO Review*, No. 6, (1973), p. 31; Eurogroup Communique, December 9, 1974, *Atlantic News*, December 11, 1974, p. 2.

35. Lord Carrington, "The Eurogroup," *NATO Review*, January-February 1972, p. 11.

36. *Policy, Troops and the NATO Alliance*, Report of Senator Sam Nunn to the Committee on Armed Services, U.S. Senate, April 2, 1974 (Washington, D.C., 1974), p. 12.

37. "Declaration on Mutual and Balanced Force Reductions Adopted by Foreign Ministers and Representatives of Countries Participating in the NATO Defense Program," June 24-25, 1968, *NATO Letter*, July-August 1968, p. 29.

38. Bernard Gwertzman, "Brezhnev Urges the West to Confer on Troop Cuts," New York *Times*, May 15, 1971.

39. Elliot R. Goodman, "Disparities in East-West Relations," *Survey*, Summer 1973, pp. 88-96.

40. Theo Sommer, "Detente and Security: The Options," *Atlantic Community Quarterly*, Spring 1971, p. 44.

41. Steven L. Canby, "Policy Implications of Restructuring NATO's Military Forces," Appendix V in Paul Thyness, rapporteur, The Security of the Alliance, Military Committee, North Atlantic Assembly, October 1973, Q 136 MC(73)16; Steven L. Canby, *NATO Military Policy: Obtaining Conventional Comparability with the Warsaw Pact*, Rand R-1088-ARPA (Santa Monica, Calif.), June 1973; Kenneth Hunt, *The Alliance and Europe: Part II, Defense with Fewer Men*, Adelphi Papers, No. 98, IISS (London), Summer 1973; R. W. Komer, "Treating NATO's Self-Inflicted Wound," *Foreign Policy*, Winter 1973-74; Steven L. Canby, *The Alliance and Europe: Part IV, Military Doctrine and Technology*, Adelphi Papers, No. 109, IISS (London), Winter 1974.

42. Marshall D. Shulman, *Beyond the Cold War* (New Haven, 1966), p. 101.

43. Ibid., pp. 101-2.

44. Anthony Eden, Earl of Avon, "A New Diplomatic Role for NATO," New York *Times*, October 14, 1967.

45. Clyde H. Farnsworth, "Belgium Seeking Disarmed Europe," Ibid., January 25, 1967.

46. Final Communique, NATO Ministerial Meeting, June 3-4, 1971, *NATO Review*, July-August 1971, p. 26.

47. "High Level NATO Meeting on MBFR," October 5-6, 1971, Ibid., November-December 1971, p. 24.

48. Cleveland, "The Transformation," *NATO Letter*, November 1967, p. 6.

49. Ibid., pp. 6-7.

50. Address by Ambassador Harlan Cleveland at Paris, July 19, 1966, Department of State *Bulletin* 55, no. 1419: 345.

51. "NATO and East-West Contacts," *NATO Letter*, November 1966, p. 25.

52. Peyton V. Lyon, *NATO as a Diplomatic Instrument* (Toronto, 1970), p. 7.

53. "Report on the Future Tasks of the Alliance," adopted December 16, 1967, *NATO Letter*, January 1968, pp. 26-27. For an insider's account of the writing of the Harmel report, see Harlan Cleveland, *NATO: The Transatlantic Bargain* (New York, 1970), pp. 138-47.

54. Comments by NATO Secretary General Joseph Luns on the Recommendations and Resolutions Adopted at the Eighteenth Session of the North Atlantic Assembly, April 1973, Q 28, SC (73), p. 3.

55. Press Conference of German Federal Foreign Affairs Minister Walter Scheel at Copenhagen, June 15, 1973, *Relay from Bonn*, June 18, 1973.

56. Address by Deputy Secretary of State Kenneth Rush at Atlanta, May 22, 1973, Department of State *Bulletin* 68, no. 1773: 867-68.

57. Alastair Buchan, *Crisis Management* (Boulogne-sur-Seine, France, 1966), p. 47.

58. "Martino's Answer to State Department on Atlantic Union Bill," *Freedom & Union*, October 1967, p. 3.

59. Cleveland, "The Transformation," op cit., pp. 6-7.

60. Theodore C. Achilles, "Whither the Atlantic Alliance," *Orbis*, Summer 1965, p. 496.

61. Alastair Buchan and Philip Windsor, *Arms and Stability in Europe*, (New York, 1963), p. 221.

62. Buchan, op. cit., pp. 37-39, 49.

63. Eugene V. Rostow, "The Future of the Atlantic Community," *Atlantic Community Quarterly*, Winter 1969-70, p. 478.

64. Buchan, op. cit., pp. 37-39,49.

65. "Atlantic Policy Advisory Group of NATO meets in United States," Department of State *Bulletin* 48, no 1245: 721.

66. George W. Ball, *The Discipline of Power* (Boston, 1968), pp. 64-65.

67. Address by President Richard M. Nixon at Washington, D.C., April 10, 1969, Department of State *Bulletin* 60, no. 1557: p. 353.

68. *Atlantic News*, November 4, 1969, p. 2.

69. Final Communique, NATO Ministerial Meeting, June 3-4, 1971, *NATO Review*, July-August, 1971, p. 26.

70. "High Level NATO Meeting on MBFR," October 5-6, 1971, *NATO Review*, November-December 1971, p. 24.

71. *Atlantic News*, February 27, 1974, p. 1; March 15, 1974, p. 1.

72. Address by President Richard M. Nixon at Washington, D.C., April 10, 1969, Department of State *Bulletin* 60, no. 1557: 353-54.

73. "Environment: The Third Dimension of NATO," Georges Mundeleer, rapporteur, Scientific and Technical Committee, North Atlantic Assembly, October 1969, pp. 7-8.

74. The initial meeting of CCMS in December 1969 as well as the pilot projects accepted by the North Atlantic Council in January 1970 are fully reported in the February 1970 issue of *NATO Letter*, which was entirely devoted to the activities of CCMS. Further reporting is contained in subsequent issues of *NATO Letter* (After May-June 1971 *NATO Review*.) See also James R. Huntley, *Man's Environment and the Atlantic Alliance*, NATO Information Service (Brussels, 1971).

75. Address by Daniel P. Moynihan at Brussels, October 21, 1969, Department of State *Bulletin* 61, no. 1586: 419.

76. General Report of the Scientific and Technical Committee. Georges Mundeleer, rapporteur, North Atlantic Assembly, October 1970, pp. 18-19.

77. Address of NATO Secretary General Manlio Brosio at Brussels, December 8, 1969, *NATO Letter*, February 1970, p. 4.

78. Address by NATO Secretary General Joseph Luns at Ottawa, April 10, 1973, *NATO Review*, May-June 1973, p. 19.

79. Address by Moynihan, op. cit., pp. 418-19.

80. "Atlantic Political Problems," Erik Blumenfeld, rapporteur, Political Committee, North Atlantic Assembly, October 1970. The Council of Europe Convention procedure and other mechanisms that might be applied on an Atlantic scale are examined further in "New Possibilities of Atlantic Cooperation," Eric Blumenfeld, rapporteur, Political Committee, North Atlantic Assembly, September 1971.

81. Dirk U. Stikker, *Men of Responsibility* (New York, 1965), pp. 341-42, 382-86. See also the comments of SACEUR's Chief of Staff, 1952-63, General James E. Moore, "The Military Effectiveness

of NATO," in *NATO in Quest of Cohesion*, eds. Karl H. Cerny and Henry W. Briefs, (New York, 1965), pp. 162-65.

82. "German Is Given a Key NATO Post," New York *Times*, June 5, 1964.

83. Final Communique, NATO Ministerial Meeting, May 22-24, 1963, *NATO Letter*, June 1963, p. 16.

84. Communique, NATO Defense Ministers' Meeting, July 25, 1966, *NATO Letter*, September 1966, p. 25.

85. Final Communique, NATO Ministerial Meeting, December 14, 1967, *NATO Letter*, January 1968, p. 25. Subsequent decisions have extended this operation, as for example when the Defense Ministers in 1968 adopted force goal plans for 1969 through 1973. See Final Communique, NATO Defense Ministers' Meeting, May 10, 1968, *NATO Letter*, June 1968, p. 28.

86. Henry Tanner, "NATO's Ministers Change Strategy," New York *Times*, May 10, 1967.

87. William Beecher, "Strategy Change Adopted by NATO," New York *Times*, December 13, 1967; Final Communique, NATO Ministerial Meeting, December 14, 1967, *NATO Letter*, January 1968, p. 25.

88. Richard E. Mooney, "U.S. Offers NATO Radio Satellites to Bypass France," New York *Times*, September 29, 1966; Anne Sington, "NATO 'Satcom.' " *NATO Letter*, March 1968, pp. 14-21; Gerard van Rossum, "NATO Communications Satellite Launched," *NATO Letter*, April 1970, pp. 1-6; "NATO's Second Communications Satellite in Orbit," *NATO Letter*, March-April 1971, pp. 16-17.

89. William Beecher, "NATO Building New Data Center," New York *Times*, May 16, 1967; Hanson W. Baldwin, "NATO's New Centers: Command Post for Vast Areas," New York *Times*, January 24, 1969; Peter Jenner, "NATO-Wide Communications Improved," *NATO Letter*, April 1970, pp. 7-8.

90. Harlan Cleveland, "NATO After the Invasion," *Foreign Affairs*, January 1969, p. 257.

91. Final Communique, NATO Ministerial Meeting, December 15 and 16, 1966, *NATO Letter*, January 1967, p. 13.

92. Final Communique, NATO Ministerial Meeting, December 14, 1967, *NATO Letter*, January 1968, p. 25; "STANAVFORLANT: NATO's First Standing Naval Force," *NATO Letter*, April 1968, pp. 14-19: "STANAVFORLANT," *NATO Review*, No. 1 (1973), pp. 16-17.

93. "MARAIRMED," *NATO Letter*, January 1969, pp. 20-23.

94. "NATO's Defense Chiefs Agree on Flotilla for Mediterranean," New York *Times*, January 17, 1969; " 'NAVOCFORMED' is Operational," *Atlantic News*, May 12, 1970, pp. 2-3.

95. "Establishment of a Standing Naval Force, Channel," *NATO Review*, May-June 1973, p. 24.

96. Stikker, op. cit., pp. 328-29.

97. Ibid., pp. 291-93.

98. Ibid., p. 343.

99. Letter of Ambassador Thomas K. Finletter, February 13, 1968, *Atlantic Community Quarterly*, Spring 1968, pp. 95-96. See also Finletter testimony of May 5, 1966, in *The Crisis in NATO: Hearings before the Subcommittee on Europe of the Committee on Foreign Affairs*, House of Representatives 89th Cong., 2d sess. (Washington, D.C., 1966), p. 130.

100. Quoted in "Non-Military Functions of NATO," Report of the NATO Committee of the Atlantic Council of the U.S., *Atlantic Community Quarterly*, Winter 1965-66, p. 436.

101. Cleveland, *NATO*, pp. 191-92. See also W. Randolph Burgess and James R. Huntley, *Europe and America* (New York, 1970), pp. 191-94.

102. Interview of German Federal Minister of Finance Helmut Schmidt by Frank Vogl, *The Times* (London), January 26, 1973.

103. Address by German Federal Minister of Finance Helmut Schmidt at Newberry, S.C., January 11, 1973, *The Bulletin*, Press and Information Office of the German Federal Government, January 16, 1973, p. 9.

104. "Schmidt Urges NATO's Scope Be Enlarged to Embrace Economic Cooperation," *ibid.*, April 10, 1973, p. 97.

105. Economic Committee, Recommendation 26, adopted by the Eighteenth Annual Session of the North Atlantic Assembly, November 1972, Bonn, in *Texts Adopted, NAA, 1972*, pp. 24-26.

106. *Atlantic News*, April 11, 1973, p. 3.

107. Address by NATO Secretary General Joseph Luns at the Europe-America Conference, Amsterdam, March 26, 1973, p. 4.

108. Address by Henry A. Kissinger, Assistant to the President for National Security Affairs, at New York, April 23, 1973, Department of State *Bulletin* 68, no. 1768: 594-95.

109.   See, for example, "Evolution of Relations between Europe and the United States," Michael Stewart, rapporteur, Document 602, May 3, 1973, Assembly, WEU, *Proceedings*, June 1973, I, p. 133.

110.   Address by Secretary of State Henry A. Kissinger at London, December 12, 1973, Department of State *Bulletin* 69, no. 1801: 778.

111.   Declaration on Atlantic Relations, June 19, 1974, Department of State *Bulletin* 71, no. 1828: 44.

112.   Address by Professor Johan Holst at the Europe-America Conference, Amsterdam, March 27, 1973, p. 8.

113.   Address by Kissinger, April 23, 1973, op. cit., pp. 593, 598.

CHAPTER

7

POLITICAL ISSUES
FACING THE
ATLANTIC ALLIANCE

Broadly speaking, four types of problems will continue to confront an Atlantic Alliance that turns its attention to long-range political issues.

The first essentially concerns the internal organization of the Atlantic Community. As the nations of Western Europe move toward union, and therefore toward a position of parity with the United States, it will be necessary to readjust the trans-Atlantic relationship as well. Care must be taken to modernize and adapt Atlantic institutions like NATO so that increasing European cohesion does not become disruptive of Atlantic unity. Since we have already emphasized the importance of this problem, and have speculated briefly about possible future trans-Atlantic political configurations, it would seem unnecessary to dwell upon it further at this point.

The remaining three long-term political issues might be viewed as the external relations of the Atlantic Community: namely, the problem of ending the estrangement between Eastern and Western Europe; the regulation of the arms race and the strategic relationship, which primarily concerns the positions of the superpowers of East and West; and finally the challenge of concerting the policies of the West beyond the confines of the NATO Treaty area.

There will obviously be an intimate connection between the unfolding of these internal and external relations. The scope, cohesion, and timing of greater unity in Western Europe will interact with the nature of the ties that might be developed between Western and Eastern Europe. This, in turn, will affect the character of any arms control arrangements that might become possible in Europe so as to provide the European continent with a new security system. Such an arrangement could not be viewed apart from the superpower relationship, which finds its sharpest differences in the heart of Europe. The superpowers will be influenced by the way they might respond to new European security arrangements in part by the type of strategic relationship they had established with each other. And a combination of these factors, that is, the nature of an emerging West European union, and the character of East-West relations both within Europe and beyond it, will affect the ability of the West to concert global policies. It is assumed that all these policy threads will be interwoven, but for simplicity of discussion it will be convenient to consider them separately.

MAKING EUROPE WHOLE AND
REUNITING GERMANY

The problem of mending a riven European continent is, at its core, intra-European in nature. It involves breaking down the barriers between the nations of Europe, East and West, and creating new pan-European ties that can create military security, political stability, and economic prosperity. An integral part of this mending process, although perhaps coming as its culmination, would be some form of reunifying Germany. This bundle of intra-European problems can only find resolution, however, if the extracontinental superpowers of the Soviet Union and the United States are also integrally associated with the terms of settlement. From the Western side, NATO can be an important and useful instrument for relating American and European aims and evolving the procedures to pursue them.

The German problem will be both the most difficult and the most important to resolve, since any improvement in the relations between the nations of Eastern and Western Europe will always remain tentative and capable of disruption, so long as the instabilities and tensions of a divided Germany are implanted in the center of the continent. NATO must constantly keep under review the prospects and possible terms of a German settlement, not because it can be expected to materialize in the near future, but because the West must identify itself with the legitimate aim of self-determination for the entire German nation. If Bonn's NATO allies should disavow this goal, or even lose interest in supporting Bonn's efforts to move toward it, the West German bond with NATO will wear thin and likely break down completely. The result would be to push Bonn toward unilateral negotiations with Moscow, which could only forebode ill for the West.

Moreover, German disillusionment with the West might also place intolerable strains on the democratic institutions of the Federal Republic. It might be felt that a regime in the autocratic tradition of Bismarck could more easily play off East against West for the purpose of achieving German national objectives. If frustrated rage should again become the controlling mood of the German people, it is conceivable that the overpowering irrationality of another Hitler might come to the fore. The postwar democratic record of West Germany is infinitely better than many people had anticipated. Yet the roots of this experiment are still tender, and a strong authoritarian strain remains in German life. If, as happened in the past, Western democracy should become identified with impotence, a turn toward the pursuit of German goals through a policy of unbridled national force could produce cataclysmic results. Among these might be German denunciation of the pledge not to manufacture atomic, biological, or chemical weapons, which the Federal Republic assumed in 1954 in connection with German rearmament and membership in NATO. For its part, NATO simultaneously pledged itself to support the peaceful reunification of Germany. Abandonment of the Western commitment to Bonn would leave open the real possibility that Bonn would feel released from its part of the basic "contract."[1]

Ever since its admission to NATO, the Alliance has been an indispensable mechanism for a collective management of the German problem. The security that NATO supplied to Western Europe against the threat from the East also provided the East with security against stirrings from a resurgent, free-wheeling West Germany. What would be the prospect for Europe of a West Germany that had broken its NATO bond because it had concluded that it could only hope to overcome its division by its own resources? It could either seek to accomplish this end by coming into conflict or cooperation with the Soviet Union. Either course could bring catastrophe: either a European war, in case of conflict, or the projection of Soviet power into the heart of Western Europe, in case of cooperation on lines set by Soviet policy.

Future arrangements must not cut loose the Federal Republic but seek to pursue its legitimate goal of a reunited German people within the larger institutional policy-making framework of the West. Franz-Josef Strauss, who is frequently considered one of the most assertive West German political figures, has nevertheless cautioned against German initiatives that would set West Germany adrift: "What we can do is to help to create a framework, a European architecture in an Atlantic Community in which the German problem can be absorbed, in which the Germans become predictable because they are no longer in a position to be unpredictable."[2]

CHANGES IN THE APPROACH TO GERMAN REUNIFICATION

Over time the West German approach to reunification has changed radically, and it would seem that, in some quarters at least, the concept of reunification itself has been basically transformed. The rigid assumption of the Adenauer era that any movement toward East-West detente must be made conditional upon progress toward reunification was gradually undermined by the hard fact that no progress on reunification was made; nor would it be, on terms acceptable to the West, so long as the Communists adamantly rejected the principle of national self-determination expressed by a free vote of the German people. Moreover, the building of the Berlin Wall in 1961 both stabilized the East German regime and shattered any remaining illusions about the ease of reunifying Germany.

The effort to impart movement to Bonn's *Ostpolitik* and work toward reconciliation with East Germany by indirect means led to an explicit reversal of the earlier position by the Kiesinger grand coalition government. In 1967 Foreign Minister Willy Brandt declared: "We do *not* make our policy of detente dependent on progress with the German question."[3] Instead, emphasis was placed on efforts to increase intra-German contacts and to foster liberalization of East Germany in the hope of alleviating its living conditions.

This policy of "small steps," undertaken for commendable humanitarian aims, was based on a calculated gamble. Each West German overture to the G.D.R. unavoidably enhanced the political status of the East German regime. Yet such concessions, which might acquire an irreversible momentum, were made without solid assurance that the desired response would be forthcoming from the East. The hope that an increasingly liberalized East Germany might facilitate reunification has therefore remained unproven. As Melvin Croan observed, even Ulbricht had introduced significant changes in the G.D.R., especially innovations that encouraged the operation of a more rational and efficient economic system. "With the further consolidation of the regime postulated by proponents of the formula 'reunification through liberalization,'" the East German leaders "might well grant more and more concessions to the population without necessarily sacrificing their own control or proving more pliable on the national issue. On the contrary, such a sequence of events, by enhancing the popularity of the regime at home, might only serve to render it more truculent towards the Federal Republic."[4]

Furthermore, the greater size and strength of the Federal Republic relative to the G.D.R. may only be an illusory bargaining advantage for Bonn. The obvious vulnerability of the East German leaders in their confrontation with the West has made them acutely aware of the threat to their power positions. Paradoxically, generous West German offers of collaboration stimulate East German intransigence. "No amount of West German assurance or economic aid is really sufficient on this score. Rather, to the extent to which West German concessions may tend to increase the self-confidence of the East German leaders by lending them a greater degree of domestic consolidation, their propensity to challenge the Federal Republic, far from being diminished, would probably increase."[5]

Ultimately, the East German leaders could press for their version of reunification, without endangering the basis of their Communist regime by subjecting it to the perils of a free vote. They could revive their long-proposed plan for a confederation between the two legally recognized German states, under which they would maintain intact their relatively closed society in the East, while intervening freely in the open democratic processes of West Germany. Even without formal confederation, Croan speculated that an East German regime "might find its political support sought by the opposition to any existing West German government. The more its support was sought, the higher its demands would probably be. The results might well include the paralysis of West German government and the discrediting of democracy in the Federal Republic, as well as a steady weakening of West Germany's ties to the West." Should such a confederation finally be consummated, it would continuously offer to the East German leaders numerous possibilities "to demoralize West German politics and destroy its ties to the West."[6]

Such a scenario may seem alarmist, but developments along these lines cannot be entirely discounted. In January 1971 Brandt remarked before the Bundestag: "No other state in the world receives as much detailed and active attention from the G.D.R. as the Federal Republic. I do wonder: Is this not the interference in the internal affairs of another state which the G.D.R. leadership is otherwise so eager to denounce? Do they not often try even to instigate our citizens to revolt against the law of their state?"[7]

In the spring of 1972 Brandt's slim parliamentary majority was so badly eroded during the Bundestag's consideration of the ratification of the Moscow and Warsaw Treaties that it soon became necessary to dissolve the Bundestag and hold new elections. In this instance Brandt was decisively returned to power in November 1972 and the domestic crisis was surmounted without imperiling the democratic nature of the regime. Yet this prolonged parliamentary paralysis was nevertheless caused by the sharp divisions of opinion within the Federal Republic on how to regulate its relations with the Communist East, and it is conceivable that another such domestic crisis arising from its Ostpolitik might not have the same happy outcome.

The Moscow Treaty and the Basic Treaty subsequently signed with the G.D.R. have unavoidably made the Kremlin and East Berlin important factors in West German political life and have given the Communist East direct leverage over the internal policies of the Federal Republic. The Bonn regime has been deeply marked by international forces and events ever since its inception, and there is every prospect that this will remain true in the future. Its relations with the Soviet bloc expose West Germany to the perpetual danger of having its internal fabric torn apart by the activity of external agents that seek to refashion it and to detach it from the West.

REUNIFICATION REDEFINED

As the grand coalition under Chancellor Kiesinger attempted to widen its contacts with the East, the search for detente seemed only remotely related to the goal of reunification as traditionally conceived. Theo Sommer, an editor of the influential *Die Zeit,* summed up the rationale for the new approach: "It is of little import whether the two parts of Germany will be united within the borders of a single national state or whether they will be united in a more pragmatic fashion that would permit the Germans to get together without actually living together under one flag." According to this view, "what ails the Germans is not so much that their nation is divided: It is rather that seventeen million of them have to live under an oppressive regime. If that regime became less oppressive, if it were democratized and liberalized, though remaining Communist, partition would be less unbearable than it is now."[8]* Such a rapprochement between the divided parts of the German people reduced "reunification" to some sort of an institutionalized or regulated coexistence between two separate but increasingly amicable German states.

This emasculated version of reunification was based upon the sanguine vision of two German states converging upon liberal principles of government. But this hope soon received a rude rebuff by events in Czechoslovakia. The Soviet-led invasion of August 1968, which forcibly reversed the liberalization process in Czechoslovakia, also strengthened those elements that sought to resist liberalization in East Germany. As we have observed, the East German leaders might, over time, permit limited liberalization in some areas if it proved to be

---

*Sommer subsequently reformulated this view: "The object is not to move borders but to change their nature; it is not to annul the division of Germany but to make it tolerable for human beings; not to reduce Soviet power in Europe but to break down barriers between East and West. The rest must be left to the course of history. The final stage could be the division of Germany if it appeared bearable to the Germans, or reunification if it was accepted by the Europeans."[9]

a way of consolidating their rule. But there would always be limits to such liberalization so as to avoid sacrificing their own political control. To submit their rule to legitimation by any genuinely democratic process, the East German leaders would have to assume foolhardy risks. This would be true for the leadership of any of the bloc states, whose rule is maintained by reliance on Soviet power, since any valid expression of self-determination would instantly reveal the lack of popular support and the fragility of the political regimes that have been imposed on the various peoples.

This general condition is aggravated in East Germany by the special fact that the East German people look longingly toward union with their more numerous, more powerful, and more prosperous West German brothers, who at the same time live in a condition of political freedom. All attempts of the Communist East German leaders to generate loyalty to a separate East German state must therefore remain shallow. By the same token, the more that freedom of movement is allowed between East and West Germany, the more the Communist leaders expose themselves to odious comparisons. A genuinely popular East German regime that could withstand the test of free and easy contacts with West Germany is not the kind of regime that felt compelled to build the Berlin Wall. When the East Germans tear down the Berlin Wall, the West German partisans of "reunification through liberalization" will have a more reasonable basis for their policy.

In November 1972 East German Party chief Erich Honecker anticipated the influx of the West Germans across the frontier and through the Berlin Wall as a result of the intra-German accords with the observation that nonetheless "the frontier and the Wall remain as existing realities." Moreover, the increased contacts implied "no possibility of ideological convergence," since the two systems were based on "totally different fundamental principles" that "mutually exclude each other."[10] In order to preserve those differences and shield the East Germans from the contagion of West German ideas, Honecker contrived the policy of "delimitation," which might well prove easier to decree than to enforce. Some 2 million of East Germany's 17 million people who comprised the ruling elite—the ranking Party and government officials, members of the armed forces and police units—were forbidden to have Western visitors at home and were required to have special permission to meet with them at other places. Several hundred thousand non-Party members who held what were considered to be sensitive jobs in the economy, the transport network, and social services were also included in this ruling.[11]

Such precautions must be expected as part of the process of normalizing relations with the West. In the Soviet lexicon, in fact, "normalization" has several special meanings. The forcible imposition of a Soviet-controlled regime in Prague was called the normalization of life in Czechoslovakia. It was only when these political forces were once again firmly under the Kremlin's control that the Soviet leaders felt free to resume their detente policies aimed at "normalizing" relations with the West. Similarly, the East German leaders had to assure the safeguarding of their Communist orthodoxies so as to maintain "normalcy" at home while they undertook to normalize relations with the Federal Republic. As Egon Bahr, the principal architect of Bonn's Ostpolitik, was reluctantly obliged to admit: "I fear that relations between Bonn and the G.D.R. will not be 'truly normal' in the sense of smoothness such as the ties between Austria and the Federal Republic—as long as the G.D.R. is the G.D.R.; as long as it belongs to another system."[12]

THE BREZHNEV DOCTRINE AND GERMAN REUNIFICATION

The Soviet assault on Czechoslovakia decisively confirmed the vision of "reunification" as relations between two separate German states. The rationale for sanctioning the unlimited right of Soviet intervention in bloc states was authoritatively expounded by Soviet Party General Secretary Leonid Brezhnev in his speech to a Congress of Polish Communists on November 12, 1968. But the essence of the Brezhnev Doctrine, as Chancellor Kiesinger recalled, had already been formulated in a letter of July 15, 1968 to the Czechoslovak Communist Party sent by the Soviet Union and its four Warsaw Pact allies who were to join in the armed intervention. "We shall never permit imperialism to force a breach in the socialist system," the letter warned, "either by peaceful or unpeaceful means, or from inside or outside, and thus change the balance of power in its favor."[13]

Following the invasion, Soviet Ambassador Tsarapkin called upon the West German Chancellor on September 2 and delivered a harsh statement that related the German question to the Soviet action in Czechoslovakia. Explaining that the invasion had been undertaken to preserve the solidarity of the socialist commonwealth, which was supposedly threatened by counterrevolutionary forces that had been encouraged from abroad, the Soviet note asserted: "Nobody would ever be allowed to break as much as a single link away from the community of socialist countries." Since Moscow considered East Germany to be a member of the socialist commonwealth, the Chancellor asked whether this doctrine was meant "to infer that a new element had been introduced into Soviet foreign policy, i.e., that the Soviet Union regarded the division of Germany as definitive and considered every attempt to end that division by peaceful means as a hostile policy against the Soviet Union?" To this query, "Ambassador Tsarapkin replied that . . . the present situation in Europe . . . would have to be recognized by the Federal Government."[14]

The day after Kiesinger reported this exchange to the Bundestag, *Pravda* published a detailed doctrinal elaboration of this tough assertion to intervene, by force if necessary, in any Communist state where the "socialist gains" were presumably endangered by creeping counterrevolutionary influences. Arguments that have been raised about the sovereignty of the states of the socialist commonwealth and their rights of national self-determination, *Pravda* asserted, are "untenable primarily because they are based on an abstract, nonclass approach to the question of sovereignty and the right of nations to self-determination." In exercising the power to govern socialist countries, Communist Parties "must neither damage socialism in their own country nor the fundamental interests of the other socialist countries nor the worldwide workers' movement, which is waging a struggle for socialism." This view of sovereignty "means that every Communist Party is responsible not only to its own people but also to all the socialist countries and to the entire Communist movement. Whoever forgets this by placing emphasis on the autonomy and independence of Communist Parties lapses into one-sidedness, shirking his international obligations." Each ruling Communist Party must be reminded that its country "retains its national independence thanks precisely to the power of the socialist commonwealth—and primarily to its chief force, the Soviet Union—and the might of its armed forces. The weakening of any link in the world socialist system has a direct effect on all the socialist countries, and they cannot be indifferent to this."[15] Peking's acid repudiation of this

Soviet verbiage contained an element of refreshing candor. "The Soviet revisionist renegade clique," the Chinese Communists said, "trumpets the so-called theory of 'limited sovereignty,' the theory of 'international dictatorship' and the theory of 'socialist community.' What does all this stuff mean? It means that your sovereignty is 'limited,' while his is unlimited."[16]

When Foreign Minister Gromyko echoed the Brezhnev Doctrine before the U.N. General Assembly,[17] Walter Ulbricht interpreted it as a pledge of Soviet protection for the separate status of East Germany into the indefinite future. "We welcome the statement of the Soviet Union," Ulbricht said, "that never and nowhere will it be permitted to tear off a state from the commonwealth of socialist states."[18] Assessing the impact of this doctrine nearly a year after it had been developed, Chancellor Kiesinger bluntly told the Bundestag: It is "evident that according to the intentions of the Soviet Union and the overlords in the other part of Germany, our countrymen separated from us would have to remain against their will within the Communist camp forever. Under this doctrine, the reunification of Germany could not become a reality unless the Federal Republic, too, would be included in the socialist camp."[19]

When Willy Brandt became Chancellor in October 1969, he pledged to continue the search for German unity, but "without illusions." Consequently, he spoke realistically of the existence of "two states in Germany" which are nevertheless members of one German nation and therefore "are not foreign countries to each other."[20] This new realism also led to a change of vocabulary. When asked, "Why don't you talk about reunification any more?" Chancellor Brandt explained:

> The term "reunification" stems from the time directly after World War II. Until somewhere in the mid-1950s, it seemed still to be possible on the basis of free elections to reunite the parts of Germany that had been separated from each other by the occupation powers. That would have required an agreement between the three Western powers and the Soviet Union. Such a happy solution to the German question was not achieved. . . . Since then, years have gone by, and the world has changed. In Germany two states with quite different political and social systems have come into

existence, systems that do not easily lend themselves to unification. Nor is there any prospect today that the world powers would be able to agree about such a reunification. . . . We must recognize that the reunification of Germany in the original sense is no longer possible. And a Chancellor has the duty to tell his people the truth, even when it is bitter.[21]

The reunification of Germany, Brandt warned, must now be relegated to the distant future. Accepting Germany's division "does not mean that we have abandoned our aim of making it possible for our own people one day—if they then so want—to live together again. But this has now been embedded in the major task of all Europeans: reuniting our divided continent."[22]

RESTRUCTURING THE ALLIANCE SYSTEMS AS A MEANS OF OVERCOMING THE DIVISION OF GERMANY

The ultimate goal of reunifying the German nation within a single state will doubtless linger on, although its realization would require a restructuring of the alliance systems that divide Europe. At present, reunification of the German nation within a single state would only be conceivable upon two contingencies: either a collapse of Soviet power and with it the East German regime, so that reunification would come on Western terms, or a collapse of Western unity, emptying NATO of its meaning if not ending its existence, so that reunification would come on Eastern terms. If neither of these contingencies seem likely, the German problem will have to be lived with within the existing alliance systems. On the Western side, NATO must continue to be an instrument for collective management of this problem in which the West Germans would be expected to take the lead in evolving relations with the East that they could find tolerable, but always with the feeling that their difficulties are understood by their NATO partners who could coordinate supportive policies.

The Ostpolitik of the grand coalition that actively sought detente with the East was thought to be consistent with a vigorous Atlantic Alliance, although the West German sponsors of this policy did envision the possibility of NATO's dissolution in the far future. In

March 1968 Chancellor Kiesinger held that the "Alliance is not in contradiction to our peace policy, on the contrary; it is this very Alliance which gives us the possibility of pursuing a policy of detente without carrying any unacceptable security risks." At the same time he did not want the Federal Republic to be tied so tightly and exclusively to NATO that it would negate the long-run aim of reunification. Picking up the Gaullist image of NATO, Kiesinger asserted that "strong as our links in the Atlantic Alliance, as our relations with the United States may be, we should not seek our own future and, we believe, that of united Western Europe within the firm framework of a North Atlantic imperium. Such a solution would turn the demarcation line dividing Germany and Europe into a permanent frontier wall."[23] This was a gratuitous remark since NATO had continually and repeatedly, though perhaps unconvincingly, pledged itself to pursue German reunification. Such a statement did, however, reveal doubts about how long-run German aims and those of NATO might diverge. It might also serve as a warning that if NATO is to remain relevant to the Germans, it must in good faith seek to help the Germans overcome their division.

Foreign Minister Brandt reflected a somewhat similar ambivalence about NATO in 1967. "Our policy of detente must not be interpreted as underestimating or neglecting the role of the Alliance." The value of NATO was not only military but diplomatic. "Nothing could be further from the truth than to assume that we now believe in an isolated settlement of the German question." Instead, "we have warned against bilateralism in East-West relations being allowed to prevail." As to the future when the basis for a firm detente might hopefully be laid, Brandt speculated that "a European security system could be based on one of two different patterns: Either the present alliances continue and are brought into some relationship with each other, or the pacts are gradually abolished and replaced with something new."[24] This statement was wholly unobjectionable, since NATO was never intended as an end in itself. It was designed to create conditions of political stability and military security, which were the necessary prerequisites for overcoming the division of Europe that resulted from World War II and for negotiating a general European settlement. The problem, once again, was one of priorities; namely, that NATO not be replaced *before* some new arrangement could come into being that could dependably provide for European security.

The effects of the Soviet invasion of Czechoslovakia only gave renewed emphasis to the abiding nature of the Kremlin's commitment to hold on to the Warsaw Pact states. It also caused to recede into an even more distant future the prospect of the disappearance of the alliances that divide Europe, and to dampen expectations about the restructuring of European security arrangements that might have been entertained prematurely.

Although Chancellor Brandt was willing to tell his people the bitter truth about reunification, his accession to power also intensified the active search for better relations with the East that had been begun under the Ostpolitik of the grand coalition. The openly acknowledged limitations upon a successful resolution of the German problem were thus combined with a more active, independent West German policy, and this held potential dangers both for the Federal Republic and its NATO allies. As an outcome of Bonn's initiatives toward the East, Moscow and East Berlin gained recognition for the existence of a separate East German state that was an inseparable part of the Soviet bloc, while Bonn might find disappointment and frustration in its attempts to foster liberalization within the G.D.R. and sufficiently ease contacts among Germans so as to prevent the two parts of Germany from drifting even further apart. "There is a risk of failure in any 'policy of movement,' " either the failure to ease tense relations with the East, or "the lesser (but no less frustrating) failure of better relations that merely consecrate the division of Europe at a lower level of hostility." The result, as this commentator observed, could be a crisis in West Germany's relations with its allies. "West Germany, treated as and having behaved as a dependent for so many years, might be persuaded to blame failure not on an impossible situation, but on allies that failed to keep their promises." Should this occur, the Federal Republic could become unhinged from NATO and set adrift toward the East. "The Soviet Union might try to tempt West Germany into what would be, in effect, a disguised recognition of the East European status quo and a disruption of the West European one; West Germany, disappointed with its allies, might be lured out of the Alliance, in exchange for some vague offer of German confederation." Thus, "West Germany's excessive reliance on the United States yesterday and its growing self-reliance today mean, paradoxically enough, possibly excessive dependence on the Soviet Union tomorrow."[25]

There are latent fissures in the Western Alliance that the Kremlin could conceivably play upon to bring about this result. For Bonn's allies, the West German treaties with the Soviet bloc states might appear to constitute a settlement of outstanding issues that would assure that the Federal Republic could henceforth be unambiguously integrated into a political federation of Western Europe, while fully retaining a place in the Atlantic Alliance. But perhaps the long-range view from Bonn might be different. Egon Bahr, the chief theoretician and negotiator of Brandt's Ostpolitik, as early as 1963 argued that the aim of this policy should be to promote "change through rapprochement" with the East so as someday to allow for German reunification.[26] His concept of detente is essentially dynamic in that it anticipates the gradual evolution of policy in East Germany and the Soviet bloc generally in order to bring reunification within reach. But might this not also require important changes in the Federal Republic's relations with the West? At some point in the future might not the needs of the German nation be asserted at the expense of West Germany's ties with a European Union and the Western Alliance system? Some of Bahr's pronouncements would seem to indicate that this might be so.[27]

Thus it is quite conceivable that a Soviet stance that at first appeared to have the defensive aim of consolidating a divided Germany into the Soviet bloc would be transformed into a Soviet political offensive that would fundamentally alter the political balance in Western Europe. An Atlantic Alliance that had suffered the defection of West Germany would likely be in no position to resist further Soviet pressure aimed at pushing Western Europe toward a pro-Soviet "neutrality" and driving the United States and Canada out of Western Europe. The key to preventing this chain of events from being set in motion is to reinforce the political mechanism of NATO so as to provide for a constant and candid examination of the risks and benefits of all proposed policies in the hope that such a dialogue would permit the close and continuous association of the Federal Republic's Ostpolitik with the policies of its NATO allies. Only in this manner can one hope to avoid the estrangement of Bonn from the West and the disintegration of the West itself.

Chancellor Brandt was obviously alive to these dangers when he proclaimed: "The Federal Republic of Germany is not 'wandering between two worlds.' Without the background and the security afforded by proven friendships and proven alliances there could be no active German contribution towards the policy of detente at all." The nub of the problem is to translate policy declarations into the formulation of compatible policies between Bonn and its NATO partners. This problem becomes infinitely more difficult because it must be conceived in a very long time frame. The solution of the German problem, in effect, means the solution of the problems of a divided Europe and the complete reordering of the existing political and security systems that span the continent. Chancellor Brandt clearly recognized this when he said that Bonn's dealings with the East must be based upon "the striving for national unity and freedom within the framework of a European peace arrangement." And when he asked, "How can these objectives be achieved today by German policy?" he replied, "They cannot be attained any longer by the traditional means of the nation-state, but only in alliance with others. In future there will be no political settlements of significance any more outside of alliances, security systems or communities. In future German problems of importance can be dealt with not in terms of the nation-state and in traditional fashion, but only through gradual endeavors for a European peace arrangement."[28] Until its dissolution into some new European peace arrangement, NATO has before it a long-term and indispensable role. Since moves toward German unity automatically involve basic changes in the international system, this inevitably requires the closest collaboration among the NATO partners and the summoning of their collective wisdom.

THE SEARCH FOR ACCOMMODATION BETWEEN THE SUPERPOWERS

Another set of political problems that will continue to bear upon the political interests of the NATO members essentially revolves around superpower relations. The strategic capabilities and global reach of Soviet and American power has opened a gap between themselves and all Europeans, East and West, and has made European concerns seem parochial by comparison. Until Europe, or at least some part of Europe, takes shape politically, there is every indication that the gap will grow increasingly wider. Obviously, negotiations between the superpowers over measures that seek to regulate the arms race, and in particular to control the contest over nuclear weapons, will unavoidably affect the security and political interests of the Europeans and require the closest coordination between superpower and European diplomacy. Once again on the

Western side, NATO can be a logical, central forum for thrashing out conflicts in the positions of the different Western states and in arriving at a coordinated approach to the East.

There is a constant temptation for Washington to try to settle arms control and related issues directly with Moscow, with only minimal consideration for the views of its European allies. Since in many respects the United States and the Soviet Union are unique among the nations of the world in their capacities to organize and employ power, including nuclear power, Washington can easily fall prey to a superpower complex. This represents a perilous and simplistic tendency to assume that if only the United States could deal directly with the Kremlin, without bothering about the tiresome complications of the various European interests, we could strike a deal that could solve many issues, including perhaps those of Europe's future. Peking has seized upon manifestations of Soviet-American collaboration dealing primarily with arms control and has elaborated them into a full-fledged political plot of a superpower duopoly aimed at ruling the world. This is, of course, pure paranoia, since the substance of such Soviet-U.S. agreements have dealt essentially with ways of preventing nuclear war, rather than with joint programs of a positive political content. A more realistic assessment of a superpower duopoly would reveal other dangers: the tendency for agreement on Soviet and American spheres of influence that would perpetuate the present division of Europe, including the perpetuation of the division of Germany; the tendency for the superpowers to keep the Europeans in an inferior position by cutting them out of their dealings and refusing, for example, to share in the advantages of nuclear power; and finally the tendency to foster the illusion that a European settlement would be capable of easy solutions if left to the superpowers, and that it might somehow be accomplished without full European participation.

Soviet-American discussions on a variety of issues over the years have always raised these specters, whether the topic be a scheme for assured access routes to Berlin, for a demilitarized or a nuclear-free zone in Central Europe, or arms inspection plans to safeguard against surprise attack. In each case, East-West relations assumed the existence of a political and territorial stability that confirmed a status quo that was repugnant to the aim of dismantling East-West barriers in general, and to the reunification of Germany in particular.

THE IMPACT OF THE NON-PROLIFERATION
TREATY ON ALLIANCE SOLIDARITY

Perhaps the negotiation of the Non-Proliferation Treaty (NPT) to prevent the dissemination of nuclear weapons, which was finally signed in 1968, offers the clearest example of how superpower relations gave rise to a cluster of fears among America's European partners and stimulated resentment in Europe against the United States. Soviet and American motives for the treaty coincided only insofar as both parties hoped that the NPT would reduce the likelihood of nuclear warfare. However, Washington was primarily concerned with the possibility of nuclear weapons becoming available in the third world, while Moscow was clearly preoccupied with hampering the role of the Federal Republic. Not only did it seek to bar every sort of West German access, however indirect, to nuclear weapons, but the Kremlin conceived of the NPT as a political device to alienate Bonn from Washington, and in general as a way of driving a wedge into NATO so as to separate the United States from Western Europe.[29] In these respects, the Kremlin managed to score a substantial success.

German fears about Alliance solidarity were explicitly and officially confirmed by a principal American advocate of the NPT. William C. Foster, Director of the U.S. Arms Control and Disarmament Agency, recorded in 1965 that a possible cost of the treaty "could be the erosion of alliances resulting from the high degree of U.S.-Soviet cooperation which will be required if a non-proliferation program is to be successful." Moreover, he acknowledged that "within NATO there could be concern that the detente would lead to a weakening of our commitment to Western Europe. The problem will be particularly acute in Germany where there will be the added concern that the amelioration of the East-West confrontation could lead to an increased acceptance of the status quo in Central Europe."[30]

The Soviet Union grasped the occasion of the treaty negotiations to attack NATO plans for nuclear sharing, as in the then-proposed Multilateral Force (MLF), since Moscow claimed this would be incompatible with an NPT. The U.S. draft of an NPT, submitted in

August 1965, defined nonproliferation in clear and precise terms. Its aim was simply to prevent an increase in the number of nuclear weapon centers. According to the American draft, each party to the treaty would refrain from transferring nuclear weapons "into the national control of any nonnuclear state, either directly, or indirectly through a military alliance." This provision in no way upset the Germans, since no one had proposed creating a West German national deterrent, and, indeed, the West German government had explicitly and repeatedly rejected this possibility.

In addition, the American draft pledged each party to the treaty "not to take any other action which would cause an increase in the total number of states and other organizations having independent power to use nuclear weapons."[31] A NATO nuclear deterrent, such as the MLF, would not have increased the total number of states or organizations having the power independently to use nuclear weapons since the United States and Britain as MLF members would have had a veto over the use of the collective force. Nonnuclear NATO states such as West Germany, Italy, and the Netherlands, however, would have had a share in the ownership and management of the force, and its operation could have formed a tangible, joint strategic link holding the two sides of the Atlantic together. It was this prospect of reinforcing the Alliance that the Soviet leadership found so unacceptable, not the idea that the MLF would have been a form of proliferation, as Moscow contended. Generally overlooked in the furor raised over the prospect that Germany might share in the operation of a MLF was the fact that West Germany was already the world's third largest nuclear power by virtue of sharing tactical nuclear weapons on German soil with the United States under the two-key system. While Moscow would have been pleased to remove such indirect German access to nuclear weapons, which it had on a bilateral basis with the United States, realistically there was little chance of doing so. The main Soviet thrust in negotiating the NPT was therefore to prevent any further moves toward integration and cohesion within NATO which might have arisen out of new plans for nuclear sharing.

The Soviet counterproposal for an NPT, advanced in September 1965, staked out the maximum conceivable prohibitions. It sought to obstruct any type of nuclear sharing, either within the Atlantic Alliance as it then existed or within some possible Atlantic or European defense community in the future. According to the Soviet draft, nuclear weapons could not be transferred "in any form, directly or indirectly, through third states or groups of states," nor could an NPT "accord to such states or groups of states the right to participate in the ownership, control or use of nuclear weapons." This prohibition would extend to the armed forces or personnel of nonnuclear states, "even if such units or personnel are under the command of a military alliance."[32]

The United States successfully rebuffed this far-reaching Soviet attempt to disrupt the existing NATO nuclear arrangements whereby nonnuclear allies participated in planning and training exercises involving nuclear weapons and owned delivery vehicles for which the United States held the nuclear warheads. The United States, in effect, managed to uphold the status quo by resisting Soviet efforts to unravel the degree of nuclear collaboration that had been achieved within NATO. But some European members of NATO expressed the fear that the United States would not resist further Soviet pressure that was aimed at blocking any sort of nuclear sharing within the Alliance. West German NATO Ambassador Wilhelm Grewe warned in January 1967: "The Soviet Union apparently aims to divide the members of the Atlantic Alliance by preventing them from making arrangements for allied or European nuclear agreements." In the future negotiation of the NPT, "concessions made to further this Soviet interest can only have a demoralizing effect on the NATO partners. This would happen mainly if they would give in to Soviet demands to exclude future nuclear community solutions."[33]

The United States, in fact, did yield to such Soviet pressure and agreed that the NPT should forbid the creation of any sort of a jointly owned NATO nuclear force. The crucial treaty changes that affected nuclear sharing within NATO appeared in the identical texts submitted by the Soviet Union and the United States in August 1967. They remained intact in the amended identical Soviet-American draft presented in January 1968, as well as in the final draft of the NPT as signed in June 1968.[34] The language of this approach, which accommodated Soviet demands, specified that nuclear weapon states would undertake "not to transfer to any recipient whatsoever nuclear weapons or other nuclear explosive devices or control over such weapons or explosive devices directly, or indirectly," as well as "not in any way to assist, encourage or induce" the acquisition of nuclear devices by nonnuclear states. The scope of this commitment was obviously much broader than the original American concept, which simply sought to avoid the creation of any additional, independent centers disposing of nuclear weapons.

Under the provisions of the NPT as adopted, various types of Western institution building with important military and political implications had been foreclosed. As Secretary of State Dean Rusk explained to the Senate Foreign Relations Committee when it was considering ratification of the NPT, "the treaty would bar transfer of nuclear weapons (including ownership) or control over them to any recipient, including a multilateral entity."[35] This burial of the MLF idea gave substance to William Foster's prediction about the possible "erosion of alliances resulting from the high degree of U.S.-Soviet cooperation which will be required if a non-proliferation program is to be successful."

The final form of the NPT treaty also conspicuously omitted the "European clause" that would have sanctioned the building of a European nuclear deterrent that might have come into existence as part of the protracted process of forming a European Union. The Kremlin thus succeeded in asserting its opposition to various conceivable forms of strengthening Western institutions, either on an Atlantic or European scale, however hypothetical these plans might have appeared at the time. Washington reassured its European partners that, in its view, a European federation could become a successor state that would inherit the nuclear status of any of its constituent parts, such as Britain or France, which were formerly independent nuclear powers. While a future federated Europe could thus become a nuclear state, under the terms of the NPT, the United States was pledged not to assist any form of a multilateral European defense agency short of a fully developed European federation that had established control over all aspects of its defense, including all matters of foreign policy that related to external security. This effectively whittled down Europe's chances of ever becoming a nuclear power and demonstrated to America's European allies that when faced with a choice, it gave priority to its superpower relations with Moscow over issues involving Western unity. It might be added that the Soviet Union has not publicly acknowledged even this limited interpretation of how a European nuclear force might be created.

With the options for a MLF or European deterrent ruled out, and with the uncertainty then prevailing over NATO's future as a result of the defection of France, the Federal Republic was prompted to ask the United States for a special guarantee against nuclear attack. Instead, the United States joined the Soviet Union in offering a resolution, attached to the NPT, that nations seeking security against the threat or the use of nuclear weapons could turn to the procedures of the U.N. Security Council. It is scarcely surprising that Bonn did not feel reassured against the possibility of Soviet nuclear blackmail by the prospect of turning for protection to a body that could be paralyzed by a Soviet veto.[36]

The Germans also became acutely aware of the opportunities that the NPT provided the Soviet Union to intervene in the future activities of the Federal Republic or of other nonnuclear weapon states. In contrast to the clear and explicit notion of nonproliferation that was in the original American draft, the Soviet-inspired changes contained important ambiguities. The final treaty prohibited the transfer of control over nuclear weapons either "directly or indirectly," but nowhere was there an agreed definition on what indirect control means. Soviet spokesmen have denounced, for example, German participation in NATO's consultative bodies on nuclear planning as an indirect form of control, and the future German role in any new method of allied deliberations about nuclear policy could bring similar charges and offer the Kremlin the rationale to interfere in the internal operations of NATO.

Moreover, the treaty did not provide an effective way of distinguishing between nuclear military technology, which is forbidden to nonnuclear weapon states, and nuclear civil technology, which is to be encouraged. Again, Soviet pronouncements have accused the Federal Republic of engaging in a variety of civil nuclear programs, which are alleged to be preparing or actually initiating production of nuclear weapons both inside and outside West German borders. Since the technological achievements involved in the peaceful uses of nuclear energy have potential military value, a restrictive interpretation of the treaty would make almost any civil nuclear program impossible. On the other hand, the uncertainty inherent in the distinction between military and nonmilitary activity could permit the Soviet Union to give a broad interpretation to civil nuclear programs for those states that Moscow wishes to favor.[37] As in the case of defining direct or indirect control over nuclear weapons, the NPT established no arbitrator to provide an authoritative judgment about these ambiguities. Technical and scientific processes could therefore easily be transformed into bitter political disputes.

The agreed Soviet-American draft of the NPT certainly underestimated the issue of realizing the economic potential of nuclear power for peaceful purposes. It therefore quickly created dissension among the nonnuclear states, including America's NATO allies, on the grounds that they might be permanently consigned a second-class status, deprived of the economic benefits of nuclear power.

The enormous promise of generating electricity from nuclear energy was not, at first, widely appreciated. The first generation of nuclear thermal reactors was rather inefficient and was dependent upon a supply of slightly enriched uranium, which had to be imported from a few countries, like the United States, which also had isotope separation facilities. But starting about 1980, a number of countries will have in operation fast breeder reactors that first convert modest amounts of uranium into plutonium and then "breeds" more plutonium than they consume in generating electricity. This will render numerous countries relatively independent of uranium suppliers, make unnecessary the construction of their own isotope separation facilities, and provide an inexpensive method for generating electrical power.[38] Given this enormous economic potential, it is understandable why the nonnuclear weapon states insisted upon revisions in the joint Soviet-American draft of the NPT so as to assure them of greater access to the nuclear technology that would be involved in the future uses of nuclear power for peaceful purposes. The bargaining between the two groups, however, often assumed the unhappy spectacle of the Soviet Union and the United States (with Britain as a junior partner) standing on one side, with the nonnuclear states, including the rest of the NATO nations, standing on the other.

The basic provisions of the NPT, as U.S. NATO Ambassador Harlan Cleveland testified, were "worked out bilaterally toward the end of 1966 around the edges of the U.N. General Assembly in New York. Only several weeks later were the NATO allies brought up to date." When the matter was finally introduced into the NATO forum, even those allies that were in sympathy with the aims of the treaty "were so unhappy about the procedure that they made difficulties about the substance as a matter of principle. . . . In the end the treaty was considered word by word and phrase by phrase in the North Atlantic Council." Different aspects of the NPT were under Council review for nearly a year before a NATO consensus was reached. This permitted Cleveland to declare that "without the intensive

consultation in NATO there would have been no treaty."[39] The fact
nevertheless remained that allied consultation was in the nature of a
tardy effort to make amends for oversights in a deal originally struck
by the superpowers. Again in terms of priorities, the superpower
complex had overwhelmed the requirements of Western solidarity.

ASSESSING THE LIMITATIONS OF THE NPT

It would be a mistake to expect that the NPT might permanently
prevent the dissemination of nuclear weapons. Consider, for
example, the ominous fact that the widespread use of fast breeder
reactors will spread staggering amounts of plutonium over the face of
the globe. Plutonium, as it happens, is the element commonly used
for making nuclear weapons. States producing plutonium for the
generation of electricity will be in a position to enrich and compress it
into weapons-grade material at very little cost. Nor can international
inspection provide a satisfactory answer to the gradual, clandestine
diversion of plutonium during the normal operation of fast breeder
reactors. Given the uncertainties inherent in inspection procedures,
an expert notes that "a two per cent range of error is inevitable" in
monitoring plutonium production.[40]* Moreover, even those

---

*Representative Craig Hosmer, a member of the Joint Committee on
Atomic Energy, disparaged the ability of the International Atomic Energy
Agency (IAEA) to provide "effective safeguards" against the diversion of
plutonium, as anticipated under the terms of the NPT. "Neither the IAEA
inspection staff, nor anyone else, for that matter, has the remotest notion of
what constitutes a normal loss of uranium or plutonium in the industrial
process—therefore, there is not the slightest possibility of any inspector
spotting illegal diversions because he can't even be told when his suspicion
should be aroused. Even should a suspicion be aroused for other reasons,
IAEA procedures need never bring it to anyone's attention. IAEA's
Inspector General is not obliged to tell IAEA's Director General about it,
and if he does, the latter is under no obligation to tip off anyone else."[41]
Another close student of the NPT remarked in 1971: "It now seems clear that
intra-IAEA politics and the Agency's conception of its safeguards role are
combining to make that role more modest than proponents hoped and than
skeptics feared. These characteristics are discernible in the agreed-upon
guidelines for NPT accords and in the description of the IAEA safeguards by
the Agency's own Inspector General."[42]

monitored plutonium stockpiles, which were presumably stored for peaceful purposes, could be quickly converted to military use.

If only a small portion of such plutonium were diverted for military purposes, there would still be an ample supply to do considerable mischief. According to the calculations of Bruce Smith, West Germany and Japan, as the two most powerful industrial states without nuclear weapons, will by 1980 be producing enough plutonium to make 800 nuclear bombs a year.[43] Under Secretary of State Nicholas Katzenbach had estimated that "nuclear power reactors in operation by 1985 . . . will also be producing enough plutonium to make 20 bombs a day."[44] Albert Wohlstetter's projections are even more astronomical. By the end of the 1970s, civilian reactors might have as a "byproduct about 10,000 bombs worth of plutonium; in the following twenty or thirty years, perhaps a million bombs worth, doubling every ten years."[45]

In a somewhat different vein, but hardly less disturbing, is the prospect of Mafia-type or terrorist groups stealing, hijacking, or otherwise capturing small amounts of plutonium. "Once groups like these get hold of enough plutonium," one commentator observed, "their method of exploding it need not be very efficient—but it still would be a nuclear explosion in the order of the Hiroshima bomb."[46]

There is, moreover, the possibility of producing weapons-grade enriched uranium by the gas centrifuge process. While this process cannot produce the enormous amounts of enriched uranium that came from the huge gaseous diffusion plants that were originally built to provide fissile material for bombs, by the same token the centrifuge process might well prove to be a cheaper way of producing smaller quantities of fissile material. It has been estimated that "the minimum practical plant using centrifuges probably would require about 100 times *less* in dollar investment, electric power and size of structure" than that required to build and operate the older gaseous diffusion plants.[47] Therefore, the "gas centrifuge process . . . could provide small would-be nuclear powers with bomb fuel on the cheap."[48] Following several years of negotiation, a British-Dutch-West German agreement for the joint operation of several centrifuge plants was signed in 1970.[49] One uranium enrichment plant is located at Capenhurst, England, the other at Almelo, Holland, while the headquarters for the joint operation is in the Federal Republic. The agreement was framed with the hope that other European countries might also join, if they so desired. There is a strong incentive to build such facilities elsewhere, since this reduces the need for the producing states to import enriched uranium from the United States. While the signatories of the first tripartite centrifuge operation pledged themselves to observe the NPT, such a pledge might not always be fulfilled in the future. In any event, the capability for creating relatively inexpensive facilities to produce fissile material that could be diverted to making nuclear weapons is clearly proliferating.

It would appear that the NPT has been vastly oversold to the general public. It is, after all, a treaty among sovereign states. Basically the decision as to whether a nation will or will not produce nuclear weapons is too important to be effectively regulated by a treaty of this sort. (One cannot help recalling that the Kellogg-Briand Pact had "abolished" war.) The NPT takes cognizance of this fact by providing that the sovereign parties to it may withdraw upon three months notice if a state decides that "extraordinary events" warrant denunciation. The fashion in recent times, however, has not been for states to announce their official intent to go to war, or formally to declare war, but simply to start fighting. The comfort of the denunciation clause, which is small in any case, is not very reassuring.

Treaties may also be viewed as binding by the contracting governments, but within a relatively short period may be repudiated, either formally or informally, by successor governments, which can plead that they face wholly new and different circumstances. This argument, which has ample historical precedent, could lead states to abandon their treaty obligation not to obtain or make nuclear weapons, while remaining in possession of large supplies of plutonium. Leonard Beaton had suggested as a remedy that nuclear fuel for civilian reactors be owned from the start by an international agency, which would lease out the uranium and buy back the surplus plutonium.[50] This arrangement, though sensible, may already be too late to implement, and in any event would require endowing an international body with such enormous power as to be politically unacceptable. Even in the pristine days of atomic development, when the United States was the sole possessor of atomic power, Soviet intransigence prevented the United Nations from adopting the Baruch Plan, which had offered to vest ownership and control of all atomic facilities in an international authority.[51]

The NPT shunned the approach of an international agency owning nuclear fuel, and instead relied wholly upon international inspection of nationally owned fuel and reactors as a safeguard against diversion to military purposes. Here again, if there were to be ironclad security arrangements, the international inspectorate would have to become an extremely large and competent agency, powerful enough to force its will upon national bureaucracies that are imbued with patriotic motives. Such patriotism would likely take the form of preparing and keeping secretly at the ready nuclear bombs, the designs for which are by now well known, but without actually inserting the weapons-grade plutonium into them. The value of the NPT would then be reduced to verifying the fact that many nations had accumulated enough plutonium to become nuclear weapons powers, but that, so far as could be discovered, the plutonium and the bombs had not actually been brought together, nor had the bombs been tested. (Testing is hardly necessary in reproducing well-known bomb designs.) The crucial question then becomes how many days, or perhaps hours, it would take to assemble an operational bomb once a nation had decided to become a nuclear weapons state.[52]

In view of the fact that the NPT is scarcely a panacea for preventing the spread of nuclear weapons, while at the same time it has doubtless fostered illusions in world opinion as to the security it might provide against future dangers, one may be permitted to ask whether it was worth all the damage that it inflicted upon American-European relations. It must be acknowledged that the NPT has some value in helping potential nuclear weapons states to communicate their intentions to each other, so that each one will not rush headlong into weapons production for fear that the others are doing so. On this account alone the treaty would be worthwhile in slowing down the dissemination of nuclear weapons. The objection is not to this achievement, but to the manner in which it was brought about. Surely this end could have been accomplished by a different mode of netogiation that would not have permitted the Soviet Union to inject itself into Western defense arrangements that had widespread political and military repercussions. The original American negotiating position should have been stoutly maintained: namely, that a MLF-type nuclear sharing among NATO states did not constitute proliferation, nor would a broad option for some future European deterrent.

If a MLF agreement had been consummated in the early 1960s as a result of steady, high-level American sponsorship, which could have proved decisive, instead of languishing in a protracted state of agonizing indecision, as was the case, the Soviet Union could have been presented with the fait accompli of a MLF treaty to which it would have grudgingly accommodated itself. With the MLF in hand, the West could then have proceeded to negotiate an NPT, and the Soviet leaders would likely have taken up a fresh position that could have permitted the conclusion of this objective.

Dean Acheson recalled how the Kremlin repeatedly assumed uncompromising stands, only to abandon them in the face of determined Western policies. The Soviet Union tried to prevent the formation of a viable West German state with the Berlin blockade, but gave this up when it proved ineffective. Later when the Western powers moved to end their occupation of West Germany and to associate it with NATO, Moscow assumed harsh and threatening postures that were likewise given up when it became obvious that they would be fruitless. "What one may learn from these experiences," Acheson commented, "is that the Soviet authorities are not moved to agreement by negotiation—that is, by a series of mutual concessions calculated to move parties desiring agreement closer to an acceptable one. Theirs is a more primitive form of political method. They cling stubbornly to a position, hoping to force an opponent to accept it. When and if action by the opponent demonstrates the Soviet position to be untenable, they hastily abandon it—after asking and having been refused an unwarranted price—and hastily take up a new position, which may or may not represent a move toward greater mutual stability."[53]

The prolonged delays that prevented action on the MLF never forced the Soviet Union to abandon its specious argument that the MLF was a form of proliferation. Instead, by making the demise of the MLF a part of its price for signing the NPT, Moscow could exploit Western differences over this issue, and it did cause NPT partisans in the U.S. Arms Control and Disarmament Agency and elsewhere to step up their attacks on the idea of any sort of a NATO nuclear force in the hope of removing Soviet objections on this score. Past experience suggests that this was a needless concession, given as a result of Western vacillation and hesitation to move ahead in an area where it had the capacity to act.

Furthermore, when it came to discussing the terms of the NPT that related to the economic implications of using nuclear power for peaceful purposes, these sensitive issues should have been confronted fully and at an early stage within the appropriate organs of the Atlantic Alliance. The basic flaw in the negotiation of the NPT was the absence from the beginning of an adequate frame of reference that integrated the deepest concerns of America's allies. The initial approach was that of a superpower dialogue, which frequently pitted Moscow and Washington against the nonnuclear states in NATO. The Atlantic Alliance was used for extensive consultation on the NPT, but it came too late and regretably took the form in many instances of an effort to modify details or soothe embittered feelings that had already been aroused within the Alliance.

SALT AND OTHER SOVIET-AMERICAN ACCORDS AT THE SUMMIT

The Strategic Arms Limitation Talks (SALT), which finally got under way in 1969, presented another instance of a superpower dialogue. In this case, the United States appeared to have learned from past experiences, since it made a determined effort to use the forum of the North Atlantic Council to consult with its colleagues fully and frequently and apparently succeeded in dispelling, or at least in minimizing, the inevitable fears of a deal that might be struck with Moscow affecting the vital interests of Europe's military and political future. When the SALT I agreements were signed in May 1972, West German Defense Minister Helmut Schmidt declared that these "agreements became possible not despite the existing Western Alliance, but because the negotiations were conducted in closest possible consultation with and in the interest of all partners in the Alliance."[54]

The European members of the Alliance were particularly fearful that Washington might accept the Soviet definition of "strategic" weapons, which the Kremlin held were weapons systems capable of reaching the Soviet Union or the United States. This would have included the forward-based systems (FBS) of the U.S. aircraft stationed in Western Europe or on aircraft carriers plus some ground missiles in Europe, all of which NATO considered as tactical nuclear weapons. While some FBS would be capable of striking western regions of the Soviet Union, the United States viewed the retention of these weapons as necessary for the defense of NATO Europe. The Soviet negotiators, for their part, staunchly opposed bringing into SALT I the Soviet intermediate- and medium-range missiles that were deployed west of the Urals and were targeted on Western Europe.[55]

At some point in future negotiations both of these weapons systems, which vitally affect the security of Western Europe, will likely be subject to further arms control accords. The French and British national nuclear deterrents would also presumably have to be included in these wider agreements. When negotiations proceed to this stage the United States will have to use extreme caution in its dealings with the Kremlin in order to ensure that its negotiating positions are responsive to the needs and special concerns of its European allies.

SALT I, which was concluded at the first Nixon-Brezhnev summit, was better received by NATO Europe than several other accords reached at Soviet-American summit meetings.

The declaration of "Basic Principles of Relations" between the United States and the Soviet Union signed in May 1972 was drawn up on the American side by the White House staff under Henry Kissinger without the knowledge of America's allies in the North Atlantic Council, where a similar set of principles to guide allied relations with Moscow was then also under consideration. American spokesmen on the Council were particularly embarrassed, since they too were unaware of the White House initiative and took positions in the NATO forum that were at odds with the text of the Soviet-American declaration. Not only was the procedure unfortunate, but the bilateral agreement yielded points of substance to Moscow to which most NATO allies strongly objected. The Soviet-American text, for example, omitted mention of the need for freer movement of people and ideas between East and West, nor did it include the right of peoples to self-determination. It did adopt, however, the phrase "peaceful coexistence," which has special meaning in Soviet terminology including, among other things, the continued sanctioning of ideological warfare. Soviet spokesmen can even stretch these Communist code words to endorse the Brezhnev Doctrine.[56]

Subsequently, Soviet Foreign Minister Andrei Gromyko visited several Western European capitals and indicated that he would not accept any statement of principles from other Western states that went further than the joint Soviet-American declaration. This only complicated the task of the West when these issues were later introduced into the CSCE forum in Helsinki. It also damaged the delicate fabric of mutual confidence and trust that was so badly needed on the eve of a new phase of extensive East-West negotiations.

Similar American high-handedness was exhibited by the "Agreement on the Prevention of Nuclear War," concluded at the Soviet-American summit of June 1973, which again was drafted bilaterally with the Kremlin with only the barest pretence of consultation with America's NATO allies. The caution that this accord pledged the superpowers to display with regard to situations that could lead to the use of nuclear weapons evoked a widely felt response in NATO Europe that the American nuclear guarantee had been uncoupled from the defense of Europe. The Europeans feared that the Kremlin would think that the United States would withhold the use of nuclear weapons if the Russians attacked Western Europe by conventional means. This agreement therefore intensified Western Europe's feeling of vulnerability to the immensely superior Soviet conventional forces, which might not actually have to be used to gain political dividends, since their continued presence and heightened importance might be manipulated as an instrument of political blackmail.

A West German observer commented typically that since "the agreement on the prevention of nuclear warfare, NATO countries in Europe have known for a fact what they have hitherto merely feared might be the truth. America is no longer prepared to regard a threat to the security of Europe as tantamount to a threat to the United States and take appropriate action. . . . What has changed is the political quality of America's military commitments in Europe."[57]

American spokesmen attempted to explain that this accord did not in any way undermine the credibility of the U.S. nuclear guarantee to Europe, and that in fact it amounted to little more than a formal pledge to use the Moscow-Washington "hot line" as the need arises. However, the Soviet press repeatedly interpreted the text in a broader way. "Some of these commentaries," Flora Lewis noted, "imply that the United States and the Soviet Union promised not to use nuclear weapons against each other if either was in combat with third countries—an interpretation that would collapse Western Europe's nuclear umbrella."[58] Deterrence is, in essence, a state of mind: to what extent the enemy believes and the allies trust in one's professions of faith to respond promptly when the allied cause is in danger. U.S. preoccupation with the superpower relationship had apparently damaged the credibility of the U.S. deterrent for foe and friend alike.

The United States was admittedly pulled in two opposite directions. On the one hand it wished to have a superpower accord on preventing nuclear war, which included a provision for urgent consultations with the Soviet Union in the event of a crisis. On the other hand it wanted to uphold its obligations to its NATO partners if they came under Soviet attack. Some Europeans, fearing the worst, had come to the bizarre conclusion that the United States had agreed to consult with the Russians before helping defend a European ally that was threatened, or had actually been attacked, by the Soviet Union.

Put another way, the United States both wanted an agreement with the Soviet Union on preventing nuclear war and a NATO Alliance that involved the pledge to fight the Soviet Union in a nuclear war, should the situation demand it.

In an effort to dispel misinterpretations of its agreements with the Soviet Union, the United States consented to include in the NATO Declaration on Atlantic Relations of June 1974 several phrases that were meant to reassure NATO Europe that the United States would defend it with nuclear weapons if necessary. The members of the Alliance affirmed that since the purpose of a defense policy "is to deny to a potential adversary the objectives he seeks to obtain through an armed conflict, *all necessary forces would be used* for this purpose." Thus while the NATO states appreciated the efforts of agreements that seek to reduce the risk of war, "they also state that such agreements will not limit their freedom to *use all forces at their disposal* for the common defense in case of attack."[59] Hopefully this renewed pledge might relieve some of the anxieties afloat in Western Europe.

THE PROBLEMS OF CONCERTING
GLOBAL POLICIES

There is, finally, the broad category of political problems that will continue to occupy the attention of NATO which relates to the desirability of concerting policies of the member countries in far-flung regions of the world. Events beyond the NATO Treaty area inevitably reverberate upon European-Atlantic relationships. Sharp policy differences relating to the Middle East, for example, strain the fabric of cooperation among NATO partners in all their dealings with each other. Thus consider the trauma to the Alliance that resulted from the Suez crisis of 1956 and from the repercussions of the Yom Kippur war in 1973 when the United States and Europe approached these events from diametrically opposed perspectives. To the extent that Western positions can be brought into alignment anywhere, the West will benefit everywhere.

The North Atlantic Council has frequently been used for the explanation of national policies in all parts of the world, but positive results in harmonizing these policies by means of such deliberations have been discouragingly meager. Yet these problems will not go away, and as NATO increasingly deals with political issues, efforts should continually be made to prevent disagreement where it is unnecessary and avoidable, to minimize the impact of the policy differences that remain, and generally to strive for mutual understanding that can produce increased harmony.

In the more distant future, the function of concerting policies beyond the NATO Treaty area will acquire new importance and different dimensions, as conditions ripen for a genuine East-West detente. The time element involved would naturally depend heavily upon the internal transformation of the Soviet regime so as to render it a more cooperative member of the family of nations. As that point is reached, not only the West as a whole, but the East and West together will be faced with elaborating joint ventures to relieve the oppressive misery and explosive pressures building up in the underdeveloped world. The end of East-West conflict might thus open the way for a more fruitful North-South relationship. While NATO alone cannot be expected to deal adequately with many aspects of questions that should be entrusted to international economic agencies, close contact among NATO partners on broad policy questions could nonetheless build up a reservoir of experience in grappling with issues that will increasingly come to the fore as East-West detente becomes more of a reality.

U.S. officials have repeatedly recognized the value of concerting global policy and have offered a number of suggestions for making this type of political consultation more effective. Speaking as Chairman of the State Department's Policy Planning Council, Walt W. Rostow told a European audience in June 1964 that "we must consult with a new intensity over a much wider range than in the past, understanding that consultation means assumption of responsibility and of risk as well as the mutual giving of advice. We are anxious to see the agenda of the Atlantic Alliance expanded in ways which would permit us increasingly to grip these problems on a communal rather than a separate basis." Among the methods that might facilitate such communal policy consideration in NATO, Rostow suggested bringing together "policymaking officials from home governments, who are directly concerned with the problems under discussion," as well as measures designed to "strengthen the role of the Secretary General and the international staff." It might also be useful to borrow or adapt practices found in other international bodies. "We are all impressed with the role played by the Commissions in the European Communities, and by the Secretary General in the U.N. as catalytic agents in the process of agreement." Finally, consultation should be structured so as to "enable Europe to achieve growing influence as it moves toward unity. The consultation we envisage would do just this. To the extent that European nations could concert among themselves about the issues under disscussion, their ability to affect the agreed outcome would surely be enhanced."[60]

NATO Secretary General Brosio responded to Rostow's proposals with mixed feelings. He agreed that "an extremely useful purpose would be served should the Atlantic Council become a center for coordinating and promoting member countries' activities throughout the world." NATO itself need not be involved in many of the operational aspects of these problems. "This coordinated policy could easily be implemented through various world political and economic organizations . . . and other international associations and institutions which count NATO countries among their members." Regretably, however, Brosio added, "It is clear that this possibility is far from materializing." Therefore, "we should not expect too much of the method of consultation." In particular there would be difficulties with Rostow's suggestion that "consultation should imply not only an exchange of ideas but also the acceptance of responsibilities and risks."[61]

EUROPEAN UNION AND MORE EFFECTIVE CONSULTATION ABOUT GLOBAL POLICIES

While the requirements of diplomacy prevented Brosio from allocating blame to the member states, the reasons for failure of the existing mode of NATO consultation to achieve concerted policies throughout the world are clear enough. On the one hand, the strong impulse of the United States to act unilaterally, springing from its superpower complex, has often overcome the best American intentions to consult adequately with its allies. On the other hand, this propensity for unilateralism is easily given encouragement by the nature of the global consultations that are encouraged. The medium-sized and smaller NATO powers may engage in consultation with the United States about global policies, hoping that they might thereby exercise influence over American policy positions. Individual states may also wish to contribute special knowledge of particular regions, based on past ties with former colonial countries or arising out of an exposed strategic position. At the same time, the states that are willing to offer advice are, in general, extremely reluctant to accept responsibilities or risks for any extended commitments that might result from a broadening of the consultative process. In addition, the diversity in their own foreign policies and the different degrees of concern that each state has in various areas makes it difficult to arrive at a meaningful consensus. The United States, consequently, often does not feel greatly constrained to modify its policies. Should the United States be faced with a coherent stand by a united Europe that was capable of exercising effective power outside Europe, the situation would be fundamentally altered. The creation of a powerful European entity would stimulate American responses and exert an influence for policy innovation that is currently lacking. Duncan Sandys, a leading figure among the British Conservatives, perhaps overstated the matter when he bluntly warned his fellow European parliamentarians: "If the nations of Europe are unwilling to assume the responsibilities and are not capable of coordinating their views, they will have to accept that any consultation by the United States will continue to be a matter of courtesy rather than of right."[62] It is clear that most Europeans look forward to the day when they can not only offer advice but also assume responsibility for the advice given. Advice without responsibility, however well-intended, can often appear to be irresponsible or irrelevant, and the consultation process can seem frustrating to both parties.

Modest steps toward the formulation of a responsible European foreign policy became possible as soon as de Gaulle had departed from the political scene. The new impetus given to the European movement by the Hague summit conference of December 1969 was reflected in the establishment of the Davignon Committee in 1970, which aimed to coordinate the activities of the Foreign Ministries of the members of the European Community. Working cautiously and pragmatically as a sort of permanent intergovernmental conference, the Committee has undertaken systematic prior consultations on a wide range of topics in order to harmonize views and, if possible, to take common decisions and actions on foreign policy matters affecting not only Europe but other areas around the world.

As Europeans increasingly find it possible to speak with one voice, the European voice will again be heard in world councils where it had fallen silent. The widely felt European sense of withdrawal and drift arose from a feeling of helplessness in dealing with the great issues of world politics. The preoccupation with seemingly parochial affairs was a logical consequence of trying to effect the small concerns that could be changed, rather than dwell on the larger ones that seemed out of reach. As former Under Secretary of State George Ball observed, Americans have not very often acknowledged even to themselves that "Europeans are unlikely to see their interests in the same global terms in which we see ours because of the structural factor—the disparity in size and resources."[63] Reflecting upon his efforts to stimulate political consultations within NATO about global issues, Ball found that the difference in the scale of political power among the participants was crucial. He concluded regrettably that "European feelings of vexation in relations with America are bound to increase so long as Europe, because of her anachronistic structure, is unable to translate her economic strength and prosperity into political terms giving her a single effective voice in world affairs." Therefore, while "Europe remains in its present fragmented state, Europeans will shy away from a wholehearted participation in efforts to make decisions through Atlantic institutions—particularly decisions that relate to matters outside the Atlantic area."[64]

Others who have been intimately involved in the effort to coordinate global policies among NATO states seem to agree. Livingston Merchant, who served as Under Secretary of State for Political Affairs, recalls that he "sat in on at least twenty Ministerial Council meetings and heard hours of wide-ranging frank exchange on formulation and exposition of policies relating to problems around the globe." The results, nevertheless, were unspectacular. "The root of the trouble," he agreed with Ball, consists "in the great disproportion of power and responsibility possessed by the United States compared to that possessed by its partners." Some measure of effective union in Europe is therefore required. Merchant, however, went beyond the need for unity in Europe, which in any event would probably only include a part of the European NATO states. "In the complicated, dangerous world in which we live, we of NATO cannot afford two, three, or five significantly different foreign policies or fiscal policies or commercial policies. We can never adequately harmonize our policies by consultation alone." What then stands beyond consultation with some form of European Union? "What is the real remedy? In my view, the ultimate and only valid answer lies in the development of an Atlantic Community." Specifically, this means "the gradual but conscious, progressive development of a political union—entailing further individual sacrifices of national sovereignty." He added that he knew well that "this Atlantic Community can be only a goal in the years immediately ahead, but if we are ultimately to reach it we must start working towards it now."[65]

Thus we return to a familiar theme: namely, that as Europe is restructured so as to achieve greater unity, Atlantic relationships must also be restructured so as to achieve greater unity. It would appear premature, viewed from the present perspective, to adapt to an Atlantic scale the idea of the Commission of the European Community, which could propose initiatives transcending national viewpoints, accompanied perhaps by some form of weighted majority voting among representatives of the constituent nations. Yet ideas such as these are worthy of consideration and careful study, in preparation for the day when they might be appropriate subjects for action. Without some form of political community, however rudimentary, the very real national differences on various issues will simply continue to assert themselves. This would remain true even if the petty nationalisms of Europe coalesce into a large "European nationalism." In this event, the potential power behind different policies would be greater and the potential for conflict would increase. In order to form communitywide appraisals of problems so as to approach common policies, it is essential to go far beyond the formal diplomatic interchanges of foreign offices. It is simply not enough to say that Europe and America face common problems and that common sense dictates that common and reasonable solutions will be arrived at. What is needed is a political process that engages representatives of the NATO nations in working at concrete issues, under the spur of community-minded organs that are designed to initiate, formulate, and keep alive proposals that would not likely otherwise emanate from national foreign offices.

The problems of the future will, of course, be different, but they will have evolved out of the past. In all likelihood they will be more severe and more threatening, given the crushing growth of population in store and the easy accessibility of weapons that will lead to increasing levels of violence, just to cite two factors. It will be more essential than ever to reduce the anarchy that is a natural byproduct of the nation-state system, so as to ensure military security and political stability, and to maximize the use of resources for human welfare through common supranational institutions. The nationalism that is today so obviously antiquated for Europe will also become obviously antiquated for the conduct of European-Atlantic affairs. Hopefully other regional areas will move in the same direction. The common market idea, for example, is becoming increasingly accepted in Latin America. Such organizational superstructures can only be successfully erected upon a foundation of shared values, and therefore, despite their advantages, they will only arise slowly. One would hope that there is sufficient congruence in the value systems of the European-Atlantic civilization to provide a model for transcending nationalism and contributing to the growth of a more stable world order.

NOTES

1. James L. Richardson, *Germany and the Atlantic Alliance* (Cambridge, Mass., 1966), pp. 359-60.

2. Quoted in Max Kohnstamm, "Utopia in a Nuclear Age," *Interplay*, August-September 1967, p. 13.

3. Foreign Minister Willy Brandt, "Detente over the Long Haul," *Aussenpolitik*, August 1967; reprinted in *Survival*, October 1967, p. 312. (Italics added.)

4. Melvin Croan, "Party Politics and the Wall," *Survey*, October 1966, p. 43.

5. Ibid., pp. 43-44.

6. Ibid., p. 45.

7. Address by Chancellor Willy Brandt to the Bundestag, January 28, 1971, *Supplement to the Bulletin*, Press and Information Office of the German Federal Government, February 2, 1971, p. 5.

8. Theo Sommer, "Will Europe Unite?" *Atlantic Community Quarterly*, Winter 1967-68, p. 557.

9. *Die Zeit*, March 28, 1969; reprinted in *Survival*, June 1969, p. 194.

10. Interview of Erich Honecker by C. L. Sulzberger, New York *Times*, November 23, 1972.

11. New York *Times*, November 19, 1972, December 7, 1972, and April 1, 1973.

12. "Bahr: Basic Treaty Offers New Chance for German Nation," *The Bulletin*, Press and Information Office of the German Federal Government, March 13, 1973, p. 67.

13. Quoted in Address by Chancellor Kurt Kiesinger to the Bundestag, October 16, 1968, *Supplement to the Bulletin*, Press and Information Office of the German Federal Government, October 22, 1968, p. 2.

14. Address by Chancellor Kurt Kiesinger to the Bundestag, September 25, 1968, *Supplement to the Bulletin*, Press and Information Office of the German Federal Government, October 1, 1968, pp. 4-5.

15. S. Kovalev, "Sovereignty and the International Obligations of Socialist Countries," *Pravda*, September 26, 1968.

16. Lin Piao, "Report to the Ninth National Congress of the Communist Party of China," April 1, 1969, *Peking Review*, April 28, 1969, p. 27.

17. Address by Foreign Minister Andrei A. Gromyko to the United Nations General Assembly, New York, October 3, 1968, *Pravda*, October 4, 1968.

18. Address by SED First Secretary Walter Ulbricht, marking the nineteenth anniversary of the G.D.R., East Berlin, October 7, 1968, *Neues Deutschland*, October 8, 1968.

19. Address by Chancellor Kurt Kiesinger to the Bundestag, June 17, 1969, *Supplement to the Bulletin*, Press and Information Office of the German Federal Government, June 24, 1969, p. 2.

20. Address by Chancellor Willy Brandt to the Bundestag, October 28, 1969, *Supplement to the Bulletin*, Press and Information Office of the German Federal Government, November 4, 1969, p. 3.

21. Interview of Chancellor Willy Brandt in *Welt am Sonntag*, February 1, 1970; quoted in *The Bulletin*, Press and Information Office of the German Federal Government, February 3, 1970, pp. 21-22.

22. Chancellor Willy Brandt, "The Old World, the New Strength," New York *Times*, April 29, 1973.

23. Address by Chancellor Kurt Kiesinger to the Bundestag, March 11, 1968, *Supplement to the Bulletin*, Press and Information Office of the German Federal Government, March 19, 1968, pp. 3-4.

24. Brandt, "Detente over the Long Haul," op. cit., p. 312.

25. Stanley Hoffman, *Gulliver's Troubles* (New York, 1968), pp. 434-38.

26. Walter F. Hahn, "West Germany's *Ostpolitik*: The Grand Design of Egon Bahr," *Orbis*, Winter 1973, pp. 862-63.

27. Ibid., pp. 874-80. See also description by Craig R. Whitney, New York *Times*, September 27, 1963, of Bahr's 1968 report, which envisioned German reunification as a result of the dissolution of NATO and the Warsaw Pact.

28. Address by Chancellor Willy Brandt to the Bundestag, January 14, 1970, *Supplement to the Bulletin*, Press and Information Office of the German Federal Government, January 20, 1970, pp. 5-6.

29. The anti-German, anti-NATO motivations are well documented in Gerhard Wettig, "Soviet Policy on the Nonproliferation of Nuclear Weapons, 1966-1968," *Orbis*, Winter 1969, pp. 1058-84.

30. William C. Foster, "New Directions in Arms Control and Disarmament," *Foreign Affairs*, July 1965, p. 600.

31. Text of the American draft for an NPT of August 1965, *Survival*, October 1965, pp. 268-69.

32. Text of the Soviet draft for an NPT of September 1965, *Survival*, December 1965, pp. 336-38.

33. Address by Ambassador Wilhelm G. Grewe at Bonn, January 24, 1967, *Europa-Archiv*, No. 3 (1967), p. 94.

34. Text of the American draft for an NPT of August 1967, which was identical to the Soviet draft of the same date, *Survival*, November 1967, pp. 347-48; text of the identical Soviet-American draft for an NPT of January 1968, ibid., March 1968, pp. 81-83. This was slightly amended and signed by both states in June 1968. For the final text and a perceptive account of the many issues raised in the course of the negotiations, see Elizabeth Young, *The Control of Proliferation: The 1968 Treaty in Hindsight and Forecast*, Adelphi Papers, No. 56 (London, 1969).

35. Testimony of Secretary of State Dean Rusk before the Senate Committee on Foreign Relations, July 10, 1968, Department of State *Bulletin* 59, no. 1518: 133.

36. For the text of the Resolution on Security Assurances attached to the NPT, see *Survival*, August 1968, pp. 269-70.

37. Wettig, op. cit., pp. 1065-69.

38. V. Gilinsky, *Fast Breeder Reactors and the Spread of Plutonium*, The Rand Corporation, RM-5148-PR, March 1967.

39. Harlan Cleveland, *NATO: The Transatlantic Bargain* (New York, 1970), pp. 68-69.

40. George H. Quester, "Israel and the Nuclear Non-Proliferation Treaty," *Bulletin of Atomic Scientists*, June 1969, p. 45. See also George H. Quester, "Is the Nuclear Nonproliferation Treaty Enough?" ibid., November 1967, pp. 35-37.

41. *Nonproliferation Treaty, Hearings before the Committee on Foreign Relations, United States Senate*, 90th Cong., 2d Sess., July 10-17, 1968, p. 168.

42. Jon McLin, "The Peaceful Atom Comes of Age," American Universities Field Staff, West Europe Series, 6, no. 1, (1971), p. 8.

43. Bruce L. R. Smith, "The Non-Proliferation Treaty and East-West Detente," *Journal of International Affairs*, No. 1 (1968), p. 98. See also Victor Gilinsky and Bruce L. R. Smith, "Civilian Nuclear Power and Foreign Policy," *Orbis*, Fall 1968, pp. 819-22.

44. Address by Under Secretary of State Nicholas de B. Katzenbach at Washington, D.C., April 26, 1968, Department of State *Bulletin* 58, no. 1508: 647.

45. Albert Wohlstetter, "Strength, Interest and New Technologies," in *The Implications of Military Technology in the 1970s*, Adelphi Papers, No. 46, (March 1968), pp. 1-2.

46. "A-Armed Terrorists, Thugs a Possibility, Say Scientists," *International Herald Tribune*, September 18, 1972. Mason Willrich likewise agreed that "most experts consider the design and manufacture of a crude nuclear explosive device without previous access to classified data to be no longer an extremely difficult task technically." (Anthony Ripley, "More Safeguards on A-Bombs Urged," New York *Times*, November 15, 1972.) See also Mason Willrich and Theodore B. Taylor, *Nuclear Theft: Risks and Safeguards* (Cambridge, Mass., 1974).

47. Walter Sullivan, "Three Countries Plan Two Nuclear Plants," New York *Times*, October 28, 1969.

48. Christopher Layton, *European Advanced Technology* (London, 1969), p. 120.

49. "Statement by Mr. Scheel, Federal German Minister for Foreign Affairs, on Signing the Tripartite Agreement on the

Production of Enriched Uranium by the Ultra-centrifuge Process,"
March 4, 1970, Assembly, WEU, *Monthly Note*, No. 3 (March 1970),
p. 7.

50. Leonard Beaton, "Nuclear Fuel-For-All," *Foreign Affairs*,
July 1967, pp. 664-69.

51. For an evaluation of the Baruch Plan and the Soviet
response to it, see Elliot R. Goodman, *The Soviet Design for a World
State* (New York, 1960), pp. 399-407.

52. Quester, "Is the Nuclear Nonproliferation Treaty Enough?"
Bulletin of Atomic Scientists, November 1967, pp. 35-36.

53. Dean Acheson, *Present at the Creation* (New York, 1969),
pp. 274-75.

54. Statement by German Federal Minister of Defense Helmut
Schmidt at Bonn, May 31, 1972, *Relay from Bonn*, German
Information Center, New York, June 2, 1972.

55. Briefing to Congressional Leaders on SALT Agreements by
Henry A. Kissinger, Assistant to the President for National Security
Affairs, at the White House, June 15, 1972, Department of State
Bulletin 67, no. 1724: 44.

56. Flora Lewis, "Soviet-American Accord Embitters NATO
Officials," New York *Times* July 26, 1972; *Atlantic News*, September
22, 1972, p. 2. For the text of the "Basic Principles of Relations,"
signed in Moscow, May 29, 1972, see Department of State *Bulletin*
66, no. 1722: 898-99.

57. Gunther Gillessen, "Europe's Father Image No Longer
Holds Good," *Frankfurter Allgemeine Zeitung*, June 28, 1973;
reprinted in the *German Tribune*, July 12, 1973. See also Hermann
Bohle, "U.S.-U.S.S.R. Nuclear Agreement Worries NATO
Partners," *Munchner Merkur*, July 3, 1973; reprinted in the *German
Tribune*, July 19, 1973. For the text of the "Agreement on the
Prevention of Nuclear War," signed in Washington, June 22, 1973,
see Department of State *Bulletin* 69, no. 1778: 160-61.

58. Flora Lewis, "Soviet Bid for Police Role with the U.S. Is
Reported," New York *Times*, July 22, 1973.

59. Declaration on Atlantic Relations, June 19, 1974,
Department of State *Bulletin* 71, no. 1828: 43. (Italics added.)

60. Address by Counselor Walt W. Rostow at Rome, June 24,
1964, Department of State *Bulletin* 51, no. 1307: 42-43.

61. Address by Secretary General Manlio Brosio at Paris,
November 16, 1965, Assembly, WEU, *Proceedings*, November 1965,
IV, p. 99.

62. "State of European Security," Duncan Sandys, rapporteur, Document 354, October 25, 1965, Assembly, WEU, *Proceedings*, November 1965, III, p. 66.

63. George W. Ball, *The Discipline of Power* (Boston, 1968), p. 63.

64. Ibid., pp. 66-67.

65. Livingston T. Merchant, "North America and the Atlantic Community," *Atlantic Community Quarterly*, Winter 1964-65, pp. 523-26.

8

THE NETTLE OF
MULTILATERAL
NUCLEAR SHARING

No single issue has been the subject of so much confusion and complex dissension within the West as the control of nuclear weapons. While the disposition of the nuclear forces has obvious military dimensions, it is also unavoidably a political matter of the first magnitude since it poses the ultimate question about a nation's existence: Who will have the power to decide who will die for whom and under what circumstances? Unfortunately, the West has not been able to develop a single coherent answer, or even several different but compatible answers. Instead, three general approaches to the management of nuclear weapons have coexisted uneasily: (1) nuclear nationalism, (2) plans for nuclear partnership of a bilateral nature between the United States and a uniting or a united Europe, and (3) a variety of multilateral schemes that would extend nuclear sharing to various depths between the United States and those European allies that would form some joint nuclear enterprise.

The American, French, and British nuclear forces are all different expressions of nuclear nationalism. The huge U.S. deterrent has remained under ultimate American control, although over time America's NATO allies have come to share more information about it and have increasingly participated in some aspects of its management. Moreover, it has always been committed to the defense of the Atlantic Alliance so that Europe as well as North America have been brought under its protection. Since Europe is, in fact, dependent upon the U.S. nuclear guarantee, the essential problem is to make that dependence as tolerable as possible. This has been the object of various plans for nuclear sharing, whether they be of the hardware or nonhardware variety.

THE FUTURE OF SMALL NATIONAL
NUCLEAR FORCES

The French and British nuclear forces have been minuscule, compared to the American deterrent, and despite brave talk to the contrary they have never been intended for independent use. While it has been argued that their independent use would inflict substantial damage ("tearing an arm off" the enemy is the Gaullist terminology), it is also true that the price for such independent use would be totally unacceptable, since it would amount to national suicide for France or Britain. Given this fact, these small national forces, taken alone, can scarcely be considered credible deterrents.

Nevertheless they have continued to exist. De Gaulle's military justification for his force de frappe found its classic formulation when he said: "No one in the world—particularly no one in America—can say if, where, when, how and to what extent the American nuclear weapons would be employed to defend Europe."[1] British spokesmen have sometimes sounded the same sentiment, although perhaps phrased in more diplomatic language. In both cases the nagging doubt remained that the U.S. nuclear guarantee might not be dependable. National forces might therefore serve as a form of insurance, if not for independent use, then as detonators of the American force.

While the triggering function remains a remote possibility, it would be perilous for the Europeans to rely upon it since, if true, it would place an intolerable strain on U.S.-European relations and make imperative the withdrawal of the American nuclear umbrella from Europe. The triggering of the U.S. deterrent, in any event, has been rendered much less likely by such developments as the Moscow-Washington "hot line" that was established in 1963. This was amplified by two U.S.-Soviet agreements of September 1971, one of which improved the nature of the communications link itself, while the other aimed to reduce the risk of nuclear war through measures such as informing the other party if their warning systems were interfered with or if they detected a possible missile attack. They also undertook to give advance notice of any missile flights beyond one's national territory in the direction of the other party and to destroy or render harmless any unauthorized or accidental nuclear launching. These commitments were reinforced by the June 1973 U.S.-Soviet accord on the prevention of nuclear war, which elaborated their understanding to enter into urgent consultations under circumstances that might endanger international peace.

Both superpowers obviously share an interest in not becoming the prisoner of their own huge nuclear arsenals, nor of permitting themselves to become hostage to the designs of some third party. Thus the United States might use the "hot line" to avoid becoming entangled willy-nilly in a war not of its making by warning Moscow in time that any action by France or Britain would be taken on their own initiative, without American approval or support.

The superpowers have established a formidable technological lead over the small nuclear states, who have long been in danger of being priced out of the strategic nuclear arms competition. Militarily, therefore, the prospect for the small nuclear forces is uncertain at best. Conceivably they might even be counterproductive, by introducing an element of instability into the nuclear equation, since they might appear to be provocative and invite a preemptive attack. In theory, this situation might apply both to the French and British forces, but in practice it has only applied to France since the British force has always been operationally integrated with the larger American deterrent.

Politically, the retention of the French and British nuclear forces has continued to seem attractive, since it endows these states with the prestige and status of a great power—or at least greater power than the nonnuclear medium-sized states. Thus while the force de frappe might not be brandished seriously against a superpower, it might prove useful someday in dealing with West Germany in the event that the Germans might seek to become the senior partner in the Franco-German entente that was founded by de Gaulle in 1963. Both Britain and France might also be skeptical of the ability of the Non-Proliferation Treaty to prevent other states such as India, Japan, or Israel from acquiring nuclear weapons in the future. Indeed, India detonated a nuclear device in May 1974. Although this was presumably intended for peaceful purposes, the fact remains that there is no basic difference in the design of such a device for peaceful or military uses. With other less-developed nations on the brink of "going nuclear,"

Britain and France would diminish their comparative political status in the councils of the world if they would abandon their limited nuclear capabilities. Moreover, until such time as a genuine form of sharing U.S. nuclear power with Europe is devised, which would provide an adequate substitute for the British and French national deterrents, the intangible political benefits of these small national forces will doubtless cause them to remain in existence.

Their prolonged life will obviously be an increasing luxury. The narrow economic base upon which the force de frappe has rested was clearly revealed by the upheaval of the French economy in May-June 1968, as well as by the subsequent trials of the franc in the world monetary market. These difficulties caused de Gaulle to abandon his ambitious plans for an ICBM force. Instead, the farthest reach of any element of the force de frappe rested with intermediate-range weapons. The 36 Mirage IV A, each carrying only one 60-kiloton bomb, are short-range aircraft that must be refueled in the air in order to be able to return home from a mission. It was anticipated that they would go out of service sometime in the mid-1970s. Eighteen land-based IRBMs (instead of the 27 originally planned) have been installed in Central France. The last component of the French deterrent, the nuclear ballistic missile submarine, has only about half the range of the British Polaris submarines. Of the projected fleet of five French nuclear submarines, two were commissioned in the early 1970s, a third is anticipated in about 1975, and two more are planned before the end of the 1970s. During the mid-1970s it would still only be possible to keep one such submarine permanently on firing station. In addition to the limited range of their missiles, these French vessels are also vulnerable to the large fleet of Soviet hunter-killer submarines. Moreover, France lacks a MIRV capability, and it is uncertain when, if ever, it will obtain it. Since it is highly questionable if such a force de frappe would be able to survive a Soviet first strike, its credibility as a deterrent must remain open to serious doubt.

The strain of trying to build a strategic deterrent upon the limited economic resources of Britain has been even clearer. The obsolescent V-bomber force was to be replaced in the mid-1970s by a joint Anglo-French swing-wing or variable geometry aircraft. But in July 1967 this project collapsed when France withdrew from it. As an interim delivery system, Britain had meanwhile placed all its hopes in the British-built TSR-2, a supersonic, low-flying, all-purpose aircraft. After sizable expenditures for development, London decided to abandon this as too costly, and in its place contracted to buy 50

American F-111A aircraft. But in January 1968 this contract was also canceled because of the excessive expense. There remained only four British submarines (instead of the five originally planned), each armed with 16 Polaris missiles supplied by the United States as a result of the Nassau agreement of December 1962. During 1965 the United States began development of the Poseidon missile, which was twice as powerful and twice as accurate as the Polaris, and in addition could be fitted with independently targeted multiple warheads. In June 1967 Prime Minister Harold Wilson casually announced that Britain would not follow suit in replacing Polaris with Poseidon, again due to cost. Subsequent British governments have shown little inclination to spend the money needed to install Poseidon missiles, even though this could conceivably be done by renegotiating the nuclear accord with the United States as it comes up for renewal.* The British strategic nuclear force therefore has come down to four submarines equipped with increasingly outmoded missiles. And of these four submarines, British operational procedures for refitting and overhaul only permit one or sometimes two to be fully on station at any given moment.

The argument is frequently heard that Europe could be better protected if France and Britain pooled their resources and built a joint nuclear force. Closer examination also makes this seem unpromising. The French relationship to NATO would first of all have to be substantially modified before any kind of British-French nuclear collaboration would be feasible. Britain insists that such collaboration would have to occur within the framework of NATO and its Nuclear Planning Group (NPG) so that a British-French force would be targeted in coordination with the U.S. deterrent and be operated upon principles that were compatible with Alliance strategic doctrine. Other members of NATO Europe, and particularly the West Germans, would also surely protest strenuously if it appeared that such a force would be formed outside NATO. France, however, has refused to join the NPG, nor has it resumed its former military collaboration with NATO.

So long as France retains this attitude, the United States would scarcely assist a joint British-French force. American aid is essential

---

*In 1974 Britain tested an improved warhead for its Polaris missiles. This suggested that Britain had decided to rely indefinitely on Polaris rather than spend millions to convert to Poseidon.[2]

to this project, since under the terms of the U.S.-U.K. agreements on the uses of atomic energy, Britain must obtain U.S. approval before it can pass on to a third country any of its nuclear information that was derived from American sources. Since the American contribution to the U.K. deterrent has been thoroughly intermixed with the British, Britain would find it extremely difficult to share its knowledge with France without American consent, which must be forthcoming not only from the executive branch but also from the Congress.

Moreover, a British-French force would not be a European force, but quite simply a British-French force in Europe. Such an arrangement would only heighten discrimination against the other nonnuclear European states, and especially against the Federal Republic. Not only would it create new strains within Europe, it might well raise doubts about the character of the American nuclear guarantee to Europe. The Germans would be anxious to preserve this guarantee, since they would likely view the American force as a more credible deterrent than a British-French force. The only sound foundation for creating a joint nuclear force in Europe would be to build it upon the political base of a European federation in which all of the West European states could participate as equals.[3]

Should a European Union someday arise, it is conceivable that a European deterrent might be created. Under the terms of the Non-Proliferation Treaty as finally signed, however, the United States could not render aid in building this force, short of the creation of a fully fledged European federation. The Europeans would therefore have to support all of the painfully expensive intermediate stages of its development by their own resources. Should this come to pass, one would then be faced with the many imponderables of a nuclear partnership between Europe and the United States which have previously been examined as part of the general discussion of the partnership concept. At best, nuclear partnership appears to be a distant prospect with uncertain consequences.

THE ORIGIN AND AGONIES OF THE MULTILATERAL FORCE IDEA

One is therefore left with the option for increased sharing of the American deterrent on a multilateral basis with a number of individual NATO partners.

Proposals to this effect were first advanced in 1960 by General Lauris Norstad who, as SACEUR, wanted to create a NATO force of medium-range ballistic missiles (MRBMs) to counter the threat of similar Soviet missiles that were targeted on Western Europe. On March 2, 1960 Norstad suggested the formation of a multinational NATO "fire brigade," armed with both conventional and nuclear weapons, which could give an Atlantic political coloration to any response to an enemy intervention.[4] The concept of placing a stockpile of American nuclear warheads under Alliance control was then discussed informally at a September 9 meeting of General Norstad, NATO Secretary General Paul-Henri Spaak, Chancellor Konrad Adenauer, and Dirk Stikker, then Dutch Ambassador to NATO and soon to be Spaak's successor as NATO Secretary General. It was agreed to explore the idea with other allied leaders, although even at that time Adenauer reported de Gaulle's disturbingly negative attitude.[5]

On October 12 Norstad publicly launched the phrase that NATO should become "the fourth atomic power" in the West, conceiving of this NATO deterrent primarily as a mobile land-based MRBM force. The State Department had meanwhile circulated a study, directed by Robert Bowie, which recommended the creation of a commonly owned and operated NATO fleet of submarines armed with Polaris missiles.[6] During November Norstad elaborated his theme of NATO as the fourth atomic power within the forum of the NATO parliamentarians. "How do we meet a growing desire for a broader sharing in the control of nuclear weapons?" he asked; by committing nuclear weapons to NATO for the life of the Alliance. "For the Alliance to have continuing life and meaning, it needs increasing authority; it needs power of some form. If politically feasible, action to pass to the Alliance greater control over atomic weapons and to subject their use more directly to the collective will could be a great and dramatic new step."[7] The State Department proposal was formally presented to the NATO Ministerial meeting on December 16, 1960 when Secretary of State Christian Herter offered to explore with the allies the creation of a special MRBM force, "which would truly be multilateral, i.e., under multilateral ownership, financing and control and with mixed manning insofar as this seemed desirable."[8] Mixed manned crews were advocated as a means of strengthening the bond of the allied force by making it impossible to withdraw national contingents for separate use.

The idea of an allied Multilateral Force (MLF) was raised in a tentative manner in Ottawa by President Kennedy in May 1961. There he suggested that the Alliance "look to the possibility of eventually establishing a NATO seaborne force, which would be truly multilateral in ownership and control, if this should be desired and found feasible by our allies."[9] There was no note of urgency in this approach, however, which placed higher priority upon first fulfilling NATO's nonnuclear force goals. Nor was there any explanation of what truly multilateral "control" might consist. Ensuing allied discussions did little to clarify the control issue or advance the idea generally.

The loss of impetus was in large measure due to the policies introduced by the Kennedy administration. The doctrine of flexible response placed greater emphasis on the buildup of conventional forces, while it was judged that no new nuclear forces need be made available to NATO. "McNamara looked upon the MLF as an accounting problem," one high Defense Department official commented to this writer. Viewed strictly from the number of nuclear weapons already available, Secretary McNamara could see no justification for another deterrent in the West. This assessment, however, missed the fundamental reason for multilateral nuclear sharing. Schemes like the MLF should not have been viewed as a purely technical military matter, but as an eminently political problem since nuclear weapons possess enormous political significance. A properly conceived plan of nuclear sharing could have increased the political cohesion of the Alliance by making the collective security of the West responsive to some form of collective control.

The new strategic doctrine enunciated by McNamara in 1962 completely neglected this essential political factor. He condemned the continued existence of "relatively weak national nuclear forces" since their "limited nuclear capabilities, operating independently, are dangerous, expensive, prone to obsolescence, and lacking in credibility as a deterrent."[10] On the other hand, "the United States nuclear contribution to the Alliance is neither obsolete nor dispensable." Again, as a military judgment this appeared entirely sound. What he omitted was the consideration that Britain and France would have little political incentive to abandon their small deterrents until there was some new repository to which these forces could be transferred and in which they could share control. If the United States was unwilling to provide for this kind of nuclear sharing, it was of little use to call these small forces names, however well deserved.

The general nuclear strategy that McNamara laid down reflected the same inadequacy. He emphasized "the importance of unity of planning, concentration of executive authority and central direction. There must not be competing and conflicting strategies to meet the contingency of nuclear war. . . . Our best hope lies in conducting a centrally controlled campaign against all of the enemy's vital nuclear capabilities." Since the size and nature of the American deterrent permitted it alone to cover all enemy targets, the United States must be the repository for the centralized command and control arrangements for the entire West. "The United States is as much concerned with that portion of Soviet nuclear striking power that can reach Western Europe as with that portion that can also reach the United States. In short, we have undertaken the nuclear defense of NATO on a global basis." Once again, the military logic of the demand for the centralization of operational control was faultless. McNamara could properly claim that "this mission is assigned" to the American deterrent "because the character of nuclear war compels it."[11] Completely overlooked in this analysis was the political logic of the Alliance that called for a sharing in the formulation of nuclear policy and control of the nuclear capability of the West.

McNamara was asking the allies to entrust their nuclear defense to the United States and accept on faith that their interests would be adequately protected. This policy could be made politically acceptable if a decision by the President of the United States also represented a decision of the commonly elected government of America's allies. In its ultimate form this would require the creation of an Atlantic Union, in order to escape from the threat of what Arnold Toynbee called "annihilation without representation." Short of this type of political legitimation, there were other measures that could have been taken to alleviate the pressures for nuclear sharing, of which the MLF was only a limited gesture. As late as the NATO Ministerial meeting of December 1962, however, the United States tried to discourage the MLF idea, since McNamara held that there was no military requirement for it.[12]

President Kennedy, with whom the ultimate decision rested, was subjected to conflicting advice but he was always heavily influenced by McNamara. George Ball, who at the time was Under Secretary of State, recalled with regret that the MLF project was allowed to languish "largely because our own government failed to take a sufficiently decisive position during 1961 and 1962. . . . The core of the difficulty was that President Kennedy never made up his mind that the Multilateral Force was a good thing. He never fully convinced himself that it might prevent the building up of conflicts and feelings of inequality and irresponsibility that flow from impotence among the Europeans."[13] During 1963 Kennedy seemed to give the MLF his personal backing when he instructed the U.S. Ambassador to NATO, Thomas Finletter, to set up a working group at NATO headquarters to draft, with other interested allied states, the necessary political guidelines and legal documents required to put the MLF concept into effect. "This detailed and complicated work" Finletter recorded, "was well under way, with substantial agreement and support from the other members of the working group, at the time of President Kennedy's death."[14] In addition, a special section in the State Department was created to foster the development of the MLF. But even given this encouragement, the project could never take off politically, because as Ball noted, "the President was continually having second thoughts about the idea. . . . Because of the President's hesitancy, we were precluded from presenting the plan to Congress and the natural enemies of the scheme were left in full command of the field. The result of this inaction was to leave the field open for an intellectually squalid treatment of an important subject."[15]*

Two events conspired to resurrect the MLF: the Nassau agreement of December 21, 1962, and de Gaulle's brusk rejection of it along with his veto of Britain's Common Market entry bid on January 14, 1963.

The Nassau meeting between President Kennedy and Prime Minister Harold Macmillan was precipitated by the American decision to cancel the further development of the Skybolt missile, upon which Britain was depending in order to prolong the life of its V-bomber aircraft as an independent nuclear force. The cancellation arose from a Pentagon "computer decision," which could be justified on military grounds. But again characteristically, "the political consequences for Britain and for U.S. relations with London and Paris were overlooked or underestimated." As Robert Kleiman aptly commented: "It was a decision that should have been postponed until

---

*In line with this view, Kennedy is recorded as having said to Paul-Henri Spaak in the spring of 1963: "The whole debate about an atomic force in Europe is really useless, because Berlin is secure, and Europe as a whole is well protected. What really matters at this point is the rest of the world."[16]

new arrangements could have been made with the British that would not have endangered vital U.S. objectives abroad; the bill for a six- or twelve-months postponement would have been cheap compared with the political losses that later ensued."[17]

Although the British had warnings of the difficulty in developing Skybolt, they could not face the prospect of abandoning it, since they had staked the future of their national deterrent upon its success. Macmillan felt that the survival of his government hung upon returning from Nassau either with a renewed pledge for Skybolt or for some adequate substitute for it. Moreover, he was bent upon defending any new agreement as upholding the independent status of the British nuclear force. Kennedy wanted to placate Macmillan in order to avoid a wave of anti-American feeling in Britain, and so offered to sell Britain submarine-launched Polaris missiles as well as provide assistance for the construction of the British submarines. At the same time, Kennedy sought to use the occasion to reduce the dangers and folly of small national deterrents by having the British Polaris force committed irrevocably to NATO. This would help satisfy the centralized command and control requirements of McNamara's strategic doctrine. Kennedy also wanted to use the opportunity to offer de Gaulle the same terms of assistance as Macmillan, thereby integrating the force de frappe into NATO. Such an offer would, at least, be a clear test of de Gaulle's intentions, about which there was still much speculation.

Macmillan could not agree to commit the British deterrent irrevocably to NATO, but he did consent to subscribe part of the British nuclear force as a contribution to a NATO nuclear force, along with elements of the American deterrent, subject to the right of withdrawal if supreme national interests dictated. Moreover, Macmillan and Kennedy agreed that the purpose of creating the force armed with "Polaris missiles must be the development of a multilateral NATO nuclear force in the closest consultation with the other NATO allies." In response to Kennedy's suggestion that the agreement be left tentative until de Gaulle had an opportunity to consider it, Macmillan insisted that he return to London with a final deal. Kennedy agreed, although this presented de Gaulle with the appearance of an "Anglo-Saxon" fait accompli from which France had been excluded. This facilitated both de Gaulle's rejection of the Nassau accord and provided him with a convenient pretext for vetoing Britain's attempt to enter the Common Market.[18]

While it is true that de Gaulle had no part in shaping the Nassau agreement, Kennedy and Macmillan secretly contacted de Gaulle before its terms were made public and offered France nuclear assistance on the same conditions that had been extended to Britain. It was clear that France would require more than the Polaris missile, since at the time it lacked both the missile warheads and the submarine technology. The American and British ambassadors in Paris were instructed to enter into urgent consultations with de Gaulle in order to inform him that such additional assistance would be made available and to sound out de Gaulle's response. For a brief period de Gaulle hesitated, since this was an attractive offer that would have greatly shortened the process of developing his force de frappe and of making it the equal of Britain's.[19]

It would also have brought Britain and France together inside the NATO framework. But his is precisely what de Gaulle did not want. He was determined to move away from and not toward NATO. He was also unwilling to promote greater intimacy with Britain, since under no conditions would he accept the challenge of British membership in the European Community. Just prior to going to Nassau Macmillan had met with de Gaulle at Rambouillet, where Macmillan had found de Gaulle's "unshakable resistance to British membership." Nevertheless, de Gaulle encouraged the myth, which became widely accepted, that his decision to veto British entry was determined by Nassau.[20] While Nassau provided de Gaulle with a plausible occasion for administering this blow, it would be a gross misunderstanding of de Gaulle to assume that Nassau was the reason for the veto.

In the same fateful press conference of January 14, 1963 in which he announced his veto, de Gaulle also explained that he would refuse to enter into any arrangement that might modify the total and complete independence of his force de frappe. He upheld the principle "of disposing in our own right of our deterrent force. To turn over our weapons to a Multilateral Force, under a foreign command, would be to act contrary to that principle of our defense and our policy." "For us," de Gaulle added, "integration is something that is unimaginable."[21]

While the Nassau agreement did mention the prospect of a multilateral nuclear force, no one at the time had a clear idea of what that might mean. Moreover, the explanation of the terms given to de Gaulle by Kennedy's and Macmillan's emissaries was reportedly confined to the "assignment" of the French deterrent to NATO for targeting purposes, with the privilege, also extended to Britain, to withdraw such a force from NATO in the event that "supreme national interests" were judged to be involved. In effect, France could regain full control of its force in time of emergency or war, while it was not asked to participate in any of the multilateral aspects of the Nassau agreement that would have diluted French control. This did not demand a great deal of de Gaulle, but it was still more than he was willing to concede.[22]

There nevertheless remained a commitment to form what Nassau had variously called "a NATO nuclear force" or "a multilateral NATO nuclear force." Following de Gaulle's press conference, the MLF idea promptly attained an importance it had not hitherto possessed, since it could serve as a concrete project to bind together the other allies so as to counteract the damage de Gaulle had done to the attempt to move Britain into Europe and bring Europe and the United States closer together in NATO. The position of West Germany was crucial in this respect. When de Gaulle followed his rebuffs with the signing of the Franco-German Treaty on January 23, 1963, it was feared that the Germans might become tied to French policy. The Germans, therefore, should be offered the opportunity of reinforcing their bonds to NATO by cooperating in building a Multilateral Force.

What precisely had been so hurriedly agreed upon at Nassau was much in doubt. The British began using "multilateral" to mean the composition of a multinational nuclear force, to which NATO countries could assign national contingents, while the Americans reverted to their earlier concept of a commonly owned and operated, mixed-manned, integrated seaborne force. Ambassador Gerard Smith, who was later to head an office in the State Department devoted to the MLF project, remarked pointedly that "Polaris missiles were promised in exchange for some verbiage about multilateral and multinational forces." Following Nassau, "President Kennedy observed to an aide: 'We didn't even know what those words meant.' "[23]

In the course of 1963 it was agreed that the term "multilateral" in MLF would embody the American interpretation. The British never showed enthusiasm for this approach, since it was thought that participation in a commonly owned and operated, mixed-manned fleet would destroy what was left of Britain's special relationship with the United States by reducing Britain to but one of several states cooperating in a joint enterprise. Macmillan's Conservative government sought to preserve one of the last remnants of a great world power in the form of a British nuclear force, which might, however, be contributed as a separate, identifiable contingent to an interallied or multinational fleet.

The MLF idea finally took the shape of a proposal for 25 surface ships armed with 200 Polaris missiles. (The objections of Admiral Hyman Rickover about the possible loss of American submarine secrets prevailed, so that surface ships were substituted for submarines.) At one point, eight NATO states participated in the MLF talks, and the technical feasibility of operating a mixed-manned fleet was proven by an 18-month trial run during 1964-65 on the guided missile destroyer, *U.S.S. Claude V. Ricketts,* which was staffed by 335 crewmen from various NATO countries. As the complex negotiations proceeded, rumors arose about President Johnson's resolve to see the MLF project through. Ambassador Finletter sought clarification and reported that in an interview of April 10, 1964 the President privately gave the MLF proposal his "full support." This pledge was repeated publicly ten days later.[24] Further encouragement was found in the joint statement issued after the June 12, 1964 meeting between President Johnson and Chancellor Erhard, in which the two leaders praised the proposed MLF and affirmed that "efforts should be continued to ready an agreement for signature by the end of the year."[25]

Yet difficulties lay ahead. The military feasibility of the project might have been established, but the depth of the political commitment proved to be too shallow. And the MLF was a supremely political undertaking. On purely military grounds, the addition of this joint force might be considered unnecessary. Rather the MLF was a military instrument designed to solve the political problem of satisfying the European need for a greater sense of participation in managing the nuclear defense of the West. The crucial political problem of how the MLF would be jointly controlled was never met head-on, however. Instead, the State Department assumed an evasive stance. Policy planner Walt Rostow considered the questions: "Whose finger will be on the trigger, whose finger on the safety catch? Could the European forces fire their atomic weapons without the agreement of the United States? Could the United States fire without the agreement of Europe? Could individual nations within the Alliance veto firing by others?" To such queries he answered: "It has been our view that these ultimate questions could not and should not now be settled immediately and finally." Once the MLF was in operation the process of shared experience and consultation would justify "our faith that a rational and sensible resolution of the control issue would emerge."[26]

With luck and sufficient momentum behind the negotiations, a MLF agreement could conceivably have come into force without definitely resolving the control issue. But it was scarcely correct to consider this an "ultimate" question. Instead, it was a primary, basic question, upon whose solution hung the success or failure of the project.

A number of control plans circulated in the NATO diplomatic community: That each participant would have a veto over the MLF's use; that there would be two vetoes, an American one and a collective European one; that the United States would abandon its veto after a trial period of five years or so; that the United States might be persuaded to enter the agreement without a veto. It made a great deal of difference which option was taken in attempting to launch the MLF. As long as the United States insisted on retaining its veto, the Europeans widely viewed the MLF as a facade (or as a "gimmick" as one European Ambassador to NATO remarked to this writer) for perpetuating U.S. control over nuclear weapons. There was not much incentive to spend a good deal of money on a militarily superfluous deterrent if this would only increase European political dependence on the United States.

One of the principal aims of the MLF was to head off a possible future German demand for nuclear weapons by placing German control over a nuclear force within the safe context of a widely shared allied deterrent. From the point of view of preventing independent German action, a five- or seven-member allied nuclear force would considerably dilute the German role and even be an improvement on the then-existing two-key system of controls over tactical nuclear weapons shared with the United States. Everyone conceded at the time that there was no demand on the part of the Germans for a national nuclear force, although former Defense Minister Franz-Joseph Strauss had pressed for specific assurances about keeping stockpiles of American nuclear weapons on German soil, as well as granting West Germany some sort of joint control so as to assure the timely firing of tactical nuclear weapons that the Americans held in Germany. The Germans were keenly concerned that any allied force be viewed as a credible deterrent by the Kremlin and were therefore opposed to making its use dependent upon unanimous consent. It was feared, for example, that a neutralist-inclined government might come to power in Italy, and that its potential veto would paralyze the force.

The Germans were also caught between the pulls of Washington and Paris. In 1963 Defense Minister Kai-Uwe von Hassel repeatedly emphasized that the object of the MLF should be to induce France at some future time to join the allied force. "We must recognize," von Hassel said, "that the French will never join this force so long as the effectiveness of its nuclear capabilities can be degraded by the veto."[27] He realized that this would require an important modification in French policy, which might also permit the strengthening of European unity. Since this was not an immediate prospect, he did not wish to push for the abandonment of an American veto, but he did recommend that the door clearly be left open to revision of MLF control procedures, so that at some point in the future the United States would relinquish its veto.[28]

The prospect of German participation in any sort of allied nuclear force generated strong resistance in some quarters, and the possibility that the MLF might turn out to be essentially a German-American arrangement was scarcely acceptable to anyone. Here the position of Britain was critical. The resistance of the Conservative government to the MLF proposal has already been noted. In the political campaign preceding the British election in the fall of 1964, the Labor Party also attacked the MLF, but it went further by suggesting that Britain entirely abandon its role as a nuclear weapons power. Harold Wilson ridiculed the contention that the British independent deterrent was either British or a deterrent, since the Polaris missiles were furnished by the United States and the force was too small to be employed by itself as a credible deterrent.[29] Wilson broadly hinted that a Labor victory would bring a renegotiation of the Nassau agreement and the phasing out of the British nuclear force.

THE BRITISH COUNTERPROPOSAL OF AN ATLANTIC NUCLEAR FORCE

When Labor won the 1964 election, the new government developed its own proposal for nuclear sharing, which it viewed as an alternative to the MLF. While there were ambiguities in the British position that required clarification, the outlines of the Labor government initiative contained the following elements: Reduce the size of the MLF mixed-manned surface fleet from 25 to 10 or 12 ships; exclude British participation in the MLF element altogether, if possible, by leaving its composition to the nonnuclear NATO nations plus the United States; constitute a new, more inclusive Atlantic Nuclear Force (ANF) that would be composed of contingents of all existing nuclear delivery systems in Europe, except small tactical nuclear weapons. This aspect of the proposal, which had originally been suggested by the Conservative government, would consist of transferring land-based missile sites and nuclear aircraft squadrons to an interallied force under NATO command. Labor spokesmen sought to satisfy the demand for mixed-manning by suggesting that some of these crews might be composed of mixed nationalities, while other components could consist of strictly national contingents. In contrast to the Conservatives, Labor was willing to assign all these forces to NATO irrevocably. By giving up the right of withdrawal in time of national emergency, Labor argued that it would have abandoned all pretense of possessing an independent, British national deterrent. In addition, Britain would irrevocably assign to NATO the Polaris submarines whose construction was agreed upon at Nassau, provided the United States matched this with a comparable American submarine fleet. While the submarines would be nationally manned, they and the other weapons systems involved would be commonly financed, owned, and operated by the NATO states composing the ANF. The collective owners would operate the ANF in accordance with approved NATO strategy and procedures, so that it would become a unified system forming an integral part of the defense of the entire Alliance. Decisions on the use of the ANF would either be by the unanimous agreement of the participating states or at the least the United States and Britain would retain a veto.[30]

The net effect of the proposal would have been to upgrade the British contribution and voice in an allied nuclear force, while sharply downgrading the German contribution and influence. This could also be done without spending large additional sums, since the weapons systems were already at hand or under construction, and they could be financed internationally. This stood in contrast to the MLF proposal, which called for building a new fleet of surface ships and anticipated that West Germany might pay about 40 percent of the cost and have a comparable share of the command posts. Therefore, while the British proposal could be conceived as a vehicle for creating allied unity, it also reflected an anti-German feeling still widespread in Britain. Wilson's express desire to keep an American veto in an ANF demonstrated a fear for what the Germans might do at some point in the future without a built-in restraint from the United States.*

By the fall of 1964 the stage was finally set for a resolution of these questions about nuclear sharing. President Johnson and Chancellor Erhard had agreed that a MLF Treaty should be signed by the end of the year. As discussions intensified and this prospect seemed likely to materialize, President de Gaulle abruptly stepped up his attack on the MLF by vaguely threatening reprisals against NATO members that might join. Similarly, Soviet invective against the MLF reached new heights. Meanwhile, the British had advanced their own alternatives of an ANF and were prepared to discuss it with the Americans.

It was the impending visit to Washington of Prime Minister Harold Wilson that finally forced President Johnson to focus on the MLF problem. Johnson assembled his advisors and heard arguments on all sides, but he concluded that the project was not worth the trouble pursuing. He came to this decision not on the merits of its impact on international relations, but on the domestic ground that it

---

*Ferenc Vali notes the effect of British Germanophobia on the problem of nuclear sharing: "English public opinion is much less concerned by actual French bombs than by the slight chance the Germans might have them"— even in a diluted form of joint ownership, one might add. In Britain, "Vanstittartite and other, less violent anti-German sentiment is still widespread within the circle of elites and policy-makers. Propensities to neutralism, denuclearization, and pacifism go hand-in-hand with anti-German sentiment in British politics and affect large segments of the British public. All those forces continue, in the words of Sir Lewis Namier, 'to fight ghosts'; that is, Nazism and aggressive German nationalism, which now have ceased to be a danger." Namier pointed out that "in Britain, fear of Spain survived deep into the seventeenth century, and of France deep into the nineteenth, after neither was any longer dangerous; this misdirection of fears favored the rise of that nation which, in turn, became a menace. He indicates that a similar situation arose after World War II with regard to Germany, in neglect of the Russian menace."[31]

would require a considerable battle to get a MLF treaty approved by the Senate.[32] There is little doubt that the absence of steady presidential sponsorship of the MLF, both on the part of Kennedy and Johnson, had not permitted proper preparation for its reception by Congress. On the record, President Johnson was still in favor of concluding an MLF agreement, and conceivably he could have worked to get the necessary congressional assent, but he chose not to try. Ambassador Finletter sharply rejects the thesis "that Congress might have refused to follow the presidential lead to bring the MLF into being. This is impossible. Rarely has a President been in such a strong position with Congress as President Johnson was in 1964." Not only did he possess great experience and skill in dealing with Congress, but his crushing victory in the 1964 elections swept into office strong congressional support, which he used successfully to push through a mass of legislation. "Such congressional opposition as was reported in the various soundings which were made was the result of the failure of the President to ask for congressional approval of the MLF project. The later reluctance of the President to go through with MLF was the result, not the cause, of his failure to ask the Congress for what they would never have refused him."[33] As a result of the attitude Johnson assumed, the MLF was doomed even before the British talks opened.

The denouement of the drama came on December 8, 1964, when Prime Minister Wilson arrived at the White House. According to a high State Department official who participated in the Wilson-Johnson discussions, Wilson showed that he was willing to make a serious bid toward nuclear sharing in the form of his ANF proposal and even to consider some aspects of a scaled-down version of the MLF. The elements were present for some sort of compromise formula, but there were also many unresolved details that required hard bargaining before a jointly agreed position could have emerged. In order to bring those negotiations to a successful conclusion, however, determined presidential leadership was necessary on the American side. As in the past, this is precisely what was lacking on this issue. The result was that President Johnson removed all deadlines for arriving at a treaty on nuclear sharing. As the above-cited State Department official remarked to this writer, once Wilson grasped Johnson's relaxed attitude, the British began backing away from the entire project. For months following the meeting, Johnson and other American officials insisted that the MLF-ANF idea was still the subject for serious discussion, but in fact the whole enterprise was dead.

The Labor Party felt compelled to devise the ANF proposal after its election campaign denouncing the Conservatives' policy on nuclear weapons. But once it had been put forward, Wilson felt that he had fulfilled his commitment, and that the difficulties involved in pursuing it did not justify the effort involved. Not only would any scheme for nuclear sharing have stirred up anti-German feeling in Britain, which was especially strong in his own party, but he would have been mired in a highly complicated issue that the public could scarcely be expected to comprehend. Consequently, during 1965 the British openly admitted that they had lost interest in their own proposal.[34] This left NATO without the prospect for some sort of allied nuclear force and Britain with a national nuclear force, which the Labor government frankly acknowledged was neither independent nor credible, yet one which they themselves refused to abandon.

The scuttling of this attempt at nuclear sharing let down the expectations of those allies who had supported the MLF idea, and personally damaged the reputations of the European statesmen who had become identified with it. André Fontaine recalls being in Bonn when President Johnson pigeonholed the project. "This did not prevent his decision, taken without consulting or warning anyone, from having a catastrophic effect in Germany, Italy and the Netherlands. . . . I can personally testify to the bitterness of the German leaders, in whom a certain spring of confidence in the United States was, in some manner, smashed. As Washington's decision greatly pleased the Russians, the fear, always latent in the Federal Republic, of being sacrificed to Soviet-American good feeling, was thereby aroused."[35] This suspicion was subsequently given genuine substance when the United States, in its eagerness to arrive at a Non-Proliferation Treaty with the Russians, agreed to the Soviet proposal that explicitly forbade assistance by nuclear weapons states to any sort of MLF-type project for nuclear sharing in NATO. Although the United States did not formally advance this version of the NPT until August 1967, a decision to give priority to the conclusion of the NPT with the Soviet Union over establishing a NATO nuclear force had apparently been made as early as June 1965.[36]

De Gaulle too was pleased, although he was not appeased. Johnson's decision to abandon the MLF was undertaken, in part, in the belief that de Gaulle might thereby be placated and that he might remain a faithful NATO ally, if only he were not antagonized too much. At the time some analysts argued in vain that this view did not reflect an understanding of Gaullism, which was not susceptible to such appeasement, since it did not take account of de Gaulle's stubborn determination to go his own way once it was clear that he could not reorganize the whole Alliance on his own terms. De Gaulle's desire to destroy NATO was as profound as that of the Soviet leaders, although each pressed this policy for different reasons. As events proved, de Gaulle pulled France out of NATO and expelled NATO from French soil in 1966, even though the MLF concept had been thoroughly buried. In retrospect, it is clear that what de Gaulle did with regard to NATO he was going to do in any event, with or without an MLF. But if some sort of a NATO nuclear force had been brought into being, it is also clear in retrospect that its creation would surely have been cited erroneously as the reason for de Gaulle's defection.

Looking back at the might-have-beens, what policy, on balance, would have been most fruitful? A strong case can be made for bringing a NATO nuclear force into being, undeterred by Gaullist intimidation. For such an allied force to be meaningful, however, it would have been necessary to undercut the Gaullist contention that the proposed MLF was a "multilateral farce," since it retained an American veto. As long as this control arrangement remained, the Gaullist claim that no one "can say if, where, when, how and to what extent the American nuclear weapons would be employed to defend Europe" would continue to fall on fertile ground. The strength of the Gaullist argument was therefore directly dependent upon an American willingness to provide a control formula for genuine nuclear sharing. Indeed, President Kennedy admitted that "the MLF was something of a fake. Though he was willing to try it, he could not see why Europeans would be interested in making enormous financial contributions toward a force over which they had no real control."[37] At the same time, to be acceptable an allied nuclear force that was freed of an American veto should not have been disruptive of an overall NATO command structure and a NATO strategy. What was required, in short, was a thoroughly integrated Atlantic nuclear force without an American veto.

The MLF contained bold ideas, such as the concept of a commonly owned and operated allied force with mixed-manned crews. Yet the MLF failed because it was not bold enough, especially on the central issue of political control. Perhaps if it had been given the firm, high-level sponsorship required to bring it into being, it could have been the beginning of daring developments leading toward some sort of Atlantic integrated institutions at a later date. In order to manage and service the MLF, for example, it might have been necessary to create something like an integrated Navy Department for the West. Moreover, the sizable European investment in such an ongoing institution would logically have led to European pressures to modify or abandon the American veto. Political control over such an allied deterrent would also logically have required institutional innovations on the political level for the elaboration of a commonly agreed strategy and for the joint management of political policy on related defense matters. Once such a political executive authority could have begun to function, it might also have been used for dealing with other lesser political and military problems that have continually dragged on unresolved in the cumbersome diplomatic processes of the North Atlantic Council and its committees. In short, this might have provided the nucleus for upgrading a diplomatic forum into a political entity with limited but important powers, which in turn could have led to further growth of political integration in the American Community.

THE DUYNSTEE CONCEPT OF AN INTEGRATED ATLANTIC DETERRENT

In the name of historical accuracy, it should be noted that a plan for a NATO nuclear deterrent with precisely these implications was carefully elaborated in the Defense Committee of the Assembly of Western European Union, under the guidance of the Dutch parliamentarian, A. E. M. Duynstee.[38] Beginning in the fall of 1962 and continuing for several years thereafter, Duynstee developed a proposal for a substantial Atlantic nuclear force in which the Europeans would have an incentive to participate, while simultaneously reinforcing the interdependence of Europe and the United States so as to make the indivisibility of the West's defenses not only a slogan but an accomplished and irreversible fact.

Duynstee embraced the idea of joint ownership and management of a mixed-manned force, as contained in the MLF proposal, but he wanted to extend the application of this principle beyond a fleet of surface ships bearing Polaris missiles. It would also have included Polaris submarines, a segment of Minuteman strategic missiles based in the United States, and tactical nuclear weapons located in Europe. He suggested mixed-manning of submarines, which he was convinced was feasible, the integration of European crews with American personnel on the Minuteman sites, and replacement of the U.S. custodian corps, responsible for guarding nuclear warheads for the European-based tactical weapons, by a mixed-manner NATO custodian corps. The political decision for the release of those warheads, as well as for the use of other integrated nuclear forces, would pass to a NATO nuclear executive authority. Moreover, as third and fourth generation nuclear weapons would come into being, they could be produced on a communal Atlantic basis and be incorporated into this force on similar conditions.

When the British Labor government advanced its ANF proposal in the fall of 1964, Duynstee showed a willingness to take account of this approach as well, as long as it did not imply an abandonment of the vital principle of multilateral, integrated forces. The Assembly of Western European Union, voting on December 2, 1964, adopted a recommendation arising from the Duynstee report that urged "all member governments of WEU and NATO to support the principle of an Atlantic nuclear force on a multilateral basis, allowing for mixed-manned participation," and providing, among other things, that "strong political control of the force" should be exercised by the participating countries. This recommendation passed the WEU Assembly by a vote of 37 to 9, with 15 abstentions, indicating a reasonably broad consensus of the parliamentary opinion from the seven WEU member nations (the Six plus Britain).[39] This sampling of sentiment came immediately before the crucial meeting between President Johnson and Prime Minister Wilson and showed that if Johnson had exercised leadership in pursuing the MLF-ANF concept, important support could have been forthcoming from influential European circles.

The heart of the Duynstee plan rested, not in its hardware aspects, however, but in his concept of political control. The adopted WEU Assembly recommendation affirmed that "every effort must be made to institute a system of joint political control over nuclear forces assigned to the Alliance." While Duynstee accepted this general proposition, he proceeded to elaborate specific ideas on the touchy and all-important subject of control. A Nuclear Council with a membership of some ten countries would formulate general nuclear policy, while a smaller Nuclear Executive would be entrusted with the actual management of the integrated deterrent, including an authorization to fire. Duynstee suggested that the Nuclear Executive take decisions for an initial trial period of 18 months on the basis of unanimity, after which control procedure would be determined by weighted majority vote.

The central concern in governing an integrated Atlantic force was the problem of representation. The Europeans did not feel that their views were represented on the use of a deterrent taken by the President of the United States, whom they had no voice in choosing. On the other hand, the United States had reason for concern about the possible separate use of independent, national nuclear forces in Europe, about whose disposition they ultimately had no voice. Duynstee sought to resolve both problems by combining the European national forces with elements of the U.S. deterrent under the control of an integrated NATO Nuclear Executive that would take decisions by a system of weighted majority votes, in which the United States would have the most important position but still not have a veto.

He argued that there would be no hope of Britain or France abandoning control of their national nuclear deterrents until there first existed a new repository to which these forces could be transferred, and in which these powers could genuinely share control and take decisions effectively. This approach to the problem of political control was the opposite of that employed by the MLF advocates, who sought to evade these hard political decisions by concentrating upon the hardware aspects of the force, with only a vague promise of some future evolution of the control formula. Like the MLF, the Duynstee proposal was also thinking ahead to the possibility of satisfying future German or other European demands for a share in the direct control of a nuclear deterrent, without having to create other national nuclear forces in Europe. Again, the prospect of joining an integrated NATO nuclear deterrent without an American veto would have been more attractive to other Europeans than the MLF format.

Both of these proposals originated before the advent of the Non-Proliferation Treaty, which has, in theory, eliminated the possibility of new national nuclear forces, such as a German one, from arising in Europe. Only the future political evolution of Europe will tell whether this is a realistic premise, since treaty commitments, and especially those in the NPT with its right of easy withdrawal, have seldom been a barrier to asserting national action that could be justified on other grounds. German and other European participation in an integrated Alliance deterrent would have elminated the continuing feeling of discrimination against those who are excluded from taking part in the management of a nuclear force, which is inherent in the NPT. Other Alliance mechanisms for dealing with the nuclear problem may prove to be adequate substitutes for such direct participation. Or, again, over time they may not be. This disquieting prospect would not arise if other Europeans had been locked into an integrated NATO nuclear force in which they felt satisfied that they had a meaningful voice in shaping their own destinies. The concept of a common, integrated force, it might be noted, was itself a nonproliferation device, since it was intended to absorb the small national nuclear forces in Europe and prevent others from appearing.

The Duynstee formula for a weighted majority vote in the Nuclear Executive also sought to take account of the predominant U.S. nuclear strength in NATO by providing adequate protection for American interests. He suggested several schemes to illustrate how votes in the executive authority might be weighted. Under one plan there could be a five-member Nuclear Executive, in which the United States would have five votes, Britain and France two votes each, and two rotating members one vote each. This five-member executive would have a total of 11 votes. Or a seven-member Nuclear Executive might be constituted in which the United States would have ten votes, with Britain and France given three each, the Germans two, and three nonpermanent alternating members one vote apiece. This seven-member executive would have a total of 21 votes. In both cases the principle was the same. Whether the United States had five out of a total of 11 votes, or ten out of a total of 21, the Americans would not have a veto, while at the same time they would have ample safeguards for their undeniably important position. In either case, the integrated allied force could be used without American consent only if all the European members on the executive authority could agree to act in common, whereas if the United States wanted to employ the force, it could be done with the agreement of any one European member.* Given this situation, former NATO Secretary General Stikker expressed the view to this writer that the Duynstee plan amounted to a "modification," not an elimination of the American veto, since in practice the differences among the various European states would make it most improbable that the European members on the executive authority would all agree with each other while, at the same time, they would all disagree with the United States.

Furthermore, American interests would be protected in other ways. While this plan envisaged progressively larger elements of the U.S. deterrent coming under the control of the integrated allied force along with increased European contributions, nevertheless the sheer bulk and disproportionately larger size of the U.S. nuclear forces would always leave important elements outside the NATO deterrent in strictly American hands, although these forces would be pledged as before to the defenses of NATO. In practice, this inevitably would have required an intimate meshing of the policies of the NATO Nuclear Executive, on which the United States would exercise a powerful influence, with the operation of the forces in the U.S. Strategic Arms Command. That is, realistically, the NATO force would not go into action unless SAC went, since it would be suicidal for the Europeans to set off the NATO forces against American wishes and without SAC support. The resulting policies governing all the nuclear forces in the West would therefore likely be based on a solid consensus that would take fully into account the predominant American nuclear capabilities, while simultaneously permitting a meaningful European role in the formulation of these policies and in the control of the commonly owned and operated NATO nuclear force. The benefits of such nuclear sharing would not have been confined to some hypothetical future military crunch; rather it could

---

*Compare this formula for weighted majority voting with the proposal of Livingston Hartley, noted in Chapter 1. Duynstee's proposal was still within the realm of reality, in terms of arguing for American accession to such a scheme, whereas Hartley's suggestion for taking decisions in the North Atlantic Council by a two-thirds majority, in which the United States would have less than one-third of the total votes, was clearly beyond the bounds of what could realistically be imagined.

have relieved present persistent political tensions within the Alliance and significantly strengthened political cohesion within the West.

This design for nuclear sharing hopefully held out a place for France on the executive authority, and yet Duynstee recognized that so long as France remained Gaullist, the French seat would remain empty. Since this was a long-range plan that sought to undercut the Gaullist rationale for the force de frappe, it was hoped, in time, that France might join. In the interim, the other European members could have readjusted the voting mechanism among themselves, while maintaining the same basic weighted voting principle between the United States and Europe.

At one point Duynstee also made allowance for the emergence of a European political federation.[40] His concept of a nuclear partnership between Europe and the United States differed significantly from the usual image of two powerful, relatively self-sufficient deterrents, tied together by some tenuous contractual relationship. Nuclear partnership, rather, should come to mean the pooling of resources in an integrated Atlantic deterrent, in which the vital interests of both sides were so intertwined that it would minimize the dangers of each partner going along separate paths. In this case, authorization to fire nuclear weapons in the commonly owned and operated NATO force would be taken by the concurring and equal votes of the United States and a united Europe. On less vital matters, such as the management of the force and the approval of its budget, decisions could be taken by perhaps two-thirds of the members on the executive authority, regardless of their national origin. Purely as a theoretical matter, this option remains open, since the NPT allows for a European Union to dispose of a nuclear force as it sees fit. In reality, this remains a dim prospect, however, since the impetus behind the formation of a European deterrent by a future federal Europe would most likely be to assert its separate identity and sense of independence from the United States. But if the various European states had previously had a successful experience with nuclear sharing along the lines that Duynstee had projected, the evolution of a nuclear partnership with a European Union might have taken place within the context of an integrated Atlantic deterrent that could have dispelled the possibility of the major segments of the West pursuing conflicting, and even perhaps mutually destructive policies.

On what shoals did such an imaginative project for nuclear sharing go aground? An objection was frequently raised that this idea of a Nuclear Executive lacked credibility, since it would be unable to reach a decision rapidly in times of crisis. Duynstee had specified that in case of an all-out Soviet strategic nuclear attack there would be no need for joint consultation. As soon as the nature of the attack was properly verified, retaliation by the NATO nuclear force would be instantaneous, as provided for by previously agreed guidelines, while authorization to unleash the retaliatory strikes could be left to a single NATO authority such as the Secretary General. However, in the case of minor probing actions or a conventional Soviet attack, there would be time to consult and to arrive at a majority decision on whether or not to escalate the conflict. To argue that a majority decision could not be taken in time gets down to the argument that a majority view could not be found—which would be unlikely. Once a majority had coalesced, it would insist on a vote being taken, since it would be apparent that its view would prevail. Conceivably, the nature of the military conflict could easily dictate a unanimous decision, so that the whole problem of weighted majority voting would become academic. The fact that the members of the executive authority would necessarily have to be officials of senior status with direct and immediate access to heads of government in crisis situations would also have enhanced the reality of this proposal for taking effective action.

A related objection was that the U.S. Congress would not consent to being "voted into war" by a NATO executive authority. However, such a force, by its nature, would not be adapted to a preemptive strike by the Europeans alone. As previously noted, it would be extremely improbable that all the European members would agree to launch a nuclear war without American agreement and support. Thus the voting procedure was not designed to decide the issue of peace or war, but only to decide whether or not to escalate a conflict that had already broken out, and if so, to what degree. This basic point was not really grasped by the sampling of congressional opinion conducted by this writer. Rather, there was the simple instinctive response not to participate in any scheme that involved any type of majority voting that would have eliminated the American veto. If the U.S. Congress was poorly prepared to receive the MLF proposal, the same would apply with greater force to this modification of the MLF idea. This does not reflect upon the merits of the proposal so much as it demonstrated a lack of willingness on the part of important elements of the American government, both in the Executive and in Congress, to face up to the issues of engaging in genuine nuclear sharing. It was not generally recognized, for example, that the formal abandonment of an American veto over a NATO deterrent was largely irrelevant, since the United States already had no veto over the French force, nor to a lesser degree did it have one over the British force. The same would apply to any future national nuclear forces that might arise in Europe, should the NPT prove ineffective. Might it not have been better for the United States to have a powerful and nearly decisive voice inside an integrated Alliance deterrent than to have no voice in the operation of purely national forces outside the NATO deterrent?

Presuming for the moment that the groundwork for a sympathetic reception had been laid in American opinion, the most vulnerable aspect of the Duynstee plan probably rested with the need to abandon the American veto to a collection of weak European states. To many in Congress, this might have seemed a gratuitous, if not presumptuous, demand. In politics such concessions are generally made to partners who already possess formidable power. Advocates of European Union have argued that Congress might be willing to make concessions to a sizable political entity like a European federation. Its very strength and capability for independent action would make it appear essential for the United States to avoid the dangers of working at cross purposes with it, and so a substantial modification or elimination of the American veto would seem to be an intelligent and necessary choice that would become politically acceptable to Congress. Moreover, by starting with the existing European states, as Duynstee did, one would be forced to raise constitutional issue of sovereignty at once, while by the time a European Union had come into being the issue of merging sovereignty might be easier to accomplish. But by then the momentum for an integrated Atlantic deterrent might have been so thoroughly dissipated, and a European deterrent might have come into being to such a large extent as a symbol of a new European "nationalism," that the prospects of merging it with an American force would be entirely beyond reach.

British participation would also have been crucial in the creation of an integrated Atlantic deterrent without an American veto. No one knows what shape the British project for an Atlantic Nuclear Force might finally have taken or how it might have become modified over time, since negotiations over it were abandoned before it could be brought to life. At the time the ANF was proposed, however, Prime Minister Wilson rejected "the totally unacceptable nature of any scheme in which, either at the outset or at a later date, there was any question of the American veto on the use of the strategic weapon being withdrawn, or made subject to any system of majority voting. For any combination of NATO alliances by a majority vote to override either the United States or Britain would ... involve proliferation which would be unacceptable."[41] It is understandable that the British might have wished to salvage something of their "special relationship" in nuclear affairs with the United States, which set them apart from the other European states, by insisting that both the United States and Britain retain a veto in any NATO nuclear force. But to have argued that majority voting such as was proposed by the Duynstee formula amounted to proliferation was clearly incorrect. Wilson either did not understand, or perhaps did not want to understand, what was involved.

The Western definition of proliferation, as it appeared in the American draft of an NPT treaty in August 1965, simply prohibited "an increase in the total number of states or other organizations having independent power to use nuclear weapons."[42] This phrase was intended to sanction the formation of a MLF, which would not have created a new independent nuclear power, by virtue of the American and other vetoes that would have applied to its operation. The same could be said for the Duynstee proposal for taking decisions by weighted majority votes. Here a decision to fire could have been made either by the United States and any one European member of the executive authority or by all the European states combined, including Britain. In either case, the affirmative vote of either the United States or Britain would have been required for a majority decision, so that no proliferation of new centers capable of taking decisions independently of the existing nuclear states would have been created. Wilson's rejection of a scheme for majority voting probably reflected the widely held British bias against bringing German participation into any plan for nuclear sharing, as was evident in his distaste for the MLF. If some ANF-MLF force had actually been created, the experience in working with the Germans in such a joint venture might have caused these fears to fade away. Moreover, once the European states had become intimately involved in the operation of a common Atlantic deterrent, with men, material, and important financial contributions, it would have been a natural development over a period of time for the European members to press on for the elimination or modification of the American veto.

In its broadest terms, the Duynstee proposal was conceived as a way of moving NATO toward a higher degree of cohesiveness in all its functions. Hopefully, the creation of such a commonly owned and controlled allied deterrent would have generated "political fallout" that would have gone far beyond the mechanics of the decision making for pushing the nuclear button. The very existence of a Nuclear Executive, staffed by senior representatives with direct access to heads of state, would have facilitated the resolution of numerous other problems that otherwise tended to linger on endlessly at lower-level NATO committees without the prospect of decisions. A necessary and logical accompaniment of concerting national policies on nuclear matters would have been the strengthneing of the civil-military international staff of NATO for the formulation of an agreed allied strategic posture and a more effective system of allied contingency planning for the joint conduct of policy in crises. The aim was to formulate a genuine NATO policy by having it "first elaborated in the international NATO framework and then referred back for consideration by national authorities before its final adoption in the NATO Council." Such a procedure would not only "reduce conflicts of views which now arise where initial planning takes place at the national level," but it would "also give all countries of the Alliance a feeling of much greater participation in the planning, and, hence, of commitment to the final policy." Such an evolution should logically have led to "the establishment of a NATO Defense Ministry. All proposals for international executives of this nature must also take account of the need for international parliamentary control at the same level."[43] The vision, in sum, was for the movement of the Atlantic Community toward the growth of supranational institutions in a number of areas.

THE TRUSTEE FORMULA FOR
NUCLEAR SHARING

Even though the hardware approach to nuclear sharing in NATO came to nothing, and the ambitious proposals for the institutional development of the Alliance associated with it remained unrealized, some aspects of this of this high-level approach to policy making as it related to nuclear weapons reappeared in a different form.

Both European and American officials acknowledged that European dependence on U.S. strategic protection was an unhealthy relationship that could generate resentment and misunderstanding. As long as NATO Europe could not participate in the ownership and final decision to use nuclear weapons, such tensions and suspicions of U.S. strategic policy would be inevitable. Constructive arrangements could be devised, however, to minimize these sources of friction by bringing America's NATO partners into intimate contact with those who framed U.S. strategic thought and by encouraging Europeans to take part in the planning process that governed the deployment of the U.S. deterrent that was dedicated to Europe's defense. If the relationship could develop into a genuine strategic dialogue that could be maintained through institutional arrangements, the Europeans could in turn conceivably influence U.S. strategic policy in the planning stages. This would no longer be a one-sided relationship, but rather one of mutual benefit with results that could more nearly satisfy all NATO powers. Ideally, under this concept of nuclear management, Washington would serve as the trustee for the commonly agreed interests of the Alliance. The disposition and targeting of U.S. nuclear weapons would be based upon an allied understanding, and their possible use would be founded upon a commonly accepted strategic doctrine. The outcome would be to reduce to a technicality the ultimately decisive role of the President of the United States, since he would presumably be acting as the agent of the collective will of the Alliance upon previously agreed guidelines that had been formulated in common.

This idyllic view of the trustee arrangement does not, of course, deal with the basic problem of the political legitimation of the American President, who was not elected by the Europeans. As long as the collective governance of the U.S. deterrent sidesteps the issues of common ownership and the actual decision making on the use of such a nuclear force, the Europeans are dependent upon the good faith, if not upon the personal idiosyncrasies, of the American President who has been entrusted to carry out the commonly agreed plans. From this point of view, it must be recognized that the trustee formula can never be fully satisfying to many Europeans. The smaller European states may find the trustee formula quite acceptable since they have historically come to rely upon the protection of a larger neighbor for their ultimate security. The medium-sized European powers that have a tradition for looking after the strategic dimension of their defense, and today in the case of Britain and France maintain their own nuclear forces, would more likely find the trustee formula unnatural and disagreeable. Nevertheless, comprehensive allied involvement in the nuclear planning processes can be a useful and welcome device for allaying fears and creating a better basis for confidence in the arrangements that sustain the U.S. nuclear umbrella for the common protection of the Alliance.

The first allied effort to share previously withheld information about American and British nuclear weapons (the French, as might be expected, refused to participate) took place in Athens at the NATO Ministerial meeting of May 1962. The United States, for example, provided detailed information about the size and location of its nuclear stockpile in Europe. Furthermore, the "Athens guidelines" on nuclear policy were adopted. As Secretary McNamara later recalled, the "Athens guidelines" did "set forth some general guidelines for circumstances in which nuclear weapons might be used and some general principles on consultation about the use of nuclear weapons, but these principles did not seem to affect the debate in any substantial way."[44] These gestures were supported by the decision of the NATO Ministerial meeting in May 1963 at Ottawa to make "arrangements for broader participation by officers of NATO member countries in nuclear activities in Allied Command Europe and in coordination of operational planning at Omaha," where the U.S. Strategic Air Command headquarters was located. It was also agreed to the installation "by SACEUR on his staff of a deputy responsibile to him for nuclear affairs."[45] This nuclear deputy post was subsequently given to a European officer.

McNAMARA'S INITIATIVES AND THE WORK OF THE SPECIAL COMMITTEE

Further efforts along this line were held in abeyance while the MLF debate raged during 1963 and 1964, but when the Johnson-Wilson meeting of December 1964 effectively killed the MLF, the nonhardware approach to nuclear sharing revived. At a meeting of

NATO Defense Ministers in Paris on May 31, 1965, McNamara suggested the formation of a "Select Committee" of four or five members who would develop better methods for strategic planning and nuclear consultation within NATO. This ad hoc group was not considered permanent, although it was thought that it might lead to the creation of some permanent institution. Although McNamara was willing to include the Netherlands in this select group as a representative of the smaller powers, "to the surprise and annoyance of the Americans, the Dutch led the opposition among the smaller members to the establishment of any committee which did not contain *in principle* the possibility for participation by any NATO nation."[46] Consequently, when the matter was taken up by the North Atlantic Council on November 27, 1965, it was decided to transform the "Select Committee" into the "Special Committee" with a membership of ten.[47] In addition to the nuclear powers of the United States and Britain, the Special Committee consisted of Belgium, Canada, Denmark, Germany, Greece, Italy, the Netherlands, and Turkey. While Norway and Portugal chose not to be members, in July 1966 they sent observers to the committee proceedings.[48] This left outside only the two smallest states, Luxembourg and Iceland (which had no armed forces), and Gaullist France whose nationalist doctrine did not even sanction an exchange of information about nuclear matters or joint consultation on nuclear strategy.

The Special Committee had the broad aims of discovering how best nuclear planning could be conducted in peacetime by including the interested nonnuclear NATO powers and of setting up the procedures and informational networks through which consultation could take place in times of crisis on the use of nuclear weapons. In order to study these problems, the Special Committee was broken down into three working groups on (1) nuclear policy planning, (2) intelligence and data exchange, and (3) communications. The first dealt with the substance of nuclear consultation, while the other two dealt with the creation of effective procedures and techniques for obtaining the information needed for consultation. Each working group consisted of five members, with the United States and Britain represented on all three groups. Initially it was expected that Defense Ministers would sit on all groups, but this proved to be unrealistic. Only the nuclear planning working party met at the level of Defense Ministers, while their deputies comprised the other two working parties.

The intelligence and data exchange group recommended the establishment of a Situation Center to provide an adequate data base for nuclear consultation. This recommendation was subsequently accepted and acted upon. Similarly, the communications group recommended the creation of a redundant, militarily secure, classified teletype network between NATO headquarters and the capitals of the member states, as well as a satellite communications systems between SHAPE and its key military commands. These suggestions were also followed up and successfully implemented.

The Defense Ministers who formed the nuclear planning working group, as Secretary McNamara explained, "examined and discussed the strategic nuclear resources of the Alliance, the tactical nuclear weapons of the Alliance, the potential circumstances and consequences of their use, and the way in which the Alliance should organize to carry on future discussions of these subjects. Most importantly," McNamara added, "we have begun to deal with these matters pragmatically, realistically and in detail. I have been struck by how beneficial these discussions have been—how much better we do in communicating in a small group of responsible national officials with adequately detailed preparation."[49]

CREATION OF THE NUCLEAR DEFENSE AFFAIRS COMMITTEE AND THE NUCLEAR PLANNING GROUP

As the Special Committee had completed its ground-breaking functions in 1966, it was dissolved and replaced by two new permanent nuclear organs by a decision of a NATO Ministerial meeting (without French participation) on December 14, 1966.[50] A general policy body, the Nuclear Defense Affairs Committee (NDAC), was formed and opened to every NATO state. In practice its membership comprised all NATO powers with the exception of Luxembourg and Iceland and, of course, France. Subordinate to the NDAC there was created the Nuclear Planning Group (NPG), which was designed to carry on the substantive, detailed work on allied nuclear matters. In order to keep the NPG from becoming unwieldy, the United States first proposed that its membership be restricted to five. The United States, Britain, Germany, and Italy would be permanent members, while one smaller state would be chosen at random from the NDAC. Interest was so keen and competition for this one seat was so intensive that it became necessary to expand the NPG to seven, with the three places for the smaller states rationed out on a rotating basis of 18-month terms. Practically, this assured that one seat would alternate between the Netherlands and Belgium, one between Canada and Denmark, and one between Greece and Turkey.[51] The rivalry between Greece and Turkey, both of which wanted to participate from the start, gave rise to an odd compromise. Turkey originally won the seat, but only for half of the first 18-month term. After that Greece took office for a full 18-month term, followed by Turkey for a full 18-month term. Yielding to the political pressures of this rivalry caused their rotation to be thrown out of cycle with the other nonpermanent members.

Finally, Norway belatedly decided to join the inner circle of nuclear planning, and so beginning January 1, 1970 took a seat on the NPG. This added another rotating nonpermanent member and further complicated the arithmetic, since the rotating members now alternated in teams of three and four, thereby giving the NPG at one time seven members and at another time eight members. While this was also a rather awkward arrangement, it testified to the importance that had become attached to the work of the NPG. It was even more significant in view of the fact that Norway had never agreed to the stationing of American nuclear weapons on its territory and had always tried to deal with nuclear matters at arms length.

The NDAC and the NPG are exceptional among the committees functioning under the aegis of the North Atlantic Council in that countries are represented upon these two bodies directly by Defense Ministers. In addition, they meet at the ambassadorial level of Permanent Representatives, and all meetings, whether at the ministerial or ambassadorial level, take place under the chairmanship of the NATO Secretary General. These arrangements ensure that the proceedings receive the close attention of the responsible defense officials in the NATO capitals as well as among the international staff at NATO headquarters. Finally, NDAC and NPG member countries meet together at the delegation staff level to prepare meetings for the higher levels. It was further decided at the NPG Ministerial meeting at the Hague in April 1968 that the outgoing members of the NPG could continue to participate in the NPG proceedings at the staff and ambassadorial levels in the periods between the NPG meetings of

Defense Ministers. This permits rotating members of the NPG whose terms have expired to maintain continuity of work on nuclear matters and it softens the blow of temporary exclusion from the deliberations of the NPG Ministers.[52]

The character of the meetings of Defense Ministers on the NPG is unique among the most senior officials who participate in NATO gatherings. It has been the practice for the NPG Ministers to convene two or three times a year, in turn in the various member countries— often at some quiet retreat. Their deliberations are carefully prepared, with all documents circulated in advance in the expectation that discussion might begin at a sophisticated level. To facilitate understanding of what is often complicated material, these meetings have simultaneous translations in all of the languages of the members attending, instead of the usual NATO practice of translations only in English and French. Uninhibited exchange of views is encouraged by always holding closed meetings, with delegations limited to five officials from each country. The Chairman of the Military Committee, SACEUR, and SACLANT also attend as observers. Other than a minute and a brief final communique, there is no formal record kept of the proceedings. The NPG has the broad charter to consider any subject related to nuclear weapons, and each Minister is free to raise the topics that are of particular interest to his country. The terse communiques issued after each NPG Ministerial meeting have revealed frankly what aspects of nuclear policy have been discussed.

The aim of drawing Defense Ministers directly in a continuous dialogue about all the possible contingencies for the disposition and use of nuclear weapons is best fulfilled when the Ministers and their aides engage in a searching, scholarly analysis of the problems under discussion. This requires the Defense Ministers to be depoliticized, and this is frequently difficult, since they often rose to become Ministers by being successful politicians. Their instincts for political survival have taught them to fuzz positions, shade the truth, and avoid a frank confrontation of sharply delineated choices. The clarification of positions and the laying bare of objective facts needed for successful NPG deliberations require another mentality. McNamara was essentially nonpolitical by training and instinct. Indeed, at times he was sadly lacking in a political sensitivity when dealing with allies. Yet he performed a valuable service in giving the NPG its initial impetus by the careful, precise, frank manner in which he prepared for NPG discussions, as well as by his willingness to place vital information before America's allies. Authoritative sources informed this writer that McNamara told the NPG Ministers as much as he told congressional committees in executive session. At first it was found that the United States was about five years ahead of its NATO partners in strategic thought, but the gap has been continually narrowed, in large measure because of the operation of the NPG. McNamara, incidentally, was also in the habit of presenting "sanitized" versions of classified nuclear papers in public statements or speeches so as to communicate these ideas to the Kremlin, since deterrence only exists if it exists in the minds of the enemy.

Among other Ministers whose background suited them for service on the NPG, one might mention Denis Healey, the former British Labor Minister of Defense. Healey's aptitude for the NPG came by virtue of his academic career at Oxford and his expertise in strategic thought. He had close contacts with the strategic community in which, for example, he helped found the Institute for Strategic Studies in London. By way of contrast, former U.S. Secretary of Defense Melvin Laird was a completely political animal. Although he was familiar with defense problems, his previous experience scarcely prepared him to think like an academician.

Political considerations have, of course, intruded upon the work of the NPG. The most flagrant case ironically came when McNamara, presumably under domestic political pressures, announced in a San Francisco speech of September 18, 1967 the intention of the United States to build a "thin" ABM. This was unfortunate timing, since this question was scheduled to be discussed by the NPG Ministers just ten days later. The NPG had previously considered the ABM problem at its April 1967 meeting,[53] but the indecent haste of the American announcement on the eve of another NPG meeting appeared to undermine the value of nuclear consultation within NATO. Healey was known to have expressed Britain's unhappiness about this incident.[54]

One of the most notable achievements of the NPG arose from a collaborative British-German effort to draw up detailed guidelines on the crucial question of the possible use of tactical nuclear weapons in Europe. Faced with the staggering figure of some 7,200 tactical nuclear weapons, one wonders if any plan for their controlled use in time of war could be meaningful. The explosion of only a small percentage of these weapons might unleash such devastation that command and control arrangements and policy guidelines for the use of the remaining weapons might prove fanciful. Nevertheless, Denis Healey undertook the initiative of working out the basis of an agreement on the projected use of tactical nuclear weapons during 1968 with German Defense Minister Gerhard Schroeder. This project was formally concluded, after the change of government in Bonn, with Defense Minister Helmut Schmidt. The substance of the Healey-Schmidt understanding was presented to the NPG Ministerial meeting in November 1969, where it also received the essential U.S. approval.[55] The NDAC and then a full NATO Ministerial meeting, minus France, formally accepted the NPG recommendations as Alliance policy. This took the form of two documents: One provided guidelines for faster political consultation regarding tactical nuclear weapons, the other sought to define a common political rationale for the resort to their use.[56] The difficulties raised by these studies are so great that one must reserve judgment as to whether politically useful guidelines on the employment of tactical nuclear weapons have actually been achieved. Nevertheless within the space of two years, the NPG had been able to create the basis for a consensus on an extremely sensitive and complicated subject, which had previously been surrounded by widely divergent views and misunderstanding.

Healey explained the intent behind the NPG directives. What "has now been achieved has been to get away from an automatic tripwire strategy for NATO in favor of a strategy of more flexible response . . . and to devise guidelines for the initial tactical use of nuclear weapons which would reduce the risk that, if they ever were used, there would be an automatic escalation to strategic nuclear war." This means that "NATO gave up planning the very large scale and indiscriminate use of tactical nuclear weapons in a defensive role." Hopefully this would fulfill the basic purpose of such weapons, which "is to restore the credibility of the overall deterrent in a situation in which a large scale conventional attack shows that credibility has disappeared."[57]

General Kielmansegg of the Federal Republic likewise hailed this achievement. While tactical nuclear weapons had existed in Europe for a number of years, "how they might be used was a purely military speculation with no political guidelines for it. There was nothing more than the American nuclear monopoly and thus a constant strain on NATO, because these weapons were stored in Europe and would only be fired on European soil." The significance of the agreement reached "after protracted negotiations in the Nuclear Planning Group rests in the fact that the previously one-sided teacher-pupil process of the U.S.A. vis-a-vis the Europeans concerning the use of nuclear weapons has been transformed into a mutual process. It also means that for the first time the Americans have pledged themselves to certain considerations valid for all and not just for themselves, and not dictated alone by American interests."[58] There is no doubt that the Healey-Schmidt exercise served as a watershed in allied nuclear affairs, since it was undertaken on European initiative and upset the previous teacher-pupil relationship. The growth of a common body of allied understandings that has evolved within the NPG has reflected the maturing of trans-Atlantic nuclear deliberations.

The NDAC and particularly the NPG have undeniably been vehicles for progress in managing the problem of nuclear weapons within the Alliance. These two bodies, it might be noted in passing, bear a certain resemblance to Duynstee's proposals for a Nuclear Council of about ten members that would have supervised general nuclear policy and a Nuclear Executive of five or seven members, some of whom would be permanent while the others would sit for fixed terms on a rotating basis. Duynstee first elaborated these proposals nearly three years before the creation of the Special Committee, out of which came the NDAC and the NPG.[59]

The NPG, like Duynstee's envisioned Nuclear Executive, has been designed to handle the substantive management of Alliance nuclear policy and to have as its working members national representatives of cabinet-level status with easy access to their heads of government. Unlike the Duynstee proposal, of course, the NPG does not manage a commonly owned Alliance deterrent, nor does it take decisions by weighted majority vote. Intervening between the launching of the Duynstee plan and the creation of the NPG came the debate over the Multilateral Force and then its demise, both practically and legally, when the United States accepted the Soviet provision in the Non-Proliferation Treaty that banned further attempts to form a commonly owned and operated allied nuclear force. As long as the treaty remains in effect, for better or for worse NATO is obliged to consider the NPG as the highest form of nuclear sharing attainable.

THE PROSPECTS FOR ALLIED
NUCLEAR SHARING

There are disquieting prospects for the development of the trans-Atlantic relationship that must be sustained by the trustee formula for nuclear sharing. A shift in the nuclear equation between the superpowers provides one important change in context. The United States could credibly threaten massive retaliation against an attack from the East at a time when the United States maintained an overwhelming preponderance of nuclear weapons. European willingness to rely upon the pledge of U.S. nuclear response may seem less convincing under the present conditions of Soviet-American nuclear parity.

The strategy of massive retaliation born in the era of American superiority has been officially replaced by the doctrine of flexibility in response, and this requires the retention of substantial ground forces, including a significant American contingent, in NATO Europe. But the movement is in the direction of a drawdown of U.S. ground forces in Europe, with all the disruptive influence this implies for an effective allied fighting force. The defection of France from NATO deprived SACEUR of reliance upon French ground forces as well as the loss of allied infrastructure and support facilities in France. It also created more exposed communication and logistical support lines for NATO forces in Germany. Such cumulative strains on NATO conventional capabilities could upset the conventional force balance to the point where it could dissolve the political cement of the Western Alliance. The European allies would become more susceptible to Soviet political pressures including nuclear blackmail, moving them to accommodate Soviet demands by weakening, if not fatally impairing, the Alliance. Should a military conflict arise out of some incident, the absence of substantial ground troops would necessarily require the lowering of the nuclear threshold by a prompt resort to tactical nuclear weapons. Thus the drawdown of conventional forces in NATO Europe would not only diminish the flexibility in a NATO response, but as Alastair Buchan has aptly remarked, "the security of Western Europe would be even more dependent on the deployment, threat, or use of American nuclear weapons—either tactical in Europe or strategic outside it. Therefore, the control of a European crisis would be concentrated more than ever in the hands of American decision makers."[60]

What would be the likely European response to such increased dependence upon the United States in its role as nuclear trustee for the West? Would there be renewed interest in building up the British and French nuclear forces, even though they had become increasingly obsolete as a result of the gap that had developed between their nuclear capabilities and those of the superpowers, and even though it was recognized that the small national nuclear forces were not designed for use independently of the American deterrent? Would this condition create pressures for some more tangible form of access to nuclear weapons in West Germany, with all the adverse consequences this might entail? Would this involve a breakdown in the Non-Proliferation Treaty? If the NPT were broken, would there be a renewed effort at multilateral nuclear sharing of a commonly owned and operated force? Allied nuclear sharing may well move to the fore again, although in a different setting from the MLF days. Or would the strain on European-U.S. relations serve as spur to the creation of a European deterrent? But when will its prerequisite of a political union in Europe come into existence? And if it did finally come to pass, how would such a European force relate to the American deterrent? All these and other questions remain unanswered. The nettle of nuclear sharing has still not been grasped.

NOTES

1. President de Gaulle's seventh press conference, January 14, 1963, Ambassade de France, New York, Speeches and Press Conferences, No. 185, p. 10.

2. Alvin Shuster, "Britain Atom Test in U.S. Disclosed," New York *Times*, June 25, 1974.

3. On the problems and prospects of forming a European nuclear deterrent out of the British and French national nuclear forces, see Ian Smart, *Future Conditional: The Prospect for Anglo-French Nuclear Cooperation*, Adelphi Paper No. 78 (London, 1971); Andrew J. Pierre, "Nuclear Diplomacy: Britain, France and American," *Foreign Affairs*, January 1971, pp. 283-301; Sir Bernard Burrows and Christopher Irwin, *The Security of Western Europe*

(London, 1972), pp. 70-79; Paul C. Davis, "A European Nuclear Force: Utility and Prospects," *Orbis*, Spring 1973, pp. 110-31.

4. *Keesing's Contemporary Archives*, Vol. 13, January 1-7, 1961, p. 17846.

5. C. L. Sulzberger, "The Crucial Compact of Como," New York *Times*, November 23, 1960.

6. "NATO Atom Arms Weighted by U.S.," New York *Times*, October 13, 1960.

7. Address by General Lauris Norstad at Paris, November 21, 1960, *Addresses by Speakers*, Sixth NATO Parliamentarians' Conference (Paris, 1960), pp. 34-35.

8. *Keesing's*, op. cit., p. 17845.

9. Address by President John F. Kennedy at Ottawa, May 17, 1961, Department of State *Bulletin* 44, no. 1145: 841.

10. Address by Secretary of Defense Robert S. McNamara at Ann Arbor, Michigan, June 16, 1962, Department of State *Bulletin* 47, no. 1202: 67-68.

11. Ibid., p. 68.

12. Robert Kleiman, *Atlantic Crisis* (New York, 1964), p. 113.

13. George W. Ball, *The Discipline of Power* (Boston, 1968), pp. 207-8.

14. Thomas K. Finletter, *Interim Report* (New York, 1968), pp. 93-94.

15. Ball, op. cit., p. 209.

16. Quoted in Arthur M. Schlesinger, Jr., *A Thousand Days* (Boston, 1967), p. 797.

17. Kleiman, op. cit., pp. 52-53.

18. Ibid., pp. 47-61, for a good discussion of the Skybolt controversy and the Nassau meeting. For the text of the Nassau agreement of December 21, 1962, see Department of State *Bulletin* 48, no. 1229: pp. 43-45.

19. John Newhouse, *De Gaulle and the Anglo-Saxons* (New York, 1970), pp. 222-26.

20. Ibid., pp. 210-11, 226-27.

21. President de Gaulle's seventh press conference, January 14, 1963, pp. 10-12.

22. Newhouse, op. cit., p. 225.

23. Gerard Smith, "The United States," *Interplay*, November 1968, p. 10.

24. Finletter, op. cit., pp. 91, 94.

25. Joint Communique of President Lyndon B. Johnson and Chancellor Ludwig Erhard, Washington, D.C., June 12, 1964, Department of State *Bulletin* 50, no. 1305: 993.

26. Address by Walt W. Rostow, Chairman of the Policy Planning Council, at Philadelphia, March 28, 1963, Department of State *Bulletin* 48, no. 1242: 533.

27. Quoted in Wallace C. Magathan, Jr., "West German Defense Policy," *Orbis*, Summer 1964, p. 304.

28. Ibid., pp. 305-6.

29. See, for example, New York *Times*, February 20, 1964.

30. The most authoritative expositions of the ANF proposal are found in the speeches of Prime Minister Harold Wilson on December 16, 1964, and of Defense Minister Denis Healey on December 17, 1964 in the course of a debate in the House of Commons. (See Documents T. 54 and T. 55, December 1964, British Information Services, New York.)

31. Ferenc A. Vali, *The Quest for a United Germany* (Baltimore, 1967), pp. 251-53.

32. Philip Geyelin, *Lyndon B. Johnson and the World* (New York, 1966), pp. 159-180.

33. Finletter, op. cit., pp. 95-96.

34. New York *Times*, October 12, 1965.

35. Andre Fontaine, "Has America Had Enough of Europe?" *Interplay*, June-July 1968, p. 9.

36. New York *Times*, July 1, 1965, gave details of the presumably top-secret report on the subject by a Presidential panel headed by Roswell L. Gilpatric. When Chancellor Erhard met President Johnson in Washington on December 21, 1965, their joint communique did not ever mention the MLF although it emphasized the need for nonproliferation of nuclear weapons. (Ibid., December 22, 1965.)

37. Schlesinger, op. cit., p. 797.

38. The Duynstee proposal for an integrated, Atlantic nuclear force was developed in the following comprehensive reports of the Committee on Defense Questions and Armaments of the Assembly of Western European Union: Document 251, October 16, 1962; Document 268, April 26, 1963; Document 290, October 30, 1963; Document 320, October 20, 1964. See also Duynstee's speech of November 6, 1964, Official Report, Consultative Assembly, Council of Europe, 16th Ordinary Session, 15th sitting, pp. 571-75.

39. Recommendation 110, "On the State of European Security: Aspects of Western Strategy," Assembly, WEU, *Proceedings*, December 1964, IV, p. 23. This volume also contains the very interesting debates that preceded the vote. The opposition came, as expected, from the Gaullists, while many of the abstentions came from Social Democrats of several countries, some of whom said they wished to reserve judgment pending the outcome of the Johnson-Wilson negotiations.

40. NATO Parliamentarians' Conference, Tenth Plenary Session, Paris, November 20, 1964, Verbatim Report, pp. 14-15.

41. Speech by Prime Minister Harold Wilson in a debate in the House of Commons, December 16, 1964, Document T. 54, British Information Services, New York, p. 15.

42. Text of the American draft for an NPT of August 1963, *Survival*, October 1965, p. 268.

43. "State of European Security: The NATO Nuclear Force," A. E. M. Duynstee, rapporteur, Document 290, October 30, 1963, Assembly, WEU, *Proceedings*, December 1963, III, p. 122.

44. Testimony of Secretary of Defense Robert S. McNamara, June 21, 1966, *Hearings before the Subcommittee on National Security and International Operations*, U.S. Senate, 89th Cong., 2d sess., Part 6 (Washington, D.C., 1966), p. 192.

45. Text of Communique, May 24, 1963, NATO Ministerial Meeting, Department of State *Bulletin* 48, no. 1250: 895.

46. Robert W. Russell, "The Atlantic Alliance in Dutch Foreign Policy," *Atlantic Community Quarterly*, Summer 1970, pp. 178-79.

47. Henry Tanner, New York *Times*, November 28, 1965.

48. David Halberstam, New York *Times*, July 27, 1966.

49. Testimony of Secretary of Defense Robert S. McNamara, June 21, 1966, op. cit., p. 192.

50. Text of Final Communique, December 16, 1966, NATO Ministerial Meeting, Department of State *Bulletin* 56, no. 1437: 50-51.

51. Russell, op. cit., pp. 180-81.

52. Arthur Hockaday, "Nuclear Management in NATO," *NATO Letter*, May 1967, p. 7: W. F. van Eekelen, "Development of NATO's Nuclear Consultation," ibid., July-August 1970, p. 4.

53. Text of Communique of the NATO Nuclear Planning Group, April 7, 1967, Department of State *Bulletin* 56, no. 1453: 687.

54. Terrence Smith, New York *Times*, September 29, 1967.

55. William Beecher, New York *Times*, November 13, 1969.

56. Text of Final Communique, December 5, 1969, NATO Ministerial Meeting, Department of State *Bulletin* 61, no. 1592: 628.

57. Press Conference of Minister of Defense Denis Healey, February 23, 1970, *NATO Letter*, May 1970, p. 26.

58. General Johann Adolf Graf Kielmansegg, "What's to Become of NATO?" *Aussenpolitik*, English ed., No. 1 (1970), p. 40.

59. "State of European Security: A NATO Nuclear Force," A. E. M. Duynstee, rapporteur, Document 251, October 16, 1962, Assembly, WEU, *Proceedings*, December 1962, III, p. 150; "State of European Security: The NATO Nuclear Force after the Nassau Agreement," A. E. M. Duynstee, rapporteur, Document 268, April 26, 1963, Assembly, WEU, *Proceedings*, June 1963, I, pp. 67, 69. The Special Committee was formed on November 27, 1965, and the NDAC and NPG were created on December 14, 1966.

60. Alastair Buchan, "The Future of NATO," *International Conciliation*, No. 565 (November 1967), pp. 39-40.

9

THE ECONOMICS OF
THE ATLANTIC
COMMUNITY

The forces that will shape the future political and military institutions of the Atlantic Community will be deeply affected by the grid of economic relations that connects these nations, and which has already for good or ill inseparably bound their fates together.

These trans-Atlantic relations bear little resemblance to the ties that hold the Soviet Union to its East European client states. In the East the basic force that binds the Soviet imperium is the military might of the Soviet Union. The natural tendency of the nations of Eastern Europe to express themselves economically, culturally, and to some extent politically is to be drawn toward the West and to resist domination from the East. Historically, states like Poland, Czechoslovakia, Hungary, and Rumania have had intimate connections with their West European brothers and in many respects they had reached economic and cultural levels of achievement that surpassed their Russian mentors. The same is obviously true of the East Germans, who represent a special situation because of the complications of the German problem. Yugoslavia and Albania have moved beyond the pale of Soviet military domination, although its shadow still lurks menacingly, and Yugoslavia has rebuilt substantial economic and cultural relations with the West. This leaves only little Bulgaria that might naturally look to Moscow, but even here latent anti-Russian forces have been building up and the economic and cultural attraction of the West has, over time, been growing. In short, the Soviet imperium is a highly artificial construct that will be condemned to remain in a condition of perpetual tension. The repeated rebellions of the various East European states against Soviet control, which in several cases had to be reimposed by the massive use of Soviet armed force, bears witness to the unnatural and essentially fragile community of nations that the Communists rule in the East.

The fundamental setting of the Atlantic Community is precisely the opposite. Its military and political arrangements rest upon consent, not coercion. When de Gaulle pulled out of NATO, the United States did not invade France. And the other West European states desperately sought to keep American armed forces committed in Europe, while the United States steadily moved in the direction of a military disengagement. Underlying these shifting political and military policies, however, has been an intense economic and cultural interpenetration among the nations of the Atlantic Community which has produced a natural, broadly based sense of cohesion. This multifaceted community of interests has helped to minimize the divergencies in political and military policies and hopefully can help keep such differences in the future within manageable bounds. The Atlantic Community is therefore not an artificial and fragile structure. Basically, it rests upon the sound and resiliant inter-dependence of nations with a common heritage and is sustained by the interaction of numerous forces that transcend the nation-states that comprise the larger community.

This truth is nowhere more apparent than in the complex web of economic ties that bind the nations of the Atlantic Community together. Since the end of World War II, "the Atlantic nations have achieved among themselves a degree of international economic integration and cooperation which is unique both historically and in the contemporary world."[1] This has been facilitated by the increasing compatibility of the economic systems of the advanced industrial countries and by their shared economic objectives. Broadly speaking, there is agreement upon the desirability of a mixed economy, comprising both private enterprise and economic intervention by the state. Although there are different mixtures in the various states, the constant experiments in running a mixed economy have been guided to a remarkable extent by a quiet pragmatism that has left behind as irrelevant the rigid ideological argument about "capitalism" and "socialism." There is broad agreement that the various systems should achieve sustained economic growth, high levels of employment, price stability, and should undertake welfare policies for the disadvantaged. Since the countries of the Atlantic Community are concerned with a common and interrelated set of problems, it is natural for them to share an interest in each others' economic policies while given the fact "that the problems are interdependent compels such interest. These countries are closely and increasingly linked by ties of trade, technology, and capital. Knowledge of each others' institutions and practices has increased enormously, and the level of mutual confidence in national economic policies has risen to the point of greatly reducing psychological barriers to the movement of capital and the location of production. In short, the major industrial countries are becoming more closely 'integrated.' "[2]

The level of economic integration among these countries is obviously not as high as that achieved within the separate national entities, nor is there a uniform degree of interaction among all the states concerned, since regional groupings like the European Common Market have drawn some national economies closer together than others. One should also not be too literal in believing that the advanced industrial countries of the Atlantic Community are all washed by the waters of the Atlantic: Switzerland is landlocked, Italy is in the Mediterranean, and the attainment of a highly developed economic status by Japan has quite properly made it a member of an otherwise exclusively Euro-American organization like OECD. Given these qualifications, it nevertheless remains true that the advanced industrial countries of the world have become increasingly sensitive to an intensified economic interaction among themselves and that the central strand in this network of ties lies in the North Atlantic basin. In this sense "Atlantic Community" remains a meaningful term, since the countries on either side of the Atlantic have become progressively interlocked and have shrunk the ocean that separates them to the dimensions of a pond.

THE MULTINATIONAL ENTERPRISE AS A RADICALLY NEW ECONOMIC FORCE

The nature of this economic interaction is in some important respects radically different from the way classical economists thought the international economic system would operate. Indeed, the nations of the Atlantic Community are still burdened with obsolete economic theories that have not yet taken account of their actual economic behavior. Traditionally, the classical economists conceived of international economic activity primarily in terms of international trade. Each trading partner was supposed to organize the various factors of production within the borders of its nation and then export the resulting products to other nations. Ideally, in a world trading pattern that was free of artificial obstructions such as tariffs and quotas, each nation would specialize in the production of those commodities in which it had a comparative advantage. It was taken for granted that the nation-state was the only legitimate point of reference for all such economic activity: Not only was production organized nationally, but the purpose of exchanging products was to maximize the welfare of each nation by exporting more than it imported and thereby acquire a favorable balance of payments.

The difficulty with this conventional wisdom is that it ignores the startling growth in the activities of the multinational enterprise, which organizes the factors of production across national borders. Instead of exporting products, the multinational enterprise exports such factors of production as capital, technology, and management. Ideally, in such operations national boundaries become irrelevant; in actual practice the attempts of nations to regulate these activities are often viewed as annoyances by the multinational corporation, which clearly does not view the nation-state as the only legitimate point of reference.

While the concept of a multinational enterprise is admittedly imprecise, we might do well to accept the definition offered by Raymond Vernon of "a cluster of corporations of diverse nationality joined together by ties of common ownership and responsive to a common management strategy."[3] The importance of the multinational enterprise lies in the fundamental but little-appreciated fact that by 1967, U.S.-owned multinational corporations produced abroad four times the value of U.S. exports, and by 1969 this rate had increased to five to one.[4] That is, the value of the foreign production derived from the direct investments of U.S.-based multinational corporations was five times greater than that of American exports; the most important link in international economic transactions for the United States was through the multinational corporation, not through foreign trade. Not only was the net income to the United States from its direct investments abroad many times larger than the net income from international trade, but the multinational enterprises were, in general, growing at twice the rate of the various national economies.[5] Between 1960 and 1969 the annual rate of increase of repatriated earnings from foreign affiliates of U.S.-owned multinational corporations was 11.1 percent, compared to 6.1 percent for the total U.S. corporate profits after taxes. There was every reason to believe that the higher growth rates and earnings of these multinational enterprises would continue through the 1970s.[6]

It is often mistakenly thought that the bulk of the wealth generated by U.S.-owned multinational corporations comes from extracting mineral and petroleum products from underdeveloped countries. The facts show that by the end of 1969, mining and smelting only accounted for 8 percent of such activity, while oil amounted to 28 percent of the total of U.S. direct investments abroad through multinational corporations. By way of contrast, two-thirds of such direct investments were in nonextractive industries, like manufacturing and mercantile enterprises, and almost all of that was located in Western Europe.[7] The fate of the U.S.-based multinational corporation is therefore predominantly tied to that of the Atlantic Community.

The new dimensions of this economic interdependence have frequently been overlooked by governments that persist in thinking about international economic transactions in the Atlantic Community in outmoded economic categories. The American government sought to rectify the U.S. balance-of-payments deficit with Europe, which became endemic during the 1960s, by placing controls on the outflow of U.S. capital to Europe. This reflected the traditional view that the balance-of-payments problem was primarily the function of international trade.

Such a policy was not only misguided but largely ineffective. It neglected taking into account the connection between freedom of capital movement over national frontiers and use of much of this capital to create new production abroad, in large part through the multinational enterprise. As noted, the rate of earnings repatriated from foreign affiliates of U.S.-owned multinational corporations during the 1960s was about twice as high as domestic earnings, and therefore if controls on capital outflow from the United States had succeeded in choking off the growth of foreign affiliates it would have had the effect over time of reducing the inflow of earnings from abroad. This would only have aggravated the position of the U.S. balance of payments.

The annual investment income from U.S.-based multinational corporations, a U.S. official noted, is far greater than their annual capital exports. "In 1971 the profits remitted to U.S. parent corporations as well as large patent and trademark royalties totaled about $10 billion, twice their capital outflow in that year."[8] This net inflow of $5 billion was increased to $7.2 billion by the beginning of 1973.[9]

Such figures demonstrate how fortunate it was that the U.S. efforts to prevent the flow of capital movements over national borders were circumvented by the multinational corporations. In this case, the prohibition against the outflow of dollars from the United States gave birth to the phenomenon of the Eurodollar market that achieved such phenomenal growth during the 1960s. The development of this new money market and the rapid expansion of European branches of U.S. banks, plus the use of the resources from foreign banks, permitted the multinational corporations to raise capital abroad for plant construction in Europe. These new international facts of economic life clearly demonstrated the manner in which the economic strategy of the multinational enterprise could not be identified with any given nation-state, not even its "native" one. Rather, it looked upon the Atlantic Community, and in some cases the entire globe, as its home.

What is manifestly required is a new definition of balance of payments which takes account of the new impulses that the multinational corporation has given to international economic activity. As Neil Jacoby points out, the deficit in U.S. balance of payments that investment controls were designed to curtail "vanishes when international transactions are measured on an assets basis rather than on a liquidity basis." When a U.S.-owned multinational corporation invests in Europe it acquires a long-term asset, in return for which it pays dollars, which is considered a short-term liability of the United States. "Although the transaction enlarges the U.S. deficit on the liquidity basis, it does not change the value of the assets owned in the two countries." If one looked to "the value of assets held, the financial position of the United States is strong and growing stronger."[10]

The United States finally recognized the lack of wisdom, if not the futility, of trying to control capital outflows when Treasury Secretary George Schultz announced in February 1973 that all restraints on capital would be phased out by the end of 1974. In practice it was found possible to end such control in January 1974.[11]

THE AMERICAN CHALLENGE AND THE
EUROPEAN RESPONSE

It was the growing economic strength of U.S.-owned multinational corporations in Europe that gave rise to the anguished cries of *The American Challenge,* which was so effectively publicized by J.-J. Servan-Schreiber. It is true that American corporations have led the movement toward multinationalism because the size and wealth of the U.S. economy permitted them to use their enormous savings for investment in foreign markets where there was an attractive rate of return. The American capital market was better organized than those of Europe, while the advanced managerial techniques of American enterprises generally surpassed the more tradition-bound management found in Europe. Those factors, among others, combined to give the United States an advantage in *direct* corporate investment in Europe. This situation has often obscured the fact that "Europeans hold almost exactly the same amount of private investments in the United States as Americans on the old continent. In the case of Europe, however, the investors are American corporations; in the case of the United States, on the other hand, about two-thirds of the investors are the European savers" who have invested in American securities without obtaining control over American corporations.[12]

The early lead that the United States held in direct investments abroad has steadily been eroded by growing European strength. "Since 1967 European companies have for the first time increased their direct investments in America more rapidly than American firms increased theirs in Europe."[13] By 1969, "the value of net assets owned by Europeans in the United States rose by a fifth, while the value of United States [direct] investments in Europe increased by just over a tenth." It is interesting, as Joseph Greenwald, the American Ambassador to OECD, pointed out, that "most of this European investment appears to be financed by raising funds in the United States markets, just as United States firms are financing an increasing amount of their foreign direct investment by resort to foreign sources." By 1970 American direct investment in Europe was still twice as much as European direct investment in the United

States, "but the trend is clearly shifting from a one-way flow. The result is even greater economic interdependence" among the nations of the Atlantic Community.[14]

The growth in the number of foreign subsidiaries of European-based multinational corporations during the decade 1960-70 was nothing short of astonishing. In the period 1962-64, they established 676 such subsidiaries. In the period 1965-67 the figure of newly-established subsidiaries nearly doubled to 1,159, while in the period 1968-70 this figure again nearly doubled to 2,083. Meanwhile, the U.S.-based multinational growth of foreign subsidiaries was steady, but much less rapid.[15] By 1970 the sales volume of foreign manufacturing subsidiaries of European-based multinational corporations reached more than $82 billion, which is very close if not equal to the estimated business done by U.S.-based foreign manufacturing subsidiaries.[16] Thus surprisingly the sales and foreign assets of U.S. and European-based multinational corporations are roughly equal. American direct investment in Europe still exceeds European direct investment in the United States, since the bulk of such foreign investments by European multinationals is in other European countries, as well as in their former colonies. If the Nine someday becomes One, the cross-European investment within the European Community would no longer be "foreign." But the strength of the remaining Europeanwide multinational corporations would be formidable indeed.

As European integration gathers momentum, it can be expected that the European Community will establish a European company law that will facilitate international mergers within the Community. Harmonization of taxes on corporate amalgamations is also a clearly recognized need that will accompany measures to permit large corporate units to function effectively across national frontiers. But even now in the absence of such supranational European arrangements, the whole structure of industry is already being reformed on a Europeanwide basis. "For U.S. firms operating in Europe, this means tougher competitors whose horizons no longer end at the national border. . . . As the number of mergers multiplies and European entrepreneurs meet the new technical, production, and market demands, U.S. firms may find that they in turn must evolve new methods to meet the '*défi européen.*' "[17] The merger movement of European companies has also significantly stimulated the "flow of investment to the United States beyond that thought possible only a decade ago," one American observer remarked in 1970. "Some foreign firms are beginning to look at the country with the biggest market in the world less as a threat and more as the new land of corporate opportunity."[18] The devaluation of the dollar in 1971 and again in 1973 greatly accelerated the pace of direct foreign investment, since it lowered the price of real American assets and permitted Europeans to acquire American companies at bargain rates. European export industries also had the incentive of trying to keep their competitiveness in the U.S. market by establishing American manufacturing branches and even of using the United States as a manufacturing base for exports.[19]

European corporations increasingly have been in a better position to compete with American giant enterprises on both sides of the Atlantic, not only by virtue of the trend toward mergers, but also by adopting managerial and research techniques once thought to be the monopoly of Americans. "Management has been the driving force behind U.S. industrial expansion abroad. More than any other factor, it will continue to determine success or failure in international business. Europe's somewhat tardy appreciation of this fact should not be allowed to obscure the effectiveness of measures now being taken to correct past deficiencies. With all the zeal of the newly converted, European legislators, educators and a host of public and private organizations have turned to the promotion of management education." Ironically, among the most effective of such management institutions is the U.S. foreign subsidiary in Europe. "The many 'graduates' produced by these subsidiaries now constitute an increasing pool of management talent in the very skills which fueled the international expansion of U.S. firms."[20]

The presumed "technological gap" between the United States and Europe was, in large measure, a "managerial gap," so that increasing European sophistication in management has helped to reduce this disparity. Another aspect of the "technological gap" was found in the differing patterns of research and development (R and D) conducted by American and European corporations. It has long been recognized that Europe was not lacking in technological talent, which has produced a number of major discoveries. Nor has Europe expended an appreciably smaller amount of resources on technological development than has the United States. Nevertheless, the results produced in Europe have lagged behind those of the United States. This difference can largely be accounted for by the manner in which such technological talent and resources have been organized. Much of the lag can be attributed to "the fragmented character of the European R and D effort, a condition which European companies are now aware of and are going to great lengths to correct. Efforts are being made at both the national and international levels to eliminate the waste of duplication and to secure the efficiencies of coordinated programs. Indeed, in certain research-intensive industries, such as space, nuclear energy and aircraft, product development in Europe today is almost entirely the result of a de facto industrial integration encompassing the resources of many countries."[21] The European Economic Community is promoting this coordination in R and D, which will doubtless improve as economic unity increases.

Even where separate European countries have tried to give assistance to industries considered essential to the national interest, such as nuclear energy, electronics, or aerospace, it has become apparent that programs cannot be supported economically if they are confined within national borders. The benefits of large expenditures, including R and D, comes from sharing facilities that are geographically dispersed over different countries. Thus even purely national endeavors are likely to move toward multinational ones.[22]

The picture that emerges is one of much greater equality between European and American multinational enterprises than was previously supposed, and an ever-increasing economic inter-penetration between Europe and the United States.

There is also the certain prospect of the rapidly expanding role of multinational enterprises in the world's economy. The growth rate of multinational corporations is greater than the average increase in GNP of the various national economies in which they operate, since such multinational enterprises are normally in the more technically advanced industries. As a consequence of this growth rate and the constant entrance of new companies into the multinational category, "the free world faces a substantial shift in ownership and control of industry from local nationals to foreigners." Jack Behrman thinks it is reasonable to project growth rates for these ever-expanding multinational corporations at 10 to 20 percent, compared to less than 5 percent for an average GNP. Looking ahead toward the end of the century, such accelerated economic activity on the part of the multinational enterprise would mean that "by the year 1990, at recent rates of growth, free-world GNP should reach $4,000 billion, of which nearly half could be owned by foreign companies or residents."[23] Even more radical is the figure provided by Howard Perlmutter, who has estimated "that by 1985 some 300 giant multinational firms will produce more than half of the world's goods and services."[24]

Moreover, Charles Kindleberger has conjectured that the large multinational corporations will be one of the most effective means available for equalizing salaries, income, and interest rates throughout the area in which they operate, much as the large American corporations did for the development of the American economy after 1880.[25] Economically, the eggs of the Atlantic Community will be so thoroughly scrambled that a retreat to purely national economic policies will become an absurdity.

THE IMPACT OF MULTINATIONAL ENTERPRISES ON THE NATION-STATE SYSTEM

What effects will such transnational economic developments likely have upon the political structure of the nation-state system? Over time one can be fairly certain that they will be substantial, but forecasts of any precision will be hazardous. It seems clear from the broad sweep of human history that mankind has been moving steadily toward larger-scale forms of political life under the pressures of economic, scientific, and technological forces. The multinational corporation epitomizes the development of modern technology. Sidney Rolfe argues that

> at least since the Middle Ages, man's technological capabilities have outpaced his social and political organizing ability. The compass, the gun, the steam engine, the jet, the computer, even the missile and the H-bomb are no more than stations on the technological way; more will come. So too have there been political way stations—the city-state, the duchy, the confederation, the nation-state, and now haltingly in several areas, common markets. As technology for trade or war pressed then-prevailing political

boundaries, those boundaries have historically expanded to incorporate and use the new dimensions technology made possible. Wider markets, wider defense areas, mean wider political dimensions.[26]

Movement toward larger political entities will not be an easy, uninterrupted flow of events, since Rolfe properly acknowledges the contradictory and often dominant theme of our times that "the world is not yet ready to abandon the nation-state for a broader organization." There is little point denying the refractory nature of modern nationalism, nor the difficulty in shifting loyalties to a political unit beyond the nation-state. Nevertheless, one should not ignore the fact that "the international corporation and international investment are part of an international dimension of life which would seem likely to call forth some form of international political organization." Despite the efforts of national governments to protect their parochial political interests that appear threatened by transnational forces beyond their control, it may in time become apparent that such larger forces are undeniably increasing the welfare of a larger community of which the nation is a part. At this point a new sense of community may become sufficiently strong to permit the growth of political institutions. As Rolfe suggests, such larger communities may be defined in various ways. "Surely Europe is such a community; it is defensible that the Atlantic Community is such a community."[27]

While such new loyalties are in the process of developing, the nation-state may not only be able to obstruct political evolution, but even to hamper economic growth. George Ball warns that "unless we can make faster progress in modernizing the world's political structure, the multinational corporation may find itself increasingly harassed by obstacles and restrictions that will seriously reduce its potential." The contrast between the economic and political forces involved is sharply counterposed: "While the structure of the multinational corporation is a modern concept, designed to meet the requirements of a modern age, the nation-state is a very old-fashioned idea and badly adapted to serve the needs of our present complex world."[28]

Basically, the transnational perspective is in conflict with the national one. The multinational corporation seeks to locate its various factors of production wherever they can be employed most economically, without regard for the borders of the nation-state. Officers of multinational corporations publicly proclaim that they are "good citizens" of whatever nation they happen to find themselves in, and there is every reason that they should try to adhere to high standards of citizenship so as to avoid needless interference in their business on the part of national officials. Yet inherently the multinational corporation must carry multiple loyalties deriving from its transnational operations which find expression in a decision favorable to the parent government on one occasion and to the host government on another. This is so since their essential criterion for decision making is economic, not political. The nationally oriented leaders of the various governments, on the other hand, are more likely to judge events by their political impact, although they must also be mindful of the economic consequences. In particular, "the host government," as Behrman explains, "is caught in a 'love-hate' syndrome. It wants the contributions to wealth and economic growth that the multinational enterprise can provide because they add to its power within the country, as well as internationally. At the same time it dislikes and fears the results: the incursions on national sovereignty and technological dependence. The host government finds multinational enterprises difficult to live with, but, so long as it seeks to increase national power, equally unpleasant to live without." This presents the host nation with the paradox: "To gain power, a country needs the added wealth-generation of the multinational enterprise, which may entail giving up the ability to exercise the power gained."[29]

In the pulls and tugs of the various forces at play between the multinational corporation and the nation-state, what likely patterns of evolution might one expect? In the short run a given nation-state may seek to regulate the economic activity that would otherwise escape its jurisdiction by imposing nationalistic controls that could hamper the economic operation of the multinational corporation, even if this would also impoverish the economic welfare of the nation. As Vernon observes: "One marvels at the tenacity with which man seeks to retain a sense of differentiation and identity, a feeling of control, even when the apparent cost of the identity and the control seems out of all proportion to its value."[30] But such controls would most likely only be effective for brief periods, since the multinational corporation retains the advantages of a broader scope of operations and of transactions between affiliates "whose relationships are long term and organic in character." In this confrontation, it would appear certain that "the regulatory capabilities of an intervening state inevitably decline. . . . Given the complexity of multinational institutions and the presence of so many alternative channels for the legitimate international movement of funds and other resources, the regulating sovereign seems increasingly at a disadvantage."[31]

At this point, how might the nation-state seek to reassert a measure of its control? Here Vernon suggests that the various governments concerned might feel obliged to coordinate their monetary, fiscal, and other economic policies on an intimate and continuous basis so that their joint scope of regulatory activity might substantially embrace the scope of the multinational enterprise. This could lead to a number of joint policy agreements and even joint institutions to implement them. One might envision, for example, agreements among states on principles of taxation and on avoiding jurisdictional disputes over subsidiaries of multinational corporations. Controversies that would inevitably arise from the application of such international agreements would require "some kind of international adjudicating mechanism in order to be operative." This approach to regulating the activity of the multinational enterprise, in Vernon's view, "would have a somewhat greater chance of being launched among the advanced countries alone than on a global basis."[32] That is, we are again talking about the creation of some sort of political institution in what is essentially the Atlantic Community.

Furthermore, as the parties to such international agreements would be relinquishing their previous claims to control overseas subsidiaries, the nations involved "would probably wish to protect themselves from the risks that the subsidiaries' new-found freedoms would imperil some important national objective. Accordingly, there might well be a need for a joint commitment on the part of the countries concerned to launch on a continuous, nonstop process of policy harmonization in the fields in which they were accepting restraints upon their exercise of sovereign power." But even the de facto limitation of sovereignty through policy harmonization would not be able to surmount those aspects of the operation of multinational enterprises that would still lie outside the scope of these agreements. "For instance, national employment policy and national monetary policy would still be subject to the actions of the multinational enterprises to a degree that might prove intolerable for the nations concerned." Here the de facto limitations of sovereignty, might lead to a de jure one. Vernon concludes that "one way to 'solve' a difficult problem is to submerge it into an even larger one. In this case, the larger problem is already waiting in the wings. The threat to national policies will be mounting from many directions: not alone from the existence of the multinational enterprise, but also from the shrinkage of trade barriers, the improvement in transport and communication, and so on. These are likely to raise issues of sovereignty that may, in the end, dwarf the multinational enterprise problem. Perhaps when that occurs, the resulting institutional adjustments will deal with the multinational enterprise as well."[33] While it is too early to state with assurance that new institutions will arise in the Atlantic Community to which sovereign powers over basic economic policies can be transferred, neither should one say that the logic of the movement of economic forces should rule out this eventuality.

It is, of course, only too easy to fall into the trap of an economic determinist, and to assert with assurance that the movement of economic forces will be sufficiently powerful to remold the political forms of the Atlantic Community. "Although the economic and technical substructure partially determines and interacts with the political superstructure," Robert Gilpin cautions, it is the "political values and security interests" that are the "crucial determinants of international relations."[34] History repeatedly demonstrates that "the contradiction between the economic and political organization of society is not always resolved in favor of economic rationality." It is therefore not inevitable that politics will adjust to technology. In the confict between the multinational enterprise and the nation-state, "the determining consideration will be the diplomatic and strategic interests of the dominant powers," rather than the economic relations among these powers.[35] The Pax Britannica provided the security and political framework for the expansion of nineteenth-century transnational economic activity, while in the twentieth century the security arrangements and political ties that the United States has created with Western Europe through NATO as well the treaty arrangements it has with Japan have created a congenial political environment within which the United States could integrate economic factors of production across national boundaries through the medium of the multinational corporation. However, Gilpin warns, "just as a particular array of political interests and relations permitted this system of transnational economic relations to come into being, so changes in these political factors can profoundly alter the system and even bring it to an end." Since it is conceivable over time that Western Europe and Japan would arrive at different political and security alignments that would no longer tie them closely to the United States, or that the United States might retreat into isolationism, the resolution of the contradiction between the nation-state and transnational economic activities "may very well be in favor of the nation-state, or more likely, of regional arrangements centered on the dominant industrial powers: Japan, the United States, and Western Europe."[36] By the same token, of course, if the modifications in the political and security arrangements the United States has with its allies are not of sufficient magnitude to unhinge these essential connections, then the multinational enterprise, based not only in the United States but in other developed countries, will have considerable freedom to operate. In these circumstances, it is likely that the multinational enterprise will eventually prevail over the anachronistic structures of the nation-state, and new transnational economic and even political institutions will arise in their stead.

THE ORGANIZATION FOR ECONOMIC COOPERATION AND DEVELOPMENT

The intertwining of the economies of the advanced industrial states has already been recognized by the creation of a number of international organizations, of which the broadest is perhaps the Organization for Economic Cooperation and Development (OECD).[37] It, in turn, was an outgrowth of a recognition of the need to concert a broad range of economic policies among the European nations that were recipients of Marshall Plan aid and that joined together to form the 18-member Organization for European Economic Cooperation (OEEC). Within OEEC, procedures were devised for examining all aspects of the domestic economies of the European states which required harmonization in order to make most effective use both of American aid and of their own national economic resources. Each member country submitted a detailed statement on its economic status and policies in an annual review, which was subjected to careful scrutiny by its fellow members. This confrontation process took place in closed meetings where full and frank disclosures could avoid the embarrassment of publicity or needlessly dilate issues involving national prestige. It proved to be influential in shaping a variety of economic policies in their formative stages so that something like a European consensus frequently emerged.

By 1960 OEEC had lost much of its rationale. American aid had ended; indeed the dollar shortage in Europe had turned into a dollar deficit in the U.S. balance of payments. By 1958 the Europeans had achieved free convertibility of their currencies, and they then broke into two trading groups with the creation of the Six of the Common Market and the Seven of the European Free Trade Association (EFTA). Acting largely upon American initiative, the OEEC members agreed in December 1960 to a new convention by which they transformed themselves into the OECD. The United States and Canada had been associate members in the old organization and now became full members in the new one. Following the required ratifications, OECD began functioning in September 1961.

OECD not only broadened its scope from a European to an Atlantic body, but the "D" in its title denoted the new activity of development aid by the advanced industrial countries to the under-developed world. A Development Assistance Committee (DAC) was created to carry on this work. OECD's other activities, broadly speaking, were to foster the economic growth of its members and expand their world trade on a nondiscriminatory basis. Under these general rubrics, a panoply of committees and working parties was established to consider on a continuous basis such problems as balance-of-payments trends, economic policies relvant to growth such as cost and price stability, employment, restrictive business practices, the impact of science, and other related questions. All of these activities have been serviced by an impressive process of gathering and processing a huge flow of statistical material and detailed studies on the widest range of economic subjects.

The Atlantic nature of OECD was modified somewhat when Japan, which had already participated in DAC, became a full member of OECD in 1964. This was followed by the accession to full membership of Finland in 1969, which had previously taken part in certain selected activities, and of Australia in 1971, which had previously maintained a membership in DAC. In 1973 New Zealand became an OECD member. (In addition, Yugoslavia has maintained a special limited status in several OECD bodies.) OECD remains an expression of the basic economic concerns of the Atlantic Community insofar as the core of highly industrialized nations of the non-Communist world is found in the North Atlantic basin. As other nations that are geographically removed from this core area, like Japan, have achieved the industrialized status so as to share these common concerns and are able to contribute to the work of OECD, it is entirely logical that they should also participate in its activities.

The OECD members, after all, still constitute a relatively cohesive and unique group of the developed nations in the world. Taken together they comprise only 20 percent of the world's population, yet they account for 64 percent of the world's industrial production, nearly 70 percent of world trade, and provide 90 percent of development aid. There is an urgent need for them to coordinate their policies on major questions like industrial and agricultural trade and the functioning of the international monetary system so as to avoid fratricidal trade wars or the collapse of confidence in monetary arrangements that could set off a disastrous chain reaction that would not only impoverish each of them but the rest of the world as well.

By now it should be clear that no industrialized country, even a powerful one like the United States, nor any economic area like the European Community can hope to solve its own economic problems at another's expense. Only through concerted policies and agreements can each member hope to sustain its own economic welfare. Furthermore, the affluent, developed countries cannot effectively help the poor, underdeveloped ones unless the OECD nations solve their own common economic problems. The fact remains that wealth is primarily generated by the mutual economic prosperity of the rich, and unless this prosperity is put on a firm footing of multilateral cooperation, the rich will not do much for the poor. Access to the flourishing markets of the OECD nations on the part of the developing ones, buttressed by unilateral tariff concessions to the poor, will prove more important in the long run than direct grants and loans, although these are important as well. Viewing such economic transactions, both among the rich as well as between the rich and the poor, one cannot escape the fundamental conclusion that all the economic processes of the world are inter-related and that no one problem can be solved in isolation.

OECD is founded upon the premise that there is a seamless web connecting all the economic problems of its members. It is further assumed that it is impossible to partition off domestic from foreign economic policies. The list of examples is as long as the topics constantly kept under consideration by the various OECD bodies. Interest rates that are higher in Europe than in the United States attract an outflow of dollars to Europe, exacerbating the U.S. balance-of-payments problem; the elimination of tariff barriers raises the importance of nontariff barriers, which are rooted in the fabric of the domestic economic structure of each member country; even efforts to control environmental pollution in one country cannot be safely undertaken without comparable efforts by its trading partners so that the country with the lowest environmental standards does not reap an unfair competitive advantage. In short, there cannot be effective harmonization of foreign economic policies without adjustments in domestic economic policies.

In order to pursue these complex tasks OECD has retained the methods of work that were used with such success by its predecessor, OEEC. Formally, OEEC might have been viewed simply as a permanent intergovernmental conference that could only take binding action by unanimity. In practice, it often proved able to work out a consensus on policy, or at least an acceptable compromise, by focusing attention on elements of national policy making in their formative stages through the mechanism of policy confrontation. The OECD charter is even weaker than that of OEEC, since in deference to the sensitivities of the U.S. Senate any reference to binding decisions, even by unanimity, was omitted. Moreover, OEEC yielded more spectacular results since it was concerned with the urgent problems of economic recovery in Europe, whereas OECD represents wider, less coherent membership with a broader scope of global economic concerns. In this sense a strict comparison between the achievements of the two organizations must be somewhat unfair.

Taking these differences into account, one must acknowledge that a great deal of useful work has been accomplished in OECD, in large measure by reliance upon the confrontation process. This involves both the periodic critical examination of the national economic situation and policies of a member nation by its partners and the personal confrontation of senior policy makers with their counterparts from the various national capitals who are frequently brought together to supplement the continual contact of the Permanent Representatives and their staffs in the many OECD committees. It is generally conceded that such mutual scrutiny of each other's problems and plans as well as the evident formation of a fraternal bond among the various national elites who are responsible for the execution of policy have had a perceptible influence on the way in which national policies are formulated and implemented. National policy making is not only viewed within the traditional national frame of reference, but also in terms of the impact such policies will have upon other member countries. If a state finds support for its policies it may proceed with greater confidence than otherwise; if it does not accept the admonition and advice of its partners, at least it has foreknowledge of the probable risks and consequences it will encounter by pursuing an independent policy. Often a discordant policy can be modified in a national capital by the weight of reasoned opinion that is brought to bear by the views expressed in an OECD forum, especially if some national policy makers are convinced of the validity of such criticism and are seeking justification for a change of policy. Accommodation is always facilitated by the confidential nature of the consultations among decision makers, who are not required to make changes in their views in the glare of a public spotlight. Frequent, private consultation on different policy approaches still in the making is infinitely more useful than infrequent, widely publicized meetings on decisions already frozen at the national level and therefore very difficult to modify.

Upon the creation of OECD, the Kennedy administration sought to enhance its effectiveness by the consistent dispatch of delegations that included key officials in the Treasury and State Departments as well as members of the Federal Reserve System and the President's Council of Economic Advisers, among others. After several years of such experience, Assistant Secretary of State for European Affairs William Tyler spoke approvingly of OECD's work that had produced "increasingly frank consultation and close collaboration on matters of economic growth, fiscal and monetary policy, and balance of payments. The consultative process has made it possible to compare alternative approaches to common problems and to explore the interaction of programs and expectations in different countries. It has yielded sharpened awareness of the international impact of domestic policy and of means for insulating others from possible adverse effects of change in policy."[38] The fact that busy officials of the cabinet and subcabinet level have continued to travel steadily to such "club" meetings, not only from the United States but from other member countries as well, is testimony to the contribution

OECD has made to the economic cooperation among the non-Communist, industrialized states of the world.

One should not, of course, overstate the potential of a body whose mandate is limited to consultation, no matter how wide the range of problems it surveys. It would be infinitely more effective if it were also capable of reaching binding decisions based on some sort of majority voting and then had some executive function for implementing agreed policy. But such a structure, however desirable, seems beyond reach for the foreseeable future. For the moment, OECD, like NATO, is reliant upon policy harmonization, which is always difficult in a collection of sovereign states. Since concerted action is dependent upon the voluntary consent of its members, in theory any one member could paralyze the functioning of the group by its veto. In the actual procedures of both organization, however, there is considerable flexibility in conducting business and the veto is seldom used. As is the case in NATO, various activities are often undertaken by partial agreement among those who are willing to move ahead on a given program. OECD in particular retained the practice inherited from OEEC that a member may abstain from a specific undertaking so that the action taken by others would not apply to it. When broader agreement is required, OECD tends to proceed with caution. Before a formal meeting is held, a recalcitrant state often has pressure brought to bear on it by a variety of officials who may persuade it to abandon or modify its position of isolation. If this cannot be done, the matter is likely to be postponed until further pressures can be built up so as to make the problem ripe for reconsideration and the unanimous adoption of a solution. Furthermore, unanimous agreement may be possible in principle on a certain topic, but it may not be possible for all states to implement the agreement in the same way or at the same time. Here states enter "reserves" noting their inability to fulfill an agreement in all respects. These reserves either have a time limit to them or are stated in terms of lifting them "as soon as possible." The international staff conducts periodic surveys to see if the reserves are still justified or if they should be ended, and this serves as a further prod to full implementation of an agreement. In this way the unanimity principle permits all states to partake in undertakings as they are able to do so.

OECD has also shown itself capable of modifying its structure to conform to new functions as the need arose. For example, although the expansion of world trade was one of the principal aims set forth in Article 1 of the OECD convention, it was deliberately played down during the initial years of OECD's existence, due to fears in the U.S. Congress that this might infringe upon American legislative prerogatives, as well as the American view that trade matters should be pursued primarily through the negotiating forum of the General Agreement on Tariffs and Trade (GATT). However, the pressing need to coordinate trade policies soon changed the American attitude. A decade after OECD's founding it was recognized that the world trade situation no longer conformed to the GATT image of an economically powerful United States and a congeries of other states. Instead, the European Community and Japan played as important roles as the United States, and all three faced the prospect of potentially disastrous conflicts in their trade policies. Consequently, at a Ministerial meeting of the OECD Council in June 1971 Secretary of State William Rogers strongly endorsed a proposal by the Secretary General of OECD for the creation of a High Level Group on Trade and Related Problems, which could provide a select consultative body that could deliberate upon this urgent problem. The prompt adoption of this proposal by OECD showed the manner in which the organization could assume new responsibilities. Further evolution of OECD can reasonably be expected as new tasks arise.

While it would be a mistake to inflate the capabilities of OECD in solving the delicate and complex tasks under its jurisdiction, neither should one dismiss its promise. "The potential uses of the OECD," Henry Aubrey aptly judged, "range from consultations to avoid mutual harm to a joint search for a more common political will; from a better application of agreed principles in actual practice to the conception of new and concerted policies leading to parallel action if joint action is not yet politically feasible; from the crystallization of a felt need for the better use of scarce resources (such as aid or credit) to coordination and harmonization of broad national policies which remain de jure autonomous, yet are de facto becoming increasingly interdependent."[39]

Movement toward a de jure interdependence is a matter that cannot be safely predicted. Moreover, the forces pushing in this direction are broader and more deeply rooted than the formal organizational life of OECD. In the interim, it is still possible to envision a number of limited steps of an evolutionary nature that could make OECD a more useful forum.

OECD's Secretariat has the ability to propose ideas, although it does not have the powers of initiative nor the planning functions entrusted to the Commission of the European Community. While it would be unrealistic to expect the OECD Secretariat to be given those powers in the near future, it could be expected to assume a more positive leadership role similar to that exercised by the OEEC Secretariat. It was widely recognized that the OEEC international civil servants exerted greater influence over the events in that organization than did a similar group in OECD in the beginning years of that body, due in part to the change in personnel in the Secretariat and in part to its enlarged and more diffuse membership. Yet there is good reason to believe that with the appointment of Emile van Lennep as OECD Secretary General in 1969 the possibility exists for the creation of a more forceful Secretariat. This writer was assured by members of several delegations, including the American one, that as the Secretariat proved itself increasingly competent to handle more tasks, there would be a willingness to turn more responsibilities over to it. This, in turn, could build confidence and lead to a further expansion of the Secretariat's scope of influence. National sovereignty will not likely be renounced in a dramatic gesture, but it might be expected to be eroded gradually by the inherent logic of an intertwining relationship. The potential value of OECD is considerable, since the breadth of its subject matter plus its relatively limited membership opens the way toward harmonization of the foreign economic policies of the major industrialized nations of the free world.

Since OECD has such a comprehensive competence, a number of its functions are also pursued in other organizational forums. Thus discussion of trade policies in OECD has been accompanied by trade negotiations primarily among the developed nations within GATT, while a dialogue on trade problems between the developed and developing nations has been conducted within the United Nations Conference on Trade and Development (UNCTAD). In the area of international monetary policy and development aid, OECD has shared its concerns with a variety of bodies, often with a large measure of overlapping membership. Such proliferation of international organizations may appear wasteful, but it would seem to be inevitable when the tasks are so broad and complex, and it may even be useful when adequate coordination is maintained among different groups that seek to attack the same problem from different perspectives. The one conclusion that emerges from an examination of the major problem areas is that success in formulating solutions depends in each instance upon the joint efforts of the advanced industrialized nations, whose core is found in the Atlantic Community.

INSTITUTIONS OF THE INTERNATIONAL MONETARY SYSTEM

The groups entrusted with the supervision of the international monetary system are clearly built around this core area. The Bretton Woods agreement that established the International Monetary Fund (IMF) was drawn up by the principal non-Communist industrial nations in 1944. While it has nearly universal membership, aside from the Communist states, its Executive Directors and its weighted voting system reflect the reality that decisive power in monetary affairs was traditionally concentrated in the hands of a few nations around the North Atlantic basin, plus Japan. The IMF provides a pool of funds that can be lent to deficit countries for their medium-term needs, usually on a three- to five-year basis. In addition, the able leadership first provided by the IMF management under Per Jacobson and his staff, and maintained by their successors, has made it a respected source of analysis and advice on international monetary problems. Studies sponsored by the IMF are read with great care in all the financial capitals of the world, and the annual meetings of the governors of the IMF are faithfully attended by financial officials of cabinet rank. This reflects the deeply ingrained habits of cooperation and the feelings of fraternity that have grown up in the non-Communist financial community since the founding of the IMF, and it is tangible recognition of the economic and financial interdependence of the IMF members who are determined not to revert to the disastrous go-it-alone, beggar-my-neighbor policies that characterized the 1930s.

In a number of respects the IMF did not operate as originally envisioned, nor did its rules provide adequate answers to the classic monetary problems of confidence, liquidity, and adjustment. Consequently, monetary experts from the leading financial powers devised a bewildering array of expedients to bolster the international monetary system. A network of ingenious multilateral and bilateral agreements for increased credit facilities, greater liquidity, and better protection for the mediums of international exchange (gold, the dollar, and the pound) were forthcoming, almost always in response to some actual or threatened monetary crisis. While these schemes reflected the ingenuity of their inventors, they also inadvertently reflected the fragility of the international monetary system and the need to continue the intimate collaboration of its collective managers so that the system might function on a durable basis over the long haul.

A few instances of recent monetary innovations will suffice to demonstrate the growing trend of collaboration among the key countries to overcome the crises that could shatter their delicate monetary mechanisms.

The normal capital resources of the IMF available for lending were increased by more than 50 percent in 1959. Still faced with the threat that the IMF would run short of funds, a further $6 billion of standby credits were negotiated in 1961-62 among the newly formed Group of Ten.[40] Though the Group of Ten came into being as a special lending facility for the IMF, it soon developed a life and identity of its own, quite independent of the larger organization that it was designed to serve. The membership of the Group of Ten was revealing, since it was virtually identical with that of Working Party Three of OECD. The latter is the inner group in OECD, consisting of high-level officials from the central banks and finance ministries, that was originally charged with constantly surveying the balance-of-payments problem, although it later extended its purview to other related areas. Both bodies had as members Britain, Canada, France, Germany, Italy, Japan, the Netherlands, Sweden, and the United States. Belgium belong to the Group of Ten, but not Working Party Three. Switzerland was a full member of Working Party Three, but only an associate member of the Group of Ten, since Switzerland was not a member of the IMF. The financial strength of the Group of Ten was reflected in the fact that it held about 80 percent of the world's reserves of gold and foreign exchange, and with Switzerland added it represented an even greater proportion of the world's wealth. The fate of the international monetary system therefore rested in these relatively few hands, and the joint action of these states would obviously prove decisive on any issue.

In October 1963 the Group of Ten turned its attention to the liquidity problem.[41] The world needed a dependable and orderly way of providing the additional cash resources required for financing the growing volume of world trade and for settling other international transactions. Yet the availability of reserves for these purposes depended upon a number of haphazard factors: the accidental discoveries of gold, the dollars or pounds temporarily held abroad (in large measure because of U.S. payments deficit or the precarious British balance-of-payments situation), and finally the crisis financing for various countries having payment difficulties through special credit lines. During the 1960s the single greatest factor pumping liquidity into the international monetary pipeline was the dollar that resulted from the U.S. balance-of-payments deficit. All parties agreed that this condition should be corrected, and yet it was evident that if the United States brought its balance of payments into equilibrium there would necessarily be a drastic shortage of liquidity.

Consequently the Group of Ten and later the Executive Directors of the IMF commissioned studies on the liquidity problem. For half a dozen years, from 1963 through 1969, the major financial powers engaged in a series of complicated and delicate negotiations that involved not only the technical monetary aspects of the problem but also the profoundly political questions that are necessarily attached to the creation of international money. These negotiations succeeded in producing agreement on the so-called Special Drawing Rights (SDRs), which permitted the deliberate creation of a centralized reserve asset in the form of internationally guaranteed claims on the IMF that could be accepted and used by all countries in their balance-of-payments settlements.[42] On January 1, 1970 the IMF created its first issue of $3.4 billion of SDRs, and further installments of SDRs have been placed into circulation since then. The conscious and systematic creation of this international money, sometimes referred to as "paper gold," represented a decisive advance in bringing stability into the international monetary system. It was also evidence of the ability of the major powers to surmount their differences for the common good, since the creation of SDRs requires a multilateral decision.

Cooperative arrangements in the Atlantic monetary community have also developed in the forum of the Bank for International Settlements (BIS) in Basel. Founded in 1930 by European central banks to manage the financial transactions involved in German reparations payments, it evolved in the post-World War II era into a major center of intimate and intricate financial dealings. The United States became associated when its Federal Reserve System assumed observer status, since the Federal Reserve was not strictly speaking a central bank in the European sense. For all practical purposes, however, U.S. participation has amounted to that of a full member. The members of this exclusive club remain in contact with each other almost daily by phone inside Europe and across the Atlantic, and once a month the governors of the central banks or their high-ranking associates meet in person at Basel to conduct their negotiations in an atmosphere of complete secrecy so as to preserve confidence in their sensitive dealings. The world only gets a glimpse of BIS activities at its annual meeting, when certain public business is transacted and its highly respected annual report on the state of the world's finances is issued.

Over the years BIS has performed a number of valuable functions. Its statistical research on monetary matters has been the basis for discussions both in the Group of Ten and Working Party Three of OECD. In such matters as the financing of surpluses and deficits in international accounts, the three organizations formed close functional links.[43] This was logical in view of their nearly identical membership and concern with the same set of problems. The BIS has also extended loans to central banks, settled debts, bought and sold gold, and acted to stabilize financial markets, as for example when it has sought to relieve strains in the markets for foreign-held dollars in Europe by its intervention in the so-called Eurodollar market.[44] Among its noteworthy contributions was the Basel Agreement of March 1961, which was used on a number of occasions thereafter to rescue the pound when large speculative funds flowed out of Britain. Under this agreement the central bankers extended short-term emergency loans to Britain until it could mobilize its second line of defense by drawings upon the IMF. Such action was important not only for Britain but for all countries that held sterling as a reserve currency.

The BIS likewise became the center for the multilateral supervision of a network of bilateral currency "swaps" among its members.* Swaps consist of reciprocal credit lines extended between central banks, and between central banks and the BIS, that take the

---

*A report of the Group of Ten issued in August 1964 stated that the BIS would henceforth institute a system of "multilateral surveillance" of the various bilateral swaps. While group permission was not required before negotiating swaps, all bilateral transactions would be reported to the BIS, and their impact on balance-of-payments situations would be discussed within the BIS.[45]

form of a mutual exchange of currencies for the purpose of combating short-term speculative attacks on any one of the currencies involved. In the case of the dollar, swaps have also provided a temporary alternative to the enlargement of dollar holdings abroad beyond the point that conversion into gold would have been likely. Swap agreements, which can be activated almost instantly, generally run for limited periods of three to six months, although they have been made renewable by mutual consent. The huge amounts of currency involved in these deals since their inception has testified to their usefulness. In 1962-63 the United States initiated swap agreements with the central banks of the countries found in the Group of Ten and Working Party Three, plus Austria and the BIS itself.[46] The United States supplemented swaps by issuing Treasury securities of various redemption periods that were denominated in foreign currencies. This was a way of protecting the dollar and enhancing the balance-of-payments position by borrowing abroad in a country's own currency instead of dollars. (These were the so-called Roosa bonds, named after their originator, Under Secretary of the Treasury Robert V. Roosa.)

The BIS was also involved in the creation of the "gold pool." A sudden rush on the London gold market in the fall of 1960 sent the price of gold soaring and frightened the central banks of the West into joining together to subscribe agreed quotas of gold to a common fund in order to stabilize its price. The eight members of the gold pool again formed a familiar group: Belgium, Britain, France, Germany, Italy, the Netherlands, Switzerland, and the United States. The pool officially came into existence in 1961 and was managed in London by the Bank of England. For six years its operation sought to control price fluctuations by offering gold to the open market in periods of demand and purchasing gold for distribution to its members in slack periods. The pool also discouraged the accumulation of gold hoards in the hands of private speculators by channeling a maximum flow of newly produced gold into the official reserves of the gold-pool members. But this arrangement proved insufficient to prevent a determined run on gold by speculators, which began in the fall of 1967. Within a short six-month period, from October 1967 to March 1968, the pool lost $3.7 billion worth of gold and there was no end in sight.[47] The monetary authorities of the gold pool gathered in Washington for an emergency meeting on March 17 and shut off the hemorrhage by a tour de force that divided the gold market into a two-tier arrangement. It was agreed to sever the connection between the private and official gold markets by stopping all trading in gold in the private market and by pledging that gold sales among central banks would remain at $35 per ounce regardless of the free market price. This effectively ended the wild specualtion by private traders and their indirect access to the U.S. gold stock, while perserving, at least in theory, the official connection between gold and the dollar. The gold pool thereupon ceased operation.

The gold rush of March 1968 illustrated once again how precariously the international monetary system is based and how dependent it is on a variety of strategms and palliatives in order to keep it functioning. While the decision to create SDRs is doubtless a major step of lasting importance in meeting one of the basic needs of the system, the other measures reviewed above have, in effect, comprised a patchwork of stopgap measures that have shored up the system's perimeter defenses so as to avoid its collapse. The long-range task of constructing the central core of a stable monetary system remains to be built. This will be complicated but imperative, and there is no question but that this will require the willing cooperation of the principal members of the monetary community who were embodied in the Group of Ten.

DE GAULLE'S "GOLD WAR AGAINST THE ANGLO-SAXONS"

Even concerting policies among the Ten on the various expedients described frequently found Gaullist France as odd man out. Such a stubbornly held position of isolation was de Gaulle's monetary counterpart to his political offensive against NATO or his determined exclusion of Britain from the Common Market. In retrospect it is surprising that it took de Gaulle so long to launch "the gold war against the Anglo-Saxons."[48] Perhaps this can be accounted for by the esoteric nature of monetary affairs as well as de Gaulle's general disdain for economics.*

---

*It might be argued that de Gaulle was interested in economics since he used economic arguments to keep Britain out of the EEC. Again in retrospect it should be clear that this exclusion was primarily a matter of politics, not economics. In the absence of political will to make the needed accommodation, de Gaulle made use of economic pretexts to disguise his political animus.

It was not until the beginning of 1965 that de Gaulle openly sought to undermine the status of the dollar and the pound as reserve currencies by insisting that the world return to a pure gold standard as the sole medium of international exchange. In his press conference of February 4, 1965, de Gaulle extolled the pre-World War II dependence on gold. "We consider that international exchanges must be established, as was the case before the great world wide disasters, on an unquestionable monetary basis which does not bear the mark of any individual country. What basis? Actually it is difficult to envision in this regard any other criterion, any other standard than gold. Yes, gold, which does not change in nature, which can be made either into bars, ingots or coins, which has no nationality, which is considered in all places and at all times the immutable and fiduciary value par excellence."[49] De Gaulle's attachment to gold was one of those turn-of-the-century verities that he had imbibed in the formative years of his education and which, like his exaggerated sense of national glory, he never outgrew or abandoned.

This led France to begin converting all of its new dollar assets into gold as of January 1, 1965. It also stepped up its regular monthly purchases of gold that were begun the previous year and which continued until October 1966, when 88 percent of French reserves consisted of gold.[50] (It was found that a small cash cushion of dollars was still required for some transactions). The French taxpayer may not have been aware of the cost of this campaign that was undertaken for reasons of high politics, since the most unproductive possible way to hold reserves is by storing gold. Ordinarily reserves held in dollars are invested in interest-bearing securities, whereas gold is a sterile metal that pays no interest.* In addition, when nations convert dollars into gold they generally leave the gold in their vaults in the Federal Reserve Bank of New York, whereas de Gaulle decreed that French gold be transported back to Paris. This consideration of

---

*It was estimated, for example, that if France converted $500 million of its dollars to gold in 1965, it would cost the French treasury $18.4 million in lost investment revenue for 1965 alone. Over time the loss would be much greater, of course, since this sum represented only a fraction of French gold holdings, and such interest would be lost each year that France continued to hold substantial reserves in gold.[51]

prestige added the needless costs of gold shipping and insurance to his conversion policy.[52] Such dramatic acts were undertaken with the hope that other central banks would follow suit and that depleting the U.S. gold reserves would cause a devaluation of the dollar and a consequent shattering of the leading position of the United States in the world monetary system.

But de Gaulle's initiatives did not cause a stampede in imitation. The alternatives of returning to a pure gold standard were singularly unappealing. One could either propose transacting business in gold at its present value, with the certain result of a catastrophic shrinkage in international liquidity and a crushing squeeze on the world economy, or one could create adequate liquidity by doubling, or perhaps tripling, the price of gold. The latter course, however, would have had very uneven results. At one stroke, countries like France that held a high proportion of their reserves in gold would suddenly double or trible the worth of their reserves, while countries that loyally stuck by the dollar, like Germany and Japan, would be severely penalized and would doubtless ask the United States to transfer gold to them in order to compensate them for their past policy of holding dollars instead of gold. However the scenario would be played out, the U.S. gold stock would be quickly drained away, and there would be nothing to put in its place. But this was the prospect that de Gaulle anticipated with pleasure. There was the further consideration of giving special rewards to the principal gold mining countries, which happened to be South Africa and the Soviet Union.

De Gaulle's attack on the dollar also extended to the pound. While there were reports that the French did not like the 11-country credit package put together under the Basel Agreement in November 1964 to support the pound, France nevertheless participated in it. Once again it was in 1965 that an open change of policy occurred. When Britain was forced to return to its creditors in September 1965 for additional help, de Gaulle bluntly refused to join in. This did not prevent the other ten from helping Britain; it only highlighted the French position of isolation.[53] Similarly, when Britain devalued the pound in November 1967, France refused to join the other nations in the Basel club in extending short-term credits through their central banks. In the delicate negotiations that preceded British devaluation, France was also alone in refusing to give an assurance that it would not devalue its currency. If France had devalued as well this most likely would have set off a chain reaction of devaluation on the continent and have wiped out the gains of the British move.[54]

Gaullist obstructionism also extended to the workings of the gold pool that was set up in 1961 to control speculation in gold. France opened its offensive by renouncing its subscription to the gold pool in June 1967. (The United States picked up the French quota.) The ensuing months of mounting gold speculation were marked by a consistent pattern of inspired leaks from the French Treasury to *Le Monde*, in which confidential conversations among governments about highly sensitive monetary matters were always given the most disruptive possible interpretations. As a result, when the gold pool members met in emergency session in March 1968, the French were not invited since there was no assurance that the confidential nature of the talks would be respected. France need not have been invited, of course, since it had already dropped out of the gold pool, yet some wished to include the French as a matter of courtesy, since parallel negotiations on the creation of the SDRs were then in the final stages and French cooperation in monetary matters was still being sought.

Just prior to the decisive gold pool meeting of March 17, 1968, all European gold markets were closed down, with the exception of Paris. The Bank of France was officially instructed to keep the gold market open in the hopes of fostering the wild speculation then in progress and through it attacking the dollar and complicating a decision for the gold-pool members. In Washington the gold pool reached several important decisions. On the one hand, there was the formation of the two-tier gold system previously noted, which ended government intervention in the private market and so tamped down private speculation in gold. On the other hand, a quiet understanding of even greater importance was concluded among the governments to the effect that in their official dealings they would no longer threaten the dwindling U.S. gold stock by demanding the exchange of substantial quantities of dollars for gold.[55] Disbanding the gold pool thereby both reduced the incentive for speculation in gold in the private market and effectively demonitized gold as an official medium for exchange among central banks. France was naturally not bound by this agreement and so remained the sole major financial power that continued to convert large-scale dollar holdings into gold. The sweep of events thus moved in precisely the opposite direction from that set out by de Gaulle: Instead of a return of the gold standard there was a dramatically decreasing reliance upon the use of gold for any monetary purpose.*

The use of "paper gold" in the form of SDRs as an additional substitute for metallic gold was likewise anathema to de Gaulle. When the negotiations on the liquidity problem began in 1963, the French Minister of Finance, Valery Giscard d'Estaing, advanced his version of a proposal for a composite reserve unit (CRU) as a way of creating international liquidity. As he envisioned it, the CRU would join gold but replace the dollar and the pound as a new major reserve unit. But de Gaulle's personal intervention into the monetary debate with his pronouncement of February 1965 obliged Giscard d'Estaing to repudiate his own proposal, since de Gaulle insisted upon nothing less than reversion to the nineteenth-century gold standard.[56] From that point on, as Stephen Cohen, a careful chronicler of the SDR negotiations, noted: "The French preoccupation with gold and their repetitious attempts to force the rest of the Group of Ten and the IMF, against their wills, to consider changing the role and price of gold as a means of 'reforming' the gold-exchange standard, produced a state of near-total isolation of the French in the monetary reform talks."[57]

The essential decision to implement the SDR proposal was taken at Stockholm in March 1968 by the ministers of the Group of Ten. Here a confrontation occurred between France, which withheld its assent, and the other nine that proceeded without France to subscribe to the final agreement. In an effort to placate de Gaulle, an opting-out procedure was written in the agreement, as well as an opting-in clause, should the French later decide to join, as in fact they eventually did. Also as a concession to France, a provision was inserted that permitted a country to refuse to finance a predetermined portion of SDRs. Finally, de Gaulle had been trying to mobilize the

----

*The two-tier gold system of March 1968 became obsolete when the United States abandoned the convertibility of dollars into gold in August 1971. Finally, in November 1973 the 1968 agreement was formally buried when the participants of the agreement declared their willingness to sell officially held gold on the open market under conditions when the market price was above the official price, as had long been the case. Such reduced holdings of gold by central banks thus further demonitized gold.

Six of the Common Market against the "Anglo-Saxons," and so a voting procedure for creating SDRs was included that gave the EEC a veto if all members voted together. The United States had accepted the principle of Common Market unity on monetary matters, but it was de Gaulle who broke it. "France apparently had crossed a threshold which required its five partners to place national interests before community interests. Although the EEC had been endeavoring for well over a year to achieve a common position in the Group of Ten, the political pride and leverage associated with such unity could not in the end survive France's defiant determination to go it alone."[58]

French splendid isolation in monetary matters quickly proved to be rather unsplendid. The upheaval of the May-June 1968 "events" in France demonstrated how meaningless it was for de Gaulle to store huge amounts of gold. The political riots, general strike, and subsequent wage increases shook the French economy to its foundations and gravely weakened confidence in the franc. The brittle state of the economy was in part due to de Gaulle's obsession with hoarding gold, since the price of its accumulation was a substantial lowering of the annual economic growth rate, with expenditures on goods and services that might have been distributed to the French people going instead to the United States in exchange for gold.

In order to meet a massive attack on the franc, de Gaulle was obliged to sell large quantities of gold for hard currencies, chiefly dollars. The dollar was the world's intervention currency, and it was the dollar that de Gaulle needed to support the price of the franc.[59] In addition, de Gaulle was forced to seek the cooperation of the same major monetary powers that he had just rebuffed in the recently concluded negotiations over the gold pool and SDRs. In July 1968 France obtained short-term credits of $1.3 billion in the form of swaps with the U.S. Federal Reserve Bank and several European central banks. Then in November the Group of Ten extended France a $2 billion loan package, the largest component of which was furnished by the United States and Germany. American concern about the fragile and interdependent nature of the whole monetary system properly came before pique over past Gaullist policy toward the United States. By the end of November 1968, French reserves, which had amounted to more than $6 billion before the May-June upheaval, had decreased by 50 percent.[60] Chastened by these events, de Gaulle was not in a position to return to his frontal attack on the dollar, and soon thereafter he was out of power.

THE EFFECTS OF THE DOLLAR CRISIS ON
THE INTERNATIONAL MONETARY SYSTEM

Although the Gaullist version of an international monetary system lay in ruins, there was still no generally agreed, viable alternative to put in its place. The world remained on the dollar-gold exchange standard, but the position of the dollar was rapidly deteriorating.

The United States was confronted with an uncontrolled inflation stemming in good measure from the effects of monetary and fiscal management in paying for the costs of the Vietnam war. Beginning in 1969 there was also serious unemployment accompanied by a worsening position in foreign trade, where an overvalued dollar made U.S. exports uncompetitive. In addition, the U.S. balance-of-payments deficit, which had been chronic throughout the 1960s, suddenly began increasing to alarming proportions.

The crisis in the dollar developed from the existence of a huge pool of unwanted dollars in Europe, in the form of the Eurodollar market.* Eurodollars are essentially dollars that went to Europe and remained there because of the persistent U.S. balance-of-payments deficit. The single largest item in this capital outflow, although not often recognized by Europeans, undoubtedly arose from the military expenditures undertaken to fulfill America's NATO commitment. The balance-of-payments figures show that from 1955 through 1970 the United States lost nearly $26 billion on its military balance-of-payments account with Europe, and even after deducting offsetting European military purchases from the United States, the net deficit

---

*Eurodollars are stateless in the sense that they do not show up in the reported money supply of any country. They are thus a transnational currency that has expanded beyond the reach of the nation-state system. In this respect they have much in common with the multinational corporation, which makes abundant use of Eurodollars both for short-term money flows and for longer-term borrowing.

for this period was still about $19 billion. Since one must assume that such a sum created approximately an equal amount of credit, U.S. military expenditures in Europe had created a pool of nearly $40 billion, which accounted for the bulk of the estimated $50 billion Eurodollars at the time of the 1971 crisis.[61]

By 1971 Europe was surfeited with dollars coming from the flow of short-term capital that had been attracted to Europe by high interest rates. The temptation was strong to cash in these surplus dollars for gold, and to a limited extent this took place. But the basic fact became apparent to all that the U.S. gold stock could not possibly cover the potential claims against it. Dollars then held by foreign governments were about three times higher than the U.S. gold reserves, and in Germany where the crisis was most acute the Bundesbank alone owned more dollars than there was gold in Fort Knox. The assumption that the dollar was "as good as gold" was obviously hollow.

In May 1971 speculators bet on the revaluation of the mark, and the inflow of "hot" money into Germany accelerated. After trying to support the fixed parity of the mark to the dollar through huge Bundesbank purchases of the dollar, Germany was forced to cut the mark loose so that it could float upward. The Dutch also floated their currency, while the Austrian and Swiss currencies were upvalued at one stroke.

It was in this setting that President Nixon on August 15, 1971 suspended the dollar's convertibility into gold and other reserve assets and conceded a de facto devaluation of the dollar by permitting it to float downward in relation to other currencies. He also announced several protectionist measures, such as a 10 percent surcharge on all imports and an intensified "buy America" policy. The European exchange markets responded by closing for a week, and when they reopened on August 23, Austria, Belgium, Denmark, Italy, and Britain joined Germany and the Netherlands in floating their currencies against the dollar. France adopted a two-tier exchange market in which only one part was allowed to float.

It might be argued that Nixon's unilateral actions were justified by the circumstances, but the manner in which his administration proceeded struck a heavy blow at all of the cooperative practices and principles that had so carefully been built up the international monetary community since Bretton Woods. For the first time since the end of World War II the United States abandoned multilateral negotiations to correct its monetary and trade problems in favor of unilateral edicts. One had the uncomfortable feeling of witnessing American Gaullism. De Gaulle's brand of nationalism was characterized by unilateralism, tactical surprise, and treating one's ally as an enemy. Nixon, who had often expressed his admiration for de Gaulle, now employed these weapons from the Gaullist armory. American Gaullism during this period was expressed most acutely by John Connally who, as Secretary of the Treasury, was entrusted with leading the United States in international negotiations on the monetary front. Connally is said to have described himself, accurately in this case, as "the bully boy on the manicured playing fields of international high finance."[62]

The bitter, adversary-type negotiations in the fall of 1971 culminated in the Smithsonian Agreement of December 18, in which the leading monetary powers sought to repeg their parities in a multilateral realignment of currencies. The dollar was now devalued de jure an average of about 10 percent against European currencies and 15 percent against the yen. The United States promised to devalue the dollar against gold and to phase out the protectionist measures taken in August. All parties also agreed on the urgent need to reform the entire international monetary system. Nixon hailed this achievement as "the most significant monetary agreement in the history of the world."[63] but his enthusiasm was misplaced. Only six months later, in June 1972, Britain could no longer sustain the parities fixed by the Smithsonian Agreement and so floated the pound once again. Then after another six months, in January 1973, the Swiss were forced to float their franc rather than support the dollar against the pressure of speculators. The dollar itself was next subjected to a significant change when on February 13, 1973, the United States, in agreement with its principal monetary partners, again devalued the dollar by 10 percent against European currencies. The dollar was also again devalued in terms of gold. At this point Japan floated the yen against the dollar. The Smithsonian Agreement was obviously finished.

The international monetary crisis, however, was not. A month later, on March 12, 1973, six of the European Community currencies (all except Britain, Ireland, and Italy) announced that they would jointly float against the outside world. This brought about the float of the dollar once again, with the announcement that the U.S. Treasury stood prepared to intervene in the money markets to support the dollar only on a flexible, ad hoc basis. Thus by the spring of 1973 all of the major currencies of the world were floating against each other.

THE GROUP OF TEN AND THE
COMMITTEE OF TWENTY

Efforts to reform the international monetary system had meanwhile been set in motion. Secretary Connally expressed his displeasure at the Group of Ten as the forum for these deliberations since he noted that in the negotiations that led to the Smithsonian Agreement the voting was all too often nine against the United States. He therefore suggested some new forum containing from 12 to 20 states.[64] After toying with several suggestions, it was finally agreed that a Ministerial-level Committee of Twenty of the Board of Governors of the IMF be appointed to conduct the negotiations on monetary reform. The Group of Ten was not disbanded under this new arrangement however, since the Committee of Twenty consisted of the Group of Ten plus Australia and nine developing nations. The Finance Minister of Indonesia, Ali Wardhana, was made Chairman, but the Committee selected as head of the group of deputies, where the real spadework would be done, Jeremy Morse of the Bank of England. The Committee of Twenty was convened for the first time in September 1972 in connection with the annual assembly of the IMF Governors.[65] It was envisaged that its work in redesigning the international monetary system would take about two years. In fact the Committee of Twenty delivered its final report in June 1974, after which it ceased functioning.

Even after the Committee of Twenty had begun its work, however, the old Group of Ten continued to operate, although in a slightly modified form. During the monetary upheaval of March 1973, for example, 14 Finance Ministers and central-bank Governors met and issued two statements that were intended to reopen the money markets under orderly conditions.[66] This assemblage represented the old Group of Ten, plus Switzerland, which had always participated as an observer, and as a gesture toward European solidarity, the three small states of the enlarged European Community, Denmark, Ireland, and Luxembourg, which had previously not taken part in such meetings. Finance Minister Wardhana of Indonesia was also invited as an observer representing the Committee of Twenty. Thus the real locus of monetary power as represented in the Group of Ten continued to assert itself.

U.S. Secretary of the Treasury George Shultz, who had meanwhile replaced John Connally, told the annual meeting of the

IMF Governors in September 1973 that in the future the IMF "should have available a forum of workable size . . . at which responsible national officials can speak and negotiate with both flexibility and authority." This might be achieved, he suggested, "by keeping in being a streamlined Committee of Twenty."[67] It was his view that 20 was too large a body for effective negotiation. However, the pressure for representation in such a forum was sufficiently great that it proved impossible to reduce its membership. Consequently, when the Committee of Twenty was dissolved, it was succeeded by a Council of the Board of Governors of the IMF with a membership of 20 Finance Ministers, who in turn represented all of the member countries of the IMF. The mandate of the new, permanent Council was to advise the Board of Governors in supervising the management and adaptation of the international monetary system in light of the recommendations for reform proposed by the Committee of Twenty.

OUTLINE OF A REFORMED INTERNATIONAL MONETARY SYSTEM

A consensus gradually emerged from the deliberations of the Committee of Twenty on some key issues. The liquidity problem had basically been resolved during the debates of the 1960s, which ended with the agreement to create SDRs. Perhaps relabeled so as to reflect more accurately its function as "paper gold," the "SDR will become the principal reserve asset" while the "role of gold and reserve currencies will be reduced." In accordance with its increased importance, it was further agreed that "the SDR will also be the numeraire in terms of which par values will be expressed."[68]

The value of the SDR would no longer be related to the price of gold,* and its dependence upon the dollar was greatly reduced. It was

---

*In an action coincident with the final report of the Committee of Twenty, the Group of Ten agreed that gold could be used as collateral for loans at a price agreed upon between the lender and the borrower. Such a price would clearly be far beyond the unrealistic official price of gold. While this action was helpful to nations with large gold stocks which were in balance-of-payments difficulties, it did not restore gold to its former central position in the world monetary system.[69]

decided to compute the value of the SDR daily on the basis of the market value of a "basket" of 16 national currencies. In making this calculation each national currency was alloted a different weight. Thus the U.S. dollar, though no longer the sole determinant, was still given the single greatest weight since its value accounted for one-third of the value of the 16-nation composite. In order to make the SDR a more attractive asset, it was also given a higher interest rate, which would fluctuate over time.[70]

There was no agreed solution to the adjustment problem, that is, the process whereby countries correct their imbalance of payments by adjusting the value of their currency relative to one another. Bretton Woods made the problem of adjusting the U.S. payments imbalance unique, since under it all currencies were tied to the value of the dollar, which, as the linchpin of the entire international monetary system, could not be changed through devaluation. This arrangement ultimately became untenable and was buried when the dollar's tie to gold was broken and the dollar was allowed to float in August 1971. It was agreed that in the future the United States would have the possibility of changing the parity of its currency in the same way as other countries. The dollar would undoubtedly retain an important position, perhaps as the chief vehicle currency for the conduct of international trade and as the chief intervention currency, but otherwise it would play a far less central role than it had before. Moreover at some point in time there would be a return to the convertibility of one reserve asset into another.

There was considerable disagreement within the Committee of Twenty on how the adjustment mechanism should operate in the future. One school of thought, led by the French, insisted upon the return to a system of fixed parities.* It was acknowledged that when changes in valuation would be made there should be procedures for making small, timely, and appropriate changes in exchange rates instead of the old system where adjustments came in jolts because the changes in valuation were large and generally long overdue. This situation also encouraged speculation and "hot money" flows.

----

*France did not practice what it preached, however, since on January 19, 1974 it cut the franc loose from the joint currency "snake" of six members of the European Community and let the franc float by itself. This was done abruptly, without consultation with its European Community partners.

Should a system of "stable but adjustable par values" be reintroduced, it was agreed that the rules for adjustment would apply symmetrically to all countries, both those in surplus and in deficit with sanctions levied against countries not complying. It was further generally agreed that currencies should be able to fluctuate within wider bands on either side of par before a devaluation or revaluation would take place. Under this concept countries might still find the escape hatch of adopting "floating rates in particular situations, subject to Fund authorization, surveillance and review."[71]

The United States at first seemed to approve some variant of this proposed reformed adjustment system, but eventually came to the conclusion that currencies should legally be allowed to float indefinitely if a country so chose. The dire predictions uttered in some quarters about the consequences of the floating of all of the major currencies, which had begun in March 1973, had not been realized. On the contrary, the sudden and huge increases in oil prices in 1973-74, which vitally affected the balance-of-payments positions of all the industrialized countires, were absorbed by a system of floating rates without any monetary upheaval. "Think of the crises we would have had," Treasury Secretary Shultz remarked, "if nations were still trying to defend par values and fixed exchange rates."[72]

The consequences for the international monetary system of the quadrupling of the price of oil were so enormous and the uncertainties about the future were so great that it was decided to abandon the attempt to work out a definitive set of monetary reforms based on fixed exchange rates. Instead, the temporary tended to become permanent. Thus the Committee of Twenty turned its attention to the problems associated with permanently floating exchange rates. Unlimited floats did not mean the free operation of the market mechanism. Rather, the use of national interventions, controls and manipulations had produced a system of "dirty" floats. The Committee of Twenty recognized the danger of unregulated national behavior, and so it worked out and approved a code of good conduct in the form of detailed guidelines for the management of floating rates.[73]

The trauma of the energy crisis also prompted the Executive Board of the IMF to establish an "oil facility," which was designed to help countries soften the impact on their balance-of-payments positions that had arisen as a result of the increases in the cost of oil and oil-based products.[74] A number of underdeveloped countries were especially badly hurt by this development. Accordingly, a special Group of Twenty-Four was commissioned to study ways of staving off disaster for those less developed countries that had no oil of their own. In June 1974 the IMF set up for this purpose "an extended fund facility" that was designed to make loans at longer terms and in larger amounts than had evern been done before.[75]

THE CREATION OF A EUROPEAN MONETARY UNION

The shape of the future international monetary system will be significantly influenced by whether or not the European Community can implement its ambitious pledge to create a European Monetary Union by December 31, 1980.

Skeptics abound regarding the ability of the European Community to reach this goal. There are not only the traditional differences in viewing national interests to be overcome, but the adoption of economic and monetary integration and the creation of a common currency presuppose extensive harmonization and coordination of economic growth rates and fiscal, wage, and other policies, all of which go far beyond the realm of monetary affairs and reach deeply into the social and economic fabric of each member country.

Moreover, some critics maintain that the proper evolution for such integration should, at a minimum, be on an Atlantic scale, since the scope of a European monetary union may already be too narrow to encompass the forces that bind all the advanced countries together.*

---

*For example, Charles Kindleberger holds that the economic ties, through the multinational corporation, international capital movements, and to a lesser extent trade, which Europe has with the outside world, "bind more tightly than those within the Common Market. The same would be true if Europe were to try to fashion one capital market, one money market, one central bank, and one money. Just as Benelux intergration had to be put aside over the tough nut, agriculture, until it could be subsumed into the wider problem, so the development of effective integrated economic institutions, however attractive as an idea, poses insoluble problems. North America cannot be left out of defense, political, or economic solutions of the New Europe."[76]

Nevertheless, the impulse toward "building Europe" may be sufficiently great so that a European currency and a European political union (necessarily closely tied to the currency), may evolve— not perhaps by 1980, but at some point in the future. One of the principal thrusts behind the drive for a European monetary union is the familiar European aim to achieve a condition of equality with the United States. In 1970 Rinaldo Ossola of the Bank of Italy, one of the most authoritative European spokesmen on monetary matters, articulated the widely held view that the purpose of the Community should be "one of reaffirming the individuality of the Community area vis-a-vis the large economic areas outside it, and in particular of making European currencies more independent of the U.S. dollar. This is certainly the most important immediate goal which a reinforced and enlarged Community should set itself."[77] Once the European Community had progressed to the point of a monetary union, its common currency would be an even more powerful countervailing force to the dollar.

Such a new European unit of account could also be expected to serve as a reserve asset in international transactions. It should certainly be as useful as the dollar for most international purposes. This development would be entirely logical, since the European Community would represent an area of enormous economic strength as well as being the single largest trading unit in the world.

The question would naturally arise as to the relationship between the European currency and other reserve units such as the dollar and SDRs. A European monetary union would necessarily reshape the whole context of the international monetary forums, with the IMF increasingly becoming dependent upon U.S.-European agreements. The impact of American or European monetary policies would then be so great upon each other and upon the rest of the world that special precautions and new institutional arrangements would doubtless be required to assure that these concentrations of economic and monetary power would be used constructively. Any reform of the international monetary system would therefore have to start with the recognition of the existence of these two principal monetary centers and of the interaction between them. In the view of an American economist, C. Fred Bergsten, this condition of parity could be the basis for a healthy relationship, since "dominance by one area over the other would be a dubious basis for lasting reform."[78]

By the same token, such parity of power could present a serious threat to the economic welfare and stability of the entire non-

Communist world if the requisite coordination and harmonization of policies were lacking. As in the case of other types of power, whether it be political, military, or whatever, the greater unity Europe achieves the greater the need for evolving common Atlantic arrangements and institutions in order to minimize trans-Atlantic policy conflicts. In monetary affairs, a major problem would arise in connection with the adjustment of exchange rates and the settlement of accounts between the dollar area and that of the European currency. New mechanisms for interbloc adjustment and a medium of interarea liquidity would likely have to be created. Among other things, it would be entirely logical if something like an Atlantic central bank would grow up as part of a network of new trans-Atlantic accords. Whatever the specific institutional arrangements might be, the guiding principle should be clear: Just as Europe's past subservience to the dollar area proved to be a source of irritation and conflict, so European Union, taken alone, will be a potential danger. Developments on either side of the Atlantic require the most careful scrutiny for their repercussions across the Atlantic. The interdependence of the Atlantic Community is not some abstract theory or empty slogan but an ineluctable fact of life.

THE FURTHER LIBERALIZATION OF WORLD TRADE

The whole structure of international trade is dependent upon a smoothly functioning monetary system. The Ministerial meeting of GATT of September 1973, which officially launched a new round of trade negotiations, noted the linkage between trade and monetary reform. "The Ministers recognize . . . that the new phase in the liberalization of trade, which it is their intention to undertake, should facilitate the orderly functioning of the monetary system. . . . The policy of liberalizing world trade cannot be carried out successfully in the absence of parallel efforts to set up a monetary system which shields the world economy from the shocks and imbalances which have previously occurred."[79] The outcome of efforts at further trade liberalization is also dependent upon agreements among essentially the same states—the United States, the European Community, and Japan—that are simultaneously engaged in negotiating monetary reform. The interaction between trade and monetary policies requires that progress be made in both areas.

The renewed efforts at trade liberalization differ in important respects from the negotiations under the Kennedy Round.[80] By focusing upon tariffs in industrial goods, the Kennedy Round neglected the equally troublesome problem of trade in agricultural products, as well as the whole range of obstacles to trade known as nontariff barriers.

Nor was the problem of preferential trade areas given the attention it deserves. With the enlargement of the European Community and the association of Britain's former partners in the European Free Trade Association (EFTA) with the European Community into an all European free-trade area, the United States was confronted with a huge trading area in which it did not enjoy equal privileges. This discrimination was heightened by the even broader association of a number of Mediterranean and African countries with the European Community. It has been widely suggested that the best way to solve the preference problem is through the gradual elimination of tariffs among the industrial countries over the period of perhaps a decade. Preferential trading blocs would thus disappear with the elimination of tariff preferences. This method of tearing down tariff barriers on a timetable has worked well both for the EC and EFTA, and there is no reason why this same process could not be extended to all the industrialized countries. This would also throw the markets of all of the industrialized countries open to the entire underdeveloped world, which is presently divided along the lines of trading blocs.

Going beyond the tariff problem is the more difficult but no less essential attack on nontariff barriers, which often lie at the roots of protectionism. This complex maze of restrictions, often disguised in terms of qualitative standards, safeguards for health, import procedures and quotas, export subsidies, and the like, form equally important obstacles to trade and should be subjected to multilateral negotiations in all their multifarious details so that they can be drastically reduced over a given period of time.

The new round of trade talks initiated in 1973 was pledged to confront these problems, as well as the thorny issues of trade in agricultural products, which had hitherto been put aside because of the special difficulties associated with it. The creation of the Common Agricultural Policy (CAP) of the European Community has been the subject of especially sharp recriminations. While it is true that American agricultural exports to the European Community have, in general, increased, those items subject to the CAP variable levy system have decreased, and the United States fears that one of its major sources for earning foreign exchange may be further threatened by the extension of CAP. Moreover, CAP has had the disadvantage of raising food prices for the European consumer by supporting a level of prices far above world market levels, as well as creating huge surpluses that have been dumped abroad under EC subsidies, thereby disrupting markets in third countries.

At the root of the problem is the existence of too many inefficient European farmers, whose livelihood must somehow be protected during the transitional period when some of them are moved out of agriculture into other pursuits. In 1970 13 percent of the European working population was engaged in agriculture, compared with 4.5 percent for the United States. By 1980 it is hoped that only 6 percent of the European workers will be farmers. As this point is approached, it will be infinitely more rational and less costly to supplant the variable levy system with direct income support to individual farmers. This would largely remove the threat to U.S. agricultural exports and significantly lower the cost of food for European consumers.

Needless to say, American agricultural price supports and regulations are not free of absurdities either. Indeed, there is no country that does not employ some harmful protectionist practices in agriculture.

In order to scale down such practices it is necessary to deal with the social problems within each nation which give rise to protectionism. It may well be easier to make the necessary changes in domestic support systems as part of a comprehensive international agreement than to wait for each country to act unilaterally. Concessions and adjustments made in the course of multilateral negotiations could be made more acceptable if they appeared to be part of a general tradeoff of benefits among all the negotiators. Similarly, political leaders in each country could be assisted in their efforts to provide safeguards against the sudden loss of jobs dependent upon trade if there were international guidelines for the temporary protection of exposed industries, so that domestic adjustment techniques could gradually foster trade liberalization. Unless temporary safeguard measures conformed to international standards, however, they could become permanent and provide another excuse to obstruct trade.

The general guiding principle for all trade should be that the burden of solving the social problems within each country remains a domestic responsibility, and that the problem of the uneconomic use of resources must not be passed on to the outside world in the form of protectionist trade practices. But this "domestic" problem is also unavoidably an international one that can best be attacked in a concerted manner within an international setting.

THE ATLANTIC COMMUNITY AND JAPAN

Japan, as one of the world's major industrialized democracies, has appropriately assumed its place in the inner councils of the organizations that have dealt with the economy of the non-Communist world. Soon after its founding, Japan became a full member of OECD. In monetary affairs, Japan has been a member of OECD's Working Party Three, the Group of Ten, and IMF's Committee of Twenty. In trade matters, it has played an active part in the work of GATT.

Yet the sentiment has gained ground that such connections with members of the Atlantic Community are not sufficiently comprehensive to respond to the challenges that jointly face the America-Europe-Japan triangle of industrialized democracies. "Japan, as an important member of the 'economic triangle,' has not yet found the kind of interlocutors or partners with whom it can exchange views multilaterally on all major issues," John Tuthill, Director General of the Atlantic Institute, asserted in 1972. "Hence the need for a broader and regular dialogue with its Western counterparts. Above all, such a dialogue should be put in a commonly agreed framework, encompassing more than the purely technical and more than specific trade and monetary questions. Ways should be found to allow Japan to participate in a more meaningful fashion in the general debate on problems that concern it and all the Western democratic countries."[81] Included in such broader debate should be general security-political concerns and a shared interest in coordinating policies toward the Communist world and the underdeveloped countries.

Similar thoughts led David Rockefeller, Chairman of the Chase Manhattan Bank, to organize the Trilateral Commission—composed of influential private individuals from North America, Western Europe, and Japan—as a mechanism for focusing attention on and recommending solutions to essential common problems that must be dealt with by this golden triangle, if they were to be dealt with at all. "While it is important to develop greater cooperation among all the countries of the world," the Executive Committee of the Trilateral Commission asserted at its first meeting in October 1973, "Japan,

Western Europe and North America, in view of their great weight in the world economy and their massive relations with one another, bear a special responsibility for developing effective cooperation, both in their own interests and in those of the rest of the world. They share a number of problems which, if not solved, could cause difficulties for all. They must make concerted efforts to deal with the challenges of interdependence they cannot manage separately."[82] The debates and reports of the various task forces of the Trilateral Commission, though advanced by private individuals, were intended to present the various governments concerned with a working basis for taking official action.

Zbigniew Brzezinski, who was appointed the first Director of the Trilateral Commission, would carry the process further. He would develop on a regular and formal basis political consultations among the governmental units of the three areas, which could engage in common planning with regard to problems of mutual interest. This would include annual trilateral cabinet meetings among members of the Council of Ministers of the European Community and the American and Japanese cabinets, a standing secretariat to service these meetings which could form a common policy planning and review staff, the promotion of more frequent meetings of OECD foreign ministers so as to involve states outside the formal confines of the triangle with their planning processes, and the holding of regular three-way meetings of the parliamentarians of the "cooperative triangle" on as wide a parity basis as possible.[83]

These ambitious proposals deserve thoughtful consideration, but they also require careful scrutiny of the nature of the triangle upon which such relations would be based. Upon examination, it is apparent that the links in the trilateral relationship are of very uneven strength.

Culturally and historically the European-American ties form a much older and stronger connection than those of either of these two entities with Japan. The U.S.-Japan ties are of a special character, since Japan became accustomed to dealing with the outside world in the post-World War II period through the United States. Japan was abruptly shaken out of this dependence by the "Nixon shocks": first by the unilateral U.S. economic measures of August 1971 and then by the deceitful manner in which Washington established relations with Peking in 1972 without any consultation whatever with Tokyo. The future of American-Japanese relations remains dangerously uncertain. The relationship between Europe and Japan, on the other hand, is merely in its infancy and no one can yet venture a reliable prediction about its course.

While the Western democracies all need to improve their ties with Japan, it should be evident that if the most fundamental and venerable trans-Atlantic connection cannot be kept in good repair, then any talk of trilateralism will only be an empty geometrical abstraction.

NOTES

1. Harold van B. Cleveland, *The Atlantic Idea and Its European Rivals* (New York, 1966), p. 155.

2. Richard N. Cooper, *The Economics of Interdependence* (New York, 1968), p. 8.

3. Raymond Vernon, "Economic Sovereignty at Bay," *Foreign Affairs,* October 1968, p. 114.

4. Judd Polk, "The New World Economy," *Columbia Journal of World Business,* January-February, 1968, p. 8; Arthur Ross, "The Multinational Corporation in the Grand Design of Internationalism," Information Document prepared for the Political and Economic Committees of the North Atlantic Assembly, September 1971, p. 3.

5. Address by Richard F. Pederson, Counselor, Department of State at Washington, D.C., February 17, 1971, Department of State *Bulletin* 64, no. 1655: 324.

6. A. A. Groppelli, "U.S. Investments Abroad," Lionel D. Edie and Co. Report, October 2, 1970, p. 2; Assistant Secretary of State for Economic Affairs Philip H. Trezise, in an address of May 3, 1971 at Racine, Wisc., reported: "The rate of return on U.S. foreign direct investment has averaged about 12.5 per cent in recent years." Department of State *Bulletin* 64, no. 1665: 670.

7. Pederson, op. cit., p. 325; Neil H. Jacoby, "The Multinational Corporation," *The Center Magazine,* May 1970, p. 39.

8. Testimony of Peter M. Flanigan, Executive Director, Council of International Economic Policy, before the Senate Subcommittee on International Trade, February 26, 1971, Department of State *Bulletin* 68, no. 1761: 363. Another, unofficial estimate

placed the profit remittances for 1971 at $9 billion. See International Economic Policy Association, *The United States Balance of Payments* (Washington, D.C., 1972), p. 36.

9. Address by Under Secretary for Economic Affairs William J. Casey at Harriman, N.Y., March 10, 1973, Department of State *Bulletin* 68, no. 1764: 449. See also International Economic Policy Association, *Priority Program Objectives* (Washington, D.C., 1973), p. 9.

10. Jacoby, op. cit., pp. 47-48. See also Raymond Vernon, "A Skeptic Looks at the Balance of Payments," *Foreign Policy,* Winter 1971-72, pp. 52-65. On suggestions for a new, more realistic definition of balance of payments, see Charles P. Kindleberger, *Balance of Payments Deficits and the International Market for Liquidity,* Essays in International Finance, No. 46 (May 1965), Princeton University.

11. "Statement by Secretary Shultz on Devaluation of the Dollar," New York *Times,* February 14, 1973; Edwin L. Dale, Jr., "U.S. Terminates Curb on Lending Dollars Abroad," New York *Times,* January 30, 1974.

12. Rainer Hellmann, *The Challenge to U.S. Dominance of the International Corporation* (New York, 1970), p. 306.

13. Ibid., p. 306. Dr. Hellmann supplied this writer with the following data: In 1967 the growth rate of U.S. assets in Western Europe was 10.5 percent, while the growth rate of Western European assets in the United States was 11.6 percent.

14. Ambassador Joseph A. Greenwald, "International Trade Policies," address of October 30, 1970, *Survival,* February 1971, p. 57.

15. James W. Vaupel and Joan P. Curhan, *The World's Multinational Enterprises: A Sourcebook of Tables* (Boston, 1973), pp. 71, 79.

16. Ibid., pp. 4-5, 47. The U.S. figure could only be estimated, Vaupel explained to this writer, since the Harvard Business School data on U.S.-based multinational corporations only went up to January 1, 1968. See also, "Europe's Got Its Tentacles Too," *Vision,* October 15, 1973, pp. 85-86.

17. Francis M. Goldmark, "Europe Catches the Merger Fever," *Columbia Journal of World Business,* March-April 1969, p. 54.

18. James Leontiades, "The European Challenge: A Response," *Columbia Journal of World Business,* July-August 1970, p. 13.

19. Richard Howe, "Europe Invades the American Dream," *Vision,* September 15, 1973, pp. 73-75.

20. Leontiades, op. cit., p. 12.

21. Ibid., pp. 11-12.

22. Ibid., p. 15.

23. Jack N. Behrman, *National Interests and the Multinational Enterprise: Tensions Among the North Atlantic Countries* (Englewood Cliffs, N.J., 1970), p. 10.

24. Harvey D. Shapiro, "The Multinationals: Giants Beyond Flag and Country," New York *Times Magazine,* March 18, 1973, p. 20.

25. Kindleberger quoted in Roberto de Oliveira Campos, "Multinational Enterprise—Friend or Foe to Latin America," *Interplay,* March 1971, p. 36.

26. Sidney E. Rolfe, "The International Corporation in Perspective," in *The Multinational Corporation in the World Economy,* eds. Sidney E. Rolfe and Walter Damm (New York, 1970), p. 32.

27. Ibid., pp. 32-35.

28. George W. Ball, "The Promise of the Multinational Corporation," *Fortune,* June 1, 1967, p. 80.

29. Behrman, op. cit., pp. 7-8.

30. Vernon, "Economic Sovereignty," op. cit., p. 122.

31. Ibid., p. 119.

32. Raymond Vernon, "Future of the Multinational Enterprise," in *The International Corporation,* ed. Charles P. Kindleberger (Cambridge, Mass., 1970), pp. 397-98.

33. Ibid., pp. 399-400.

34. Robert Gilpin, "The Politics of Transnational Economic Relations," *International Organization,* Summer 1971, p. 403.

35. Ibid., p. 417.

36. Ibid., p. 413.

37. For a good survey of the origin and early functioning of OECD, see Henry G. Aubrey, *Atlantic Economic Cooperation: The Case of the OECD* (New York, 1967).

38. Address by Assistant Secretary of State for European Affairs William R. Tyler at Detroit, April 27, 1964, Department of State *Bulletin* 50, no. 1299: 780.

39. Aubrey, op. cit., pp. 147-48.

40. On the $6 billion General Arrangements to Borrow negotiated by the Group of Ten, announced by the IMF on January 8, 1962, see Department of State *Bulletin* 46, no. 1185: 187-88.

41. For the seminal statement of the Group of Ten of October 2, 1962, which ultimately led to the creation of Special Drawing Rights, see Department of State *Bulletin* 49, no. 1269: 615.

42. Stephen D. Cohen, *International Monetary Reform, 1964-69* (New York, 1970), provides a good account of the negotiations over the SDRs.

43. See the testimony of Federal Reserve Chairman William McChesney Martin, Jr. on August 30, 1965 in *Hearings before the Subcommittee on National Security and International Operations of the Committee on Government Operations,* U.S. Senate, 89th Cong., 1st sess., Part 4 (Washington, D.C.), pp. 193-94.

44. Clyde H. Farnsworth, "Joining Basel Club Is Easy: Be a Central Banker," New York *Times,* January 24, 1968.

45. Edwin L. Dale, Jr., "Studies Seek Rise in Monetary Fund," New York *Times,* August 11, 1964.

46. On the initiation of swap agreements, see the articles by Charles A. Coombes, Vice President, Foreign Department, New York Federal Reserve Bank in the *Federal Reserve Bulletin,* September 1962, March 1963, and September 1963.

47. Robert Triffin, "The Thrust of History in International Monetary Reform," *Foreign Affairs,* April 1969, p. 487.

48. The felicitous phrase is that of Guy de Carmoy, *The Foreign Policies of France, 1944-1968* (Chicago, 1970), p. 444.

49. President de Gaulle's eleventh press conference, February 4, 1965, Ambassade de France, New York, Speeches and Press Conferences, No. 216, p. 6. On March 20, 1968 de Gaulle informed his cabinet that the existing monetary system was "henceforth inapplicable" and again demanded in its place "a monetary system based on gold, which alone has the character of immutability, impartiality, and universality." ("France Calls Money System 'Henceforth Inapplicable,'" *Wall Street Journal,* March 21, 1968.)

50. Richard E. Mooney, "Paris Bids Debts Be Paid with Gold," New York *Times,* February 12, 1965; Richard E. Mooney, "France Quits Buying U.S. Gold as Her Inflow of Dollars Ebbs," New York *Times,* October 28, 1966.

51. Edward T. O'Toole, "France Is Loser in Gold Program," New York *Times,* April 7, 1965.

52. "France Takes Gold," New York *Times,* July 22, 1965.

53. Richard E. Mooney, "Ten Nations Extend Aid to the Pound; France Abstains," New York *Times,* September 11, 1965.

54. John M. Lee, "Gold-Buying Wave Swells, Battering Dollar in Europe," New York *Times,* November 24, 1967; Henry Tanner, "Paris Didn't Pledge Firm Franc on Eve of London's Devaluation," ibid., November 25, 1967.

55. H. Erich Heinemann, "Members of Gold Pool Said to Agree Not to Draw from U.S. Stock," New York *Times,* March 19, 1968.

56. Cohen, op. cit., pp. 32, 51-54.

57. Ibid., p. 59. De Gaulle later elaborated his opposition to any new reserve unit when he denounced "the pressure exerted by the Americans and the British to bring Europe over to accepting, at its expense and to the profit of the Anglo-Saxon balance of payments deficits, the creation of artificial monetary resources called liquidity. These resources, actually, no longer being pegged to gold, would add a boundless source of international inflation to those that already exist under the cover of the 'gold-exchange standard,' arbitrary and excessive issuings and exports of the dollar." (President de Gaulle's fifteenth press conference, May 16, 1967, Ambassade de France, New York, Speeches and Press Conferences, No. 260A, p. 8.)

58. Cohen, op. cit., pp. 149-51.

59. Edwin L. Dale, Jr., "$100 Million in Gold Sold by France to Get Dollars," New York *Times,* July 13, 1968.

60. De Carmoy, op. cit., p. 450. Although de Gaulle refused in a statement of November 24, 1968 to devalue the franc, for reasons of prestige and in defiance of economic realities, devaluation came anyway in August 1969. At that time, French reserves, mostly held in gold, which had amounted to $6.6 billion at the beginning of May 1968, had dwindled to less than $3.5 billion. ("Devaluation of the Franc," Lionel D. Edie and Co. Report, August 12, 1969.)

61. Timothy W. Stanley, "Atlantic Security in the Seventies," Atlantic Treaty Association, London, September 1971, pp. 21-22.

62. Robert Kleiman of the New York *Times* maintains that this was the way that Connally proudly described himself.

63. New York *Times,* December 20, 1971.

64. New York *Times,* March 16 and 29, 1972.

65. On the membership and structure of the Committee of Twenty, see *IMF Survey,* October 9, 1972, pp. 65, 72-73. See also Edwin L. Dale, Jr., "Monetary Groups Elect Chairmen," New York *Times,* September 29, 1972.

66. For the communiques of the expanded Group of Ten of

March 9 and 16, 1973, see Department of State *Bulletin* 68, no. 1764: 454-55.

67. Address by Secretary of the Treasury George P. Shultz at Nairobi, Kenya, September 25, 1973, ibid., 69, no. 1792: 546.

68. Committee of Twenty, "First Outline of Reform," September 24, 1973, *IMF Survey, Annual Meetings Issue Supplement,* October 8, 1973, p. 308.

69. Edwin L. Dale, Jr., "Accord Set on Use of Monetary Gold," New York *Times,* June 13, 1974.

70. "SDR Valued by 16 Currencies," *IMF Survey,* June 17, 1974, pp. 177, 185.

71. Committee of Twenty, "First Outline of Reform," op. cit., p. 307.

72. Quoted in Edwin L. Dale, Jr., "Monetary Stand Is Shifted by U.S.," New York *Times,* January 10, 1974.

73. "Guidelines for Management of Floating To Be Used by Board in Consultations," *IMF Survey,* June 17, 1974, pp. 181-83.

74. "Board Agrees on Oil Facility," ibid., pp. 177, 185-86.

75. "Communique of the Intergovernmental Group of 24 on International Monetary Affairs," ibid., p. 184.

76. Charles P. Kindleberger, *Power and Money* (London, 1970), p. 226.

77. Rinaldo Ossola, "Aim Is To Be Independent of the Dollar," *European Review,* Winter 1970-71, p. 24.

78. C. Fred Bergsten, "Taking the Monetary Initiative," *Foreign Affairs,* July 1968, p. 731.

79. "Text of Tokyo Declaration," GATT Ministerial Meeting, September 14, 1973, Department of State *Bulletin* 69, no. 1789: 451.

80. For a brief, well-balanced treatment of the trade problem, see Karl Kaiser, *Europe and the United States: The Future of the Relationship* (Washington, D.C., 1973), pp. 10-27, 44-52.

81. John W. Tuthill, *The Decisive Years Ahead,* Atlantic Papers, No. 4 (1972) (Paris, 1973), pp. 61-62. See also, Curt Gasteyger, ed., *Japan and the Atlantic World,* Atlantic Papers, no. 3 (1972) (Paris, 1972).

82. "Statement of Purposes," Executive Committee of the Trilateral Commission, October 23, 1973, *Trialogue,* No. 2 (November 1973), p. 1.

83. Zbigniew Brzezinski, "U.S. Foreign Policy: The Search for Focus," *Foreign Affairs,* July 1973, p. 724.

10

THE NORTH-SOUTH
RELATIONSHIP

The highly industrialized non-Communist societies around the North Atlantic basin plus several distant islands of advanced technology, notably Japan and Australia, have jointly shared a special responsibility for assisting the bulk of humanity who live in the industrially undeveloped or underdeveloped lands of Africa, Asia, and Latin America. In addition, the less developed countries (LDCs) have the responsibility for helping themselves.

Alleviating the problems of world poverty is not simply a matter of transferring economic resources from the rich nations to the poor, while developing the economic resources within the poor countries. What is at stake is the modernization of the entire fabric of industrially backward societies. This entails far-reaching transformations in the political, social, and economic structures of these countries and involves the abandonment of time-honored institutions and patterns of behavior that are highly resistant to change. The problem, in short, is of enormous complexity and is not subject to short-term solutions.

Much of the current disillusionment with foreign aid in the developed countries arose from the unfounded assumption that the process of economic development in the LDCs would be comparable to that of Western Europe under the Marshall Plan. Such an analogy missed the essential fact that the countries of Western Europe were already modern industrial societies, and though devastated by war, nevertheless had in place the political and social infrastructure that was needed to make good use of economic aid so as to produce striking results in a short order. The LDCs not only lack, in varying degrees, the necessary political and social infrastructure, but their problems are more intractable and more desperate than were those of Western Europe.

The gravity of the situation is concealed by an optimistic bias in the statistics that, as Gunnar Myrdal has convincingly demonstrated, are systematically used by the advocates of foreign aid, both among the officials in the LDCs and among those in the developed countries who seek to support aid programs.[1] But deception or self-deception can only add complications, breed new illusions, and prevent one from coming to grips with the problem. Candor requires us to acknowledge the unmistakable fact that, generally speaking, the condition of the LDCs is genuinely desperate. Whether their condition is so desperate as to be hopeless is an open question. The answer will, in large measure, doubtless depend upon the exertions made on behalf of the development process, both by the rich and poor countries.

It is at least evident that the effort must be made. The reasons are both moral and practical. Every advanced, industrial society has recognized the imperative within its own borders to alleviate the suffering of its poor and disadvantaged by transferring wealth from the affluent to those in need. Feelings of human solidarity no longer permit the rich to turn a blind eye to persistent conditions of abject poverty. The same impulse to affirm the principle of human solidarity has found expression in the idea of foreign aid, which was only given systematic form as recently as the end of World War II. Not only are these aid programs of recent origin, but the humanitarian impulse is much weaker across state boundaries than within them. Nevertheless, the humanitarian impulse exists on a transnational scale, and the ever-closer contact and interdependence of nations unavoidably created by modern societies requires an intensification of human concern on the part of the rich nations for poor ones.

Elementary considerations of a very practical nature also compel the rich countries to assume an abiding interest in the welfare of the poor on a global scale. Too much is at stake to permit the bulk of mankind to stagnate in a condition of grinding poverty, while the advanced industrial countries leap ahead in their own self-contained development. There is, of course, no way to guarantee the growth of harmonious North-South relations, since the problems facing the LDCs are complex and immense and the modernization process is itself very disruptive to organized society. Yet if the effort of development assistance is not made, one can absolutely guarantee that mounting waves of discontent will find an outlet in disruption and violence that will spill over into the isolated sanctuaries of the privileged. The perception by the global poor of an ever-widening gap between their condition of life and that of the rich will create feelings of intolerable frustration and hatred that could easily be aggravated by racial strife. With the exception of Japan, the modern industrial nations are all white Western societies that jointly comprise a distinct minority of the world's population. The bulk of humanity is not only poor but largely colored and the specter of race warfare would loom over the relationship between these segments of mankind.

There are other valid, practical motives as well. Turbulent, low-income areas have neither the economic resources to become valuable trading partners with the advanced industrial states, nor would they have the political will to help construct a viable political order in the world. Rather, they would only offer Communists targets of opportunity to create regimes that would be openly hostile to Western man. Such considerations springing from enlightened self-interest could reinforce the humanitarian impulse so as to put the question of development aid in the proper perspective.

GIVING AID FOR THE RIGHT REASONS

Experience tells us that aid will only be given over the long term if it is given for the right reasons. The Pearson Commission report sponsored by the World Bank wisely cautioned against expecting results from aid given for the wrong reasons. The relationship between the donor and the recipient "should not be pursued for the express purpose of transforming it into a political alliance, or of securing short-term political advantage. An aid relationship is difficult in the best of circumstances. It become untenable if conditions requiring political support are attached to it."[2] It was recognized that much foreign aid had been granted "to enable some countries to maintain large armed forces rather than promote economic growth." It was therefore hardly surprising that "hopes of satisfactory development progress were disappointed or that aid given as 'defense support' has on occasion led to greater involvement in a deteriorating security situation" in the recipient country.[3]

Nor should aid be given in order to provide immediate economic assistance to the donor, as is often done through tied aid that can only be spent in the donor country and which has the effect of financing export sales.

The sorry state into which the U.S. foreign aid program degenerated can be directly attributed to just such practices. Traditionally economic aid and military assistance were put before the Congress in a single package, and frequently the appeal of short-term political gains presumably accruing from military assistance was relied upon in order to get congressional approval of economic aid. This resulted in a thoroughly debased rationale for development aid, in which humanitarian instincts had to be disguised as unworthy of consideration. Over time foreign aid became suspect to many since it seemed to involve the United States in political and military commitments that were implied in the aid giving. And so the strategy of linking development aid to military and political objectives worked in reverse. This interaction is vividly illustrated by the American experience in Vietnam. The more economic aid became tainted by Vietnam the smaller it became. Its rapid decline in the late 1960s coincided precisely with the deepening U.S. military involvement in Vietnam. Also while Vietnam became the largest U.S. commitment in the third world, aid to other countries was also tied to short-term American political and strategic goals. Again the result was self-defeating. Insofar as such goals were not achieved, it became more difficult to sustain support for further aid.

Ultimately this caused long-term supporters of foreign aid, such as Senator Frank Church, to shift to the position of outspoken congressional critics. Church recalled that "foreign aid, economic as well as military, was sold to Congress as a national security measure." Consequently, "well over a half of our aid to the so-called developing countries has been military and paramilitary assistance." Under the guise of fighting communism, American aid was "used not to promote development but for quite the opposite purpose of supporting the rule of corrupt and stagnant—but vociferously anti-Communist—distatorships." In such recipient countries, "the rewards of development are grabbed up by a small privileged caste while the majority of people are left hopeless, debilitated and demoralized." Church quite properly emphasized the need for basic reforms in the structure of the underdeveloped country if aid would become meaningful. "If the bulk of the people are to make the concerted effort and accept the enormous sacrifices required for lifting a society out of chronic poverty, they have got to have some belief in the integrity of their leaders, in the commitment of those leaders to social justice, and in the equality of sacrifice required of the people."

Finally Church complained that the economic impact of American aid was largely self-serving. In arguing the case for American aid in 1968, for example, the director of the U.S. Agency for International Development emphasized the fact that "93 percent of AID funds are spent directly in the United States. . . . Some 4,000 American firms in fifty states received $1.3 billion in AID funds for products supplied as part of the foreign aid program."[4] A good measure of "foreign aid" was really domestic aid.

Until the issues raised by such protests are honestly dealt with, there is little prospect that the United States will assume its proper role in alleviating the explosive pressures generated in the North-South encounter. There is first of all the way in which the issue of communism has been used or, more properly, misused. It would be a grave error to go to the other extreme of saying that communism in the third world never was and will never be a threat to Western democratic societies. In this respect, reformed liberals like Senator Church tend to throw the baby out with the bath water in the disavowal of their past support for mistaken programs. Clearly, Communist regimes, whether pro-Moscow, pro-Peking, or of some more exotic variety, are organized on the lines of a dictatorship dedicated to purposes that are inimical to basic Western values. While it is, of course, a travesty to support anti-Communist dictatorships in the name of defending the "free world," it is nonetheless in the genuine interests of the liberal democracies to do what is possible to forestall the growth of communism in the third world, as elsewhere.

It should also be clear that the most effective way to do this is by assisting regimes in the underdeveloped world which display some commitment to social justice and are endeavoring to restructure their societies for the benefit of the many in need instead of hoarding outside assistance for the advantage of a privileged few. Only in this way can the alienation of the masses from their rulers be overcome and a reasonable degree of identification between ruled and rulers be created. The absence of such conditions of societal cohesion provide a fertile breeding ground for all sorts of drastic solutions, communism included.

As previously noted, the industrially advanced, non-Communist countries do have a vital stake in the political development of the LDCs, but it must be conceived as a long-term one. Rather than trying to foster discredited satellites for short-term advantages by bribing oppressive and unpopular regimes, the donor states should encourage the emergence of self-reliant, self-respecting developing societies that are interested in joining a cooperative network of international institutions that will be needed to underpin the free world community.

The economic abuse of aid for the benefit of the donor as symbolized in the practice of aid-tying also deserves, and has been getting, closer attention. The practice was begun to aid donor countries in balance-of-payments difficulties, but it is generally recognized that it has gone far beyond this requirement. The additional costs to the recipient country of being forced to take goods and services from the donor, instead of being able to use the funds to shop around for the best bargain, vary from case to case, but frequently such costs have exceeded 20 percent.[5]

All of the developed non-Communist donor nations share the problem with the United States of giving aid for the right reasons. The foreign aid programs of the others, however, have not met with the disaster that has befallen American aid, doubtless because they managed to escape the trauma of the Vietnam adventure and all the political fallout that it entailed. Their various aid programs also reflect a mixture of motives, some purer than others. France and Britain, for example, have directed aid to their former colonies in order to protect their remaining investments and trade ties. France, in particular, has also allocated large sums, designated as foreign aid, to perpetuate its *mission civilisatrice* in Africa and elsewhere by subsidizing instruction in the French language and culture. "Part of the expenditure for aid has also been lost in corruption, or, more often, in what could be called the 'collective corruption' of providing inordinately high salaries and all sorts of excessive amenities to a ruling oligarchy, kept allegiant to French policy."[6]

Sweden presents another picture. Without an empire in modern times, it has not been tempted to use aid to serve Swedish military or strategic interests abroad. Nor have the Swedes been inclined to use aid as an excuse to spread subsidies haphazardly to domestic business concerns. Among the Swedes, Myrdal affirms, "there cannot be any other reason for giving aid than the simple humanitarian impulse to feel solidarity with those who are poor, hungry, diseased and illiterate, and who meet difficulties in their efforts to rise out of poverty." Based on this motivation, Swedish aid has steadily *increased* and public pressure for further annual increases remains strong. This experience, Myrdal insists, clearly demonstrates the conquering strength of the moral imperative in aid giving "when it is not confused in opportunistic duplicities and then buried in failure and frustration, as in the United States."[7]

Several other smaller, highly developed countries without important overseas commitments to defend have also followed the Swedish example and have proceeded to increase aid as they have relied more strongly upon moral grounds. This has been the case in Canada and the Netherlands, and a similar trend has developed to a lesser extent in Switzerland, Denmark, Austria, Finland, and Norway.[8]

Perhaps the smaller countries cannot be models for the larger ones, precisely because they lack important foreign interests. Also in the case of Sweden, in particular, we encounter a uniquely homogeneous society where it may be possible to adopt certain policies that would not be feasible with a large, heterogeneous population like the United States. Yet there would still seem to be a lesson to be learned by contrasting Sweden, where aid has increased when it was given for the right reasons, with the United States, where aid has decreased when it was given for the wrong reasons. The moral factor can be a powerful element in the aid relationship, and it is a mistake to disguise or ignore it.

An important consequence of the Swedes giving aid for moral reasons has been to liberate them from extraneous policy interests that might distort the use of aid while permitting them to try to influence the governments of the underdeveloped countries in order to assure that the aid will achieve its humanitarian aims. At the same time, mounting public pressure has been "exerted to steer the aid to progressive underdeveloped countries carrying on radical reforms."[9]

It might be objected that even aid given for moral reasons becomes immoral when it has the effect of interfering in the domestic affairs of the recipient country. However, no aid is neutral, whatever its nature or for whatever reasons it is given. Aid is always a scarce, much-prized commodity that inevitably strengthens the hand of some element and some policy trend in the underdeveloped country. The question is really what element and what policies will benefit by it. Aid given for the wrong reasons inescapably has imperialist implications since it is given in an attempt to buy allies and bring economic benefits to the donor. Such aid seldom, or only incidentally, has the effect of producing humanitarian benefits. Aid based upon moral purposes permits and indeed requires that, insofar as possible, it be channeled into the hands of those most in need of it. This, in turn, most often can only be accomplished by working with those reformist elements that are bent upon fundamental changes in the recipient society.

THE DEFINITION OF "UNDERDEVELOPED" STATES

A survey of the problems facing most LDCs is a disheartening experience, since every major aspect of life is in need of significant, often drastic, alterations that will not easily be forthcoming.[10] In varying degrees, all underdeveloped countries are what Myrdal calls "soft states." Corruption is extraordinarily widespread in the conduct of official business and this has a demoralizing effect upon all social, economic, and political transactions. The administration of law is arbitrary and its enforcement generally poor, since public officials frequently act in collusion with powerful persons or groups whom they are presumably assigned to regulate.

Social and economic inequality is everywhere grossly apparent, and despite governmental policy declarations that condemn such inequities, the gap between the indigenous rich and poor is generally getting wider. Social and economic inequalities hinder development, since malnutrition and deplorable living conditions impair the ability to work intensively while fostering attitudes of fatalism, hopelessness, and despair.

Land reform is at the heart of alleviating inequalities and producing incentives for development. Absentee land ownership and sharecropping provide very low yields and deprive the toiler of the feeling that he has a stake in the future of his society. While land reform can assume different patterns, in each case it can result in a healthy relationship between man and his land, which will create the incentive to work harder and more effectively and to invest in a meaningful future. The recent "Green Revolution," arising from the availability of high-yielding grain seeds, has not made the need for land reform obsolete. On the contrary, since the only group to benefit by it were the wealthy farmers who could afford to irrigate their land and to buy fertilizers and implements needed for such intensive agriculture, the inequalities and disparities in rural life have been aggravated. Everywhere land reform has been given lip service, but almost everywhere it has remained an empty slogan and a fading goal. Even where partial land reforms have been legislated, they have seldom been carried out effectively.

Illiteracy and lack of proper education have been the handmaidens of massive poverty and social and economic inequalities. Developed societies demand universal literacy and widespread education. Again, despite frequent official pledges to erase illiteracy and provide educational opportunities for the masses, actual developments in education have been twisted for the benefit of already educated classes. Adult education to abolish illiteracy has been almost universally neglected, and a priority for increasing elementary education has given way to emphasis upon secondary and tertiary schooling. Even so, the performance of elementary education has been exceedingly poor with a great percentage of dropouts or repeaters. This massive waste of human resources has been the greatest in the poorest countries that could least affort it.

Bearing down upon all these problems is the unprecedented and seemingly unstoppable increase in population. Again it is the poverty-stricken countries with the smallest economic base that must support the huge increases in population growth, even though they cannot presently provide a decent life for their existing populations. Efforts at birth control have been introduced by various underdeveloped countries, but it is an immensely difficult task to reach down to the village level and implement effective programs. Even if there were now completely adequate birth control programs in effect, the age groups already born will continue to enter the labor force for decades to come and apply unwanted pressure on the already scarce resources. The prospect would seem to be that of a rising tide of ever-increasing unemployed or underemployed rural labor and a continued swelling of the stream of rural refugees to abominable urban slums.

Given this array of staggering and deep-rooted problems, one wonders what prospect there is for properly conceived aid to make any significant inroads upon the patterns of life that require change.

Certainly one should not expect too much. At the same time it is important not to be immobilized by an overwhelming sense of defeatism. If, as has been argued, the stakes in the North-South relationship are too high to be ignored and we feel compelled to act for reasons of morality and enlightened self-interest, then the aid relationship must be sustained and strengthened.

MAKING AID CONDITIONAL

Effective aid is dependent upon both improving the performance of the donors as well as improving the performance of the recipients. Both aspects of this aid relationship are interlocked, since neither the donors nor the recipients alone can assure satisfactory progress in the development process. Different tasks can be apportioned to each, but both must cooperate toward agreed goals. And these goals, it cannot be sufficiently emphasized, involve nothing less than basic structural reforms in the underdeveloped countries. The advanced countries must provide the right kind of assistance, but it must be conditioned upon efforts by the recipients to put such aid to the right uses.

If aid is given for valid purposes, the donor has every right to make it conditional upon needed reforms. Otherwise the absence of such reforms can undermine the rationale for giving aid. Take, for example, the case of tax reforms in the LDCs. Typically, their tax systems are highly regressive. Not only are the tax laws written to favor the ruling oligarchies, but the rich, and sometimes they are fabulously rich, often manage to escape existing taxation by means of corruption and collusion with the governmental authorities. The rich are also frequently in a position to control the disbursement of foreign aid so that it ends up lining their own pockets.[11] Under these circumstances, it is possible to envisage aid going from citizens in the developed countries to persons overseas who are richer than they. Aid should therefore "not be given to strengthen reactionary regimes that are bent upon resisting reform." Instead, donors should "demand that aid be given to countries making serious efforts toward social reform and even that it be given on condition that such reforms are undertaken; indeed, the aid may be given to make such reforms more possible."[12]

Just how much leverage conditional aid can provide is open to question. Robert Asher, one of the more thoughtful commentators on the aid question, makes some of the necessary distinctions about when leverage might or might not be effective. Efforts to keep a recipient on too short a leash can be a disincentive to orderly planning. Also while performance can and should be continually reviewed, it is often illusory to expect certain specified actions to be taken within a limited time frame in return for the release of certain supplies. In the granting of project aid, it is entirely proper to require such things as site and feasibility studies, the allocation of the necessary local currency, and the availability of the needed materials and personnel, including qualified management. However, broad reforms of the social and economic system, such as tax or land reforms, which are only indirectly related to a specific project, cannot plausibly be demanded as a quid pro quo. On such larger issues the recipient may appropriately be asked to take action in return for program aid, as distinguished from project aid—that is, assistance that is broadly gauged to support the general budgetary aims of the underdeveloped country.[13]

Experience has shown that there is "very limited leverage inherent in a technical assistance program," while "capital assistance in substantial volume does carry leverage." However, aid that may appear to be very substantial to a small underdeveloped country might make very little impact on a huge country like India. The size of the aid in relation to the size of the country is therefore an important factor. Asher cautions that as the volume of aid rises "it encourages arrogance on the part of the donors and stimulates fears and resistance among receivers. Consequently, the peak is never very high and hopes of obtaining or maintaining vast amounts of leverage through foreign aid are unlikely to be realized."[14]

Sometimes the networks of economic controls that are erected by the ruling oligarchies in the underdeveloped countries benefit principally the rich, while facilitating corruption and hampering the development effort. Such controls may "be pierced by foreign aid in the right amounts at the right time." Moreover, such governmental barriers can be circumvented in cases when "foreign aid can perhaps be channeled directly to the urban and rural poor, by providing small amounts of credit and technical assistance to organized community groups, or by partial financing of major programs of public works."[15]

In most cases there will be a variety of contradictory forces at work inside the recipient country. Conditional aid will therefore only be effective to the extent that the donors can identify and then ally themselves with those recipient groups that are already inclined to carry out reforms. This results in the paradox that reforms are carried out best by those countries that need to make reforms the least; that is, the leverage is most effective when one really does not need to use it. Applying leverage through giving aid is therefore both a difficult and a deliberate process. If successful, conditional aid can nudge the recipient in the desired direction. Massive pressure will likely be counterproductive. "The more bluntly the aid instrument is used the less effective it becomes."[16]

In order to surmount the sensitivities and allay the suspicions that are aroused by conditional aid it is necessary to broaden the basis of the aid relationship beyond that of a bilateral dealing between governments. "The less reason the receiver has to suspect the motives of the foreign adviser, the more likely it is that the advice will be judged on its merits."[17] In this regard, high-caliber consultants from academic institutions or private groups are frequently more valuable than governmental emissaries.

Moreover, bilateral aid is more inclined to be suspect of ulterior motives than is multilateral aid. The likelihood of imperialist implications in a direct confrontation between a rich donor and a poor recipient is largely avoided when there are a number of donors jointly operating through an international agency. It is not, as is frequently asserted, that multilateral aid "takes the politics out of aid." As previously noted, aid giving is always a highly political act, since it involves giving someone power to control a scarce commodity. But by making aid giving a multilateral process it reduces the possibility of aid serving the short run political aims of any single donor.

It also changes the context of the aid relationship in several important respects. The larger forum allows the recipient to participate in the policymaking of an international organization, and by so doing not only permits it to help shape decisions that affect its own future but also bestows a sense of responsibility upon the recipient to implement the agreed program. Furthermore, expert advice is more readily accepted when it comes from civil servants of diverse nationalities in an international organization. When dealing with large and complex development projects, even the bigger bilateral aid programs would not likely have the necessary documentation, experience, and expertise that would be available to many international organizations. Multilateral aid also provides an opportunity for the donors to avoid competitive, uncoordinated bilateral programs and to concert and maximize their contributions so that the total aid package becomes more than the sum of its otherwise disparate parts. Finally, the global or regional scope of international agencies permits them to foster cooperation and regional integration among the aid users in the underdeveloped world.

THE MULTILATERAL AID INSTITUTIONS

There are a number of multilateral instruments available, each of differing value. Perhaps the most respected, experienced, and dynamic is the World Bank Group, consisting of the World Bank itself (officially the International Bank for Reconstruction and Development), which loans to "credit worthy" countries; the International Development Association, the "soft loans" affiliate, which loans money to governments on concessional terms; and the International Finance Corporation, which promotes development in the private sector by lending to and investing in privately owned enterprise.

Regional development banking institutions include the Inter-American Development Bank, the Central American Bank for Economic Integration, and the Asian and African development banks. They differ from each other in their experience, level of competence, and lending operations, but all could provide the promise of channeling multilateral aid to the LDCs within the rational context of regional development. The World and regional banks also add an element of rationality to planning by putting aid on a long-term basis.

Finally among the multilateral programs there is a whole complex network of U.N. bodies. They are gathered together under the U.N. Development Program, which works in association with a number of U.N. specialized agencies that are concerned with various aspects of the development problem. In an officially sponsored U.N. study, Sir Robert Jackson concluded that the U.N. development system was really a "nonsystem."[18] While the separate vested interests of the different U.N. aid agencies will doubtless inhibit their overhauling and streamlining, as Sir Robert has proposed, they will still continue to make valuable contributions, particularly as a source of preinvestment aid and technical assistance.

Standing somewhere between a multinational and a bilateral aid relationship are the aid consortia and consultative groups. Consortia have brought a group of donors together for the purpose of aiding a particular recipient. A high degree of policy harmonization and coordination is achieved in the process of assessing the scope and nature of aid needed, and then in soliciting contributions from the donors. Consortia have had some institutional sponsorship, for example as in the case of the World Bank guiding the consortia for India and Pakistan, while the ones for Greece and Turkey were formed under the aegis of OECD. Consultative groups, also sponsored by some international body, are much like consortia in that they bring donors together for mutual consultation over aid to some specific country, but they do not involve financial commitments or fund raising.

An institutionalized form of a consultative group was created in Latin America in connection with the Alliance for Progress. There the United States and Latin American countries formed the Inter-American Committee for the Alliance for Progress. It has conducted annual reviews of the economic performances of Latin American countries by submitting them to multilateral scrutiny and then presumably linking aid to the commitments to carry out needed social and economic reforms. Myrdal maintains that while this was sound in principle, it has been thoroughly abused in practice. Members of the ruling oligarchies only gave half-hearted assurances of reforms they never intended to implement. The whole land reform effort for example, was effectively sabotaged. American business interests that dealt with the ruling oligarchies also showed little support for reforms, and ultimately the U.S. government abandoned most of the objectives of the Alliance for Progress.[19] This illustrates the truism that organizational structures can become empty forms if there is a lack of political will to fill them with the necessary social and economic content.

All of the major industrially developed nations in the non-Communist world have sought to deal collectively with the aid problem through the Development Assistance Committee (DAC) of OECD. When DAC began functioning in September 1961 the core of its membership was drawn from the NATO nations: Belgium, Canada, Denmark, France, Germany, Italy, the Netherlands, Norway, Portugal, the United Kingdom, and the United States. The Commission of the European Economic Community was also given a seat. Japan, although outside the Atlantic Community, nevertheless became a founding member. Subsequently the three European neutrals—Austria, Sweden, and Switzerland—overcame their hesitation to associate themselves with this group and assumed membership. Australia, a developed non-Atlantic country like Japan, likewise later joined this donors club.

DAC, as a corporate body, has no funds to distribute, but since 90 percent of all public and private capital going to the LDCs in the past has come from DAC members it was thought that much could be done through mutual consultation to improve and harmonize their bilateral aid programs. DAC was therefore seen as multilateralizing bilateral aid, or at least placing all the important bilateral aid efforts within a multilateral framework.

At the time of its founding, some observers expressed the hope that DAC might develop into a major international agency with substantial authority. "We might consider," Senator J. William Fulbright suggested in the fall of 1962, "the elevation of the Development Assistance Committee at an appropriate time in the future from a policy-coordinating body to a *policy-making* body. Conceivably, the Committee could be empowered to make its decisions under a system of 'qualified majority' voting like that of the Common Market Commission. Under this system it might be authorized to determine amounts and conditions of aid to be extended and also to determine appropriate contributions by the Atlantic countries." He recognized that such "assessments" could not be legally binding "for obvious constitutional reasons." Nevertheless, the "determinations of the Committee might be expected to carry the same *moral* obligation as the system of national contributions to the United Nations."[20] Subsequent events have shown that these aspirations outran the possibility of actual developments, and so they have remained unfulfilled.

Similarly, in their careful study of DAC, Milton Esman and Daniel Cheever remarked that "the circumstances of its origin suggest that it was expected by some of its founders, particularly the United States, to be a politico-economic forum to consider all major aspects of the development process." However, the record has demonstrated "little public evidence that development policies are considered in the DAC in terms of a coordinated free world political strategy." The scope of DAC activities have in practice been "limited pretty much to economics and development technology."[21] DAC deliberations in these areas have been extremely useful, but such consultations have been more narrowly focused than some had once hoped.

Nor have DAC proceedings engaged officials at a sufficiently high level to make an adequate impact on the common aid effort. Key operating officials responsible for the administration of the various national aid programs have come together regularly at DAC meetings, and within these confines much has been accomplished to rationalize the otherwise multiple and chaotic individual aid programs. Moreover, the scrutiny and confrontation of each donor's aid effort by the other DAC members at the Annual Aid Review has produced probing and sophisticated enquiries that have tended to raise the general level of performance. Yet the realm of DAC's influence has been too limited. Goran Ohlin, who closely observed DAC's operations as a member of OECD's Development Center, noted that "it is probably on the technical level and among aid administrators that DAC's influence has been greatest. Beyond that level DAC does not easily reach. But the basic decisions about aid policy, decisions about its volume and direction, are made elsewhere—in high echelons of ministries of finance and foreign affairs or in cabinets."[22] It might be added that since DAC's work is not subject to substantial review by an international parliamentary assembly, it also lacks adequate access to legislators who appropriate aid money.*

AID LEVERAGE THROUGH MULTILATERAL INSTITUTIONS

How might the various multilateral aid organizations be used to make aid efforts more effective? In particular, in what ways could these agencies exert influence upon the social and economic patterns in the underdeveloped countries so as to foster the necessary

---

*The Chairman of the Ministerial Council of OECD does present an annual report to the Consultative Assembly of the Council of Europe, in which DAC activities are summerized. However, the Council of Europe does not have as members DAC's extra-European donors, that is, the United States, Canada, Japan, and Australia.

structural reforms. A brief, illustrative survey of the different problem areas might suggest some lines of action.

In dealing with the syndrome of societal disorders associated with "soft states," the donors can at least seek to attain greater accountability in the use of funds so as to ensure that they go for the intended purposes and are used with reasonable efficiency. The different agencies of the World Bank Group have tried to make recipients of their loans increasingly accountable, but this practice should be vigorously strengthened and extended to other multilateral organizations where it is not seriously in use.

Western business interests frequently contribute to dishonesty in government by promoting corruption among politicians and officials in the LDCs. Bribery is often justified as a necessary business expense required in order "to get things done." However a conspiracy of silence surrounds this entire problem. It is time for such pernicious practices to be aired publicly and an enforceable code of good behavior to be drawn up. Logically this could be done in DAC where all the important industrially developed countries consult about common problems of both public and private transactions in the LDCs. By facing up to their responsibilities candidly it would become clear that bribe giving not only substantially increases the cost of doing business but also introduces an element of uncertainty and irrationality in all economic planning. It also frequently aligns Western business interests with reactionary and exploitative dictatorships and so blackens the image of the West in the minds of important segments of the population in the LDCs.

Business practices vary not only between companies but also between nationalities. As matters stand, those who refuse to engage in bribery and graft are put at a competitive disadvantage. It should be possible through DAC, or perhaps some other channel, to make a collective effort to stamp out the malignancy of such unfair competition. Just as bribing officials is considered a crime within the home country, and no exemptions are allowed there for bribery as a business expense, so these practices could be punished when engaged in abroad. This would involve having all the developed countries collectively extend the scope of their commercial law, with sanctions against bribery applied equally in each country in accordance with the agreement negotiated. While such a code of good behavior would obviously benefit the business interests in the developed countries, it would also help efforts at political reform in the LDCs so as to make their governments more honest and more responsive to the urgent needs of their own people.[23]

The gross social and economic inequality everywhere evident in the LDCs could be significantly altered by land reforms that created a more equitable basis of land tenure. The landowning class has traditionally sought to sabotage land reforms in large part because it has feared that such a redistribution might be associated with expropriation, inadequate payment, or the acceptance of government bonds that were of questionable value. Multilateral financial agencies of unquestioned integrity, like the World Bank or the various regional banks, could step in and guarantee that bonds issued for land would, in fact, be honored. This could be done either through supplying a direct guarantee of the bonds in question, or of a guarantee of an adequate sinking fund used to retire the bonds. The guaranteeing agency could also support a program of related measures of agricultural services and credits that could make funds available for tools, irrigation needs, etc.

When land reforms have been well executed, as in Mexico, Bolivia, Japan, South Korea, and Taiwan for example, experience has demonstrated convincingly how the whole fabric of a nation can be transformed and social justice enhanced. Land ownership for the toiler immediately supplies an incentive to increase agricultural production. The peasants' income grows rapidly, some of which is reinvested in a more productive agriculture, while other parts of the surplus income flow to the cities to stimulate urban and export markets. Meanwhile the landlords have invested substantially in urban industry, which increasingly grows as demands rise from the prosperous countryside. Other portions of the surplus go for social infrastructure, like building schools and hospitals. Wider educational opportunities produce greater literacy. This, together with the elevated social status of the new landowners, gradually fosters broader political activity and permits great segments of the population that were formerly excluded from political life to participate in it for the first time. Land reform thus not only produces a significant increase in economic prosperity, but it also promotes democratic social changes that can over time remold the social and political power structure. The amounts of money required to set such a mechanism of land reform in motion are modest and well within the capacity of the donors, while its many and varied benefits are almost beyond calculation. Perhaps there is no other single means in the modernization process that the developed countries can take that is likely to have such far-reaching consequences for such a small input.[24]

Basic changes are also required in the educational systems of LDCs if the benefits of society are to flow to the voiceless multitudes instead of being used to defend the narrow self-interests of the ruling elites. The possibilities of achieving dramatic results from outside efforts to assist education would appear to be much more limited than in the case of land reform. Nevertheless, insofar as aid that is earmarked for education can be given through multilaterial agencies, it may be possible to make its use conditional and exert some influence in the needed directions.

As a rule, the educational systems of LDCs are oriented toward preserving the social and political status of the minority of the population that has already been educated. The children of this favored group receive a higher education that can prepare them for administrative desk jobs, rather than practical field work. Hence swollen, ineffective state bureaucracies are found everywhere in the third world, alongside the "overeducated" unemployed. Meanwhile the needs of the peasantry are unattended, since there is a contempt for manual work and a loss of status if one dirties one's hands with the practical problems of the illiterate masses. The entire educational system is thus antidevelopmental. Adult education for the illiterate and primary education for the masses are needed above all, but instead there is higher schooling for the educated elite who look down on the masses and do little through their education to help them. The most astonishing experience of the educated elite has been to meet members of the Peace Corps, and similar groups from European countries, who are both well educated and dedicated to getting their hands dirty at the rice roots level.[25] It is doubtful, however, to what extent such examples will be picked up and copied by the indigenous elites. Perhaps radical educational reforms might eventually be forthcoming from the greater upward mobility that would surely issue from serious land-reform efforts.

Basic to a solution of all developmental problems is the population question. In the judgment of the Pearson Commission, "no other phenomenon casts a darker shadow over the prospects for international development than the staggering growth of population. . . . It is clear that there can be no serious social and economic planning unless the ominous implications of uncontrolled population growth are understood and acted upon."[26]

Even in those LDCs that had achieved a good rate of economic growth, population increases largely and sometimes totally negate such advances, so that there is little if any actual per capita rate of improvement. This creates a treadmill economy in which scarce capital funds must be diverted from essential development projects to basic human needs simply to keep an increasing population alive. Increased food production is eaten up by an expanding population with the result that there is more hunger and malnutrition. The same paradox is evident everywhere: There are increased educational facilities, but more uneducated, more job openings are met by a rising army of underemployed and unemployed, more health and other social services are accompanied by deteriorating health and social conditions, more housing finds increasing hordes being jammed into slum areas, and so on.

The appalingly high abortion rates in the LDCs are silent testimony to the demand for population control. In addition, as the Pearson Commission reports, "numerous field surveys of parents in developing countries indicate that birth rates would be reduced by one-third if parents had the knowledge and means to plan the size of their families."[27] The developed world has an obligation to respond to these urgent needs, and again the most appropriate and effective mechanisms are through multilateral agencies.

In his inaugural presidential address to the World Bank in September 1968, Robert McNamara laid heavy stress upon the responsibility of the World Bank to finance family planning programs and to assist research into the most effective methods of controlling population growth.[28] The World Bank has since taken the lead in judging loan applications in terms of a country's population policy and the effective measures that have been taken to implement it. The World Bank has also jointly sponsored with the World Health Organization field missions to assist in family planning operations. Other multilateral financial institutions should follow the World Bank's example and aid population control efforts wherever opportunities exist. A United Nations Fund for Population Activities was set up in July 1967, but for a long time it remained bogged down with bureaucratic inertia.[29] Financing its operations on a major scale would be a logical opportunity to expand work in this area. Programs could be developed through the various multilateral agencies both to intensify research into all methods of birth control as well as to help finance incentive plans in the LDCs that would reward those who participated in family planning schemes.

However much the developed world cooperates to foster birth control programs, the hard task of carrying them into effect remains with the underdeveloped countries themselves. This requires building a vast administrative apparatus that can effectively reach down to the village household or urban slum dwelling. It means training a large corps of medical and paramedical workers, who are already in very short supply. And all this must be done by indigenous personnel, since a delicate job of this nature cannot be undertaken by outsiders. Furthermore, family planning is more difficult to explain and to implement where the population has not had the benefit of education, but is living by traditional superstitions and prejudices that impede rational family planning. Here the need to erase illiteracy and bring primary education to the masses is directly related to the widespread success of birth control programs.

The problem is immense and urgent, but perhaps not totally unmanageable, given a serious commitment to master it. Already Taiwan, South Korea, Hong Kong, and Singapore have had their birth rates drop markedly.[30] The other underdeveloped countries have no choice but to follow suit. However, time is not on their side, nor is there much time left.

POSSIBLE INITIATIVES BY THE DEVELOPED COUNTRIES

The radical domestic transformations and structural reforms sketched out above are far more important requisites for rapid and sustained development than foreign aid, although as has been demonstrated in cases like land reform, external aid can be a most important catalyst in speeding up domestic reforms. Nevertheless, the underdeveloped countries must assume the primary responsibility for saving themselves or they will not be saved.

There are, however, a few areas in which the developed countries, acting on their own, might make significant contributions to the efforts of the LDCs to help themselves. Robert McNamara, speaking as head of the World Bank but with the added perspective of a former Secretary of Defense, has pointedly commented on the disproportionate amounts of money spent on arms and foreign aid. "That twenty times more should be spent on military power than on constructive progress appears to be to be the mark of an ultimate, and I sometimes fear, incurable folly." The difficulty of diverting funds from arms to aid is that the arms race is a function of East-West tensions and until they are resolved there will be few dividends forthcoming that could be used to ease the North-South confrontation. However, McNamara continued, "if there were only a five percent shift from arms to development we would be within sight of the Pearson target for development assistance," that is, one percent of the donor's GNP. "And who among us, familiar with the methods and audits of arms planning, would not admit that such a margin could be provided from convertible waste alone?"[31] The idea that waste in defense spending should be converted into development aid is one of those eminently sensible proposals that probably has little chance of adoption.

Less dramatic and more work-a-day measures that might be taken on the initiative of the developed countries form the daily agenda of DAC. Here measures are constantly under review to improve the terms, conditions, and administration of aid. Typical subjects might be proposals to ease the burden of debt-servicing, to untie aid, and to funnel more aid through multilateral channels. Frequently these subjects are interdependent. The more aid is untied, for example, the easier it is to place in multilateral agencies. DAC policy positions are also closely related to action taken in other institutions. The problem of reducing the service charge on loans could be materially helped, for instance, if the developed countries substantially increased their contributions to the International Development Association, which was created to loan money on liberal terms.

The developed countries could have a major impact on the ability of the LDCs to increase their revenues for development purposes if they would stop discriminating against the trading interests of the poor nations. Trade has supplied the LDCs with from three-fourths to four-fifths of their total foreign exchange flow.[32] Viewed in this manner, trade is much more important than aid. It is sometimes suggested that if existing trade barriers disappeared, the LDCs could earn their way to development without any foreign aid. Perhaps this is valid as a long-term objective, but for the forseeable future the needs of the LDCs are so immense that aid is a necessary supplement to revenue from trade. There is little doubt, however, that the poor countries could greatly increase their foreign exchange earnings if trade barriers were abolished, and that a portion of this revenue might be used to replace some foreign aid. It is in the interests of both the donors and recipients of aid to move in this direction, since earnings from exports put the LDCs on the road to self-sufficiency while avoiding the stigma of charity attached to grants or the future burden of repayment as in the case of loans.

It is not simply the existence but the structure of tariffs in the developed countries that works a hardship on the export efforts of the LDCs. Many raw materials that do not compete with products from the developed countries have little or no tariff duties placed on them. But as these materials reach progressively higher stages of processing, the tariff scale also rises sharply until the levy on many finished goods is prohibitive. That is, the tariffs of the developed world are systematically rigged so as to discourage the industrialization of the underdeveloped world and to keep it underdeveloped. So long as this remains true, the developed world must be held responsible in large measure for preventing the LDCs from moving toward a condition of self-sufficiency.

Bitter complaints about this situation have been made repeatedly at the various sessions of the U.N. Conference on Trade and Development, as elsewhere, and various parts of the developed world have made limited progress in unilaterally reducing tariffs on goods from the LDCs. Continued resistance to lowering or abolishing tariffs in the developed countries has remained so strong, however, that, as the Pearson Commission put it, "aid has sometimes been termed a 'soft option' compared to the measures which are indicated in the field of trade."[33]

If one were to follow the law of comparative advantage, the LDCs should be permitted to concentrate upon exporting their natural resources and building up labor-intensive industries. These aims are frequently frustrated by subsidies the developed countries give to their agricultural products that compete with agricultural exports from the poor countries and by protective tariffs and quotas the advanced countries use to shelter their labor-intensive (and generally low-wage) industries. Not only do the LDCs suffer but these practices are not in the interests of the consumers of the developed countries, who must pay for the subsidies with their taxes and spend more than is necessary for goods from uneconomic domestic industries. It is only rational for the developed countries to shift their resources out of low-wage and low-technology industries to high-wage and high-technology ones.*

Politically powerful special interest groups, both in management and labor, have succeeded in preventing much of this necessary movement. Considerable resistance to change might be overcome, however, by use in the developed countries of trade adjustment assistance to provide relief, retraining, and relocation of industry and labor where imports have been found to cause injury. Vigorous action of this type is increasingly urgent, for as Harald Malmgren, the U.S. trade negotiator, has remarked: "A way out of our present dilemma in domestic and international policy must be found, because in the long run it will not be possible to continue to repress the large majority of the world's population, keeping them in unemployment and poverty in order to benefit a relatively small number of workers in the developed countries."[34]

A final area in which the developed countries could make a substantial addition to the resources of the poor countries centers on the possible use of Special Drawing Rights (SDRs) in a reformed international monetary system. SDRs (or "paper gold") have been issued by the International Monetary Fund as a way of assuring an orderly growth in the world monetary reserves that are needed to sustain world trade and other international transactions. Since the developed countries dominate the IMF, by virtue of their larger contributions, which are reflected in the weighted voting formula, it was the developed countries that obtained the lion's share of the SDRs. For example, of the $9.5 billion worth of SDRs created during the first three distributions beginning January 1, 1970, 73 percent went to 25 developed countries while only 27 percent was alloted to 86 poor countries.

A proposal that has received increasingly wide support would have the developed countries relinquish a portion of their quotas of

---

*This call for economic rationality should not be interpreted as a return to the classical doctrine of comparative advantage in which the trading units were nation-states. As indicated in the discussion about the multinational enterprise, traditional trading units have given way, in many instances, to the transnational activities of the multinational corporation. This situation would also hold for many instances of production by labor-intensive industries in the LDCs, which are carried on by affiliates of multinational companies.

future SDR distributions to the International Development Association of the World Bank. The SDRs so allocated would establish a link between development aid and world liquidity. The needs of the poor countries would not dictate the amount of additional liquidity required, but when such SDRs were created they would do the double duty of adding to the purchasing power of the poor countries by way of soft loans from IDA. Since these SDRs would largely be used to import development equipment from the industrialized countries, they would mostly wind up, as before, in the reserves of the developed world. But in the meantime real resources needed for development would have been transferred from the rich to the poor countries.

There are a number of impressive advantages in this proposal. Since SDRs are created by an agreement in the IMF, the reserves made available to the poor countries in this way would not have to be appropriated by Congress or any other parliamentary body in the developed world. Nor would government budgets have to show any such expenditures. Given the increasingly difficult task of getting foreign aid money from the annual legislative battles in the donor countries, this is a considerable asset. Moreover, the poor countries would have access to a sizable flow of untied, long-term grant-like aid channeled through a competent multilateral agency. Finally, it would be an important step in integrating the underdeveloped world into an evolving international monetary and trading system.[35]

The question of establishing a link between SDRs and development aid has been given urgent, high-level attention in the councils of the IMF, where the underdeveloped countries have been unanimous in insisting upon its adoption. The resistance to such a scheme on the part of some developed states has been gradually giving way to these pressures, since the LDCs have made the acceptance of this link a condition for their approval of various items of monetary reform wanted by the developed countries. As a result one might expect some type of positive action by the IMF in which the issuance of SDRs will be tied to development aid.

THE IMPACT OF THE ENERGY CRISIS ON DEVELOPMENT AID

The quadrupling of the price of oil in the fall of 1973 provided a profound shock to all those who are dependent upon this vital source of energy. While this act was deeply disturbing to oil consumers everywhere, its impact was nevertheless uneven. The industrialized countries were severely affected, yet they have sufficient resources to work out some sort of long-term adjustments. But for the nonoil-producing underdeveloped countries, especially for the poorest of them, the effect will be utterly devastating.

The oil-importing LDCs paid $5 billion for oil in 1973. In 1974 this bill jumped to $15 billion. The increase of $10 billion exceeded the value of all foreign aid received by these underdeveloped states in 1973![36] Thus by a single blow the oil-producing states, many of which are otherwise LDCs themselves, have wiped out the efforts of the developed countries to aid the poorest people on earth. Moreover, the inability to afford the importation of oil will have numerous, disastrous side effects. The lack of oil translates in part, for example, into a lack of fertilizer, which, in turn, contributes to extensive starvation.

Where will the surplus oil funds likely go? Oil money, in search of sound investments, will predominantly flow back to the well-organized money markets of the developed countries. Those that need help the most will thus be bypassed and hurt the most. Some of these resources might find their way back to the nonoil-producing LDCs when the latter borrow from the financial markets of the West. Similarly, oil money can be funneled into various multilateral institutions like the IMF which can make funds available through its newly created "oil facility," or the World Bank, through a development fund that would be built on oil revenue, as has been proposed by World Bank President Robert McNamara. Unless such loans were on highly concessional terms approaching outright grants, however, they would not meet the needs of the poorest countries that would now be unable even to service their debts on conventional loans.

Basically the answer to the desperate needs of the LDCs is as simple as it is logical. The oil-rich states, most of which will be accumulating income at a faster pace than they can possibly absorb it at home, will be obliged to give away a small fraction of their surplus funds to the poor LDCs. Nothing short of this can reach the heart of the problem.

The oil-producing states could arrive at the same end by selling oil to the LDCs at the pre-1973 prices. There are potential difficulties in policing such a two-tier price system, since it might be possible to divert low-priced oil to countries that are otherwise paying the higher costs. Or perhaps the oil-importing LDCs could buy oil on concessional terms or simply receive it without charge, similar to the way in which they had obtained surplus agricultural products from the United States under Public Law 480. As always, if there is a will there is a way.

A place should also be made for the oil-producing states in the Development Assistance Committee, and their voting shares should be enlarged in the IMF and World Bank, as they use their resources to assume greater financial responsibility for the operation of these institutions' efforts to satisfy the needs of the oil-importing countries.

Shah Reza Pahlavi of Iran quickly demonstrated an awareness of the obligations that have accompanied his newly acquired wealth. He offered large sums toward the establishment of the special World Bank fund for the nonoil-producing LDCs. He also showed a willingess to contribute to other IMF and World Bank initiatives that were likewise designed to relieve the financial plight of oil-importing states.

The response of other oil-producing countries, however, particularly those Arab lands on the Persian Gulf, has been extremely disappointing. The richest and at the same time the least populated states, like Saudi Arabia, Kuwait, Qatar, and Abu Dhabi, have thus far refused to join in any multilateral aid enterprise.[37]

The oil-rich Arab states have given financial assistance on a bilateral basis for nonoil-producing Arab states like Egype and Jordan. This money was not really conceived of as development aid, but rather as a subsidy to carry on the Arab struggle against Israel. It is worth recalling that in the Arab-Israeli confrontation practically all of the LDCs have rallied behind the Arab cause. It would not seem unreasonable if these same underdeveloped countries should now turn to the Arab oil producers for help. The Arabs might display, if not gratitude, at least a measure of solidarity with their supporters who are now in such dire need.

The basic difficulty, it would seem, is that foreign aid comes as a new and alien idea to the Arab rulers. They might get accustomed to the concept over a period of time, but unfortunately the desperately poor countries cannot wait. The oil-rich Arabs are clearly called upon to act without delay in a collaborative effort with the industrially advanced countries to resolve some of the urgent problems of the underdeveloped world that otherwise threaten widespread disaster.

NOTES

1. This point is repeatedly made throughout Myrdal's monumental study, *Asian Drama: An Inquiry into the Poverty of Nations* (New York, 1968), 3 vols., which is concerned principally with South Asia. For a condensed, updated version that adds policy conclusions and extends the analysis to Latin America, see Gunnar Myrdal, *The Challenge to World Poverty: A World Anti-Poverty Program in Outline* (New York, 1970).

2. Lester B. Pearson, *Partners in Development* (New York, 1969), p. 9.

3. Ibid., p. 4.

4. *Congressional Record*, 92d Cong., 1st sess., 117, no. 162 (October 29, 1971), pp. S17179-86.

5. Pearson, op. cit., pp. 172-76.

6. Myrdal, *The Challenge to World Poverty,* p. 357.

7. Ibid., pp. 359-62.

8. Ibid., p. 363. These other smaller countries, however, do tie aid.

9. Ibid., p. 362.

10. The brief survey presented here is painstakingly documented in Myrdal's *Asian Drama* and *The Challenge to World Poverty*.

11. Myrdal, *The Challenge to World Poverty*, pp. 220, 369-70.

12. Ibid., p. 372.

13. Robert E. Asher, *Development Assistance in the Seventies* (Washington, D.C., 1970), pp. 50-51.

14. Ibid., pp. 54-55.

15. Ibid., p. 92.

16. Ibid., p. 51.

17. Ibid., p. 54.

18. Sir Robert Jackson, *A Study of the Capacity of the United Nations Development System* (Geneva, 1969), UN Document DP/5, 2 vols.

19. Myrdal, *The Challenge to World Poverty,* pp. 465-66.

20. Address by Senator J. William Fulbright, Bonn, November 19, 1962, p. 10 (mimeo).

21. Milton J. Esman and Daniel S. Cheever, *The Common Aid Effort* (Columbus, Ohio, 1967), p. 145. For a shorter essay on DAC by a former U.S. Representative to DAC, see Seymour J. Rubin, *The Conscience of the Rich Nations* (New York, 1966).

22. Goran Ohlin, "The Organization for Economic Cooperation and Development," *International Organization*, Winter 1968, p. 239.

23. Myrdal, *The Challenge to World Poverty*, pp. 232-33, 249-51, 264-65. Myrdal suggested action on this issue through the International Chamber of Commerce, but this got nowhere. The present writer has suggested the use of DAC.

24. Roy L. Prosterman, "Land Reform as Foreign Aid," *Foreign Policy*, Spring 1972, pp. 128-41.

25. Myrdal, *The Challenge to World Poverty*, pp. 164-207.

26. Pearson, op. cit., pp. 55, 58.

27. Ibid., p. 57.

28. Address by World Bank President Robert S. McNamara, Washington, D.C., September 30, 1968, New York *Times*, October 1, 1968.

29. Kathleen Teltsch, "UN Officials are Encouraged by Birth Control Project," New York *Times*, March 11, 1970.

30. Asher, op. cit., p. 119.

31. Address by World Bank President Robert S. McNamara, Copenhagen, September 21, 1970, *Assembly, Western European Union, Monthly Note*, No. 9 (September 1970), p. 17.

32. Harald B. Malmgren, *Trade for Development* (Washington, D.C., 1971), p. 4.

33. Pearson, op. cit., p. 80.

34. Malmgren, op. cit., p. 75.

35. James W. Howe, *Distributing the Benefits of Special Drawing Rights Among Nations Rich and Poor*, Overseas Development Council Occasional Paper No. 4 (March 1972). See also the three articles by James W. Howe, Harry G. Johnson, and Imanuel Wexler addressed to the topic "SDRs and Development: $10 Billion for Whom?" *Foreign Policy*, Fall 1972, pp. 100-28.

36. Walter J. Levy, "World Oil Cooperation or International Chaos," *Foreign Affairs*, July 1974, p. 696.

37. Juan de Onis, "$1 Billion for Poor Lands Is Pledged by Shah of Iran," New York *Times*, February 22, 1974; Chester L.

Cooper, "Oil Billions for the Few, Sand for the Starving," ibid., April 4, 1974; Juan de Onis, "Oil Nations Fail to Agree on Aid," ibid., April 8, 1974.

11

PARLIAMENTARY ASSEMBLIES IN THE ATLANTIC COMMUNITY

The problems confronting the Atlantic Community have so far been considered largely within the context of intergovernmental bodies such as NATO, OECD, IMF, and DAC. Business is transacted within these organizations by persons who are appointed and instructed by their respective governments. Negotiations conducted by such bodies are normally ponderous, since governments tend to keep their agents on a short leash and require them to seek frequent, fresh instructions from their national capitals at each stage of a discussion. Moreover, such national representatives are insulated from the direct impact of public opinion, since they are beholden to their governments, which, in turn, are responsible to the electorate.

THE VALUE OF PARLIAMENTARY ASSEMBLIES

In the democracies of the Atlantic Community it is also essential to involve in policy making the members of Congress and Parliaments who are the directly elected representatives of the people. When parliamentarians meet with each other they not only speak with a fresher awareness of the public temper, but they are also free to speak their minds as uninstructed delegates. Debate among them can be spontaneous and wide ranging, transcending the diplomatic interchanges of foreign offices. It can stimulate legislators of one country to think about problems that concern the lawmakers of another. And in addressing problems together, they educate themselves about the needs of the wider international community of which they are a part. This awareness is then transmitted to their national Parliaments and the public that elects them.

The people are the ultimate resource of the Atlantic democracies; much can be done with popular support and very little without it. International parliamentary assemblies thus have the double function both of educating the parliamentarians who participate in such gatherings and of serving as a conduit for molding opinion back home in order to inform, help educate, and mobilize support for transnational objectives.

Bringing members of national Parliaments together is the logical counterpart of coordinating the activities of the executive arm of governments in intergovernmental organizations. After all, every advance in the further integration of the members of the Atlantic Community requires supportive legislation in every participating nation. When the Parliament of one country is involved in deciding a given issue, it should be aware of the likely attitudes and actions of other nations on the same issue, and constant contact through international parliamentary assemblies can facilitate this interchange. Moreover, parliamentarians participating in an international assembly can criticize the activities and bring pressure to bear on a related intergovernmental organization in an effort to improve its performance. Thus the European Parliament scrutinizes the work of the Commission and Council of Ministers of the European Community, and the North Atlantic Assembly addresses recommendations to the North Atlantic Council in NATO. Even though such parliamentary oversight is frequently lacking in legal sanctions and is only imperfectly developed, it is a useful function that deserves encouragement.

Within the Atlantic Community there are four principal parliamentary assemblies: the European Parliament of the European Communities and the Consultative Assembly of the Council of Europe, both of which meet in Strasbourg, although the European Parliament sometimes meets in Luxembourg; the Assembly of Western European Union in Paris; and the North Atlantic Assembly whose International Secretariat is in Brussels but whose plenary sessions have in recent years met in the various capitals of its member states. For the record, one should also note the existence of the parliamentary assemblies for the Benelux Economic Union and the Nordic Council, but their limited scope does not require consideration in any detail.[1]

The four principal assemblies all have to some extent overlapping memberships and a history of interlacing jurisdictions. It is clear that a final determination of their functions and competence is yet to be made, since several of them are still in a transitional stage of development. The logical, although perhaps untidy, way to consider them is therefore to trace some of the threads that have woven them together. Before examining these interrelationships, however, perhaps a thumbnail sketch of the origin and growth of each assembly would be useful.

THE EUROPEAN PARLIAMENT

The European Parliament evolved from the Common Assembly for the European Coal and Steel Community (ECSC), which began functioning in 1952. When the Six of the ECSC brought the European Economic Community and the European Atomic Energy Community into being by the Treaty of Rome of 1957, the Common Assembly was expanded to service all three European Communities and in 1958 became the European Parliamentary Assembly. In 1962 its title was changed to the European Parliament. Its work has been principally confined to the complex and often highly technical economic activities first of the Six and then of the Nine member states of the European Community.

In the conduct of Community business the Parliament was primarily designed to oversee the workings of the Community bureaucracy directed by the Commission. The Parliament not only has regularly been consulted on the policies of the Commission, but it has also reviewed the work of the Council of Ministers. In addition, it has recommended policies of its own. Members of the Parliament address both oral and written questions to these two executive organs and hold debates on the reports and performances of the executives. There is also the practice of an annual colloquy in which members of the Commission and Council enter into a joint debate with the Parliament. The Treaty of Rome gives the Parliament the right to censure the Commission, but to date it has not been used, largely because the Parliament and the Commission have been natural allies in representing a more "European" point of view and together tend to apply pressure against the Council of Ministers, which primarily reflects the different national interests of the individual member states. The Treaty of Rome also makes provision for the direct election of members of the European Parliament, but nationalist sentiment in several countries, especially France, has so far made this impossible. From the beginning the Parliament had the right to be consulted on budgetary matters, but in 1971 it received an increase in its powers to control that part of the budget that deals with the functioning of the Community's institutions. In the beginning these sums only amounted to above five percent of the total budget, but over time this percentage seems likely to grow.

THE CONSULTATIVE ASSEMBLY
OF THE COUNCIL OF EUROPE

The Consultative Assembly of the Council of Europe was established in 1949 as a broadly based forum for members drawn from the national Parliaments of 18 European democracies. During the first period of its existence there were heated debates between those who wished to move this larger Europe toward federalism, or at least some closer form of integration, and those who resisted this trend. In the end the opponents of federalism prevailed, and the Six of the European Community proceeded to go outside the Council of Europe in order to set up their own Community organs, including the European Parliament. The scope of the Consultative Assembly has also been restricted by the membership of Austria, Sweden, Ireland, and Switzerland (which joined only in 1963), whose neutral status prevented the Council of Europe from dealing with military questions. In actual practice military subjects have unavoidably arisen in the course of the Assembly's proceedings, with the result that the original prohibition has given way to the practice of dealing with the political aspects of defense questions. However the Consultative Assembly avoids framing any resolutions or recommendations that refer to specifically military topics.

The Assembly debates political, economic, social, scientific, legal, and cultural questions and regularly receives reports from

OECD (and before it OEEC) as well as other intergovernmental bodies like the International Labor Organization and the World Health Organization. The work of the Assembly has especially fostered the protection of human rights through its role in founding the European Court and Commission of Human Rights. The Consultative Assembly has also helped initiate and draft a large number of European Conventions on a wide variety of topics, many of which have subsequently been adopted and ratified by its member states. In its consideration of economic questions, the Consultative Assembly has annually held a brief joint session with the European Parliament. An official, if somewhat stilted, relationship exists between the Consultative Assembly and a Council of Ministers, to which it addresses recommendations and questions. While the Council of Europe has not exercised any significant political authority, it has made useful contributions in a number of nonpolitical fields.

THE ASSEMBLY OF WESTERN
EUROPEAN UNION

The Assembly of Western European Union arose as part of an effort to salvage the wreckage of the European Defense Community, which met with defeat in 1954. In place of a supranational body that could control an integrated European army, Britain proposed to amend and enlarge the Brussels Treaty of 1948 which had joined Britain to France, Belgium, the Netherlands, and Luxembourg in a military alliance. As amended at Paris in October 1954, the treaty extended membership to Italy and West Germany, and in associated documents restored full sovereignty to Germany while providing for German rearmament within the context of NATO. Provision was made for controlling the type of rearmament the Germans could undertake, as well as guaranteeing that the British would keep a specified number of troops on the continent.

The supervision of these tasks was in the first instance entrusted to a Council of Ministers. But then the Belgian Foreign Minister, Paul-Henri Spaak, intervened with "*et maintenant, Messieurs, la coiffure parlementaire!*" ("and now, gentlemen, the parliamentary finishing touch!"), and Western European Union was unexpectedly endowed with a parliamentary assembly.[2] Article 9 of the amended Brussels Treaty simply provided that the WEU Council of Ministers shall make an annual report on its activities, including arms control measures, to an Assembly composed of the parliamentary delegations from the seven member countries who also attend the Consultative Assembly of the Council of Europe. The assemblies for WEU and the Council of Europe were thus closely associated from the beginning, although they each had a different focus of interest. There was a substantial overlap in some areas, however, so that from 1960 on the WEU Assembly gave up its work in social and cultural affairs to the Consultative Assembly in Strasbourg while retaining its competence in other fields.

Even when concentrating upon political and military matters, the WEU Assembly found itself in a peculiar position. Since all the WEU countries were members of NATO, a meaningful discussion of political and military problems could only be found within the larger NATO context. Therefore WEU Assembly reports and recommendations invariably examined NATO affairs, even though eight NATO allies were absent from the WEU Assembly meetings. Moreover, the WEU Council of Ministers could frequently refuse to answer questions put to it by the Assembly on the grounds that the subject matter was within the jurisdiction of NATO and the WEU Council was therefore not competent to make a reply. This, among other reasons, has made the dialogue between the WEU Council and the Assembly rather sterile.

THE NATO PARLIAMENTARIANS' CONFERENCE

As time has demonstrated, there was an obvious need for a NATO parliamentary assembly, but when the NATO Treaty was drafted in 1949 no one had the foresight to give it a "parliamentary coiffure." In retrospect, the sense of commitment generated by the founding of the Atlantic Alliance would have easily allowed a clause providing for a parliamentary assembly to have been inserted in the Treaty of Washington. But the chance was missed, and when the question of an official parliamentary body matured a dozen years later, the political forces in the Alliance had so changed, especially in

Gaullist France, that any effort to alter the treaty risked weakening, not strengthening, it.

The movement toward a NATO assembly began informally in the 1950s by a number of individuals on both sides of the Atlantic who exchanged views on this subject. Finally in 1955 leading parliamentarians of NATO Europe and North America met in Paris to hold what was called "The Conference of Members of Parliament from the NATO Countries." Subsequently this cumbersome title was shortened to the NATO Parliamentarians' Conference, and then in 1966, as part of a general reorganization and upgrading of its functions, the name was altered to the North Atlantic Assembly. Though not established by treaty and having no official status as a NATO body, the Assembly from its beginning was given NATO headquarters to use for its proceedings and was regularly addressed and briefed by the NATO Secretary General, SACEUR, and other NATO officials. Over the years the North Atlantic Assembly has made an important, if limited, contribution to disseminating an understanding of NATO and the problems associated with it.

With such an array of four different but closely related parliamentary bodies, it was not surprising that various plans were advanced to coordinate their activities, or even to merge some of them, so as to reduce confusion and duplication of effort and make the resulting arrangements more effective. In parliamentary jargon this effort was called the "rationalization" of the assemblies.

A rapid survey of the different rationalization schemes will focus on proposals that encompass the Atlantic Community, instead of purely intra-European arrangements, although it will be necessary to relate the process of movement toward greater unity in Europe to the development of trans-Atlantic ties.

THE BRITISH "GRAND DESIGN"

The first scheme aimed at remodeling all four assemblies into a coherent whole was the "Grand Design" of the British, launched by Foreign Secretary Selwyn Lloyd before the NATO Ministerial Council on December 12, 1956. He commended the just-adopted report of the "Three Wise Men" on nonmilitary cooperation in

NATO and suggested means for consolidating European unity within the larger Atlantic Community. The Atlantic pact should provide overall political and military direction, with the seven-nation WEU functioning within NATO. Economic cooperation should be strengthened between such bodies as OEEC, the six-nation common market, and a wider European free trade area. Finally, there should be "one Assembly on parliamentary lines with powers and functions to be assigned to it, which would complete the Atlantic Community."[3]

The British Minister of State for Foreign Affairs, David Ormsby-Gore, elaborated the "Grand Design" before the Consultative Assembly of the Council of Europe on May 1, 1957. In it he spoke of creating "a single Assembly of Parliamentarians for Europe" that would have "direct relations with all the inter-governmental associations: that is to say with NATO, and WEU, and OEEC" and so on.[4] That this was intended to be an Atlanticwide assembly was made clear by a subsequent official explanatory memorandum that stated: "The British Government's proposal is to establish a General Assembly of Parliamentarians, which would replace the existing Consultative Assembly of the Council of Europe, the Assembly of WEU and the Conference of NATO Parlia-mentarians, but would *not* encroach on the special nature and activities of the Six-power Assemblies" of the European Communities.[5] (At that time the Six were considering the creation of assemblies for the EEC and Euratom, in addition to the one that already existed for the ECSC. Ultimately all three European Communities were serviced by a single European Parliament.) In the British view, the parliamentary assemblies for the Six should also join "the General Assembly for joint debate of the broad problems of European cooperation, including their own, and for the sharing of administrative facilities. But there would be no question of the Six being overruled in the larger Assembly, because the latter would be a purely consultative body," while the parliamentarians of the Six would be endowed with powers of censure over executive institutions with supranational intentions.[6]

Under the broad umbrella of the General Assembly of Parliamentarians, different semiautonomous commissions would be established on a functional basis, each with its own membership and rule of procedure to suit its particular role. Thus the European neutrals would not participate in the Defense Commission, and the defense secretariat would be set apart from the others so as not to compromise their neutrality. The explicit character of the Six would be respected by special arrangements, while they would still participate as an entity in the various commissions that would cover the different aspects of European and Atlantic cooperation.

Despite the admirable goal of rationalizing European and Atlantic parliamentary activities, the "Grand Design" aroused suspicions about British ulterior purposes; this, plus other considerations, caused it to fail. The supporters of the supranational ambitions of the Six were not convinced by British disclaimers. Rather there was a widespread feeling that the British had devised a clever formula that would permit them to be part of Europe without committing themselves to the political integration of the Six. That is, their formula did not take adequate account of the political reality separating the Six from those states that were not interested in building a federal Europe. This same factor had likewise caused the failure of the 1952 proposal of British Foreign Secretary Anthony Eden, which would have remodeled the Council of Europe so that it could also serve the institutions of the Six.[7]

Neither did the "Grand Design" sufficiently allay the sensitivities of the neutrals who would have participated in a General Assembly with the NATO states, even though military affairs would have been considered in a separate commission. Moreover, there was a strain of thought among some Europeans, expressed in a WEU Assembly recommendation, "that any proposal for an Atlantic Assembly, before European unity has been further developed, should be examined with caution."[8] Specifically it was feared that the United States would overwhelm the separate smaller European states, and that an Atlantic Assembly should therefore await the time when Europe could speak to the United States as an equal partner.[9]

Finally there were unresolved organizational problems. While the "Grand Design" would have rationalized the parliamentary assemblies, it left untouched the overlapping functions of the existing political, military, and economic intergovernmental agencies that would presumably have reported to the General Assembly. The informal relations between the intergovernmental organizations and the General Assembly would have superseded the rights and functions that had already been guaranteed by the treaties that had established the assemblies of the Council of Europe and WEU, and these bodies did not wish to abandon their powers, however meager, for something of lesser substance.

The Italian government advanced a variation on the British plan, first in a note to the Council of WEU in early 1957 and then to the Consultative Assembly in Strasbourg in May 1957. It suggested retaining the existing assemblies for the Council of Europe, WEU, and for the Six, but providing them with an organic link by means of identical membership in the national parliamentary delegations to these assemblies. All three assemblies would also hold joint annual sessions and be serviced by a common secretariat. Belgian Senator Fernand Dehousse suggested to a Congress of the European Movement in June 1967 that neither the British nor the Italian proposals made a sufficiently clear separation between the supranational ambitions of the Six and the other intergovernmental institutions. Accordingly, he advanced the idea of one assembly for the Six, and one common assembly for all others, including the Council of Europe, WEU, and a proposed parliamentary body for OEEC. Perhaps ultimately these two assemblies could merge by means of identical membership.[10] Neither of these plans fared any better than the British "Grand Design."

OECD AND THE CONSULTATIVE ASSEMBLY
OF THE COUNCIL OF EUROPE

The idea of providing an official parliamentary assembly to review the economic activities of OEEC had long been pursued by the Consultative Assembly of the Council of Europe, and a number of liaison procedures had in fact been worked out between the two bodies. When OEEC was reorganized and expanded into OECD in 1960, with the inclusion of the United States and Canada as full members, the question arose as to whether OECD should not be given a trans-Atlantic parliamentary assembly. OECD Secretary General Thorkil Kristensen proposed in June 1962 that OECD should convene a special parliamentary conference, which he hoped would later be institutionalized so as to provide OECD with its own distinct parliamentary body.[11]

The Consultative Assembly of the Council of Europe quickly rejected this idea as a needless proliferation of parliamentary assemblies. Instead, it felt that it should be responsible for providing the bulk of the European parliamentarians to any such forum. While OECD was being established in 1960, the Consultative Assembly adopted a recommendation proposing that members drawn from its own Assembly meet with other parliamentarians who were members of OECD states but not members of the Council of Europe in order to provide a parliamentary body for OECD affairs.[12] In 1961 the Consultative Assembly renewed its offer to participate in giving OECD an assembly, while reaffirming its opposition to any proposal "which would in effect create a new parliamentary Assembly, whether official or unofficial, largely European in character."[13] Meanwhile, in February 1962 the Council of Europe concluded a detailed arrangement with OECD, setting forth the modalities of cooperation in a number of activities between officials of the two organizations.[14]

Then, following the Kristensen proposal of June 1962, the Consultative Assembly adopted another recommendation stating "the most serious objections to the creation of a special new assembly" for OECD. Instead, it should be the function of the Consultative Assembly "in some way or other, to represent, on the European side, the member countries of the Council of Europe—the United States, Canada, and other European countries being represented as they think most convenient."[15] Finally at the beginning of 1963 the Consultative Assembly passed a resolution urging the Committee of Ministers and member governments of the Council of Europe "to enter into negotiations with the United States and Canadian governments with a view to carrying into effect the arrangements proposed by the Assembly." It was further suggested that this be followed by direct contacts with U.S. and Canadian parliamentarians in order to implement this plan.[16]

The arguments for bringing this plan to fruition were set forth by the rapporteurs of the Assembly's Political Committee, Alois Zimmer and Pierre Pflimlin, in the fall and winter of 1962-63, and elaborated upon by Pflimlin in 1963, when he became the President of the Consultative Assembly.[17] It was suggested that such an assembly would be a logical successor to the one-time conference between 20 European parliamentarians and 14 members of Congress which was held at Strasbourg in November 1951. These discussions had been judged extremely useful, and now a permanent assembly would prove of greater value for trans-Atlantic exchange of views on OECD affairs, as well as on other problems of common interest. The Consultative Assembly had the advantage of already existing and of representing the largest number of European countries, including the neutrals. It would be logical to adopt it as an OECD forum since the Consultative Assembly was the only European assembly that was specifically committed to concern itself with OECD. Also since the Consultative Assembly did not discuss military questions and was not associated with NATO, it could inspire greater confidence in the underdeveloped countries in which OECD was interested than could an assembly emanating from the NATO Parliamentarians' Conference (NPC). From the political and legal points of view the OECD assembly should be quite separate from the NPC, although for practical purposes the two conclaves could be held in close succession so as to take advantage of the presence in Europe of parliamentarians from North America who were attending the NPC.

PLANS TO BROADEN THE NPC

During the same period that the Consultative Assembly at Strasbourg was advancing these proposals, the NATO parliamentarians began exploring ways of broadening their competence and of associating non-NATO states with their work in an enlarged assembly that would consider all aspects of Atlantic Community activity. The Declaration of Paris of the Atlantic Convention of NATO Nations of January 1962 recommended that the NPC "be developed into a consultative Atlantic Assembly . . . to receive reports regularly transmitted to it by the Secretaries General of other Atlantic bodies; to raise questions for and to consider, debate and review the work of all Atlantic institutions, and make recommendations to other Atlantic bodies and governments on questions of concern to the Atlantic Community."[18]

The Political Committee of the NATO parliamentarians, with Congressman John Lindsay as rapporteur, responded to this call by agreeing in its draft report of October 1962 that "only by the establishment of a wide, strong, parliamentary body provided with access to needed information and empowered to advise the executive bodies, not merely of NATO, not merely of OECD, but of all Atlantic institutions, only so may the energies of the separate national democracies be directed toward common goals under a system of open debate and popular representation." The Lindsay report also ventured a bold effort at parliamentary rationalization when it asserted that "two assemblies and two only are in fact needed, namely a European Parliament and an Atlantic Assembly."[19]

The Political Committee of the NPC further urged that a special subcommittee drawn from the NPC be appointed to study and recommend possible formulas for developing the NPC into an Atlantic Assembly in accordance with the views set forth in the 1962 Declaration of Paris. This subcommittee should examine the essential aspects of such a hypothetical assembly by considering its constitution, powers and functions, composition (including the difficult problem of associating the neutrals), membership and voting procedures, sessions, the secretariat, and the budget.[20] The final report of the Political Committee, accepted by a plenary session of the NPC in November 1962, incorporated these views,[21] and the NPC also recommended that a special subcommittee be set up to carry out the task of studying and making recommendations on a charter for a consultative Atlantic Assembly, as well as examining the question of its precise powers and functions.[22]

Thereafter, until the next plenary meeting of the NPC in November 1963, the Political Committee with Lindsay as rapporteur went its way, while the Special Subcommittee (thereafter known simply as the Special Committee) went in its own quite different direction. Lindsay's draft report for the Political Committee meeting of November 1963 took an affirmative stance: A single consultative Atlantic Assembly encompassing both NATO and OECD nations should and could be established. The neutrals would not take part in political and military matters pertaining to NATO by virtue of dividing the work of the Assembly into different committees that would meet in two separate plenary sessions: one for NATO affairs, the other for economic and social matters in which the OECD neutrals would take part. The membership, voting, powers, and functions of this Assembly were also considered in some detail.[23]

The Special Committee's report, also submitted for the consideration of the Political Committee and the plenary assembly of the NPC, assumed the position that political sounding taken by its Working Group had revealed that it was not feasible at that time to change the status of the NPC. "Consequently the [Special] Committee did not feel obliged to submit a draft constitution or charter for an Atlantic Consultative Assembly, as it had been requested to in its initial terms of reference." One reason transforming the NPC "was not at the moment practicable" was that "such a change of status would involve the signing of an additional protocol to the North Atlantic Treaty." Moreover, on the question of rationalizing assemblies, the Special Committee concluded "that the schemes for merging some existing assemblies, or for some North American and European members to attend a session of an existing body have not at present materialized." Instead it held that the NPC "*is* an Atlantic Assembly" and that its operation could be made more effective by doing such things as improving the work of its committees, holding plenary assemblies twice a year, and recruiting additional staff for its international secretariat.[24]

Faced with two completely contradictory reports, the matter was referred to the Standing Committee of the NPC, the permanent executive body that exercises significant control over the operation of the entire assembly. In all these deliberations the voice of Congressman Wayne Hays was clearly heard. He was both an active member of the Special Committee and its Working Group and of the Standing Committee, where he had continuously represented the United States since the founding of the NPC. Hays was also an influential member of the Political Committee where he took the lead in dismantling Lindsay's draft report. It was possible to sense an element of personal rivalry in the Hays-Lindsay confrontation, which Hays clearly won.* As a result, Lindsay's draft report was entirely rewritten to reflect the views of the Special Committee, and it was this version that the Political Committee finally accepted.[25]

Lindsay's draft report was, of course, vulnerable to criticism, since his proposal for a single Atlantic Assembly with separate

---

*At the 1963 NPC Hays and Lindsay faced each other without the possible moderating influence of any delegation from the U.S. Senate, which was detained in Washington by a vote on foreign aid. Thereafter the 1964 NPC assembly was the last one Lindsay attended. He retired from the Congress when he was elected Mayor of New York in November 1965. Meanwhile, Hays has been continually reelected to the Standing Committee and was reelected president of the entire assembly in 1969-70, after having previously served as NPC president in 1956-57. In 1974-75 Hays was elected president of the assembly for a third time.

plenary sessions appeared to be a complete nonstarter with the neutrals, who felt that their neutral status would be compromised by this form of association with the NATO nations. At least there was, as one observer commented, "no systematic attempt . . . to determine what degree of isolation from discussions of security affairs, or what variant of the two-tier formula, might in fact be acceptable."[26] Also, Lindsay's assertion that only two assemblies were needed, the one a European the other an Atlantic, might prove possible over the very long run, given very considerable changes within the Atlantic Community. But in the near or even medium range this idyllic condition appeared beyond realization for the same reason that the British "Grand Design" had failed: The different assemblies often serve different and incompatible needs. In addition, Lindsay had not given adequate weight to the change in political atmosphere between November 1962 and November 1963, which was noted by the Special Committee. In the interim de Gaulle had thrown a pall over all efforts to strengthen European and Atlantic unity by his exclusion of Britain from the Common Market, his refusal to consider any form of an allied nuclear deterrent, and his increasingly open attacks on NATO.

On the other hand, it could be argued that conditions had not changed drastically enough for the Special Committee to disregard its charge to draw up a provisional charter for an Atlantic Assembly. Nor did the Special Committee have to consult primarily OECD and NATO officials and members of NATO governments, as it said it did, instead of consulting primarily with parliamentarians, who should have been the parties most immediately concerned. And it was surely not true that changing the status of the NPC would involve an additional protocol to the North Atlantic Treaty. The NPC was not brought into being by that treaty and it could be modified by an international agreement, which in the case of the United States, for example, would only require a simple majority vote in both houses of Congress. Presumably the agreement's implementation would be possible by some given number of assenting states so as not to have all action blocked by the veto of a single dissenter. The suggestion of the Special Committee to strengthen the internal operation of the NPC was, of course, a positive step, although its suggestion of two annual plenary assemblies has never been put into practice.

Lindsay's final report for the Political Committee in November 1964 took note of the failures of the previous two years and yet restated the "convinction that the creation of an Atlantic Parliamentary Assembly would be a desirable and productive step."

It further held that "now would seem to be the right moment for setting in motion the preparations for such an institution."[27] The Political Committee was persuaded to recommend "that discussions among parliamentarians be undertaken looking toward the creation of an Atlantic Consultative Assembly, or *assemblies* meeting concurrently, embracing to the greatest degree possible the membership" of NATO and OECD.[28] The idea of Atlantic "assemblies" has generally been attributed to Karl Czernetz, then Chairman of the Committee for Foreign Affairs of the Austrian Parliament. It was his thought that if two juridically separate Atlantic assemblies could meet, either concurrently or consecutively, then the neutrals found in one assembly could be sufficiently insulated from NATO business in the other to satisfy public opinion in the neutral states. For all practical purposes the same, or at least largely the same, parliamentarians from NATO countries could participate in both assemblies.

Quiet political soundings among responsible officials and parliamentarians of the European neutrals during 1965 showed solid support for the Czernetz two-assembly formula, which had also received the somewhat ambivalent approval of the NPC Political Committee in November 1964. The question then became one of bringing these Atlantic Assemblies into being. To this end the suggestion was made by Lindsay, among others, to assemble a small group of distinguished parliamentarians drawn from the NATO and OECD countries and entrust them with the elaboration of the charter or charters that would then be submitted to the interested governments for agreement. These parliamentarians, aided by a competent staff selected by the Atlantic Institute, would act in their personal capacities and in no way represent their Parliaments, governments, or international assemblies. Thus while the new assemblies would not be an outgrowth of the NPC, it was intended that they would absorb and supersede the NPC. But high hopes that this approach at circumventing and replacing the NPC with a more inclusive body or bodies were disappointed.*

---

*Since cordial relations existed between Pierre Pflimlin, President of the Consultative Assembly of the Council of Europe, and Senator Fulbright, Chairman of the Senate Foreign Relations Committee, a proposal that gained some support would have had Pflimlin, from the European side,

NORTH AMERICANS AT THE
CONSULTATIVE ASSEMBLY OF THE
COUNCIL OF EUROPE

Meanwhile, Pflimlin, as President of the Consultative Assembly in Strasbourg, had publicly distributed his aide-memoire concerning the creation of an assembly for economic and social questions for OECD countries, based on the Council of Europe plus parliamentarians from nonmember states, including those from the United States and Canada.[29] In order to establish preliminary contact toward this end, Representative Hays accepted an invitation to address the Consultative Assembly in November 1964, where his remarks stimulated lively discussion.[30] It was then agreed that Hays would return with a congressional delegation including Senator Fulbright to engage in debate with the Assembly in May 1965. Hays and Fulbright both addressed the Assembly at that time,[31] and in a meeting with Pflimlin both agreed to return to Strasbourg a year later, namely in May 1966.

When the NPC held its plenary assembly in New York in October 1965, a Council of Europe delegation led by Pflimlin met informally with members of Congress in New York and agreed that future meetings between a congressioal delegation and the Consultative Assembly would be regularized and that they would occur back-to-back with the NPC meetings in the fall of each year. In this way the Americans could go to Strasbourg without great difficulty either before or after the NPC plenary assembly, which was ordinarily held in Europe. This would require a special short session for the Consultative Assembly, most likely in November since its three regular sessions were held in January, April-May, and September. The Strasbourg delegation, however, was willing to make the extra effort required.

In May 1966 Hays and several other House members returned to the Consultative Assembly as scheduled, but Fulbright reneged on his

---

invite half a dozen prominent parliamentarians from different countries, and Fulbright, from the American side, invite another half dozen. Together they would form an independent working group on Atlantic Assemblies. While Fulbright had the prestige to launch such a project, he withheld his support.

promise to appear. Nor did he get any other Senator to come in his stead. Fulbright's refusal created considerable ill will in Strasbourg, especially since he had been publicly on record since 1963 as an advocate of a broader Atlantic Assembly to encompass both NATO and OECD affairs, and presumably he held the contacts with Consultative Assembly as a useful step in this direction.*

At their May 1966 meeting Hays and Pflimlin agreed that future meetings of the U.S. delegation with the Council of Europe would be held in Strasbourg in May, instead of November. This would eliminate the need for a special session of the Consultative Assembly, which would likely not be well attended, and it would give the Americans exposure to a European audience in the spring as well as in the fall. Hays suggested that by coming in May the views expressed would be fresher than those repeated in November, if the Strasbourg session were held within a few days of the NPC assembly. This new agreement, however, effectively buried the back-to-back meetings of the NPC and Consultative Assembly and with it the prospect for developing two Atlantic Assemblies meeting consecutively: one for political and military affairs, the other for economic and social affairs.

Events demonstrated that the two-assemblies idea was a highly arbitrary and contrived arrangement in any case. The stuff of political life is too intertwined to separate out some aspects neatly from others. Moreover the NPC had already set up committees discussing not only political and military, but also economic, scientific, and cultural

---

*At one of his Clayton lectures at Tufts University in 1963 Fulbright said: "An Atlantic Assembly of parliamentarians superseding the NATO Parliamentarians' Conference should be constituted to serve as a consultative organ for the Organization for Economic Cooperation and Development as well as for NATO. It should embrace the full scope of Atlantic relations. . . . One can envision a body authorized to submit recommendations to both NATO and the OECD, which would be expected to reply to all proposals either in writing or by the appearance of authorized representatives before the parliamentary body or any of its subsidiary organs. In addition, the delegates to the Assembly might be empowered to express their confidence or lack of confidence in specific actions or decisions of the two executive bodies. To accommodate those countries who are members of OECD but not of NATO, procedures might be devised for separate consideration of OECD and NATO matters so that the neutrals would be able to abstain entirely from all questions of the military alliance."[32]

affairs, and it seemed reasonable for the NPC to continue to be multidimensional in character. Experience also showed that parliamentarians would talk about what was foremost on their minds at the time and not be constrained to discuss other topics simply for the sake of some abstract organizational plan.

This was clearly illustrated by the debates at the Consultative Assembly of May 4, 1966 in which Hays concentrated upon the political and military implications of Gaullist policy, followed by a sharp and entertaining exchange of views with the Gaullist deputy Edmond Nessler. The presumed rationale for bringing the Americans to Strasbourg, at least from the European point of view, was to have a forum in which OECD affairs could be discussed in the presence of the neutrals. But what actually happened hardly conformed to this aim. After the Americans had addressed the Assembly they departed from Strasbourg. Thereafter, but in their absence, the Consultative Assembly considered the annual OECD report presented by OECD Secretary General Thorkil Kristensen![33]

Hays returned to Strasbourg with a small congressional delegation in April 1967 and May 1968.[34] Thereupon the U.S. relationship with the Consultative Assembly lapsed. The Europeans thereafter invited Canadian parliamentarians to carry on this trans-Atlantic dialogue. In May 1969 a seven-member Canadian delegation led by Donald Macdonald went to Strasbourg, and in March 1971 six parliamentarians from the Consultative Assembly paid the Canadians a return visit in Ottawa. As in the case of the exchanges with the Americans, the discussions with the Canadians were wide-ranging and were not confined to OECD affairs.

The experience of these exchanges with the North Americans was instructive in several respects. It clearly demonstrated that the idea of an assembly specifically for OECD questions held little attraction for the North Americans. Even when the Consultative Assembly itself considered the annual OECD report, the Europeans found that many of the topics were so highly technical that it was difficult to sustain debate for more than a day. It was also perceived that the Economic Committee of the NPC could serve as a forum for discussing broad economic policies. Over the years the activity of this Committee has grown in importance.

Economic and other nonmilitary questions could not, of course, be discussed in the NPC in the presence of the neutrals. However, the elaborate and cumbersome special arrangements required to accommodate the neutrals, who comprised less than five percent of the people of the Atlantic Community, hardly seemed justified. Hence the two Atlantic Assemblies concept was stillborn.

Moreover, creating one of the Atlantic Assemblies by attaching parliamentarians from North America to the nucleus provided by the Council of Europe did not appear very promising. In effect, the North Americans would have joined the Council of Europe for this limited purpose. The Americans who traveled to Strasbourg said on several occasions that the United States could not become a member of the Consultative Assembly since it was essentially a European body, not a trans-Atlantic one. In 1955, just as the initial steps for creating the NPC were in progress, Sir Geoffrey de Freitas formally had proposed that the Council of Europe become a Council of the Atlantic and that the Consultative Assembly become an Atlantic Assembly.[35] However, this idea rallied little support. As the Council of Europe emerged it was both European based and European oriented, and its most appropriate role seemed to be as a forum for Greater Europe in which the members of the European Community could discuss problems with those Europeans outside the Nine. Many have suggested that its future role might be as a meeting place for European states both West and East as Communist ties loosen and it is possible to edge the East back into the European family of nations. In effect, the Council of Europe would become something like a EURESCO.

THE EFFORTS TO "INSTITUTIONALIZE" THE NATO PARLIAMENTARIANS

With the two Atlantic Assemblies idea cast aside, the most promising prospect remained to upgrade the status and enlarge the activities of the NATO parliamentarians. This approach was often put in terms of making the NPC "official."

Even though the NPC came into existence entirely by parliamentary sponsorship, and not through a treaty or international agreement among governments, it had become at least semiofficial in character. Its delegates were elected legislators appointed by their respective national Parliaments, which also supplied the funds for the NPC budget. Very soon after its founding the NPC established an informal yet real and rewarding working arrangement with NATO. When NATO headquarters were in Paris, NATO made those facilities available for committee meetings and plenary assemblies of the NPC. The NATO Secretariat also helped in some respects to service the NPC meetings. A tradition quickly developed by which the NATO Secretary General as well as major NATO military figures addressed the plenary meetings of the NPC. In addition, such NATO officials have also regularly appeared before closed NPC committee meetings, or have briefed NPC delegations on a variety of topics. The NATO parliamentarians have also made numerous field trips, arranged by the NATO staff, to inspect and learn first hand of NATO military operations.

Yet all such activities still did not make the NPC "official," since there was no legal document that placed it in an official relationship with the North Atlantic Council in the same way, for example, as the WEU Assembly stood in an official relationship to the WEU Council. This assured an official dialogue between the two bodies by which the Assembly would receive reports from the Council as well as address written questions to it, or put oral questions to a Minister representing the Council in an Assembly session. That is, the Assembly's questions, views, and recommendations would be carefully considered and answered in some fashion. The dialogue between the WEU Council and Assembly has generally been rather barren, in part because a Council reply represents the lowest common denominator of agreement among the representatives of the governments in the WEU Council. This organizational handicap would also likely afflict a dialogue between the North Atlantic Council and an Atlantic Assembly. However in another respect this relationship would be quite different. The WEU Council is a ministerial body with few meaningful functions, since at the inception of WEU it was decided that the defense of Europe could only be planned within the larger context of NATO, and hence all major questions put to the WEU Council are referred to NATO. A dialogue between the North Atlantic Council and an Atlantic Assembly would touch upon all these vital questions, and so despite some bureaucratic obstructionism it would still be possible to mount a meaningful interchange of views.

As early as 1961 French parliamentarian Arthur Conte tabled a draft constitution before the NPC for "the Assembly of the Atlantic Alliance." He would have given this assembly official status by adding a protocol to the North Atlantic Treaty.[36] Tampering with the Treaty of Washington, especially in the era when de Gaulle was in power, only opened up the prospect of weakening, not strengthening, NATO. Hence the route of a protocol to the treaty seemed unlikely and ill-advised. As previously noted, the November 1963 report of the Special Committee of the NPC also rejected this method, although it erroneously held that a change of status for the NPC would necessarily involve signing an additional protocol.[37]

Renewed impetus to the effort to make the NPC "official" was given by a resolution adopted by the NPC plenary session in October 1965, which instructed "the Political Committee to prepare a report on the possibility of converting the NATO Parliamentarians' Conference into a Consultative Assembly of NATO, in an official relationship to the North Atlantic Council."[38] The initiative for this move came from the leader of the British delegation, Sir Geoffrey de Freitas, who was then appointed by the Political Committee as special rapporteur on the question of institutionalizing the NPC. De Freitas quickly set to work to draft a Charter for what he called simply "The Atlantic Assembly" that would stand in an official, consultative capacity to the North Atlantic Council.[39]

The next plenary session of the NPC in November 1966 accepted the report of the Political Committee, which declared that "an Atlantic Consultative Assembly with full status under the NATO Treaty should be established," and that it "should be empowered to discuss all Atlantic matters, economic and political alike."[40] The de Freitas Charter, accepted by the Political Committee, was also approved by the plenary session, and the report of the Political Committee and the charter were both forwarded to the North Atlantic Council for consideration. The NPC also recommended that member governments "draw up and adopt an agreement establishing such an Assembly as soon as possible."[41]

The idea of relying upon an international agreement thus took the place of adding a protocol to the North Atlantic Treaty. It was subsequently suggested that an official Atlantic Assembly could be brought into being simply by the passage of a resolution in the North Atlantic Council. The difficulty with this proposal, of course, was that it required unanimous approval of the member governments, as was the case with a protocol. The U.S. and Dutch governments strongly urged favorable action by the Council, but as could be expected, the French took the lead in opposing any move that would strengthen an institution associated with NATO. The British also were less than enthusiastic, although this position softened over time. Nevertheless, with unanimity required, there was no prospect for results through this avenue.

THE NORTH ATLANTIC ASSEMBLY AND ITS RELATIONS WITH NATO

As a final act at its November 1966 session, the NPC, seeking to endow itself with a more formal status than a "conference," changed its name from the NPC to the North Atlantic Assembly (NAA). It also pledged to enlarge and upgrade its International Secretariat.

When NATO Secretary General Brosio addressed the North Atlantic Assembly in November 1967, he revealed that during the preceding year the question of bringing the Assembly into an official, consultative relationship "has been discussed repeatedly by both the Council and the Political Committee with all the attention your initiative certainly deserves." From these deliberations it became apparent that some governments "felt strong reluctance to move toward institutionalizing the relations between the Treaty Organization and an Atlantic Assembly. . . . In brief, although the Political Advisers and the Permanent Representatives have devoted a great amount of time and much earnest thought to this matter of the Assembly, I must admit that they were unable to make any appreciable advance in the direction of institutionalization." Brosio reported, however, that "all NATO delegations were unanimous in their wish to achieve an improvement of the practical relations between NATO and yourselves. It is, therefore, my intention to invite your next Chairman to examine with me without delay the best method to clarify the problems, so as to achieve a better working arrangement between the Organization and the parliamentarians."[42]

The NAA responded to this offer of cooperation by urging "the North Atlantic Council to take appropriate action to establish an improved and strengthened relationship with this Assembly as soon as possible."[43] The Ministerial meeting of the North Atlantic Council of December 1967 accordingly announced that "the Council discussed proposals presented by the 'North Atlantic Assembly' of Parliamentarians at their recent meeting for closer cooperation between themselves and the Council. The Secretary General was authorized to study ways and means for this purpose and to submit suggestions to the Council."[44]

Given this authorization, a number of concrete improvements in relations were negotiated during 1968 between Brosio and the newly appointed Secretary General of the Assembly, Philippe Deshormes. A closer working relationship was facilitated by the removal during 1968 of the Assembly's Secretariat from Paris to Brussels, where NATO headquarters had also been relocated.

The new arrangements were approved by the North Atlantic Council on May 24, 1968, "subject to reservations by the Permanent Representative of one country" (that is, by France). They stipulated that the NATO Secretary General would be the intermediary between the Assembly and NATO. Within NATO, the Political Division of the NATO Secretariat was charged with attending to these relations. The NATO Secretary General reaffirmed the long-established practice of presenting an oral report to the Assembly's annual session. He indicated a willingness to participate in other Assembly meetings and to brief the Assembly's parliamentarians. Other high NATO officials were authorized to appear before committee or other meetings of the Assembly. It was stipulated, however, that they should be the judge of what they were free to answer, especially if information was covered by security regulations. Perhaps the biggest innovation was the willingess of the North Atlantic Council to discuss and report back to the Assembly the Council's views on resolutions and recommendations passed by the Assembly. The various divisions of the NATO Secretariat would take a position on each issue before the Council discussion. The attitudes adopted by the individual national delegations in the Council would not, however, be made public.[45]

In 1968 the Council first commented on the Assembly's resolutions and recommendations that had been adopted the preceding year. This procedure has been followed in succeeding years, with the Council's comments progressively becoming more explicit and more meaningful. When the 1968 Assembly said that it had received "inconclusive comments" on several points raised the previous year and asked the Council for fuller explanations,[46] the Council obligingly furnished detailed answers in its next round of comments.[47] The Council, however, refused the request to admit the Assembly's President and Secretary General as observers to several Council meetings. The Council also declined to suggest subjects for the Assembly's work and studies, as had been requested. A liaison was successfully established, however, between the Assembly's Scientific and Technical Committee and NATO's Committee on the Challenges of Modern Society (CCMS), which permitted a member of the Assembly and his aide from the Assembly's staff to attend CCMS meetings as observers.[48]

The Assembly still had not obtained the full measure of institutionalization sought, although it had explored several methods. In 1969 the Assembly resolved that its members "should initiate appropriate action in their own Parliaments to bring about the recognition of the North Atlantic Assembly as a parliamentary consultative body of the North Atlantic Alliance."[49] It was hoped that the different states that had looked favorably upon insti-tutionalization, when the question was debated in the North Atlantic Council, would individually pass legislation bestowing official recognition upon the Assembly. This cumbersome and piecemeal approach did not seem very promising, but it appeared that it was the only approach left open.

Meanwhile, the Assembly has concentrated upon perfecting its own rules of procedure and structure so that it might function on a level comparable to several other well-run international assemblies.[50] By improving its own functioning, the Assembly could command greater respect and increased authority, so that it could more easily qualify as an official body, since that status remained as its goal.

FUTURE PROSPECTS FOR THE NORTH ATLANTIC ASSEMBLY

The fact is that the Assembly has already registered a number of improvements in its status without formal institutionalization, and others should be possible as well. A larger budget to provide for a bigger, more competent staff and better services should be within reach, although this would doubtless be easier to achieve if the Assembly had become official. Nevertheless the sums involved are not large, and forceful initiative on the part of the Assembly's leaders might well prod governments into raising their contributions.

The staff and operation of the Assembly of Western European Union could serve as a proper model. The new staff acquired by the NAA Secretariat, following its removal to Brussels, has decidedly upgraded the professional standards of its performance, and while the staff has gradually added personnel, it still needs enlarging, at least to the level maintained by the WEU Assembly. It is important to have well-qualified staff members who can assure properly sustained committee work by providing a continuity of well-researched, well-drafted reports for all committees. Such reports help the Assembly's more sophisticated members, in particular, to participate more meaningfully in debates that are focused on issues that are well defined in advance. Moreover, it would be well to emulate WEU's documents policy. WEU's committee documents and verbatim records of debates in the plenary sessions are published and easily accessible, unlike the similar documents and records from the North Atlantic Assembly, which are only available in mimeographed form.* Experience has shown that some of the concrete proposals found in WEU reports, which have received wide circulation, have taken on a life of their own. Over time, these ideas have influenced a much wider audience by reaching foreign offices, the press, scholars, and others who were not in the first instance concerned with the WEU debates for which the reports were originally prepared.

As in the case of the WEU Assembly, it should also be possible for the North Atlantic Assembly to hold two plenary sessions a year, since this would give more continuity and momentum to the Assembly's work. It might be recalled that in 1963 the NPC had voted to hold plenary sessions twice a year, and presumably that pledge could still be redeemed. It is true that there are real obstacles, since some parliamentarians, especially members of Congress, would not easily be able to devote the additional time required. On the other hand, there is a noticeable tendency on the part of some of the veteran NATO parliamentarians who have long held leadership positions to look upon their assembly as a pleasant, intimate club that would not be too demanding and that they can continue to control. In time a renewal of leadership might help the North Atlantic Assembly to broaden its activities and widen its impact.

Now that the two Atlantic Assemblies idea has died, it would seem logical and feasible to expand the work of the NAA's Economic

---

*The NAA, like the NPC before it, only published addresses to the plenary sessions and the final committee reports, resolutions, and recommendations. In 1971 the NAA took a step backward by ceasing to print final committee reports and addresses to the plenary sessions.

Committee. It has addressed itself to basic economic and monetary problems for some time, but its performance could be improved by receiving the OECD annual report currently sent to the Council of Europe. While the neutrals in OECD might prevent the OECD Secretary General or the President of the OECD Ministerial Council from appearing in person before the NAA's Economic Committee, it should certainly be possible to use OECD documents that could help in the preparation of Assembly reports and debates. This should be especially true in the case of aid to underdeveloped countries, which is scarcely discussed, but should be, in the North Atlantic Assembly. This Assembly would certainly be a more appropriate parliamentary forum to consider aid and development policy than the Council of Europe, however useful that exercise might be. Since the OECD's Development Assistance Committee is a relatively autonomous body, with its own permanent chairman, it might well be possible to have DAC's chairman appear before the Assembly's Economic Committee, or if not that, at least make use of his annual report.

In widening the scope of work in the Assembly's Economic Committee, ways should be found to bring members of the Japanese Diet into its deliberations. Japan has become an increasingly important factor in the economic and monetary transactions of the developed world, as well as playing a larger part in development aid. (Japan is a full member of OECD and DAC.) Each NAA committee is free to arrange its own proceedings as it sees fit, and there is nothing to prevent Japanese parliamentarians from participating in the NAA's consideration of broad economic policies both for the developed and underdeveloped worlds. The West badly needs to build reliable bonds of common interest with the emerging power of Japan, and such a special parliamentary association could be very useful.

In one respect, the North Atlantic Assembly might profitably follow a practice developed in the Council of Europe. Since 1961 leading parliamentarians of the Consultative Assembly have met annually with the Committee of Ministers in a format known as "the colloquy," a confidential yet informal meeting between the two sides in which a free and frank exchange of views could take place on a wide range of topics.[51] The parliamentarians of the North Atlantic Assembly have established a satisfactory relationship with the NATO Secretary General, and through him a working arrangement with the Permanent Representatives on the North Atlantic Council. Yet the one is still an international civil servant (although admittedly an important one), while the others are Ambassadors who cannot write their own instructions or make policy, except in narrow ways. The elected politicians need an opportunity, on a regular basis, to confront Ministers who can make policy and often can speak with considerable freedom. A colloquy between leading parliamentarians and Ministers could be arranged perhaps twice a year, to coincide with the two NATO Ministerial meetings, at which NATO Defense and Foreign Ministers, and at times other Ministers, are conveniently assembled.

The North Atlantic Assembly moved in this direction at its 1974 session when it requested its Standing Committee to hold a yearly colloquy with the Permanent Representatives of the North Atlantic Council. The Standing Committee was also instructed to send a delegation of about 20 members chosen from among the Assembly's committee officers and chairmen of national delegations to join in a colloquy with the NATO Foreign Ministers at the spring Ministerial meeting of the North Atlantic Council. In addition, the Standing Committee was asked to hold one of its own meetings at the same time and place as a Ministerial session of the North Atlantic Council, so as to facilitate contact between the two bodies. Council approval would be required for these arrangements to be put into practice.[52]

At the seventeenth annual session of the North Atlantic Assembly in Ottawa in September 1971, the Assembly adopted the proposal of Senator Jacob Javits to appoint a committee of nine prominent parliamentarians of member countries of the Alliance who would be charged with the mission of conducting a thorough study of the future of the Atlantic Alliance, including an assessment of the role to be played by the North Atlantic Assembly. The Committee of Nine, of which Javits was made chairman, deliberated diligently for two years and submitted its final report to the nineteenth annual session in Ankara in October 1973.[53] The work of the Committee of Nine provides an excellent example of the kind of contributions parliamentarians can make to an ongoing dialogue on Atlantic problems. Its conclusions were widely circulated and discussed, and in so doing it served to focus the attention of governments and international bodies like NATO and OECD on the issues raised. Subsequent efforts by Assembly members to follow up the work of the Committee of Nine also permitted parliamentarians to prod their governments to act upon a series of issues.

In an effort to define the Assembly's future, the Committee of Nine commissioned a report by Peter Dobell, an advisor to the

Canadian parliamentarians.[54] It also set up a subcommittee under Sir Geoffrey de Freitas to consider the Dobell report and other related materials.

The principal thrust of Dobell's argument was that the Assembly had to change its public image of being NATO-oriented so as to be able to attract parliamentarians interested in the broader range of other trans-Atlantic issues. In order to do this he advocated that the Assembly renounce its long-sought goal of having a consultative status with NATO. Essentially this was a replay of the old but futile attempt to find a formula for accommodating the neutrals and others who wished to avoid the NATO "stigma" so as to be able to associate OECD affairs with the NATO parliamentarians. Now, however, Dobell would have brought neutral-minded Europeans into direct contact with the North Atlantic Assembly without even the protection of a legal fiction of two juridically separate bodies as had previously been proposed.

The de Freitas subcommittee and ultimately the Committee of Nine firmly rejected the Dobell thesis. While both committees recognized the value of, and indeed urged, the extension of the Assembly's activity into as many areas as possible, they insisted upon retaining the carefully nurtured contacts between the Assembly and NATO. The loss of this close association, it was argued, could only lessen the authority of the Assembly's conclusions. It would also tend to weaken, not strengthen, delegations from member countries, since parliamentarians would be less "likely to be attracted to an Assembly which had no links with Ministers. . . . This would mean that they would, in effect, be merely talking to each other and would see no prospect of their views being translated into action by governments."[55]

The de Freitas subcommittee and the Committee of Nine instead recommended continuing the pursuit of greater institutionalization while enhancing the Assembly's activities and making them better known. It was suggested that the Assembly should discuss the reports of the political, security, and economic committees in relation to each other. To do this might require a plenary session of longer duration, and if this were not feasible, then two plenary sessions might be devoted to this purpose, one of which would be held in North America. A small delegation of distinguished delegates from both sides of the Atlantic might also usefully visit major capitals so as to convey the substance of the Assembly's recommendations personally to national legislative figures, as well as to heads of governments, appropriate ministers, and other important public officials. Meanwhile, the Assembly might seek a more established status by drawing up a protocol or declaration for adoption by member nations that would accord the Assembly official recognition.[56] For its part, the U.S. State Department commented: "We would sympathetically consider specific proposals for more formal recognition which could gain the support of all Alliance members."[57]

In the longer term the North Atlantic Assembly could logically become the body to exercise a measure of parliamentary oversight over NATO defense expenditures. It is a basic democratic principle that executive acts should be subject to parliamentary supervision. However, the decisions taken in NATO on an Alliancewide basis do not come under Alliancewide parliamentary supervision. There is, instead, the anomaly of individual national Parliaments seeking to exercise control over a whole alliance of which their government is only one partner among many others. At the same time, the discussion of defense problems and defense budgets in the national Parliaments becomes increasingly unreal, especially for the smaller powers, since decisions about NATO policy are often made on an international level.

The most appropriate place for the Assembly to begin to develop parliamentary oversight is where the gap of political scrutiny is the most obvious: namely, in the expenditures for the common NATO infrastructure.

National Parliaments supervise the national military budgets that provide their contribution to the Alliance effort, even though they lack an Alliancewide perspective and are not as sovereign in making their national decisions as they sometimes think they are. Yet beyond the national level there are jointly financed military expenditures for which no nation is solely responsible. These involve infrastructure installations constructed with funds voted by all NATO nations, such as allied airfields, missile sites, air warning systems, telecommunication networks, fuel pipelines, ammunition dumps and storage depots, command posts for military headquarters, and military agencies, etc. In addition there are all the facilities for the civil agencies of NATO and for the NATO International Secretariat. As Dutch parliamentarian J. J. Fens complained, the national Parliaments "are not able to check whether the amounts requested for international military usage are correct, or whether the voted money is spent in the most effective way."

Moreover, "the audit of expenditure on NATO infrastructure is carried out by an international board of auditors who are responsible to the NATO Council. This means that the sums are spent and audited under the authority of the same executive organ and that there is no control by an outside independent body. This gap should be filled by an international parliamentary assembly with genuine responsibility."[58]

British M.P. Robert Edwards added that "parliamentarians are accustomed to going behind the figures and bookkeeping of public accounting. In doing so they can sometimes discover and draw attention to important facts which it is not the business of auditors and accountants to comment on."[59] Politicans, for example, are more likely to complain of unduly large profits made by contractors. And in the case of NATO infrastructure, where the completed installations belong to the host country, it is a political judgment as to whether or not the expenditures best serve the collective purposes of NATO rather than give disproportionate benefits to an individual country.[60] Moreover, as Edwards pointed out, "the joint defense planning and the joint financing of commonly established infrastructure programs are the outstanding examples of that integration of separate national defense capabilities which distinguishes NATO from out-dated military alliances. . . . It is precisely the importance of these activities" that requires "a greater degree of informed public discussion of the issues involved."[61] Even though the cost of NATO infrastructure represents only a small percentage of overall expenditures for NATO purposes, their unique function justifies the special attention of an international parliamentary assembly of the NATO nations. One could also add that in absolute terms and in the aggregate over a period of time the amounts appropriated for this purpose have been significant enough to demand political scrutiny. The total cost of NATO common infrastructure since 1951, including expenditures planned for 1970-74, is more than $5.3 billion, while the single largest infrastructure project, the NADGE air defense system, has come to $308 million. These sums, stated in terms of the 1971 predevaluation dollar, would be somewhat larger if one took into account the dollar's subsequent devaluations.[62]

In order to perform its job of parliamentary supervision, the North Atlantic Assembly would have to get access to the appropriate auditing records. Presumably this could be done through an agreement between the Assembly and the North Atlantic Council.

Naturally this would be easier to conclude if the Assembly had achieved an official status. But even without full institutionalization the Assembly has begun to open up a dialogue with the Council and conceivably this relationship could be expanded to permit budgetary oversight for NATO infrastructure. In any event, in 1972 the North Atlantic Assembly formally requested the Council to publish the economic and financial data on defense capabilities contained in the NATO Review as well as details of cost-sharing arrangements relating to the infrastructure program and to transmit this information annually for the Assembly's comments.[63]

From this beginning, the Assembly could gradually assume a broader function with regard to defense spending. The logic of defense economics (although perhaps not of national politics) should lead to an increasing integration or at least a more effective coordination of defense efforts. Unless savings can be made through common procurement programs and greater standardization of logistic support systems, the individual national defense efforts will not be able to keep pace with constantly rising military costs. The price of duplicating and competing weapons designs manufactured for small- and medium-sized national markets is a luxury that can no longer be afforded, except eventually through drastic reductions in force levels that may be politically unwise. A more rational use of resources requires the strengthening of the NATO international machinery for taking broader, perhaps Alliancewide, decisions on military procurement and standardization. However, the increasing delegation of authority to an international staff operating within the framework of sovereign states is not only difficult, but if achieved, potentially dangerous, since the ability to make decisions would be placed in the hands of an international technocracy that would not be subject to the democratic safeguards of parliamentary supervision and control. The only realistic and safe method of strengthening the NATO international staff would be to create, simultaneously, an international parliamentary organ for the Alliance that could supply the necessary democratic accountability. As NATO agencies attained a greater voice in procurement and standardization policies, the North Atlantic Assembly would be needed to review all defense expenditures for NATO purposes. In this area NATO would assume at least the supranational coloration originally intended for the Commission of the European Economic Community. The parallel here might be close, since the more prominent the role of the

Commission, the more necessary is a European Parliament with increased supervisory authority.

Even if NATO did not move significantly in the direction of supranationalism, an Atlantic Assembly that constantly reviewed all NATO expenditures could still play a useful role in stimulating more coordinated defense efforts. Fens suggested that "when the Assembly in a Resolution or a Recommendation expressed its views on a certain item in the contributions for joint defense, the governments would remain free to reject the views, but would be expected by the national Parliaments to put forward sound arguments for doing so in the explanatory memorandum to their defense budget."[64] Thus even though the Assembly could not exercise constitutional control, it could still exert considerable influence over the attitudes and plans of national governments, as well as over the NATO international staff. The consensus arrived at in the Assembly could be carried back to the separate national Parliaments for supporting action, while the proposals of the NATO staff would be subjected to scrutiny and debate. Through such an interaction the Assembly could modify importantly the manner of employing the defense funds that would still be appropriated by national Parliaments.

The Assembly could also act as a catalyst for the member states of NATO to collaborate more extensively in the joint procurement and standardization programs proposed by various NATO agencies. Just as the Assembly should have a special concern for the common NATO infrastructure, so it should feel a special responsibility to foster joint equipment programs, beginning with common funding for NATO feasibility and design studies. With NATO given the right to orginate its own studies on feasibility and design of military equipment, rather than being forced to rely upon those coming from different national origins, as had so long been the accepted practice, NATO could then proceed to develop the viable projects through consortium arrangements, such as the one created for NADGE.[65] There is little doubt that Assembly activity in prodding the NATO members into collaborative enterprises of this sort could augment the defense potential of the whole Alliance and at considerable budgetary savings.

As joint ventures in defense spending increased, it would become necessary for the member states to bring various aspects of their own military legislation into greater uniformity. Here again a NATOwide assembly could be of considerable assistance. Fens illustrated the way this might work by drawing upon the experience of the parliamentary assembly for the Benelux countries. Over a period of years it has successfully drawn up draft agreements for its member states which were designed to unify national legislation on a number of topics.[66] While it is admittedly easier to bring the national laws of three states into conformity than those of a large Alliance like NATO, the North Atlantic Assembly could nevertheless be a very useful parliamentary forum for this purpose.

THE PLACE OF WEU IN THE EFFORT TO RATIONALIZE ASSEMBLIES

Much of the above discussion about the usefulness of a parliamentary assembly that would help NATO perform its common tasks originated in the debates of the Assembly of Western European Union. But an anomaly was at once apparent: The seven-member WEU Assembly excluded the other European NATO members as well as its two important trans-Atlantic partners. As a Minister speaking on behalf of the WEU Council noted in his efforts to resist the demands of the WEU Assembly, "The WEU Assembly and WEU itself represents only some of the European members of the NATO Alliance. It would be difficult to expect non-WEU countries to allow criticisms of them, of auditors' and other reports, to be made public to a small section of the Alliance as a whole."[67] Logically the North Atlantic Assembly should provide the parliamentary scrutiny for NATO activities. What, then, would become of WEU?

It was sometimes claimed by those who wished to keep WEU intact that WEU had been entrusted with several specialized functions that required its continued existence. The WEU Treaty prohibited West Germany from producing atomic, biological, and chemical weapons. Verification of German arms manufacture as well as of weapon stocks held by other WEU countries was assigned to an Agency for Control of Armaments. Britain also pledged through the WEU Treaty to maintain certain force levels on the European continent, and this was subject to check. A Standing Armamanets Committee was supposed to help member countries standardize their military equipment. Finally, Article 5 of the WEU Treaty pledged more automatic mutual assistance to an ally that became the object of armed attack in Europe than the more loosely worded commitment found in the North Atlantic Treaty.

Those who looked upon WEU as superfluous noted that its work in relation to force levels and the control and production of armaments was so intimately connected with the functions of NATO that these tasks could be done equally well within NATO. When WEU was called upon to express an opinion on British requests to withdraw troops from Germany, for example, WEU found that it had to turn to NATO's SACEUR for advice. The information of the arms control agency was also largely dependent upon data supplied by NATO. Weapons' standardization was, in reality, handled by various NATO agencies and there were provisions for partial agreements among different European members for purely intra-European efforts. If, however, certain functions could best be performed by the continued work of the WEU Council, the ambassadors to NATO from the seven WEU countries could meet in a restricted session of the North Atlantic Council in order to transact WEU business.[68] As to the wording on mutual assistance found in the two treaties, NATO had created an integrated command structure and other comon agencies that intimately enmeshed the fate of all its member countries. This has gone far to dispel fears that there would not be an immediate, common response to an armed attack. On a parliamentary level, the discussion of military, political, and economic questions that engaged the WEU Assembly could easily, and more appropriately, take place in the North Atlantic Assembly.

Various plans have been advanced to merge WEU with NATO, and the WEU Assembly with the NATO Parliamentarians' Conference. In 1959 Belgian Foreign Minister Pierre Wigny sketched out a plan for a general reallocation of functions among European-Atlantic bodies that would have reduced WEU to a skeleton organization. Discussion of military and general political questions would have been transferred from the WEU Assembly to the NPC, while social and economic matters would have gone to the Council of Europe. The status of the NATO parliamentarians would also have been upgraded so as to be on a legal par with the Consultative Assembly and the WEU Assembly. In his view the WEU Assembly would then remain only as a parliamentary forum for verifying the arms control activities specified in the WEU Treaty.[69]

The draft protocol to the North Atlantic Treaty which Conte proposed to the NPC in 1961 envisioned a partial merger of the WEU

Assembly with an institutionalized NPC. The parliamentarians from the seven WEU countries who would attend the NPC would meet either before or after the full NPC assembly and would constitute a restricted session of the assembly for the purpose of considering purely WEU matters.[70] Similarly, in 1966 the de Freitas Charter for an official Atlantic Assembly stipulated that the specialized functions of the WEU Assembly could be performed within the framework of an Atlantic Assembly by the delegates from the seven WEU members, and the WEU Assembly would cease to exist as a separate body.[71]

All these plans for absorbing the WEU Assembly into a larger Atlantic Assembly were premised upon the latter (whether the NPC or, after November 1966, the NAA) attaining an officially recognized status. As long as such official status is lacking, it appears most unlikely that the WEU Assembly would merge with another body that is less official than itself. As British parliamentarian Peter Kirk warned, the WEU Assembly should treat proposals for its demise "with great caution, and under no circumstances give up its present position until the new position was embodied in strict constitutional terms."[72] The North Atlantic Assembly has moved in the direction of obtaining the benefits of an official status without formal institutionalization. Unless it obtains statutory protection equal to that of the WEU Assembly, however, it would seem that no merger will occur between the two. The rationalization of the European-Atlantic parliamentary bodies dealing with essentially the same NATO-oriented issues will continue to be frustrated. Both parliamentary forums will continue to overlap in many of their functions and in many cases draw upon the same parliamentarians in doing so.

Standing in contrast to the thrust to absorbe the WEU Assembly into an Atlantic parliamentary body, there is another strand of thought that has sought to emphasize the purely European composition of WEU and has looked forward to the merger of the WEU Assembly with the European Parliament. In June 1962 the WEU Assembly, anticipating the accession of Britain to the European Community, approved in principle its own dissolution and the absorption of its functions in the political and defense fields by the European Parliament.[73] Given this broader competence, the European Parliament could then consider the annual report of the WEU Council, which would still be speaking to the same seven nations as had formerly comprised the WEU Assembly. It was further assumed that a European executive agency dealing with political and military affairs would emerge in the near future and that the European Parliament would acquire genuine democratic control over those activities. The proposal made it quite clear that while the European Union would make its own distinctive contribution to the Atlantic Alliance, it would do so by maintaining its ties inside NATO and not by going outside it. There would be no attempt, for example, to set up an independent European chain of military command, but rather continue to rely upon the integrated command structure that NATO had set up.[74]

De Gaulle obstructed the realization of these plans, first by vetoing Britain's entry into the European Community, and then by doing more than his share to prevent the Community from developing into a political and military entity. It was only after de Gaulle's death that plans for merging the WEU Assembly into a strengthened European Parliament were actively considered again.

The "relaunching of Europe," symbolized by the Hague summit meeting of the Community heads of government in December 1969, reopened the debate among those who held differing views on the future roles of the two parliamentary bodies. The Foreign Ministers of member governments of the European Community clearly indicated their own preference. On July 20, 1970 they approved a report of a committee of the heads of the political departments of their ministries, chaired by Etienne Davignon, political director of the Belgian Foreign Ministry, which promised to develop widespread political consultation within the framework of the European Community rather than WEU and proposed a larger role for the European Parliament in the process.[75] And as a prospective Community member in 1971, a spokesman for the British government told the WEU Assembly that his government welcomed the arrangements projected by the Davignon Committee and accepted the fact that the future discussions within the European Community and European Parliament "will replace political consultation in WEU."[76]

Since WEU had specific treaty obligations to fulfill, especially those related to arms control and force levels in Europe, while the European Community and the European Parliament were not soon likely to step into those fields, the WEU Assembly, according to this scenario, would concentrate its attention almost entirely upon its defense functions. Eventually the WEU Assembly might be attached to the European Parliament as a special committee charged with supervising WEU military activities. In the longer-range future, when the European Parliament was ready to develop its own capabilities in defense questions, the special WEU committee could then be absorbed into the larger body, accompanied by the necessary amendments in the various treaties concerned. As the WEU Assembly moved toward a closer association with the European Parliament, it would also be necessary to modify the WEU Treaty in order to change the basis for selecting the members of the Assembly. Instead of a personal union existing between the members of the WEU Assembly and the Consultative Assembly of the Council of Europe, as was originally provided for, members of the WEU Assembly would have to be composed of members of the European Parliament. This would be of special importance following the introduction of direct elections to the European Parliament. Those who accepted this image of a European Parliament that was competent to deal with foreign policy and defense viewed the transformations involved as part of gradual and lengthy process.

Other "good Europeans," expressing a greater sense of urgency about the future development of Europe, favored the early establishment of a European political and defense community. Lord Gladwyn, in particular, advocated this view in the deliberations of the WEU Assembly. Ideally he would have had the whole WEU organization taken over by the newly expanded Eruopean Community. This would include the prompt merging of the WEU Assembly with the European Parliament. But acknowledging that it might be expecting too much to accomplish this merger in a single step, he fell back to the proposition that WEU (both Council and Assembly) should be built up in parallel with the institutions of the European Community so that WEU could articulate a single, strong European voice in foreign policy and defense matters, pending the day when the ultimate merger might take place. Gladwyn granted that the existence of the Eurogroup within NATO had helped a European consensus to emerge on defense policy. Yet this could only be considered a provisional arrangement, since it was flawed by the fact that France did not belong to the Eurogroup (since its goals were too closely identified with those of NATO), while the Eurogroup did include Greece and Turkey, neither of which was a member of the European Community or of WEU. In Gladwyn's view, a European political and defense community should be based on a WEU that presumably would be expanded to match the membership of the enlarged European Community.[77]

The Gladwyn scenario presented several difficulties of its own. It ran counter to the views expressed by the Davignon Committee, and agreed to by Britain, that WEU should have less, not more, to do as time went on. There were membership problems here as well. It seemed that, as a new Community member, Denmark (and for a time it was assumed Norway), would not likely adhere to the WEU system of military guarantees and obligations, and it seemed quite evident that neutral Ireland would not do so. In fact, Ireland's participation in any Western military grouping remains in doubt. In 1972 Prime Minister John Lynch stated that Irish neutrality would not prevent Ireland from participating in the move toward European political union. However, any request for the acceptance of a military commitment would have to be submitted to the Irish people in a referendum. As for the foreseeable future, he did not expect the institutions of the European Community to become involved in defense policies.[78]

There was also a danger in bypassing or superseding the Eurogroup in NATO in order to form a European defense community based on WEU that would be acceptable to France. As long as French hostility to NATO remains, any European defense community that was congenial to France might well be destructive to NATO and therefore unacceptable to the other European states. High French officials have, in fact, repeatedly indicated that they would like to maintain WEU intact, precisely as a possible future European defense arrangement that would be an alternative to the Eurogroup in NATO.[79]

Whatever evolution is in store for WEU, both as an intergovernmental body at the level of the Council and at the parliamentary level of the Assembly, it seems likely that it will progressively focus on expressing the European element in the trans-Atlantic dialogue. While it is too early to foresee precisely how the WEU Assembly will be tied to the European Parliament, and both related to the growth of a European political union, it is at least clear that both bodies will increasingly become absorbed in European problems and in the construction of a larger European entity. Under these circumstances, those institutions that are designed to deal with *Atlantic* problems, like NATO and the North Atlantic Assembly, will become more essential then ever before, lest the Europeans consumed with their own internal affairs drift away from their trans-Atlantic partners.

NORTH AMERICAN TIES WITH THE
EUROPEAN PARLIAMENT

An additional, useful trans-Atlantic parliamentary link was forged in 1972 between members of the U.S. Congress and the European Parliament. In January a number of House members from the Ways and Means Committee and two subcommittees of the House Committee on Foreign Affairs (those on Europe and on International Organizations and Movements) toured the institutions of the European Community and met with members of the European Parliament. From these contacts it became evident that there was urgent need for improved communication between the legislators of the world's two biggest trading units. Misunderstandings on both sides, it was acknowledged, had accounted in part for the mounting tensions associated with E.C.-U.S. trade policies. There was also the feeling that while genuine differences in economic and monetary policies existed, there was a still wider area of common interest that bound the fate of both sides inseparably together. It was therefore agreed that intensified and regular parliamentary contacts were required if viable solutions were to be worked out.[80]

In May-June 1972 the European Parliament sent an official delegation to Washington, at the invitation of Congressmen Benjamin Rosenthal and Donald Fraser, the chairmen of the two subcommittees of the House Foreign Affairs Committee that had participated in the initial contacts in Europe. Following several days of meetings with members of Congress and administration officials concerned with European policies, both sides issued a joint statement emphasizing the crucial nature of the relationship between the United States and the European Community in the years to come and the need for parliamentarians on both sides of the Atlantic to support continuing efforts to improve it. In June the European Parliament unanimously adopted a resolution authorizing future working meetings with members of Congress, to be held in principle twice each year, alternately in Europe and the United States.[81] Although members of the U.S. Senate did not take part in these original arrangements, their participation was sought and it seems reasonable that they should contribute to these assemblies at some point in the future.

In March 1973 delegations from the European and Canadian Parliaments met for the first time in Brussels. In accordance with their agreement on the desirability of further such meetings, the delegation of the European Parliament that visited Congress in the fall of 1973 proceeded on to Ottawa, where the first European-Canadian conclave of parliamentarians took place on Canadian soil. Arrangements for regular, annual exchanges of Canadian-European parliamentary visits were subsequently concluded.[82]

These periodic meetings between members of the European Parliament and their U.S. and Canadian counterparts should provide a valuable supplement to other European-North American dialogues in progress elsewhere. While the Economic Committee of the North Atlantic Assembly is competent to discuss E.C.-U.S. trade and monetary issues, for example, its consideration of these topics would not likely be as well focused or as thorough as the Congressional-European Parliament deliberations. By tradition, the NAA Economic Committee has emphasized the impact of economic policies upon the functioning of the political and military aspects of the Atlantic Alliance. Moreover, the members of the European Parliament can represent the collective interests of the European Community in a way that separate spokesmen from its member countries cannot. This relationship will also be tangible expression of the cardinal principle that movement toward European Union must be accompanied by a continual process of strengthening trans-Atlantic ties.

NOTES

1. For a description of the Benelux and Nordic parliamentary assemblies, see Kenneth Lindsay, *European Assemblies* (New York, 1960), pp. 32-38, 252-67.

2. Quoted in J. J. Fens, "The Influence of The Assembly of WEU in the Field of Western Defense," in *Ten Years of Seven-Power Europe* (WEU, Paris, 1964), p. 98.

3. Records of NATO Ministerial Council proceedings are secret, but a British press briefing to Reuters outlined the proposal.

See Assembly, WEU, Information Document, December 13, 1956, A/WEU/GA (56) 19.

4. Speech of Minister of State for Foreign Affairs, the Rt. Hon. David Ormsby-Gore, M.P., to the Consultative Assembly of the Council of Europe, May 1, 1957, British Information Service, T. 23, May 28, 1957, pp. 3-4.

5. "The 'Grand Design' for Europe," Information Office, British Embassy, Washington, May 20, 1957, p. 2.

6. Ibid., p. 3.

7. On the Eden Plan, see A. H. Robertson, *The Council of Europe* (New York, 1956), pp. 99-100; Oliver Crawford, *Done This Day: The European Idea in Action* (London, 1970), pp. 70-72.

8. Recommendation No. 20, "On the Rationalization of European Assemblies," Assembly, WEU, *Proceedings*, October 1957, V, p. 31.

9. "The Unification of European Assemblies," M. van der Goes van Naters, rapporteur, Document 62, September 21, 1957, Assembly, WEU, *Proceedings*, October 1957, IV, p. 68.

10. *Designs for Europe*, Political and Economic Planning, No. 414, September 16, 1957, pp. 192-93.

11. Memorandum by the Secretary General of the Council of Europe, "Organization of Parliamentary Meetings on OECD Affairs," March 15, 1963, Council of Europe SG (63) 1, pp. 3-4.

12. Consultative Assembly of the Council of Europe, Twelfth Ordinary Session, Recommendation 245, adopted April 29, 1960.

13. Consultative Assembly of the Council of Europe, Twelfth Ordinary Session, Recommendation 273, adopted March 3, 1961.

14. Arrangement between the Council of Europe and the Organization for Economic Cooperation and Development, adopted February 1, 1962, pp. 1-13.

15. Consultative Assembly of the Council of Europe, Fourteenth Ordinary Session, Recommendation 336, adopted September 25, 1962.

16. Consultative Assembly of the Council of Europe, Fourteenth Ordinary Session, Recommendation 241, adopted January 17, 1963.

17. Consultative Assembly of the Council of Europe, Report of the Political Committee, Alois Zimmer, rapporteur, September 1962, Doc. 1478; Report of the Political Committee, Pierre Pflimlin, rapporteur, September 1962, Doc. 1479; Report of the Political

Committee, Pierre Pflimlin and Alois Zimmer, rapporteurs, January 1963, Doc. 1546; Speech by Alois Zimmer to the Council of OECD on December 18, 1962, AS/Pol (14) 70, Council of Europe, January 4, 1963; Aide-Memoire by Pierre Pflimlin, President of the Consultative Assembly of the Council of Europe, September 20, 1963, Doc. 1721.

18. "Declaration of Paris," Atlantic Convention of NATO Nations, January 8-20, 1962, *Freedom & Union*, February-March 1962, p. 14.

19. Draft Report of the Political Committee, NPC, agreed at its Meeting on October 1, 1962, John V. Lindsay, rapporteur, Paris, p. 4.

20. Ibid., pp. 2-4.

21. Report of the Political Committee, adopted by the Eighth Annual Conference of NATO Parliamentarians, November 1962, Paris, in *Reports and Recommendations, NPC, 1962*, pp. 7-10.

22. Political Committee, Recommendation 1, adopted by the Eighth Annual Conference of NATO Parliamentarians, November 1962, *Reports and Recommendations, NPC, 1962*, pp. 47-48.

23. Draft Report of the Political Committee, NPC, November 1963, John V. Lindsay, rapporteur, Paris, pp. 3-5.

24. Report of the Special Committee of the Conference Charged with the Study of its Institutionalization, adopted by the Ninth Annual Conference of NATO Parliamentarians, November 1963, Paris, in *Reports and Recommendations, NPC, 1963*, pp. 7-12.

25. Report of the Political Committee, adopted by the Ninth Annual Conference of NATO Parliamentarians, November 1963, Paris, in *Reports and Recommendations, NPC, 1963*, pp. 15-19.

26. J. Allan Hovey, Jr., *The Superparliaments* (New York, 1966), p. 167. See also pp. 170-73.

27. Report of the Political Committee, adopted by the Tenth Annual Conference of NATO Parliamentarians, November 1964, Paris, in *Reports and Recommendations, NPC, 1964*, pp. 12-13.

28. Recommendation I, Political Committee, *Reports and Recommendations, NPC, 1964*, p. 53. (Italics added.)

29. Consultative Assembly of the Council of Europe, Doc. 1721, February 10, 1964, Aide-Memoire concerning the Organization of Parliamentary Debates among Representatives of the Member Countries of OECD. This made public Pflimlin's previous Aide-Memoire of September 20, 1963 on the same subject.

30. Consultative Assembly of the Council of Europe, Official

Report, Sixteenth Ordinary Session, Third Part, November 6, 1964, AS (16) CR 14 and AS (16) CR 15.

31. Consultative Assembly of the Council of Europe, Official Report, Seventeenth Ordinary Session, First Part, May 4, 1965, AS (17) CR 3.

32. Address by Senator J. William Fulbright, Medford, Mass., April 30, 1963, p. 9. Again in a Munich speech of the following year, Fulbright reaffirmed this idea. (New York *Times*, November 20, 1964).

33. Consultative Assembly of the Council of Europe, Official Report, Eighteenth Ordinary Session, First Part, May 4, 1966, AS (18) CR 4; Order of Business for the First Part of the Eighteenth Ordinary Session of the Consultative Assembly, 2nd to 6th May 1966.

34. Consultative Assembly of the Council of Europe, Official Report, Nineteenth Ordinary Session, First Part, April 26, 1967, AS (19) CR 4; Official Report, Twentieth Ordinary Session, First Part, May 8, 1968, AS (20) CR 5 and May 9, 1968, AS (20) CR 6.

35. Geoffrey de Freitas, "The Case for an Atlantic Assembly," in *NATO is Not Enough: Two Approaches to an Atlantic Assembly* (London, 1955), pp. 17-24.

36. Draft Additional Protocol to the North Atlantic Treaty, tabled by Arthur Conte to the Seventh Annual Conference of NATO Parliamentarians, November 1961, Paris.

37. Report of the Special Committee of the Conference Charged with the Study of its Institutionalization, adopted by the Ninth Annual Conference of NATO Parliamentarians, November 1963, Paris, in *Reports and Recommendations, NPC, 1963*, p. 7.

38. Political Committee, Recommendation III, adopted by the Eleventh Annual Conference of NATO Parliamentarians, October 1965, New York, in *Reports, Resolutions and Recommendations, NPC, 1965*, pp. 75-76.

39. Conversion of the NATO Parliamentarians' Conference into a Consultative Assembly of NATO, Draft Report by Sir Geoffrey de Freitas, Special Rapporteur of the Political Committee on the Need for an Atlantic Assembly, Political Committee, NPC, February 1966.

40. Report of the Political Committee, adopted by the Twelfth Annual Conference of NATO Parliamentarians, November 1966, Paris, in *Reports, Resolutions and Recommendations, NPC 1966*, p. 10.

41. Political Committee, Resolution II, adopted by the Twelfth Annual Conference of NATO Parliamentarians, November 1966, Paris, *Reports, Resolutions and Recommendations, NPC, 1966*, p. 81.

42. Address by NATO Secretary General Manlio Brosio, November 20, 1967, to the Thirteenth Annual Session of the North Atlantic Assembly, Brussels, in *Addresses by Speakers, NAA, 1967*, p. 19.

43. Political Committee, Recommendation II, adopted by the Thirteenth Annual Session of the North Atlantic Assembly, November 1967, Brussels, in *Reports, Resolutions and Recommendations, NAA 1967*, p. 101.

44. NATO Ministerial Meeting Final Communique, December 14, 1967, Brussels, *NATO Letter*, January 1968, p. 25.

45. Philippe Deshormes, Report of the Secretary General to the Plenary Assembly, International Secretariat, North Atlantic Assembly, November 1968, Brussels, pp. 2-3. L. 167 SC. (68) 45.

46. Political Committee, Recommendation VI, adopted by the Fourteenth Annual Session of the North Atlantic Assembly, November 1968, Brussels, in *Addresses, Reports and Recommendations, NAA, 1968*, pp. 132-33.

47. Comments of the North Atlantic Council on the Recommendations adopted at the Fourteenth Session of the North Atlantic Assembly, International Secretariat, NAA, April 1969, pp. 8-9. M36.

48. Deshormes, op. cit., pp. 3-4.

49. Political Committee, Resolution III, adopted by the Fifteenth Annual Session of the North Atlantic Assembly, October 1969, Brussels, in *Addresses, Reports and Recommendations, NAA, 1969*, p. 213.

50. Political Committee, Order I, adopted at the Sixteenth Annual Session of the North Atlantic Assembly, November 1970, The Hague, in *Addresses, Reports and Texts Adopted, NAA, 1970*, p. 261. Institutionalization of the Assembly, Suggested Changes to the Rules of Procedure and Interpretation of the Rules, Sir Geoffrey de Freitas, rapporteur, April 1970, International Secretariat, North Atlantic Assembly, N 22 SC (70) 6 Rev. 1. Subsequent Assembly documents have continued to refine the points raised in this draft report.

51. Michael Palmer, John Lambert et al., *European Unity* (London, 1968), pp. 130-31.

52. *Texts Adopted by the North Atlantic Assembly*, Twentieth Annual Session, November 1974, London, Political Committee, Recommendation 44 On Extending Assembly Relations with the North Atlantic Council, pp. 8-9; Political Committee, Resolution 23 On Expanding Assembly Relations with Member Governments of the North Atlantic Alliance, pp. 17-18; Political Committee, Order 14 On Expanding Relations with Member Governments of the North Atlantic Alliance, p. 27.

53. Report of the Committee of Nine, International Secretariat, North Atlantic Assembly, September 1973, Brussels, Q 119.

54. Peter C. Dobell, "Trans-Atlantic Interparliamentary Links and the Future of the North Atlantic Assembly," International Secretariat, North Atlantic Assembly, October 1972, Brussels, P 130 SC(72)49.

55. Sir Geoffrey de Freitas, Chairman of the Sub-Committee Appointed to Study the Appendix to the Interim Report of the Committee of Nine on the Future Prospects of the North Atlantic Assembly, Draft Report Prepared for the Washington Meeting of April 4, 1973, International Secretariat, North Atlantic Assembly, March 1973, Brussels, Q 34 PC/C9(73) 4, p. 4. See also de Freitas reports by same subcommittee, May 1973, Q 67 PC/C9(73) 7 rev. 1; September 1973, Q 117 PC/C9(73) 8; October 1973, Q 202 PC/C9(73) 11 rev. 1.

56. Report of the Committee of Nine, op. cit., pp. 25-26.

57. Comments by the Department of State on the Committee of Nine Report for the North Atlantic Assembly, June 1974, Washington, D.C., p. 68.

58. "The State of European Security, 1956-1961," J. J. Fens, rapporteur, Document 215, November 10, 1961, Assembly, WEU, *Proceedings*, December 1961, III, pp. 120-21.

59. Assembly, WEU, *Proceedings*, June 1967, I, p. 97.

60. Assembly, WEU, *Proceedings*, December 1966, IV, p. 75.

61. Assembly, WEU, *Proceedings*, June 1967, I, p. 98.

62. *NATO Facts and Figures*, NATO Information Service, October 1971, p. 138; the NADGE figure came from a communication with the NATO Secretariat of November 1972. All figures originally given in IAU (infrastructure accounting units) based on one pound sterling before the 1967 devaluation, or $2.80 to one IAU.

63. Military Committee, Recommendation VI, adopted by the

Eighteenth Annual Session of the North Atlantic Assembly, November 1972, Bonn.

64. "The State of European Security, 1956-1961," op. cit., p. 121.

65. See Robert Rhodes James, "Standardization and Common Production of Weapons in NATO," monograph no. 3 of the Institute for Strategic Studies series, *Defense, Technology and the Western Alliance* (London, 1967); Draft Report on Standardization and Common Production in NATO, Philip Goodhart, rapporteur, NATO Parliamentarians' Conference, Military Committee, K. 53 (Rev. 1) MC (67) 3, October 1967. Finally in 1972 some first steps were taken in the direction of common funding for NATO feasibility and design studies.

66. "The State of European Security, 1956-1961," op. cit., p. 122.

67. Assembly, WEU, *Proceedings*, June 1967, II, p. 119.

68. A. H. Robertson, *European Institutions* (New York, 1959), pp. 238-39.

69. Pierre Wigny, "Rationalization of European Institutions Other Than Those of the Six," Aide-Memoire transmitted by the Belgian Government to the Member States of the Council of Europe, February 6, 1959. Assembly, WEU, Document CP (59) 6, May 15, 1959.

70. Draft Additional Protocol to the North Atlantic Treaty, tabled by Arthur Conte to the Seventh Annual Conference of NATO Parliamentarians, November 1961, Paris.

71. Conversion of the NATO Parliamentarians' Conference into a Consultative Assembly of NATO, Draft Report by Sir Geoffrey de Freitas, Special Rapporteur of the Political Committee on the Need for an Atlantic Assembly, Political Committee, NPC, February 1966.

72. Assembly, WEU, *Proceedings*, December 1966, III, p. 75.

73. Recommendation 77, "The Future Organization of Western Defense on the Executive and Parliamentary Levels," Assembly, WEU, *Proceedings*, June 1962, II, p. 38.

74. "The Future Organization of Western Defense," F. J. Goedhart and Raffaele Cardona, rapporteurs, Document 231, May 3, 1962, Assembly, WEU, *Proceedings*, June 1962, I, pp. 109-58.

75. "Political Union: First, Timid Steps," *European Community*, No. 137, August 1970, p. 13. See also "The Political

Consequences of Relaunching Europe," Hubert Leynen, rapporteur, Document 509, May 11, 1970, Assembly, WEU, *Proceedings*, June 1970, I, pp. 127-29, 132. For the debate, see WEU, *Proceedings*, June 1970, II, pp. 59-75.

76. "The Future Organization of Western Defense," James Boyden, rapporteur, Document 557, November 16, 1971, Assembly, WEU, *Proceedings*, December 1971, III, pp. 121, 126. See also draft recommendation of the report, "Europe and Present-day Economic and Political Problems," James Scott-Hopkins, rapporteur, Document 577, May 23, 1972, Assembly, WEU, *Proceedings*, June 1972, I, p. 222: "In due course, the European Parliament should become the main parliamentary forum for debate and decision on economic, political and financial matters, but . . . in the meantime the [WEU] Assembly must retain to the full its terms of reference in the political, defense and technological fields."

77. "The Brussels Treaty and the European Institutions (Prospects for Western European Union)," Lord Gladwyn, rapporteur, Document 554, November 4, 1971, Assembly, WEU, *Proceedings*, December 1971, III, pp. 61-75. In his report Gladwyn advanced a number of possible courses of action without firmly approving any one. In the joint debate on the Boyden and Gladwyn reports, however, Gladwyn made his preference quite clear. See WEU, *Proceedings,* December 1971, III, pp. 121, 126. See also draft

78. Joe Carroll, "EC Goals and Irish Neutrality: Are They Compatible?" *European Community*, August-September 1972, p. 16.

79. *Atlantic News*, November 9, 1971, February 25, 1972, June 7, 1972.

80. Clyde Farnsworth, "House Unit Supports a United Europe," New York *Times*, January 13, 1972; *The European Community and the American Interest*, Report of Special Study Mission to Europe, January 1972 by Benjamin S. Rosenthal, Chairman, Subcommittee on Europe, and Donald M. Fraser, Chairman, Subcommittee on International Organizations and Movements, Committee on Foreign Affairs, 92d Cong., 2d sess. (Washington, D.C., 1972).

81. *A Growing Bond: The European Parliament and the Congress*, Report on the First Official Visit to Congress by a Delegation of the European Parliament, May 1972, by Benjamin S. Rosenthal, Chairman, Subcommittee on Europe, and Donald M. Fraser, Chairman, Subcommittee on International Organizations

and Movements, Committee on Foreign Affairs, 92d Cong., 2d sess. (Washington, D.C., 1972); *European Parliament Working Documents, 1972-1973,* Document 82/72, July 1, 1972, Report on Parliamentary Relations Between the European Community and the United States of America, Willem J. Schuijt, rapporteur.

82. Joint Communique of the Meeting Between the Delegation of the European Parliament and the Delegation of the Canadian Parliament, Ottawa, November 1, 1973; Resolution of the European Parliament on Relations with the Canadian Parliament, Strasbourg, April 1974.

EPILOGUE:
A LOOK AHEAD

It is fashionable to view the future of the Atlantic Community with pessimism—and with good reason. "The correlation of forces," as the Soviets would say, seem to be shifting against the West.

Even before the trauma of the quadrupling of oil prices, many of the economies of the industrialized, non-Communist countries were moving toward double digit inflation. The erosion of buying power made it extremely difficult to maintain, let alone improve, NATO's defense requirements in the face of the increasingly sophisticated and constantly growing forces of the Warsaw Pact. This disability was frequently reinforced by a detente euphoria in the West, which rested upon the dangerous assumption that the Soviet leaders had basically altered their purposes.

The Kremlin labored under no similar burdens. Inflation was not a problem, and neither were illusions of public opinion to which the Soviet leaders had to trim their policies. Furthermore, when the world price of oil skyrocketed, the Soviet Union reaped the benefit of being, for the time at least, a net oil exporter.

At some point in the future there will be economically viable energy substitutes for oil. The problem, however, is to get from here to there. In the transition period there will be an entirely unprecedented magnitude of change in the functioning of industrial civilization and a massive transfer of wealth to the oil producers. The response to these new circumstances, to be adequate, must also be unprecedented in scope.

Managing balance-of-payments difficulties arising from the oil crisis, or recycling petrodollars are tasks that are simply beyond the capabilities of the traditional private banking system. Take, for example, the case of Italy, which is tottering on the brink of bankruptcy. If Italy were to declare a moratorium on the repayment of its borrowings, there would be disastrous consequences for a number of key financial institutions in other Western countries.

Clearly what is required is for the OECD countries as a group to innovate institutional arrangements that will build upon present economic and monetary practices, but go beyond them where needed to supply new answers to grave new problems. And this inventiveness must be undertaken, not singly and in isolation, but with a full appreciation of the profound interdependence of all of the countries of the Atlantic Community.

When under severe pressure, the natural tendency will be for each country to adopt a *sauve qui peut* attitude and go its own way. Nothing could be less effective in bargaining with the oil exporting countries, nor more disastrous in working out solutions for the common good. Indeed, no solutions are likely unless they are jointly elaborated.

A breakdown in the intimate collaboration that has characterized so much of the post-war practices of Western societies would now have catastrophic ramifications, not just for economic order, but for the political and social structures associated with it. In a word, the Atlantic Community is entering a truly critical period and its gravest tests lie ahead.

ABOUT THE AUTHOR

ELLIOT R. GOODMAN is currently Professor of Political Science at Brown University. He has been at Brown since 1955, teaching courses in Soviet politics, world communism, and the politics of the Atlantic Community. Research for this book was supported by a Guggenheim Fellowship and a NATO Research Fellowship.

Professor Goodman is the author of *The Soviet Design for a World State*, which was also translated into Spanish and Portuguese. He has published articles in several books and in numerous scholarly journals, including *Journal of Politics, Russian Review, Current History, International Organization, Journal of International Affairs, Orbis, NATO Letter,* and *Atlantic Community Quarterly,* and a number of foreign journals including *Survey, Osteuropa, Internationale Spectator,* and *Affari Esteri.* His articles have been published abroad in ten languages.

Dr. Goodman received an A.B. (Phi Beta Kappa) from Dartmouth College and an M.A., a Certificate of the Russian Institute, and a Ph. D. from Columbia University.

EAST EUROPEAN PERSPECTIVES ON EUROPEAN SECURITY AND COOPERATION
edited by Robert R. King and
Robert W. Dean

THE EUROPEAN COMMUNITY IN THE 1970s
edited by
Steven Joshua Warnecke

THE FUTURE OF INTER-BLOC RELATIONS IN EUROPE
edited by Louis J. Mensonides
and James A. Kuhlman

QUANTITATIVE TECHNIQUES IN FOREIGN POLICY ANALYSIS
Michael K. O'Leary and
William D. Coplin, with
the assistance of Howard
B. Shapiro

REGIONAL ECONOMIC ANALYSIS FOR PRACTITIONERS:
An Introduction to Common Descriptive Methods (revised edition)
Avrom Bendavid